MOSAICS

FOCUSING ON SENTENCES IN CONTEXT

SECOND EDITION

KIM FLACHMANN

California State University, Bakersfield

Prentice
Hall

Upper Saddle River, New Jersey 07458

D1417023

Library of Congress Cataloging-in-Publication Data

Flachmann, Kim.
   Mosaics, focusing on sentences in context / Kim Flachmann.—2nd ed.
      p. cm.—(Mosaics)
   Rev. ed. of: Mosaics, focusing on sentences in context / Kim Flachmann . . . [et al.]. c1998.
   Includes bibliographical references and index.
   ISBN 0-13-016314-7
      1. English language—Sentences—Problems, exercises, etc. 2. English
   language—Rhetoric—Problems, exercises, etc. I. Title: Focusing on sentences in context.
   II. Mosaics, focusing on sentences in context. III. Title. IV. Mosaics (Upper
   Saddle River, N.J.)

   PEI441 .F48 2001
   808'.042—dc21

2001050079

VP/Editor in Chief: Leah Jewell
Sr. Acquisitions Editor: Craig Campanella
Editorial Assistant: Joan Polk
Development Editor in Chief: Susanna Lesan
Development Editor: Harriett Prentiss
AVP/Director of Production and Manufacturing:
   Barbara Kittle
Project Manager: Maureen Richardson
Sr. Managing Editor: Mary Rottino
Manufacturing Manager: Nick Sklitsis

Prepress and Manufacturing Buyer: Ben Smith
Creative Design Director: Leslie Osher
Interior Design: Kathryn Foot
Cover Design: Kathryn Foot
Cover Art: Wolfgang Kachler Photography
Director of Marketing: Beth Mejia
Marketing Manager: Rachel Falk
Marketing Assistant: Christine Moodie
Copyeditor: Bruce Emmer
Proofreader: Rainbow Graphics

This book was set in 11/13 Goudy by Interactive Composition Corp. and was printed and bound by
Courier Companies, Inc. The cover was printed by Phoenix Color Corp.

For permission to use copyrighted material, grateful acknowledgment is made to the copyright holders listed on
pages 682–683, which are considered an extension of this copyright page.

© 2002, 1999 by Pearson Education, Inc.
Upper Saddle River, New Jersey 07458

Printed in the United States of America
10 9 8 7 6 5 4 3 2 1

ISBN 0-13-016314-7 (Student Edition)
ISBN 0-13-094213-8 (Annotated Instructor's Edition)

Pearson Education LTD., *London*
Pearson Education Australia PTY, Limited, *Sydney*
Pearson Education Singapore, Pte. Ltd
Pearson Education North Asia Ltd, *Hong Kong*
Pearson Education Canada, Ltd., *Toronto*
Pearson Educacion de Mexico, S.A. de C.V.
Pearson Education—Japan, *Tokyo*
Pearson Education Malaysia, Pte. Ltd

For
Laura

BRIEF CONTENTS

CONTENTS

PREFACE

PREFACE TO THE INSTRUCTOR

Experience tells us that students have the best chance of succeeding in college if they learn how to respond productively to the varying academic demands made on them throughout the curriculum. One extremely important part of this process is being able to analyze ideas and think critically about issues in many different subject areas. *Mosaics: Focusing on Sentences in Context* is the first in a series of three books that teach the basic skills essential to all good academic writing. This series illustrates how the companion skills of reading and writing are parts of a larger, interrelated process that moves back and forth through the tasks of prereading and reading, prewriting and writing, and revising and editing. In other words, the *Mosaics* series shows how these skills are integrated at every stage of the writing process.

THE *MOSAICS* SERIES

This second edition of the *Mosaics* series consists of three books, each with a different emphasis: *Focusing on Sentences in Context*, *Focusing on Paragraphs in Context*, and *Focusing on Essays*. The first book highlights sentence structure, the second book paragraph development, and the third the composition of essays. Each book introduces the writing process as a unified whole and asks students to begin writing in the very first chapter. Each volume also moves from personal to more academic writing. The books differ in the length and level of their reading selections, the complexity of their writing assignments, the degree of difficulty of their revising and editing strategies, and the length and level of their student writing samples.

This entire three-book series is based on the following fundamental assumptions:

- Students build confidence in their ability to read and write by reading and writing.

- Students learn best from discovery and experimentation rather than from instruction and abstract discussions.
- Students need to discover their personal writing process.
- Students learn both individually and collaboratively.
- Students profit from studying both professional and student writing.
- Students benefit most from assignments that actually integrate thinking, reading, and writing.
- Students learn how to revise by following clear guidelines.
- Students learn grammar and usage rules by editing their own writing.
- Students must be able to transfer their writing skills to all their college courses.
- Students must think critically and analytically to succeed in college.

HOW THIS BOOK WORKS

Mosaics: Focusing on Sentences in Context teaches students how to write effective sentences. For flexibility and easy reference, this book is divided into four parts:

Part I: The Writing Process
Part II: Writing Effective Sentences
Part III: Paragraphs: Sentences in Context
Part IV: From Reading to Writing

Part I: The Writing Process   All six chapters in Part I demonstrate the cyclical nature of the writing process. They begin with the logistics of getting ready to write and then move systematically through the interlocking stages of the process by following a student essay from prewriting to revising and editing. Part I ends with a quiz that students can take to identify their "Editing Quotient"—their strengths and weaknesses in grammar and mechanics.

Part II: Writing Effective Sentences   Part II, the heart of the instruction in this text, is a complete handbook—including exercises—that covers eight main categories: Sentences, Verbs, Pronouns, Modifiers, Punctuation, Mechanics, Effective Sentences, and Choosing the Right Word. These categories are coordinated with the Editing Checklist that appears periodically throughout this text. The chapters provide at least four types of practice after each grammar concept, moving the students systematically from identifying exercises to writing their own sentences. Within each chapter, students read professional paragraphs, write their own paragraphs, edit another student's writing, and finally edit their own writing. Each unit ends with practical editing exercises that ask students to use the skills they just learned to edit a paragraph written by another student and then edit the paragraph they wrote earlier in the chapter.

Part III: Paragraphs: Sentences in Context   The next section of this text helps students move from writing effective sentences to writing effective paragraphs. It systematically explains how to recognize, write, revise, and edit a paragraph. Then it shows paragraphs at work in both professional and student examples. Part III ends with a series of writing assignments and workshops designed to encourage your students to write, revise, and edit a paragraph (or essay) and then reflect on their own writing process.

Part IV: From Reading to Writing   Part IV of this text is a collection of readings arranged by rhetorical mode. Multiple rhetorical strategies are at work in most of these essays, but each is classified according to its primary rhetorical purpose. Each professional essay is preceded by prereading activities that will help your students focus on the topic at hand and then is followed by 10 questions that move students from literal to analytical thinking skills as they consider the essay's content, purpose, audience, and paragraph structure.

APPENDIXES

The appendixes will help your students keep track of their progress in the various skills they are learning throughout this text. References to these appendixes are interspersed throughout the book so that students know when to use them as they study the concepts in each chapter:

Appendix 1: Critical Thinking Log
Appendix 2: Revising and Editing Peer Evaluation Forms
Appendix 3: Editing Quotient Error Chart
Appendix 4: Error Log
Appendix 5: Spelling Log

OVERALL GOAL

Ultimately, each book in the *Mosaics* series portrays writing as a way of thinking and processing information. One by one, these books encourage students to discover how the "mosaics" of their own writing process work together to form a coherent whole. By demonstrating the interrelationship among thinking, reading, and writing on progressively more difficult levels, these books promise to help prepare your students for success in college throughout the curriculum.

UNIQUE FEATURES

Several unique and exciting features separate this book from other basic writing texts:

- It moves students systematically from personal to academic writing.
- It uses both student writing and professional writing as models.
- It demonstrates all aspects of the writing process through student writing.
- It integrates reading and writing throughout the text.
- It teaches revising and editing through student writing.
- It features culturally diverse reading selections that are of high interest to students.
- It teaches rhetorical modes as patterns of thought.
- It helps students discover their own writing process.
- It includes a complete handbook with exercises.
- It offers worksheets for students to chart their progress in reading and writing.

INSTRUCTOR'S TEACHING PACKAGE

Annotated Instructor's Edition—ISBN 0-13-094213-8. For the first time, *Mosaics* has an *Annotated Instructor's Edition*. Written by Kim Flachmann and Cheryl Smith, the *AIE* contains in-text answers and marginal annotations to help instructors prepare thoroughly for class. The *AIE* gives both experienced and new instructors ideas about how to get the most out of the text, providing teaching tips, summaries of the readings, readability levels for the essays, additional writing activities, ideas for incorporating the Internet into class, and much more. This supplement is *free* to adopters.

Instructor's Resource Manual—ISBN 0-13-097522-2. Also written by Kim Flachmann and Cheryl Smith, the *Instructor's Resource Manual* contains sample syllabi, additional teaching strategies, sample quizzes, journal assignments, additional grammar and writing assignments, rubrics for marking paragraphs and essays, and much more. It is available in print or electronic format and is *free* to adopters.

Instructor's Resource CD. This CD contains video clips of the author discussing how to best use the *Mosaics* series in class. Designed with the new instructor in mind and organized around specific parts of each text in the series, this CD will provide instructors with concrete teaching strategies taken from Kim Flachmann's own classroom. It is *free* to adopters. Contact your local Prentice Hall representative for a copy.

STUDENT'S LEARNING PACKAGE

Prentice Hall WORDS. An Internet-based assessment tool like no other in the Developmental English market, *PH WORDS* provides students with summary instruction and practice on each element of writing as presented in the *Mosaics* series. *PH WORDS* includes over 200 learning modules covering the writing process, paragraph and essay development, and grammar. For each module, students have access to the following online features:

- *Watch Screens* that provide an audio and animated summary of the content,
- *Recall Questions* that test their comprehension of the content,
- *Apply Questions* that test their ability to apply the concepts to existing writing, and
- *Write Questions* that prompt students to generate their own prose using the concepts.

This technology solution frees up class time by allowing students to work individually on their areas of weakness. The software measures and tracks students' progress through the course with an easy-to-use management system. *PH WORDS* is available at a discount when packaged with the text. Contact your local Prentice Hall representative for more information and a demonstration.

Companion Web Site: www.prenhall.com/flachmann. The Companion Web Site allows students to gain a richer perspective and a deeper understanding of the concepts and issues discussed in *Mosaics: Focusing on Sentences in Context.* This site is *free* to all students. Features of this site include the following:

- Chapter learning objectives that help students organize key concepts,
- On-line quizzes which include instant scoring and coaching,
- Essay questions that test students' critical thinking skills, and
- Built-in routing that gives students the ability to forward essay responses and graded quizzes to their instructors.

The New American Webster Handy College Dictionary, Third Edition—ISBN 0-13-032870-7. With over 1.5 million Signet copies in print and over 115,000 definitions, this dictionary is available *free* to your students when packaged with the text.

The New American Roget's College Thesaurus—ISBN 0-13-045258-0. With over 17 million Signet copies in print, this latest edition of the classic paperback thesaurus contains over 20,000 new words and phrases and over 1,500 additional entries. This thesaurus is available *free* to your students when packaged with the text.

English on the Internet 2001: Evaluating On-line Resources—ISBN 0-13-019484-0. This completely revised guide helps students develop the critical thinking skills needed to evaluate on-line sources critically. This supplement is available *free* when packaged with the text.

The Prentice Hall ESL Workbook—ISBN 0-13-092323-0. This 138-page workbook is designed for use with a developmental English textbook to improve English grammar skills. Divided into seven major units, this workbook provides thorough explanations and exercises in the most challenging grammar topics for non-native speakers. With over 80 exercise sets, this guide provides ample instruction and practice in nouns, articles, verbs, modifiers, pronouns, prepositions, and sentence structure. The *PH ESL Workbook* also contains an annotated listing of key ESL Internet sites for further study and practice, an answer key to all the exercises so students can study at their own pace, and a glossary for students to look up difficult words and phrases. Contact your local Prentice Hall representative for a copy.

The Prentice Hall Grammar Workbook—ISBN 0-13-042188-X. This 21-chapter workbook is a comprehensive source of instruction for students who need additional grammar, punctuation, and mechanics. Covering topics like subject-verb agreement, conjunctions, modifiers, capital letters, and vocabulary, each chapter provides ample explanations, examples, and exercises. The exercises contain enough variety to ensure students' mastery of each concept. This supplement is available to students packaged by itself or with the text at a discount.

The Prentice Hall TASP Writing Study Guide—ISBN 0-13-041585-5. Designed for students studying for the Texas Academic Skills Program test, this guide prepares students for the TASP by familiarizing them with the elements of the test and giving them strategies for success. The authors, both from Prairie View A&M, provide practice exercises for each element of the writing and multiple-choice portions of the exam, and the guide ends with a full-length practice test with answer key so that students can evaluate their own progress. Contact your local Prentice Hall representative for a copy.

Ask your local Prentice Hall representative for information about our ever-growing list of supplements for both instructors and students.

ACKNOWLEDGMENTS

I want to acknowledge the support, encouragement, and sound advice of several people who have helped me through the development of the *Mosaics* series. First, Prentice Hall has provided guidance and inspiration for this project through the wisdom of Craig Campanella, Senior Acquisitions Editor; the insights and vision of Harriett Prentiss, Development Editor; the diligence and clairvoyance of Maureen Richardson, Project Manager; the foresight and prudence of Leah Jewell, Editor in Chief; the creative inspiration of Rachel Falk, Marketing Manager; the brilliant observations of Charlyce Jones-Owen, Editorial Director for Humanities; the hard work and patience of Celeste Parker-Bates, Permissions Editor; the guidance and fortitude of Bruce Emmer, Copyeditor; and the common sense and organization of Joan Polk, Administrative Assistant for Developmental English. Also, this book would not be a reality without the insightful persistence of Phil Miller, Publisher for Modern Languages.

I want to give very special thanks to Cheryl Smith, my consultant and advisor for the duration of this project and author of the margin annotations and the *Mosaics Instructor's Resource Manual*. I am also grateful to Valerie Turner, Rebecca Hewett, Brad Ruff, and Kelly Osdick for their discipline and hard work and to Monique Idoux, Matt Woodman, Thomas Board, Victoria Bockman, and Li'i Pearl for their dedication and expertise. I want to also thank Rebecca Juarez, Heather Morgan, Richard Marquez, Lynette Betty, Barbara Mitchell, Marilyn Cummings, Jessica Sanchez, Jolene Christie, Katie Greer, Beth Olson, Kathy Angelini, and Misty Kuykendall for their assistance and support.

In addition, I am especially grateful to the following reviewers who have guided me through the development and revision of this book: Lisa Berman, Miami-Dade Community College; Patrick Haas, Glendale Community College; Jeanne Campanelli, American River College; Dianne Gregory, Cape Cod Community College; Clara Wilson-Cook, Southern University at New Orleans; Thomas Beery, Lima Technical College; Jean Petrolle, Columbia College; David Cratty, Cuyahoga Community College; Allison Travis, Butte State College; Suellen Meyer, Meramec Community College; Jill Lahnstein, Cape Fear Community College; Stanley Coberly, West Virginia State University at Parkersville; Jamie Moore, Scottsdale Community College; Nancy Hellner, Mesa

Community College; Ruth Hatcher, Washtenaw Community College; Thurmond Whatley, Aiken Technical College; W. David Hall, Columbus State Community College; and Marilyn Coffee, Fort Hays State University.

I also want to express my gratitude to my students, from whom I have learned so much about the writing process, about teaching, and about life itself. I am especially grateful to Cheryl Smith's classes, who class-tested the book and gave me good ideas for revising in Spring 1999, in Fall 2000, and in Winter 2001, and to Rebecca Hewett's classes for doing the same in Spring 1999. Thanks especially to the students who contributed paragraphs and essays to this series: Josh Ellis, Jolene Christie, Mary Minor, Michael Tiede, and numerous others.

Finally, I owe a tremendous personal debt to the people who have lived with this project for the last two years; they are my closest companions and my best advisers: Michael, Christopher, and Laura Flachmann. To Michael, I owe additional thanks for the valuable support and feedback he has given me through the entire process of creating and revising this series.

Kim Flachmann

P · A · R · T

I

THE WRITING PROCESS

Writing and rewriting are a constant search for what it is one is saying.

—JOHN UPDIKE

The primary goal of this first section of *Mosaics* is to show you how important good sentences are as building blocks to good writing. Clear, effective sentences are the result of clear thinking, and clear thinking will get you good grades and good jobs. Sentences are the foundation of all of your writing—whether it is a history essay exam, a writing assignment for English, a memo asking for a raise, or an editorial for the newspaper. Your sentences represent you everywhere you go.

CHAPTER 1

Writing Successful Sentences

The fact that a person writes every day makes that person a writer. Whether you make a list of chores to do, e-mail a friend, do your English assignment, or write a note to your boss, you are part of a community of writers. In fact, you *are* a writer.

The more you know about writing sentences, the better you can communicate and get what you want out of life. You can figure out what you want to say and then state it in the best way possible so that you reach your audience and achieve your purpose. For example, if you want to tell your parents how serious you are about school, you might write, "I am adjusting well to college. I study every day. I hardly go out at all, and I am really serious about school." To a friend, however, you might write the same message with a slightly different slant: "I hope this adjustment period is over soon. I have to study all the time to survive. I have no social life to speak of, and my classes are killing me." Since your purpose is slightly different in these two cases, you choose different words to convey your message.

All writing starts with good sentences. In fact, any piece of writing more formal than a grocery list is usually the result of a series of activities that we call *the writing process.* On the surface, some of these activities may seem to have very little to do with the act of writing itself. But learning to use this process to help you communicate your ideas is part of learning to write well.

YOUR APPROACH TO WRITING

Everyone approaches writing in a different way. At the same time, some general guidelines apply to all writers—students and professionals alike. They include setting aside a time and place for your writing task, gathering the necessary supplies, and thinking of yourself as a writer.

1. *Set aside a special time for writing, and plan to do nothing else during that time.* The bills will wait until tomorrow; your car doesn't have to be washed today; your room can be cleaned some other time; and the dirt on your bike won't turn to concrete overnight. When you first get a writing assignment, a little procrastination is good because it gives your mind time to plan your approach to the task. The trick is to know when to quit procrastinating and get down to work so that you can make your deadline. Don't wait until the day before your paper is due to begin.

2. *Find a comfortable place with few distractions.* You need to set up your own place for writing, one that suits your individual needs. Ideally, it should be where you are not distracted or interrupted. Some people work best sitting at a table or desk, while others write best on the floor or on a bed. The particular place doesn't matter, as long as you feel comfortable writing there. Also, some people write best with noise in the background, while others need complete silence. Some snack and wear their favorite jeans while they write, and others sip coffee in their pajamas. Whatever your choices, you need to set up a writing environment that is comfortable for you.

3. *Gather your supplies before you begin to write.* Who knows what great idea you might lose while you search for a pen that writes or a disk that's formatted. Gather in advance all the supplies and/or equipment that will bring out your best writing. Some writers use paper and a pen to get started, and others go straight to their computers. One of the big advantages of writing on a computer is that once you type in your ideas, it is easy to change them or move them around. In any case, whatever equipment you choose, make sure it is ready when you want to write.

4. *Think of yourself as a writer.* Now that you have a time and place for writing and all the supplies you need, you are ready to learn more about yourself as a writer. Understanding your individual writing habits and taking yourself seriously are extremely important to your growth as a writer. So take a minute now to do Practice 1, and record some of your own preferences when you write.

TEACHING ON THE WEB

Exploring and Discussing: Have students find Web sites where other students talk about their fears, hopes, or desires about writing. Where did they find these testimonials? Did they get any tips for overcoming their fears? Were any of these sites inspiring? In what way?

TEACHING ON THE WEB

Mosaics Web Site: To learn more about successful sentences, students can go to www.prenhall.com/mosaics.

Practice 1   Explain the routine you naturally follow as you prepare to write. Where do you write? What time of day brings out your best work? Do you like noise? Quiet? What other details describe your writing environment? What equipment do you use to write?

WRITING ASSIGNMENTS

In this text, you will be writing sentences and paragraphs. A **paragraph** is a group of sentences on a single topic. The first line of each paragraph is indented to show that a new topic or sub-topic is starting. Although paragraphs vary in length, typical paragraphs average about 100–125 words.

You will get writing assignments of all different lengths in college. They will vary from paragraphs to full essays and research papers. All writing longer than a sentence has a beginning, a middle, and an end.

Here are the parts of a paragraph:

Paragraph
Topic Sentence
Supporting Sentences
Concluding Sentence

No matter what the length, however, all writing is made up of sentences. Successful sentences lead to successful writing—whatever your purpose. So to develop a good writing project of any length, you have to start with individual sentences.

The following writing assignment is typical of what you will be doing throughout this book. You will be working on this assignment over the next five chapters, so you can apply what you are learning about the writing process to a specific assignment. At the same time, you will follow the work of a student named Darryl Jarvis so you can see how he approaches and completes the same assignment. By the end of Chapter 6, you will have an understanding of the entire writing process, which is essential to your success as a writer.

Writing a Paragraph

Think about your life so far, and recall an incident or event that made you feel a strong emotion, such as happiness, sadness, anger, joy, power, weakness, fear, or pride. It does not have to be a major incident. It can be something as ordinary as going for a walk with a grandparent, losing a favorite toy, fighting with a best friend, or just being 11 or 16 years old—just as long as the event was important enough to have made a lasting impression on you. Write a paragraph explaining this event to someone who was not with you.

Understanding the Writing Process

Your writing process begins the minute you get a writing assignment. It involves all the mental and physical activities you do from choosing a subject to turning in a final draft. The main parts of the process are outlined here.

Prewriting

Prewriting refers to any activities that help you explore a subject, generate ideas about it, settle on a specific topic, establish a purpose, and analyze the audience for your assignment. Your mission at this stage is simply to stimulate your thinking.

Writing

When you have generated lots of ideas to work with, you are ready to begin writing. Writing involves expanding your best ideas, organizing your thoughts, and writing a first draft.

Revising

The process of writing is not finished with your first draft. You should always revise your work to make it stronger and better. Revising involves rethinking your content and organization so that your writing says exactly what you want it to. The purpose of your paper should be clear, your main ideas should be supported with details and examples, and your organization should be logical.

Editing

When you have made all the changes in the content of your writing that you plan to make, the final step in the writing process is editing. Read your

TEACHING
UNDERSTANDING
THE WRITING
PROCESS
Have students draw a picture of their writing process. Be sure to tell students to include all steps of the writing process. How do they get from assignment to deadline? This can take any form—a cartoon, an abstract drawing, a flowchart. Then have the students explain their writing process to the class with their pictures. The purpose of this exercise is to get students thinking about what they do every time they get a writing assignment.

■ For additional material about teaching the writing process, for journal entries, and for various tests, see the *Instructor's Resource Manual*, Section II, Part I.

TEACHING ON THE WEB

Exploring and Discussing: Have students find the Web site of their favorite author. How does this author prepare to write? How long does it take for the author to finish a project? How many drafts does the author go through? What can students learn from the advice of such authors?

TEACHING ON THE WEB

Mosaics Web Site: To learn more about the writing process, students can go to www.prenhall.com/mosaics.

writing slowly and carefully to find any errors in grammar, punctuation, mechanics, or spelling. Such errors distract your reader from the message you are trying to communicate. Some errors can even cause communication to break down altogether. Editing means cleaning up your draft so that your writing is clear and precise.

Practice 1

1. Explain prewriting in your own words.

   Answers will vary.

   _____

2. What does "writing" consist of?

   Writing involves expanding your best ideas, organizing your thoughts, and writing a first

   draft.

3. What is the difference between revising and editing?

   Revising involves rethinking your content and organization, and editing involves finding

   any errors you made in grammar, punctuation, mechanics, and spelling.

PICTURE THE PROCESS

Even though we talk about the stages of writing, writing is actually a cyclical process, which means that at any point you may loop in and out of other stages. In other words, writing is not a lockstep, straight line activity. Instead, a writer moves among all the stages of the process in no particular order. The sketch on the next page shows how the stages of the writing process can overlap.

Generally, the writing process moves from prewriting to writing to revising and, finally, editing. Once you start on a writing project, however, you will loop in and out of the different stages of writing. For example, you may change a word in the very first sentence that you write (revising), think of a new detail to add to a sentence (prewriting), and cross out and rewrite a misspelled word (editing) all in the first two minutes of your writing time.

Although you may approach every writing project in a different way, we hope that in Part I of this text you will settle on a writing process that you follow with each writing task while you find your comfort zone as a writer.

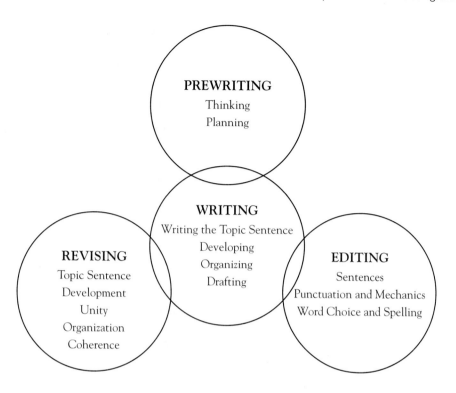

🌿 Practice 2

1. List the two parts of prewriting.
   Thinking and planning

2. List the four parts of writing.
   Writing the topic sentence, developing, organizing, and drafting

3. List the five parts of revising.
   Topic sentence, development, unity, organization, and coherence

4. List the three parts of editing.
   Sentences, punctuation and mechanics, and word choice and spelling

5. In what ways do the various parts of the writing process overlap?
   You might revise, prewrite, and edit at the same time that you are writing.

Prewriting

Would you be surprised to find out that a number of steps in the writing process have to occur before you can actually put words on paper? All writing tasks involve some sort of *prewriting*—or thinking and planning. The more you know about these two aspects of prewriting—thinking and planning—the more control you have over your writing process and the more efficient your process will be.

Specifically, prewriting refers to the following activities:

- exploring a subject
- generating ideas about it
- settling on a specific topic
- establishing a purpose
- understanding your audience

We will begin this chapter by looking at activities that many writers use to stimulate their thinking as they approach a writing task.

THINKING

Thinking is always the first stage of any writing project. It's a time to explore your topic and the material you have to work with. The following five activities promise to stimulate your best thoughts: reading, freewriting, brainstorming, clustering, and questioning. You will see how Darryl Jarvis, the student writer, uses each strategy, and then you can try your hand at the strategy yourself.

Reading

A good way to start your thinking and your writing process is to surf the Net or read an article on your topic.

TEACHING
PREWRITING
Give students a topic for each of the prewriting strategies, and have them practice each one. For example, give them "father" for reading and note taking (you will need to provide a short reading), "mother" for freewriting, "family" for brainstorming, "relatives" for clustering, "holidays" for questioning, and "brothers or sisters" for discussing.

Once students discover which prewriting strategy they are most comfortable with, have them use this strategy for future essays.

■ For additional material about teaching prewriting, for journal entries, and for various tests, see the *Instructor's Resource Manual*, Section II, Part I.

📝 Darryl's Reading   Darryl read the following paragraph from an essay titled "The Sissy" by Tobias Wolff. Wolff describes a fight two sixth graders get into, and it reminds Darryl of some of his own arguments on the playground. He jotted several notes to himself in the margins.

> *This reminds me of a time I was attacked in fourth grade*
>
> His first swing caught me dead on the ear. There was an <u>explosion inside my head</u>, then a continuous rustling sound as of someone crumpling paper. It lasted for days. When he swung again, I turned away and took his fist on the back of my head. He threw punches the way he threw balls, sidearm, with a lot of wrist, but he somehow got his weight behind them before they landed. <u>This one knocked me to my knees.</u> He drew back his foot and kicked me in the stomach. The papers in my bag deadened the blow, but I was stunned by the fact that he had kicked me at all. I saw that <u>his commitment to this fight was absolute.</u>
>
> *Ouch!*
>
> *great details*
>
> *This kid is mad and serious*

Later, Darryl wrote this entry in his writing journal, a notebook he keeps to jot down ideas for writing and reactions to his reading.

> I like the way Tobias Wolff talks about this fight. He seems so calm as he writes. Being attacked is really awful. I remember many times when I thought I was going to be in a fight, but I wasn't. Until one time I was chased into the corner of the playground by a big bully. I was really afraid. I thought he was going to destroy me. But then I got the courage to yell at him, and he walked away. He never bothered me again.

🌿 Your Reading   Read the following paragraph from "Casa: A Partial Remembrance of a Puerto Rican Childhood," an essay by Judith Ortiz Cofer on page 593, and write your thoughts in the margins as you read.

> It was on these rockers that my mother, her sisters, and my grandmother sat on these afternoons of my childhood to tell their stories, teaching each other, and my cousin and me, what it was like to be a woman, more specifically, a Puerto Rican woman. They talked about life on the island and life in *Los Nueva Yores*, their way of referring to the United States from New York City to California—the other place, not home, all the same. They told

real-life stories though, as I later learned, always embellishing them with a little or a lot of dramatic detail. And they told *cuentos,* the morality and cautionary tales told by the women in our family for generations: stories that became a part of my subconscious as I grew up in two worlds, the tropical island and the cold city, and that would later surface in my dreams and in my poetry.

Freewriting

Writing about anything that comes to your mind is the way to freewrite. You should write without stopping for five to ten minutes. Do not worry about grammar or spelling. If you get stuck, repeat an idea or start rhyming words. Just keep writing constantly because the act of writing will actually help you think of other ideas.

Darryl's Freewriting   Darryl wasn't sure if he could freewrite. He had never done anything like this before. But he followed directions and just started in.

> My teacher told us to freewrite for a few minutes on anything we want to, but I don't know what to write about. It's hard for me to just sit here and start writing, especially when I have nothing to say. Nothing, nothing, nothing, and still nothing to say. I wonder what all these other people are writing about. Are they writing about their families? Their boyfriends or girlfriends? School? I guess I could write about how my family is proud of me for going to college. I don't know why—it's always been expected. I don't even think I realized college was not an option. I just always knew that after high school came college—no exceptions. I can't imagine not going to college, though. Where else could I learn about freewriting?

 Your Freewriting   Try to freewrite following the directions given here.

Brainstorming

Like freewriting, brainstorming draws on free association—letting one thought naturally lead to another. But brainstorming usually takes the form of a list. Write down whatever comes into your mind on a topic—ideas, memories, examples, facts. As with all prewriting strategies, don't worry about grammar or spelling.

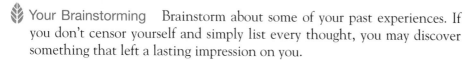 **Darryl's Brainstorming**   Here is Darryl's brainstorming on some of his past memories:

> Alaska—finally away from home
>
> I could see green everywhere
>
> Started working in the factory
>
> worked with fish all day long
>
> spent the evenings with my sister
>
> earned money for school

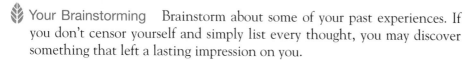 **Your Brainstorming**   Brainstorm about some of your past experiences. If you don't censor yourself and simply list every thought, you may discover something that left a lasting impression on you.

Clustering

Clustering is like brainstorming, but it illustrates how your thoughts are related. To cluster, take a sheet of blank paper, write a key word or phrase in the center of the page, and draw a circle around it. Next write down and circle any related ideas that come to your mind. As you add ideas, draw lines to the thoughts they are related to. Try to keep going for two or three minutes. When you finish, you'll have a map of your ideas that can help you write a good paragraph.

Darryl's Cluster   Here is Darryl's cluster.

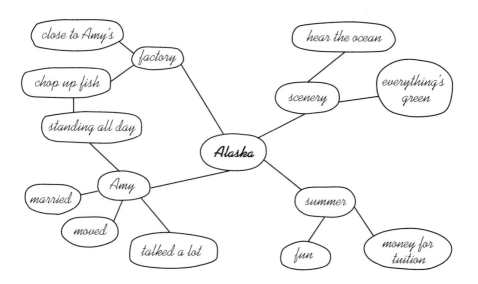

🌿 Your Cluster   Write "my past" in the middle of a piece of paper, and draw a cluster of your own personal associations with this word.

Questioning

Journalists use the questions known as the "five *W*'s and one *H*"—Who? What? When? Where? Why? and How?—to check that they've covered all the important information in a news story. You can use these same questions to generate ideas on a writing topic.

🍃 Darryl's Questions   Here is how Darryl used questioning to generate ideas on his topic:

Who?	Me, Amy, and her husband
What?	My summer job in a fish factory
When?	Last summer
Where?	At my sister's in Alaska
Why?	Because I wanted to see my sister and earn some extra money
How?	By living with my sister and working in the fish factory

🌿 Your Questions   Answer these six questions about an event that left a lasting impression on your life: Who? What? When? Where? Why? How?

🌿 Practice 1A   Now that you have been introduced to several prewriting strategies, which is your favorite? Why do you like it best?

_____

_____

_____

_____

🌿 Practice 1B   Using two prewriting strategies on one assignment is often a good idea. What is your second favorite prewriting strategy? Why do you like this strategy?

_____

_____

_____

_____

PLANNING

Writing a paragraph takes not only thinking, but also planning. You need to decide on your subject, purpose, and audience. These decisions will, in turn, affect all the rest of the decisions you make about your writing assignment.

Subject

A paragraph focuses on a single subject or topic. So your first decision is about your *subject*: What are you going to write about? Sometimes your topic is given to you—for example, your history instructor may assign a paper on the causes of the Civil War. But other times, you choose your own topic. In such cases, choosing a subject that interests you is the best approach. You will have more to say, and you will enjoy writing much more if you know something about your topic.

Purpose

Your *purpose* is your reason for writing. Your purpose could be to explore your feelings on a topic (*to do personal writing*), to tell a friend about something funny that happened to you (*to entertain*), to explain something or share information (*to inform*), or to convince others of your position on a controversial issue (*to persuade*). Whatever your purpose, deciding on it in advance makes writing your paragraph much easier.

Audience

Your *audience* is made up of the people who will read your writing. The more you know about your audience, the more likely you will accomplish your purpose. The audience for your writing in college is usually your instructor or your classmates, who represent what is called a "general audience"— people with an average amount of knowledge on most subjects. A general audience is the group to aim for in all your writing unless you are given other instructions.

Darryl's Plans   Darryl made the following decisions before beginning to write about his past:

Subject:	my summer in Alaska
Purpose:	personal—to reflect on something in my past that has made a lasting impression on me
Audience:	general—I want people who read this to think about a similar experience and remember how important it is to them

Your Plans   Identify the subject, purpose, and audience of the paragraph you will write on your past experience.

Subject: _____

Purpose: _____

Audience: _____

Writing

The writing phase is made up of several steps that lead you to your first draft. At this point, you have been given a topic (a memorable experience) and worked through many different prewriting techniques with that subject. You have also produced a number of ideas and decided on a purpose and audience.

In this chapter, you will learn how to write a topic sentence for your paragraph. Then you will add some specific, concrete details to your paragraph and put your ideas in a logical order. Finally, you will be ready to write your paragraph. The rest of this chapter will guide you through your first draft, which you will then revise and edit in Chapters 5 and 6. Again, you will be working alongside Darryl, who is learning about the writing process with you.

WRITING THE TOPIC SENTENCE

The decisions you made about subject, purpose, and audience will lead you quite naturally to your topic sentence. The *topic sentence* of a paragraph is its controlling idea, the sentence that tells what the paragraph is about. A typical paragraph consists of a topic sentence and details that support the topic sentence. Although a topic sentence can be the first or last sentence in a paragraph, it usually functions best as the first sentence.

A topic sentence has two parts—a topic and a statement about that topic. The topic should be limited enough that it can be developed in a paragraph.

Topic	Limited Topic	Statement
Reading	Leisure reading	can improve your grades.
Politics	Politics in the United States	is difficult to follow.
Sports	Watching sports events	is a relaxing pastime for many people.
Anger	Hate crimes	are tearing our community apart.

TEACHING WRITING
To encourage students to compose directly on the computer, conduct class in a computer lab, and have students write e-mails, join chat rooms, and send instant messages to each other. On another day, have students practice typing directly into a word processing program. Show students how to turn the automatic spell-check and grammar-check off so that the red and green underlines don't interfere as students generate ideas. In this way, you are also showing students that they should not focus on revision and editing errors as they write a first draft.

■ For additional material about teaching writing, for journal entries, and for various tests, see the *Instructor's Resource Manual*, Section II, Part I.

🌿 **Practice 3A**   Limit the following topics. Then develop them into statements that could be topic sentences. *Answers will vary.*

Topic	Limited Topic	Statement
1. The environment	_____	_____
2. Work	_____	_____
3. Malls	_____	_____
4. Writing	_____	_____
5. Summer	_____	_____

🌿 **Practice 3B**   Complete the following topic sentences. Make sure they are general enough to be developed into a paragraph, but not too general. *Answers will vary.*

1. The Internet _____.

2. _____ is the best vacation spot.

3. Becoming a lawyer _____.

4. Cars _____.

5. _____ is a rough and tough macho sport.

🌿 **Practice 3C**   Write topic sentences for the following paragraphs. *Answers will vary.*

1. *Finding the right college is very important and should be taken seriously.* _____

First, people need to look at what different schools have to offer in the field they think they might pursue. Then, they should look into different scholarship or financial aid packages that might help them with paying for college. Location is also something people should look into, and, if possible, they should visit schools they are considering. A lot of decisions need to be made before choosing the school that's just right.

2. *My sister and I get along well as long as we are far apart.* _____

We fought for years while we were growing up. I often denied even having a sister. She was only two years older and we went to the same school, but I just said, "No, I am not related to that person." I don't remember why we disliked each other so. Now she has moved to

Connecticut with her new husband, and we talk to each other all the time. It's as if we were always friends. The distance makes it easier, I guess. I hate to think about what would happen if we lived in the same city again.

3. _I want to be a prosecutor._ _____

It's what I've wanted to be since I was little. I believe there are too many defense lawyers out there, so I prefer the District Attorney's office. I think I can make a big difference by prosecuting defendants. I'm not saying there is anything wrong with defense attorneys; it's just not the job for me. I just couldn't look at myself in the mirror if I got a guilty person off. So I'll try to be the best and fairest prosecutor I can be.

✎ Darryl's Topic Sentence   Darryl writes a sentence that he believes will represent his whole paragraph. It introduces the beginning of his summer.

Limited Topic	**Statement**
I landed	in Alaska last summer.

🌿 Your Topic Sentence   Write a topic sentence that can serve as the controlling idea for your paragraph.

Limited Topic	**Statement**
_____	_____

DEVELOPING

After you write a topic sentence, you are ready to add specific details that will make up the rest of your paragraph. These must be concrete, supporting details and examples that are directly related to your topic. Concrete words refer to anything you can see, hear, touch, smell, or taste, like _dogs_, _tractors_, _fire_, _relatives_, _car_, _alarm_, and _popcorn_. Concrete words make writing come alive because they help us picture what the writer is talking about.

🌿 Practice 4   For each of the following topic sentences, list five details and/or examples to develop them. _Answers will vary._

1. E-mail is the best way to keep in contact with friends who live far away.

   _____

   _____

   _____

   _____

   _____

2. Jokes are a good way to brighten someone's day.

   _____

   _____

   _____

   _____

   _____

3. Weddings are a day to celebrate.

   _____

   _____

   _____

   _____

   _____

4. Swimming is a good way to work every muscle in the body.

   _____

   _____

   _____

   _____

   _____

5. Vegetarians need to follow a special diet in order to receive the nutrients their bodies need.

   _____

   _____

_____

_____

_____

Darryl's Development   To come up with concrete details and examples that will support his topic sentence, Darryl goes back to the cluster he did during his planning stage. Then, to generate more ideas, he uses the questioning technique.

Who?	Me and my sister Amy
What?	away from mom and dad
	ocean and green mountains
	new job--stand all day long
	talking with Amy
	earned money for college
When?	last summer
	evenings with Amy
Where?	Alaska
	in a fish factory
	in my sister's house
Why?	to be on my own
	to be with my sister
	to earn some money for college
	to get out of my hometown for a while
How?	being responsible without parents
	spending time with my sister

 Your Development   Choose one of the prewriting activities, and use it to generate more specific details and examples about your topic sentence.

ORGANIZING

At this point, you are moving smoothly through the writing process. You have tried several prewriting strategies. You have determined your subject, purpose, and audience, and you have written your topic sentence. You have also thought of additional details, examples, and facts to develop your topic sentence. Now you are ready to organize your ideas. How do they fit together logically? What should come first? What next?

A working outline is the best way to see how your ideas work together. All your ideas should support your topic sentence and be related to each other. With a working outline, you can visually check to see if the supporting ideas are related to the topic sentence or if any idea is not connected to the others.

For example, if you are describing your car, you can help the reader follow your train of thought by describing the exterior design first, then the interior, and, finally, its performance. In other words, you move from the outside to the inside and then under the hood. This is much better than hopping around from the color of the car to the stereo system to the gas mileage and back outside to the tires. An outline lets you see how your ideas are arranged.

Sometimes the most logical order is according to time order. Stories are organized by time order: *The spy was given his assignment. That evening, he flew to Paris, where he met with a secret agent from the Kremlin*, and so on. Time order is also important in giving directions: *First pour 2 cups of milk into a bowl. Add the pudding mix. Then beat with a wire whisk for two minutes. Pour the pudding into individual cups and refrigerate.*

If you are providing facts and reasons as supporting details, the logical organization may be from least important to most important. That way, your most important point will be in your reader's mind at the end of your paragraph. You could also put the most important point first to pull in your reader at the beginning.

Practice 4   Put the following groups of sentences into logical order in a rough outline. Then write a topic sentence for each group.

1. **Topic Sentence:**   *Arranging flowers is an easy process.*

5   Go back inside and find a vase that is big enough to fit all the flowers you have cut and picked.

1   First, put on gardening gloves.

4   Cut the stems long enough that they fit in the vase.

2   Grab scissors, and make sure they are sharp.

6   Fill the vase with lukewarm water, not too hot or too cold, which will kill the flowers.

3   Go out in your yard and cut all the flowers that you like.

8   Finally, put the flowers where everyone can see and enjoy them.

7   Arrange the flowers in the vase.

2. Topic Sentence: _My garage is neatly arranged so my car can fit nicely._

2   On the left of my car is a door that opens into the backyard. We keep the garden tools here.

4   Next to the door to the house are the air hockey table and bicycles.

1   My car is located in half of a two-car garage.

3   To the right of my car is the door to the house, where we keep the recycling boxes.

3. Topic Sentence: _I love spending time with my family._

5   My parents and I don't get to talk often enough, so this is perfect for us.

1   I especially love it when we have family days together.

3   We go to the beach, to the mountains, or into the city.

2   I don't get to spend too much time with them.

4   My favorite is going to the beach because we seem to do a lot of talking there.

Darryl's Organization   Darryl decides to organize his paragraph from the least important part of his summer to the most important part. He first talks about the scenery in Alaska. Then he plans to describe his summer job (working in a fish canning factory, chopping up fish). He wants to end by talking about his sister, Amy. He outlines his ideas in this order and then lists as many concrete details as he can under each category.

General: I went to Alaska last summer.

  Least important: Scenery

    Specific Details: green mountains

                           hear the ocean

  More important: Job

    Specific Details: fish canning factory

                           stand all day

                           chop up fish

                           everywhere I looked there was fish

  Most important: Amy

    Specific Details: her nice, comfortable house

                           house six blocks from work

moved to Alaska two years ago

we talked every night

Concluding thoughts: that was my summer

Specific Details: working in a fish place was fun for me

beautiful scenery

became closer to Amy

had a lot of fun

 Your Organization   What is the best way for you to organize your ideas about your past experience? Why do you think this order will be best?

DRAFTING

Drafting is writing your thoughts on paper. At this point, you have completed your prewriting activities, written a topic sentence, developed supporting details, and decided how you will organize these details. Now you are ready to write a draft of your paragraph in complete sentences—no more lists and outlines. At this stage, don't worry too much about grammar or spelling. You'll deal with those details when you edit your writing.

 Darryl's First Draft   Darryl tries to get down all his ideas in his first draft.

I went to Alaska last summer. I was glad to finally be away from Mom and Dad for a while. I looked around. Everything was green. I could here the ocean. I was really glad to see my sister, Amy. I only had one day before I started my new job. I just walked to and from work. My new job was in a factory. I had to stand up all day, I had to chop up fish as fast as possable. My friend back home worked in a sardine factory. Every night, I would go home to my sister's house. She just lived about six blocks away from the factory. Since my sister Amy got married. I hardly ever see her. She moved to Alaska right after her wedding. But we made up for lost time last summer. We talked every night. It was great. So that was my summer. Working in a fish canning factory may not sound exotic. It was for me. A river rafting guide sounds exotic. I earned enough money too pay for my tuition. I also became very close to my sister. We spent so much time together. I had fun.

Your First Draft   Write a draft of your paragraph about a memorable experience.

_____

_____

_____

_____

_____

_____

_____

_____

_____

_____

Revising

Revising your writing means working with it until it says exactly what you want it to say in the best way possible. Revising is changing words and phrases in your writing until you are sure you have communicated your message clearly to your audience. Revision involves both *content* (what you are trying to say) and *form* (how you deliver your message). When you revise, you should look closely at the five main elements that are listed here in the Revising Checklist.

Working Together   An important part of revising is working with others. This *collaborative work* might be in groups, in pairs, with a tutor, or with a friend. Asking someone to read your writing is always a good idea when you are working toward a final draft. Your readers can tell you which parts of your paragraph are most effective. They can also tell you if any parts are confusing, if you need more supporting details, or if the details could be organized in some clearer way.

Revising Checklist

TOPIC SENTENCE
✔ Does the topic sentence convey the paragraph's controlling idea and appear as the first or last sentence?

DEVELOPMENT
✔ Does the paragraph contain *specific* details that support the topic sentence?

✔ Does the paragraph include *enough* details to explain the topic sentence fully?

UNITY
✔ Do all the sentences in the paragraph support the topic sentence?

TEACHING REVISING
Divide students into groups of three or four, and have them exchange papers. Have the first student read his or her paper aloud while the other students listen for and take notes on suggested revisions. When the reader finishes, have each listener explain his or her suggestions; make sure the reader does not talk or try to clarify any points during this interchange. After all suggestions have been relayed, have the next writer read his or her paper, and so on. Allow only 10 minutes per paper.

■ For additional material about teaching revising, for journal entries, and for various tests, see the *Instructor's Resource Manual*, Section II, Part I.

ORGANIZATION
- ✔ Is the paragraph organized logically?

COHERENCE
- ✔ Do the sentences move smoothly and logically from one to the next?

Let's look at these questions one by one.

Topic Sentence

- ✔ Does the topic sentence convey the paragraph's controlling idea and appear as the first or last sentence?

As you learned in Chapter 3, every paragraph should have a topic sentence that states the paragraph's main idea. This sentence gives direction to the rest of the paragraph. It consists of two parts: a limited topic and a statement about that topic. Generally, the topic sentence is the first sentence in a paragraph.

Practice 1A   Revise the underlined topic sentences of the following paragraphs so that they introduce all the details and ideas in their paragraphs.

1. <u>My mom tried to discourage me from going to college</u>. I like to learn, and I love my classes. My professors are great and they are all interesting and unique individuals. The professors make the classes fun and not boring like some I've had in the past. All of my classes I find easy because I'm putting myself into them, and I'm not fooling around. I like the campus, too. It's really nice and easy to get around because all of the facilities are really close. I really look forward to going to school everyday.

Revised Topic Sentence: *Going to college was the best decision I ever made.*

2. <u>It is hard to make a living by painting</u>. First, I make sure I have all the supplies I need. I check to make sure I have the right kind of paper and the right brushes. Then, I need to get a bowl full of lukewarm water. Hot water and cold water will break down the brushes, and then the brushes will be unusable. I also have to make sure I have a towel or paper towels because I have to wipe off the water and paint once I'm done with a particular

color. Finally, I can decide what I'm going to paint. Sometimes I have a plan, but most of the time, I will just place my brush on the paper and let my imagination take over.

Revised Topic Sentence: *I love to paint, and I always want to be prepared before I start.*

3. <u>Not many people believe in horoscopes.</u> But I like to learn what the sun and the moon have to do with a person's moods and how the signs of the zodiac interact with one another. The moon phases are what fascinate me the most. Each phase of the moon affects each sign a different way and at different times. I also find it fascinating how a horoscope can be so closely related to what I do every day. I always read it every night before I go to bed so I can see how the prediction matches with the day I had.

Revised Topic Sentence: *Horoscopes are fun when you know how to predict them.*

🌱 Practice 1B   Write a topic sentence for each of the following paragraphs.

1. *Volunteering is very rewarding.*

I feel as if I have given a part of myself to someone, and I always get lost in what I do. I put so much of myself into volunteering that it gives me a feeling of self-worth. I love helping both elderly people and helpless animals that need the help that they don't get. I believe that the animals can tell someone is there helping them. I also think that volunteering makes elderly people feel better about themselves because it shows them that someone cares.

2. *I love the feeling of waking up after camping in the mountains.*

As I look out the tent door, I see the ground covered in dew from the night before, and the smell of pine is everywhere. I can hear the birds chirping as the sun begins to rise. I step out into the crisp summer air and realize how refreshing and clean mountain air can be. I turn in a circle slowly and see the mountains in the distance with a bit of snow on the tops. I walk over to the fire pit and light a fire for the relaxing day that lies ahead.

3. *Long-distance relationships are difficult to maintain.*

If you go to a college in one state and your girlfriend or boyfriend goes to school in a different state, it will be a challenge to stay together. No matter how strong the feelings you have for each other, being far apart can be lonely. Eventually, one person meets someone who is very interesting. The two might start out being friends, but the friendship may develop into more than that. Before long, the long distance relationship is stressed to the breaking point.

Darryl's Revision   When Darryl looks back at his topic sentence, he realizes it does not accurately introduce what he talks about in his paragraph. His topic sentence only tells readers that he went to Alaska, not that he was on his own in a new place with his sister.

Topic Sentence: I went to Alaska last summer.

He decides to expand his topic sentence so that it introduces all the details that will follow in his paragraph:

Revised Topic Sentence: **When** I went to Alaska last summer, **I was relieved to be on my own to work and happy to be with my sister.**

He feels that this topic sentence introduces the general idea of his summer with Amy and will let him talk about what he did while visiting his sister.

Your Revision   With these guidelines in mind, revise your topic sentence.

Your Topic Sentence: _____

_____

Your Revised Topic Sentence: _____

_____

Development

> ✔ Does the paragraph contain *specific* details that support the topic sentence?
> ✔ Does the paragraph include *enough* details to explain the topic sentence fully?

Details are the building blocks of a paragraph. The details in your paragraph should be as specific as possible, and you should provide enough details to support your topic sentence. If you keep both of these guidelines in mind, you will develop your paragraphs adequately and specifically.

How can you know if your details are specific enough? What is a specific detail, as opposed to a general detail? Look at the following examples, and see how they move from general to specific and from abstract to concrete. As you learned in Chapter 3, concrete words refer to items you can see, hear, touch, smell, or taste. Abstract words, on the other hand, refer to ideas and concepts like *companionship* and *shelter*.

companionship (general, abstract)
> animal
>> dog
>>> golden retriever
>>>> friendly golden retriever
>>>>> friendly golden retriever named Portia (specific, concrete)

shelter (general, abstract)
> apartment
>> one-bedroom apartment
>>> one-bedroom apartment with a swimming pool and rec room
>>>> one-bedroom apartment with a swimming pool and rec room near campus
>>>>> one-bedroom apartment with a swimming pool and rec room near campus for $500 per month (specific, concrete)

❉ Practice 2A   Underline the most specific word or phrase in each group.

1. newspaper, crossword puzzle, advertising, <u>The Sunday Sun</u>, articles

2. animals, cat, fur, <u>Persian cat</u>, domestic animal

3. West Edmonton Mall, shopping mall, food court, <u>hot dog on a stick</u>, food

4. sports, <u>home run</u>, baseball, plays, team

5. entertainment center, surround sound, living room, home, <u>Bose speakers</u>

✳ Practice 2B   Fill in the blanks so that each sequence moves from the general and abstract to the specific and concrete. *Answers will vary.*

1. homework

   _____

     _____

       _____

2. _____

     love

       _____

         _____

3. nature

     _____

       _____

         _____

4. _____

     _____

       _____

         contact lenses

5. _____

     _____

       picture frame

         _____

🖉 Darryl's Revision   When Darryl looks at his first draft, he realizes that he can make his details much more specific and concrete. Here are three sentences that he revises (with concrete details in bold type):

Revised: Everything was green, **especially the lush mountains and open fields.**

Revised: My new job was in a **fish canning** factory.

Revised: Every night, I would go home to my sister's **small white** house, **which was always neat and comfortable.**

In addition to providing specific, concrete details, you also need to furnish *enough* details to support the main idea of your paragraph. Without enough details, the main idea of a paragraph is not adequately developed, and you may not be communicating your point.

❦ Practice 3A   List three details that could support each of the following sentences. *Answers will vary.*

1. Boats seem to disappear in the Bermuda Triangle.

    _____

    _____

    _____

2. Limousines are a great way to travel around.

    _____

    _____

    _____

3. I hope that I have enough money for the trip.

    _____

    _____

    _____

4. Computer hackers can get into any program they want to.

    _____

    _____

    _____

5. Miracles can happen when people believe they can.

    _____

    _____

    _____

❦ Practice 3B   Develop two of the following topic sentences into paragraphs with enough specific details. *Answers will vary.*

1. Soft music is good background music while studying.

2. MTV should provide more music videos.

3. When I rearrange my room, I feel calm.

4. Swordfish are the most wanted fish among fishermen.

5. Los Angeles is a top vacation spot for young families.

Darryl's Revision   The sentences in Darryl's paragraph need *more* details and *more specific* details to communicate his message as effectively as possible. He accomplishes this by adding more details about his job in the fish canning factory. He writes about how he was able to talk with his sister every night; and he thinks about how he learned something important by the end of the summer.

> When I went to Alaska last summer, I was relieved to be on my own to work and happy to be with my sister. I was glad to finally be away from Mom and Dad for a while. I looked around. Everything was green, **especially the lush mountains and open fields.** I could here the ocean. I was really glad to see my sister, Amy. **She is the reason I went to Alaska.** I only had one day before I started my new job. I just walked to and from work. My new job was in a **fish canning** factory--**Great Northern Packing Company.** I had to stand up all day, I had to chop up fish as fast as possable. **There were lots of new tasks to learn.** My friend back home worked in a sardine factory. Every night, I would go home to my sister's **small white** house, **which was always neat and comfortable.** She just lived about six blocks away from the factory. Since my sister Amy got married. I hardly ever see her. She moved to Alaska right after her wedding. But we made up for lost time last summer. We talked every night. **We talked about everything in our lives.** It was great. So that was my summer. Working in a fish canning factory may not sound exotic. It was for me. A river rafting guide sounds exotic. I earned enough money too pay for my **college** tuition. I also became very close to my sister. We spent so much time together. I had **lots of** fun. **The whole summer taught me something. I was happy and extremely proud of my sister and myself.**

Your Revision   Add more details to your paragraph to make your sentences as interesting as possible.

Unity

> ✔ Do all the sentences in the paragraph support the topic sentence?

A paragraph has *unity* when its topic sentence and supporting details focus on only one idea. All the sentences in the paragraph should relate directly to the paragraph's controlling idea or topic sentence. Information that does not expand on the main idea is not relevant and therefore does not belong in the paragraph.

Practice 4A   Cross out the three irrelevant sentences in the following paragraph.

> My Grandpa was a wonderful man. He was a man who did everything he could for his community. He helped built the local mall, which to this day still stands. He also built the movie theatre. ~~I love to watch movies~~. He also built the drive-in theatre, which still shows movies every summer. He was also the mayor of the town for many years. ~~Mayors have difficult jobs~~. He was always involved and very active in the community. ~~Volunteer work is an admirable pastime~~. He will be remembered and loved for always and forever.

Practice 4B   Rewrite the following paragraph, deleting the three irrelevant sentences.

> I believe that adoption is wonderful. Adoption gives a child a chance to live a better lifestyle. ~~Adopted parents are required to have a background check on them to prove that they are financially stable and will provide a good home. Everyone should watch their finances~~. Children who are adopted are lucky. They are given a home full of love and support. ~~Family life is very important~~. They may not have been given that opportunity for a better home if it weren't for the birth parents. It is hard for birth parents at times because they are giving up their child, but adoption is often best for the child.

Darryl's Revision   Darryl sees now that some of his supporting sentences are not directly related to his topic sentence. The comments about his friend back home and river rafting guides do not support his topic sentence. If these details were dropped, the revised paragraph would read as follows:

> When I went to Alaska last summer, I was relieved to be on my own to work and happy to be with my sister. I was glad to finally be away from Mom and Dad for a while. I looked around. Everything was green, especially the lush mountains and open fields. I could here the ocean. I was really glad to see my sister, Amy. She is the reason I went to Alaska. I only had one day before I started my new job. I just walked to and from work. My new job was in a fish canning factory--Great Northern Packing Company. I had to stand up all day, I had to chop up fish as fast as possable. There were lots of new tasks to learn. ~~My friend back home worked in a sardine factory.~~ Every night, I would go home to my sister's small white house, which was always neat and comfortable. She just lived about six blocks away from the factory. Since my sister Amy got married. I hardly ever see her. She moved to Alaska right after her wedding. But we made up for lost time last summer. We talked every night. We talked about everything in our lives. It was great. So that was my summer. Working in a fish canning factory may not sound exotic. It was for me. ~~A river rafting guide sounds exotic.~~ I earned enough money too pay for my college tuition. I also became very close to my sister. We spent so much time together. I had lots of fun. The whole summer taught me something. I was happy and extremely proud of my sister and myself.

 Your Revision   Read your paragraph carefully, and cross out any irrelevant words, phrases, or sentences.

Organization

> ✔ Is the paragraph organized logically?

How you organize your paragraph depends to a great extent on your topic and your purpose. What are you trying to accomplish? What order will help you accomplish your purpose?

🌾 Practice 5A   Reorganize the following sentences so that they are in a logical order.

5   Many get into cars after they've been drinking at parties, sometimes causing fatal accidents.

4   They attend parties and don't think about the consequences of drinking.

1   Binge drinking is a growing problem among college students.

3   When college students get drunk, they may have unprotected sex.

2   Some college students have died from alcohol poisoning.

🌾 Practice 5B   Reorganize the following sentences so they are in a logical order.

6   They can recycle and use products wisely on a daily basis.

1   Pollution in California is a growing problem.

2   It is affecting people, animals, and the atmosphere.

3   The earth is being destroyed, and it can't be repaired.

5   But even individuals can help.

4   The state is trying to control pollution.

✎ Darryl's Revision   In Chapter 4, Darryl decided that the best way to organize his paragraph was from the least important point to the most important. But now he needs to make sure that every detail is in the right place. He notices a sentence about the distance from Amy's house to her work that is out of order, so he moves the sentence to the part of the paragraph that focuses on Amy's house.

General Statement   When I went to Alaska last summer, I was relieved to be on my own to work and happy to be with my sister. I was glad to finally be away from *More Specific* Mom and Dad for a while. I looked around. Everything was green, especially the lush mountains and open fields. I could here the ocean. I was really glad to see my sister, Amy. She is the reason I went to Alaska. I only had one day before I started my new job. ~~I just walked to and from work.~~ My new job *Concrete examples* was in a fish canning factory--Great Northern Packing Company. I had to stand up all day, I had to chop *Specific details* up fish as fast as possable. There were lots of new tasks to learn. Every night, I would go home to my sister's small white house, which was always neat and comfortable. She just lived about six blocks away from the factory. **I just walked to and from work.** Since my sister Amy got married. I hardly ever see her. She moved to Alaska right after her wedding. But we made up for lost time last summer. We talked every night. We talked about everything in our lives. It was great. So that was my summer. Working in a fish canning factory may not sound exotic. It was for me. I earned enough money too pay for my college tuition. I also became very close to my sister. We spent so much time together. I had lots of fun. The whole summer taught me something. I was happy and extremely proud of my sister and myself.

Concrete details

Specific references

🌿 Your Revision   Look again at the order you chose in Chapter 4: Is it best for accomplishing your purpose? Are all your details in their proper place?

Coherence

> ✔ Do the sentences in the paragraph move smoothly and logically from one to the next?

A *coherent* paragraph is smooth, not choppy, and readers move logically from one thought to the next. They can see a clear relationship between the ideas. In other words, the ideas "cohere" or stick together to make their point. The most successful technique for making paragraphs coherent is well-chosen transitions.

Transitions   *Transitional words and phrases* are like bridges or links between your thoughts. They show your readers how one idea is related to another or when you are moving to a new point. Good use of transitions makes your writing smooth rather than choppy.

Choppy: Working in a fish canning factory may not sound exotic. It was for me.

Smooth: Working in a fish canning factory may not sound exotic. **But it** was for me.

Transitions have very specific meanings, so you should take care to use the most logical one.

Confusing: Working in a fish canning factory may not sound exotic. **Meanwhile,** it was for me.

Here is a list of some common transitional words and phrases that will make your writing more coherent. They are listed by meaning.

Some Common Transitions

Addition:	*moreover, further, furthermore, besides, and, and then, likewise, also, nor, too, again, in addition, next, first, second, third, finally, last*
Comparison:	*similarly, likewise, in like manner*
Contrast:	*but, yet, and yet, however, still, nevertheless, on the other hand, on the contrary, after all, in contrast to, at the same time, otherwise*
Emphasis:	*in fact, indeed, to tell the truth, in any event, after all, actually, of course*
Example:	*for example, for instance, in this case*
Time:	*meanwhile, at length, immediately, soon, after a few days, now, in the meantime, afterward, later, then, sometimes, other times, still*
Place:	*here, there, beyond, nearby, opposite, adjacent to, near*
Purpose:	*to this end, for this purpose, with this objective*
Result:	*hence, therefore, accordingly, consequently, thus, as a result, then, so*
Summary:	*to conclude, to sum up, to summarize, in brief, on the whole, in sum, in short, as I have said, in other words, that is*

For more information on transitions, see pages 79–80.

Practice 6A   Using the list above for reference, *underline any transitions you see* in the following paragraphs. Not all transitions are on the list here.

1. One summer I went with my friend Liz to my Uncle's cabin. We decided that we would take the motorbike around the lake and maybe check out new trails. I was ahead of her when we did find a new trail. I was

going as fast as the motorbike would let me. But I know I should have been going slower because there were huge tree roots sticking out of the middle of the track. Finally, the tree roots caught up with me, and my motorbike flipped upside down. All I can remember is waking up underneath the motorbike with Liz calling my name. I guess I passed out for about five minutes. Luckily I had my helmet on because I could have been hurt. Consequently, I did learn a lesson on that journey: slow down when I don't know a trail.

2. I once worked for an incompetent manager. As a result, I found my job difficult to deal with. My manager was constantly taking credit for work I had performed, and I became more and more resentful of the way I was treated. The manager refused to give me a raise for my good work, yet she continually received raises in pay based upon my performance. I finally decided enough was enough and walked out the door one day. Afterward, a friend who still worked for the company told me the manager was no longer praised for a job well done.

3. Maintaining a household is difficult when people lead such busy lives. When people are busy with school, work, and extracurricular activities, the last thing on their minds is how long the grass is or whether the laundry has been done. There just isn't enough time in the day to take care of all the responsibilities. Therefore, the little, but necessary, jobs pile up and become enormous jobs. On the whole, it's better to just keep up with the jobs as they are still small.

🌿 Practice 6B   Fill in the blanks in the following paragraphs with logical transitions. The list on page 36 can guide you in your choices, but it is not a complete list of all transitions. *Answers may vary.*

1. Watching TV can be addicting. Anytime I turn on the TV, I feel compelled to watch it. It doesn't even matter what's on—I just watch and watch and watch. __*However*__, I get very little accomplished when I turn on the TV. __*Sometimes*__ I have to restrain myself from turning the TV on; __*nevertheless*__, the TV usually wins. I think I'm just going to have to get rid of the TV.

2. I work two full-time jobs and go to school full-time. __*Therefore*__, I get very little sleep. At the end of each school term, I try to catch up on sleep; __*however*__, because of the two jobs, that doesn't always happen. It's funny.

I think people actually get used to living on so little sleep. ___*In fact*___, I think people can train themselves to get by, which is why I'm still able to function after all these years with very little sleep.

3. Staying in shape is not difficult as long as people choose to work out and eat right. The problem is that most people can't get motivated to exercise and don't want to give up their eating habits. ___*Therefore*___, most people don't stay in shape. Once people decide that their health is important, ___*however*___, they become motivated and try to stay on a work-out and diet schedule. Once people get past the two- or three-week mark, the schedule is stuck in their routines, and they ___*finally*___ discover how easy it is to keep on track.

✎ Darryl's Revision   When Darryl checks his paragraph for transitions, he decides his writing would be much clearer and smoother if he added more signal words to help the readers. So he adds two more transitions that show the relationship between his ideas and make his paragraph more readable.

> When I went to Alaska last summer, I was relieved to be on my own to work and happy to be with my sister. I was glad to finally be away from Mom and Dad for a while. I looked around. Everything was green, especially the lush mountains and open fields. I could here the ocean. I was really glad to see my sister, Amy. **In fact,** she is the reason I went to Alaska. I only had one day before I started my new job. My new job was in a fish canning factory--Great Northern Packing Company. I had to stand up all day, I had to chop up fish as fast as possable. There were lots of new tasks to learn. Every night, I would go home to my sister's small white house, which was always neat and comfortable. She just lived about six blocks away from the factory. I just walked to and from work. Since my sister Amy got married. I hardly ever see her. She moved to Alaska right after her wedding. But we made up for lost time last summer. We talked every night. We talked about everything in our lives. It was great. So that was my summer. Working in a fish canning factory may not sound exotic. **But** it was for me. I earned enough money too pay for my college tuition. I also became very close to my sister. We spent so much

time together. I had lots of fun. **As a result,** the whole summer taught me something. I was happy and extremely
proud of my sister and myself.

In addition to *but*, what transitions did Darryl add to his paragraph?

In fact, as a result

List the meaning of all three transitions in Darryl's paragraph:

1. Transition: *in fact*   Meaning: *emphasis*
2. Transition: *but*   Meaning: *contrast*
3. Transition: *as a result*   Meaning: *result*

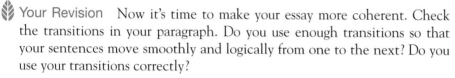 **Your Revision** Now it's time to make your essay more coherent. Check
the transitions in your paragraph. Do you use enough transitions so that
your sentences move smoothly and logically from one to the next? Do you
use your transitions correctly?

Darryl's Revised Paragraph After revising his topic sentence, his development, his unity, his organization, and his coherence, Darryl wrote the following revised paragraph. All of his revisions are in bold type.

> **When** I went to Alaska last summer, **I was relieved to
> be on my own to work and happy to be with my sister.** I
> was glad to finally be away from Mom and Dad for a while.
> I looked around. Everything was green, **especially the lush
> mountains and open fields.** I could here the ocean. I was
> really glad to see my sister, Amy. **In fact, she is the reason
> I went to Alaska.** I only had one day before I started my
> new job. ~~I just walked to and from work.~~ My new job was
> in a **fish canning** factory--**Great Northern Packing Com-
> pany.** I had to stand up all day, I had to chop up fish as fast
> as possible. **There were lots of new tasks to learn.**
> ~~My friend back home worked in a sardine factory.~~ Every
> night, I would go home to my sister's **small white** house,
> **which was always neat and comfortable.** She just lived
> about six blocks away from the factory. **I just walked to
> and from work.** Since my sister Amy got married. I hardly
> ever see her. She moved to Alaska right after her wedding.
> But we made up for lost time last summer. We talked every
> night. **We talked about everything in our lives.** It was

great. So that was my summer. Working in a fish canning factory may not sound exotic. **But** it was for me. ~~**A river rafting guide sounds exotic.**~~ I earned enough money too pay for my college tuition. I also became very close to my sister. We spent so much time together. I had **lots of** fun. **As a result, the whole summer taught me something. I was happy and extremely proud of my sister and myself.**

Your Revised Paragraph   Now that you have applied all the revision strategies to your own writing, write your revised paragraph here.

_____

_____

_____

_____

_____

_____

_____

_____

_____

_____

_____

_____

_____

Editing

After you revise your paragraph, it's time to edit it. Editing involves finding your grammar, punctuation, mechanics, and spelling errors and correcting them. (*Mechanics* refers to capital letters, numbers, and abbreviations.) The choices you make in editing communicate just as much as your words. They help your reader move from one idea to the next in your writing.

For easy reference, we divide editing into three categories: sentences, punctuation and mechanics, and word choice and spelling. See the Editing Checklist below. This checklist doesn't cover all the grammar and usage problems you may find in your writing, but it focuses on some of the main errors college students make.

 Editing Checklist

SENTENCES

✔ Does each sentence have a main subject and verb?

✔ Do all subjects and verbs agree?

✔ Do all pronouns agree with their nouns?

✔ Are modifiers as close as possible to the words they modify?

PUNCTUATION AND MECHANICS

✔ Are sentences punctuated correctly?

✔ Are words capitalized properly?

WORD CHOICE AND SPELLING

✔ Are words used correctly?

✔ Are words spelled correctly?

YOUR EQ (EDITING QUOTIENT)

Editing is finding and correcting errors in your individual sentences. Since sentence skills are the heart of this book, you might want to start the editing stage by finding your EQ (or editing quotient). Knowing your EQ will tell you which errors you recognize and which errors you need to study. Use Practice 1 to determine your EQ.

Practice 1 EQ Test   In the following paragraphs, underline and label (a, b, c) the errors you find from the following list. Then list each error by name on the lines below the paragraph. Do not make any corrections. At this time, all you want to do is find the errors. The number of lines represents the number of errors in the paragraph. The first couple errors are done for you. *Answers are in Practice 2.*

abbreviation	fragment	pronoun reference
capitalization	modifier error	run-on
comma	number	subject-verb agreement
confused word	pronoun	verb form
end punctuation	pronoun agreement	

1. Rambo is my playful dog. ⓐMy dad wanted a big ferocious dog, my mom and I wanted a cute fluffy dog. We decided to get the cute fluffy dog but give it a ferocious name, Rambo. Rambo is 3/4 poodle and 1/4 cocker spaniel. He's the cutest dog. ⓑWith the greatest personality. He has never attacked a person or another animal he is one of the gentlest dogs that I know. He does get an attitude sometimes and wont listen. If you have food. Then he'll love you forever. Rambo loves anybody and will be your best friend forever.

   ⓐ run-on _____

   ⓑ fragment _____

   ⓒ _____

   ⓓ _____

2. Jet skiing can be dangerous, as I have learned in the past. I was at a lake one summer day with a few friends. We brought a boat, a couple of jet skis, some water skis, knee boards, and wake boards. Since the jet skis were on the beach and it was getting dark out. One of my friends and I decided that we would take the jet skis to the loading dock. As we were

waiting to load them onto the truck, we was just fooling around and showing off. I guess we got carried away. One thing led to another we were just about going full speed. We were also getting too close to the loading dock, but there was still enough room. We were doing 360 degree turns and was a little too close—we crashed. My jet ski collided with hers. She jumped off as mine flew on top of hers, and I flew in front and over mine. Both jet skis were wrecked, but we were ok. That experience was scary and it shook us up, but we've both learned to be more careful.

(a.) _____

(b.) _____

(c.) _____

(d.) _____

3. Smoking is a dangerous and bad habit. Smoking is know to kill people in many ways, and people know that, but they don't seem to care. The majority of people who smoke are the younger generation, teens, and young adults. Tobacco companies advertising smoking so that it appeals to the young. Younger people are drawn into smoking. Because of peer pressure. They think that it's cool and that everyone will like them because they're "cool." It's not cool it's wrong. Smoking doesn't only kill you, it makes you smell and it's a dirty habit.

(a.) _____

(b.) _____

(c.) _____

(d.) _____

4. Credit cards can be deceiving. They are sent out to anyone with a bank account many people can't afford to have a credit card. A person can get a card and use it whenever they spend or buy. A person gets the bill and pays the minimum required. They may even pay it all off. If they have the money. Once a person is in a situation like this. Life can be very difficult for them. A lot of people get in debt because of credit cards, which is why anyone who is unable to financially deal with a credit card should not be allowed access.

(a.) _____

(b.) _____

(c.) _____

(d.) _____

(e.) _____

5. There are many teen idols in children's lives who are not good role models. Looking up to idols, lives can be changed. Idols today are just not what they used to be. They are dressing more daringly. Showing that dressing a certain way is cool. Some are into drugs, violence, and weapons. What does this say to children? Drugs, violence, and weapons are good. No. Society is changing it's telling children that bad is good.

(a.) _____

(b.) _____

(c.) _____

(d.) _____

6. Migraine Headaches are the worst headache that people can have. When I get a migraine I feel terrible. First, I see a black dot whenever I blink it grows bigger with each blink. Then, on either the left or right temple, it feels like someone is hammering a nail into my head. Finally, I feel queasy. To rid of this kind of headache. I usually will lie down in a dark quiet room with a cold compress over my forehead. I take an Advil to help me sleep. When I wake up, I usually feel better, but there is the odd time that the headache will last for days. I hate migraine headaches.

(a.) _____

(b.) _____

(c.) _____

(d.) _____

(e.) _____

7. There are 3 types of eating disorders: anorexia, bulimia, and compulsive eating. Although men and women of all ages are affected by eating disorders. The majority affected are adolescent females. Some situations that contribute to these diseases are low self-esteem, helplessness, and the fear of being fat. Anorexia is caused by a person starving him or herself those suffering from bulimia will purge. People battling compulsive

eating disorder will eat whenever they feel depressed or upset. These disorders are dangerous and are used as severe ways of battling emotional problems they could possible lead to death.

a. _____

b. _____

c. _____

d. _____

8. Opposite-sex best friends are friends who act like big brothers or little sisters. These kind of best friends will tease and joke they will also be their whenever you need help. They will give great advise about the opposite sex, and they will also comfort and offer a shoulder to lean on. Opposite-sex best friends will always except and never judge. Because they understand who their best friends are.

a. _____

b. _____

c. _____

d. _____

e. _____

f. _____

g. _____

h. _____

9. One of my most vivid childhood memories were the day I was introduced to my Mother and Grandmother. Although I was only four years old at the time the image is stuck in my mind like a photograph. I remember being very intimidated and frightened of my mother. Instead of going to my new mom. I first went to my grandmother. But when my new mother spoke to me, it sounded like violins playing. She was very magical she had a calm about her. She made me feel as if I was going to be safe, and my frightened feelings went away.

a. _____

b. _____

c. _____

d. _____

(e.) _____

(f.) _____

10. During the summer of 2000. I learned a life lesson. I thought that since I was 18 I was able to do what I wanted so I disobeyed my father and went to a nightclub. I did not come home that night or the next couple of nights. I thought that I was teaching them a lesson, I was actually learning one. Once I ran out of money, clean clothes, and places to stay, I finally realized that I was making a mistake. I went back home. I didn't realize until I was on my own for a few days how difficult it is in the real world. At the time, I was immature and trying to grow up the way I wanted. I now value my parents and the life their helping me lead.

(a.) _____

(b.) _____

(c.) _____

(d.) _____

❈ Practice 2 Answers   Use the following answer key to score your answers to Practice 1.

1. Rambo is my rambunctious dog. (a)My dad wanted a big ferocious dog, my mom and I wanted a cute fluffy dog. We decided to get the cute fluffy dog but give it a ferocious name, Rambo. Rambo is 3/4 poodle and 1/4 cocker spaniel. He's the cutest dog. (b)With the greatest personality. (c)He has never acted against a person or another animal he is one of the gentlest dogs that I know. He does get an attitude sometimes and won't listen. (d)If you have food. Then he'll love you forever. Rambo loves anybody and will be your best friend forever.

(a.) run-on _____

(b.) fragment _____

(c.) run-on _____

(d.) fragment _____

2. Jet skiing can be dangerous, as I have learned in the past. I was at a lake one summer day with a few friends. We brought a boat, a couple of jet skis, some water skis, knee boards, and wake boards. (a)Since the jet skis were on the beach and it was getting dark out. One of my friends and I decided that we would take the jet skis to the loading dock. As we were

waiting to load them onto the truck, ᵇwe was just fooling around and showing off. I guess we got carried away. ᶜOne thing led to another we were just about going full speed. We were also getting too close to the loading dock, but there was still enough room. We were doing 360 degree turns and ᵈwas a little too close—we crashed. My jet ski collided with hers. She jumped off as mine flew on top of hers, and I flew in front and over mine. Both jet skis were wrecked, but we were ok. That experience was scary, and it shook us up, but we've both learned to be more careful.

a. fragment _____

b. subject-verb agreement _____

c. run-on _____

d. subject-verb agreement _____

3. Smoking is a dangerous and bad habit. Smoking is ᵃknow to kill people in many ways, and people know that. But they don't seem to care. The majority of people who smoke are the younger generation, teens, and young adults. Tobacco companies ᵇadvertising smoking so that it appeals to the young. Younger people are drawn into smoking. ᶜBecause of peer pressure. They think that it's cool and that everyone will like them because they're "cool." ᵈIt's not cool it's wrong. Smoking doesn't only kill you, it makes you smell and it's a dirty habit.

a. verb form _____

b. verb form _____

c. fragment _____

d. run-on _____

4. Credit cards can be deceiving. ᵃThey are sent out to anyone with a bank account many people can't afford to have a credit card. ᵇA person can get a card and use it whenever *they* spend or buy. ᶜA person gets the bill and pays the minimum required. *They* may even pay it all off. If *they* have the money. ᵈOnce a person is in a situation like this. Life can be very difficult for ᵉthem. A lot of people get in debt because of credit cards, which is why anyone who is unable to deal with a credit card should not be allowed to have one.

a. run-on _____

b. pronoun agreement _____

c. pronoun agreement _____

(d.) fragment _____

(e.) pronoun agreement _____

5. There are many teen idols in children's lives ⓐwho are not good role models. ⓑLooking up to idols, lives can be changed. Idols today are just not what they used to be. They are dressing more provocatively. ⓒShowing that dressing a certain way is cool. Some are into drugs, violence, and weapons. What does this say to children? Drugs, violence, and weapons are good. No. ⓓSociety is changing it's telling children that bad is good.

(a.) modifier error _____

(b.) modifier error _____

(c.) fragment _____

(d.) run-on _____

6. Migraine ⓐHeadaches are the worst headache that people can have. When I get a migraineⓑ, I feel terrible. ⓒFirst, I see a black dot whenever I blink it grows bigger with each blink. Then, on either the left or right temple, it feels like someone is hammering a nail into my head. Finally, I feel queasy. ⓓTo get rid of this kind of headache. I usually will lie down in a dark quiet room with a cold compress over my forehead. I take an Advil to help me sleep. When I wake up, I usually feel better, but there is the odd time that the headache will last for days. I hate migraine headaches ⓔ?

(a.) capitalization _____

(b.) comma _____

(c.) run-on _____

(d.) fragment _____

(e.) end punctuation _____

7. There are ⓐ3 types of eating disorders: anorexia, bulimia, and compulsive eating. ⓑAlthough men and women of all ages are affected by eating disorders. The majority affected are adolescent females. Some situations that contribute to these diseases are low self-esteem, helplessness, and the fear of being fat. ⓒAnorexia is caused by a person starving him or herself those suffering from bulimia will purge. People battling compulsive eating disorder will eat whenever they feel depressed or upset.

[ⓓ]<u>These disorders are dangerous and are used as severe ways of battling emotional problems they could possibly lead to death</u>.

(a.) number _____

(b.) fragment _____

(c.) run-on _____

(d.) run-on _____

8. An opposite-sex best friend is a friend who acts like a big brother or little [ⓐ]sis. [ⓑ]<u>These kinds of best friends will tease and joke</u> [ⓒ]<u>they will also be</u> [ⓓ]<u>their whenever help is needed</u>. They will give great [ⓔ]<u>advise</u> about the opposite sex, and they will also comfort and offer a shoulder to lean on. Opposite-sex best friends will always [ⓕ]<u>except</u> and never judge. [ⓖ]<u>Because they understand who</u> [ⓗ]<u>there best friends are</u>.

(a.) abbreviation _____

(b.) pronoun reference _____

(c.) run-on _____

(d.) confused word _____

(e.) confused word _____

(f.) confused word _____

(g.) fragment _____

(h.) confused word _____

9. [ⓐ]One of my most vivid childhood memories <u>were</u> the day I was introduced to my [ⓑ]<u>Mother</u> and [ⓒ]<u>Grandmother</u>. Although I was only four years old at the time [ⓓ]<u>,</u> the image is stuck in my mind like a photograph. I remember being very intimidated and frightened by my mother. [ⓔ]<u>Instead of going to my new mom</u>. I first went to my grandmother. But when my new mother spoke to me, it sounded like violins playing. [ⓕ]<u>She was very magical she had a calm and collected aura about her</u>. She made me feel as if I was going to be safe, and my frightened feelings went away.

(a.) subject-verb agreement _____

(b.) capitalization _____

(c.) capitalization _____

(d.) comma _____

(e.) fragment _____

(f.) run-on _____

10. [ⓐ]<u>During the summer of 2000</u>. I learned a life lesson. I thought that since I was 18 I was able to do what I wanted [ⓑ]<u>,</u> so I disobeyed my father and went to a nightclub. I did not come home that night or the next couple of nights. [ⓒ]<u>I thought that I was teaching them a lesson. I was actually learning one</u>. Once I ran out of money, clean clothes, and places to stay, I finally realized that I was making a mistake. I went back home. I didn't realize until I was on my own for a few days how difficult it is in the real world. At the time, I was immature and trying to grow up the way I wanted. I now value my parents and the life [ⓓ]<u>their</u> helping me lead.

(a.) fragment _____

(b.) comma _____

(c.) run-on _____

(d.) confused word _____

🌿 **Practice 3 Find Your EQ**   Turn to Appendix X, and chart the errors you didn't identify. Then record your errors on the second EQ chart, and see what pattern they form.

HOW TO EDIT

Editing is a two-part job: First, you must locate the errors. Then you must know how to correct them.

Finding Your Errors

Since you can't correct errors until you find them, a major part of editing is proofreading. *Proofreading* is reading to catch your sentence-level errors. If you do not proofread carefully, you will not be able to find and correct the errors that interfere with your message.

When we proofread, we often read what we think we wrote instead of what we actually wrote. The best way to overcome this problem is to read your writing out of logical order. For example, you might read your paragraph backwards, starting with the last sentence first. This helps you concentrate on your sentences rather than your ideas.

Another technique is to keep an Error Log, in which you list the mistakes you make. An Error Log is provided for you in Appendix 6. To use this log in proofreading, read your paper for one error at a time. For example, if you often write fragments and run-on sentences, read your paper once to catch fragments and a second time to find run-ons. Then read it again to find other types of errors.

You can also use Grammar Check on your computer, which will point out possible grammar errors and make suggestions for rewording some of your sentences. We all make errors in our writing, but part of the writing process is to find and correct these errors before we turn in written work.

Working Together

Just as working with others—or collaboration—is important when you revise, it is also important in editing. You might work in groups, in pairs, with a tutor, or with a friend. But having someone read your writing is always a good idea when you are preparing a final draft because that person might find errors that you missed. Collaborative work is built into every chapter in Part II.

When others read your writing, they might want to use the Editing Symbols on the inside back cover to highlight your errors for you. You can then use the page references on the chart to guide you to the part of this textbook that explains how to correct those errors.

Correcting Your Errors

After you find your errors, you need to correct them. Part II of this text will help you do just that. It is a complete handbook. You can use it along with the Editing Symbols on the inside back cover.

As you proofread, record your errors in the Error Log and Spelling Log. If you do this regularly as you write, these logs will eventually help you get control of the most common errors in your writing.

Finally, use the Editing Checklist at the beginning of this chapter to help you edit your writing. Work with your writing until you can answer *yes* to every question on the checklist.

Practice 4 Using the Handbook   Using the instruction in Part II, list the page references for the 14 different types of errors you worked with in Practice 1.

abbreviation   page _____

capitalization   page _____

comma   page _____

confused word	page _____
end punctuation	page _____
fragment	page _____
modifier error	page _____
number	page _____
pronoun	page _____
pronoun agreement	page _____
pronoun reference	page _____
run-on	page _____
subject-verb agreement	page _____
verb form	page _____

Practice 5 Using the Error Log and the Spelling Log   Turn to Appendixes 6 and 7, and start an Error Log and a Spelling Log of your own with the errors you didn't identify in Practice 1. For each error, write out the mistake, the Handbook reference, and your correction.

Practice 6 Using the Editing Checklist   Use the Editing Checklist at the beginning of this chapter to edit two of the paragraphs from Practice 1. Rewrite the entire paragraphs.

Darryl's Editing   When Darryl proofreads his paper for grammar, punctuation, mechanics, and spelling, he finds five errors. He looks them up in Part II and makes the corrections.

The first error is a run-on sentence:

Run-on: I had to stand up all day, I had to chop up fish as fast as possable.

Darryl realizes that this sentence has too many subjects and verbs without any linking words or end punctuation between them. He looks up "run-on" on page 128 of Part II and corrects the error by putting a comma and a co-ordinating conjunction (*and*) between the two sentences.

Correction: I had to stand up all day, **and** I had to chop up fish as fast as possable.

He also finds a sentence that doesn't sound complete:

Fragment: Since my sister Amy got married.

When he looks up the problem in Part II (page 108), he remembers this error is called a *fragment*. It is easily corrected by connecting it to another sentence.

Correction: Since my sister Amy got married/, I hardly ever see her.

Darryl records these two errors in his error log (Appendix 6).

Next, he checks his paragraph for spelling errors. He is unsure about five words:

1. I could **here** the ocean
2. as fast as **possable**
3. **There** were lots of new tasks
4. **too** pay for my college tuition
5. **extremely** proud

He uses spell-check and a dictionary and finds out that *possable* is wrong, are all the rest right? He remembers the chapter on confused words (Chapter 30). He looks up *here*, *there*, and *too* and discovers that *there* is correct but *here* and *too* are not used correctly. So he makes the following corrections:

1. I ~~here~~ **hear** the ocean
2. as fast as ~~possable~~ **possible**
3. **There** were lots of new tasks **CORRECT**
4. ~~too~~ **to** pay for my college tuition
5. **extremely** proud **CORRECT**

He records these errors in the Spelling Log (Appendix 7).

Darryl's Edited Draft   All five of these errors are corrected in Darryl's edited draft.

> When I went to Alaska last summer, I was relieved to be on my own to work and happy to be with my sister. I was glad to finally be away from Mom and Dad for a while. I looked around. Everything was green, especially the lush mountains and open fields. I could **hear** the ocean. I was really glad to see my sister, Amy. In fact, she is the reason I went to Alaska. I only had one day before I started my new job. My new job was in a fish canning factory—Great Northern Packing Company. **I had to stand up all day, and I had to chop up fish as fast as possible.** There were lots of new tasks to learn. Every night, I would go home to my

sister's small white house, which was always neat and comfortable. She just lived about six blocks away from the factory. I just walked to and from work. **Since my sister Amy got married/, I hardly ever see her.** She moved to Alaska right after her wedding. But we made up for lost time last summer. We talked every night. We talked about everything in our lives. It was great. So that was my summer. Working in a fish canning factory may not sound exotic. But it was for me. I earned enough money **to** pay for my college tuition. I also became very close to my sister. We spent so much time together. I had lots of fun. As a result, the whole summer taught me something. I was happy and extremely proud of my sister and myself.

🌿 Your Editing   Proofread the sentences in your paragraph carefully. Use at least two of the methods from this chapter to help you find the errors you made in your paragraph. Record your errors and their corrections here.

_____

_____

_____

_____

_____

_____

_____

_____

_____

🌿 Your Edited Draft   Now write out a corrected draft of your paragraph.

_____

_____

_____

_____

_____

_____

_____

_____

_____

_____

Review of the Writing Process

Clues for Review

- The **writing process** is a series of cyclical tasks that involves prewriting, writing, revising, and editing.
- **Prewriting** consists of generating ideas and planning your paragraph.

  Thinking: Reading, freewriting, brainstorming, clustering, questioning, discussing

  Planning: Deciding on a subject, purpose, and audience
- **Writing** includes writing a topic sentence, developing your ideas, organizing your paragraph, and writing a draft.

  Writing a topic sentence: A limited topic and a statement about that topic

  Developing: Making details more specific; adding details and examples

  Organizing: Arranging ideas from general to particular, particular to general, chronologically, spatially, or from one extreme to another.

  Drafting: Writing a first draft
- **Revising** means "seeing again" and working with organization and development. Check these features of your paragraph:

  Topic sentence

  Development

  Unity

  Organization

  Coherence
- **Editing** involves proofreading and correcting your grammar, punctuation, mechanics, and spelling errors.

⁂ Review Practice 1

1. What are the four main parts of the writing process? *The four parts*
   are prewriting, writing, revising, and editing.

2. What is your favorite prewriting activity? Why is it your favorite?
   Answers will vary.

3. How do you prepare yourself for a writing project?
   Answers will vary.

4. Where do you usually do your academic writing? Do you write your
   first draft on a computer? What time of day do you do your best
   writing?
   Answers will vary.

5. What is the difference between revising and editing? *Revising involves con-*
   tent and organization; editing deals with grammar, punctuation, mechanics, and spelling.

6. What are the five main categories of revising?
   Revising means reviewing your topic sentence, development, unity, organization, and
   coherence.

7. Explain editing. *Editing involves grammar, punctuation, mechanics, and spelling.*

8. What are the three main phases of editing? *Editing phases are finding*
   your errors, working together, and correcting your errors.

9. Why are revising and editing so important to the final draft?
   Revising and editing work together to make what you have to say as good as it can be.

10. Do you try to get someone to read your writing before you turn it in?
    Explain your answer. _Answers will vary._ _____

    _____

🌾 **Review Practice 2**   Write a topic sentence for each of the subjects below. Then develop one topic sentence into a paragraph. _Answers will vary._

1. Award ceremonies
2. Fourth of July
3. Beautiful colors
4. Chocolate
5. Gas stations
6. My best friend
7. My future plans
8. My dream car
9. Political campaigns
10. My favorite class

🌾 **Review Practice 3**   Revise the paragraph you wrote for Review Activity 2, using the checklist on pages 24–25.

🌾 **Review Practice 4**   Edit the paragraph you wrote for Review Activity 2, using the checklist on page 41.

P · A · R · T

II

WRITING EFFECTIVE SENTENCES

This section consists of an Introduction and eight units:

The Editing Symbols (inside back cover) and the Error and Spelling Logs (Appendix 6 and 7) can help you tailor this section to your own needs.

Introduction

This handbook uses very little terminology. But sometimes talking about the language and the way it works is difficult without a shared understanding of certain basic grammar terms. For that reason, your instructor may ask you to study parts of this introduction to review basic grammar—parts of speech, phrases, and clauses. You might also use this Introduction for reference.

This section has three parts:

Parts of Speech
Phrases
Clauses

PARTS OF SPEECH

Every sentence is made up of a variety of words that play different roles. Each word, like each part of a coordinated outfit, serves a distinct function. These functions fall into eight categories:

1. Verbs
2. Nouns
3. Pronouns
4. Adjectives
5. Adverbs
6. Prepositions
7. Conjunctions
8. Interjections

Some words, such as *is*, can function in only one way—in this case, as a verb. Other words, however, can serve as different parts of speech, depending on how they are used in a sentence. For example, look at the different ways the word *paint* can be used:

Verb: We **paint** our house every five years.

(*Paint* is a verb here, telling what we do.)

Noun: The **paint** needs two days to dry.

(*Paint* functions as a noun here, telling what needs two days to dry.)

Adjective: My dog knocked over the **paint** can.

(*Paint* is an adjective here, modifying the noun *can*.)

Note how the following paragraph by Jo Goodwin Parker uses all eight of the different kinds of words to deliver a message.

> But you say to me, there are schools. Yes, there are schools. My children have no extra books, no magazines, no extra pencils, or crayons, or paper and most important of all, they do not have health. They have worms, they have infections, they have pink-eye all summer. They do not sleep well on the floor, or with me in my one bed. They do not suffer from hunger, my seventy-eight dollars keeps us alive, but they do suffer from malnutrition. Oh yes, I do remember what I was taught about health in school. It doesn't do much good. In some places there is a surplus commodities program. Not here. The county said it cost too much. There is a school lunch program. But I have two children who will already be damaged by the time they get to school.

Verbs

The **verb** is the most important word in a sentence because every other word depends on it in some way. Verbs tell what's going on in the sentence.

There are three types of verbs: action, linking, and helping. An **action verb** tells what someone or something is doing. A **linking verb** tells what someone or something is, feels, or looks like. Sometimes an action or linking verb has **helping verbs**—words that add information, such as when an action is taking place. A **complete verb** consists of an action or linking verb and all its helping verbs.

Action: The boy **hiked** up the hill.

Action: Jeremy **watches** the birds.

tape to the front of each index card (so each can be removed and placed back into position many times). Place the index cards, word side down, on the paper in the order of their number. For instance, 1–10 in the first row, 11–20 in the second row, and so on.

Have students break into teams of three or four and try to find the matching words. When a team uncovers two words that match, they must identify the part of speech before they get credit for the match. Otherwise, the pair goes back onto the board for another team to uncover and label.

The team that gets the most cards wins.

■ For more sample words, see the *Instructor's Resource Manual*, Section II, Part II.

Linking:	Myra **looks** lonely.
Linking:	I **was** happy to be chosen.
Helping:	They **will be** leaving when the job is finished.
Helping:	Jennifer **has been** taking piano lessons.
Complete Verb:	They **will be leaving** when the job is finished.
Complete Verb:	Jennifer **has been taking** piano lessons.

REVIEWING VERBS

Define each of the following types of verbs, and give an example of each.

Action: Tells what someone or something is doing. Examples will vary.

Linking: Tells what someone or something is, feels, or looks like. Examples will vary.

Helping: Adds information such as when action is taking place. Examples will vary.

What is a complete verb? Give an example with your definition.

A complete verb consists of an action or linking verb and all the helping verbs.

Examples will vary.

🌿 Practice 1 Identifying   In each of the following sentences, identify the underlined verbs as action (A), linking (L), or helping (H).

1. __L__ The baby <u>is</u> asleep.

2. __H__ We <u>have</u> looked for the best deal.

3. __A__ The outfielder <u>saw</u> the ball coming toward him.

4. __A__ Most college students <u>want</u> lower tuition.

5. __H__ Geoffrey <u>should have</u> paid for my dinner.

6. __A__ The orchestra <u>played</u> music by Bach.

7. __L__ He <u>looks</u> happy today.

8. __A__ Every Sunday, we <u>give</u> money to charity.

9. __L__ This <u>seems</u> like the best choice.

10. __H__ Marci <u>had been</u> swimming for an hour.

🌿 **Practice 2 Identifying**   Underline the complete verbs in the following sentences. Some sentences have more than one verb.

1. I <u>feed</u> my fish every morning.
2. The banker <u>forgot</u> his money.
3. My favorite restaurant <u>is</u> Steak 'n Shake.
4. This instructor <u>seems</u> strict.
5. I <u>was planning</u> a party this weekend.
6. Janelle <u>feels</u> ignored.
7. My friends <u>had been dancing</u> all night.
8. Mario <u>wished</u> for a new car.
9. Tiffany <u>has</u> five dollars.
10. The lady <u>walked</u> to the bench and <u>sat</u> down.

🌿 **Practice 3 Identifying**   List five complete verbs from the paragraph by Jo Goodwin Parker on page 61. *Answers will vary.*

_____

_____

_____

_____

_____

🌿 **Practice 4 Completing**   Fill in each blank in the following paragraph with a complete verb. *Answers will vary.*

Yesterday I (1) _____ to the radio when the disc jockey (2) _____ a new contest. He (3) _____ a music question and said he (4) _____ the tenth caller. I immediately (5) _____ the telephone and (6) _____ for the DJ to answer. The phone (7) _____ several times, and it (8) _____ like I was waiting forever. When he finally (9) _____ my call, I (10) _____ $50 and tickets to an upcoming concert.

❋ Practice 5 Writing Your Own

A. Write a sentence of your own for each of the following verbs. *Answers will vary.*

1. were growing _____

2. ran _____

3. looks _____

4. had been singing _____

5. draw _____

B. Write five sentences of your own, and underline all the verbs. Remember that sentences can have more than one verb. *Answers will vary.*

_____

_____

_____

_____

_____

Nouns

People often think of **nouns** as "naming words" because they identify—or name—people (*teacher, Jimmy, brother, clerk*), places (*town, lake, Phoenix*), or things (*flower, car, desk, pants*). Nouns also name ideas (*freedom, liberty*), qualities (*honesty, kindness*), emotions (*sadness, happiness*), and actions (*competition, agreement*). A **common noun** names something general (*singer, hill, water, theater*). A **proper noun** names something specific (*Britney Spears, Grand Canyon, Sprite, McDonald's*).

HINT: To test whether a word is a noun, try putting *a*, *an*, or *the* in front of it:

Nouns: a dog, an apple, the courage
NOT Nouns: a silly, an under, the sing

This test does not work with proper nouns:

NOT   *a Jeffrey* or *the Washington.*

> ### Reviewing Nouns
>
> *What is a noun?*
>
> *A noun names people, places, things, ideas, qualities, emotions, and actions.*
>
> *What is the difference between a common noun and a proper noun? Give an example of each.*
>
> **Common noun:** *A common noun names something general. Examples will vary.*
>
> **Proper noun:** *A proper noun names something specific. Examples will vary.*

Practice 6 Identifying   In each of the following sentences, identify the underlined nouns as common (C) or proper (P).

1. __P__ There are many tourists at <u>Niagara Falls</u>.
2. __C__ My last <u>girlfriend</u> was a model for Calvin Klein.
3. __P__ This is the last gas station before we get to <u>Tulsa</u>.
4. __C__ Give me a <u>dollar</u> for lunch.
5. __C__ Is Elizabeth ready for her big <u>date</u>?
6. __P__ I can't find my pencil from <u>Disneyland</u>.
7. __C__ Jack is having a <u>hamburger</u> for dinner.
8. __P__ While I was at the office, I met <u>Michael Jordan</u>.
9. __C__ Can you take me to <u>school</u> today?
10. __P__ The <u>Beale Library</u> is closed for remodeling.

Practice 7 Identifying   Underline the nouns in the following sentences. Some sentences have more than one noun.

1. We will be going to <u>San Francisco</u> next <u>week</u>.
2. My coin <u>collection</u> is very important to me.
3. <u>Travis</u> is my <u>nephew</u>.
4. <u>George</u> is going to see a <u>movie</u> this <u>afternoon</u>.
5. The most popular TV <u>show</u> is <u>West Wing</u>.

6. I am tired of this hot <u>weather</u>.

7. My <u>grandma</u> makes the best <u>cookies</u>.

8. The basketball <u>player</u> has broken several <u>records</u>.

9. <u>Steve</u> is writing an <u>essay</u> about *Gulliver's Travels* by <u>Jonathan Swift</u>.

10. <u>Melissa</u> grew up in <u>New York City</u>.

🌱 Practice 8 Identifying   List five nouns from the paragraph by Jo Goodwin Parker on page 61. *Answers will vary.*

_____

_____

_____

_____

_____

🌱 Practice 9 Completing   Fill in each blank in the following paragraph with a noun. *Answers will vary.*

In the month of (1) _____, I had two vacations planned. The first was a short visit to (2) _____, and the other was a five-day cruise in (3) _____. I had to travel by (4) _____ to get to both places, and I was excited about the (5) _____. My younger (6) _____ was going with me on the first trip, and we hadn't been getting along very well. To make sure there was (7) _____ between us, I brought along some old (8) _____ from our younger days. My mom also gave me (9) _____ that brought back lots of funny memories. By the end of our trip, we had become so close that we vowed to be (10) _____ forever!

🌱 Practice 10 Writing Your Own

A. Write a sentence of your own for each of the following nouns. *Answers will vary.*

1. pastor _____

2. Sea World _____

3. strength _____

4. audience _____

5. actions _____

B. Write five sentences of your own, and underline all the nouns. Remember that sentences can have more than one noun. *Answers will vary.*

_____

_____

_____

_____

_____

Pronouns

Pronouns can do anything nouns can do. In fact, **pronouns** can take the place of nouns. Without pronouns, you would find yourself repeating nouns and producing boring sentences. Compare the following sentences, for example:

Matt rode **Matt's** bike to **Matt's** house because **Matt** was late for dinner.

Matt rode **his** bike to **his** house because **he** was late for dinner.

There are many different types of pronouns, but you need only focus on the following four types for now.

Most Common Pronouns

Personal (refer to people or things)

Singular:	First Person:	*I, me, my, mine*
	Second Person:	*you, your, yours*
	Third Person:	*he, she, it, him, her, hers, his, its*
Plural:	First Person:	*we, us, our, ours*
	Second Person:	*you, your, yours*
	Third Person:	*they, them, their, theirs*

Demonstrative (point out someone or something)

Singular:	*this, that*
Plural:	*these, those*

Relative (introduce a dependent clause)

who, whom, whose, which, that

Indefinite (refer to someone or something general, not specific)

Singular:	*another, anybody, anyone, anything, each, either, everybody, everyone, everything, little, much, neither, nobody, none, no one, nothing, one, other, somebody, someone, something*
Plural:	*both, few, many, others, several*
Either Singular or Plural:	*all, any, more, most, some*

HINT: When any of these words are used with nouns, they become adjectives instead of pronouns.

Adjective:	My brother wants to borrow **some money.**
Pronoun:	My brother wants to borrow **some.**
Adjective:	The dog wants **that bone.**
Pronoun:	The dog wants **that.**

REVIEWING PRONOUNS

What is a pronoun?

A pronoun is a word that can take the place of a noun.

Define the four most common types of pronouns, and give two examples of each:

Personal: Refer to people or things. Examples will vary.

Demonstrative: Point out someone or something. Examples will vary.

Relative: Introduce a dependent clause. Examples will vary.

Indefinite: Refer to someone or something general. Examples will vary.

🌿 **Practice 11 Identifying**   In each of the following sentences, identify the underlined pronouns as personal (P), relative (R), demonstrative (D), or indefinite (I).

1. __P__ This drink is <u>his</u>.
2. __P__ <u>It</u> doesn't matter what you wear to the game.
3. __R__ I think the person <u>who</u> broke the lamp should pay for it.
4. __D__ Tiffany gave me <u>that</u> for my birthday.
5. __I__ If <u>anyone</u> could do a better job, please tell me.
6. __P__ Jackie is taking <u>her</u> to the doctor.
7. __D__ <u>These</u> are my favorite shoes.
8. __I__ There is <u>something</u> I have to tell you.
9. __R__ I hope <u>that</u> we can meet at the movie.
10. __I__ I am donating <u>both</u> to the thrift store.

🌿 **Practice 12 Identifying**   Underline the pronouns in the following sentences. Some sentences have more than one pronoun.

1. <u>Some</u> of <u>us</u> are not happy with the results.
2. <u>These</u> are not the right answers.
3. <u>I</u> think <u>they</u> are being honest with <u>us</u>.
4. <u>Nobody</u> wants to do the work.
5. Is <u>that</u> the dress <u>I</u> loaned <u>you</u>?
6. If <u>you</u> would just study, <u>everything</u> would be easier for <u>you</u>.
7. <u>It</u> is not <u>my</u> fault that Steve broke <u>his</u> arm.
8. Kari knows <u>whose</u> job <u>that</u> is.
9. <u>Those</u> were the best appetizers at the party.
10. <u>My</u> sister believes in that theory.

🌿 **Practice 13 Identifying**   List five pronouns from the paragraph by Jo Goodwin Parker on page 61. *Answers will vary.*

_____

_____

_____

_____

_____

✺ **Practice 14 Completing**   In the following paragraph, replace the nouns in parentheses with pronouns.

Anne bought (1) ___her___ (Anne's) cat when Anne was 12. It was a kitten at the time, and (2) ___she___ (Anne) couldn't resist its cute face. When (3) ___her___ (Anne's) friends saw the cat, (4) ___they___ (Anne's friends) told (5) ___her___ (Anne) to name (6) ___it___ (the cat) Marble because (7) ___it___ (the cat) was so colorful. Anne decided to name the cat Spunky instead because (8) ___it___ (the cat) had lots of energy. Now Anne is going away to college and (9) ___her___ (Anne's) cat is going with (10) ___her___ (Anne).

✺ **Practice 15 Writing Your Own**

A. Write a sentence of your own for each of the following pronouns. *Answers will vary.*

1. anybody _____

2. those _____

3. who _____

4. both _____

5. we _____

B. Write five sentences of your own, and underline the pronouns. Remember that sentences can have more than one pronoun. *Answers will vary.*

_____

_____

_____

_____

_____

Adjectives

Adjectives modify—or describe—nouns or pronouns. Adjectives generally make sentences clear and vivid.

Without Adjectives: He took candy, a camera, and a backpack to the amusement park.

With Adjectives: He took **licorice** candy, a **digital** camera, and a **blue** backpack to the amusement park.

REVIEWING ADJECTIVES

What is an adjective?

An adjective modifies or describes a noun or pronoun. _____

Give three examples of adjectives.

Examples will vary. _____   _____   _____

Practice 16 Identifying   For each of the following sentences, if the underlined word is an adjective, write Adj in the blank.

1. __Adj__ That was an <u>ugly</u> dog.

2. __Adj__ My father is a <u>generous</u> man.

3. _____ Stan tried to <u>scare</u> Jessica.

4. __Adj__ The <u>new</u> student has been very helpful.

5. _____ I met a <u>boy</u> in the library today.

6. __Adj__ The <u>rich</u> man is giving his estate to charity.

7. __Adj__ His <u>proud</u> smile was beautiful.

8. _____ Put the <u>cup</u> in the dishwasher.

9. __Adj__ I need a <u>cold</u> drink.

10. _____ Jeremy's <u>computer</u> has a virus.

Practice 17 Identifying   Underline the adjectives in the following sentences. Some sentences have more than one adjective.

1. The <u>curly</u> hair is <u>full</u> of <u>thick</u> knots.

2. Linda plays <u>concert</u> piano in front of <u>large</u> audiences.

3. The <u>longest</u> novel I have ever read is <u>Bleak House</u> by Charles Dickens.

4. I need a <u>good</u> <u>parking</u> place today.

5. It was a <u>cold</u> day in November when we won the <u>big</u> <u>football</u> game.

6. <u>That</u> <u>cheese</u> pizza looks like a <u>great</u> meal.

7. The <u>baby's</u> <u>loud</u> cry is giving me a headache.

8. I need a cup of <u>strong</u> coffee to stay awake.

9. Kevin has to mow the <u>long</u> grass in the backyard.

10. Renee uses a <u>black</u> <u>ballpoint</u> pen to sign <u>her</u> checks.

🌿 **Practice 18 Identifying**   List five adjectives from the paragraph by Jo Goodwin Parker on page 61. *Answers will vary.*

_____

_____

_____

_____

_____

🌿 **Practice 19 Completing**   Fill in each blank in the following para-graph with an adjective. *Answers will vary.*

Last summer, my brother and I drove to a (1) _____ city in Texas. I have some (2) _____ relatives who live there, and they wanted us to visit. We stayed for a (3) _____ week and talked about (4) _____ things. I took lots of (5) _____ pictures also, because I didn't know when we would be back to see them again. All in all, it was a (6) _____ visit. We enjoyed our (7) _____ conversations, and we learned about our family's (8) _____ history. I promised to write often, and they were (9) _____ to see us leave. On the way home, we felt a little more (10) _____ about our relatives and ourselves.

🌾 Practice 20 Writing Your Own

A. Write a sentence of your own for each of the following adjectives.
Answers will vary.

1. pretty _____

2. heavy _____

3. small _____

4. fourth _____

5. loud _____

B. Write five sentences of your own, and underline all of the adjectives. Remember that sentences can have more than one adjective. *Answers will vary.*

_____

_____

_____

_____

_____

Adverbs

Adverbs modify—or describe—adjectives, verbs, and other adverbs. They do *not* modify nouns. Adverbs also answer the following questions:

How?	thoughtfully, kindly, briefly, quietly
When?	soon, tomorrow, late, now
Where?	inside, somewhere, everywhere, there
How often?	daily, always, annually, rarely
To what extent?	generally, specifically, exactly, very

HINT: Notice that adverbs often end in *-ly*. That might help you recognize them.

REVIEWING ADVERBS

What is an adverb?

An adverb modifies or describes an adjective, a verb, or another adverb.

> *What are the five questions that adverbs answer?*
>
> <u>   How?   </u>   <u>   When?   </u>   <u>   Where?   </u>   <u>   How often?   </u>   <u>To what extent?</u>
>
> *Give one example of an adverb that answers each question.*
>
> *Examples will vary*   <u>   </u>   <u>   </u>   <u>   </u>   <u>   </u>

✣ Practice 21 Identifying   For each of the following sentences, if the underlined word is an adverb, write Adv in the blank.

1. __*Adv*__ He <u>kindly</u> waited for me at the corner.
2. __*Adv*__ Jan spoke <u>softly</u>, and I couldn't hear her.
3. __*Adv*__ He was <u>outside</u> when I called her.
4. _____ Henry can <u>hop</u> on one leg.
5. __*Adv*__ That was <u>very</u> thoughtful of you.
6. __*Adv*__ Pam was <u>much</u> appreciated for her hard work.
7. _____ The <u>power</u> bill is higher this month than last.
8. _____ Peggy's <u>son</u> is a sweet boy.
9. __*Adv*__ Meet me <u>tomorrow</u> in the lobby.
10. __*Adv*__ I read it <u>quickly</u>, so I don't remember what it said.

✣ Practice 22 Identifying   Underline the adverbs in the following sentences. Some sentences have more than one adverb.

1. I <u>surely</u> <u>won't</u> be at that party.
2. They <u>almost</u> collided in the hall.
3. Tammy will come by <u>today</u> to wash the car.
4. This is the <u>very</u> last time you will make that mistake.
5. <u>Don't</u> drive <u>too</u> fast.
6. This was <u>quite</u> a good movie.
7. Jennifer <u>quickly</u> ran to the bus stop.
8. Are you <u>absolutely</u> sure you can be <u>here</u>?
9. I <u>suddenly</u> realized that I forgot my homework.
10. We went to the meetings <u>monthly</u>.

❋ Practice 23 Identifying   List five adverbs from the paragraph by Jo Goodwin Parker on page 61.

_____ *not*

_____ *well*

_____ *much*

_____ *too*

_____ *already*

❋ Practice 24 Completing   Fill in each blank in the following paragraph with an adverb. *Answers will vary.*

When the grocery store in our small town (1) _____ closed, several people were out of work. It was a (2) _____ sad situation for many people. One family, the Johnsons, (3) _____ found a solution. They opened a new grocery store with more (4) _____ priced items. They also (5) _____ employed people from the first store, and they (6) _____ donated food items for families that were (7) _____ struggling. The town was (8) _____ grateful for their generous help. The Johnsons were (9) _____ awarded a key to the city at a big dinner held in their honor. I know the Johnsons never planned to get so much recognition, but they (10) _____ deserved it.

❋ Practice 25 Writing Your Own

A. Write a sentence of your own for each of the following adverbs. *Answers will vary.*

1. often _____

2. rarely _____

3. softly _____

4. too _____

5. yesterday _____

B. Write five sentences of your own, and underline all of the adverbs. Remember that sentences can have more than one adverb. *Answers will vary.*

_____

_____

_____

_____

_____

Prepositions

Prepositions indicate relationships among the ideas in a sentence. Something is *up*, *down*, *next to*, *behind*, *around*, *near*, or *under* something else. A preposition is always followed by a noun or a pronoun called the **object of the preposition.** Together, they form a **prepositional phrase.**

Preposition	+	Object	=	Prepositional Phrase
beside		the water		beside the water
at		the meeting		at the meeting

Here is a list of some common prepositions.

Common Prepositions

about	beside	into	since
above	between	like	through
across	beyond	near	throughout
after	by	next to	to
against	despite	of	toward
among	down	off	under
around	during	on	until
as	except	on top of	up
at	for	out	upon
before	from	out of	up to
behind	in	outside	with
below	in front of	over	within
beneath	inside	past	without

HINT: *To* + a verb (as in *to go, to come, to feel*) is not a prepositional phrase. It is a verb phrase, which we will deal with later in this unit.

REVIEWING PREPOSITIONS
....

What is a preposition?

A preposition indicates relationships among the ideas in a sentence.

Give two examples: Examples will vary. _____

What is a prepositional phrase?

A prepositional phrase consists of a preposition and its object.

Give two examples: Examples will vary. _____

Practice 26 Identifying For each of the following sentences, if the underlined word is a preposition, write P in the blank.

1. __P__ The most important papers are <u>on</u> the top.
2. __P__ My cousins live <u>around</u> the corner.
3. __P__ The fisherman went <u>over</u> his limit of trout.
4. _____ I am hanging a <u>poster</u> of Ben Affleck in my room.
5. __P__ Don't walk <u>behind</u> that building at night.
6. __P__ Julie went <u>through</u> the neighborhood with fliers.
7. _____ I have been writing in my <u>diary</u> since I was eight years old.
8. __P__ The museum is <u>near</u> the community center.
9. _____ Turn off the <u>radio</u> while I'm studying.
10. __P__ Paul flew his plane <u>above</u> the clouds.

Practice 27 Identifying Underline the prepositions in the following sentences. Some sentences have more than one preposition.

1. Before getting <u>out</u> of the car, he noticed a lady <u>in</u> a white hat.
2. The house is <u>on</u> the hill <u>at</u> the end <u>of</u> the windy road.
3. The best hotels <u>in</u> San Diego are <u>beside</u> the ocean.
4. My new computer is <u>in</u> a box <u>by</u> my desk.

5. <u>During</u> the dance, I leaned <u>against</u> the table, and it fell.

6. One <u>of</u> the twins has a birthmark <u>under</u> her knee.

7. The cookie jar is sitting <u>on top of</u> the refrigerator.

8. We forgot <u>about</u> the balloons <u>in</u> the car.

9. My slip is hanging <u>below</u> my skirt.

10. Iris walked <u>through</u> the mall <u>with</u> Becky.

❀ Practice 28 Identifying   List five prepositions from the paragraph by Jo Goodwin Parker on page 61. *Answers will vary.*

_____

_____

_____

_____

_____

❀ Practice 29 Completing   Fill in each blank in the following paragraph with a preposition. *Answers may vary.*

Miguel has been walking (1) _____*on*_____ campus all day, trying to sell tickets to a car wash. He walked (2) _____*up to*_____ me this morning and asked me to buy one. He said he was raising money (3) _____*for*_____ the chess club because the club members are going (4) _____*to*_____ Disney World (5) _____*in*_____ Florida. I don't know how much money they need, but (6) _____*at*_____ the time of our conversation, they had only $50. The chess club is usually very disorganized and is always (7) _____*without*_____ money. This year, it has a new president, who went (8) _____*through*_____ the club's books and found a way to pay its bills. Miguel was the vice president, but he quit because he didn't want to be (9) _____*under*_____ so much pressure. I think he just wants to graduate (10) _____*by*_____ next year and needs more time for studying.

❦ Practice 30 Writing Your Own

A. Write a sentence of your own for each of the following prepositions.
Answers will vary.

1. below _____

2. with _____

3. around _____

4. between _____

5. toward _____

B. Write five sentences of your own, and underline the prepositions. Remember that sentences can have more than one preposition. *Answers will vary.*

_____

_____

_____

_____

_____

Conjunctions

Conjunctions connect groups of words. Without conjunctions, most of our writing would be choppy and boring. The two types of conjunctions are easy to remember because their names state their purpose: *coordinating* conjunctions link equal ideas, and *subordinating* conjunctions make one idea subordinate to—or dependent on—another.

Coordinating conjunctions connect parts of a sentence that are of equal importance or weight. Each part of the sentence is an **independent clause,** a group of words with a subject and verb that can stand alone as a sentence (see pages 88–90). There are only seven coordinating conjunctions:

Coordinating Conjunctions

and, but, for, nor, or, so, yet

Coordinating: Isaac wanted to see a movie, **and** I wanted to go to dinner.

Coordinating: I enjoy listening to music, **but** I don't know how to play any instruments.

Subordinating conjunctions join two ideas by making one dependent on the other. The idea introduced by the subordinating conjunction becomes a **dependent clause,** a group of words with a subject and a verb that cannot stand alone as a sentence (see pages 88–90). The other part of the sentence is an independent clause.

Dependent Clause

Subordinating: She will stay **until** the baby falls asleep.

Dependent Clause

Subordinating: **Unless** I am busy, you are welcome to come visit.

Here are some common subordinating conjunctions.

Common Subordinating Conjunctions

after	because	since	until
although	before	so	when
as	even if	so that	whenever
as if	even though	than	where
as long as	how	that	wherever
as soon as	if	though	whether
as though	in order that	unless	while

REVIEWING CONJUNCTIONS

What is a coordinating conjunction?

A coordinating conjunction connects parts of a sentence that are of equal

importance or weight.

Name the seven coordinating conjunctions.

and   but   for   nor   or   so   yet

> **What is a subordinating conjunction?**
>
> A subordinating conjunction joins two ideas by making one dependent on the other.
>
> **Write a sentence using a subordinating conjunction.**
>
> Answers will vary.

❋ Practice 31 Identifying   In each of the following sentences, identify the underlined conjunction as coordinating (C) or subordinating (S).

1. __C__ Polly wanted to be here, <u>yet</u> she had prior commitments.
2. __S__ <u>Before</u> you go, sign the guest book.
3. __S__ I didn't make cookies, <u>though</u> I knew you would be hungry.
4. __S__ <u>As if</u> he could read my mind, he brought me flowers.
5. __C__ Henry is allergic to chocolate, <u>so</u> he can't eat that cake.
6. __S__ Richard will do that part, <u>unless</u> he gets too busy.
7. __S__ <u>While</u> I was waiting, I read an article on computers.
8. __S__ <u>Although</u> she's never been there, Cara said Hawaii is beautiful.
9. __C__ Dean is a lawyer, <u>and</u> he's working on a big tobacco case.
10. __C__ I can make tri-tip, <u>or</u> I can call for pizza.

❋ Practice 32 Identifying   Underline the conjunctions in the following sentences.

1. We all want to go, <u>but</u> there are only ten tickets left.
2. <u>As long as</u> you're watching him, the baby can play outside.
3. I had a good time, <u>yet</u> I never did see my friends there.
4. <u>When</u> you were at the store, I worked on my essay.
5. I know it's going to be hot today, <u>for</u> the forecast predicted mid-90s.
6. <u>Although</u> it's only June, stores are selling Halloween costumes.
7. We can begin the meeting <u>as soon as</u> Peter arrives.
8. Stephanie will buy the donuts <u>even though</u> she lost her job.

9. I made a special card for Amber, <u>so</u> I hope you will sign it.

10. <u>Whenever</u> you come to town, you should call me.

❊ Practice 33 Identifying   List five conjunctions from the paragraph by Jo Goodwin Parker on page 61. *Answers will vary.*

_____

_____

_____

_____

_____

❊ Practice 34 Completing   Fill in each blank in the following paragraph with a conjunction. *Answers will vary.*

Cooking is not fun for me, (1) _____ I have been learning a lot about it. (2) _____ I usually make my girlfriend do the cooking, last night it was my turn. I planned to make a pasta dish, (3) _____ I forgot a couple of things at the store, (4) _____ I decided to make chef salads instead. (5) _____ I was doing the cooking, my girlfriend was surfing on the Internet in the back room. (6) _____ she wasn't paying attention to me, she didn't notice how many times I licked my fingers or dropped things on the floor. I think the salads were just fine, (7) _____ I did notice a cat hair had somehow landed in mine. (8) _____ there was anything strange in my girlfriend's salad, she didn't bring it to my attention. I think she was just glad to have the night off, (9) _____ the next time I have to cook, I will get take-out. (10) _____ I've heard that cooking is an expression of love, I still think it is too much work.

❊ Practice 35 Writing Your Own

A. Write a sentence of your own for each of the following conjunctions. *Answers will vary.*

1. but _____

2. until _____

3. so _____

4. wherever _____

5. as long as _____

B. Write five sentences of your own, and underline the conjunctions. Remember that sentences can have more than one conjunction. *Answers will vary.*

_____

_____

_____

_____

_____

Interjections

Interjections are words that express strong emotion, surprise, or disappointment. An interjection is usually followed by an exclamation point or a comma.

Interjection: **Hey!** You're standing on my foot.

Interjection: **Wow,** that was scary!

Other common interjections include *aha, alas, great, hallelujah, neat, oh, oops, ouch, well, whoa, yeah,* and *yippee.*

REVIEWING INTERJECTIONS

What is an interjection?

An interjection expresses strong emotion, surprise, or disappointment.

Write a sentence using an interjection.

Answers will vary.

Practice 36 Identifying   For each of the following sentences, if the underlined word is an interjection, write I in the blank.

1. ____*I*____ <u>Ouch</u>, I hit my finger!
2. ____*I*____ <u>No</u>! That's the wrong house.
3. ____*I*____ <u>Oops</u>, I didn't mean to say that.
4. _____ <u>Thank you</u> for taking me home.
5. ____*I*____ I can't believe you made it! <u>Wow</u>!
6. ____*I*____ <u>Yes</u>! I got an A on that paper.
7. _____ <u>Please</u> take me to the dance.
8. _____ <u>Can</u> you hand me the salt?
9. ____*I*____ The car didn't run out of gas. <u>Thank goodness</u>!
10. ____*I*____ <u>Well</u>, I think I can find time.

❊ Practice 37 Identifying   Underline the interjections in the following sentences.

1. <u>My goodness</u>! That was a terrible storm.
2. The boys' team, <u>alas</u>, has beaten the girls' team again.
3. <u>Yeah</u>! We are going to the semifinals!
4. <u>Wow</u>, do you know how much that costs?
5. My mom is paying my tuition! <u>Hallelujah</u>!
6. <u>Man</u>, this is a steep hill.
7. <u>Oh</u>, guess who's having another baby!
8. <u>Hooray</u>! We won a new car.
9. That was a great save! <u>Neat</u>!
10. <u>Hey</u>! Am I the only one who knows how to take out the trash around here?

❊ Practice 38 Identifying   List two interjections from the paragraph by Jo Goodwin Parker on page 61.

_____*Yes*_____

_____*Oh yes*_____

❊ Practice 39 Completing   Fill in each blank in the following paragraph with an interjection. *Answers will vary.*

(1) __________, we were almost late for the plane! (2) __________! We thought it was departing at 11:00 a.m., but our tickets actually said 9:30 a.m. (3) ____________, I can't believe we were that careless. Fortunately, we left for the airport two hours early because we were going to buy lunch there. (4) ____________! During the drive, I looked at the ticket and, (5) ____________, it said 9:30 a.m. in bold. I can't believe I didn't see it before. (6) ____________! We ran and ran through the terminal, and when we got to the gate, they told us there were only two seats left. (7) ____________! (8) ____________, there were only two of us traveling that day. We found our seats on the plane, and (9) ____________, was it stuffy! At least we made it to Denver on time. (10) ____________!

Practice 40 Writing Your Own

A. Write a sentence of your own for each of the following interjections. *Answers will vary.*

1. yikes ____
2. wow ____
3. yeah ____
4. ouch ____
5. mercy ____

B. Write five sentences of your own, and underline the interjections. *Answers will vary.*

____

____

____

____

____

PHRASES

A **phrase** is a group of words that functions together as a unit. Phrases cannot stand alone, however, because they are missing a subject, a verb, or both.

TEACHING PHRASES
Divide students into two groups, and provide them with a series of cards

containing phrases that can be made into five different sentences. For example,

running in the morning / is causing / long days
my best friend / has enjoyed / her new job / in my father's sporting goods store
my father / has owned / a sporting goods store / for many years
running a store / has been / a challenge / for my father
my mother / has been trying / to get me / to work in the store

The sentences should all focus on the same theme.

Give students the cards in random order, and have them try to create five sentences that all make sense. For instance, if they create the sentence *My best friend has enjoyed her new job running a store* and if they get the other three sentences correct, they will be left with *in my father's sporting goods store has been a challenge for my father.* Obviously, this does not make sense, so they will have to figure out how to make all the sentences work. The first group to get all five sentences in a logical order wins. Remember that the sentences can be rearranged and still be logical.

The major objective of this exercise is to show students how phrases work as part of a larger whole—a sentence.

■ For more sample phrases and sentences, see the *Instructor's*

Look at how groups of words function as single units in the following paragraph by Scott Russell Sanders.

> I climbed out of the car with a greeting on my lips, but the sky hushed me. From the black bowl of space countless fiery lights shone down, each one a sun or swirl of suns, the whole brilliant host of them enough to strike me dumb. The Milky Way arced overhead, reminding me of froth glimmering on the dark surface of a mountain creek. I know the names of a dozen constellations, but I wasn't thinking in words right then. I was too busy feeling brimful of joy, without need of any props except the universe. The deep night drew my scattered pieces back to the center, stripped away clutter and weight, and set me free.

Phrases come in several varieties. But all are missing a subject, a verb, or both. Look at the following examples:

Phrases: the new reality TV show, my best friend (missing verbs)
Phrases: had been working, can jump (missing subjects)
Phrases: without any money, near the bank (missing both)
Phrases: helping other people, to be listening (missing subjects)

Phrases function as single parts of speech in their sentences.

REVIEWING PHRASES

What is a phrase?

A phrase is a group of words that function together as a unit. They cannot stand alone.

Give two examples of phrases.

Examples will vary.   _____

❋ **Practice 1 Identifying**   In each of the following sentences, identify the underlined phrase as missing a subject (S), missing a verb (V), or missing both (B).

1. __V__   <u>A new car</u> is parked in my driveway.

2. __B__   James is transferring <u>to a new college</u>.

3. __S__   Mabel and Sarah <u>should have been exercising</u> instead of sleeping.

4. __V__   <u>A very high ladder</u> was leaning against the wall.

5. ___B___ We wanted to swim <u>under the bridge</u>.

6. ___B___ Rachel asked <u>for directions</u> when she was lost.

7. ___B___ We became friends <u>in this dorm room</u>.

8. ___B___ I don't know how to find a pet <u>with a good personality</u>.

9. ___V___ The bald <u>plumber</u> stopped to get some milk on his way home.

10. ___S___ All of us <u>were willing</u> to help her with her math homework.

Resource Manual,
Section II, Part II.

❀ **Practice 2 Identifying**   Underline the phrases in each sentence. Every sentence has more than one phrase.

1. <u>The Harris family</u> <u>will be vacationing</u> <u>in the mountains</u> <u>for two weeks</u>.

2. <u>Driving home</u> <u>from school</u>, Jack remembered <u>about his wallet</u> <u>on his dresser</u>.

3. <u>During the blackout</u>, no one <u>could find</u> <u>the candles</u>.

4. We <u>should have been paying</u> <u>more attention</u> <u>to the time</u>.

5. <u>Tired and exhausted</u>, Maria <u>was thankful</u> when <u>her shift</u> ended.

6. <u>The car</u> sped <u>down the street</u> <u>despite the speed limit signs</u>.

7. <u>Pam and Cecilia</u> <u>have been</u> <u>best friends</u> since they were <u>in elementary school</u>.

8. It was foolish <u>to lie</u> <u>to the instructor</u>.

9. <u>Kevin and I</u> talked <u>for hours</u> sitting <u>underneath the stars</u>.

10. I <u>would have accepted</u> <u>that job offer</u>.

❀ **Practice 3 Identifying**   List five phrases from the paragraph by Scott Russell Sanders on page 86. *Answers will vary.*

_____

_____

_____

_____

_____

❀ **Practice 4 Completing**   Fill in each blank in the following paragraph with an appropriate phrase to complete the sentence. *Answers will vary.*

Ever since Sam applied for vacation time at (1) _____, he found that he was very excited about (2) _____. As he walked (3) _____, he heard that his roommate, Tony, also got (4) _____. Sam learned that (5) _____ were coming for a surprise visit and (6) _____ in their apartment. Even though Sam had tried hard to get ahead (7) _____, he knew he was going to have to (8) _____ in order to keep up with his classes. In only three hours, he got most of his homework done (9) _____. Now he has to (10) _____. His friends were arriving today.

❋ Practice 5 Writing Your Own

A. Write a sentence of your own for each of the following phrases. *Answers will vary.*

1. tapes, CDs, and videotapes _____

2. around town _____

3. should have been ready _____

4. the man sitting in the front row _____

5. to qualify for the Olympics _____

B. Write five sentences of your own, and underline all the phrases. *Answers will vary.*

_____

_____

_____

_____

_____

TEACHING CLAUSES
For about five minutes, have students write down as many song titles as they can think of—no made-up titles allowed. Be sure they write down the full titles. After they

CLAUSES

Like phrases, clauses are groups of words. But unlike phrases, a **clause** always contains a subject and a verb. There are two types of clauses: *independent* and *dependent*.

Let's begin by looking at how some clauses, or subject-and-verb sets, work in a paragraph by Mike Rose:

have completed their lists, have them cross out all song titles that are only phrases, leaving titles that are clauses. The student with the most titles that are clauses wins.

All the hours in class tend to blend into one long, vague stretch of time. What I remember best, strangely enough, are the two things I couldn't understand and over the years grew to hate: grammar lessons and mathematics. I would sit there watching a teacher draw her long horizontal line and her short, oblique lines and break up sentences and put adjectives here and adverbs there and just not get it, couldn't see the reason for it, turned off to it. I would hide by slumping down in my seat and page through my reader, carried along by the flow of sentences in a story. She would test us, and I would dread that, for I always got Cs and Ds. Mathematics was a bit different. For whatever reasons, I didn't learn early math very well, so when it came time for more complicated operations, I couldn't keep up and started day-dreaming to avoid my inadequacy. This was a strategy I would rely on as I grew older. I fell further and further behind. A memory: The teacher is faceless and seems very far away. The voice is faint and is discussing an equation written on the board. It is raining, and I am watching the streams of water form patterns on the windows.

An **independent clause** contains a subject and a verb and can stand alone and make sense by itself. Every complete sentence must have at least one independent clause.

Independent Clause: Tracy loved to watch sunrises.

Now look at the following group of words. It is a clause because it contains a subject and a verb. But it is a **dependent clause** because it is introduced by a word that makes it dependent, *because.*

Dependent Clause: **Because** Tracy loved to watch sunrises.

This clause cannot stand alone. It must be connected to an independent clause to make sense. Here is one way to complete the dependent clause and form a complete sentence.

                    Dependent   Independent
Because Tracy loved to watch sunrises, she always woke up early.

HINT: Subordinating conjunctions (such as *since, although, because, while*) and relative pronouns (*who, whom, whose, which, that*) make clauses dependent. (For more information on subordinating conjunctions, see page 80; for more on relative pronouns, see page 68.)

REVIEWING CLAUSES

For a group of words to be a clause, it must have a ___subject___ **and a**
___verb___.

What is an independent clause?

An independent clause contains a subject and a verb and can stand alone and

make sense by itself.

What is a dependent clause?

A dependent clause contains a subject and a verb but cannot stand alone.

Name the two kinds of words that can begin a dependent clause.

subordinating conjunctions   _relative pronouns_

Name five subordinating conjunctions. _Answers will vary._

_____ _____ _____ _____ _____

Name the five relative pronouns.

who   _whom_   _whose_   _which_   _that_

🌱 Practice 1 Identifying   Identify the following clauses as either independent (I) or dependent (D).

1. __I__ Karen was late for class.

2. __D__ Because her car wouldn't start.

3. __D__ What I really don't know.

4. __I__ The Grand Canyon is one of the Seven Wonders of the World.

5. __I__ I only buy name-brand clothes.

6. __D__ When Walt visited me last month.

7. __I__ Tirana wears beautiful clothes and is self-confident.

8. __D__ Although Angela bought a new computer.

9. __I__ The next-door neighbor is ready to go overseas.

10. __D__ When they are first born.

✻ Practice 2 Identifying Underline the clauses in the following sentences, and label them independent (I) or dependent (D). Some sentences have more than one clause.

    1. Dawn started playing soccer *(I)* when she was six years old. *(D)*

    2. His plans had been changed, *(I)* and he didn't mind. *(I)*

    3. Even though Martin liked roller coasters, *(D)* he didn't want to try the new one. *(I)*

    4. All of my relatives want to stay forever *(I)* when they visit me. *(D)*

    5. My brothers and sisters created a company, *(I)* but they got help from our mom and dad. *(I)*

    6. The coach put the girl back in the game *(I)* after she rested. *(D)*

    7. Children's books have great pictures in them. *(I)*

    8. The number of homeless people in the United States is growing. *(I)*

    9. Alternative rock music is for people *(I)* who like a heavy beat. *(D)*

   10. I saw Margaret running on the track *(I)* that is across from the dorms. *(D)*

✻ Practice 3 Identifying List two independent clauses and three dependent clauses from the paragraph by Mike Rose on page 89. *Answers will vary.*

_____

_____

_____

_____

_____

✻ Practice 4 Completing Make the following dependent clauses into independent clauses by crossing out the subordinating word (either a subordinating conjunction or a relative pronoun).

    1. ~~Before~~ I got into the car.

    2. The waiter ~~who~~ made $50 in tips every night.

    3. Each one of the beautiful gardens ~~that~~ contained fresh herbs and flowers.

    4. ~~While~~ my brother stayed in Salem, Oregon, and I lived off the Puget Sound in Washington State.

5. ~~When~~ you can earn a living.

6. ~~After~~ they were ten years old.

7. The shark ~~that~~ lingered near the boat.

8. ~~Although~~ he bought a Chevy Tahoe.

9. ~~Since~~ I passed my final exam.

10. The party ~~that~~ got out of control.

Practice 5 Writing Your Own

A. Add a dependent clause to the following independent clauses. *Answers will vary.*

1. The cat is sleeping on the sofa.

   _____

2. My brother borrowed my computer.

   _____

3. This test covers five chapters in our textbook.

   _____

4. I can't come over until after lunch.

   _____

5. The box is filled with candy.

   _____

B. Write five independent clauses. Then add at least one dependent clause to each independent clause. *Answers will vary.*

_____

_____

_____

_____

_____

Unit 1 Sentences

Complete sentences are one of the staples of good writing. But sometimes our thoughts pour out of our heads faster than we can get them all down. As a result, we write sentences that need to be corrected in the editing stage. This is a natural part of writing. Always get your ideas down first, and edit your sentences later.

To help you start editing your writing, we will focus on the following sentence elements:

Chapter 7: Subjects and Verbs
Chapter 8: Fragments
Chapter 9: Run-Ons

Writing complete, correct sentences is one of the most difficult tasks for college writers. It involves understanding the transition from oral to written English. Students have to make decisions about sentences that they don't have to deal with when they speak, such as what makes up a sentence and how to punctuate it. What is important, however, is that students address these issues. This unit will help your students start making the transfer from oral to written English.

Subjects and Verbs

✐ Checklist for Identifying Subjects and Verbs

> ✔ Does each of your sentences contain a subject?
>
> ✔ Does each of your sentences contain a verb?

A sentence has a message to communicate, but for that message to be meaningful, the sentence must have a subject and a verb. The subject is the topic of the sentence, what the sentence is about. The verb is the sentence's motor. It moves the message forward to its destination. Without these two parts, the sentence is not complete.

Notice how subjects and verbs work together in the following paragraph by Garrison Keillor.

> A hydrant was open on Seventh Avenue above 23rd Street last Friday morning, and I stopped on my way east and watched people hop over the water. It was a brilliant spring day. The water was a nice clear creek about three feet wide and ran along the gutter around the northwest corner of the intersection. A gaggle of pedestrians crossing 23rd went *hop hop hop hop hop* over the creek as a few soloists jaywalking Seventh performed at right angles to them, and I got engrossed in the dance. Three feet isn't a long leap for most people, and the ease of it permits a wide range of expression. Some hoppers went a good deal higher than necessary.

In this paragraph, Garrison Keillor describes some unusual observations he made one spring morning. Before continuing in this chapter, take a moment to record some of your own observations. Save your work because you will use it later in the chapter.

Writing Assignment: Unusual Observations

What are some of your funniest observations? Some of your saddest observations? Some of your most memorable observations? Write a paragraph describing one of your most unusual observations. See if you can make it come alive like Keillor does in his paragraph.

Revising Your Writing

Revise the first draft of your paragraph before you focus on editing. Use the Revising Checklist on pages 24–25 to help you with your revision. Make sure your paragraph has a good topic sentence and is well developed. Then check your paragraph for unity, organization, and coherence.

story or essay on the Internet and print it out. Then have them underline the subjects once and the verbs twice in one of the paragraphs. How difficult was it for students to identify the subjects and verbs?

TEACHING ON THE WEB

Mosaics Web Site: To learn more about subjects and verbs, students can go to www.prenhall.com/ mosaics.

SUBJECTS

To be complete, every sentence must have a subject. The **subject** tells who or what the sentence is about.

Subject

The **students** study for their tests.

Computers solve many problems.

Compound Subjects

When two or more separate words tell what the sentence is about, the sentence has a **compound subject.**

Compound Subject: **Dogs** and **cats** are fun to play with.
Compound Subject: The **cars** and **trucks** were on display.

HINT: Note that *and* is not part of the compound subject.

Unstated Subjects

Sometimes a subject does not actually appear in a sentence but is understood. This occurs in commands and requests. The understood subject is always *you*—meaning either someone specific or anyone in general.

Command:	Move away from the fire.
	s
Unstated Subject:	(You) move away from the fire.
Request:	Help me open the jar, please.
	s
Unstated Subject:	(You) help me open the jar, please.

Subjects and Prepositional Phrases

The subject of a sentence cannot be part of a prepositional phrase. A **prepositional phrase** is a group of words that begins with a **preposition,** a word like *in, on, under, after,* or *from.* Here are some examples of prepositional phrases:

in the street	**next to** the wall	**before** lunch
on the bus	**behind** the car	**instead of** the subway
under the water	**around** the mess	**across** the alley
after work	**into** the boat	**for** the children
from the left side	**during** the storm	**at** the intersection

(See page 76 for a more complete list of prepositions.)

If you are looking for the subject of a sentence, first cross out all the prepositional phrases. Then figure out what the sentence is about.

~~During the flood~~, the **men** and **women** helped block the water.

The **phone** ~~around the corner~~ was working fine.

Some ~~of the water~~ leaked ~~into our boat~~.

REVIEWING SUBJECTS

What is a subject?

The subject tells who or what the sentence is about.

What is a compound subject?

A compound subject is two or more separate words that tell what the sentence is

about.

What is an unstated subject?

An unstated subject does not appear in the sentence but is understood.

How can you find the subject of a sentence?

First, cross out all the prepositional phrases, and then figure out what the sen-

tence is about.

Practice 1 Identifying Underline the subjects in each of the following sentences. Cross out the prepositional phrases first.

1. <u>Bob</u> and <u>Jolene</u> got married last weekend.
2. The <u>author</u> was proud ~~of her work~~.
3. <u>*The Andy Griffith Show*</u> is still my favorite show.
4. <u>Each</u> ~~of the students~~ is responsible ~~for bringing an essay~~.
5. A popular <u>actor</u> visited our school today.
6. <u>I</u> am getting a better car ~~in September~~.
7. Sometimes <u>Lavonne</u> doesn't tell the truth.
8. The <u>boys</u> and <u>girls</u> ~~in the first grade~~ have learned to add and subtract.
9. ~~At Christmas dinner~~, my <u>brother</u> will be announcing his engagement.
10. <u>I</u> think that you will make an excellent doctor.

Practice 2 Identifying Put an X next to the sentence if the underlined portion is not a subject. Cross out the prepositional phrases first.

1. _____ The <u>dogs</u> ate their food.
2. __X__ Good musicians practice <u>every day</u>. *(musicians)*
3. __X__ Manuel was a talented <u>baseball player</u>. *(Manuel)*

4. _____ ~~After June~~, I will take a vacation.

5. __X__ Every month, Ioana gets money ~~from her parents~~. (Ioana)

6. _____ The television blared all night.

7. __X__ The fountain ~~in the plaza~~ was built by my uncle. (fountain)

8. _____ Shawna wants an interview ~~with you in the near future~~.

9. _____ Money doesn't grow ~~on trees~~.

10. __X__ I am applying ~~for a new job~~. (I)

Practice 3 Correcting   Correct the errors in Practice 2 by listing the correct subjects here. *See Practice 2.*

_____

_____

_____

_____

_____

Practice 4 Completing   Fill in each blank in the following sentences with a subject that is not a person's name. *Answers will vary.*

1. _____ took a trip to Hawaii last summer.

2. _____ is a beautiful place in the winter.

3. _____ has been working out every day.

4. _____ is in the shoe department.

5. _____ just finished her medical residency.

6. _____ and _____ have been best friends since kindergarten.

7. Under the umbrella, _____ was staying nice and dry.

8. _____ has a black belt in karate.

9. In two days, _____ will have earned all of his tuition money.

10. Sometimes _____ makes me laugh at myself.

✹ Practice 5 Writing Your Own

A. Write a sentence of your own using each of the following nouns as a subject. *Answers will vary.*

1. shirt _____

2. teacher _____

3. courage _____

4. award _____

5. computer _____

B. Write five sentences of your own, and underline the subjects in each sentence. *Answers will vary.*

_____

_____

_____

_____

_____

VERBS

To be complete, a sentence must have a verb as well as a subject. A **verb** tells what the subject is doing or what is happening.

Verb
↓

The students   **study** for their tests.

Computers   **solve** many problems.

Action Verbs

An **action verb** tells what a subject is doing. Some examples of action verbs are *skip, ski, stare, flip, breathe, remember, restate, sigh, cry, decrease, write,* and *pant.*

Action Verb: The lobsters **scurried** across the ocean floor.

Action Verb: The car **swerved** out of the way.

Linking Verbs

A **linking verb** connects the subject to other words in the sentence that say something about it. Linking verbs are also called **state-of-being verbs** because they do not show action. Rather, they say that something "is" a particular way. The most common linking verb is *be* (*am, are, is, was, were*).

Linking Verb: The water **is** in the gutter.
Linking Verb: I **am** worried about the presentation.

Other common linking verbs are *remain, act, look, grow,* and *seem.*

Linking Verb: The woman **remained** concerned about her clothes.
Linking Verb: Firefighters **act** proud.
Linking Verb: The cliff **looks** tall.
Linking Verb: The stream **grew** wide.
Linking Verb: Children **seem** happy about going to Six Flags Magic Mountain.

Some words, like *smell* and *taste*, can be either action verbs or linking verbs.

Action Verb: I **smell** flowers.
Linking Verb: This house **smells** like flowers.
Action Verb: She **tasted** the soup.
Linking Verb: It **tasted** too salty.

Compound Verbs

Just as a verb can have more than one subject, some subjects can have more than one verb. These are called **compound verbs.**

Compound Verb: She **skips** and **hops** over the cracks in the sidewalk.
Compound Verb: He **laughs** when he's happy and **cries** when he's sad.

HINT: A sentence can have both a compound subject and a compound verb.

s   s   v   v

Men and **women avoided** the crowds and **dashed** to their cars.

Helping Verbs

Often the **main verb** (the action verb or linking verb) in a sentence needs help to convey its meaning. **Helping verbs** add information, such as when an action took place. The **complete verb** consists of a main verb and all its helping verbs.

Complete Verb: The snow **will be** gone tomorrow.

Complete Verb: You **should** not go outside today.

Complete Verb: You **might** fall in the ditch.

Complete Verb: We **should have** fixed the faucet.

Complete Verb: City workers **have** checked the stoplights.

Complete Verb: The repair technician **will be** coming to fix the problem.

HINT: Note that *not* isn't part of the helping verb. Similarly, *never, always, only, just,* and *still* are never part of the verb.

Complete Verb: I **have** always **liked** hot weather.

The most common helping verbs are

be, am, is, are, was, were
have, has, had
do, did

Other common helping verbs are

may, might
can, could
will, would
should, used to, ought to

REVIEWING VERBS

What is a verb?   _A verb tells what the subject is doing or what is happening._

What is the difference between action and linking verbs?

An action verb tells what the subject is doing. A linking verb connects the subject

to other words in the sentence.

Give an example of a compound verb. _Examples will vary._____

Give an example of a helping verb. _____

What is the difference between a subject and a verb?

The subject tells who or what the sentence is about, and the verb tells what the sub-

_ject is doing or what is happening._____

❊ Practice 6 Identifying   Underline the complete verb in each of the following sentences.

1. That book is hard to read.

2. The jurors stayed in the courtroom.

3. Thomas is going to the movies.

4. We waited by the phone and hoped for a call.

5. Martha screamed at the top of her lungs.

6. Until last night, we had never won a game.

7. I cook and eat only healthy foods.

8. Bob and Melissa turned down the wrong street.

9. Every June, we spend a week in the mountains.

10. Ricky was waiting for a ride to work.

❊ Practice 7 Identifying   Put an X next to the sentence if the underlined portion is not a verb.

1. _____ I gave you my best advice.

2. __X__ Cammy wrote a paper about *The Tempest*. *(wrote)*

3. _____ Next year, I will take piano lessons.

4. __X__ Jill just filed her income taxes. *(filed)*

5. __X__ The child jumped into the pool. *(jumped)*

6. _____ Water is better for you than soft drinks.

7. _____ My father walked to the car and opened the door.

8. __X__ Edgar's car is definitely totaled. *(is totaled)*

9. __X__ Doctors and lawyers buy big houses. *(buy)*

10. _____ Abby does not want that cookie.

Practice 8 Correcting   Correct the errors in Practice 7 by listing the correct verbs here. *See Practice 7.*

_____

_____

_____

_____

_____

Practice 9 Completing   Fill in each blank in the following sentences with a verb that makes sense. Avoid using *is, are, was,* and *were* by themselves. *Answers will vary.*

1. The doctor _____ my forehead.

2. My grandmother _____ me a check for my birthday.

3. We always _____ bottled water on camping trips.

4. They _____ happy soon.

5. My friend _____ jigsaw puzzles.

6. Sometimes college _____ solutions to difficult problems.

7. Most of the time, my uncle _____ the dishes.

8. I _____n't _____ to leave.

9. We _____ a midnight flight to Las Vegas.

10. I _____ often _____ magazines in bed.

Practice 10 Writing Your Own

A. Write a sentence for each of the following verbs, and label the verb as either action or linking. *Sentences will vary.*

1. grow _action_ _____

2. should have been asking _action_ _____

3. appears _linking_____

4. will pay _action_____

5. has gone _action_____

B. Write five sentences of your own, and underline the complete verbs in each sentence. Remember that sentences can have more than one complete verb. *Answers will vary.*

_____

_____

_____

_____

_____

CHAPTER REVIEW

You might want to reread your answers to the questions in the review boxes before you do the following exercises.

Review Practice 1 Reading   Refer to the paragraph by Garrison Keillor on page 94 to do the following exercises.

A. List five subjects. *Answers will vary.*

1. _____

2. _____

3. _____

4. _____

5. _____

B. List the five complete verbs that go with the subjects listed in A. *Answers will vary.*

1. _____

2. _____

3. _____

4. _____

5. _____

🌿 Review Practice 2 Identifying   Underline the subjects once and the verbs twice in each of the following sentences.

1. The dogs barked at the door.
2. My neighbor has tropical fish.
3. We watched *Survivor* last night.
4. Rocky swam in the lake.
5. Janine and Wallis went to the movies.
6. I ran to the car and unlocked the door.
7. You have been driving all night.
8. Marny is not feeling well today.
9. The TV is fuzzy.
10. They will never see her again.

🌿 Review Practice 3 Correcting   List any subjects and verbs you didn't identify correctly in Review Practice 2. *Answers will vary.*

_____

_____

_____

_____

_____

✎ EDITING A STUDENT PARAGRAPH

Following is a paragraph written and revised by Ralph McKensey in response to the writing assignment in this chapter. Read the paragraph, and underline his subjects once and complete verbs twice.

When I was in sixth grade, I came home from school one day to fire engines in front of my house. Smoke was pouring out of the kitchen window. There was a police car, and I could see my mom and my dog sitting in the back of the car. My mom was holding one hand over her mouth and was petting the dog with her other hand. I ran to my mom as if I was moving in slow motion. It seemed like it took forever to get to the police car. Finally, she put her arms around me and told me that things would be all right. My family and I will never forget that day.

Collaborative Activity

Team up with a partner, and list Ralph's subjects and their verbs in two columns. There are 14 subjects and 15 verbs. *See student paragraph for answers.*

EDITING YOUR OWN PARAGRAPH

Now return to the paragraph you wrote and revised at the beginning of this chapter.

Collaborative Activity

Exchange paragraphs with your partner, and underline the subjects once and the complete verbs twice in your partner's paragraph.

Individual Activity

To complete the writing process, make sure each of your sentences has at least one subject and verb.

CHAPTER 8

Fragments

 ## Checklist for Identifying and Correcting Fragments

✔ Does each sentence have a subject?
✔ Does each sentence have a verb?

One of the most common errors in college writing is the fragment. A fragment is a piece of a sentence that is punctuated as a complete sentence. But it cannot stand alone. Once you learn how to identify fragments, you can avoid them in your writing.

Notice how all the complete sentences work in the following paragraph by Bailey White.

> There is only one paved street in the town, with buildings on only one side of that street. Big oak trees shade the storefronts, and their roots have humped up the sidewalk and crumbled the asphalt of the street. In the middle of the row of buildings is an abandoned municipal garage. It still has its brick walls with the arched openings of doorways and windows, but the roof is gone, and limbs of the oak trees hang over the walls and drop acorns into the Model A Ford roadster that is parked inside, rusting away under a rotten tarpaulin. The other buildings, once hardware stores and drugstores and feed stores, have given over to the peculiar and the exotic.

In this paragraph, Bailey White is recording interesting details about an old town. Before continuing in this chapter, take a moment to record details about your hometown. Save your work because you will use it later in the chapter.

TEACHING
FRAGMENTS
Buy blank flash cards in an educational supply store, and on each card, put parts of a sentence: subordinating conjunctions, relative pronouns, phrases, subjects, verbs, and so on. Give each student a certain number of flash cards. Then have the students create sentences out of the words and then stand in front of the class in order so as to form complete sentences. For instance, three students might hold up the sentence *the car/was swerving/on the street.* Have another student add *because* to the beginning of the sentence to show how one word can create a fragment.

Have students make other sentences in the same way. Then add and subtract words from these sentences so that students can see the way fragments are both formed and fixed.

■ For suggested words, phrases, and clauses, see the *Instructor's Resource Manual*, Section II, Part II.

TEACHING ON THE WEB

Exploring and Discovering: Have students explore different Web sites to see how often site authors use fragments. When are they used? Why are they used? Are they used more when something is being advertised? Are the fragments effective on the Web sites?

TEACHING ON THE WEB

Mosaics Web Site: To learn more about fragments, students can go to www.prenhall.com/mosaics.

Writing Assignment: Hometown Highlights

What kind of town were you brought up in? What are some of your most vivid mental pictures of this town? In a paragraph, describe your town's downtown area for someone who has never been there. What are its physical features? What is its general atmosphere? Do you feel that you fit in this town?

Revising Your Writing

Revise the first draft of your paragraph before you focus on editing. Use the Revising Checklist on pages 24–25 to help you with your revision. Make sure your paragraph has a good topic sentence, is well developed, and is well organized. Then check your paragraph for unity and coherence.

ABOUT FRAGMENTS

A complete sentence must have both a subject and a verb. If one or both are missing or if the subject and verb are introduced by a dependent word, you have only part of a sentence, a **fragment.** Even if it begins with a capital letter and ends with a period, it cannot stand alone and must be corrected in your writing. The five most common types of fragments are explained in this chapter.

Type 1: Afterthought Fragment

He works at the garage. **And the bank.**

Type 2: *-ing* Fragment

Breaking the sidewalk. The oak tree is old large and strong.

Type 3: *to* Fragment

Some people have moved. **To live in the heart of town.**

Type 4: Dependent-Clause Fragment

Because there are no malls here. We go to another city to shop.

Type 5: Relative-Clause Fragment

The hardware store is on the corner. **Which is a good location.**

WAYS TO CORRECT FRAGMENTS

Once you have identified a fragment, you have two options for correcting it. You can connect the fragment to the sentence before or after it or make the fragment into an independent clause:

Correction 1.   Connect the fragment to the sentence before or after it.
Correction 2.   Make the fragment into an independent clause:
          (a) add the missing subject and/or verb, or
          (b) drop the subordinating word before the fragment.

REVIEWING FRAGMENTS

What is a sentence fragment?

A sentence fragment is punctuated like a sentence but is missing a subject and/or

verb or is introduced by a dependent word.

What are the five types of fragments?

afterthought fragment

-ing fragment

to fragment

dependent-clause fragment

relative-clause fragment

What are the two ways to correct a fragment?

1. Connect it to the sentence before or after it.   2. Make it into an independent clause.

IDENTIFYING AND CORRECTING FRAGMENTS

The rest of this chapter discusses the five types of fragments and the corrections for each type.

Type 1: Afterthought Fragments

Afterthought fragments occur when you add an idea to a sentence but don't punctuate it correctly.

Fragment: He works at the garage. **And the bank.**

The phrase *And the bank* is punctuated and capitalized as a complete sentence. Because this group of words lacks a subject and a verb, however, it is a fragment.

Correction 1:   He works at the garage **and** the bank.

Correction 2:   He works at the garage. **He also works** at the bank.

REVIEWING AFTERTHOUGHT FRAGMENTS

What is an afterthought fragment? An idea added to a sentence but not punctuated correctly

Give an example of an afterthought fragment.
Examples will vary.

What are the two ways to correct an afterthought fragment?

1. Connect it to the sentence before or after it.

2. Make it into an independent clause by adding the missing subject and/or verb to it.

🌱 **Practice 1 Identifying**   Underline the afterthought fragments in each of the following sentences.

1. I applied for a credit card. <u>But was turned down.</u>

2. Tim looked into the room and saw his keys. <u>On the end table.</u> He was very frustrated.

3. Sharla is sleeping in class today because she stayed up late. <u>With her homework.</u>

4. Spring is my favorite time of year because flowers are growing. <u>And blooming.</u>

5. Carlene turned in her paper by the deadline. <u>But received a poor grade.</u>

6. Jerome ate pizza. <u>With anchovies on it.</u> His breath smelled disgusting.

7. Juana sits next to me. <u>In class.</u> And tries to copy my homework.

8. The best books I ever read were *Gulliver's Travels.* <u>And *Lord of the Flies.*</u> *The Slave Dancer* is good too.

9. The boy bumped his head. <u>On the bedpost.</u> <u>And cried loudly until his mother heard him.</u>

10. My air conditioner isn't working. <u>Or blowing out any cold air.</u>

✸ Practice 2 Identifying   Underline the afterthought fragments in the following paragraph.

The best day of my life was July 6, 2001. <u>A Monday.</u> My sister helped me move into my new apartment. <u>On the east side of town.</u> I loved living with my parents, but I felt it was time to move on. When I found this apartment, I knew it was perfect. <u>And just my style.</u> The apartment has a big living room and kitchen. <u>But only one tiny bedroom.</u> While we were moving my stuff, my sister said she was jealous. She had no job. <u>And couldn't move out on her own yet.</u> I almost felt sorry for her. Then I remembered how nice it was to have my own place. <u>And stopped worrying about her.</u>

✸ Practice 3 Correcting   Correct the afterthought fragments in Practice 1 by rewriting them, using both correction methods. *Answers will vary.*

1. _____

2. _____

3. _____

4. _____

5. _____

6. _____

7. _____

8. _____

9. _____

10. _____

🌾 **Practice 4 Correcting**   Rewrite the paragraph in Practice 2, correcting the fragments. *Answers will vary.*

_____

_____

_____

_____

_____

_____

🌾 **Practice 5 Writing Your Own**

A. Write five afterthought fragments of your own, or record five from your papers. *Answers will vary.*

1. _____

2. _____

3. _____

4. _____

5. _____

B. Correct these fragments, using both correction methods. *Answers will vary.*

1. _____

2. _____

3. _____

4. _____

5. _____

Type 2: *-ing* Fragments

Words that end in *-ing* are formed from verbs but cannot be the main verbs in their sentences. For an *-ing* word to function as a verb, it must have a helping verb with it (see pages 101–102).

Fragment: **Breaking the sidewalk.** The oak tree is large and strong.

Breaking is not a verb in its sentence because it has no helping verb. Also, this group of words is a fragment because it has no subject.

Correction 1:   **Breaking the sidewalk,** the oak tree is large and strong.

Correction 2:   **The oak tree is breaking the sidewalk.** The oak tree is large and strong.

HINT: When you connect an *-ing* fragment to a sentence, insert a comma between the two sentence parts. You should insert the comma whether the *-ing* part comes at the beginning or the end of the sentence.

The oak tree is large and strong, **breaking the sidewalk.**

Breaking the sidewalk, the oak tree is large and strong.

REVIEWING *-ing* FRAGMENTS

How can you tell if an -ing word is part of a fragment or is a main verb?

If the -ing verb has a helping verb, it is part of the main verb. Otherwise, it could be

part of a fragment.

Give an example of an -ing fragment.

Examples will vary.

What are the two ways to correct an -ing fragment?

1. Connect it to the sentence before or after it.

2. Make it into an independent clause by adding the missing subject and/or verb to it.

What kind of punctuation should you use when you join an -ing fragment to another sentence?

Use a comma when joining an -ing fragment to another sentence.

Practice 6 Identifying   Underline the *-ing* fragments in each of the following sentences.

1. <u>Driving to the store</u>. I wore my seat belt.

2. The boy is coloring. <u>Breaking the crayons in half</u>.

3. <u>Sleeping in the corner</u>. The cat is curled into a ball.

4. Something has leaked on the floor. <u>Making a big mess</u>.

5. I hear soft music in the background. <u>Setting the tone of the movie</u>.

6. <u>Eating a large pastrami sandwich</u>. Nick got a stomachache.

7. When this term is over, I'm going home. <u>Starting my big vacation</u>.

8. <u>Reading at night</u>. Travis fell asleep on his books.

9. The last time we went to that restaurant, we were unhappy. <u>Waiting twenty minutes for drink refills</u>.

10. <u>Playing in the swimming pool all afternoon</u>. I got a sunburn.

Practice 7 Identifying   Underline the *-ing* fragments in the following paragraph.

When my brother joined the Navy, he was very excited. <u>Wanting to travel around the world and meet new people</u>. The reality was not so entertaining. He did get to travel, but he wasn't always stationed in exotic places. <u>Lying on the beach or visiting famous landmarks</u>. He also had a pretty boring job. <u>Washing jet planes</u>. <u>Working the graveyard shift</u>. When he was in high school, he was quite rebellious. <u>Making bad choices in friends</u>. He was often in trouble for breaking his curfew and staying out too late. Overall, the Navy was good for him. <u>Forcing him to grow up</u>. Though it wasn't the paid vacation that he expected, it did give him the taste of responsibility that he needed.

Practice 8 Correcting   Correct the *-ing* fragments in Practice 6 by rewriting them, using both correction methods. Remember to insert a comma with correction 1. *Answers will vary.*

1. _____

2. _____

3. _____

4. _____

5. _____

6. _____

7. _____

8. _____

9. _____

10. _____

❋ **Practice 9 Correcting**   Rewrite the paragraph in Practice 7, correcting the fragments. Remember to insert a comma with correction 1. *Answers will vary.*

_____

_____

_____

_____

_____

_____

❋ **Practice 10 Writing Your Own**

A. Write five *-ing* fragments of your own, or record five from your papers. *Answers will vary.*

1. _____

2. _____

3. _____

4. _____

5. _____

B. Correct these fragments, using both correction methods. *Answers will vary.*

1. _____

2. _____

3. _____

4. _____

5. _____

Type 3: *to* Fragments

When *to* is added to a verb (*to see, to hop, to skip, to jump*), the combination cannot be a main verb in its sentence. As a result, this group of words is often involved in a fragment.

Fragment: Some people have moved. **To live in the heart of town.**

Because *to* + a verb cannot function as the main verb of its sentence, *to live in the heart of town* is a fragment as it is punctuated here.

Correction 1:   Some people have moved **to live in the heart of town.**

Correction 2:   Some people have moved. **They live in the heart of town.**

HINT: A *to* fragment can also occur at the beginning of a sentence. In this case, insert a comma between the two sentence parts when correcting the fragment.

To live in the heart of town, some people have moved.

REVIEWING *to* FRAGMENTS

What does a to fragment consist of?

A to fragment consists of to plus a verb.

Give an example of a to fragment.

Examples will vary.

What are the two ways to correct a to fragment?

1. Connect it to the sentence before or after it.

2. Make it into an independent clause by adding the missing subject and/or verb to it.

Practice 11 Identifying   Underline the *to* fragments in each of the following sentences.

1. My neighbors drive an expensive car. To look like they are rich.

2. Harry is going with me. To help me buy a car. He is a good negotiator.

3. Breanne makes her own clothes. To save money.

4. To be more prepared for the test. I will devote my weekend to studying.

5. To grow tomatoes in your backyard. You need a big garden area.

6. This is the last time we will call you. To ask you for a donation.

7. <u>To finish wallpapering the living room</u>. My husband will take tomorrow off work.

8. This morning I got up at 5 a.m. <u>To jog around the block before I got in the shower</u>.

9. Julie was getting her nails done. <u>To be in a wedding on Saturday</u>.

10. Put your feet up and relax. <u>To watch this movie with me</u>.

🌿 Practice 12 Identifying   Underline the *to* fragments in the following paragraph.

My parents are finally putting in a swimming pool. <u>To keep us from bothering the neighbors</u>. We have been telling them for years that we need a pool, but they always complained about money. <u>To avoid the discussion</u>. Last weekend, my dad learned from a friend about a company that installs swimming pools at a reasonable price. We were so happy. <u>To finally get a pool of our own</u>. The contractor said it would take six to eight weeks. <u>To finish the pool</u>. In the meantime, our back fence has been pulled down. <u>To make room for the big backhoe</u>. It is exciting for my brother and me. <u>To watch the construction</u>. We can't wait to go swimming in our own backyard.

🌿 Practice 13 Correcting   Correct the *to* fragments in Practice 11 by rewriting them, using both correction methods. *Answers will vary.*

1. _____

2. _____

3. _____

4. _____

5. _____

6. _____

7. _____

8. _____

9. _____

10. _____

🌿 Practice 14 Correcting   Rewrite the paragraph in Practice 12, correcting the fragments. Rearrange the sentences if necessary. Remember to

insert a comma when you add the *to* fragment to the beginning of a sentence. *Answers will vary.*

_____

_____

_____

_____

_____

_____

❧ Practice 15 Writing Your Own

A. Write five *to* fragments of your own, or record five from your papers.
Answers will vary.

1. _____

2. _____

3. _____

4. _____

5. _____

B. Correct these fragments, using both correction methods. *Students should connect the fragment to the sentence before or after it and should make it into an independent clause.*

1. _____

2. _____

3. _____

4. _____

5. _____

Type 4: Dependent-Clause Fragments

A group of words that begins with a **subordinating conjunction** (see the list on the next page) is called a **dependent clause** and cannot stand alone. Even though it has a subject and a verb, it is a fragment because it depends on an independent clause to complete its meaning. An **independent clause** is a group of words with a subject and a verb that can stand alone. (See pages 88–90 for help with clauses.)

Here is a list of some commonly used subordinating conjunctions that create dependent clauses.

Subordinating Conjunctions

after	because	since	until
although	before	so	when
as	even if	so that	whenever
as if	even though	than	where
as long as	how	that	wherever
as soon as	if	though	whether
as though	in order that	unless	while

Fragment: **Because there are no malls here.** We go to another city to shop.

This sentence has a subject and a verb, but it is introduced by a subordinating conjunction, *because*. As a result, this sentence is a dependent clause and cannot stand alone.

Correction 1:   Because there are no malls here**, we** go to another city to shop.

Correction 2:   ~~Because~~ There are no malls here. We go to another city to shop.

HINT: If the dependent clause comes first, put a comma between the two parts of the sentence. If the dependent clause comes second, the comma is not necessary.

Because there are no malls here, we go to another city to shop.

We go to another city to shop **because there are no malls here.**

REVIEWING DEPENDENT-CLAUSE FRAGMENTS

What is a dependent-clause fragment?

A group of words with a subject and verb that cannot stand alone

What type of conjunction makes a clause dependent?

subordinating conjunction

What is an independent clause?

A group of words with a subject and verb that can stand alone

Give an example of a dependent-clause fragment.

Examples will vary.

What are the two ways to correct a dependent-clause fragment?

1. *Connect it to the sentence before or after it.*

2. *Make it into an independent clause by dropping the subordinating word before it.*

❦ Practice 16 Identifying   Underline the dependent-clause fragments in each of the following sentences.

1. <u>While my daughter slept</u>. I finished her scrapbook.

2. <u>Although my brother is in my Spanish class</u>. He will not help me with homework.

3. This winter will be very cold. <u>Since this summer was not as warm as usual</u>.

4. Jared will practice basketball every day. <u>Even if he doesn't make the team</u>.

5. <u>As soon as Maury gets here</u>. I'm going home.

6. Nelly can do the video portion of the project. <u>Unless you have a better idea</u>.

7. <u>Before the sun comes up tomorrow</u>. We will be driving through New Mexico.

8. The Dixie Chicks sang "There's Your Trouble." <u>When they gave a concert in our town</u>.

9. My computer speakers went out. <u>While I was listening to a radio show on the Internet</u>.

10. <u>As long as I am in charge</u>. This is the way we should organize the club.

❦ Practice 17 Identifying   Underline the dependent-clause fragments in the following paragraph.

    <u>While I was driving through my hometown</u>. I noticed the ice-cream parlor where I used to work. During my high school years, the

parlor was a popular hangout. <u>Even though the ice cream was a little overpriced</u>. The owners were Sam and Billy, who let my friends come by to visit with me. <u>Whenever I had to work weekends</u>. <u>Before it was an ice-cream parlor</u>. The building was used as a bank. Everyone in the town was glad to have the parlor instead. <u>So that teenagers had somewhere safe to spend time</u>. Sam and Billy were the best bosses I could have asked for. <u>Although the pay was not very good</u>. I will never forget that job. <u>Because I learned so much about myself</u>.

🌿 Practice 18 Correcting   Correct the dependent-clause fragments in Practice 16 by rewriting them, using both correction methods. *Answers will vary.*

1. _____
2. _____
3. _____
4. _____
5. _____
6. _____
7. _____
8. _____
9. _____
10. _____

🌿 Practice 19 Correcting   Rewrite the paragraph in Practice 17, correcting the fragments. When you use correction 1, remember to add a comma if the dependent clause comes first. *Answers will vary.*

_____

_____

_____

_____

_____

_____

🌿 Practice 20 Writing Your Own

A. Write five dependent-clause fragments of your own, or record five from your papers. *Answers will vary.*

1. _____

2. _____

3. _____

4. _____

5. _____

B. Correct these fragments, using both correction methods. *Answers will vary.*

1. _____

2. _____

3. _____

4. _____

5. _____

Type 5: Relative-Clause Fragments

A **relative clause** is a dependent clause that begins with a **relative pronoun:** *who, whom, whose, which,* or *that.* When a relative clause is punctuated as a sentence, the result is a fragment.

> **Fragment:**   The hardware store is on the corner. **Which is a good location.**

Which is a good location is a clause fragment that begins with the relative pronoun *which.* This word automatically makes the words that follow it a dependent clause, so they cannot stand alone as a sentence.

> **Correction 1:**   The hardware store is on the corner, **w**hich is a good location.

> **Correction 2:**   The hardware store is on the corner. **It** is a good location.

REVIEWING RELATIVE-CLAUSE FRAGMENTS

How is a relative-clause fragment different from a dependent-clause fragment?

A relative-clause fragment begins with a relative pronoun rather than a subordi-

nating conjunction.

Give an example of a relative-clause fragment.

Examples will vary.

What are the two ways to correct a relative-clause fragment?

1. Connect it to the sentence before or after it.

2. Make it into an independent clause by dropping the relative pronoun.

Practice 21 Identifying   Underline the relative-clause fragments in the following sentences.

1. The company president is Mr. Washington. <u>Who always sits with my family at church.</u>

2. My brother is taking the class. <u>That is taught by Dr. Roberts.</u>

3. Those are the neighbors. <u>Whose dogs run loose in the streets.</u>

4. I am taking a trip to Poughkeepsie. <u>Which is in New York.</u>

5. Maureen talked to the woman. <u>Whose car is for sale.</u>

6. You are the one. <u>Whom the committee selected.</u>

7. I just quit smoking. <u>Which was the hardest thing I've ever done.</u>

8. This afternoon, I have a meeting with the dean. <u>Who is in charge of admissions.</u>

9. Dennis works at the restaurant. <u>That is on Elm Street.</u>

10. Sherry is going on a date with Jack. <u>Whom she met at the coffeehouse.</u>

Practice 22 Identifying   Underline the relative-clause fragments in the following paragraph.

Last year, I celebrated Independence Day with Christine. <u>Whom I met through work</u>. She had a dinner party at her house. <u>Which is on the corner of Fourth Street and Harker Avenue</u>. Christine invited several other people as well. <u>Who brought fireworks and sparklers</u>. The food was great, the company was nice, and the fireworks were entertaining. I met one guy at the party, who drove a beautiful 1965 Mustang. <u>That was fully restored</u>. He was friendly and attractive, but he had a girlfriend. <u>Whose father happened to be the city's mayor</u>. This year, Christine is having another party, and I hope to go.

❋ Practice 23 Correcting   Correct the relative-clause fragments in Practice 21 by rewriting them, using both correction methods. *Answers will vary.*

1. _____
2. _____
3. _____
4. _____
5. _____
6. _____
7. _____
8. _____
9. _____
10. _____

❋ Practice 24 Correcting   Rewrite the paragraph in Practice 22, correcting the fragments. *Answers will vary.*

_____

_____

_____

_____

_____

_____

Practice 25 Writing Your Own

A. Write five relative-clause fragments of your own, or record five from your papers. *Answers will vary.*

1. ______________________________
2. ______________________________
3. ______________________________
4. ______________________________
5. ______________________________

B. Correct these fragments, using both correction methods. *Answers will vary.*

1. ______________________________
2. ______________________________
3. ______________________________
4. ______________________________
5. ______________________________

CHAPTER REVIEW

You might want to reread your answers to the questions in the review boxes before you do the following exercises.

Review Practice 1 Reading Refer to the paragraph by Bailey White on page 107 to do the following exercises.

A. Write one of each type of fragment based on White's paragraph:

Afterthought: ______________________________

-ing Fragment: ______________________________

to Fragment: ______________________________

Dependent Clause: ______________________________

Relative Clause: ______________________________

B. Correct the fragments that you just wrote.

_____

_____

_____

_____

_____

Review Practice 2 Identifying   Underline the fragments in each of the following sentences.

1. I went to the grocery store. <u>To buy a pound of hamburger</u>.

2. <u>Trying to get the best seats</u>. We arrived at the concert early.

3. <u>Since there was nothing we could do</u>. We decided to go home.

4. Yesterday I spoke with my grandfather. <u>Who is also my best friend</u>.

5. Mrs. Robinson teaches history. <u>And economics</u>.

6. <u>While I was walking to the mailbox</u>. I tripped on my untied shoelaces.

7. Janie got her navel pierced. <u>Thinking that would make her happy</u>.

8. <u>To find the best price on computers</u>. We searched the Internet.

9. The small boy played with the heavy door. <u>And pinched his fingers</u>.

10. We invested in the alarm system. <u>That also comes with a paging service</u>.

Review Practice 3 Correcting   Correct the fragments in Review Practice 2 by rewriting each incorrect sentence. Use the methods that you learned in this chapter. *Answers will vary.*

✎ EDITING A STUDENT PARAGRAPH

Following is a paragraph written and revised by Marty Rhodes in response to the writing assignment in this chapter. Read the paragraph, and underline the subjects once and complete verbs twice.

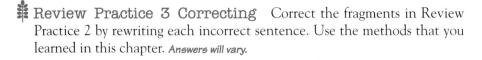

Our downtown <u>center</u> <u><u>was</u></u> just <u><u>renovated</u></u>. <u>It</u> <u><u>has</u></u> bricks down the center of the street.[And lights on the trees all year long.][A beautiful sight.]<u>I</u> never <u><u>thought</u></u> that <u>I</u> <u><u>would enjoy</u></u> downtown so much. Every <u>building</u> <u><u>is</u></u> also <u><u>being</u></u>

replastered and repainted. [So that the buildings stay in good shape.]The bars are now reopening. Downtown is attracting new people. [And bringing in a lot of money.]

Collaborative Activity

Team up with a partner, and put brackets around the four fragments in Marty's paragraph. Then, working together, use what you have learned in this chapter to correct these errors using both correction methods. Rewrite the paragraph with your corrections. *See student paragraph for errors. Corrections will vary.*

EDITING YOUR OWN PARAGRAPH

Now return to the paragraph you wrote and revised at the beginning of this chapter. Underline your subjects once and main verbs twice.

Collaborative Activity

Exchange paragraphs with your partner, and put brackets around any fragments that you find in your partner's paragraph. Watch especially for clauses with an implied *that*.

Individual Activity

On the Error Log in Appendix 6, record any fragments that your partner found in your paragraph. To complete the writing process, correct these fragments by rewriting your paragraph.

Run-Ons

 Checklist for Identifying and Correcting Run-Ons

> ✔ Are any sentences run together without punctuation?
> ✔ Are any sentences incorrectly joined with only a comma?

When we cram two separate statements into a single sentence, we create what is called a **run-on.** Run-on sentences generally distort our message and cause problems for our readers. In this chapter, you will learn how to identify and avoid run-ons in your writing.

Before you study run-on sentences, look at the well-constructed sentences in the following paragraph by Tim O'Brien.

> I drank some chocolate milk and then lay down on the sofa in the living room, not really sad, just floating, trying to imagine what it was to be dead. Nothing much came to me. I remember closing my eyes and whispering her name, almost begging, trying to make her come back. "Linda," I said, "please." And then I concentrated. I willed her alive. It was a dream, I suppose, or a daydream, but I made it happen. I saw her coming down the middle of Main Street, all alone. It was nearly dark and the street was deserted, no cars or people, and Linda wore a pink dress and shiny black shoes. I remember sitting down on the curb to watch. All her hair had grown back. The scars and stitches were gone. In the dream, if that's what it was, she was playing a game of some sort, laughing and running up the empty street, kicking a big aluminum water bucket.

In this paragraph, O'Brien is writing about an emotional daydream he once had. Before continuing in this chapter, take a moment to record a time you relied on your imagination. Save your work because you will use it later in the chapter.

> ### Writing Assignment: A Fantasy
>
> Have you ever used your imagination to get you through a tough situation? Have you ever just pretended to be somewhere else? Write a paragraph that describes one time when your imagination worked for you. Give as many details about the situation as you can.

> ### Revising Your Writing
>
> Revise the first draft of your paragraph before you focus on editing. Use the Revising Checklist on pages 24–25 to help you with your revision. Make sure your paragraph has a good topic sentence, is well developed, and is well organized. Then check your paragraph for unity and coherence.

IDENTIFYING RUN-ON SENTENCES

Whereas a fragment is a piece of a sentence, a **run-on** is two sentences written as one. A run-on just runs on—the first sentence runs into the next without the proper punctuation between the two. There are two types of run-ons: *fused sentences* and *comma splices*.

Fused Sentence: The movie ended I went home.

Comma Splice: The movie ended, I went home.

Both of these sentences are run-ons. The difference between them is one comma.

A **fused sentence** is two sentences "fused" or jammed together without any punctuation. Look at these examples of run-on sentences:

Fused Sentence: I was lying on the sofa I had just eaten lunch.

This example consists of two independent clauses with no punctuation between them:

1. I was lying on the sofa.
2. I had just eaten lunch.

Fused Sentence: I began to think about my brother I felt good.

Students will invariably choose the longer sentence as the run-on because of its length. Showing students that even very short sentences can be run-ons forces students to look at the grammar of the sentence and not the length.

■ For more sample run-ons, see the *Instructor's Resource Manual*, Section II, Part II.

TEACHING ON THE WEB
Exploring and Discussing: Have students find articles from newspapers on line (like the *New York Times* or *Washington Post*) that contain run-ons. How hard were the run-ons to find? What type of run-on appears most frequently?

TEACHING ON THE WEB
Mosaics Web Site: To learn more about run-ons, students can go to www.prenhall.com/mosaics.

This run-on also consists of two independent clauses with no punctuation between them:

1. I began to think about my brother.
2. I felt good.

Like a fused sentence, a **comma splice** incorrectly joins two independent clauses. However, a comma splice puts a comma between the two independent clauses. The only difference between a fused sentence and a comma splice is the comma. Look at the following examples:

Comma Splice: I was lying on the sofa, I had just eaten lunch.
Comma Splice: I began to think about my brother, I felt good.

Both of these sentences consist of two independent clauses. But a comma is not the proper punctuation to separate these two clauses.

REVIEWING RUN-ON SENTENCES

What are the two types of run-on sentences?

_____fused sentence_____   _____comma splice_____

What is the difference between them?

A fused sentence has no punctuation between the run-together sentences, and a

comma splice has a comma between them.

Practice 1 Identifying   Identify each run-on in the following sentences as either fused (F) or comma splice (CS). Put a slash between the independent clauses that are not joined correctly.

1. ___F___ Devon wanted to join the swim team/he had been practicing all summer.

2. ___CS___ The car stalled in the middle of the road,/two men helped push it out of traffic.

3. ___CS___ I don't know why you weren't there,/I'm sure you had a good excuse.

4. ___F___ Henrietta ran quickly to the phone/she didn't want to miss the call.

5. ___CS___ Summer is coming,/the children are ready for a vacation from school.

6. ___CS___ The team practiced for the tournament,/it was three weeks away.

7. ___F___ The book is on the table/it is collecting dust.

8. ___F___ Journals are on the third floor of the library/the copy machines are there too.

9. ___F___ I like to see movies during my free time/the last movie I saw was *Shrek.*

10. ___CS___ Kimber is getting married in August,/she has already found her wedding dress.

Practice 2 Identifying   In each of the following sentences, put a slash between the independent clauses that are not joined correctly.

1. This class is being taught by Dr. Smith,/she is the best professor in the department.

2. I am doing a report on Rudolfo Anaya/there are five books about him in our library.

3. We are leaving this morning and should arrive by midafternoon,/it is a six-hour drive.

4. Manny's computer has a virus/I hope he doesn't send me any e-mail.

5. My grandmother has the prettiest roses in her garden/she said they are 80 years old.

6. Olivia called the bank to check on her account,/she had more money than she thought.

7. My campus is organizing a drug awareness program,/it will be an outreach for elementary students.

8. We are entering an art contest/it is held at the fairgrounds.

9. Yvonne made my favorite dessert/it was a chocolate cream pie.

10. The geraniums on the counter are wilting,/they need some water.

Practice 3 Identifying   Label each run-on in the following paragraph as either fused (F) or comma splice (CS).

(1) _____F_____ My girlfriend and I rented a movie last night it was *Proof of Life*. (2) _____CS_____ We ordered a pizza and put on the show, within 15 minutes I was falling asleep. (3) _____CS_____ I guess I stayed up too late the night before, there was a big test in my math class. Boy, was I embarrassed when I couldn't stay awake! (4) _____F_____ My girlfriend nudged me about five times, trying to wake me up I just couldn't keep my eyes open. (5) _____CS_____ Finally, she gave up and let me sleep, just as the movie was ending, I woke up.

Practice 4 Identifying   Put a slash between any independent clauses that are not joined correctly.

I went to an antique store yesterday/I was looking for an old tricycle. I wanted to put it in the corner of my bedroom,/I have the perfect teddy bear to sit on the seat. Unfortunately, the antique store didn't have any tricycles,/it did have a little wagon. It was red and just the right size/it said "Radio Flyer" on the side in chipped white paint. I talked to the store owner about the price/he wanted $50 for it. I told him that was too expensive/I didn't want to spend that much money. He wouldn't lower his price, so this weekend I'm going to look at yard sales,/maybe I can find something there.

Practice 5 Writing Your Own

A. Find five run-on sentences in your writing or in another student's writing. *Answers will vary.*

1. _____
2. _____
3. _____
4. _____
5. _____

B. Write five new run-on sentences of your own. *Answers will vary.*

1. _____
2. _____

3. _____

4. _____

5. _____

CORRECTING RUN-ON SENTENCES

You have four different options for correcting your run-on sentences:

1. Separate the two sentences with a period, and capitalize the next word.
2. Separate the two sentences with a comma, and add a coordinating con-junction (*and, but, for, nor, or, so,* or *yet*).
3. Change one of the sentences into a dependent clause with a subordinat-ing conjunction (such as *if, because, since, after,* or *when*) or a relative pronoun (*who, whom, whose, which,* or *that*).
4. Separate the two sentences with a semicolon.

Correction 1: Use a Period

Separate the two sentences with a period, and capitalize the next word.

I was lying on the sofa**. I** had just eaten lunch.

I began to think about my brother**. I** felt good.

Practice 6 Correcting   Correct the run-on sentences in Practice 1 by rewriting them, using correction 1. *Students should insert a period where the slashes are and capitalize the next word.*

1. _____

2. _____

3. _____

4. _____

5. _____

6. _____

7. _____

8. _____

9. _____

10. _____

🌿 **Practice 7 Correcting**   Correct the run-on sentences in Practice 2 by rewriting them, using correction 1. *Students should insert a period where the slashes are and capitalize the next word.*

1. _____
2. _____
3. _____
4. _____
5. _____
6. _____
7. _____
8. _____
9. _____
10. _____

🌿 **Practice 8 Correcting**   Correct the run-on sentences in Practice 3 by rewriting the paragraph, using correction 1. *Students should insert periods after night, show, before, up, and sleep, and they should capitalize it, within, there, I, and just.*

_____
_____
_____
_____
_____
_____

🌿 **Practice 9 Correcting**   Correct the run-on sentences in Practice 4 by rewriting the paragraph, using correction 1. *Students should insert a period where the slashes are and capitalize the next word.*

_____
_____
_____
_____
_____
_____

🌱 Practice 10 Writing Your Own

A. Correct the five run-on sentences from Practice 5A by rewriting them, using correction 1. *Separate with a period.*

1. _____
2. _____
3. _____
4. _____
5. _____

B. Correct the five run-on sentences from Practice 5B by rewriting them, using correction 1. *Separate with a period.*

1. _____
2. _____
3. _____
4. _____
5. _____

Correction 2: Use a Coordinating Conjunction

Separate the two sentences with a comma, and add a coordinating conjunction (*and, but, for, nor, or, so,* or *yet*).

I was lying on the sofa, **for** I had just eaten lunch.

I began to think about my brother, **so** I felt good.

🌱 Practice 11 Correcting   Correct the run-on sentences in Practice 1 by rewriting them, using correction 2. *Students should insert a comma and a coordinating conjunction where the slashes are.*

1. _____
2. _____
3. _____
4. _____
5. _____

6. _____

7. _____

8. _____

9. _____

10. _____

❧ Practice 12 Correcting   Correct the run-on sentences in Practice 2 by rewriting them, using correction 2. *Students should insert a comma and a coordinating conjunction where the slashes are.*

1. _____

2. _____

3. _____

4. _____

5. _____

6. _____

7. _____

8. _____

9. _____

10. _____

❧ Practice 13 Correcting   Correct the run-on sentences in Practice 3 by rewriting the paragraph, using correction 2. *Students should insert a comma and a coordinating conjunction between night and it, show and within, before and there, up and I, and sleep and just.*

_____

_____

_____

_____

_____

_____

❧ Practice 14 Correcting   Correct the run-on sentences in Practice 4 by rewriting the paragraph using correction 2. *Students should insert a comma and a coordinating conjunction where the slashes are.*

_____

_____

_____

_____

_____

_____

❈ Practice 15 Writing Your Own

A. Correct the five run-on sentences from Practice 5A by rewriting them, using correction 2. *Separate with a comma and a coordinating conjunction.*

1. _____
2. _____
3. _____
4. _____
5. _____

B. Correct the five run-on sentences from Practice 5B by rewriting them using correction 2. *Separate with a comma and a coordinating conjunction.*

1. _____
2. _____
3. _____
4. _____
5. _____

Correction 3: Create a Dependent Clause

Change one of the sentences into a dependent clause with a subordinating conjunction (such as *if, because, since, after,* or *when*) or a relative pronoun (*who, whom, whose, which,* or *that*).

I was lying on the sofa **because** I had just eaten lunch.

Whenever I began to think about my brother, I felt good.

For a list of subordinating conjunctions, see page 80.

HINT: If you put the dependent clause at the beginning of the sentence, add a comma between the two sentence parts.

Because I had just eaten lunch, I was lying on the sofa.

🌱 Practice 16 Correcting   Correct the run-on sentences in Practice 1 by rewriting them, using correction 3. *Students should change one of the sentences in each run-on into a dependent clause with a subordinating conjunction.*

1. _____
2. _____
3. _____
4. _____
5. _____
6. _____
7. _____
8. _____
9. _____
10. _____

🌱 Practice 17 Correcting   Correct the run-on sentences in Practice 2 by rewriting them, using correction 3. *Students should change one of the sentences in each run-on into a dependent clause with a subordinating conjunction.*

1. _____
2. _____
3. _____
4. _____
5. _____
6. _____
7. _____
8. _____
9. _____
10. _____

🌿 Practice 18 Correcting   Correct the run-on sentences in Practice 3
by rewriting the paragraph, using correction 3. *Students should change one of the
sentences in each run-on into a dependent clause with a subordinating conjunction.*

_____

_____

_____

_____

_____

_____

🌿 Practice 19 Correcting   Correct the run-on sentences in Practice 4
by rewriting the paragraph, using correction 3. *Students should change one of the
sentences in each run-on into a dependent clause with a subordinating conjunction.*

_____

_____

_____

_____

_____

_____

🌿 Practice 20 Writing Your Own

A. Correct the five run-on sentences from Practice 5A by rewriting them,
using correction 3. *Create a dependent clause.*

1. _____

2. _____

3. _____

4. _____

5. _____

B. Correct the five run-on sentences from Practice 5B by rewriting them,
using correction 3. *Create a dependent clause.*

1. _____

2. _____

3. _____

4. _____

5. _____

Correction 4: Use a Semicolon

Separate the two sentences with a semicolon.

I was lying on the sofa**;** I had just eaten lunch.

I began to think about my brother**;** I felt good.

You can also use a **transition,** a word or expression that indicates how the two parts of the sentence are related, with a semicolon. A transition often makes the sentence smoother. It is preceded by a semicolon and followed by a comma.

I was lying on the sofa**; in fact,** I had just eaten lunch.

I began to think about my brother**; consequently,** I felt good.

Here are some transitions commonly used with semicolons.

Transitions Used with a Semicolon Before and a Comma After

also	*however*	*furthermore*	*instead*
meanwhile	*consequently*	*for example*	*similarly*
in contrast	*therefore*	*for instance*	*otherwise*
of course	*finally*	*in fact*	*nevertheless*

🌱 Practice 21 Correcting   Correct the run-on sentences in Practice 1 by rewriting them, using correction 4. *Students should put semicolons where the slashes are.*

1. _____

2. _____

3. _____

4. _____

5. _____

6. _____

7. _____

8. _____

9. _____

10. _____

❊ Practice 22 Correcting   Correct the run-on sentences in Practice 2 by rewriting them, using correction 4. *Students should put semicolons where the slashes are.*

1. _____

2. _____

3. _____

4. _____

5. _____

6. _____

7. _____

8. _____

9. _____

10. _____

❊ Practice 23 Correcting   Correct the run-on sentences in Practice 3 by rewriting the paragraph, using correction 4. *Students should put semicolons between night and it, show and within, before and there, up and I, and sleep and just.*

_____

_____

_____

_____

_____

_____

❊ Practice 24 Correcting   Correct the run-on sentences in Practice 4 by rewriting the paragraph, using correction 4. *Students should put semicolons where the slashes are.*

_____

_____

_____

_____

_____

_____

Practice 25 Writing Your Own

A. Correct the five run-on sentences from Practice 5A by rewriting them, using correction 4. *Separate with a semicolon.*

1. ____________________
2. ____________________
3. ____________________
4. ____________________
5. ____________________

B. Correct the five run-on sentences from Practice 5B by rewriting them, using correction 4. *Separate with a semicolon.*

1. ____________________
2. ____________________
3. ____________________
4. ____________________
5. ____________________

Reviewing Methods of Correcting Run-On Sentences

What are the four ways to correct a run-on sentence?

1. *Separate the two sentences with a period, and capitalize the next word.*
2. *Separate the two sentences with a comma, and add a coordinating conjunction.*
3. *Change one of the sentences into a dependent clause with a subordinating conjunction.*
4. *Separate the two sentences with a semicolon.*

Why is correcting run-ons important?

They distort a writer's message and cause readers problems.

CHAPTER REVIEW

You might want to reread your answers to the questions in the review boxes before you do the following exercises.

❧ **Review Practice 1 Reading**   Refer to the paragraph by Tim O'Brien on page 128 to do the following exercises.

1. Write a fused sentence based on Tim O'Brien's paragraph:

   _____

2. Correct the fused sentence that you just wrote using the four correction methods.

   Correction 1: _____

   Correction 2: _____

   Correction 3: _____

   Correction 4: _____

3. Write a comma splice based on Tim O'Brien's paragraph:

   _____

4. Correct the comma splice that you just wrote using the four correction methods.

   Correction 1: _____

   Correction 2: _____

   Correction 3: _____

   Correction 4: _____

❧ **Review Practice 2 Identifying**   Put slashes between the run-ons in each of the following sentences.

1. My brother wants to go with us/we'd better let him, or he'll feel bad.

2. The printer is jammed again/that's the second time this month.

3. I hope you remembered to pay the water bill/I think it's past due.

4. Tracy left the party last night,/she was crying.

5. My memory is failing/I can't remember anything anymore.

6. Loan me three dollars,/I need to bring cookies to the class party.

7. Simon sits next to me in class,/he always takes great notes.

8. The airbag inflated during the accident/it broke the driver's nose.

9. My favorite shoes are my white Nike sneakers/I wear them every day.

10. If you want to go, you should ask,/I can't read your mind.

🎋 **Review Practice 3 Correcting**   Correct the run-on sentences in Review Practice 2 by rewriting each incorrect sentence. Use the methods that you learned in this chapter. *Answers will vary.*

✎ EDITING A STUDENT PARAGRAPH

Following is a paragraph written and revised by Melanie Frazier in response to the writing assignment in this chapter. Read the paragraph, and underline each of her independent clauses.

My imagination has saved my life several times /I call on it to get me out of binds all the time. When I am depressed, it finds a way to take me away from the problem that is bothering me. My mom would call this activity daydreaming,/I call it self-defense. Usually, I just start drifting in my mind away from the trouble at hand. I remember one time in my first few weeks of college,/I got a paper back in English class with a low grade. To keep myself from crying, I started to drift. I took a journey up into my childhood tree house/I stayed up there in my mind for a long time, playing with old toys and talking to my childhood friends. I don't know what happened in class that day,/I had a great time remembering.

Collaborative Activity

Team up with a partner, and put slashes between the clauses in the two fused sentences and three comma splices in Melanie's paragraph. Then, working together, use what you have learned in this chapter to correct these errors using all four correction methods. Rewrite the paragraph with your corrections. *See student essay for answers. Corrections will vary.*

🌿 EDITING YOUR OWN PARAGRAPH

Now return to the paragraph you wrote and revised at the beginning of this chapter. Underline each of your independent clauses.

Collaborative Activity

Exchange paragraphs with your partner, and put slashes between the clauses in any run-on sentences that you find in your partner's paragraph.

Individual Activity

On the Error Log in Appendix 6, record the run-on sentences that your partner found in your paragraph. To complete the writing process, correct these run-ons using the four correction methods.

Unit 1 Review Sentences

※ **Unit Practice 1 Identifying**   Underline the fragments or put a slash between the independent clauses in run-on sentences in each of the following sentences. Remember to identify the subjects and verbs to help you find these errors.

1. Cats and dogs are often treated as children. <u>And part of the family</u>.

2. Carmen was at the public pool,/she was meeting Toby there.

3. <u>Hoping it will increase in value</u>. Many people collect old money.

4. <u>When the flowers are in bloom in spring</u>. My grandmother's garden is spectacular.

5. Driving up to Diamond Lake at midnight was a hard task/I almost fell asleep at the wheel.

6. Thomas was a fabulous tutor,/the university lost him when he became a teacher at Stockdale High.

7. Computers save us a lot of time,/they are a good way to organize bills.

8. I went through the old chest. <u>Hoping to find something from my high school days</u>.

9. My mother lives in Sacramento/I'm going to visit her this weekend.

10. The lawyers were convinced of the jury's decision. <u>After bribing a corrupt juror</u>.

11. The air pressure gauge was broken /she almost panicked underwater when she realized her problem.

12. We visited the Broken Heart. <u>A pub in rural England</u>.

13. <u>To get a better grade</u>. Shelby studied all weekend.

■ For additional material about teaching sentences, for journal entries, and for various tests, see the *Instructor's Resource Manual*, Section II, Part II.

ADDITIONAL WRITING TOPIC
Have your students expand into well-developed essays the paragraphs they wrote in one of the unit chapters.

14. If you get a chance, I would like to ask you some questions/I have a big decision to make.

15. I didn't get enough sleep last night,/now I can't think clearly.

16. I was reading a book about vampires/I had nightmares that Dracula was chasing me.

17. People are afraid of the ocean. <u>Because they think that sharks will attack them</u>.

18. <u>Sitting peacefully watching the sunset</u>. She was able to clear her mind.

19. Please carry my books for me,/my arm is about to break.

20. <u>During the afternoon that I skipped class</u>. I missed two quizzes and an in-class essay.

❊ Unit Practice 2 Correcting   Correct the fragments and run-ons in Unit Practice 1 by rewriting each incorrect sentence. *Answers will vary.*

❊ Unit Practice 3 Identifying   In the following paragraph, underline the fragments or put a slash between the independent clauses in run-on sentences. Remember to identify the subjects and verbs to help you find these errors.

    Eating fast food is not the healthiest way to go, but it sure is the cheapest. <u>And the best</u>. There are places now that serve 49-cent tacos,/others serve 59-cent hamburgers. Fast-food corporations have ensured that families of four can eat out for less than $10. <u>Which is very cheap</u>. This is appealing to many families/then they fall into the fast-food trap. <u>Eating out all the time</u>. Once people become accustomed to eating out cheaply, it's hard to return to making home-cooked meals. Sometimes this can lead to health problems /often people gain weight. Eating fast food can also cause families to become strangers, they usually don't sit down long enough to talk about what is going on in their lives. <u>Which is very sad</u>. People should take the time to slow down at least once a month. <u>To eat a meal together at home</u>. That way, families can remain happy/they will always have one night together. Therefore, families should not get used to eating fast food,/then they will never learn to eat properly. They become fast-food junkies for life/they will lose valuable time with their family members. <u>Hardly worth it</u>.

❊ Unit Practice 4 Correcting   Correct the fragments and run-ons in Unit Practice 3 by rewriting the paragraph. *Answers will vary.*

UNIT WRITING ASSIGNMENTS

1. What are the people in this picture looking at? Who are they? What has just happened? Use your imagination to fill in the details in this picture. Then explain what's going on here.

2. You have been asked to write a short statement for your English class about a fairly radical change you just made in your life or in your behavior. What did you change? Why did you make this particular change? Explain in detail this adjustment.

3. You have been asked by a friend to recommend a place for her to travel. What is your recommendation? Why do you recommend this place?

4. Describe the atmosphere of the classroom in your English class. Who sets the pace of the instruction in the class? What is the chemistry in the class? How does it compare to other classes? What is your opinion of the classroom atmosphere?

5. Create your own assignment (with the help of your instructor), and write a response to it.

Unit 2 Verbs

Verbs can do just about anything we ask them to do. Because they have so many forms, they can play lots of different roles in a sentence: The bells *ring* on the hour; I like that *ring* on your *ring* finger; we could here the clock *ringing* miles away. As you can see from these examples, even small changes, like a single letter added to a word, mean something; as a result, verbs make communication more interesting and accurate. But using verbs correctly takes concentration and effort on your part.

In this unit, we will discuss the following aspects of verbs and verb use:

Students need to understand that verbs are the heart and soul of their sentences and that using verbs correctly is a major part of communication—in college and in the workplace. Only when students realize the importance of verbs in the communication process will they take time to learn how to use them correctly.

Regular and Irregular Verbs

TEACHING REGULAR AND IRREGULAR VERBS

Have students create mnemonic devices for the irregular verbs that give them the most trouble. For instance, a silly poem based on the game of Battleship might help students remember *sink, sank, sunk:*

If you *sink* my battleship, then you *sank* it.
But I must say,
"You've *sunk* my battleship!"

Have students create as many mnemonic devices as they can to help them remember irregular verbs. Then ask them to read their devices to the class.

TEACHING ON THE WEB

Exploring and Discussing: Have students explore different Web sites in a certain time limit to find as many uses of irregular verbs as they can. How hard was it to find these types of

✎ Checklist for Using Regular and Irregular Verbs

> ✔ Are regular verbs in their correct forms?
> ✔ Are irregular verbs in their correct forms?

All verbs are either regular or irregular. *Regular verbs* form the past and past participle by adding *-d* or *-ed* to the present tense. If a verb does not form its past tense and past participle this way, it is called an *irregular verb*.

Notice how both types of verbs work in the following paragraph by Stella Sanfratello.

> I will never forget the time in fourth grade when my teacher sternly called me to stand before her desk after I had pleaded ignorance of her instructions one too many times. "I'm tired of hearing you say you don't know what you're supposed to be doing!" she said angrily. "I want you to stop saying, 'I didn't know, I didn't know, I didn't know!'" The scolding was intense and continued for several minutes. I recall feeling stunned and confused at her accusation that I had been acting intentionally. I knew it had never occurred to me to do this on purpose or to act maliciously or irresponsibly. Today as an adult, however, I understand my teacher's frustration and the fact that, as a 9-year-old, all I could do was just what I did—stand there help-lessly, filled with pain, confusion, and shame.

In this paragraph, author Stella Sanfratello explains how she felt as a hearing-impaired child trying to survive in the educational system. Before continuing in this chapter, take a moment to record some of your own childhood memories. Save your work because you will use it later in the chapter.

verbs? How many did they find within the time limit? What does the number of verbs they found tell them about the uses of irregular verbs— are they frequent or infrequent in our language?

Writing Assignment: A Childhood Memory

Do you have a vivid childhood memory? What is the memory? What happened? Who was involved? Was the memory a good or bad one? How did the situation make you feel as a child? Do you see the situation differently now that you are older? Write a paragraph describing a vivid childhood memory.

Revising Your Writing

Revise the first draft of your paragraph before you focus on editing. Use the Revising Checklist on pages 24–25 to help you with your revision. Make sure your paragraph has a good topic sentence and is well developed. Then check your paragraph for unity, organization, and coherence.

TEACHING ON THE WEB
Mosaics Web Site: To learn more about regular and irregular verbs, students can go to www.prenhall.com/ mosaics.

REGULAR VERBS

Here are the present, past, and past participle forms of some regular verbs. **Regular verbs** form the past tense and past participle by adding -d or -ed. The past participle is the verb form often used with helping verbs like *have*, *has*, or *had*.

Some Regular Verbs

Present Tense	Past Tense	Past Participle (used with helping words like *have, has, had*)
listen	listen**ed**	listen**ed**
look	look**ed**	look**ed**
receive	receiv**ed**	receiv**ed**
paint	paint**ed**	paint**ed**
call	call**ed**	call**ed**

The different forms of a verb tell when something happened—in the *present* (I *walk*) or in the *past* (I *walked*, I *have walked*, I *had walked*).

REVIEWING REGULAR VERBS

What is a regular verb?

A regular verb forms its past tense and past participle by adding -d or -ed.

Identify three forms of a regular verb.

| present | past | past participle |

🌱 **Practice 1 Identifying**   Underline the regular verbs in each of the following sentences.

1. The old man walked across the street.
2. We recalled happy memories.
3. Henry talked through the lecture.
4. I watched the birds.
5. He asks many questions.
6. The dog barked at the stranger.
7. Samantha burned her arm.
8. The children played all afternoon.
9. I believe in UFOs.
10. You skip down the sidewalk.

🌱 **Practice 2 Identifying**   Put an X next to the incorrect verb forms in the following chart.

	Present Tense		Past Tense		Past Participle	
1.	X kicked		____ kicked		____ kicked	*(kick)*
2.	____ jump		X jumpt		____ jumped	*(jumped)*
3.	____ cook		____ cooked		X cooken	*(cooked)*
4.	____ bake		X baken		____ baked	*(baked)*

5. _____ mail   _____ mailed   _____ mailed

6. __X__ played   _____ played   _____ played   *(play)*

7. _____ watch   _____ watched   __X__ watchen *(watched)*

8. _____ answer   _____ answered   __X__ answerd *(answered)*

9. _____ clean   __X__ cleant   _____ cleaned *(cleaned)*

10. __X__ typed   _____ typed   _____ typed   *(type)*

Practice 3 Correcting   List the correct form of each of the incorrect verb forms in Practice 2. *See Practice 2.*

1. _____

2. _____

3. _____

4. _____

5. _____

6. _____

7. _____

8. _____

9. _____

10. _____

Practice 4 Completing   Fill in each blank in the following sentences with a regular verb that makes sense. *Answers willl vary.*

1. We _____ to the orchestra.

2. I _____ in that play.

3. Sally, _____ some flowers out of the garden.

4. They _____ until they cried.

5. I _____ at sad movies.

6. Johnny did _____ for help.

7. The books must have _____ by themselves.

8. The horse _____ over the hedge.

9. The team members have _____ their suitcases to the train station.

10. The workers _____ the wheelbarrow with dirt.

🌿 Practice 5 Writing Your Own

A. Write a sentence of your own for each of the following verbs. *Answers will vary.*

1. place _____

2. moan _____

3. has tasted _____

4. lift _____

5. have gained _____

B. Write five sentences of your own using regular verbs, and underline the verbs in each sentence. *Answers will vary.*

1. _____

2. _____

3. _____

4. _____

5. _____

IRREGULAR VERBS

Irregular verbs do not form their past tense and past participle with *-d* or *-ed*. That is why they are irregular. Some follow certain patterns (*spring, sprang, sprung; ring, rang, rung; drink, drank, drunk; sink, sank, sunk*). But the only sure way to know the forms of an irregular verb is to spend time learning them. As you write, you can check a dictionary or the following list.

Irregular Verbs

Present	Past	Past Participle (used with helping words like *have, has, had*)
am	was	been
are	were	been
be	was	been

bear	*bore*	*borne, born*
beat	*beat*	*beaten*
begin	*began*	*begun*
bend	*bent*	*bent*
bid	*bid*	*bid*
bind	*bound*	*bound*
bite	*bit*	*bitten*
blow	*blew*	*blown*
break	*broke*	*broken*
bring	*brought* (not *brang*)	*brought* (not *brung*)
build	*built*	*built*
burst	*burst* (not *bursted*)	*burst*
buy	*bought*	*bought*
choose	*chose*	*chosen*
come	*came*	*come*
cost	*cost* (not *costed*)	*cost*
cut	*cut*	*cut*
deal	*dealt*	*dealt*
do	*did* (not *done*)	*done*
draw	*drew*	*drawn*
drink	*drank*	*drunk*
drive	*drove*	*driven*
eat	*ate*	*eaten*
fall	*fell*	*fallen*
feed	*fed*	*fed*
feel	*felt*	*felt*
fight	*fought*	*fought*
find	*found*	*found*
flee	*fled*	*fled*
fly	*flew*	*flown*
forget	*forgot*	*forgotten*
forgive	*forgave*	*forgiven*
freeze	*froze*	*frozen*
get	*got*	*got, gotten*
go	*went*	*gone*

grow	grew	grown
hang[1]	hung	hung
has	had	had
have	had	had
hide	hid	hidden
hear	heard	heard
hurt	hurt (not hurted)	hurt
is	was	been
know	knew	known
lay	laid	laid
lead	led	led
leave	left	left
lend	lent	lent
lie[2]	lay	lain
lose	lost	lost
meet	met	met
pay	paid	paid
prove	proved	proved, proven
put	put	put
read [rēd]	read [rĕd]	read [rĕd]
ride	rode	ridden
ring	rang	rung
rise	rose	risen
run	ran	run
say	said	said
see	saw (not seen)	seen
set	set	set
shake	shook	shaken
shine[3]	shone	shone
shrink	shrank	shrunk
sing	sang	sung
sink	sank	sunk
sit	sat	sat

sleep	*slept*	*slept*
speak	*spoke*	*spoken*
spend	*spent*	*spent*
spread	*spread*	*spread*
spring	*sprang* (not *sprung*)	*sprung*
stand	*stood*	*stood*
steal	*stole*	*stolen*
stick	*stuck*	*stuck*
stink	*stank* (not *stunk*)	*stunk*
strike	*struck*	*struck, stricken*
strive	*strove*	*striven*
swear	*swore*	*sworn*
sweep	*swept*	*swept*
swell	*swelled*	*swelled, swollen*
swim	*swam*	*swum*
swing	*swung*	*swung*
take	*took*	*taken*
teach	*taught*	*taught*
tear	*tore*	*torn*
tell	*told*	*told*
think	*thought*	*thought*
throw	*threw*	*thrown*
understand	*understood*	*understood*
wake	*woke*	*woken*
wear	*wore*	*worn*
weave	*wove*	*woven*
win	*won*	*won*
wring	*wrung*	*wrung*
write	*wrote*	*written*

1. *Hang* meaning "execute by hanging" is regular: *hang, hanged, hanged.*
2. *Lie* meaning "tell a lie" is regular: *lie, lied, lied.*
3. *Shine* meaning "brighten by polishing" is regular: *shine, shined, shined.*

REVIEWING IRREGULAR VERBS

What is the difference between regular and irregular verbs?

Irregular verbs do not form their past tense and past participle with -d or -ed.

What is the best way to learn how irregular verbs form their past tense and past participle?

The best way to learn them is to become familiar with them.

Practice 6 Identifying   Underline the irregular verbs in each of the following sentences.

1. The cat broke your vase.
2. The wind blew all night.
3. You tell the truth.
4. The garbage cans stink.
5. They met once before.
6. The flowers grew in the yard.
7. The children hid behind the house.
8. The criminal fled the scene.
9. I proved you wrong.
10. The moon shone brightly.

Practice 7 Identifying   Put an X next to the incorrect verb forms in the following chart.

Present Tense	Past Tense	Past Participle	
1. _____ shake	_X_ shooked	_____ shaken	(shook)
2. _X_ bound	_____ bound	_____ bound	(bind)
3. _____ am	_____ was	_X_ was	(been)
4. _____ feed	_____ fed	_X_ feeded	(fed)

5. _____ choose   _X_ chosen   _____ chosen   *(chose)*

6. _____ deal   _X_ dealed   _____ dealt   *(dealt)*

7. _____ pay   _____ paid   _____ paid

8. _____ ring   _____ rang   _X_ rang   *(rung)*

9. _X_ understood _____ understood _____ understood *(understand)*

10. _____ get   _X_ gotten   _____ gotten   *(got)*

🌿 **Practice 8 Correcting**   List the correct form of each of the incorrect verb forms in Practice 7. *See Practice 7.*

1. _____

2. _____

3. _____

4. _____

5. _____

6. _____

7. _____

8. _____

9. _____

10. _____

🌿 **Practice 9 Completing**   Fill in each blank in the following sentences with an irregular verb that makes sense. *Answers willl vary.*

1. We didn't _____ the problem.

2. We had _____ that book before.

3. Every few months, a cable station _____ a James Bond movie marathon.

4. The storm _____ away our garage.

5. Many people _____ their luggage.

6. My foot _____ after I twisted it.

7. My sister will not _____ anything but bottled water.

8. The old man _____ us fishing.

9. Kenneth and Brian _____ Sarah and Jenny to the movies last Friday.

10. My dogs have _____ time in a kennel.

🌟 Practice 10 Writing Your Own

A. Write a sentence of your own for each of the following irregular verbs.
Answers will vary.

1. draw _____

2. spread _____

3. fight _____

4. swear _____

5. lay _____

B. Write five sentences of your own using irregular verbs, and underline the verbs in each sentence. *Answers will vary.*

1. _____

2. _____

3. _____

4. _____

5. _____

USING *LIE/LAY* AND *SIT/SET* CORRECTLY

Two pairs of verbs are often used incorrectly—*lie/lay* and *sit/set*.

Lie/Lay

	Present Tense	Past Tense	Past Participle
lie (recline or lie down)	*lie*	*lay*	(*have, has, had*) *lain*
lay (put or place down)	*lay*	*laid*	(*have, has, had*) *laid*

The verb *lay* always takes an object. You must lay something down:

Lay down *what?*

Lay down *your cards.*

Sit/Set

	Present Tense	Past Tense	Past Participle
sit (get into a seated position)	*sat*	*sat*	(*have, has, had*) *sat*
set (put or place down)	*set*	*set*	(*have, has, had*) *set*

Like the verb *lay*, the verb *set* must always have an object. You must *set* something down:

Set *what?*

Set *the chair* over here.

REVIEWING *Lie/Lay* AND *Sit/Set*

What do lie and lay mean?

Lie means recline or lie down; lay means put or place down.

What are the principal parts of lie and lay?

Lie, lay, lain and lay, laid, laid

What do sit and set mean?

Sit means get into a seated position; set means put or place down.

What are the principal parts of sit and set?

Sit, sat, sat and set, set, set

Which of these verbs always take an object?

Lay and set

Practice 11 Identifying   Underline the correct verb in each of the following sentences.

1. Marci has (lay, <u>lain</u>) on the couch for an hour.
2. Will you please (<u>sit</u>, set) down?
3. The dog has (sat, <u>set</u>) his bone on the floor.
4. You (lay, <u>laid</u>) the reports on this table.
5. (Lie, <u>Lay</u>) your clothes out on the bed.

6. The shivering man (set, sat) in the hot sun.
7. Eustice has (lain, laid) a beautiful picnic on the grass.
8. He (laid, lay) on the lawn and soon began to snore.
9. That 60-pound dog (set, sat) on my foot.
10. We have (lain, laid) all the cards out on the table.

Practice 12 Identifying Put an X next to the sentence if the underlined verb is incorrect.

1. ___X___ Lie those heavy crates on the ground. *(lay)*
2. ___X___ I laid back and relaxed while the hairdresser washed my hair. *(lay)*
3. ______ You had sat on a cactus.
4. ___X___ We had set down in the cool grass. *(sat)*
5. ______ You have lain around the house all day.
6. ___X___ Please set beside me during the movie. *(sit)*
7. ___X___ The workers have lay down the concrete. *(laid)*
8. ___X___ I had sat my purse on the kitchen table. *(set)*
9. ___X___ I'm going to lay down on the bed to relax. *(lie)*
10. ___X___ Will you sit those books on the counter? *(set)*

Practice 13 Correcting Correct the verb errors in Practice 12 by rewriting each incorrect sentence. *See Practice 12.*

1. ______________________________
2. ______________________________
3. ______________________________
4. ______________________________
5. ______________________________
6. ______________________________
7. ______________________________
8. ______________________________
9. ______________________________
10. ______________________________

✴ Practice 14 Completing   Fill in each blank in the following sentences with a form of *lie* or *lay*, *sit* or *set* that makes sense.

1. You have _____set_____ your new suit in a puddle of grape juice.

2. I had _____laid_____ the hot iron down for only a minute, but it burned my shirt anyway.

3. Sara _____lay_____ down in the warm sun and fell asleep.

4. How long did you _____sit_____ in the dentist's office?

5. That lazy, overfed cat _____sat_____ in the window seat all day and night.

6. Jim gently _____set_____ the antique clock on the table.

7. Please _____sit_____ on the inside so I can have the outside seat.

8. "_____Lie_____ still while I remove these bandages," said the doctor.

9. When we were on vacation, the newspapers piled up and _____sat_____ on the driveway for a week.

10. Ouch! I just _____sat_____ on a tack.

✴ Practice 15 Writing Your Own

A. Write a sentence of your own for each of the following phrases. *Answers will vary.*

1. you just sat _____

2. Jim had lain _____

3. Mary Ann has set her _____

4. lay out your clothes _____

5. set that _____

B. Write five sentences of your own using *lie*, *lay*, *sit*, and *set*, and underline the forms of these verbs in each of your sentences. *Answers will vary.*

1. _____

2. _____

3. _____

4. _____

5. _____

CHAPTER REVIEW

You might want to reread your answers to the questions in the review boxes before you do the following exercises.

🌱 **Review Practice 1 Reading**   Refer to the paragraph by Stella Sanfratello on page 150 to do the following exercises.

A. List five regular verbs from Sanfratello's paragraph. *Answers will vary.*

1. _____

2. _____

3. _____

4. _____

5. _____

B. List five irregular verbs from Sanfratello's paragraph. *Answers will vary.*

1. _____

2. _____

3. _____

4. _____

5. _____

🌱 **Review Practice 2 Identifying**   Underline the incorrect verb forms in each of the following sentences.

1. We <u>drived</u> in the car all night long. *(drove)*

2. He <u>lays</u> down right after he gets home from school. *(lies)*

3. I called you last night, but the phone just <u>ringed</u>. *(rang)*

4. Peter was very supportive, and he said he <u>feeled</u> my pain. *(felt)*

5. Karen <u>filt</u> up the gas tank yesterday, but it's already empty. *(filled)*

6. The air conditioner <u>broked</u> yesterday. *(broke)*

7. He <u>standed</u> in my front yard and sang to me. *(stood)*

8. When I asked the question, the teacher acted like she never <u>heared</u> me. *(heard)*

9. After Jerry divorced Ruth, she never <u>forgived</u> him. *(forgave)*

10. I <u>sat</u> the fork in the sink. *(set)*

✿ **Review Practice 3 Correcting**   Correct the verb errors in Review Practice 2 by rewriting each incorrect sentence. *See Review Practice 2.*

✎ EDITING A STUDENT PARAGRAPH

Following is a paragraph written and revised by Melba Madison in response to the writing assignment in this chapter. Read the paragraph, and underline each of her verbs.

Last year, I <u>walk</u> [X] to the old shed at the edge of my grandmother's backyard. I <u>decided</u> that I would either <u>fixed</u> [X] the eyesore or <u>tear</u> [X] it down. I <u>begun</u> [X] looking through the old boxes that <u>were</u> inside, and I <u>founded</u> [X] a package of letters. I <u>set</u> [X] down and <u>read</u> them. They <u>was</u> [X] love letters dating back to the early 1900s. The writing <u>was</u> flowery and hard to read, but I eventually <u>begin</u> [X] to make out the words. I <u>set</u> [X] as the sun <u>rised</u> [X] high in the sky. I <u>sat</u> as the sun <u>descended</u> and the moon <u>rose</u>. The letters <u>were</u> from a man whom I <u>had</u> never <u>heard</u> of. He <u>poured</u> his soul out to my grandmother. And then suddenly the letters <u>stop</u> [X]. To this day I often <u>lay</u> [X] down to go to sleep and <u>wonders</u> [X] about that man. Who <u>is</u> he? What <u>happened</u> to him? Why <u>did</u> my grandmother never <u>mention</u> him? I finally <u>decide</u> [X] to leave the shed standing. I <u>couldn't</u> <u>bear</u> to tear down such a memory.

Here are the corrected verbs:
walked
fix
began
found
sat
were
began
sat
rose
stopped
lie
wonder
decided

Collaborative Activity

Team up with a partner, and place an X above the 13 verb errors in Melba's paragraph. Then, working together, use what you have learned in this chapter to correct these errors. Rewrite the paragraph with your corrections. *See student paragraph for errors. Corrections are in the margin.*

❧ EDITING YOUR OWN PARAGRAPH

Now return to the paragraph you wrote and revised at the beginning of this chapter. Underline each of your verbs.

Collaborative Activity

Exchange paragraphs with your partner, and circle any verb errors that you find in your partner's paragraph.

Individual Activity

On the Error Log in Appendix 6, record any verb errors that your partner found in your paragraph. To complete the writing process, correct these errors by rewriting your paragraph.

Verb Tense

Checklist for Correcting Tense Problems

- ☐ Are present-tense verbs in the correct form?
- ☐ Are past-tense verbs in the correct form?
- ☐ Are *-ing* verbs used with the correct helping verbs?
- ☐ Are the forms of *be*, *do*, and *have* used correctly?

When we hear the word "verb," we often think of action. We also know that action occurs in time. We are naturally interested in whether something happened today or yesterday or if it will happen some time in the future. The time of an action is indicated by the *tense* of a verb, and the ending of a verb shows its tense. This chapter discusses the most common errors in using verb tense.

Notice the different tenses and the way they communicate time in the following paragraph by Lansey Namioka.

> Father's approach to English was a scientific one. Since Chinese verbs have no tense, he was fascinated by the way English verbs changed form according to whether they were in the present, past imperfect, perfect, pluperfect, future, or future perfect tense. He was always making diagrams of verbs and their inflections, and he looked for opportunities to show off his mastery of the pluperfect and future perfect tenses, his two favorites. "I shall have finished my project by Monday," he would say smugly.

In this paragraph, author Lansey Namioka explains her father's fascination with English verbs. Before continuing in this chapter, take a moment to record some of your own unique habits or hobbies. Save your work because you will use it later in the chapter.

TEACHING VERB TENSE

Put the following grids on the board:

Past:

1 2 3 4 5 6

Present:

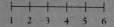

1 2 3 4 5 6

Future:

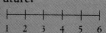

1 2 3 4 5 6

Place a picture of a horse and buggy at the 1 on the "Past" line, a car at the 1 on the "Present" line, and a spaceship at the 1 on the "Future" line.

Divide students into three teams, one for each tense. Provide students with sentences that are not in their team's tense. The first team to correctly change the sentence into their tense moves one space forward on the grid. For instance, the following sentence might be given to the Past and Present teams: "We will search for the answer." If the Past team changes the sentence to "We searched for the answer," its horse and buggy moves forward one space; if the Present team changes it to "We search for the answer," its car moves forward; and so on.

The first vehicle to reach the end of the grid wins.

■ For more sample sentences, see the *Instructor's Resource Manual*, Section II, Part II.

TEACHING ON THE WEB

Exploring and Discussing: Have students find Web sites from different countries that have translated their material into English. How many instances do students find problems with verb tense? Why do they think verb tenses are so difficult to learn for second-language speakers?

TEACHING ON THE WEB

Mosaics Web Site: To learn more about verb tenses, students can go to www.prenhall.com/ mosaics.

Writing Assignment: A Unique Hobby

Do you have a unique habit or hobby? What is it? How do you go about doing it? Why do you do it? How do others see you because of this? Write a paragraph describing a unique hobby or habit of yours.

Revising Your Writing

Revise the first draft of your paragraph before you focus on editing. Use the Revising Checklist on pages 24–25 to help you with your revision. Make sure your paragraph has a good topic sentence and is well developed. Then check your paragraph for unity, organization, and coherence.

PRESENT TENSE

One of the most common errors in college writing is reversing the present-tense endings—adding an *-s* where none is needed and omitting the *-s* where it is required. Make sure you understand this mistake, and then proofread carefully to avoid it in your writing.

Present Tense

Singular		Plural	
INCORRECT	CORRECT	INCORRECT	CORRECT
NOT *I laughs*	*I laugh*	NOT *we laughs*	*we laugh*
NOT *you laughs*	*you laugh*	NOT *you laughs*	*you laugh*
NOT *he, she, it laugh*	*he, she, it laughs*	NOT *they laughs*	*they laugh*

You also need to be able to spot these same errors in sentences.

	Error	Correction
NOT	**The black cat climb** the tree.	**The black cat climbs** the tree.
NOT	**My brother love** chocolate.	**My brother loves** chocolate.
NOT	**You speaks** beautifully.	**You speak** beautifully.
NOT	**They sings** in the choir.	**They sing** in the choir.

REVIEWING PRESENT-TENSE ERRORS

What is the most common error in using the present tense?

Reversing the present tense endings—adding -s when not needed or omitting it when

it is required

How can you prevent this error?

By learning the correct forms and proofreading carefully

Practice 1 Identifying   Underline the correct present-tense verb in each of the following sentences.

1. He (<u>misses</u>, miss) you.
2. The international finance course (<u>is</u>, will be) hard.
3. Janeen (<u>likes</u>, like) bungee jumping at the fair.
4. The cats (runs, <u>run</u>) through the neighborhood.
5. The committee members (votes, <u>vote</u>) on the amendments.
6. The boat (<u>reaches</u>, reach) the harbor at noon.
7. Most people (believes, <u>believe</u>) in justice.
8. The fire hydrant (<u>sprays</u>, spray) water into the air.
9. My friends (thinks, <u>think</u>) a lot of you.
10. They (hopes, <u>hope</u>) for a speedy solution.

Practice 2 Identifying   Put an X next to the sentence if the underlined verb is incorrect.

1. _____ Henry <u>walks</u> his dog in the park every day.
2. __X__ They <u>hopes</u> for a miracle. *(hope)*
3. __X__ A rabbit's tail <u>bring</u> good luck. *(brings)*
4. __X__ The flowers <u>smells</u> nice. *(smell)*
5. __X__ The river <u>swell</u> in the spring. *(swells)*
6. _____ My grandparents <u>visit</u> us often.

7. _____ The sun <u>dries</u> grapes into raisins.

8. __X__ All the books <u>belongs</u> to the library. *(belong)*

9. _____ Our family <u>travels</u> out of the country every year.

10. _____ You <u>need</u> to be more careful.

❋ **Practice 3 Correcting**   Correct the verb errors in Practice 2 by rewriting each incorrect sentence. *See Practice 2.*

1. _____

2. _____

3. _____

4. _____

5. _____

6. _____

7. _____

8. _____

9. _____

10. _____

❋ **Practice 4 Completing**   Fill in each blank in the following sentences with a present-tense verb that makes sense. *Answers will vary.*

1. Every spring, they _____ under the stars.

2. I _____ it when you smile.

3. The pots and pans _____ to be cleaned.

4. The professionals _____ the problem.

5. She _____ whenever he walks by.

6. Will you _____ me a song?

7. This season's new comedies _____ hilarious.

8. Martha _____ once a week.

9. Many people _____ in the supernatural.

10. This jasmine _____ only at night.

🌾 Practice 5 Writing Your Own

A. Write a sentence of your own for each of the following present-tense verbs. *Answers will vary.*

1. graduate _____

2. wastes _____

3. improve _____

4. arrests _____

5. operate _____

B. Write five sentences of your own in the present tense, and underline the verbs in each sentence. *Answers will vary.*

1. _____

2. _____

3. _____

4. _____

5. _____

PAST TENSE

Just as we know that a verb is in the present tense by its ending, we see that a verb is in the past tense by its ending. Regular verbs form the past tense by adding -d or -ed. But some writers forget the ending when they are writing the past tense. Understanding this problem and then proofreading carefully will help you catch this error.

Past Tense

Singular		Plural	
INCORRECT	CORRECT	INCORRECT	CORRECT
NOT *I call*	*I called*	NOT *we call*	*we called*
NOT *you call*	*you called*	NOT *you call*	*you called*
NOT *he, she, it call*	*he, she, it called*	NOT *they call*	*they called*

You also need to be able to spot these same errors in sentences.

	Error	**Correction**
NOT	**Janet yell** the cheer.	**Janet yelled** the cheer.
NOT	**He wander** through the store.	**He wandered** through the store.
NOT	**Those girls talk** too loudly.	**Those girls talked** too loudly.
NOT	Yes, **we want** to win the game.	Yes, **we wanted** to win the game.

REVIEWING PAST-TENSE ERRORS

What is the most common sentence error made with the past tense?

Forgetting the past tense ending (-d or -ed)

How can you prevent this error?

By learning the correct forms and proofreading carefully

❋ Practice 6 Identifying   Underline the correct past-tense verbs in each of the following sentences.

1. The plane (land, <u>landed</u>) near our house.

2. You (developt, <u>developed</u>) a wonderful presentation.

3. The stars (twinklen, <u>twinkled</u>) in the sky.

4. The children (<u>wanted</u>, will want) water balloons.

5. They (maded, <u>made</u>) a mess throughout the house.

6. Mr. Lockhart (teached, <u>taught</u>) us to rock climb.

7. Only a few people (show, <u>showed</u>) up for the party.

8. It (happen, <u>happened</u>) only yesterday.

9. The singers and dancers (<u>performed</u>, performs) a spectacular show.

10. The cars (<u>backed</u>, backt) into each other.

❋ Practice 7 Identifying   Put an X next to the sentence if the underlined past-tense verb is incorrect.

1. ___X___ Waldo <u>plans</u> the wedding a year ago. *(planned)*

2. _____ They <u>worked</u> very hard on the project.

3. _____ The witches <u>came</u> out on All Hallow's Eve.

4. ___X___ I <u>burn</u> the meal for tonight's supper. *(burned)*

5. ___X___ The teacher <u>helps</u> me with this paper yesterday. *(helped)*

6. ___X___ The neighbor's stereo <u>blares</u> last night. *(blared)*

7. _____ The flag <u>waved</u> in the wind.

8. ___X___ The politician <u>speaks</u> at the banquet yesterday. *(spoke)*

9. ___X___ Last summer, we <u>drive</u> to Yosemite. *(drove)*

10. ___X___ Hey! You <u>drink</u> my Pepsi. *(drank)*

❋ Practice 8 Correcting Correct the verb errors in Practice 7 by rewriting each incorrect sentence. *See Practice 7.*

1. _____

2. _____

3. _____

4. _____

5. _____

6. _____

7. _____

8. _____

9. _____

10. _____

❋ Practice 9 Completing Fill in each blank in the following sentences with a past-tense verb that makes sense. *Answers will vary.*

1. The baby _____ loudly.

2. The basket weavers _____ many beautiful designs.

3. The meal _____ appetizing.

4. You _____ the wrong question.

5. The Salingers _____ until morning.

6. The firecrackers _____ high in the sky.

7. It _____ me.

8. Oh, no! The cat _____ a mouse.

9. These gates _____ only once a year.

10. The thieves _____ into the school.

🌱 Practice 10 Writing Your Own

A. Write a sentence of your own for each the following past-tense verbs.
   Answers will vary.

1. regretted _____

2. swore _____

3. crashed _____

4. written _____

5. jumped _____

B. Write five sentences of your own in the past tense, and underline the verbs in each sentence. *Answers will vary.*

1. _____

2. _____

3. _____

4. _____

5. _____

USING HELPING WORDS WITH PAST PARTICIPLES

Helping words are used only with the past participle form—*not* with the past-tense form. It is therefore incorrect to use a helping verb (such as *is, was, were, have, has,* or *had*) with the past tense. Make sure you understand how to use helping words with past participles, and then proofread your written work to avoid making errors.

	Error	Correction
NOT	They **have drove** to town.	They **have driven** to town.
NOT	She **has shook** the bottle thoroughly.	She **has shaken** the bottle thoroughly.

NOT   I **have wrote** a book.   I **have written** a book.

NOT   We **had took** the test early.   We **had taken** the test early.

REVIEWING ERRORS WITH HELPING WORDS
AND PAST PARTICIPLES

....

What is the most common sentence error made with past participles?

Using a helping word with the past tense instead of the past participle
_____

How can you prevent this error?

By learning the correct forms and proofreading carefully
_____

🌿 **Practice 11 Identifying**   Underline the correct helping verbs and their past participles in each of the following sentences.

1. The walls (had shook, <u>had shaken</u>) in the earthquake.

2. Mandy (<u>had bitten</u>, had bit) her tongue.

3. The fruit (has fell, <u>has fallen</u>) to the ground.

4. I (have drove, <u>have driven</u>) my mother crazy.

5. The caterpillars (<u>have eaten</u>, have ate) all the leaves on my rose bush.

6. We (have saw, <u>have seen</u>) many strange things.

7. Many of the children (<u>had hidden</u>, had hid) behind the couch.

8. The guests (have went, <u>have gone</u>) home.

9. A cannon (has shotten, <u>has shot</u>) the clown into the air.

10. The outraged citizens (<u>have written</u>, have wrote) a letter to their representative.

🌿 **Practice 12 Identifying**   Put an X next to the sentence if the underlined verb is incorrect.

1. _____ They <u>had ridden</u> all the rides.

2. __X__ We <u>have grew</u> a garden. *(have grown)*

3. _____ My chair <u>had broken</u> before I sat in it.

4. __X__ The jeans <u>have tore</u> at the knees. *(have torn)*

5. _____ Poor Tom! He <u>has spent</u> all his money.

6. __X__ He <u>has drew</u> the pictures in black and white. *(has drawn)*

7. __X__ The children <u>have forgot</u> their coats and gloves. *(have forgotten)*

8. _____ We <u>had begun</u> to see daylight.

9. __X__ The ice <u>has froze</u> the fish solid. *(has frozen)*

10. __X__ He <u>has forgave</u> your mean comments. *(has forgiven)*

※ Practice 13 Correcting   Correct the verb errors in Practice 12 by rewriting each incorrect sentence. *See Practice 12.*

1. _____

2. _____

3. _____

4. _____

5. _____

6. _____

7. _____

8. _____

9. _____

10. _____

※ Practice 14 Completing   Fill in each blank in the following sentences with a correct past-participle verb that makes sense. *Answers will vary.*

1. The pictures have _____ off the wall.

2. The worker has _____ a break.

3. The attendant has _____ our tickets.

4. The dealer had _____ me a bad hand.

5. Cassidy had _____ her nose all morning.

6. The teacher has _____ many times the boy for his pranks.

7. They have _____ the dinner bell.

8. If we had _____ the answer, we wouldn't have asked the question.

9. The student has _____ to do his best.

10. The gum has _____ under the desk.

Practice 15 Writing Your Own

A. Write a sentence of your own for each of the following past-participle verb forms. *Answers will vary.*

1. has known _____

2. had told _____

3. have chosen _____

4. have stolen _____

5. has broken _____

B. Write five sentences of your own using helping verbs and past participles, and underline the complete verbs in each sentence. *Answers will vary.*

1. _____

2. _____

3. _____

4. _____

5. _____

USING -*ing* VERBS CORRECTLY

Verbs ending in -*ing* describe action that is going on or that was going on for a while. To be a complete verb, an -*ing* verb is always used with a helping verb. Two common errors occur with -*ing* verbs:

- Using *be* or *been* instead of the correct helping verb
- Using no helping verb at all.

Learn the correct forms, and proofread carefully to catch these errors.

	Error	**Correction**
NOT	The boys **be going** to the mall.	The boys **are going** to the maill

NOT	The boys **been going** to the mall.	The boys **were going** to the mall. The boys **have been going** to the mall. The boys **had been going** to the mall.
NOT	We **eating** a snack.	We **are eating** a snack. We **have been eating** a snack. We **were eating** a snack. We **had been eating** a snack.

R EVIEWING -*ing* V ERB E RRORS

What two kinds of errors occur with -ing verbs?

Using be or been instead of the correct helping verb

Not using any helping verb at all

How can you prevent these errors?

By learning the correct forms and proofreading carefully

 Practice 16 Identifying   Underline the correct helping verbs and -*ing* forms in each of the following sentences.

1. Many people (be planning, <u>are planning</u>) the event.

2. Marcy (<u>is going</u>, been going) to Jamaica this holiday.

3. The trinkets (<u>had been sitting</u>, been sitting) on this counter.

4. Those two teams (going, <u>are going</u>) to the playoffs.

5. Ashley (<u>has been finding</u>, has finding) ladybugs in the backyard.

6. The light (been shining, <u>had been shining</u>) all night.

7. Dean (<u>was taking</u>, taking) a swing at the ball.

8. We (<u>have been sitting</u>, have sitting) here for over an hour.

9. Those bikers (<u>are going</u>, be going) too fast.

10. The passengers (telling, <u>are telling</u>) jokes to one another.

❧ **Practice 17 Identifying**   Put an X next to the sentence if the under-lined helping verb or *-ing* form is incorrect.

1. _____ They <u>had been going</u> to college.
2. __X__ We <u>running</u> in a race. *(are running)*
3. __X__ The roof <u>been raised</u>. *(has been raised)*
4. _____ The sun <u>was rising</u> over the horizon.
5. __X__ The lawn <u>dying</u> in this hot sun. *(is dying)*
6. __X__ Spiders <u>running</u> up my arm! *(are running)*
7. _____ The motorist <u>is going</u> the wrong way.
8. __X__ We <u>be listening</u> very carefully. *(are listening, have been listening, will be listening)*
9. __X__ The clothes <u>be sitting</u> in the dryer. *(are sitting, have been sitting, will be sitting)*
10. __X__ The printer <u>printing</u> out your document now. *(is printing)*

❧ **Practice 18 Correcting**   Correct the verb errors in Practice 17 by rewriting each incorrect sentence. *See Practice 17.*

1. _____
2. _____
3. _____
4. _____
5. _____
6. _____
7. _____
8. _____
9. _____
10. _____

❧ **Practice 19 Completing**   Fill in each blank in the following sentences with a helping verb and *-ing* form that make sense. *Answers will vary.*

1. The crowd _____ for more.
2. I _____ when you called.

3. The wolves _____ at the moon.

4. Many people _____ to the movie.

5. She _____ for a walk to relax.

6. The moths _____ too close to the flame.

7. The photographer _____ still-life photos.

8. That night, we _____ to a professional performer.

9. Your help _____ me out of a lot of trouble.

10. A few weeks ago, I _____ with a friend.

❧ Practice 20 Writing Your Own

A. Write a sentence of your own for each the following verbs. *Answers will vary.*

1. is leaving _____

2. were cooking _____

3. had been writing _____

4. are feeling _____

5. have been promising _____

B. Write five sentences of your own using *-ing* verb forms, and underline the verbs in each sentence. *Answers will vary.*

1. _____

2. _____

3. _____

4. _____

5. _____

PROBLEMS WITH *be*

The verb *be* can cause problems in both the present tense and the past tense. The following chart demonstrates these problems. Learn how to use these forms correctly, and then always proofread your written work carefully to avoid errors.

The Verb *be*

Present Tense

Singular		Plural	
INCORRECT	CORRECT	INCORRECT	CORRECT
NOT *I be/ain't*	*I **am**/**am not***	NOT *we be/ain't*	*we **are**/**are not***
NOT *you is/ain't*	*you **are**/**are not***	NOT *you be/ain't*	*you **are**/**are not***
NOT *he, she, it be/ain't*	*he, she, it **is**/**is not***	NOT *they be/ain't*	*they **are**/**are not***

Past Tense

Singular		Plural	
INCORRECT	CORRECT	INCORRECT	CORRECT
NOT *I were*	*I **was***	NOT *we was*	*we **were***
NOT *you was*	*you **were***	NOT *you was*	*you **were***
NOT *he, she, it were*	*he, she, it **was***	NOT *they was*	*they **were***

REVIEWING PROBLEMS WITH *be*

What are two common errors made with be?

In the present tense, using be and ain't instead of the correct verb forms

In the past tense, confusing was and were

How can you prevent these errors?

By learning the correct forms and proofreading carefully

Practice 21 Identifying   Underline the correct forms of *be* in each of the following sentences.

1. My father (be, <u>is</u>) a taxi driver.

2. They (was, <u>were</u>) very late today.

3. You (<u>aren't</u>, ain't) happy.

4. I (be, <u>was</u>) in the middle of a project when the doorbell rang.

5. It (<u>was</u>, were) a hot day today.

6. That ice cream (be, <u>is</u>) so good.

7. She (<u>is</u>, been) the best person for this assignment.

8. A red signal (be, <u>is</u>) for danger.

9. My favorite novels (been, <u>are</u>) *Emma* and *Pride and Prejudice*.

10. You (was, <u>were</u>) a great host.

🌿 **Practice 22 Identifying**   Put an X next to the sentence if the underlined form of *be* is incorrect.

1. __*X*__ These balloons <u>be</u> the ones for the party. *(are)*

2. __*X*__ I <u>ain't</u> going to travel by bus. *(am not)*

3. __*X*__ They <u>was</u> outside in the rain. *(were)*

4. _____ I <u>am</u> switching phone services.

5. __*X*__ I <u>were</u> the one who broke the stereo. *(was)*

6. _____ You <u>were</u> the only one who showed up.

7. __*X*__ You <u>was</u> so much fun at the party. *(were)*

8. _____ The pens and pencils <u>are</u> in the supply cabinet.

9. __*X*__ Those clothes <u>was</u> for charity. *(were)*

10. __*X*__ He <u>were</u> asleep when you called. *(was)*

🌿 **Practice 23 Correcting**   Correct the verb errors in Practice 22 by rewriting each incorrect sentence. *See Practice 22.*

1. _____

2. _____

3. _____

4. _____

5. _____

6. _____

7. _____

8. _____

9. _____

10. _____

🌿 **Practice 24 Completing**   Fill in each blank in the following sentences with the correct form of *be* in the tense indicated.

1. I ___was___ a runner in school. (past)

2. You ___are___ the most generous person I know. (present)

3. Yesterday, the sheep ___were___ on that hill. (past)

4. At this moment, I ___am___ very happy. (present)

5. It ___is___ dark outside, so you had better stay home. (present)

6. He ___is___ my brother. (present)

7. The humidity and the flies ___are___ torturous in Africa. (present)

8. You ___are___ my favorite aunt. (present)

9. The dog in that picture ___was___ named Old Man Ruff. (past)

10. It ___was___ never polite to point at people. (past)

🌿 **Practice 25 Writing Your Own**

A. Write a sentence of your own for each of the following forms of *be*.
   Answers will vary.

1. am _____ _____

2. were _____

3. is _____

4. are _____

5. was _____

B. Write five sentences of your own using forms of *be*, and underline the verbs in each sentence. *Answers will vary.*

1. _____

2. _____

3. _____

4. _____

5. _____

PROBLEMS WITH *do*

Another verb that causes sentence problems in the present and past tenses is *do*. The following chart shows these problems. Learn the correct forms, and proofread to avoid errors.

The Verb *do*

Present Tense			
Singular		**Plural**	
INCORRECT	CORRECT	INCORRECT	CORRECT
NOT *I does*	*I do*	NOT *we does*	*we do*
NOT *you does*	*you do*	NOT *you does*	*you do*
NOT *he, she, it do*	*he, she, it does*	NOT *they does*	*they do*

Past Tense			
Singular		**Plural**	
INCORRECT	CORRECT	INCORRECT	CORRECT
NOT *I done*	*I did*	NOT *we done*	*we did*
NOT *you done*	*you did*	NOT *you done*	*you did*
NOT *he, she, it done*	*he, she, it did*	NOT *they done*	*they did*

REVIEWING PROBLEMS WITH *do*

What are two common errors made with do?

In the present tense, confusing does and do

In the past tense, confusing done and did

How can you prevent these errors?

By learning the correct forms and proofreading carefully

Practice 26 Identifying   Underline the correct forms of *do* in each of the following sentences.

1. I (done, <u>did</u>) my homework on time.
2. Scott (do, <u>does</u>) well at his summer job.
3. They (<u>do</u>, does) their exercises every night.
4. Jessica (do, <u>did</u>) her speech on violence.
5. She always (done, <u>does</u>) a good job.
6. You (<u>do</u>, does) eat a lot of food.
7. The doctor (do, <u>does</u>) rounds at the hospital every day.
8. My outdoor grill (<u>does</u>, done) steaks really well.
9. My sister (do, <u>did</u>) the best she could.
10. We (done, <u>did</u>) the assignment correctly.

Practice 27 Identifying   Put an X next to the sentence if the underlined form of *do* is incorrect.

1. __X__ He <u>do</u> his laundry at three in the morning. *(does)*
2. __X__ I <u>done</u> a quick patch on the tire. *(did)*
3. _____ My uncle and aunt <u>do</u> the cooking all the time.
4. __X__ Some people <u>does</u> their hair funny. *(do)*
5. _____ The young worker <u>does</u> the dishes.
6. __X__ We <u>done</u> everything we could think of. *(did)*

7. __X__ The camera <u>done</u> the work. (*did*)

8. __X__ He always <u>do</u> his work on time. (*does*)

9. _____ He <u>does</u> a hilarious comedy act.

10. _____ You <u>did</u> all the chores.

❧ Practice 28 Correcting   Correct the verb errors in Practice 27 by rewriting each incorrect sentence. *See Practice 27.*

1. _____

2. _____

3. _____

4. _____

5. _____

6. _____

7. _____

8. _____

9. _____

10. _____

❧ Practice 29 Completing   Fill in each blank in the following sentences with the correct forms of *do* in the tense indicated.

1. I ___*did*___ the jig last night. (past)

2. She ___*does*___ her papers quickly. (present)

3. They ___*did*___ the job easily. (past)

4. They ___*do*___ the weather report at 6:00 and 10:00. (present)

5. Last quarter, we ___*did*___ basic training together. (past)

6. You ___*do*___ math every night to keep up. (present)

7. She ___*does*___ wash her hair every day. (present)

8. The man ___*does*___ the books for my uncle's business. (present)

9. Thomas ___*did*___ the training for Carlos. (past)

10. I ___*did*___ the lettering on the poster. (past)

Practice 30 Writing Your Own

A. Write a sentence of your own for each of the following forms of *do*.
Answers will vary.

1. do _____

2. did _____

3. does _____

4. does _____

5. did _____

B. Write five sentences of your own using forms of *do*, and underline the verbs in each sentence. *Answers will vary.*

1. _____

2. _____

3. _____

4. _____

5. _____

PROBLEMS WITH *have*

Along with *be* and *do*, the verb *have* causes sentence problems in the present and past tenses. The following chart demonstrates these problems. Learn the correct forms, and proofread to avoid the errors with *have*.

The Verb *have*

Present Tense

Singular		Plural	
INCORRECT	CORRECT	INCORRECT	CORRECT
NOT *I has*	*I* **have**	NOT *we has*	*we* **have**
NOT *you has*	*you* **have**	NOT *you has*	*you* **have**
NOT *he, she, it have*	*he, she, it* **has**	NOT *they has*	*they* **have**

Past Tense

Singular		Plural	
INCORRECT	CORRECT	INCORRECT	CORRECT
NOT *I has*	*I had*	NOT *we has*	*we had*
NOT *you have*	*you had*	NOT *you has*	*you had*
NOT *he, she, it have*	*he, she, it had*	NOT *they has*	*they had*

REVIEWING PROBLEMS WITH *have*

What are two common errors made with have?

In the present tense, confusing has and have

In the past tense, confusing has or have and had

How can you prevent these errors?

By learning the correct forms and proofreading carefully

 Practice 31 Identifying   Underline the correct form of *have* in each of the following sentences.

1. I (has, <u>have</u>) your telephone number.
2. It (have, <u>has</u>) too many holes in it to work properly.
3. Charles (have, <u>has</u>) plenty of time.
4. The ceiling fans (has, <u>had</u>) broken.
5. We (<u>have</u>, has) the deadline in mind.
6. The clowns (has, <u>have</u>) a long day ahead of them.
7. You (<u>had</u>, has) the last laugh.
8. Madam Zoya's predictions (has, <u>have</u>) all come true.
9. Your paragraphs (has, <u>have</u>) great organization.
10. We (has, <u>had</u>) little to say to them.

 Practice 32 Identifying   Put an X next to the sentence if the under-lined form of *have* is incorrect.

1. _____ We <u>had</u> a wonderful time last night.
2. _____ Samantha <u>has</u> some good news for you.
3. __X__ I <u>has</u> the worst sinus headache. *(have, had)*
4. __X__ The nurses <u>has</u> time off. *(have, had)*
5. __X__ Yesterday, Jack <u>has</u> the most expensive outfit on. *(had)*
6. _____ I <u>have</u> everything I need for the trip.
7. _____ Brian <u>has</u> the story wrong.
8. __X__ The scarf <u>have</u> a small flaw. *(has, had)*
9. __X__ The trees in the front yard <u>has</u> no leaves. *(have, had)*
10. __X__ It <u>have</u> many inches of snow on top. *(has, had)*

Practice 33 Correcting   Correct the verb errors in Practice 32 by rewriting each incorrect sentence. *See Practice 32.*

1. _____
2. _____
3. _____
4. _____
5. _____
6. _____
7. _____
8. _____
9. _____
10. _____

Practice 34 Completing   Fill in each blank in the following sentences with the correct form of *have* in the tense indicated.

1. The boys and girls __have__ an early bedtime. (present)
2. I __had__ a strange dream last night. (past)
3. We __had__ fun at the beach. (past)
4. The invitation __has__ the directions to the party. (present)

5. We ___*have*___ an obligation to the court. (present)

6. Islands ___*have*___ many weather changes throughout the day. (present)

7. She ___*had*___ the answer all along. (past)

8. Cleo, my cat, ___*had*___ a small white star on her head. (past)

9. You ___*had*___ the bride's ring just a few minutes ago. (past)

10. Now you ___*have*___ the broken one. (present)

🌾 Practice 35 Writing Your Own

A. Write a sentence of your own for each of the following forms of *have*.
Answers will vary.

1. have _____

2. has _____

3. had _____

4. had _____

5. have _____

B. Write five sentences of your own using forms of *have*, and underline the verbs in each sentence. *Answers will vary.*

1. _____

2. _____

3. _____

4. _____

5. _____

CHAPTER REVIEW

You might want to reread your answers to the questions in the review boxes before you do the following exercises.

🌾 Review Practice 1 Reading
List five verbs from the paragraph by Lansey Namioka on page 167, and then complete the following tasks.
Answers will vary.

_____

_____

_____

_____

_____

1. Write the present tense of each verb.

_____

_____

_____

_____

_____

2. Write the past tense of each verb.

_____

_____

_____

_____

_____

3. Write the past participle of each verb with a helping verb.

_____

_____

_____

_____

_____

4. Write the *-ing* form of each verb with a helping verb.

_____

_____

_____

_____

_____

✹ **Review Practice 2 Identifying**   Underline the incorrect verb forms in each of the following sentences.

1. The children <u>laughs</u> at the clown's funny faces. *(laugh/laughed)*

2. Veronica and Mike <u>done</u> the dance moves perfectly. *(did)*

3. Maisy has <u>forget</u> her pager again. *(forgotten)*

4. Yesterday, you <u>ask</u> me the funniest thing. *(asked)*

5. We <u>been</u> the best of friends. *(are)*

6. Oh, no! You <u>has</u> a bug in your hair. *(have)*

7. The monkeys <u>plucks</u> fleas off of each other. *(pluck/plucked)*

8. I <u>were</u> filthy from the dust storm. *(was)*

9. We <u>eating</u> everything in sight. *(are eating/were eating)*

10. He <u>have</u> the worst cold ever. *(has)*

✹ **Review Practice 3 Correcting**   Correct the errors in Review Practice 2 by rewriting each incorrect sentence. *See Review Practice 2.*

1. _____

2. _____

3. _____

4. _____

5. _____

6. _____

7. _____

8. _____

9. _____

10. _____

✎ EDITING A STUDENT PARAGRAPH

Following is a paragraph written and revised by Mabel Adams in response to the writing assignment in this chapter. Read the paragraph, and underline each of her verbs.

My unique pastime, ice skating, <u>is</u> something that <u>is</u> not really popular in all parts of the country, but no matter where I <u>be</u>, I always <u>finds</u> an ice rink. I <u>been skating</u> my entire life. In fact, I <u>am skating</u> before I <u>will walk</u>. It <u>is</u> a very freeing activity. I just <u>get</u> on the ice and <u>set</u> my spirit free. I <u>will skate</u> for a half-hour and <u>feel</u> like I <u>have been relaxing</u> for a week. I <u>forget</u> all the pressures of being a student, and I <u>remember</u> what it <u>is</u> like to be a kid again when I <u>skate</u> alongside my boyfriend. Sometimes I <u>does</u> competitions. So far, I <u>have beat</u> all of my opponents. To most of my friends and family, skating <u>is</u> a strange way to relieve stress, especially since I <u>has</u> a 30-minute drive to the ice rink. But I <u>don't mind</u>. This December, I <u>will have skated</u> in my spare time for 20 years.

Here are the corrected verbs:
am
find
have been skating
was skating
could walk
will feel
am skating
do
have beaten
have

Collaborative Activity

Team up with a partner, and place an X above the 10 verb errors in Mabel's paragraph. Then, working together, use what you have learned in this chapter to correct these errors. Rewrite the paragraph with your corrections. *See student paragraph for errors. Corrections are in the margin.*

❧ EDITING YOUR OWN PARAGRAPH

Now return to the paragraph you wrote and revised at the beginning of this chapter. Underline each of your verbs.

Collaborative Activity

Exchange paragraphs with your partner, and circle any verb errors that you find in your partner's paragraph.

Individual Activity

On the Error Log in Appendix 6, record any verb errors that your partner found in your paragraph. To complete the writing process, correct these errors by rewriting your paragraph.

12

Subject-Verb Agreement

✐ Checklist for Correcting Subject-Verb Agreement Problems

> ✔ Do all subjects agree with their verbs?

Almost every day, we come across a situation that requires us to reach an agreement with someone. For example, you and a friend might have to agree on which movie to see, or you and your manager at work might have to agree on how many hours you'll work in the coming week. Whatever the issue, agreement is essential in most aspects of life—including writing. In this chapter, you will learn how to resolve conflicts in your sentences by making sure your subjects and verbs agree.

Notice how subjects and verbs in the following sentences by Maxine Hong Kingston work together in agreement.

Once in a long while, four times so far for me, my mother brings out the metal tube that holds her medical diploma. On the tube are gold circles crossed with seven red lines each—"joy" ideographs in abstract. There are also little flowers that look like gears for a gold machine. According to the scraps of labels with Chinese and American addresses, stamps, and post-marks, the family airmailed the can from Hong Kong in 1950. It got crushed in the middle, and whoever tried to peel the labels off stopped because the red and gold paint came off too, leaving silver scratches that rust. Somebody tried to pry the end off before discovering that the tube pulls apart. When I open it, the smell of China flies out, a thousand-year-old bat flying heavy-headed out of the Chinese caverns where bats are as white as dust, a smell that comes from long ago, far back in the brain. Crates from Canton, Hong Kong, Singapore, and Taiwan have that smell too, only stronger because they are more recently come from the Chinese.

In this paragraph, the author describes an old family treasure through her senses. Before continuing in this chapter, take a moment to write about an object that is important to you. Save your work because you will use it later in the chapter.

Writing Assignment: A Treasured Object

Think of some objects that are important to you or to people close to you. How do the objects look, sound, feel, taste, or smell? Do certain senses bring back specific memories? How do they make you feel? Write a paragraph describing your most treasured object for someone who has never seen it.

Revising Your Writing

Revise the first draft of your paragraph before you focus on editing. Use the Revising Checklist on pages 24–25 to help you with your revision. Make sure your paragraph has a good topic sentence and is well developed. Then check your paragraph for unity, organization, and coherence.

SUBJECT-VERB AGREEMENT

Subject-verb agreement simply means that singular subjects must be paired with singular verbs and plural subjects with plural verbs. Look at this example:

Singular: **She lives** in California.

The subject *she* is singular because it refers to only one person. The verb *lives* is singular and matches the singular subject. Here is the same sentence in plural form:

Plural: **They live** in California.

The subject *they* is plural, more than one person, and the verb *live* is also plural.

Once students understand how subjects and verbs agree, test your students by putting sentences with subject-verb agreement errors on the board and asking them to come to the board to find and correct the errors.

■ For more sample sentences, see the *Instructor's Resource Manual*, Section II, Part II.

TEACHING ON THE WEB

Exploring and Discussing: Have students find an on-line essay written by a student that deals with a topic that is similar to the current paragraph they are writing in this chapter. Then have students underline the subjects once and the verbs twice. Do all the subjects and verbs agree? Have students discuss the difficulties of finding their on-line source and the results of their subject-verb agreement search.

TEACHING ON THE WEB

Mosaics Web Site: To learn more about subject-verb agreement, students can go to www.prenhall.com/mosaics.

> REVIEWING SUBJECT-VERB AGREEMENT
>
> **What is the difference between singular and plural?**
>
> Singular refers to only one subject. Plural refers to more than one subject.
>
> **What kind of verb goes with a singular subject?**
>
> A singular verb goes with a singular subject.
>
> **What kind of verb goes with a plural subject?**
>
> A plural verb goes with a plural subject.

Practice 1 Identifying   Underline the verb that agrees with its subject in each of the following sentences.

1. Terri (run, <u>runs</u>) every morning.
2. Mike (<u>is</u>, are) a talented football player.
3. After school, she (<u>drives</u>, drive) straight home.
4. The truckers (was, <u>were</u>) helpful to the stranded motorist.
5. The Garcias (travels, <u>travel</u>) quite often.
6. My sister (<u>creates</u>, create) art from metal scraps.
7. The St. Louis Cardinals (has, <u>have</u>) many loyal fans.
8. The Army (<u>recruits</u>, recruit) at the local colleges.
9. Massage therapy (<u>is</u>, are) expensive but worth the cost.
10. My dog, Rusty, (<u>is</u>, are) my best friend.

Practice 2 Identifying   Put an X next to the sentence if its subject and verb do not agree. Underline the subject and verb.

1. __X__ <u>We envies</u> athletic ability. *(We envy)*
2. _____ Disgruntled <u>employees are</u> difficult to control.
3. _____ <u>Ian believes</u> in his girlfriend.
4. __X__ All those <u>paintings sells</u> for a lot of money. *(paintings sell)*

5. __X__ Adriana try to study hard. *(Adriana tries)*

6. __X__ The friends fights over stupid things. *(friends fight)*

7. __X__ Three new TV shows has great potential. *(shows have)*

8. __X__ Most kids loves rock music. *(kids love)*

9. _____ Stella drives very fast.

10. __X__ The play are about to begin. *(play is)*

🌾 **Practice 3 Correcting**   Correct the subject-verb agreement errors in Practice 2 by rewriting each incorrect sentence. *See Practice 2.*

1. _____

2. _____

3. _____

4. _____

5. _____

6. _____

7. _____

8. _____

9. _____

10. _____

🌾 **Practice 4 Completing**   Fill in each blank with a present-tense verb that agrees with its subject. Avoid *is*, *are*, *was*, and *were*. *Answers will vary.*

1. The nudity in the movie _____ inappropriate.

2. They _____ the trip will be exciting.

3. The computer automatically _____ the latest version of your document every few minutes.

4. After the holidays, Cassandra _____ for two weeks.

5. Cheerleaders _____ for the school's team to win.

6. Looking out my office window, I _____ a brick wall.

7. Jack _____ he got the lead for the play.

8. Race car drivers _____ at very high speeds.

9. Eating carrots _____ people's eyesight.

10. Firefighters _____ several fires in a week.

❋ Practice 5 Writing Your Own

A. Write a sentence of your own using each of the following as a subject.
   Answers will vary.

1. a backpack _____

2. Mike _____

3. the cars _____

4. his dogs _____

5. the computer _____

B. Write five sentences of your own, and underline the subject and verb in each sentence. *Answers will vary.*

1. _____

2. _____

3. _____

4. _____

5. _____

WORDS SEPARATING SUBJECTS AND VERBS

With sentences that are as simple and direct as *She lives in California,* it is easy to check that the subject and verb agree. But problems can arise when words come between the subject and the verb. Often the words between subject and verb are prepositional phrases. If you follow the advice given in Chapter 7, you will be able to find the subject and verb: Cross out all the prepositional phrases in a sentence. The subject and verb will be among the words that are left. Here are some examples:

Prepositional Phrases: The **donation** ~~for the charity center~~ is ~~in my car.~~

When you cross out the prepositional phrases, you can tell that the singular subject (*donation*) and the singular verb (*is*) agree.

s   v

Prepositional Phrases: The **stars** ~~in the sky~~ **twinkle** ~~at night~~.

When you cross out the prepositional phrases, you can tell that the plural subject (*stars*) and the plural verb (*twinkle*) agree.

REVIEWING WORDS SEPARATING SUBJECTS AND VERBS

What words often come between subjects and verbs?

Prepositional phrases often come between subjects and verbs.

What is an easy way to identify a subject and verb in a sentence?

Cross out the prepositional phrases first.

Practice 6 Identifying   Underline the verb that agrees with the subject in each of the following sentences. Cross out the prepositional phrases first.

1. There (is, <u>are</u>) so many reasons why people shouldn't smoke.
2. They usually (stays, <u>stay</u>) late.
3. Neither Jill nor Kevin (<u>was</u>, were) ready ~~for marriage~~.
4. Four ~~of the jurors~~ (was, <u>were</u>) dismissed ~~for misconduct~~.
5. Peanut butter and jelly (<u>is</u>, are) great ~~over ice cream~~.
6. My neighbor ~~of 12 years~~ (<u>goes</u>, go) ~~to the hockey game~~ every week.
7. My suitcase ~~with all my gifts~~ (<u>appears</u>, appear) to have been stolen.
8. Pizza and beer (<u>makes</u>, make) me relax ~~at night~~.
9. We sometimes (fights, <u>fight</u>) ~~during vacation~~.
10. Robert (<u>screams</u>, scream) really loudly ~~at concerts~~.

Practice 7 Identifying   Place an X next to the sentence if its subject and verb do not agree. Cross out the prepositional phrases first. Then underline the subject and verb.

1. __X__ The teacher ~~in the audience~~ seem familiar ~~with the speaker~~.
   (teacher seems)
2. _____ Roman architecture still influences architecture today.
3. __X__ Penn and Teller is famous magicians. *(Penn and Teller are)*
4. _____ The reports ~~on my desk~~ belong ~~to the finance department~~.
5. __X__ Ranch dressing ~~on a salad~~ taste the best. *(dressing tastes)*
6. __X__ The workers ~~in the yard~~ wants overtime work. *(workers want)*
7. _____ Horror films and suspense dramas ~~at the theater~~ give me night-mares.
8. __X__ The keys ~~on the sofa~~ fits the back door. *(keys fit)*
9. _____ The motorists ~~on that highway~~ drive too fast.
10. __X__ One ~~of her many~~ talents are dancing. *(One is)*

Practice 8 Correcting   Correct the subjects and verbs that do not agree in Practice 7 by rewriting each incorrect sentence. *See Practice 7.*

1. _____
2. _____
3. _____
4. _____
5. _____
6. _____
7. _____
8. _____
9. _____
10. _____

Practice 9 Completing   Fill in each blank in the following sentences with a verb that agrees with its subject and makes sense. Cross out the prepositional phrases first. *Answers may vary.*

1. Many travelers ~~on this trip~~ ____prefer____ trains ~~to planes~~.

2. Our award-winning roses ~~on the back patio~~ ____bloom____ ~~throughout the summer~~.

3. The decorative dragons ~~on this silk~~ _____bring_____ good fortune.

4. The beef and the noodles ~~on the stove~~ _____need_____ seasoning.

5. The clothes ~~in the dryer~~ _____need_____ folding.

6. A pool ~~above the ground~~ _____adds_____ value ~~to a house.~~

7. The Alamo Dome ~~in Texas~~ _____hosts_____ many sporting events and concerts.

8. The four ~~of us~~ _____love_____ watching scary movies.

9. Tom Hanks _____plays_____ many types ~~of characters.~~

10. The woman ~~with the poodle and funny glasses~~ always _____makes_____ me laugh.

Practice 10 Writing Your Own

A. Write a sentence of your own for each of the following prepositional phrases. *Answers will vary.*

1. behind the couch _____

2. around that mountain _____

3. with the red hair _____

4. in our company _____

5. on our team _____

B. Write five sentences of your own with prepositional phrases, and underline the subject and verb in each sentence. Cross out the prepositional phrases first. *Answers will vary.*

1. _____

2. _____

3. _____

4. _____

5. _____

MORE THAN ONE SUBJECT

Sometimes a subject consists of more than one person, place, thing, or idea. These subjects are called **compound** (as discussed in Chapter 7). Follow these three rules when matching a verb to a compound subject.

1. **When compound subjects are joined by *and,* use a plural verb.**

   Plural: **Maria** and **Tom were** my best friends.

The singular words *Maria* and *Tom* together make a plural subject. Therefore, the plural verb *were* is needed.

2. **When the subject appears to have more than one part, but the parts refer to a single unit, use a singular verb.**

   Singular: **Vinegar and oil is** great on a salad.

Vinegar is one item and *oil* is one item, but the one is not eaten without the other, so they form a single unit. Because they are a single unit, they require a singular verb—*is*.

3. **When compound subjects are joined by *or* or *nor,* make the verb agree with the subject closest to it.**

   Singular: Neither **bananas** nor **chicken** was available at the store.

The compound subject closest to the verb is *chicken*, which is singular. Therefore, the verb must be singular—*was*.

   Plural: Neither **chicken** nor **bananas were** available at the store.

This time, the compound subject closest to the verb is *bananas*, which is plural. Therefore, the verb must be plural—*were*.

REVIEWING MORE THAN ONE SUBJECT

Do you use a singular or plural verb with compound subjects joined by and*?*

A plural verb

Why should you use a singular verb with a subject like macaroni and cheese*?*

Because it forms a single unit

> *If one part of a compound subject joined by* or *or* nor *is singular and the other is plural, how do you decide whether to use a singular or plural verb?*
>
> Make the verb agree with the subject closest to it.

Practice 11 Identifying   Underline the verb that agrees with its subject in each of the following sentences. Cross out the prepositional phrases first.

1. Wine and cheese (<u>is</u>, are) a good appetizer.

2. Neither your smile nor your laughter (<u>cheers</u>, cheer) me today.

3. The brakes and alignment (needs, <u>need</u>) adjusting ~~on the ear~~.

4. The cupboards and refrigerator ~~in this house~~ (is, <u>are</u>) empty.

5. A hamburger and fries ~~from Burger King~~ (is, <u>are</u>) my favorites.

6. Neither man nor bullets (harms, <u>harm</u>) Superman.

7. Banshees and leprechauns (is, <u>are</u>) Irish folk characters.

8. Biscuits and gravy (<u>is</u>, are) a wonderful southern breakfast.

9. Either the gophers or the dog (<u>digs</u>, dig) ~~in the backyard~~.

10. My aunt and uncle (<u>live</u>, lives) ~~in San Diego, California~~.

Practice 12 Identifying   Put an X next to the sentence if its subjects and verb do not agree. Cross out the prepositional phrases first. Then underline the subject and verb.

1. __X__ Neither the <u>ham</u> nor the <u>fish</u> <u>were</u> cooked well. *(Neither ham nor the fish was)*

2. __X__ "<u>Ball and chain</u>" <u>are</u> an expression referring ~~to one's spouse~~. *("Ball and chain" is)*

3. _____ <u>Paper</u> and an <u>ink cartridge</u> ~~for the printer~~ <u>need</u> ~~to be ordered~~.

4. __X__ <u>Sam</u> and <u>Jim</u> ~~from my school~~ <u>draws</u> very well. *(Sam and Jim draw)*

5. _____ <u>Louisiana</u> and <u>Georgia</u> <u>are</u> humid states.

6. __X__ Either the <u>flies</u> or the <u>heat</u> ~~in the summer~~ <u>annoy</u> me. *(Either the flies or the heat annoys)*

7. __X__ <u>Sour cream</u> and <u>onion</u> ~~on chips~~ <u>are</u> my favorite dip. *(Sour cream and onion is)*

8. __X__ Either the <u>movers</u> or <u>I</u> <u>are</u> responsible ~~for packing the glasses~~. *(Either the movers or I am)*

9. _____ <u>Ham</u> and <u>cheese</u> ~~with mayonnaise~~ <u>makes</u> a great sandwich.

10. __X__ <u>Pens</u> and <u>pencils</u> <u>belongs</u> ~~in the third drawer~~. *(Pens and pencils belong)*

❋ Practice 13 Correcting   Correct the subjects and verbs that do not agree in Practice 12 by rewriting each incorrect sentence. *See Practice 12.*

1. _____

2. _____

3. _____

4. _____

5. _____

6. _____

7. _____

8. _____

9. _____

10. _____

❋ Practice 14 Completing   Fill in each blank in the following sentences with a verb that agrees with its subject and makes sense. Avoid *is*, *are*, *was*, and *were* when possible. Cross out the prepositional phrases first. *Answers will vary.*

1. The balloons and streamers ~~for the party~~ _____ ~~in the back seat of the car~~.

2. Neither the picture nor the wall hangings _____ good ~~on that wall~~.

3. Colds and flus _____ usually caught ~~in the winter~~.

4. Peanut butter and jelly _____ great ~~on crackers~~.

5. Dinner and a movie ~~with someone you like~~ _____ a good date.

6. Sun and water _____ plants grow.

7. The bosses and the staff ~~in this office~~ _____ a break.

8. Either this lotion or this oil _____ me ~~to break out~~.

9. Neither the girls nor the boys ~~from the third grade~~ _____ well.

10. The CDs and the DVDs _____ ~~in the entertainment center~~.

❋ Practice 15 Writing Your Own

A. Write a sentence of your own using the following words as subjects.
   Answers will vary.

1. beer and peanuts _____

2. neither my father nor my mother _____

3. the actors and their bodyguards _____

4. either the sweater or the pants _____

5. the rabbits and chickens _____

B. Write five sentences of your own with compound subjects, and underline the subject and verb in each sentence. Cross out the prepositional phrases first. *Answers will vary.*

1. _____

2. _____

3. _____

4. _____

5. _____

VERBS BEFORE SUBJECTS

When the subject follows its verb, the subject may be hard to find, which makes the process of agreeing subjects and verbs difficult. Subjects come after verbs in two particular situations—when the sentence begins with *here* or *there* and when a question begins with *who, what, where, when, why,* or *how.* Here are some examples:

Verb Before Subject: Here **are** the **contestants** for the game.

Verb Before Subject: There **is paper** in the filling cabinet.

In sentences that begin with *here* or *there*, the verb always comes before the subject. Don't forget to cross out prepositional phrases to help you identify the subject. One of the words that's left will be the subject. Then you can check that the verb agrees with it.

Verb Before Subject: Who **is** that crazy **man** with the funky hat?

Verb Before Subject: Where **are** the **keys** to this lock?

Verb Before Subject: When **are you graduating** from college?

In questions that begin with *who, what, when, where, why,* and *how,* the verb comes before the subject or is split by the subject, as in the last example.

> REVIEWING VERBS BEFORE SUBJECTS
>
> **Where will you find the verb in sentences that begin with *here* or *there*?**
>
> *Before the subject* _____
>
> **Where will you find the verb in questions that begin with *who, what, where, when, why,* and *how*?**
>
> *Before the subject* _____

Practice 16 Identifying   Underline the verb that agrees with its subject in each of the following sentences. Cross out the prepositional phrases first.

1. Here (stands, stand) the statue ~~of our state bird~~.
2. There ~~up the tree~~ (goes, go) our cat.
3. Who (is, are) the person responsible?
4. Where (is, are) the staples ~~for the stapler~~?
5. How (is, are) dinner coming along?
6. There (grazes, graze) a wild deer ~~in our yard~~.
7. Here (plays, play) the children.
8. What (is, are) Jim and Tanya doing ~~for Halloween~~?
9. There (is, are) a snake ~~in my boot~~.
10. Who (is, are) taking you ~~to the Bahamas~~?

Practice 17 Identifying   Put an X next to the sentence if the subject and verb do not agree. Cross out the prepositional phrases first. Then underline the subject and verb.

1. _____ There are several reasons ~~for this strategy~~.
2. __X__ Who is the nurses ~~for this procedure~~? *(are nurses)*
3. __X__ What is you doing ~~with all those leftovers~~? *(are you)*

4. _____ Here <u>sit</u> the <u>dogs</u> ~~for the parade~~.

5. ___X___ There <u>jumps</u> the <u>frogs</u> ~~from the pond~~. *(jump frogs)*

6. _____ Who <u>are</u> <u>you</u> taking ~~to the baseball game~~?

7. ___X___ Why <u>is</u> <u>you</u> wearing those clothes? *(are you wearing)*

8. _____ Here <u>is</u> the new <u>TV</u>.

9. ___X___ How <u>are</u> your <u>back</u> today? *(is back)*

10. ___X___ Here <u>is</u> the cleaning <u>people</u> ~~for your house~~. *(are people)*

🌿 Practice 18 Correcting   Correct the subjects and verbs that do not agree in Practice 17 by rewriting each incorrect sentence. *See Practice 17.*

1. _____

2. _____

3. _____

4. _____

5. _____

6. _____

7. _____

8. _____

9. _____

10. _____

🌿 Practice 19 Completing   Fill in each blank in the following sentences with a verb that agrees with its subject and makes sense. Avoid *is, are, was,* and *were* when possible. Cross out the prepositional phrases first. *Answers will vary.*

1. Here _____ our horses ~~after the ride~~.

2. There _____ the nervous father-to-be.

3. Who _____ that girl ~~with the red blouse~~?

4. What _____ Tom thinking?

5. There _____ the coals ~~from last night's fire~~.

6. How _____ the beginning ~~of the poem~~?

7. Where _____ Jane and Jill last week?

8. Here _____ the water ~~from the creek~~.

9. Here _____ the performers ~~for tonight's show~~.

10. When _____ are you going to throw out those old shoes?

⁂ Practice 20 Writing Your Own

A. Write a sentence of your own beginning with each of the following words.
   Answers will vary.

1. here _____

2. there _____

3. who _____

4. what _____

5. how _____

B. Write five sentences of your own with the verb before its subject, and underline the subject and verb in each sentence. Cross out the prepositional phrases. *Answers will vary.*

1. _____

2. _____

3. _____

4. _____

5. _____

COLLECTIVE NOUNS

Collective nouns name a group of people or things. Examples include such nouns as *army, audience, band, class, committee, crew, crowd, family, flock, gang, jury, majority, minority, orchestra, senate, team,* and *troop.* Collective nouns can be singular or plural. They are singular when they refer to a group as a single unit. They are plural when they refer to the individual actions or feelings of the group members.

                                s   v
Singular: The **orchestra plays** every Friday.

Orchestra refers to the entire unit or group. Therefore, it requires the singular verb *plays*.

s   v

Plural: The **orchestra play** different instruments.

Here *orchestra* refers to the individual members, who each play an instrument, so the plural verb *play* is used.

REVIEWING COLLECTIVE NOUNS

When is a collective noun singular?

When it refers to a group as a single unit

When is a collective noun plural?

When it refers to the individual actions or feelings of the group members

---

Practice 21 Identifying   Underline the verb that agrees with its subject in each of the following sentences. Cross out the prepositional phrases first.

1. A troupe ~~of acrobats~~ (fly, <u>flies</u>) ~~through the air~~ one by one.
2. The senate (was, <u>were</u>) looking separately at their calendars.
3. The navy (is, <u>are</u>) out having fun ~~on the town~~ tonight.
4. The class ~~of 2001~~ (experience, <u>experiences</u>) many new opportunities.
5. A crowd ~~of enthusiastic people~~ (yell, <u>yells</u>) encouragement ~~to the speaker~~.
6. The audience (clap, <u>claps</u>) wildly when he walks ~~on stage~~.
7. The army (march, <u>marches</u>) ~~in uniform lines~~.
8. The gang ~~of children~~ (scream, <u>screams</u>) together ~~in delight~~.
9. The jury (<u>was</u>, were) deadlocked.
10. The minority (<u>is</u>, are) ~~in the right~~.

Practice 22 Identifying   Put an X next to the sentence if the subject and verb do not agree. Cross out the prepositional phrases first. Then underline the subjects and verbs.

1. _____ My gang ~~of friends~~ is going ~~to Magic Mountain~~.

2. __X__ The committee ~~for finance~~ decide money issues. *(committee decides)*

3. _____ A crew ~~of sailors~~ whistles every time she walks by.

4. __X__ The majority ~~of the voters~~ plans a vote ~~on Monday~~. *(majority plan)*

5. __X__ The jury are passing the verdict ~~on the accused~~. *(jury is passing)*

6. _____ The flock ~~of birds~~ is flying ~~in formation~~.

7. __X__ The band play "Wipe Out" ~~at every game~~. *(band plays)*

8. __X__ My family visits one another ~~for every holiday~~. *(family visit)*

9. _____ A troupe of ~~entertainers~~ performs ~~in our town~~ once a year.

10. __X__ My brother's class ~~of graduating students~~ like the new caps and gowns. *(class likes)*

🌲 Practice 23 Correcting   Correct the subjects and verbs that do not agree in Practice 22 by rewriting each incorrect sentence. *See Practice 22.*

1. _____

2. _____

3. _____

4. _____

5. _____

6. _____

7. _____

8. _____

9. _____

10. _____

🌲 Practice 24 Completing   Fill in each blank in the following sentences with a verb that agrees with its subject and makes sense. Avoid *is*, *are*, *was*, and *were* when possible. Cross out the prepositional phrases first. *Answers will vary.*

1. The team ~~of football players~~ _____ silently going ~~through individual preparations for the game~~.

2. The majority _____ the voice ~~of the minority~~.

3. The committee _____ taken a break ~~from the long meeting~~.

4. Our class always _____ the most money ~~for charity~~.

5. The orchestra ~~in the pit~~ _____ playing badly.

6. The family _____ going ~~on vacation~~ this summer.

7. The army _____ ~~across the land~~.

8. Only a minority ~~of the citizens~~ _____ cheated ~~by the new tax~~.

9. The crowd ~~of onlookers~~ _____ shocked ~~by the scene~~.

10. The class ~~with the most rowdy students~~ _____ pleased ~~with the teacher~~.

Practice 25 Writing Your Own

A. Write a sentence of your own using each of the following collective nouns as subjects. *Answers will vary.*

1. crowd _____

2. army _____

3. family _____

4. senate _____

5. audience _____

B. Write five sentences of your own with collective nouns as subjects, and underline the subject and verb in each sentence. Cross out the prepositional phrases first. *Answers will vary.*

1. _____

2. _____

3. _____

4. _____

5. _____

INDEFINITE PRONOUNS

Indefinite pronouns do not refer to anyone or anything specific. Some indefinite pronouns are always singular, and some are always plural. A few can be either singular or plural, depending on the other words in the sentence.

When an indefinite pronoun is the subject of a sentence, the verb must agree with the pronoun. Here is a list of indefinite pronouns.

Indefinite Pronouns

Always Singular		Always Plural	Either Singular or Plural
another	neither	both	all
anybody	nobody	few	any
anyone	none	many	more
anything	no one	others	most
each	nothing	several	some
either	one		
everybody	other		
everyone	somebody		
everything	someone		
little	something		
much			

Singular: Something changes at home every day.

Everybody hates this hot weather.

Plural: Several made the long hike.

Many stay longer than necessary.

The pronouns that can be either singular or plural are singular when they refer to singular words and plural when they refer to plural words.

Singular: Some of Sarah's fear **was** gone.

Some is singular because it refers to *fear*, which is singular. The singular verb *was* agrees with the singular subject *some*.

                    s   v
Plural: **Some** of Sarah's friends **were** at her graduation.

Some is plural because it refers to *friends*, which is plural. The plural verb *were* agrees with the plural subject *some*.

REVIEWING INDEFINITE PRONOUNS

What is an indefinite pronoun?

A pronoun that doesn't refer to anyone or anything specific
_____

When are all, any, more, most, *and* some *singular or plural?*

They are singular when they refer to singular words and plural when they refer to
_____

plural words.
_____

Practice 26 Identifying   Underline the verb that agrees with its subject in each of the following sentences. Cross out the prepositional phrases first.

1. Many (<u>hope</u>, hopes) she will win the contest.
2. Everyone who ate ~~at that restaurant~~ (<u>is</u>, are) expected ~~to get sick~~.
3. Somebody (spike, <u>spikes</u>) the punch ~~at every concert~~.
4. Someone usually (<u>joins</u>, join) Victor ~~for dinner~~.
5. Each ~~of the cars~~ (<u>was</u>, were) too expensive.
6. None ~~of the vendors~~ (<u>has</u>, have) change ~~for a dollar~~.
7. Many kinds ~~of people~~ (visits, <u>visit</u>) Florida each year.
8. Not many ~~of the workers~~ (leaves, <u>leave</u>) the job ~~on time~~.
9. Sometimes the quietest person ~~in the class~~ (<u>becomes</u>, become) the most active.
10. The soda ~~on top of the TV~~ (<u>belongs</u>, belong) ~~to Jason~~.

Practice 27 Identifying   Put an X next to the sentence if its subject and verb do not agree. Cross out the prepositional phrases first. Then underline the subject and verb.

1. __X__ Several ~~of the diners~~ eats only vegetarian meals. *(Several eat)*

2. _____ Many ~~of the people~~ trip ~~on the first step.~~

3. __X__ Nothing ~~in this refrigerator~~ taste good ~~to me~~ today. *(Nothing*
   tastes)

4. __X__ More ~~of the wild animals~~ is invading the city. *(More are)*

5. __X__ Both ~~of the students in the class~~ tries very hard. *(Both try)*

6. _____ Everybody pretends ~~to like her~~.

7. __X__ All ~~of the money~~ are ~~for your business trip~~. *(All is)*

8. __X__ Most ~~of the crime scene~~ have been destroyed. *(Most has been de-*
   stroyed)

9. _____ No one paces the floor as much as you do.

10. __X__ Few ~~of the invited guests~~ plans to arrive late. *(Few plan)*

🌿 **Practice 28 Correcting**   Correct the subjects and verbs that do not
agree in Practice 27 by rewriting each incorrect sentence. *See Practice 27.*

1. _____
2. _____
3. _____
4. _____
5. _____
6. _____
7. _____
8. _____
9. _____
10. _____

🌿 **Practice 29 Completing**   Fill in each blank in the following sentences with a verb that agrees with its subject and makes sense. Cross out
the prepositional phrases first. *Answers may vary.*

1. A few ~~of the cats~~ __have had__ their shots.

2. Some ~~of the water~~ __is__ ~~on the carpet~~.

3. Someone __was__ eating my lunch.

4. Both ~~of the boys~~ _____*were*_____ late ~~for their appointments~~.

5. Nothing _____*is*_____ more important than your health.

6. Somebody ~~in this room~~ _____*is*_____ keeping a secret.

7. Several ~~of the videos~~ _____*were*_____ destroyed ~~in the heat~~.

8. Most ~~of the mud~~ _____*splashed*_____ ~~on me~~.

9. All ~~of the barking dogs~~ _____*belong*_____ ~~to the neighbor~~.

10. Each person _____*believes*_____ a different superstition.

❦ Practice 30 Writing Your Own

A. Write a sentence of your own using the following indefinite pronouns as subjects, and combine them with one of the following verbs: *is, are, was, were. Answers will vary.*

1. minority _____

2. Senate _____

3. several _____

4. Navy _____

5. some _____

B. Write five sentences of your own using indefinite pronouns as subjects, and underline the subject and verb in each sentence. Cross out the prepositional phrases first. *Answers will vary.*

1. _____

2. _____

3. _____

4. _____

5. _____

CHAPTER REVIEW

You might want to review your answers to the questions in the review boxes before you do the following exercises.

※ **Review Practice 1 Reading**   Refer to the paragraph by Maxine Hong Kingston on pages 194–195 to do the following exercises.

1. List five subjects and their verbs. *Answers will vary.*

   _____

   _____

   _____

   _____

   _____

2. Record the two sentences with verbs before their subjects.

   Sentences 2 and 3
   _____

   _____

   _____

   _____

   _____

3. Record the two sentences with indefinite pronouns as subjects.

   Sentences 5 and 6
   _____

   _____

   _____

   _____

   _____

※ **Review Practice 2 Identifying**   Underline the incorrect verbs in each of the following sentences. Cross out the prepositional phrases first.

1. We <u>speaks</u> in clear, forceful voices. *(speak)*

2. The rabbits and the chickens in the back shed <u>shares</u> the same feed. *(share)*

3. A few of the memos for today's meeting <u>was</u> misplaced. *(were)*

4. The committee of new employees <u>ask</u> a lot of questions. *(asks)*

5. Somebody <u>take</u> the erasers from this classroom every day. *(takes)*

6. Either the stereo or the TV ~~in the living room~~ <u>require</u> a new plug.
   (requires)

7. There <u>is</u> many books ~~on the shelf~~. *(are)*

8. Christy <u>water</u> the flowers ~~in the planters~~. *(waters)*

9. What <u>is</u> you watching ~~on the TV~~? *(are)*

10. The team ~~of synchronized swimmers~~ <u>compete</u> ~~in the finals~~ every year.
    (competes)

🌿 Review Practice 3 Correcting   Correct the errors in Review Practice 2 by rewriting each incorrect sentence. *See Review Practice 2.*

✎ EDITING A STUDENT PARAGRAPH

Following is a paragraph written and revised by Tyler Francis in response to the writing assignment in this chapter. Read the paragraph, and underline each of his subjects and verbs. Cross out the prepositional phrases first.

<u>It is</u> very strange, but <u>I loves</u> the smell ~~of oil, gas, and exhaust from cars~~. <u>Most says</u> these <u>things smell</u> like burning fumes, but ~~for me~~ <u>they smell</u> ~~of warm, carefree days~~ spent ~~with my dad~~. <u>Dad has</u> a passion ~~for fixing up old cars~~, and <u>I am</u> his assistant. <u>Dad and I spends</u> our summer days ~~in the shed out behind the house~~. Either <u>he are</u> ~~underneath the car~~ or ~~under its hood~~. Hovering nearby <u>is</u> his willing <u>assistant</u>, me, ~~with wrenches, oil, rags~~--anything <u>Dad need</u>. ~~In the summer by midday~~, the <u>shed gets</u> so hot that <u>I can</u> actually <u>see</u> the fumes ~~from the oil, gas, and exhaust in the air~~. <u>I breathe</u> deeply: There <u>are</u> the <u>smell</u> ~~of my father and me~~. My <u>gang</u> of friends <u>do</u> not <u>understand</u> why <u>I spend</u> my summer ~~in a hot shed with my dad~~. But <u>I knows</u> this: Here <u>is</u> my fondest <u>memories</u>.

Here are the corrected agreement errors:
I love
Most say
Dad and I spend
he is
Dad needs
is, smell, gang,
does, understand
I know, are,
memories

Collaborative Activity

Team up with a partner, and underline the nine agreement errors in Tyler's paragraph twice. Then, working together, use what you have learned in this chapter to correct these errors. Rewrite the paragraph with your corrections. *See the student paragraph above for errors. Corrections are in the margin.*

❧ EDITING YOUR OWN PARAGRAPH

Now return to the paragraph you wrote and revised at the beginning of this chapter. Underline each of your subjects and verbs.

Collaborative Activity

Exchange paragraphs with your partner, and circle any agreement errors that you find in your partner's paragraph.

Individual Activity

On the Error Log in Appendix 6, record the agreement errors that your partner found in your paragraph. To complete the writing process, correct these errors by rewriting your paragraph.

More on Verbs

✐ Checklist for More on Verbs

✔ Are verb tenses consistent?

✔ Are sentences written in the active voice?

Verbs communicate the action and time of each sentence. So it is important that you use verb tense consistently. Also, you should strive to write in the active, not the passive, voice. This chapter provides help with both of these sentence skills.

Notice how energetic and consistent the verb tenses are in the following paragraph by Robert Fulghum.

> I like sorting the clothes—lights, darks, in-betweens. I like setting the dials—hot, cold, rinse, time, heat. These are choices I can understand and make with decisive skill. I still haven't figured out the new stereo, but washers and dryers I can handle. The bell dings—you pull out the warm, fluffy clothes, take them to the dining-room table, sort and fold them into neat piles. I especially like it when there's lots of static electricity, and you can hang socks all over your body and they will stick there.

In this paragraph, Robert Fulghum describes a chore he enjoys because it's not complicated. Before continuing in this chapter, take a moment to write about your favorite or most dreaded chore. Save your work because you will use it later in the chapter.

TEACHING MORE ON VERBS

Create a short paragraph with inconsistent tenses. You might use words like *today* and *yesterday* to help create confusion. For example, "I am studying today for the hardest final I have ever taken. I had been studying for over two weeks, and I still will not feel like I'm prepared. The test was given tomorrow."

Have students rewrite the paragraph three times, once for each tense: past, present, and future. Make sure they adjust all words to indicate the correct time (for example, *today* and *yesterday*).

■ For more sample paragraphs, see the *Instructor's Resource Manual*, Section II, Part II.

Writing Assignment: My Favorite or Most Dreaded Chore

Do you have a favorite or most dreaded chore? What is it? How do you go about doing it? Why do you like or dislike this chore? Write a paragraph explaining this chore to your peers.

Revising Your Writing

Revise the first draft of your paragraph before you focus on editing. Use the Revising Checklist on pages 24–25 to help you with your revision. Make sure your paragraph has a good topic sentence and is well developed. Then check your paragraph for unity, organization, and coherence.

CONSISTENT VERB TENSE

Verb tense refers to the time an action takes place—in the present, the past, or the future. The verb tenses in a sentence should be consistent. That is, if you start out using one tense, you should not switch tenses unless absolutely necessary. Switching tenses can be confusing. Here are some examples:

                                           Present
Inconsistent: When the doorbell **rings** all through the evening

                                                   Present
            and the ghosts and goblins **come** out for candy, then

                    Past
            it **was** Halloween.

                                               Present
Consistent: When the doorbell **rings** all through the evening and

                                           Present
            the ghosts and goblins **come** out for candy, then it

            Present
            it **is** Halloween.

                        Past   Present
Inconsistent: They **rushed** to the hospital when they **hear** that
            you were having the baby.

	Past			Past

Consistent: They **rushed** to the hospital when they **heard** that you were having the baby.

	Future		Present

Inconsistent: We **will send** you a postcard, and we **buy** you some souvenirs from the Virgin Islands.

	Future		Future

Consistent: We **will send** you a postcard, and we **will buy** you some souvenirs from the Virgin Islands.

REVIEWING CONSISTENT VERB TENSES

Why should verb tenses be consistent?

Because time should be consistent within a sentence

What problem do inconsistent verb tenses create?

Inconsistent verbs can be confusing for the reader.

Practice 1 Identifying   Put a C next to the sentence if the underlined verb is consistent.

1. _____ The dog keeps scratching his ear and will need medical attention.

2. __C__ She is my sister and looks like me.

3. __C__ You will receive my message soon and will need to act quickly.

4. _____ The contestants will be arriving tomorrow morning and needed room assignments.

5. _____ We heard the good news yesterday, so we leave immediately to congratulate you.

6. __C__ The rules of the game were hard to understand, and they tried my patience.

7. __C__ I like the taste of cherries but hate cherry pie.

8. _____ The performers were interesting to watch and play well.

9. __C__ Your car will be ready in one hour, and you will need to pick it up then.

10. __C__ Because you are ill, the sheets on the bed need stripping.

🌣 **Practice 2 Identifying**   Put an I next to the sentence if the tenses of the underlined verbs are inconsistent.

1. __I__ You <u>need</u> to water the lawn so that the grass <u>did</u> not <u>die</u>. *(need, does)*

2. _____ The baby <u>cried</u> all last night, and I <u>paced</u> the floor.

3. __I__ The cows <u>escaped</u> from the pasture and <u>will roam</u> into town. *(escaped, roamed or will escape, will roam)*

4. __I__ *Scooby Doo* <u>is</u> my favorite cartoon, and I <u>watched</u> it every day. *(is, watch or was, watched)*

5. __I__ This dress <u>looks</u> lovely while you <u>were wearing</u> it. *(looks, are wearing or looked, were wearing)*

6. _____ Timmy <u>poured</u> milk on the carpet and <u>cleaned</u> it up with paper towels.

7. _____ You <u>are</u> the neatest person, and you never <u>leave</u> a mess.

8. __I__ The cups and saucers <u>were broken</u> during the move, but the glasses <u>are</u> not. *(were broken, were)*

9. _____ Food <u>cooks</u> quickly in the microwave, but it <u>tastes</u> better from the oven.

10. __I__ Barbie's laugh <u>is</u> very irritating, and she <u>laughed</u> all the time. *(is, laughs or was, laughed)*

🌣 **Practice 3 Correcting**   Correct the inconsistent verbs in Practice 2 by rewriting each incorrect sentence. *See Practice 2.*

1. _____

2. _____

3. _____

4. _____

5. _____

6. _____

7. _____

8. _____

9. _____

10. _____

🌣 **Practice 4 Completing**   Fill in each blank in the following sentences with a consistent verb that makes sense. *Answers will vary.*

1. I _____ over the toys in the living room and _____ my ankle.

2. The students _____ to the convention in Spain, where they _____ their presentations.

3. When Harvey _____, he _____ me his new address.

4. The papers _____ behind the desk, but I _____ them anyway.

5. Some people _____ sports, and others just _____ them.

6. I _____ over the fence and _____ into the house.

7. Most people _____ because they _____ happy.

8. Vitamin B _____ you energy and _____ your body heal faster.

9. Exercise _____ stress while it _____ the body.

10. The leaves _____ from the trees in autumn and _____ back in the spring.

❖ Practice 5 Writing Your Own

A. Write a sentence of your own for each of the following sets of verbs, making sure your tenses are consistent. *Answers will vary.*

1. love, hate _____

2. wash, clean _____

3. plant, grow _____

4. run, jump _____

5. smell, taste _____

B. Write five sentences of your own using consistent verb tenses, and underline the verbs in each sentence. *Answers will vary.*

1. _____

2. _____

3. _____

4. _____

5. _____

USING THE ACTIVE VOICE

In the **active voice,** the subject performs the action. In the **passive voice,** the subject receives the action. Compare the following two examples:

Passive Voice: The clothes **were washed** yesterday **by Valerie.**

Active Voice: **Valerie washed** the clothes yesterday.

The active voice adds energy to your writing. Here is another example. Notice the difference between active and passive.

Passive Voice: The picture **was painted** for this office **by my brother.**

Active Voice: **My brother painted** the picture for this office.

REVIEWING ACTIVE AND PASSIVE VOICE

What is the difference between the active and passive voice?

In the active voice, the subject performs the action. In the passive voice, the subject

receives the action.

Why is the active voice usually better than the passive?

Because it adds energy to your writing.

Practice 6 Identifying   Underline the active voice verbs in each of the following sentences.

1. Pamela <u>boiled</u> water for the spaghetti.

2. Cassey <u>bought</u> flowers for her father.

3. The sun <u>baked</u> the ground.

4. Mark <u>took</u> his dog to the vet.

5. My brother <u>smoked</u> a turkey for the Easter picnic.

6. The computer <u>translated</u> the French document into English.

7. The artist <u>created</u> a statue for the opening ceremony.

8. Buddy <u>beat</u> the dirt off the rug.

9. The black widow <u>weaves</u> a strong web.

10. Every morning, my mother <u>made</u> a pot of coffee.

Practice 7 Identifying   Put a P next to each sentence that is in the passive voice.

1. _____ Jarrett played with Issa today.

2. __*P*__ The flowers were sent to the wedding. *(The shop sent the flowers to the wedding.)*

3. __*P*__ A ticket was given to the driver. *(A police officer gave the driver a ticket.)*

4. __*P*__ The clothes were dried by the sun. *(The sun dried the clothes.)*

5. _____ We mailed invitations to our family and friends.

6. __*P*__ The bleach was spilled on my shirt by Jean. *(Jean spilled bleach on my shirt.)*

7. __*P*__ A message was received in secret. *(She received a message in secret.)*

8. _____ Ants invaded my kitchen.

9. __*P*__ The man was attacked by the dog. *(The dog attacked the man.)*

10. __*P*__ The new baby was placed in its mother's arms. *(The doctor placed the new baby in its mother's arms.)*

Practice 8 Correcting   Rewrite each passive voice sentence in Practice 7 in the active voice. *See Practice 7. Answers may vary.*

1. _____

2. _____

3. _____

4. _____

5. _____

6. _____

7. _____

8. _____

9. _____

10. _____

✷ Practice 9 Completing   Fill in each blank in the following sentences with an active-voice verb that makes sense. *Answers will vary.*

1. The news _____ current events around the nation.

2. I _____ calamine lotion on my mosquito bites.

3. The TV in my bedroom _____ a fuse when I turned it on.

4. Dexter _____ the presents in the car.

5. My favorite soda _____ Coca-Cola.

6. Mike _____ his appointment with time to spare.

7. The scientists _____ a new gene.

8. The winds _____ over 100 mph.

9. The computer _____ to me, "You've got mail."

10. Fifi _____ chasing the ducks in the park.

✷ Practice 10 Writing Your Own

A. Write a sentence of your own using each of the following subjects and verbs in the passive voice. *Answers will vary.*

1. my mom gives _____

2. he feels _____

3. the twins bought _____

4. the team threw _____

5. prisoners made _____

B. Rewrite each of your sentences from Practice 10A in the active voice.
Answers will vary.

1. _____

2. _____

3. _____

4. _____

5. _____

CHAPTER REVIEW

You might want to reread your answers to the questions in the review boxes before you do the following exercises.

❦ **Review Practice 1 Reading**   Refer to the paragraph by Robert Fulghum on page 219 to do the following exercises.

1. Rewrite the paragraph in the past tense, keeping verb tenses consistent.
   Answers will vary.

_____

_____

_____

_____

_____

2. Rewrite the paragraph in the passive voice. Notice how the paragraph loses energy. *Answers will vary.*

_____

_____

_____

_____

_____

❦ **Review Practice 2 Identifying**   Underline any inconsistent or passive verbs in each of the following sentences.

1. When the phone rings, I refused to answer it. *(inconsistent)*
2. The boat was tugged to shore by the fisherman. *(passive)*
3. This new recipe was created by my uncle. *(passive)*
4. They parked in the lot and walk a mile to the park's entrance. *(inconsistent)*
5. The students were taken on an off-campus outing. *(passive)*
6. Tim and Bill will fish this summer, and then they camped. *(inconsistent)*

7. Since I <u>love</u> chocolate, I <u>ate</u> it all the time. *(inconsistent)*

8. The cat <u>was cleaned</u> by its mother. *(passive)*

9. The solar panels <u>heat up</u> when the sun <u>came out</u>. *(inconsistent)*

10. The corrections <u>were made</u> by Mrs. Smith. *(passive)*

🌿 **Review Practice 3 Correcting**   Correct the verb errors in Review Practice 2 by rewriting each incorrect sentence. *See Review Practice 2.*

🖋 EDITING A STUDENT PARAGRAPH

Following is a paragraph written and revised by Mindy Holcombe in response to the writing assignment in this chapter. Read the paragraph, and underline each of her verbs.

Here are the
corrected verbs:
hate
I first empty the
    silverware
I unload all the plastic
    containers
am able
stack
I do the glasses
climb
makes

I <u>hate</u> doing household chores, but I especially <u>hated</u> emptying the dishwasher. Since I<u>'m</u> short, emptying the dishwasher <u>has</u> two basic stages: the places I <u>can reach</u> and the places I <u>can't reach</u>. The silverware <u>is emptied</u> by me first because I <u>can reach</u> the drawer where it <u>belongs</u>. Then all the plastic containers <u>are unloaded</u>, which I <u>coordinate</u> by color. I <u>put</u> these away in the bottom cupboard, which, of course, I <u>will be able</u> to reach. Last and most hated comes the dinnerware and glasses. I <u>take</u> the plates and bowls out of the dishwasher and <u>stacked</u> them on the kitchen counter. The glasses <u>are done</u> in the same manner. Then I <u>make</u> a little room on the counter and <u>will climb</u> up. This <u>is</u> the only way I <u>can reach</u> the cupboards above the kitchen counter. Since the glasses <u>are</u> on the top shelf, I <u>have</u> to stand up, which usually <u>made</u> me dizzy. One of these days, I<u>'m going</u> to look down only to find the ground rushing up to meet me. Maybe then my roommate <u>will</u> not <u>ask</u> me to empty the dishwasher anymore.

Collaborative Activity

Team up with a partner, and underline the eight inconsistent and passive-voice verbs twice in Mindy's paragraph. Then, working together, use what you have learned in this chapter to correct these errors. Rewrite the paragraph with your corrections. *See student paragraph for errors. Corrections are in the margin.*

🌿 EDITING YOUR OWN PARAGRAPH

Now return to the paragraph you wrote and revised at the beginning of this chapter. Underline each of your verbs.

Collaborative Activity

Exchange papers with your partner, and circle any verb errors that you find in your partner's paper.

Individual Activity

On the Error Log in Appendix 6, record any verb errors that your partner found in your paragraph. To complete the writing process, correct these errors by rewriting your paragraph.

Unit 2 Review
Verbs

For additional material about teaching verbs, for journal entries, and for various tests, see the *Instructor's Resource Manual*, Section II, Part II.

ADDITIONAL WRITING TOPIC

Let your students expand into well-developed essays the paragraphs they wrote in one of the unit chapters.

🌱 **Unit Practice 1 Identifying**   Underline the verb errors in each of the following sentences.

1. The boys <u>done</u> a great job with the backyard. *(did)*

2. My brother <u>cutted</u> his leg. *(cut)*

3. George and Martha <u>is</u> two characters from an Edward Albee play. *(are)*

4. When the full moon rises over the mountains, the wolves <u>howled</u>. *(howl)*

5. I flirted with the girl next to me and <u>make</u> her smile. *(made)*

6. The football players <u>has</u> run around the field 10 times. *(have)*

7. Jared has <u>ate</u> all the macaroon cookies again. *(eaten)*

8. We <u>eatted</u> dinner before the movie. *(ate)*

9. Here <u>is</u> several good reasons for this meeting. *(are)*

10. The shortest boy on the track team <u>run</u> the fastest. *(runs)*

11. She will fly into Boston on the third and <u>gave</u> her speech on the fourth. *(give)*

12. The criminals <u>fledded</u> from the scene of the crime. *(fled)*

13. The choir <u>have</u> sung that song many times. *(has)*

14. Jonathon <u>bended</u> the pipe with his car. *(bent)*

15. What <u>is</u> you doing in the garage every night? *(are)*

16. Last night, all of the food <u>will be</u> eaten by the guests. *(was)*

17. The dogs <u>been barking</u> at the tree all day. *(have been barking)*

18. The children <u>hidded</u> from their babysitter. *(hid)*

19. Jenny eats whatever she wants but <u>didn't</u> gain weight. *(does)*

20. There <u>are</u> no reason for this chaos. *(is)*

🌿 **Unit Practice 2 Correcting**   Correct the verb errors in Unit Practice 1 by rewriting each incorrect sentence. *See Unit Practice 1.*

🌿 **Unit Practice 3 Identifying**   Underline the verb errors in the following paragraph.

My mother has the most whimsical sense of style. She loves frogs. In the living room there <u>are</u> a frog lamp; a frog <u>hanging</u> from the bathroom towel rack; and in the entryway <u>will sit</u> a huge concrete frog, which everybody <u>stumble</u> over. And if <u>you looks</u> closely, you can find little figurines all over the house. Geese of various sizes <u>is</u> scattered about the entertainment center. A pack of hunting dogs <u>was placed</u> on the kitchen counters. Little rabbits, turtles, and cats <u>snuggles</u> in the warm earth in the household plants. But the most whimsical and cherished decoration of all <u>are</u> the hand-carved totem pole that stands in the living room. The thing has been passed down from generation to generation, even though nobody <u>know</u> who made it. There <u>is</u> fanciful woodland animals carved all around it. Merry little sprites and elves <u>dances</u> through the woods as a maiden rests in her bower. I have spent hours tracing the designs with my fingers, fantasizing about the story behind the maiden's smile. Someday this <u>will belong</u> to me, and I <u>passed</u> it down to my children. I hope it sparks their imagination as much as it has sparked mine.

🌿 **Unit Practice 4 Correcting**   Correct the verb errors in Unit Practice 3 by rewriting the paragraph. *Answers will vary.*

UNIT WRITING ASSIGNMENTS

1. Put yourself into the scene on the next page. What is embarrassing about it? Who is involved and what probably happened? How does the picture make you feel? Why are you reacting this way?

2. Have you ever had a misunderstanding with a friend or relative that wasn't your fault? How did the misunderstanding come about? Was anyone to blame, or was the situation simply a misunderstanding? Who was involved? What did you do? How did this event make you feel?

3. Have you ever performed an act of kindness with no thought to yourself? What did you do, and why did you do it? What kind of sacrifice, if any, did you make? How did your actions make you feel?

4. We often see things differently when we are children, like our impressions of our parents. As we grow older, we begin to see things from a more mature perspective. Is there a situation, like getting punished, or a person that you now understand differently from your childhood? What did you think as a child, and what do you think now? What has made your perceptions change? Do you have a better understanding of the situation or person?

5. Create your own writing assignment (with the help of your instructor), and write a response to it.

Unit 3 Pronouns

Pronouns generally go almost unnoticed in writing and speaking, even though these words can do anything nouns can do. In fact, much like our in-born sense of balance, pronouns work in sentences to make your writing precise and coherent. Without pronouns, writers and speakers would find themselves repeating nouns over and over, producing sentences that are unnatural and boring. For example, notice how awkward the following paragraph would be without pronouns:

> Robert wrote a rough draft of Robert's essay last night. Then Robert asked Robert's girlfriend to read over Robert's essay with Robert. After Robert's girlfriend helped Robert find errors, Robert made corrections. Then Robert set aside the essay for a day before Robert took the essay out and began revising again.

When we let pronouns take over and do their jobs, we produce a much more fluent paragraph:

> Robert wrote a rough draft of his essay last night. Then he asked his girlfriend to read over his essay with him. After she helped Robert find errors, he made corrections. Then he set aside the essay for a day before he took it out and began revising again.

Problems with pronouns occur when the words pronouns refer to aren't clear or when pronouns and their antecedents—the words they refer to—are too far apart. In this unit, we will deal with the following aspects of pronouns:

Chapter 14: Pronoun Problems
Chapter 15: Pronoun Reference and Point of View
Chapter 16: Pronoun-Antecedent Agreement

Once students understand that pronouns are substitutes for nouns, they can work with pronouns efficiently and effectively. So you might want to begin with a review of pronouns in the Introduction to this part. When you add the concepts of antecedents and pronoun-antecedent agreement to an understanding of pronouns, then your students really have all the information they need to use pronouns correctly in their writing.

Pronoun Problems

⬧ Checklist for Using Pronouns

- ✔ Are all subject pronouns used correctly?
- ✔ Are all object pronouns used correctly?
- ✔ Are all possessive pronouns used correctly?
- ✔ Are pronouns used in *than* or *as* comparisons in the correct form?
- ✔ Are the pronouns *this*, *that*, *these*, and *those* used correctly?

Pronouns are words that take the place of nouns. They help us avoid repeating nouns. In this chapter, we'll discuss five types of pronoun prob-lems: (1) using the wrong pronoun as a subject, (2) using the wrong pronoun as an object, (3) using an apostrophe with a possessive pronoun, (4) misusing pronouns in comparisons, and (5) misusing demonstrative pronouns.

Notice how a variety of pronouns help Lois Smith Brady create smooth paragraphs.

Eventually [love] even found me. At 28, I met my husband in a stationery store. I was buying a typewriter ribbon, and he was looking at Filofaxes. I remember that his eyes perfectly matched his faded jeans. He remembers that my sneakers were full of sand. He still talks about those sneakers and how they evoked his childhood—bonfires by the ocean, driving on the sand in an old Jeep—all those things that he cherished.

How did I know it was true love? Our first real date lasted for nine hours; we just couldn't stop talking. I had never been able to dance in my life, but I could dance with him, perfectly in step. I have learned that it's love when you finally stop tripping over your toes.

In this paragraph, Brady describes how she knew she had found true love from the moment of her first date. Before continuing in this chapter, take a moment to describe one of your first dates or your dream date. Save your work because you will use it later in this chapter.

For more sample paragraphs, see the *Instructor's Resource Manual,* Section II, Part II.

Writing Assignment: A Special Date

Think about your first real date or your dream date. Describe the date as fully as you can in a paragraph. Consider who, what, when, where, why, and how. Was the date a success?

Revising Your Writing

Revise the first draft of your paragraph before you focus on editing. Use the Revising Checklist on pages 24–25 to help you with your revision. Make sure your paragraph has a good topic sentence and is well developed. Then check your paragraph for unity, organization, and coherence.

TEACHING ON THE WEB

Exploring and Discussing: Have students find a Web site for a TV station and locate a summary of the last show they saw (soap operas always have week-in-review synopses). How many subject pronouns were used in the summary? Object pronouns? Possessive pronouns? How did these pronouns help the students understand the summary?

TEACHING ON THE WEB

Mosaics Web Site: To learn more about pronouns, students can go to www.prenhall.com/ mosaics.

PRONOUNS AS SUBJECTS

Single pronouns as subjects usually don't cause problems.

Subject Pronoun: **I** gave to charity.

Subject Pronoun: **They** flew to Dallas.

You wouldn't say "*Me* gave to charity" or "*Them* flew to Dallas." But an error often occurs when a sentence has a compound subject and one or more of the subjects is a pronoun.

	Error	**Correction**
NOT	The boys and **us** played ball.	The boys and **we** played ball.
NOT	**Him** and **me** rode together.	**He** and **I** rode together.

To test whether you have used the correct form of the pronoun in a compound subject, try each subject alone:

Subject Pronoun?   The boys and **us** played ball.

Test: **The boys** played ball.   **YES**

Test:	Us played ball. **NO**	
	We played ball. **YES**	
Correction:	The boys and we played ball.	

Here is a list of subject pronouns.

Subject Pronouns

Singular	Plural
I	*we*
you	*you*
he, she, it	*they*

REVIEWING PRONOUNS AS SUBJECTS

Name two subject pronouns.

Answers will include two of the following: I, you, he, she, it, we, or they.

How can you test whether you are using the correct pronoun as the subject of a sentence?

Try each subject separately in its sentence.

 Practice 1 Identifying   Underline the correct subject pronoun in each of the following sentences.

1. The parents and (them, <u>they</u>) are having a conference.

2. The previous year, you and (<u>she</u>, her) were the best of friends.

3. (Him, <u>He</u>) and she have been dating for three years now.

4. The bikers and (<u>we</u>, us) had the best time driving through the canyon.

5. From a distance, (<u>she</u>, her) and Pam looked alike.

6. During the soccer game, you and (<u>I</u>, me) yelled until we were hoarse.

7. You and (<u>they</u>, them) look funny together.

8. Christine, John, and (us, <u>we</u>) went to Disneyland separately but at the same time.

9. Hey! You and (her, <u>she</u>) ate all the Oreo cookies.

10. At the swim party, the children and (<u>they</u>, them) dived into the pool with their clothes on.

🌿 Practice 2 Identifying   Put an X next to the sentence if the underlined pronoun is incorrect.

1. __X__ Last night, <u>him</u> and I helped with the dishes. *(he)*

2. __X__ The dogs and <u>us</u> ran wild across the playground. *(we)*

3. __X__ He and <u>me</u> are going to the Madonna concert. *(I)*

4. _____ We and <u>you</u> can fit in that phone booth.

5. _____ In the spring, you and <u>I</u> are going fly-fishing.

6. _____ Last year, Jim, Tanya, and <u>we</u> car-pooled together.

7. __X__ You and <u>me</u> should be lab partners. *(I)*

8. _____ <u>They</u> and the receptionist have all gone to lunch.

9. __X__ My mother and <u>her</u> have known each other forever. *(she)*

10. __X__ <u>Him</u> and I felt that you were very kind. *(He)*

🌿 Practice 3 Identifying   Correct the pronoun errors in Practice 2 by rewriting each incorrect sentence. *See Practice 2.*

1. _____

2. _____

3. _____

4. _____

5. _____

6. _____

7. _____

8. _____

9. _____

10. _____

🌿 Practice 4 Completing   Fill in each blank in the following sentences with a subject pronoun that makes sense. *Answers will vary.*

1. Jamie and _____ decided to go to the same college and room together.

2. During the storm, Mindy, Brad, and _____ took shelter in the basement.

3. You and _____ need to come to an agreement.

4. After dinner, the students and _____ are going to the library to study.

5. She and _____ are getting married this June.

6. _____ and some of the parents have set up a reading area for the children.

7. The scientists and _____ are trying to discover a new planet in the solar system.

8. A famous graphic artist and _____ did the cover for this book.

9. The lifeguard and _____ both jumped in to save the swimmer.

10. Joseph, who is a great gardener, and _____, who is a wonderful decorator, designed my Asian garden.

❧ Practice 5 Writing Your Own

A. Write a sentence of your own for each of the following compound subjects. *Answers will vary.*

1. you and I _____

2. we and they _____

3. Sara and she _____

4. you and he _____

5. she and we _____

B. Write five sentences of your own using compound subject pronouns, and underline the subject pronouns in each sentence. *Answers will vary.*

1. _____

2. _____

3. _____

4. _____

5. _____

PRONOUNS AS OBJECTS

One of the most frequent pronoun errors is using a subject pronoun when the sentence calls for an object pronoun. The sentence may require an object after a verb, showing that someone or something receives the action of the verb. Or it may be an object of a preposition that is required (see page 76 for a list of prepositions).

	Error	**Correction**
NOT	She gave Alisha and **I** some candy.	She gave Alisha and **me** some candy.
NOT	This is just between you and **I**.	This is just between you and **me**.

Like the subject pronoun error, the object pronoun error usually occurs with compound objects. Also like the subject pronoun error, you can test whether you are using the correct pronoun by using each object separately.

Object Pronouns?	She gave Alisha and **I** some candy.
Test:	She gave **Alisha** some candy. **YES**
Test:	She gave **I** some candy. **NO**
	She gave **me** some candy. **YES**
Correct:	She gave **Alisha and me** some candy.

Here is a list of object pronouns:

Object Pronouns

Singular	Plural
me	*us*
you	*you*
him, her, it	*them*

8. __X__ Cindy can go down the water slide after John and <u>he</u>. *(him)*

9. _____ The competition is between <u>them</u> and us.

10. __X__ The doctor gave Valerie and <u>we</u> some candy after the shot. *(us)*

❧ **Practice 8 Correcting**   Correct the pronoun errors in Practice 7 by rewriting each incorrect sentence. *See Practice 7.*

1. _____

2. _____

3. _____

4. _____

5. _____

6. _____

7. _____

8. _____

9. _____

10. _____

❧ **Practice 9 Completing**   Fill in each blank in the following sentences with an object pronoun that makes sense. *Answers will vary.*

1. Jeremy took off running after Judy and _____.

2. Between you and _____, we can do anything.

3. The actor read his lines to them and _____.

4. We watched the children and _____.

5. Thanks to _____ and her, we have raised enough money for the trip.

6. Your mom is seated in the middle of _____ and the Turners.

7. The karate instructor made _____ and you perform in front of the class.

8. I was in awe of Cassandra and _____.

9. Charles gave the food not to Jimmy but to _____.

10. The high winds almost blew us and _____ over.

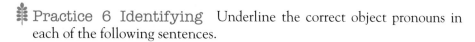

REVIEWING PRONOUNS AS OBJECTS
....

In what two places are pronouns used as objects?

After a verb and after a preposition
_____

How can you test whether you have used the correct pronoun as the object in a sentence?

Try each object separately in its sentence.
_____

Practice 6 Identifying   Underline the correct object pronouns in each of the following sentences.

1. We went to the party with Mary and (he, <u>him</u>).

2. My grandfather will give you and (I, <u>me</u>) a ride to the mall.

3. They watched you and (<u>her</u>, she) do your dance routines.

4. The professional golf teacher instructed them and (<u>us</u>, we).

5. My new girlfriend is standing beside my parents and (she, <u>her</u>).

6. The ice-cream vendor gave Cindy and (they, <u>them</u>) some free ice cream.

7. Grandmother mailed invitations to you and (he, <u>him</u>).

8. The show scared Bubba and (he, <u>him</u>).

9. My parents gave my sister and (I, <u>me</u>) $100 for the trip.

10. The spider webs were caught on (<u>them</u>, they) and Diane.

Practice 7 Identifying   Put an X next to the sentence if the under-lined pronoun is incorrect.

1. __X__ Kendra invited John and <u>I</u> to the movies. *(me)*

2. __X__ The cutest boys in the class danced with her and <u>I</u>. *(me)*

3. __X__ The baby ducks are waddling behind <u>they</u> and us. *(them)*

4. _____ Jim and George are bouncing the ball to Sandy and <u>her</u>.

5. __X__ The argument is between <u>she</u> and him. *(her)*

6. _____ I found my little sister with <u>him</u> and her.

7. __X__ The chaperones are walking in front of Mary and <u>he</u>. *(him)*

✿ Practice 10 Writing Your Own

A. Write a sentence of your own for each of the following compound object pronouns. *Answers will vary.*

1. you and me _____

2. him and her _____

3. us and them _____

4. Ben and him _____

5. Shawna and her _____

B. Write five sentences of your own using object pronouns, and underline the object pronouns in each sentence. *Answers will vary.*

1. _____

2. _____

3. _____

4. _____

5. _____

POSSESSIVE PRONOUNS

Possessive pronouns show ownership (*my* boat, *his* bed, *our* horse). (See pages 67–68 for a list of possessive pronouns.) An *apostrophe* is used with *nouns* to show ownership (Jack's cat, the worker's tools, the committee's vote). But an apostrophe is *never* used with possessive pronouns.

Possessive Pronouns

Singular	Plural
my, mine	*our, ours*
your, yours	*your, yours*
his, her, hers	*their, theirs*

	Error	**Correction**
NOT	That truck is **their's**.	That truck is **theirs**.
NOT	The apple on the counter is **your's**.	The apple on the counter is **yours**.
NOT	The cat licked **its'** paws.	The cat licked **its** paws.

REVIEWING POSSESSIVE PRONOUNS

When do you use an apostrophe with a noun?

An apostrophe is used to show ownership with a noun.

Do possessive pronouns take apostrophes?

No, possessive pronouns never take apostrophes.

Practice 11 Identifying   Underline the correct possessive pronouns in each of the following sentences.

1. I wouldn't listen to (<u>her</u>, her's) excuses anymore.
2. The winning essay was (<u>his</u>, his').
3. Glorianna is (his', <u>his</u>) girlfriend.
4. (<u>Our</u>, Our's) play was a success.
5. Those antique cars are (<u>theirs</u>, their's).
6. Are the Snoopy pajamas (<u>yours</u>, your's)?
7. That money was (mine's, <u>mine</u>).
8. The blue sweater is (<u>his</u>, his').
9. The dog chased (<u>its</u>, its') tail around and around.
10. (<u>Their</u>, Their's) garden is the loveliest on the block.

Practice 12 Identifying   Put an X next to the sentence if the underlined pronoun is incorrect.

1. _____ <u>His</u> pager went off in class.
2. __X__ <u>Her's</u> clothes are muddy. *(Her)*

3. __X__ These assignments are your's. *(yours)*

4. __X__ Those water balloons are their's. *(theirs)*

5. _____ Their gifts were the most expensive.

6. __X__ The dirty clothes on the floor are our's. *(ours)*

7. _____ His charm will not get him out of this situation.

8. __X__ The horse swished its' tail in agitation. *(its)*

9. _____ That plane behind the barn is theirs.

10. __X__ My's hair is falling out. *(My)*

🌿 Practice 13 Correcting   Correct the pronoun errors in Practice 12 by rewriting each incorrect sentence. *See Practice 12.*

1. _____

2. _____

3. _____

4. _____

5. _____

6. _____

7. _____

8. _____

9. _____

10. _____

🌿 Practice 14 Completing   Fill in each blank in the following sentences with a possessive pronoun that makes sense. *Answers will vary.*

1. This brand-new truck is _____.

2. Those punk rock clothes are definitely _____.

3. The artwork is _____.

4. _____ ghost is haunting this house.

5. _____ dog barks at everybody.

6. According to _____ notes, we should have turned left.

7. People have the right to _____ own beliefs.

8. Those are _____ goals and ambitions for the future.

9. My father rolled _____ eyes at my suggestions.

10. You spent _____ money!

🌿 Practice 15 Writing Your Own

A. Write a sentence of your own for each of the following possessive pronouns. *Answers will vary.*

1. my _____

2. theirs _____

3. hers _____

4. yours _____

5. its _____

B. Write five sentences of your own using possessive pronouns, and underline the possessive pronouns in each sentence. *Answers will vary.*

1. _____

2. _____

3. _____

4. _____

5. _____

PRONOUNS IN COMPARISONS

Sometimes pronoun problems occur in comparisons with *than* or *as*. An object pronoun may be mistakenly used instead of a subject pronoun. To find out if you are using the right pronoun, you should finish the sentence as shown here.

	Error	**Correction**
NOT	She can crochet better than **me.**	She can crochet better than **I** [can crochet].
NOT	Beatrice is as good a runner as **him.**	Beatrice is as good a runner as **he** [is].

HINT: Sometimes an object pronoun is required in a *than* or *as* comparison. But errors rarely occur in this case because the subject pronoun sounds so unnatural.

	Error	**Correction**
NOT	Elaine likes him more than she likes **I.**	Elaine likes him more than she likes **me.**

REVIEWING PRONOUNS IN COMPARISONS

What causes pronoun problems in comparisons?

Problems can occur when an object pronoun is mistakenly used instead of a subject

pronoun.

How can you test whether to use a subject pronoun or an object pronoun in a than or as comparison?

Finish the sentence to test whether to use a subject pronoun or an object

pronoun.

 Practice 16 Identifying   Underline the correct pronoun in each of the following comparisons.

1. You have more pride than (<u>they</u>, them) could ever have.
2. Her dog makes more noise than (her, <u>she</u>)!
3. I am never as jealous as (<u>she</u>, her).
4. Thelma isn't as tall as (him, <u>he</u>).
5. He always has to work later than (me, <u>I</u>).
6. We have experienced as many troubles as (them, <u>they</u>).
7. She always drives faster than (<u>he</u>, him).
8. Holly isn't as good a gymnast as (<u>she</u>, her).
9. She thinks that she is more worthy than (them, <u>they</u>).
10. Most of the time, I'm better at math than (<u>he</u>, him).

 Practice 17 Identifying   Put an X next to the sentence if the under-lined pronoun is incorrect.

1. __X__ He can read out loud better than <u>me</u>. *(I)*

2. __X__ Gabriel has more skill than <u>them</u>. *(they)*

3. _____ Cynthia is as good a race-car driver as <u>he</u> is.

4. __X__ Reyna can hold her breath longer than <u>him</u>. *(he)*

5. _____ Veronica can jump higher than <u>I</u>.

6. __X__ Carla is more popular than <u>her</u>. *(she)*

7. _____ Manuel isn't as creative as <u>she</u>.

8. __X__ He is as cold as <u>her</u>. *(she)*

9. _____ We are just as friendly as <u>they</u>.

10. __X__ Cordelia confides in you more than she confides in <u>I</u>. *(me)*

❊ Practice 18 Correcting   Correct the pronoun errors in Practice 17 by rewriting each incorrect sentence. *See Practice 17.*

1. _____

2. _____

3. _____

4. _____

5. _____

6. _____

7. _____

8. _____

9. _____

10. _____

❊ Practice 19 Completing   Fill in each blank in the following sentences with pronouns that are correct. *Answers will vary.*

1. He quits his job even more often than _____.

2. Every day, I like you more than I like _____.

3. I do believe that I am more tired than _____.

4. They are trying to recover the ball just as hard as _____.

5. Vinny and Clark are more suave than _____.

6. They push their children harder than _____ do.

7. Glenda isn't as selfish as _____.

8. Isabella likes Nolan more than she likes _____.

9. We have a better defense than _____.

10. I bet that I can play chess better than _____ can.

❊ Practice 20 Writing Your Own

A. Write a sentence of your own using each of the following pronouns in comparisons. *Answers will vary.*

1. I _____

2. they _____

3. she _____

4. he _____

5. we _____

B. Write five sentences of your own using pronouns in comparisons, and underline the pronouns in comparisons in each sentence. *Answers will vary.*

1. _____

2. _____

3. _____

4. _____

5. _____

DEMONSTRATIVE PRONOUNS

There are four demonstrative pronouns: *this, that, these,* and *those.* **Demonstrative pronouns** point to specific people or objects. Use *this* and *these* to refer to items that are near and *that* and *those* to refer to items farther away. Look at the following examples.

Demonstrative (near):	**This** is my new computer.
Demonstrative (near):	**These** are library books.
Demonstrative (farther):	**That** is the bank.
Demonstrative (farther):	**Those** are the frames for the pictures.

Sometimes demonstrative pronouns are not used correctly.

Error		**Correction**
NOT	this here, that there	this, that
NOT	these here, these ones	these
NOT	them, those there, those ones	those

Error	**Correction**
NOT **Them** are the memos she typed.	**Those** are the memos she typed.
NOT I'll give you **these here** clothes.	I'll give you **these** clothes.
NOT **Those ones** were in the garage.	**Those** were in the garage.
NOT **Those there** are the cards.	**Those** are the cards.

When demonstrative pronouns are used with nouns, they become adjectives.

Pronoun: **That** is your dog.
Adjective: **This dog** is his.

Pronoun: **Those** are memories you will always remember.
Adjective: You will always remember **those memories.**

The problems that occur with demonstrative pronouns can also occur when these pronouns act as adjectives.

Error	**Correction**
NOT Please hand me **that there** pen.	Please hand me **that** pen.

REVIEWING DEMONSTRATIVE PRONOUNS

Name the four demonstrative pronouns.

_____this_____   _____that_____   _____these_____   _____those_____

Give two examples of errors with demonstrative pronouns.

Students should choose two from this here, that there, them, these here, these ones,

those there, and those ones.

✿ Practice 21 Identifying   Underline the correct demonstrative pronoun in each of the following sentences.

1. (<u>These</u>, These here) are my favorite shows.
2. (<u>Those</u>, Them) are the people responsible.
3. Mary pushed (that there, <u>that</u>) all the way down the hall.
4. Janet gave (those there, <u>those</u>) to Manuel.
5. Are all of (<u>these</u>, these here) going in the truck?
6. (<u>Those</u>, Those ones) should be loaded first.
7. Tammy is familiar with (these ones, <u>these</u>).
8. What will you give me for (<u>this</u>, this here)?
9. (<u>That</u>, That there) is the first house ever built in this town.
10. (Them, <u>These</u>) will grow into your grass and will be hard to remove.

✿ Practice 22 Identifying   Put an X next to the sentence if the underlined demonstrative pronoun is incorrect.

1. _____ <u>Those</u> were reserved for VIPs.
2. __X__ <u>This here</u> is the best meal I've ever made. *(This)*
3. __X__ <u>Them</u> are the color swatches from the decorator. *(Those)*
4. _____ <u>These</u> are the keys you thought you'd lost.
5. __X__ Will you put <u>these here</u> in the mail? *(these)*
6. _____ <u>Those</u> were the best days of my life.
7. _____ <u>That</u> will never do.
8. __X__ Before you go, <u>these here</u> need to be fixed. *(these)*
9. __X__ <u>Those ones</u> are for you, and <u>these ones</u> are for me. *(Those, these)*
10. __X__ <u>Those there</u> on the sofa belong to my dad. *(Those)*

✿ Practice 23 Correcting   Correct the pronoun errors in Practice 22 by rewriting each incorrect sentence. *See Practice 22.*

1. _____

2. _____

3. _____

4. _____

5. _____

6. _____

7. _____

8. _____

9. _____

10. _____

Practice 24 Completing   Fill in each blank in the following sentences with a demonstrative pronoun that is correct. *Answers will vary.*

1. _____ is the old bell from the tower.

2. _____ was the worst experience I have ever had.

3. What is _____?

4. _____ of you standing at the back of the line should be patient.

5. Please take _____ to the dry cleaner.

6. Where did you find _____?

7. _____ should make the long hike more bearable.

8. Nolan stored _____ in the basement.

9. _____ are the exercises we have to have finished by Monday.

10. _____ was the longest day I've ever lived through!

Practice 25 Writing Your Own

A. Write a sentence of your own for each of the following demonstrative pronouns. Make sure you use them as pronouns and not adjectives. *Answers will vary.*

1. this _____

2. that _____

3. these _____

4. those _____

5. that _____

B. Write five sentences of your own using demonstrative pronouns, and underline the demonstrative pronouns in each sentence. Make sure you use them as pronouns and not adjectives. *Answers will vary.*

1. _____

2. _____

3. _____

4. _____

5. _____

CHAPTER REVIEW

You might want to reread your answers to the questions in the review boxes before you do the following exercises.

❊ Review Practice 1 Reading   Refer to the paragraphs by Lois Smith Brady on page 234 to do the following exercises.

1. List four different subject pronouns from the paragraphs.

Answers will vary. _____

_____

_____

_____

2. List the two object pronouns from the paragraphs.

me _____

him _____

3. List four possessive pronouns from the paragraphs.

Answers will vary. _____

_____

_____

_____

❊ Review Practice 2 Identifying   Underline the pronoun errors in each of the following sentences.

1. <u>This here</u> is a mystery. *(This)*

2. You told <u>she</u> and <u>I</u> different stories. *(her, me)*

3. These funky glasses are <u>his'</u>. *(his)*

4. Noemi isn't as good with punctuation as <u>him</u>. *(he)*

5. The whale blew air out <u>it's</u> blowhole. *(its)*

6. <u>Them</u> are definitely mine. *(These)*

7. We have to keep the surprise between you and <u>I</u>. *(me)*

8. Julianna can talk faster than <u>her</u>. *(she)*

9. The students and <u>us</u> took a rest from the examinations. *(we)*

10. Jessica, Andy, and <u>me</u> decided to eat out tonight. *(I)*

🌿 **Review Practice 3 Correcting**   Correct the pronoun errors in Review Practice 2 by rewriting each incorrect sentence. *See Review Practice 2.*

🖋 EDITING A STUDENT PARAGRAPH

Following is a paragraph written and revised by Angelina Santos in response to the writing assignment in this chapter. Read the paragraph, and underline each of her pronouns.

      <u>My's</u> first date almost turned <u>me</u> against dating forever. <u>It</u> was a blind date to an amusement park set up by <u>my</u> best friend, Claire, who was going with <u>her</u> boyfriend, Roger. <u>They</u> and <u>us</u> made small talk during the two-hour drive. Once there, Norman was a perfect gentleman, buying Claire and <u>I</u> souvenirs, holding the door open for <u>she</u> and <u>me</u>, and always saying thank you. But all of <u>that there</u> changed once <u>we</u> decided to ride the Boomerang. Norman bought a huge lemonade right before <u>we</u> got on the ride. <u>I</u> told <u>him</u> that <u>I</u> didn't think <u>it</u> was a good idea to take the drink on the ride since <u>we</u> were going to be slung up and down from one end of the ride to the other. "Don't worry," <u>he</u> said, "<u>it</u> has a lid." Sure enough, as <u>we</u> accelerated

Here are the corrected pronouns:
My
we
me
her
that
I
this

forward and upward, the lid popped off, and lemonade went everywhere. By the time the ride stopped, <u>I</u> was covered in the sweet, sticky stuff. Needless to say, <u>I</u> was angry with <u>him</u>. <u>He</u> didn't even apologize, just asked <u>me</u> what <u>my</u> problem was and told <u>me</u> that <u>he</u> was a better sport than <u>me</u>. Unfortunately, <u>this here</u> wasn't the worst part of the date. As <u>we</u> were leaving the park, <u>I</u> got attacked by a bee and was stung on <u>my</u> neck. <u>I</u> had to ride home covered in lemonade with a throbbing bee sting on <u>my</u> neck and Norman, the person responsible for <u>my</u> torment, at <u>my</u> side. <u>There</u> was no small talk <u>this</u> time.

Collaborative Activity

Team up with a partner, and place an X above the seven pronoun errors in Angelina's paragraph. Then, working together, use what you have learned in this chapter to correct these errors. Rewrite the paragraph with your corrections. *See student paragraph for errors. Corrections are in the margin.*

❧ EDITING YOUR OWN PARAGRAPH

Now return to the paragraph you wrote and revised at the beginning of this chapter. Underline each of your pronouns.

Collaborative Activity

Exchange paragraphs with your partner, and circle any pronoun errors that you find in your partner's paragraph.

Individual Activity

On the Error Log in Appendix 6, record the pronoun errors that your partner found in your paragraph. To complete the writing process, correct these errors by rewriting your paragraph.

Pronoun Reference and Point of View

⬛ Checklist for Correcting Pronoun Reference and Point-of-View Problems

✔ Does every pronoun have a clear antecedent?

✔ Are pronouns as close as possible to the words they refer to?

✔ Do you maintain a single point of view?

Any time you use a pronoun, it must clearly refer to a specific word in the sentence. The word it refers to is called its *antecedent*. Two kinds of problems occur with pronoun references: The antecedent may be unclear, or the antecedent may be missing altogether. You should also be careful to stick to the same point of view in your writing. If, for example, you start out talking about "I," you should not shift to "you" in the middle of the sentence.

Notice how the pronouns in the following paragraph by William Kowinski work with their antecedents to communicate a consistent point of view.

> The mall is a common experience for the majority of American youth; they have probably been going there all their lives. Some ran within their first large open space, saw their first fountain, bought their first toy, and read their first book in a mall. They may have smoked their first cigarette or first joint or turned them down, had their first kiss or lost their virginity in the mall parking lot. Teenagers in America now spend more time in the mall than anywhere else but home and school. Mostly it is their choice, but some of that mall time is put in as a result of two-paycheck and single-parent households and the lack of other viable alternatives.

TEACHING PRONOUN REFERENCE AND POINT OF VIEW
Provide students with a series of pictures that have a unique point of view. Ask them to study each picture to guess who they think might have taken the picture and from what point of view (for example, a young woman, trying to show the beauty of a father and child).
After the students have analyzed a few pictures, have them change their positions about who they think took the picture and what his or her point of view might be. Shifting their opinions will probably be difficult.
Point out to students that this kind of difficulty occurs when students shift point of view in their sentences or don't provide a reference for readers

when using pronouns.
Readers will experience
the same type of
confusion when pronoun
reference and point of
view shift unnecessarily
or are unclear.

**TEACHING ON
THE WEB**

Exploring and Discussing:
Have students find a
Web site that provides
lyrics to songs. Then
have students find lyrics
that use pronouns. Do
all the pronouns have
antecedents? Do any
shift in point of view?
Do students think artists
ever use unclear pronouns
on purpose? Why would
artists do this?

**TEACHING ON
THE WEB**

Mosaics Web Site: To learn
more about pronouns
reference and point of
view, students can go to
www.prenhall.com/
mosaics.

In this paragraph, the author gives examples of the things teenagers have done at a mall. Before continuing in this chapter, take a moment to write about the things people do before making a purchase. Save your work because you will use it later in this chapter.

Writing Assignment: People's Shopping Habits

Have you ever taken the time to observe people at a shopping mall? What do they do? How are they different? Do gender and age play a part in people's actions in a crowd? What can you conclude about these people from their actions?

Revising Your Writing

Revise the first draft of your paragraph before you focus on editing. Use the Revising Checklist on pages 24–25 to help you with your revision. Make sure your paragraph has a good topic sentence and is well developed. Then check your paragraph for unity, organization, and coherence.

PRONOUN REFERENCE

Sometimes a sentence is confusing because the reader can't tell what a pronoun is referring to. The confusion may occur because the pronoun's antecedent is unclear or is completely missing.

Unclear Antecedents

In the following examples, the word each pronoun is referring to is unclear.

> **Unclear:**   A box and a key lay on the beach. As Miguel reached for **it,** the surf came in.

(Was Miguel reaching for the box or the key? Only Miguel knows for sure.)

> **Clear:**   A box and a key lay on the beach. As Miguel reached for **the box,** the surf came in.

> **Clear:**   A box and a key lay on the beach. As Miguel reached for **the key,** the surf came in.

Unclear: Sandra told Denise that **she** shouldn't wear that color.

(Does *she* refer to Sandra or Denise? Only the writer knows.)

Clear: Sandra told Denise that **Sandra** shouldn't wear that color.

Clear: Speaking with Denise, **Sandra** told **her** not to wear that color.

How can you be sure that every pronoun you use has a clear antecedent? First, you can proofread carefully. Probably an even better test, though, is to ask a friend to read what you have written and tell you if your meaning is clear or not.

Missing Antecedents

Every pronoun should have a clear antecedent, the word it refers to. But what happens when there is no antecedent at all? The writer's message is not communicated. Two words in particular should alert you to the possibility of missing antecedents: *it* and *they.*

The following sentences have missing antecedents:

Missing Antecedent: In a survey, it shows that most people are happy with the president.

(What does *it* refer to? It has no antecedent.)

Clear: **A recent survey** shows that most people are happy with the president.

Missing Antecedent: **They** say that the wise know when to speak and when not to.

(Who is *they?*)

Clear: **An old saying** states that the wise know when to speak and when not to.

REVIEWING PRONOUN REFERENCE

What is an antecedent?

The word a pronoun refers to

> *How can you be sure every pronoun you use has a clear antecedent?*
>
> *Proofread carefully, and ask a friend to read your writing and tell you if your meaning*
>
> *is unclear.*
>
> _____
>
> **What two words warn you that an antecedent may be missing?**
>
>   *it*   *they*

❈ Practice 1 Identifying
Underline the pronouns with missing or unclear antecedents in the following sentences.

1. It says that you need a cup of sugar.
2. Billy and Jim drove together, yet he doesn't have his license.
3. Before Saul and Andrew left the house, he closed all the windows.
4. My checkbook and sunglasses were sitting on the counter, but when I reached for it, I tripped and fell.
5. I love to eat strawberries and chocolate, but it gives me a rash.
6. Kenny and Ed have known each other almost all their lives, but now he is moving away.
7. She bought a Coke and an ice cream and then spilled it all over herself.
8. They say a leopard never changes its spots.
9. When Tammy and Makesha decided to take a vacation, she didn't realize she was getting sick.
10. Your shorts and shirt are on your bed, but it's still too wet to wear.

❈ Practice 2 Identifying
Put an X next to each sentence with a missing or unclear antecedent.

1. __X__ They always tell me to look both ways before crossing the street.
2. _____ Talking to Tomás, Jim asked if he was interested in a job.
3. __X__ It says that we can expect a booming economy.
4. _____ My grandparents always tell me that "pretty is as pretty does."
5. __X__ Jon and Carlos decided to buy the same costume for the masquerade party, but he looks dumb in it.

6. __X__ Even though Cindy and Lena like each other, she picks fights all the time.

7. _____ According to the news, we can expect more rain.

8. __X__ Jeff told Marc that he would be leaving his job soon.

9. __X__ In last year's poll, they revealed the cause of the crises.

10. _____ When I spoke to Randy and Gage, they told me where everyone was meeting.

🌿 Practice 3 Correcting   Correct the pronoun errors in Practice 2 by rewriting each incorrect sentence. *Answers will vary.*

1. _____

2. _____

3. _____

4. _____

5. _____

6. _____

7. _____

8. _____

9. _____

10. _____

🌿 Practice 4 Completing   Fill in each blank in the following sentences with either a pronoun or a noun to make the sentence clear. *Answers will vary.*

1. César, James, and Juan have gone to pick out a new car for _____.

2. I tried to grab the coffeepot and cups, but _____ fell to the ground first.

3. When she spoke to Esther, _____ said that you couldn't go.

4. After you saw Harim and David, what did _____ have to say?

5. I looked for my lost shoe and sweater and found the _____ under my bed.

6. When Jack and Frank argue, _____ always wins.

7. When the proud parents and _____ saw the new baby, they expressed their joy.

8. The roses and the jasmine both require direct sunlight, but the _____ need more water.

9. Whenever I look at Misty and Kelly, _____ always smiles.

10. I went to the market for bread and eggs, but I forgot _____ when I got to the checkout line.

Practice 5 Writing Your Own

A. Write a sentence of your own using pronouns that refer to the following antecedents. *Answers will vary.*

1. Mary and Jane _____

2. The cash and the grocery list _____

3. Heath, Eddie, and Emilio _____

4. the news _____

5. an old saying _____

B. Write five sentences of your own using pronouns and antecedents, and underline the pronouns and antecedents in each sentence. *Answers will vary.*

1. _____

2. _____

3. _____

4. _____

5. _____

SHIFTING POINT OF VIEW

Point of view refers to whether a statement is made in the first person, the second person, or the third person. Each person—or point of view—requires different pronouns. The following chart lists the pronouns for each point of view.

Point of View

First Person:	*I, we*
Second Person:	*you, you*
Third Person:	*he, she, it, they*

If you begin writing from one point of view, you should stay in that point of view. Do not shift to another point of view. For example, if you start out writing "I," you should continue with "I" and not shift to "you." Shifting point of view is a very common error in college writing.

Shift: If **a person** doesn't save money, **you** will have nothing left for retirement.

Correct: If **a person** doesn't save money, **he or she** will have nothing left for retirement.

Shift: **I** moved to Los Angeles because **you** could meet movie stars there.

Correct: **I** moved to Los Angeles because **I** could meet movie stars there.

REVIEWING POINT OF VIEW

What is point of view?

Point of view refers to whether a statement is made in the first, second, or third person.

What does it mean to shift point of view?

A shift occurs when a writer begins in one "person" and changes to another.

 Practice 6 Identifying   Underline the pronouns that shift point of view in the following sentences.

1. We should really leave now since <u>you</u> know the traffic will be bad.

2. They can ask the administrative assistant for help if <u>you</u> have questions.

3. I decided to put my money in a CD because <u>you</u> can get a good return.

4. The dog needs to be careful in this area because <u>you</u> could easily get hit by a car.

5. I looked up at the stars; you could see them so clearly in the country.
6. Somebody keeps leaving me love notes on my desk, and you'd better confess.
7. Since I lost all my money last year on vacation, you should always carry traveler's checks.
8. We decided to get out of the hot sun, yet still they suffered.
9. People were looking around and asking questions; you were confused.
10. I've always wanted a little black dress because you know I'll look elegant in it.

Practice 7 Identifying Put an X next to the sentence if the underlined pronouns shift point of view.

1. __X__ I am nice to all strangers because you never know whom you might meet. *(I, I)*
2. __X__ People can't be too careful with our money. *(their)*
3. __X__ A body needs lots of water to keep you healthy. *(it)*
4. _____ The workers decided to cross the picket line because they wanted to end the strike.
5. __X__ People are not an island unto themselves, even if you think you are. *(they, they)*
6. __X__ I like going to rock concerts because they find it both exciting and relaxing. *(I, them)*
7. _____ A person can get a great deal right now at the car dealership if he or she has good credit.
8. _____ John ate so many cookies that he got sick.
9. __X__ One shouldn't listen at closed doors; you will never hear anything nice. *(one)*
10. __X__ A person should ask for help when you are in trouble. *(he or she—is)*

Practice 8 Correcting Correct the pronoun errors in Practice 7 by rewriting each incorrect sentence. *See Practice 7.*

1. ______________________________
2. ______________________________

3. _____

4. _____

5. _____

6. _____

7. _____

8. _____

9. _____

10. _____

❧ Practice 9 Completing   Fill in each blank in the following sentences with pronouns that stay in the same point of view.

1. I should listen to these different types of music since ___*I*___ never know what ___*I*___ will like.

2. They have had a wonderful time, and ___*they*___ plan on returning soon.

3. I buy my groceries in bulk because ___*I*___ know that ___*I*___ am getting a bargain.

4. Since you are the one in love with her, ___*you*___ should call her.

5. We have always loved this spot for picnics, and ___*we*___ intend to meet here at least once a year.

6. You can find the best sales at discount centers if ___*you*___ know how to look.

7. John ran for two miles before ___*he*___ ran out of energy.

8. They can't leave this issue alone; ___*they*___ are determined to resolve it tonight.

9. I enjoy walking in the park because ___*I*___ feel that nature relieves stress.

10. I won't admit to seeing the alien since ___*I*___ believe no one will listen.

❧ Practice 10 Writing Your Own

A. Write a sentence of your own for each of the following pronouns. Be sure the pronouns have clear antecedents and do not shift point of view. *Answers will vary.*

1. you _____

2. they _____

3. it _____

4. I _____

5. we _____

B. Write five sentences of your own using personal pronouns that have clear antecedents and do not shift point of view. Underline the pronouns and antecedents in each sentence. *Answers will vary.*

1. _____

2. _____

3. _____

4. _____

5. _____

CHAPTER REVIEW

You might want to reread your answers to the questions in the review boxes before you do the following exercises.

Review Practice 1 Reading   Refer to the paragraph by William Kowinski on page 255 to do the following exercises.

1. List the five pronouns and their antecedents from the paragraph. *Answers will vary.*

Pronoun	Antecedent
_____	_____
_____	_____
_____	_____
_____	_____
_____	_____

2. Does the paragraph shift point of view? ___No___

🌿 **Review Practice 2 Identifying**   Label each of the following sentences U if the antecedent in unclear, M if the antecedent is missing, or S if the sentence shifts point of view.

1. __U__ Both Tina and Abigail asked Jim out on a date, but he only said yes to her.

2. __M__ It says that there is a big dance tonight.

3. __M__ In a current medical study, it shows that more women are suffering heart attacks than ever before.

4. __S__ I love to read in the bathtub because it relaxes you.

5. __S__ They never send us a Christmas card because everyone is too busy.

6. __U__ I put the cell phone and the credit card right here, but now I can't find it.

7. __M__ In this poll, it says that more people are for the new law than against it.

8. __U__ Jesse told Kevin that he was going to cook dinner that night.

9. __S__ I am going to wear my fake Rolex watch and Gucci purse because everyone will think you're rich.

10. __M__ They say love is worth the pain.

🌿 **Review Practice 3 Correcting**   Correct the pronoun errors in Review Practice 2 by rewriting each sentence. *Answers will vary.*

🖊 EDITING A STUDENT PARAGRAPH

Following is a paragraph written and revised by Sergio Cardenas in response to the writing assignment in this chapter. Read the paragraph, and underline each of his pronouns.

> $\overset{X}{\underline{They}}$ say that women are gatherers and men are hunters. $\overset{X}{\underline{You}}$ never truly understood this statement until $\underline{I}$ watched a man for a good hour at the mall. $\underline{I}$ knew $\underline{he}$ was married, or at least attached, by the mounds of shopping bags--but no female--surrounding $\underline{him}$. The obviously

Here are the corrected pronouns:
People
I
A football game
The man and his son
the TV

overwhelmed man was slumped on a bench with only <u>his</u> upper torso visible due to all the shopping clutter. Eventually, the man's significant other relieved <u>him</u> of the packages, dropped off <u>their</u> 10-year-old son, and proceeded to search the mall for an outfit to match the shoes that <u>she</u> bought on sale. The bewildered yet relieved man took <u>his</u> son's hand, looked around, stood up, sat down, checked <u>his</u> watch, and yawned. Then <u>he</u> heard a sports announcer yell, "Touchdown!" <u>It</u> was on. <u>They</u> tracked the sound to a 64-inch big-screen TV just inside a department store entrance. Slowly <u>he</u> circled <u>his</u> prey, sniffing out the accessories. Then, decisively, <u>he</u> moved in for the kill. "Charge <u>it</u>!" he said.

Collaborative Activity

Team up with a partner, and put an X above the five pronoun errors in Sergio's paragraph. Then, working together, use what you have learned in this chapter to correct these errors. Rewrite the paragraph with your corrections. *See student paragraph for errors. Corrections are in the margin.*

❧ EDITING YOUR OWN PARAGRAPH

Now return to the paragraph you wrote and revised at the beginning of this chapter. Underline each of your pronouns.

Collaborative Activity

Exchange paragraphs with your partner, and circle any pronoun reference or point-of-view errors you find in your partner's paper.

Individual Activity

On the Error Log in Appendix 6, record any pronoun errors that your partner found in your paragraph. To complete the writing process, correct these errors by rewriting your paragraph.

Pronoun Agreement

Checklist for Correcting Pronoun Agreement Problems

> ✔ Do all pronouns and their antecedents agree in number (singular or plural)?
>
> ✔ Do any pronouns that refer to indefinite pronouns agree in number?
>
> ✔ Are any pronouns used in a sexist way?

As you learned in Chapter 12, subjects and verbs must agree to communicate clearly. If the subject is singular, the verb must be singular; if the subject is plural, the verb must be plural. The same holds true for pronouns and the words they refer to—their antecedents. They must agree in number—both singular or both plural.

Notice that all the pronouns and their antecedents agree with one another in the following paragraph by David Gardner, former president of the University of California.

In a world of ever-accelerating competition and change in the conditions of the workplace, of ever-greater danger, and of ever-larger opportunities for those prepared to meet them, educational reform should focus on the goal of creating a Learning Society. At the heart of such a society is the commitment to a set of values and to a system of education that affords all members the opportunity to stretch their minds to full capacity, from early childhood through adulthood, learning more as the world itself changes. Such a society has as a basic foundation the idea that education is important not only because of what it contributes to one's career goals but also because of the value it adds to the general quality of one's life. Also at the heart of the Learning Society are educational opportunities extending far

The first team to correctly match all their performer cards with pronoun cards wins.

■ For sample sentences, see the *Instructor's Resource Manual*, Section II, Part II.

beyond the traditional institutions of learning, our schools and colleges. They extend into homes and workplaces; into libraries, art galleries, museums, and science centers; indeed, into every place where the individual can develop and mature in work and life. In our view, formal schooling in youth is the essential foundation for learning throughout one's life. But without life-long learning, one's skills will become rapidly dated.

In this paragraph, the author talks about the importance of life-long learning. Before continuing in this chapter, take a moment to write about your experiences with test taking. Save your work because you will use it later in this chapter.

Writing Assignment: The Role of Education in your Life

What role does education play in your life? Is it an important aspect of your life? Or do you just want to get through school with minimum effort? What does education mean to you?

Revising Your Writing

Revise the first draft of your paragraph before you focus on editing. Use the Revising Checklist on pages 24–25 to help you with your revision. Make sure your paragraph has a good topic sentence and is well developed. Then check your paragraph for unity, organization, and coherence.

Usually, pronoun agreement is not a problem, as these sentences show:

Singular: **Mr. Parker** dropped **his** pager.

Plural: **Mirianne** and **Marvin** gave **their** opinions.

INDEFINITE PRONOUNS

Pronoun agreement may become a problem with indefinite pronouns. Indefinite pronouns that are always singular give writers the most trouble.

NOT   **One** of the contestants did **their** dance routine.

(How many contestants did the dance routine? Only *one*, so use a singular pronoun.)

Correct: **One** of the contestants did **her** dance routine.

Correct: **One** of the contestants did **his** dance routine.

NOT   **Somebody** left the lights on in **their** car.

(*How many people left their lights on? One person*, so use a singular pronoun.)

Correct: **Somebody** left the lights on in **her** car.

Correct: **Somebody** left the lights on in **his** car.

Here is a list of indefinite pronouns that are always singular.

Singular Indefinite Pronouns

another	everybody	neither	one
anybody	everyone	nobody	other
anyone	everything	none	somebody
anything	little	no one	someone
each	much	nothing	something
either			

HINT: A few indefinite pronouns can be either singular or plural, depending on their meaning in the sentence. These pronouns are *any, all, more, most,* and *some*. Here is an example:

Singular: **Most** of the senior class had **its** orientation today.

Plural: **Most** of the seniors had **their** orientation today.

In the first sentence, *class* is singular, so the singular pronoun *its* is used. In the second sentence, *seniors* is plural, so the plural pronoun *their* is used.

REVIEWING INDEFINITE PRONOUNS

Why should a pronoun agree with the word it refers to?

To communicate clearly

Name five indefinite pronouns that are always singular. Answers will vary.

_____   _____   _____   _____   _____

✿ **Practice 1 Identifying**   Underline the correct pronouns in each of the following sentences.

1. Everybody has (<u>his or her</u>, their) forms completed.

2. Each of the committee members remembered (<u>his or her</u>, their) meeting.

3. Some of the horses shook (its, <u>their</u>) heads.

4. All of the men had (his, <u>their</u>) pictures taken with the actress.

5. No one forgot (<u>his or her</u>, their) books today.

6. More of the ceramic figurines had to have (its, <u>their</u>) surface reglazed.

7. Another of the Roman statues was missing (<u>its</u>, their) arm.

8. Everything has (<u>its</u>, their) proper place and time.

9. One of the doctors dropped (<u>his or her</u>, their) stethoscopes.

10. Every one of these cats has had (<u>its</u>, their) tail bobbed.

✿ **Practice 2 Identifying**   Put an X next to the sentence if the underlined pronoun does not agree with its antecedent.

1. _____ Paula and Rebecca got help revising <u>their</u> papers.

2. _____ Any one of the sculptors will have <u>his</u> or <u>her</u> cell phone on.

3. __X__ Another of the officers turned <u>their</u> sirens on. *(his or her)*

4. __X__ Everyone had <u>their</u> immunization shots. *(his or her)*

5. __X__ All of the man's hair has lost <u>their</u> color. *(its)*

6. _____ At least one of the actresses will have <u>her</u> agent with her.

7. __X__ Someone is remembering <u>their</u> childhood. *(his or her)*

8. __X__ Nobody knows where <u>their</u> tickets are. *(his or her)*

9. _____ Each of the boys practiced <u>his</u> lessons.

10. __X__ Anybody with <u>their</u> children should board the plane first. *(his or her)*

✿ **Practice 3 Correcting**   Correct the pronoun errors in Practice 2 by rewriting each incorrect sentence. *See Practice 2*

1. _____

2. _____

3. _____

4. _____

5. _____

6. _____

7. _____

8. _____

9. _____

10. _____

❦ Practice 4 Completing   Fill in each blank in the following sentences with a pronoun that agrees with its antecedent and makes sense.

1. Somebody is playing ____*his or her*____ stereo too loud.

2. Another of the beauty queens needs ____*her*____ dress fixed.

3. All of the cars had ____*their*____ engines overhauled.

4. Everyone should listen to ____*his or her*____ elders.

5. Each of my dogs had ____*its*____ hair groomed today.

6. Some of the singers lost ____*their*____ voices.

7. Something has ____*its*____ claws in me!

8. Any of the pantsuits, with ____*its*____ matching scarf, will look good on you.

9. Most of the roads have had ____*their*____ potholes fixed.

10. Everybody has ____*his or her*____ warmest clothes on.

❦ Practice 5 Writing Your Own

A. Write a sentence of your own for each of the following indefinite pronouns and antecedents. *Answers will vary.*

1. anybody, his or her _____

2. most, their _____

3. something, its _____

4. each, its _____

5. all, their _____

B. Write five sentences of your own using indefinite pronouns as subjects and their antecedents. Underline the pronouns in each sentence. *Answers will vary.*

1. _____

2. _____

3. _____

4. _____

5. _____

AVOIDING SEXISM

In the first section of this chapter, you learned that you should use singular pronouns to refer to singular indefinite pronouns. For example, the indefinite pronoun *someone* requires a singular pronoun, *his* or *her,* not the plural *their.* But what if you don't know whether the person referred to is male or female? Then you have a choice: (1) You can say "he or she" or "his or her," or (2) you can make the sentence plural. What you should not do is ignore half the population by referring to all humans as males.

NOT	If **anyone** has questions, **they** should ask us.
NOT	If **anyone** has questions, **he** should ask us.
Correct:	If **anyone** has questions, **he or she** should ask us.
Correct:	If **people** have questions, **they** should ask us.

NOT	**Everyone** forgot to bring **their** spending money.
NOT	**Everyone** forgot to bring **his** spending money.
Correct:	**Everyone** forgot to bring **his or her** spending money.
Correct:	**All the travelers** forgot to bring **their** spending money.

Sexism in writing can also occur in ways other than with indefinite pronouns. We often assume that doctors, lawyers, and bank presidents are men and that nurses, schoolteachers, and secretaries are women. But that is not very accurate.

NOT   Each **policeman** is assigned **his** own locker.

(Why automatically assume that every member of the police force is male?)

Correct: Each **police officer** is assigned **his or her** own locker.

NOT   The **chairman** should run all department meetings.

(Since both men and women can head departments, boards, and committees, a more appropriate term is "chairperson" or "chair.")

Correct: The **chair** should run all department meetings.

NOT   A good **receptionist** keeps **her** area clear of clutter.

(Why leave the men who are receptionists out of the sentence?)

Correct: A good **receptionist** keeps **his or her** area clear of clutter.
Correct: Good **receptionists** keep **their** areas clear of clutter.

REVIEWING SEXISM IN WRITING

What is sexism in writing?

Assuming that the people in a group are all male or all female

What are two ways to get around the problem of using male pronouns to refer to both women and men?

Use he or she   Make the sentence plural

Give two examples of sexism in writing. *Examples will vary.*

Practice 6 Identifying   Underline the sexist references in each of the following sentences.

1. Each administrative assistant should leave a number where <u>she</u> could be reached.

2. A welder must always wear <u>his</u> face shield.

3. No one can complain about <u>his</u> paycheck this month.

4. Everyone has <u>his</u> own way of doing things.

5. Ask a salesman for <u>his</u> advice on this product.

6. Somebody just drove <u>his</u> car over the median.

7. With a little instruction, anyone can balance <u>her</u> checkbook.

8. Take this to your lawyer for <u>his</u> signature.

9. Each person is responsible for <u>his</u> own ride.

10. One of the receptionists didn't lock <u>her</u> file cabinet.

🌱 Practice 7 Identifying   Put an X next to the sentence if it has sexist references.

1. ___X___ A nurse left her name tag on the counter.

2. _____ Each of my co-workers was rewarded for submitting his or her ideas.

3. ___X___ A firefighter learns how to fight his way through smoke and flames.

4. ___X___ Ask a teacher if she knows the answer.

5. _____ A whistle tells the construction worker when it is time to eat his or her lunch.

6. ___X___ Each of the students passed his midterm exam.

7. ___X___ Somebody forgot to turn off her computer in the computer lab.

8. _____ Every mail carrier must deliver all the mail in his or her bag every day.

9. ___X___ A good manager always listens to his employees.

10. _____ The doctors gave their patients good advice.

🌱 Practice 8 Correcting   Correct the pronouns errors in Practice 7 by rewriting each incorrect sentence. *Answers will vary.*

1. _____

2. _____

3. _____

4. _____

5. _____

6. _____

7. _____

8. _____

9. _____

10. _____

❋ Practice 9 Completing   Fill in each blank in the following sentences with a pronoun that is correct.

1. I heard that one of the gardeners broke _____*his or her*_____ truck.

2. An opera singer can stretch _____*his or her*_____ vocal cords to many octaves.

3. No customer in our restaurant will have _____*his or her*_____ MasterCard refused.

4. Each child should bring a permission slip signed by _____*his or her*_____ parents.

5. All of the dentists have _____*their*_____ teeth checked once a year.

6. Ask one of the chefs if you can taste _____*his or her*_____ dish.

7. Scuba divers should check _____*their*_____ air tanks periodically.

8. If a mechanic wants to make more money, _____*he or she*_____ should stay open for business on the weekends.

9. Someone trimmed _____*his or her*_____ hair in the bathroom and left a mess.

10. A race-car driver's main priority is _____*his or her*_____ tires.

❋ Practice 10 Writing Your Own

A. Write a sentence of your own for each of the following antecedents. Include at least one pronoun in each sentence. *Answers will vary.*

1. politician _____

2. flight attendant _____

3. dancer _____

4. secret agent _____

6. trucker _____

B. Write five sentences of your own using antecedents and pronouns that avoid sexist references. Underline the pronouns in each sentence. *Answers will vary.*

1. _____

2. _____

3. _____

4. _____

5. _____

CHAPTER REVIEW

You might want to reread your answers to the questions in the review boxes before you do the following exercises.

✺ Review Practice 1 Reading   Refer to the paragraph by David Gardner on pages 267–268 to do the following exercises.

1. List five pronouns and their antecedents from the paragraph. *Answers will vary.*

Pronoun	Antecedent
_____	_____
_____	_____
_____	_____
_____	_____
_____	_____

2. Write two sentences with sexist references based on Gardner's paragraph. *Answers will vary.*

1. _____

2. _____

✺ Review Practice 2 Identifying   Underline the pronoun or sexist errors in each of the following sentences.

1. Everyone who wants <u>his</u> parking validated should see the receptionist. *(his or her)*

2. If a surfer isn't careful, <u>she</u> could get hit by <u>her</u> surfboard. *(he or she, his or her)*

3. Anyone can look like <u>they're</u> rich, even if <u>they</u> aren't. *(he or she is, he or she isn't)*

4. Most of the birds have built <u>its</u> nests. *(their)*

5. A good writer keeps <u>her</u> notebook close by. *(his or her)*

6. It is a law that a motorcyclist must wear <u>his</u> helmet. *(his or her)*

7. The <u>policeman</u> gave warnings to the speeding motorists. *(police officer)*

8. Somebody left <u>their</u> laundry at the laundromat. *(his or her)*

9. Each of the cherries had <u>their</u> pits removed. *(its)*

10. <u>Waitresses</u> work hard for their tips. *(servers)*

Review Practice 3 Correcting   Correct the pronoun errors in Review Practice 2 by rewriting each incorrect sentence. *See Review Practice 2. Answers will vary.*

EDITING A STUDENT PARAGRAPH

Following is a paragraph written and revised by Jarrod Cervantes in response to the writing assignment in this chapter. Read the paragraph; then underline each of his pronouns once and their antecedents twice.

<u>I</u> know how to write. <u>I</u> know how to structure <u>my</u> thoughts in an organized, cohesive manner, and <u>I</u> can convey those thoughts in written form. However, <u>I</u> cannot write on command. To say to <u>me</u>, "OK, <u>you</u> have X amount of time to answer this midterm prompt," causes instant paralysis of the brain. <u>I</u> brainstorm. <u>I</u> pray. <u>I</u> want to throw up. But <u>my</u> brain doesn't open. According to the teacher, <u>anybody</u> can pass a timed writing exam if <u>he</u>ˣ is prepared. But <u>it</u>ˣ doesn't matter how prepared <u>I</u> am for the written exam. <u>I</u> can study for a week straight, draft outlines, and remember important facts. But all of these efforts magically disappear when <u>I</u> receive the test. <u>I</u> look around and notice <u>everyone</u> with <u>their</u>ˣ heads bent, frantically writing away. <u>I</u> hear <u>somebody</u> tapping <u>his</u>ˣ pencil on the desk and wonder if <u>they</u>ˣ are as nervous as <u>I</u> am. Then the fear of

Here are the corrected pronouns:
he or she
Being prepared for the written exam doesn't matter.
his or her
his or her
he or she is
his or her
he or she is

judgment settles in. Each <u>teacher</u>, in <u>her</u>[X] infinite wis-

dom, doesn't seem to realize that <u>she</u>[X]'s passing judgment

on <u>*me*</u>, not just <u>my</u> writing, for <u>my</u> writing is a reflection of

<u>myself</u>.

Collaborative Activity

Team up with a partner, and place an X above the seven pronoun errors in Jarrod's paragraph. Then, working together, use what you have learned in this chapter to correct these errors. Rewrite the paragraph with your corrections. *See student paragraph for errors. Corrections are in the margin.*

❧ EDITING YOUR OWN PARAGRAPH

Now return to the paragraph you wrote and revised at the beginning of this chapter. Underline your pronouns once and antecedents twice.

Collaborative Activity

Exchange paragraphs with your partner, and circle any pronoun agreement errors or sexist references that you find in your partner's paragraph.

Individual Activity

On the Error Log in Appendix 6, record any pronoun errors that your partner found in your paragraph. To complete the writing process, correct these errors by rewriting your paragraph.

Unit 3 Review
Pronouns

✿Unit Practice 1 Identifying   Underline the pronoun errors in the following sentences.

1. You are just as big-hearted as <u>him</u>. *(he)*

2. I will make <u>my's</u> own destiny. *(my)*

3. I casually surveyed the room over the rim of my dark glasses, but <u>you</u> couldn't see anyone. *(I)*

4. Alyssa and Martha both ran as fast as they could, but <u>she</u> won the race. *(Alyssa or Martha)*

5. A nanny should spend some time simply playing with <u>her</u> charges. *(his or her)*

6. Jeremy and <u>her</u> are designing my furniture. *(she)*

7. Anybody can become familiar with <u>his</u> own writing process. *(his or her)*

8. <u>Them</u> in the back seat are going into storage. *(unclear "them")*

9. Somebody has <u>their</u> hand in my cookie jar! *(his or her)*

10. <u>They</u> say a bird in the hand is worth two in the bush. *(unclear "They")*

11. One of the accountants left <u>his</u> calculator behind. *(his or her)*

12. Diane loses her patience more with Jim than with <u>I</u>. *(me)*

13. In last year's books, <u>it</u> shows a marked rise in profits. *(unclear "it")*

14. You cannot eat those <u>there</u>; they will spoil your appetite. *(delete "there")*

15. During the outdoor symphony, <u>him</u> and <u>her</u> proposed to each other at the same time. *(he and she)*

16. When Julia heard Cindy and <u>he</u> yell, she went racing toward them. *(him)*

17. These lemon cakes are <u>her's</u>. *(hers)*

■ For additional material about teaching pronouns, for journal entries, and for various tests, see the *Instructor's Resource Manual*, Section II, Part II.

ADDITIONAL WRITING TOPIC
Let your students expand into well-developed essays the paragraphs they wrote in one of the unit chapters.

18. Each of the toys came with <u>their</u> own batteries. *(its)*

19. People shouldn't fear the sun altogether because <u>you</u> do get several essential vitamins from its light. *(they)*

20. These <u>here</u> were left outside and are ruined. *(delete "here")*

🌱 Unit Practice 2 Correcting   Correct the pronoun errors in Unit Practice 1 by rewriting each sentence. *See Unit Practice 1.*

🌱 Unit Practice 3 Identifying   Underline the pronoun errors in the following paragraph.

<u>They</u> say that the apple doesn't fall far from the tree, and I guess that's true. My mom is a chocolate lover. Brittany and Jennifer, my twin sisters, and <u>me</u> are chocolate lovers, too. Perhaps the word "love" isn't the right choice because this <u>here</u> is not just a craving but an obsession. We will eat any kind: dark, light, white, Swiss, German, with nuts, without nuts, and so on. I remember when Brittany and Jennifer were just five years old, Mom had given them and <u>I</u> these huge chocolate bunnies for Easter. Being the older sister, <u>you</u> know that I was entitled to a percentage of that chocolate. So I bullied the twins into giving me the ears. I fell asleep that night dreaming of all that warm, smooth, sweet stuff until I was rudely awakened by the sound of fire engines and my screaming family. Our living room was on fire. The firefighters said that the blaze had started in the fireplace. Somebody had tried to burn <u>their</u> chocolate bunny. The bubbling chocolate spilled onto the carpet and caught fire. Imagine my surprise to learn the bunny was mine. In this case, revenge wasn't so sweet. Mom and Dad denied us our chocolate for one month. From that moment on, I respected my sisters' rights to have and to hold <u>her</u> own chocolate. I have to admit that the twins have a greater passion for chocolate than <u>me</u> because <u>she</u> opened up her own chocolate shop, Sweet Chocolate, which Mom now manages. The other twin is now the chief executive officer of a top-name chocolate factory, and she loves her job. But I, too, am doing my part in this legacy: I am a wife and mother who is passing on <u>her's</u> chocolate genetics—in moderation of course—to her children.

🌱 Unit Practice 4 Correcting   Correct the pronoun errors in Unit Practice 3 by rewriting the paragraph. *Answers will vary.*

UNIT WRITING ASSIGNMENTS

1. What do you think the above picture is pointing out? Are the people related? What is the adult trying to teach the child? Is the child re-
   sponding? Why or why not? What emotions are they experiencing—are
   they happy, sad, frustrated? Use your imagination to explain the relationship between the adult and the child.

2. Your best friend has asked you to design the cover of his first rap CD,
   Incognito. What would your design be? Why this design? What colors
   would you use and why? How effective do you think your cover will be
   in marketing your friend's CD?

3. If you had to pick one word to describe your room, what would it be?
   Give examples of things in your room to help explain why you chose this
   word.

4. Most people feel there is a right way and a wrong way to do a particular
   chore, such as washing the car or mowing the lawn. Is there a particular
   chore that you insist be done a certain way? What is the chore? Explain
   the right way to go about doing it and why your way is the best.

5. Create your own assignment (with the help of your instructor), and
   write a response to it.

Unit 4 Modifiers

Words that modify—usually called adjectives and adverbs—add details to sentences, either describing, limiting, or identifying so that sentences become more vivid and interesting. They work like accessories in our everyday lives. Without jewelry, scarves, ties, and cuff links, we are still dressed. But accessories give a little extra flair to our wardrobe. Without modifiers, our writing would be bland, boring, and lifeless. However, to use adjectives and adverbs correctly, you need to learn about their different forms and functions.

In the chapters in this unit, you will learn about adjectives, adverbs, and various problems with the placement of these words in their sentences:

Chapter 17: Adjectives

Chapter 18: Adverbs

Chapter 19: Modifier Errors

The first information your students need in this unit is that modifiers are adjectives and adverbs. To prepare them for the work ahead, you might have them review the explanations of these two parts of speech in the Introduction to this part. Once your students can identify adjectives and adverbs, they are ready to work through the instruction in this unit.

The chapters that follow discuss adjectives and adverbs, their various forms, and problems with the placement of these words in their sentences.

Adjectives

Checklist for Using Adjectives Correctly

✔ Are all adjectives that show comparison used correctly?

✔ Are the forms of *good* and *bad* used correctly?

Adjectives are modifiers. They help us communicate more clearly (I have a *brown* jacket; I want a *black* one) and more vividly (the concert was *loud* and *wild*). Without adjectives, our language would be drab and boring.

Notice how the adjectives work in the following paragraph by Rebecca Zurier.

> The story of the American firehouse is part of that particular social institution, the American fire company. The buildings' size, shape, and character reflect the organization's development from a voluntary association—a cross between a lodge and a baseball team—into a branch of municipal government. Eighteenth-century firehouses were simply places to store a town's supply of fire engines, buckets, hooks, and ladders. Built in an easily accessible location, the firehouse could be a plain wooden shed or incorporated into a larger public structure— usually brick but sometimes stone—that served several functions. As responsibility for fire protection shifted from the community at large to private, fraternal companies, firehouses took on the character of clubhouses, with lavish second-story meeting rooms over the garage. Before long, the buildings themselves came to be seen as flamboyant architectural emblems—as distinctive a part of the company's regalia as its uniform.

■ For more sample sentences, see the *Instructor's Resource Manual*, Section II, Part II.

TEACHING ON THE WEB

Exploring and Discussing: Have students find a Web site that has descriptions of art work (such as a museum site). How do the descriptions use adjectives to describe the paintings, sculptures, or buildings? What happens when students remove the adjectives from the descriptions? What do adjectives add to the descriptions of the works of art?

TEACHING ON THE WEB

Mosaics Web Site: To learn more about adjectives, students can go to www.prenhall.com/mosaics.

In this paragraph, Rebecca Zurier talks about the evolution of the fire-house in the United States. Before continuing in this chapter, take a moment to write about something you would like to build or invent. Save your work because you will use it later in this chapter.

Writing Assignment: My Creation

Have you ever created something from scratch? Is there a building or product that you would like to design to make life easier? Maybe it's a walk-through aquarium or a pencil that won't run out of lead or computer software that keeps your computer from crashing. Think of a helpful invention, and write a paragraph describing it.

Revising Your Writing

Revise the first draft of your paragraph before you focus on editing. Use the Revising Checklist on pages 24–25 to help you with your revision. Make sure your paragraph has a good topic sentence, is well developed, and is well organized. Then check your paragraph for unity and coherence.

USING ADJECTIVES

Adjectives are words that modify—or describe—nouns or pronouns. Adjectives tell how something or someone looks: *dark, light, tall, short, large, small.* Most adjectives come before the words they modify, but with linking verbs (such as *is, are, look, become,* and *feel*), adjectives follow the words they modify.

Adjectives Before a Noun:	We walked down the **narrow, winding** path.
Adjectives After a Linking Verb:	The path was **narrow** and **winding.**

REVIEWING ADJECTIVES

What are adjectives?

Adjective modify or describe nouns or pronouns

> **Where can you find adjectives in a sentence?**
>
> Before a noun or pronoun or after a linking verb
> _____

Practice 1 Identifying   Underline the adjectives in each of the following sentences. Do not count possessive pronouns as adjectives. Some sentences have more than one adjective.

1. My long, white dress was caught in the car door.
2. The reunion committee is meeting at noon.
3. You are rude to say those mean things.
4. This is an important date.
5. Eugene's wedding was emotional and fun.
6. Katie got a new car for her eighteenth birthday.
7. The den carpet has brown soda stains.
8. Friskie, our tabby cat, had five kittens.
9. The weather forecast says we will have three feet of snow.
10. Harriet wrote a long list for the grocery store.

Practice 2 Identifying   Put an X next to the sentence if the underlined word is not an adjective.

1. __X__ This is a boring day. *(boring)*
2. _____ The computer was old.
3. __X__ You wrote a good essay. *(good)*
4. _____ My brother is strong and brave.
5. _____ Our last vacation was in May.
6. __X__ Could you hand me the yellow pencil? *(yellow)*
7. __X__ The new telephone rang loudly. *(new)*
8. __X__ Jimmy was nervous and worried. *(nervous, worried)*
9. __X__ My English professor would not accept my late assignment. *(late)*
10. __X__ *The Rover* is a funny play. *(funny)*

❊ Practice 3 Correcting   Correct the errors in Practice 2 by listing the correct adjectives here. *See Practice 2.*

1. _____   6. _____
2. _____   7. _____
3. _____   8. _____
4. _____   9. _____
5. _____   10. _____

❊ Practice 4 Completing   Fill in each blank in the following paragraph with an adjective that makes sense. *Answers will vary.*

Yesterday, I drove to the department store to buy a pair of (1) _____ shoes. I needed them to match my (2) _____ dress, which I bought for the (3) _____ party. The shoes looked (4) _____ and (5) _____. When I got to the store, the parking lot was (6) _____, and I had a (7) _____ time finding a place to park. Then I reached for my purse, and I was (8) _____ when I realized that I had left it in my apartment. I had to drive all the way back home to retrieve my (9) _____ purse because that's where all of my money was. When I finally got back to the store, it took me (10) _____ minutes to find another parking spot. At that point, I was determined to find that pair of shoes!

❊ Practice 5 Writing Your Own

A. Write a sentence of your own for each of the following adjectives.
Answers will vary.

1. pretty _____

2. scared _____

3. friendly _____

4. hopeful _____

5. blue _____

B. Write five sentences of your own using adjectives. Underline the adjectives in each sentence. *Answers will vary.*

1. _____

2. _____

3. _____

4. _____

5. _____

COMPARING WITH ADJECTIVES

Most adjectives have three forms: a **basic** form, a **comparative** form (used to compare two items), and a **superlative** form (used to compare three or more items).

For positive comparisons, adjectives form the comparative and superlative in two different ways.

1. **For one-syllable adjectives and some two-syllable adjectives, use -er to compare two items and -est to compare three or more items.**

Basic	Comparative (used to compare two items)	Superlative (used to compare three or more items)
large	larger	largest
cool	cooler	coolest
rainy	rainier	rainiest
happy	happier	happiest

2. **For some two-syllable adjectives and all longer adjectives, use more to compare two items and most to compare three or more items.**

Basic	Comparative (used to compare two items)	Superlative (used to compare three or more items)
loyal	more loyal	most loyal
hopeful	more hopeful	most hopeful
beautiful	more beautiful	most beautiful
trustworthy	more trustworthy	most trustworthy

For negative comparisons, use *less* to compare two items and *least* to compare three or more items.

Basic	Comparative (used to compare two items)	Superlative (used to compare three or more items)
wild	less wild	least wild
silly	less silly	least silly
enormous	less enormous	least enormous

HINT: Some adjectives are not usually compared. For example, one person cannot be "more dead" than another. Here are some more examples.

broken	final	square
empty	impossible	supreme
equal	singular	unanimous

REVIEWING ADJECTIVE FORMS

When do you use the comparative form of an adjective?

To compare two items

When do you use the superlative form of an adjective?

To compare three or more items

How do one-syllable and some two-syllable adjectives form the comparative and superlative in positive comparisons?

Add -er for the comparative and -est for the superlative.

How do some two-syllable adjectives and all longer adjectives form the comparative and superlative in positive comparisons?

With more and most

How do you form negative comparisons?

With less and least

🎋 **Practice 6 Identifying**   Identify the underlined adjectives in the following sentences as basic (B), comparative (C), or superlative (S).

1. ___S___ Ivan Rodriguez is the <u>most talented</u> catcher in professional baseball.

2. ___B___ Susan is so <u>generous</u> to let me borrow her notes.

3. ___C___ This year's talent show was even <u>funnier</u> than last year's.

4. ___B___ We ran to the <u>front</u> door and knocked loudly.

5. ___B___ There is a <u>black</u> mark on your chin.

6. ___C___ The gardens in your backyard are <u>less healthy</u> than those in your front yard.

7. ___S___ James is the <u>most spoiled</u> child I know.

8. ___S___ My friend is buying the <u>latest</u> 'N Sync album.

9. ___C___ Yvette's New Year's resolution is to be <u>less disrespectful</u> to her parents.

10. ___B___ Are you taking that <u>exciting</u> chemistry class this semester?

🎋 **Practice 7 Identifying**   Underline the adjectives in each of the following sentences. Do not count possessive pronouns as adjectives.

1. This month was <u>hotter</u> than <u>last</u> month.

2. Our hotel was <u>more expensive</u> than yours.

3. I have <u>less valuable</u> jewelry than my sister.

4. This was the <u>most stressful</u> day of the week.

5. Peter gave the <u>longest</u> presentation of anyone in the class.

6. My dad was <u>less worried</u> about my grades than about my job at the <u>department</u> store.

7. Chris's car is <u>more economical</u> than mine.

8. The <u>longest</u> line is the one for tickets.

9. I know that you are <u>richer</u> than I am.

10. Tabitha was the <u>least likely</u> person to cut class.

🎋 **Practice 8 Correcting**   Change the positive comparisons in Practice 7 to negative and the negative comparisons to positive. *Answers will vary.*

1. _____
2. _____
3. _____
4. _____
5. _____
6. _____
7. _____
8. _____
9. _____
10. _____

🌱 Practice 9 Completing   Fill in each blank in the following paragraph with the correct comparative or superlative form of the adjective in parentheses.

I was cleaning out the refrigerator when I realized that there were three packs of sandwich meat. I threw out the (1) ____oldest____ (old) one and put the other two on a shelf where I would remember to use them. The orange juice that I made a week ago tasted (2) ____more bitter____ (bitter) than I thought it should, so I threw that away also. But those were not the (3) ____grossest____ (gross) things in there. I found a piece of fruit that was (4) ____blacker____ (black) than chocolate, and I think it used to be a peach. I also found a bag of grapes that looked (5) ____more wrinkled____ (wrinkled) than raisins, a jar of jelly with furry white spots on top, and some leftover Chinese food that smelled (6) ____more rotten____ (rotten) than an old gym sock. When I opened the freezer, I found that the ice cream was (7) ____more frozen____ (frozen) than the meat, which had turned a yucky gray color. There was freezer burn on everything but the frozen burritos, which were the (8) ____most appetizing____ (appetizing) things in there. I couldn't believe it had been two months or (9) ____longer____ (long) since we had cleaned the refrigerator and freezer! When my roommate got home, she shook her head and thanked me for doing the (10) _most disgusting_ (disgusting) job in the house.

⚜ Practice 10 Writing Your Own

A. Write a sentence of your own for each of the following comparative and superlative forms. *Answers will vary.*

1. most frustrated _____

2. less hassled _____

3. more flexible _____

4. least friendly _____

5. most pleasant _____

B. Write five sentences of your own, and underline the adjectives in each sentence. *Answers will vary.*

1. _____

2. _____

3. _____

4. _____

5. _____

COMMON ADJECTIVE ERRORS

Two types of problems occur with adjectives used in comparisons.

1. Instead of using one method for forming the comparative or superlative, both are used. That is, both *-er* and *more* or *less* are used to compare two items. Or both *-est* and *most* or *least* are used to compare three or more items.

NOT   The new glue was **more weaker** than the old glue.
Correct: The new glue was **weaker** than the old glue.

NOT   Derrick was the **most smartest** employee of the company.
Correct: Derrick was the **smartest** employee of the company.

2. The second type of error occurs when the comparative or superlative is used with the wrong number of items. The comparative form should be used for two items and the superlative for three or more items.

NOT   Post-it Notes were the **newest** of the two products.
Correct: Post-it Notes were the **newer** of the two products.

NOT   Superglue was the **stickier** of the many 3M products.
Correct: Superglue was the **stickiest** of the many 3M products.

REVIEWING COMMON ADJECTIVE ERRORS

Can you ever use -er + more or -est + most?

No—you can't use both methods of comparison at the same time.

When do you use the comparative form of an adjective?

When comparing two items

When do you use the superlative form of an adjective?

When comparing three or more items

Practice 11 Identifying   Put a C next to underlined adjectives in the following sentences that are correct.

1. __C__ Which of these three brands of batteries is the <u>best</u>.
2. _____ Mikela is the <u>shorter</u> of her five sisters. *(shortest)*
3. __C__ Tiger Woods is the <u>most popular</u> golfer at the tournament.
4. _____ Today I did the <u>most craziest</u> thing. *(craziest)*
5. __C__ We are going to New York to see my mother's <u>younger</u> brother.
6. _____ This office is <u>more busier</u> than the one next door. *(busier)*
7. __C__ Mandy's coin collection is <u>older</u> than mine.
8. _____ Zack is <u>least honest</u> than Nathan. *(less honest)*

9. _____ This essay assignment is <u>more harder</u> than the last one. *(harder)*

10. __*C*__ The <u>quietest</u> person in the class is Tim.

Practice 12 Identifying   Underline the incorrect adjective forms in each of the following sentences.

1. That was the <u>most longest</u> movie I have ever seen. *(longest)*

2. My brother is the <u>shortest</u> of the two of us. *(shorter)*

3. This class is the most boring of my five classes.

4. Seth is watching his <u>most favoritest</u> cartoon. *(most favorite)*

5. Yours is the prettiest house on the block.

6. Vanity is the ugliest sin.

7. The fruit at the farmer's market was less fresh than at the roadside stand.

8. Ray is the <u>most friendliest</u> of all of my friends. *(friendliest)*

9. My voice is the <u>louder</u> among all of my family members. *(loudest)*

10. Janette likes the most confusing mystery novels.

Practice 13 Correcting   Correct the five adjective errors in Practices 11 and the five adjective errors in Practice 12 by rewriting each incorrect the sentence. *See Practices 11 and 12.*

_____

_____

_____

_____

_____

_____

_____

_____

_____

_____

🌿 **Practice 14 Completing**   Fill in each blank in the following paragraph with the correct adjective form.

Science is the (1) __*most difficult*__ (more difficult/most difficult) subject for me to understand. No matter how hard I study, I never get (2) __*higher*__ (higher/more higher) grades than C's on my exams. My sister Kimber and I usually have the same GPA, but I have always considered myself to be a little (3) __*smarter*__ (smarter/more smarter) than she is. Most subjects just come (4) __*easier*__ (easier/more easier) for me. However, when it comes to the sciences, she is definitely the (5) __*more talented*__ (more talented/most talented) one. She takes good notes, so studying is usually a lot (6) __*less stressful*__ (least stressful/less stressful) for her. I personally hate studying, but maybe that's because my notes are (7) __*more unorganized*__ (more unorganized/most unorganized) than Kimber's. I think that science itself is the (8) __*scariest*__ (scariest/most scariest) thing I've ever had to learn. If someone could find a way to make science classes (9) __*more enjoyable*__ (more enjoyable/most enjoyable), I think I would learn to be (10) __*more relaxed*__ (more relaxed/most relaxed) about them.

🌿 **Practice 15 Writing Your Own**

A. Write a sentence of your own for each of the following adjectives.
   Answers will vary.

1. kindest _____

2. more helpful _____

3. most gorgeous _____

4. smaller _____

5. more pleasant _____

B. Write five sentences of your own, and underline the adjectives in each sentence. *Answers will vary.*

1. _____

2. _____

3. _____

4. _____

5. _____

USING *GOOD* AND *BAD* CORRECTLY

The adjectives *good* and *bad* are irregular. They do not form the comparative and superlative like most other adjectives. Here are the correct forms for these two irregular adjectives:

Basic	Comparative (used to compare two items)	Superlative (used to compare three or more items)
good	better	best
bad	worse	worst

Problems occur with *good* and *bad* when writers don't know how to form their comparative and superlative forms.

NOT   more better, more worse, worser, most best, most worst, bestest, worstest

Correct: better, worse, best, worst

These errors appear in sentences in the following ways:

NOT   These over-exposed pictures are the **bestest** mistake that we ever made.

Correct: These over-exposed pictures are the **best** mistake that we ever made.

NOT   The drought got **more worse** with each dry day.

Correct: The drought got **worse** with each dry day.

REVIEWING *Good* AND *Bad*

What are the three forms of good?

_____good_____   _____better_____   _____best_____

What are the three forms of **bad?**

_____ bad _____   _____ worse _____   _____ worst _____

🏶 Practice 16 Identifying   Put a C next to underlined forms of *good* and *bad* in the following sentences that are correct.

1. _____ That was the <u>bestest</u> pie you have ever made. *(best)*

2. __C__ I need a <u>better</u> grade on this test to pass the class.

3. _____ Professional wrestling is the <u>most worst</u> sport anyone could have invented. *(worst)*

4. __C__ Washing the dog inside the house was a <u>bad</u> decision.

5. _____ Our trip to Tulsa was the <u>most best</u> vacation we have ever taken.

6. _(best)_____ I like the pink paint <u>more better</u> than the blue paint. *(better)*

7. __C__ Megan did a <u>good</u> job on her oral presentation.

8. _____ The boys' attitudes are <u>more good</u> than the girls'. *(better)*

9. __C__ My stomachache is worse than it was 20 minutes ago.

10. __C__ Our cats have taken the <u>best</u> seats in the house.

🏶 Practice 17 Identifying   Underline the incorrect adjective form in each of the following sentences.

1. This was the <u>most bad</u> day of my life. *(worst)*

2. That's the <u>bestest</u> decision I have heard so far. *(best)*

3. I liked the movie, but I thought the ending could have been better.

4. After standing out in the rain, Charity's cold got <u>worser</u>. *(worse)*

5. Carmenita likes take-and-bake pizza better than delivery.

7. I ate at the best Mediterranean restaurant in town.

8. Lee was surfing the Internet to find the <u>most best</u> deal on a Chevy Blazer. *(best)*

9. My cats always behave <u>more good</u> than my dogs. *(better)*

10. Of all my friends, Jameson has the worse handwriting.

🌿 **Practice 18 Correcting**   Correct the five adjective errors in Practice 16 and the five adjective errors in Practice 17 by rewriting each incorrect sentence. *See Practices 16 and 17.*

_____

_____

_____

_____

_____

_____

_____

_____

_____

🌿 **Practice 19 Completing**   Fill in each blank in the following paragraph with the correct form of *good* and *bad*.

Last Tuesday, I was having a really (1) _____bad_____ day. I was late to work, which made my boss think that I was the (2) _____worst_____ employee he has. While I was on my lunch break, my car broke down, and the mechanic said I had a (3) _____bad_____ transmission. To make matters (4) _____worse_____, he said it would cost $500 to replace it. I had to borrow my (5) _____best_____ friend's bicycle to get home, and then I got a ticket for not wearing a helmet. I honestly thought that day was never going to get (6) _____better_____. When I finally got home, I checked my mail and found some (7) _____good_____ news. There was a card from my grandma with a $20 bill inside, thanking me for being the (8) _____best_____ granddaughter she has. (I happen to be the *only* granddaughter she has, but that's another story.) Grandma wished me a (9) _____good_____ day and reminded me to call her. At that point, I realized that I am very lucky to have someone who wants to talk to me, even when I have nothing (10) _____*good*_____ to talk about.

❧ Practice 20 Writing Your Own

A. Write a sentence of your own using the following forms of *good* and *bad*.
Answers will vary.

1. good _____

2. better _____

3. worse _____

4. bad _____

5. best _____

B. Write five sentences of your own using forms of *good* and *bad*, and underline these forms. *Answers will vary.*

1. _____

2. _____

3. _____

4. _____

5. _____

CHAPTER REVIEW

You might want to reread your answers to the questions in the review boxes before you do the following exercises.

❧ Review Practice 1 Reading   Refer to the paragraph by Rebecca Zurier on page 283 to do the following exercises.

1. List five adjectives. *Answers will vary.*

_____

_____

_____

_____

_____

2. Provide the comparative and superlative forms of each of the following adjectives from Zurier's paragraph.

Basic	Comparative	Superlative
lavish	more/less lavish	most/least lavish
plain	plainer	plainest
accessible	more/less accessible	most/least accessible
large	larger	largest
flamboyant	more/less flamboyant	most/least flamboyant

❈ **Review Practice 2 Identifying**   Underline the incorrect adjectives in each of the following sentences.

1. The <u>bestest</u> job I ever had was at Mike's Pizza. *(best)*

2. Tiffany was <u>more lazier</u> than Sally was today. *(lazier)*

3. The <u>most biggest</u> flag flies over the gas station. *(biggest)*

4. Of the two boys, John was the <u>tallest</u>. *(taller)*

5. When Cheyenne got engaged, she couldn't have been <u>more happier</u>. *(happier)*

6. Yesterday I felt lousy, but today I feel <u>worser</u>. *(worse)*

7. We have big rats in our attic, and they're the <u>most ugliest</u> things I've ever seen. *(ugliest)*

8. There are 12 pine trees on our street, and the <u>taller</u> one is in our front yard. *(tallest)*

9. Your first essay was good, but this is even <u>more good</u>. *(better)*

10. The bananas on the counter are <u>more riper</u> today. *(riper)*

❈ **Review Practice 3 Correcting**   Correct the incorrect adjectives in Review Practice 2 by rewriting the sentences. *See Review Practice 2.*

✎ EDITING A STUDENT PARAGRAPH

Following is a paragraph written and revised by Brady Johnson in response to the writing assignment in this chapter. Read the paragraph, and underline each of his adjectives. Look specifically for comparative and superlative adjectives.

Here are the corrected adjectives:
better
thinner
longer
easiest

One thing that I have always wanted to invent is an automatic vacuum for the house. It would be like the ones used in swimming pools, only more better. Since my parents started making me vacuum our house five years ago, it has been my least favorite chore. I hate dragging the heavy vacuum up and down the stairs, and the cord is never long enough. If I could invent an automatic vacuum, it would have a more thinner body, so it could go easily down the halls. It would also have a more longer cord and more powerful suction. A person could just turn it on and let it go. Of course, it would suck up anything in its path, so a person would have to be more careful about what was left on the ground. Overall, though, I think it would make vacuuming the most easiest task.

Collaborative Activity

Team up with a partner, and mark an X above the four adjectives that are not in the correct form. Then, working together, use what you have learned in this chapter to correct these errors. *See student paragraph for errors. Corrections will vary.*

🌿 EDITING YOUR OWN PARAGRAPH

Now return to the paragraph you wrote and revised at the beginning of this chapter. Underline each of your adjectives.

Collaborative Activity

Exchange paragraphs with your partner, and circle any adjective errors that you find in your partner's paragraph. Check specifically the comparative and superlative adjectives.

Individual Activity

On the Error Log in Appendix 6, record any adjective errors that your partner found in your paragraph. To complete the writing process, correct these errors by rewriting your paragraph.

Adverbs

🖉 Checklist for Using Adverbs

✔ Are all adverbs that show comparison used correctly?

✔ Are *good/well* and *bad/badly* used correctly?

TEACHING ADVERBS
Choose a student, and
give him or her oral
directions, like "walk to
the other side of the
room." The student
should follow the
directions.

Next, add an adverb
to the sentence, and
have the student again
follow directions ("walk
slowly to the other side
of the room").

Continue changing or
adding more adverbs to
the directions so that
students can see how
adverbs can affect the
meaning of a sentence.
Don't forget to add nega-
tive as well as positive
words to remind stu-
dents of the full range of
adverbs ("do *not* walk to
the other side of the
room").

■ For more sample sen-
tences, see the *Instruc-
tor's Resource Manual*,
Section II, Part II.

Like adjectives, adverbs help us communicate more clearly (she walked *quickly*) and more vividly (he sat *comfortably*). They make their sentences more interesting.

See how the adverbs work in the following paragraphs by Russell Baker.

> Scientists have been struck by the fact that things that break down virtually never get lost, while things that get lost hardly ever break down.
>
> A furnace, for example, will invariably break down at the depth of the first winter cold wave, but it will never get lost. A woman's purse, which after all does have some inherent capacity for breaking down, hardly ever does; it almost invariably chooses to get lost.
>
> Some persons believe this constitutes evidence that inanimate objects are not entirely hostile to man and that negotiated peace is possible. After all, they point out, a furnace could infuriate a man even more thoroughly by getting lost than by breaking down, just as a glove could upset him far more by breaking down than by getting lost.

In this paragraph, Russell Baker points out that inanimate objects can let you down when you least expect it. Before continuing in this chapter, take a moment to write about an unexpected experience you have had. Save your work because you will use it later in the chapter.

Writing Assignment: The Unexpected

Unexpected events happen in life all the time—especially with inanimate objects. What unexpected experiences have you had? Who or what was involved? How did you handle the unexpected element? Write a paragraph explaining a particular event that comes to your mind.

Revising Your Writing

Revise the first draft of your paragraph before you focus on editing. Use the Revising Checklist on pages 24–25 to help you with your revision. Make sure your paragraph has a good topic sentence, is well developed, and is well organized. Then check your paragraph for unity and coherence.

USING ADVERBS

Adverbs modify verbs, adjectives, and other adverbs. They answer the questions *how? when? where? how often?* and *to what extent?* Look at the following examples.

How:	The air bag inflated **rapidly** during the accident.
When:	My car **always** breaks down when I have an important date.
Where:	Don't park your car **there.**
How often:	Maggie drives to Los Angeles **weekly.**
To what extent:	Traffic is **extremely** heavy on the weekends.

Some words are always adverbs, including *here, there, not, never, now, again, almost, often,* and *well.*

Other adverbs are formed by adding *-ly* to an adjective:

Adjective	Adverb
light	lightly
loud	loudly
busy	busily

HINT: Not all words that end in *-ly* are adverbs. Some, such as *friendly*, *early*, *lonely*, *chilly*, and *lively*, are adjectives.

REVIEWING ADVERBS

What are adverbs?

Adverbs modify verbs, adjectives, and other adverbs.

What five questions do adverbs answer?

How?   When?   Where?   How often?   To what extent?

List four words that are always adverbs.

Answers will vary.

How do many adverbs end?

In -ly

🌱 **Practice 1 Identifying**   Underline the adverbs in each of the following sentences.

1. He spoke <u>rudely</u> to me.
2. We are meeting <u>promptly</u> at 5:00 p.m.
3. Do you come to this park <u>often</u>?
4. I think I left my wallet <u>there</u>.
5. Blake decided to hold fund-raisers <u>monthly</u>.
6. Jose is <u>very</u> excited about his wife's pregnancy.
7. He did <u>not</u> attend class <u>today</u>.
8. I was <u>late</u> to my dentist's appointment.
9. The snow is falling <u>lightly</u> on the ground.
10. Roosevelt <u>proudly</u> displayed his art in the gallery.

🌱 **Practice 2 Identifying**   Put an X next to the sentence if the underlined word is not an adverb.

1. _____ I spoke <u>quietly</u> to my friend in class.

2. __X__ My girlfriend sent me <u>lovely</u> flowers on my birthday. *(no adverb)*

3. __X__ <u>Rock</u> the baby gently. *(gently)*

4. _____ Will you be able to help me <u>now</u>?

5. _____ Grace is <u>very</u> happy about her new job.

6. __X__ The CD is permanently <u>stuck</u> in the computer. *(permanently)*

7. __X__ My books got very <u>wet</u> in the rain. *(very)*

8. _____ Jason learned to type <u>quickly</u>.

9. _____ I will not make that mistake <u>again</u>.

10. __X__ Luis receives a <u>salary</u> bonus annually. *(annually)*

❧ Practice 3 Correcting   Correct the errors in Practice 2 by listing the correct adverbs here. *See Practice 2.*

1. _____   6. _____

2. _____   7. _____

3. _____   8. _____

4. _____   9. _____

5. _____   10. _____

❧ Practice 4 Completing   Fill in each blank in the following paragraph with an adverb. *Answers will vary.*

One day, I (1) _____ volunteered to take my two friends home from school. The rain was falling (2) _____ on the ground, so we ran (3) _____ to my car. It was parked on the far side of the parking lot, and I could (4) _____ remember where it was. I (5) _____ pulled out my keys, and we (6) _____ jumped inside. After we had driven around the corner, my friend (7) _____ remembered that she had (8) _____ forgotten to pick up her financial aid check. She said she (9) _____ needed the

money, and she (10) _____ begged me to go back to campus. I
(11) _____ gave in, and we turned the car around.

🌱 Practice 5 Writing Your Own

A. Write a sentence of your own for each of the following adverbs. *Answers will vary.*

1. wildly _____

2. honestly _____

3. almost _____

4. kindly _____

5. never _____

B. Write five sentences of your own, and underline the adverbs in each. *Answers will vary.*

1. _____

2. _____

3. _____

4. _____

5. _____

COMPARING WITH ADVERBS

Like adjectives, most adverbs have three forms: a **basic** form, a **comparative** form (used to compare two items), and a **superlative** form (used to compare three or more items).

For positive comparisons, adverbs form the comparative and superlative forms in two different ways:

1. **For one-syllable adverbs, use *-er* to compare two items and *-est* to compare three or more items.**

Basic	Comparative (used to compare two items)	Superlative (used to compare three or more items)
soon	sooner	soonest
fast	faster	fastest

2. **For adverbs of two or more syllables, use *more* to compare two items and *most* to compare three or more items.**

Basic	Comparative (used to compare two items)	Superlative (used to compare three or more items)
quickly	more quickly	most quickly
gently	more gently	most gently
easily	more easily	most easily

For negative comparisons, adverbs, like adjectives, use *less* to compare two items and *least* to compare three or more items.

Basic	Comparative (used to compare two items)	Superlative (used to compare three or more items)
quickly	less quickly	least quickly
gently	less gently	least gently
easily	less easily	least easily

HINT: Like adjectives, certain adverbs are not usually compared. Something cannot last "*more* eternally" or work "*more* invisibly." The following adverbs cannot logically be compared.

endlessly	eternally	infinitely
equally	impossibly	invisibly

REVIEWING ADVERB FORMS

When do you use the comparative form of an adverb?

To compare two items

When do you use the superlative form of an adverb?

To compare three or more items

How do one-syllable adverbs form the comparative and superlative in positive comparisons?

Add -er for the comparative and -est for the superlative.

How do adverbs of two or more syllables form the comparative and superlative in positive comparisons?

With more and most.

How do you form negative comparisons with adverbs?

With less and least.

Practice 6 Identifying Identify the underlined adverbs in the following sentences as basic (B), comparative (C), or superlative (S).

1. B The swimmer dived gracefully into the water.
2. C That new teacher treated us less fairly than Mrs. Wright did.
3. B The boys danced wildly on the stage.
4. B The trick-or-treaters were knocking loudly on my door.
5. S She is the most completely prepared student in the class.
6. B This newsletter is published weekly by our fraternity.
7. C I have been visiting you less often because I have no transportation to your house.
8. C My essay was more hastily written than yours was.
9. B Greta never asked me for my opinion.
10. B You are hardly ever working.

Practice 7 Identifying Underline the adverbs in each of the following sentences.

1. The river is flowing less swiftly than usual. *(more swifitly)*
2. I use the library more frequently than my roommate. *(less frequently)*
3. I like to go shopping there.
4. I was absent less often than my friend. *(more often)*
5. I am taking that class again.
6. We were both upset about the service, but Cammy spoke more angrily to the waitress. *(less angrily)*
7. They are most likely to be at the dance. *(least likely)*

8. Rachel walked <u>less gracefully</u> after her knee surgery. *(more gracefully)*

9. The other actors were brave, but I said my lines <u>more timidly</u>.
(less timidly)

10. Of all the children in day care, my son was screaming the <u>loudest</u>.
(softest)

🌾 **Practice 8 Correcting** Change the positive comparisons in Practice 7 to negative and the negative comparisons to positive. *See Practice 7.*

1. _____

2. _____

3. _____

4. _____

5. _____

6. _____

7. _____

8. _____

9. _____

10. _____

🌾 **Practice 9 Completing** Fill in each blank in the following paragraph with the correct comparative or superlative form of the adverb in parentheses.

I was 15 pounds overweight last summer because I had been eating (1) _*more foolishly*_ (foolishly) than usual. I was also exercising (2) _*less regularly*_ (regularly) because I had taken on a second job. My friend introduced me to a new diet that was the (3) _*most sensibly*_ (sensibly) organized one I had ever heard of. According to this diet, breakfast and lunch would be (4) _*more strictly*_ (strictly) planned than dinner. I could eat a piece of fruit or a bagel, but I couldn't snack between meals. I didn't really like the food options I had, but I was (5) _*more seriously*_ (seriously) worried that a piece of fruit wouldn't be enough to satisfy my appetite. Snacking between meals was my biggest problem, and I was (6) _*more often*_ (often) visiting the snack machine at work than the water fountain. In fact, that scenario had to be completely reversed. I had to drink lots and lots of water, which meant that I made visits to the bathroom (7) ___more frequently___ (frequently) than I ever had before. My co-workers cracked jokes about my trips to the bathroom, but the one who was (8) ___most genuinely___ (genuinely) supportive was Bill. Apparently, Bill wanted to start a diet too, and he was (9) ___more honestly___ (honestly) interested in the success of my weight loss than in the side effects of drinking so much water. When I eventually lost the 15 pounds, Bill hugged and congratulated me, but even (10) ___more importantly___ (importantly), he said that I looked great.

Practice 10 Writing Your Own

A. Write a sentence of your own for each of the following adverb forms.
Answers will vary.

1. the superlative form of *sweetly* ____________________
2. the positive form of *wisely* ____________________
3. the comparative form of *patiently* ____________________
4. the superlative form of *harshly* ____________________
5. the comparative form of *boldly* ____________________

B. Write five sentences of your own, and underline the adverbs in each sentence. *Answers will vary.*

1. ____________________
2. ____________________
3. ____________________
4. ____________________
5. ____________________

ADJECTIVE OR ADVERB?

One of the most common errors with modifiers is using an adjective when an adverb is called for. Keep in mind that adjectives modify nouns and pronouns, whereas adverbs modify verbs, adjectives, and other adverbs. Adverbs do *not* modify nouns or pronouns. Here are some examples.

NOT   She fastened the seat belt **tight.** [adjective]

Correct: She fastened the seat belt **tightly.** [adverb]

NOT   We were **real** frightened after the accident. [adjective]

Correct: We were **really** frightened after the accident. [adverb]

REVIEWING THE DIFFERENCE BETWEEN
ADJECTIVES AND ADVERBS

How do you know whether to use an adjective or an adverb in a sentence?

Adjectives modify nouns and pronouns. Adverbs modify verbs, adjectives, and other

adverbs.

Give an example of an adverb in a sentence.

Examples will vary.

Give an example of an adjective in a sentence.

Examples will vary.

Practice 11 Identifying   Put a C next to the sentence if the underlined word is correct.

1. _____ Handle the antiques <u>gentle</u> so they don't break. *(gently)*

2. _____ Talk to your teacher <u>nice</u>, and he'll be more willing to work with you. *(nicely)*

3. __C__ I washed my windows, and now I can see <u>clearly</u> through them.

4. _____ Polly was <u>real</u> worried about the midterm. *(really)*

5. __C__ The baby crawled <u>quickly</u> across the floor.

6. __C__ We <u>busily</u> worked until midnight.

7. _____ The laptop was <u>real</u> expensive when we bought it. *(really)*

8. __C__ He sat <u>lazily</u> on the sofa all day.

9. _____ Shannon drove <u>slow</u> during her driving test. *(slowly)*

10. _____ We painted the room <u>colorful</u> to create a cheery atmosphere.
   (colorfully)

⚘ Practice 12 Identifying   Underline the incorrect adverb form in each of the following sentences.

1. You tied your shoelaces too <u>loose</u>, and your shoes are falling off your feet. *(loosely)*
2. I set up my computer <u>real</u> quickly, and I think I missed something. *(really)*
3. She peeked quietly in the room where the baby was sleeping.
4. We sat sleepily in our chairs.
5. When we left the party, we told Joe that we had a really good time.
6. Run <u>quick</u> to the phone to call the police! *(quickly)*
7. If you want the best deal, you have to shop <u>wise</u>. *(wisely)*
8. Tina wants to go so <u>bad</u>, but she doesn't have enough money. *(badly)*
9. He signed his name sloppily on the paper.
10. If you had built the cabinet properly, it wouldn't be falling apart.

⚘ Practice 13 Correcting   Correct the five adverb errors in Practice 11 and the five adverb errors in Practice 12 by rewriting each incorrect sentence. *See Practices 11 and 12.*

_____

_____

_____

_____

_____

_____

_____

_____

_____

_____

⚘ Practice 14 Completing   Fill in each blank in the following paragraph with the correct form of the adverb in parentheses.

I (1) _____*recently*_____ (recent/recently) discovered that I am not very good at interior decorating. I had been watching a special on the Home

Improvement channel, and I saw this (2) _____really_____ (real/really) neat way to paint a wall. It's called woodgraining, and it looked very easy when the experts did it on TV. They painted the wall a dark brown and then went over it (3) _____slowly_____ (slow/slowly) with a special brush, which gave the wall a woodgrain effect. The brush has ridges in it that catch the paint and drag it (4) _____carefully_____ (careful/carefully) into lines. I just knew my dining room would look great with this paint technique, so I drove (5) _____quickly_____ (quick/quickly) to the hardware store and bought the necessary supplies. As I began the project, I (6) _____suddenly_____ (sudden/suddenly) realized that it was going to take longer than I (7) _____originally_____ (original/originally) expected. I had no idea how to control the brush, and I was (8) _____soon_____ (soon/soonly) becoming frustrated. I practiced and practiced, and it looked better (9) _____eventually_____ (eventual/eventually), but it was not (10) _____nearly_____ (near/nearly) as beautiful as the wall the experts painted. Next time, I'm hiring a professional.

✤ Practice 15 Writing Your Own

A. Write a sentence of your own using each of the following adverbs correctly. *Answers will vary.*

1. really _____
2. faithfully _____
3. poorly _____
4. happily _____
5. amazingly _____

B. Write five sentences of your own, and underline the adverbs in each sentence. *Answers will vary.*

1. _____
2. _____
3. _____

4. _____

5. _____

DOUBLE NEGATIVES

Another problem that involves adverbs is the **double negative**—using two negative words in one clause. Examples of negative words include *no, not, never, none, nothing, neither, nowhere, nobody, barely,* and *hardly.* A double negative creates the opposite meaning of what is intended.

Double Negative: I **never** had **no** seat belts in my car.

(The actual meaning is "I did have seat belts in my car.")

Correction: I **never** had seat belts in my car.

Double Negative: My brother does**n't** wear seat belts **nowhere.**

(The actual meaning is "My brother wears seat belts somewhere.")

Correction: My brother does**n't** wear seat belts **anywhere.**

Double negatives often occur with contractions.

Double Negative: There are**n't hardly** any cars in the parking lot.

(The actual meaning is "There are quite a few cars in the parking lot.")

Correction: There are **hardly** any cars in the parking lot.

Using two negatives is confusing and grammatically wrong. Be on the lookout for negative words, and use only one per clause.

REVIEWING DOUBLE NEGATIVES

What is a double negative?

Using two negative words in one sentence

List five negative words. *Answers will vary.*

_____   _____   _____   _____   _____

Why should you avoid double negatives?

They convey the opposite meaning of what is intended.

❊ **Practice 16 Identifying**   Put a C next to the sentence if the underlined negative expression is correct.

1. _____ I <u>don't never</u> want to see you again.

2. __C__ This is <u>not</u> a good idea.

3. __C__ <u>Aren't</u> you <u>ever</u> going home?

4. _____ Ada <u>couldn't hardly</u> concentrate on the test.

5. __C__ We <u>never</u> see Grandpa anymore.

6. __C__ My mother <u>wasn't anywhere</u> to be found.

7. _____ I thought my car battery was dead, but there <u>wasn't nothing</u> wrong with it.

8. _____ We <u>didn't</u> see <u>nobody</u> at the game.

9. __C__ The alarm went off, but there was <u>no</u> evidence of a burglary.

10. __C__ <u>Neither</u> of us wanted to be here.

❊ **Practice 17 Identifying**   Underline the incorrect negatives in the following sentences.

1. Nobody was <u>never</u> attending the meetings. *(ever)*

2. There <u>isn't</u> nowhere I'd rather be than here with you. *(is)*

3. My best friend <u>isn't</u> barely one month younger than I am. *(is)*

4. I didn't have <u>no</u> choice. *(any)*

5. Lara is nice, but she <u>isn't</u> no saint. *(is)*

6. Ramell can't get out of bed <u>no</u> more. *(any)*

7. Nobody left me <u>no</u> food in this house. *(any)*

8. The phone rang for ten minutes, but there <u>wasn't</u> no answer. *(was)*

9. I didn't want a date for the Christmas party, and I didn't go with <u>nobody</u>. *(anybody)*

10. That fish <u>isn't</u> hardly cooked. *(is)*

❊ **Practice 18 Correcting**   Correct the negative errors in Practice 17 by rewriting the incorrect sentences. *See Practice 17.*

1. _____

2. _____

3. _____

4. _____

5. _____

6. _____

7. _____

8. _____

9. _____

10. _____

✿ Practice 19 Completing   Fill in each blank in the following paragraph with the correct negative adverb in parentheses.

Caring for a puppy is (1) _____*hardly*_____ (hardly/not hardly) as easy as it looks. Puppies require lots of attention, and many dog owners complain that they do (2) _____*not ever*_____ (not ever/not never) have enough time to spend with their pets. It is especially important to remember that puppies need lots of training, and if they (3) _____*aren't ever*_____ (aren't never/aren't ever) given the training when they're young, they (4) _____*won't ever*_____ (won't ever/won't never) be well behaved when they get older. Also, puppies have a great deal of energy. There (5) _____*isn't anything*_____ (isn't anything/isn't nothing) they won't chew on or tear up if they get a chance. It doesn't seem to matter (6) _____*any*_____ (none/any) whether the puppy is male or female, because all puppies share those personality traits. Nonetheless, I can't think of (7) _____*anyone*_____ (anyone/no one) who couldn't benefit from a puppy's unconditional love. I haven't (8) _____*any*_____ (no/any) doubt that this is the reason people keep adopting puppies into their homes. People wouldn't (9) _____*ever*_____ (ever/never) take on the trouble of raising a dog if it wasn't so darn cute. And there isn't (10) _____*anything*_____ (anything/nothing) that compares to the feeling a person gets after being licked in the face by such a faithful friend.

❋ Practice 20 Writing Your Own

A. Write a sentence of your own using the following negative adverbs correctly. *Answers will vary.*

1. never _____

2. nobody _____

3. nowhere _____

4. barely _____

5. none _____

B. Write five sentences of your own using negative adverbs, and underline the adverbs in each sentence. *Answers will vary.*

1. _____

2. _____

3. _____

4. _____

5. _____

USING *GOOD/WELL* AND *BAD/BADLY* CORRECTLY

The pairs *good/well* and *bad/badly* are so frequently misused that they deserve special attention.

   Good is an adjective; *well* is an adverb. Use *good* with a noun (n) or after a linking verb (lv).

                                                                    n
Adjective: Wearing your seat belt is a **good** idea.

                          lv
Adjective: He looks **good.**

Use *well* for someone's health or after an action verb (av).

                          lv
Adverb: She is **well** again. [health]

                                av
Adverb: The car drives **well** since we changed the oil.

Bad is an adjective; *badly* is an adverb. Use *bad* with a noun (n) or after a linking verb (lv). Always use *bad* after *feel* if you are talking about emotions.

Adjective: n
He uses **bad** language.

Adjective: lv
I feel **bad** that I got a ticket.

Use *badly* with an adjective (adj) or after an action verb (av).

Adverb: adj
The car was **badly** damaged.

Adverb: av
He drives **badly.**

REVIEWING *Good/Well* AND *Bad/Badly*

When should you use the adjective good?

With a noun or after a linking verb

When should you use the adverb well?

For someone's health, after an action verb, or after feel for emotions

When should you use the adjective bad?

With a noun or after a linking verb

When should you use the adverb badly?

With an adjective or after an action verb

🌿 Practice 21 Identifying   Put a C next to the sentence if the underlined words are correct.

1. _____ He drives <u>bad</u> when he's upset.

2. __C__ You did a <u>good</u> job on that exam.

3. __C__ Kelly handled the awkward situation <u>well</u>.

4. __C__ I wanted to go to the movie <u>badly</u>, but I had to study.

5. _____ Jerome felt <u>well</u> about his performance last night.

6. __C__ The basketball team played <u>badly</u> in the big tournament.

7. _____ You've been sick, but now you're <u>good</u> again.

8. __C__ This is a <u>bad</u> situation.

9. __C__ Patty is doing <u>well</u> in rehearsals.

10. __C__ If I finish this project, I will feel <u>good</u> about myself.

Practice 22 Identifying   Underline the incorrect forms of *good, well, bad,* and *badly* in the following sentences.

1. If you do your job <u>good</u>, you'll probably get a raise. *(well)*

2. Tammy felt <u>well</u> about her decision. *(good)*

3. The police are often portrayed <u>bad</u> in movies. *(badly)*

4. She spoke <u>bad</u> about her parents. *(badly)*

5. Gabby was in the hospital for pneumonia, but now she is <u>good</u> again. *(well)*

6. Diane's pregnancy is going <u>bad</u>, and she has been very sick. *(badly)*

7. We feel <u>badly</u> that you can't come to our housewarming party. *(bad)*

8. Do you know that girl very <u>good</u>? *(well)*

9. I know you like Tyrone, but I think his attitude is <u>badly</u>. *(bad)*

10. Jackie is learning what sports she can play <u>good</u>. *(well)*

Practice 23 Correcting   Correct the adjective and adverb errors in Practice 22 by rewriting each incorrect sentence. *See Practice 22.*

1. _____
2. _____
3. _____
4. _____
5. _____
6. _____
7. _____

8. _____

9. _____

10. _____

❋ **Practice 24 Completing**   Fill in each blank in the following paragraph with the correct word in parentheses.

James wanted so (1) ____*badly*____ (bad/badly) to make the baseball team, he practiced long and hard all summer. When school started in the fall, he went to a really (2) ____*good*____ (good/well) baseball camp, and he spent eight weeks training with the best coaches in town. He became very (3) ____*good*____ (good/well) at pitching, and he could hit home runs (4) ____*well*____ (good/well) too. Practice finally began for baseball. James was early to every practice and tried his best, but he was so nervous that sometimes he handled the ball (5) ____*badly*____ (bad/badly). He couldn't throw the ball as (6) ____*well*____ (good/well) and was having trouble pitching fastballs. He didn't look (7) ____*good*____ (good/well) swinging the bat either. It was like something had invaded his body just to make him look (8) ____*bad*____ (bad/badly) in front of everyone. He felt so (9) ____*badly*____ (bad/badly) about his performance at practice that he made even more errors. Finally, his coach took him aside and told him to relax. He spent the weekend calming down and concentrating, and the following week he was a (10) ____*good*____ (good/well) baseball player again.

❋ **Practice 25 Writing Your Own**

A. Write a sentence of your own using the following words correctly. *Answers will vary.*

1. good _____

2. badly _____

3. well _____

4. bad _____

5. good _____

B. Write five sentences of your own using adverbs, and underline the adverbs in each sentence. *Answers will vary.*

1. _____

2. _____

3. _____

4. _____

5. _____

CHAPTER REVIEW

You might want to reread your answers to the questions in the review boxes before you do the following exercises.

Review Practice 1 Reading   Refer to the paragraphs by Russell Baker on page 302 to do the following exercises.

1. List five adverbs. *Answers will vary.*

   _____

   _____

   _____

   _____

   _____

2. Provide the comparative and superlative forms of the following adverbs from Baker's paragraphs.

Basic	Comparative	Superlative
entirely	*more entirely*	*most entirely*
thoroughly	*more thoroughly*	*most thoroughly*

3. Provide the adverb forms of the following adjectives from the model paragraphs on page 302.

Adjective	Adverb
cold	*coldly*
inherent	*inherently*

※ **Review Practice 2 Identifying**   Underline the incorrect adverb forms in the following sentences.

1. Hold on <u>tight</u> to this rope! *(tightly)*

2. I thought you did really <u>good</u> in the play. *(well)*

3. Becky made a <u>real</u> bad mistake. *(really)*

4. The groom stood <u>proud</u> at the altar, watching his bride. *(proudly)*

5. My father doesn't show me <u>no</u> respect. *(any)*

6. This soup tastes <u>badly</u>. *(bad)*

7. Listen <u>quiet</u> to the CD because I'm trying to study. *(quietly)*

8. The Rodriguez family never go <u>nowhere</u> without their dog. *(anywhere)*

9. I didn't do <u>nothing</u> to hurt you. *(anything)*

10. You drive so <u>bad</u> that other drivers are afraid of you. *(badly)*

※ **Review Practice 3 Correcting**   Correct the adverb errors in Review Practice 2 by rewriting the sentences. *See Review Practice 2.*

✎ EDITING A STUDENT PARAGRAPH

Following is a paragraph written and revised by Manuel Astonomo in response to the writing assignment in this chapter. Read the paragraph, and underline each of his adverbs.

Here are the corrected adverbs:

really

didn't have any or had no

proudly

slowly

hadn't ever or had never

awfully

I will <u>never</u> forget the day I received my driver's license. I thought I was <u>real</u> important, and I <u>honestly</u> thought I could conquer the world. Though I <u>didn't have no</u> driving experience, I convinced my parents to let me take their new convertible for a joy ride. They were reluctant at first, but they <u>most generously</u> agreed to my foolish request. I <u>immediately</u> drove to my best friend's house, and we <u>eventually</u> found three other guys. We then drove prou̇d to the burger place where students <u>often</u> gather. After visiting with some cute girls for about an hour, we decided to leave and see a movie. However, as I was backing slȯw out of my parking spot, I bumped into a post. I <u>couldn't</u> believe it! I <u>hadn't never</u> seen that post <u>before</u>, and I know I looked behind me when I put the car in reverse. Well, there was <u>only</u> minor damage to the bumper, but I knew my parents would be aẇful upset. With that in mind, we decided to see the movie and deal with the parents <u>later</u>.

Collaborative Activity

Team up with a partner and mark an X above the four adverb errors in Manuel's paragraph. Underline the two double negatives twice. Then, working together, use what you have learned in this chapter to correct these errors. Rewrite the paragraph with your corrections. *See student paragraph for errors. Corrections are in the margin.*

❧ EDITING YOUR OWN PARAGRAPH

Now return to the paragraph you wrote and revised at the beginning of this chapter. Underline each of your adverbs.

Collaborative Activity

Exchange paragraphs with your partner, and circle any adverb errors that you find in your partner's paragraph. Underline any double negatives twice.

Individual Activity

On the Error Log in Appendix 6, record any adverb errors that your partner found in your paragraph. To complete the writing process, correct these errors by rewriting your paragraph.

Modifier Errors

Checklist for Identifying and Correcting Modifier Problems

✔ Are modifiers as close as possible to the words they modify?

✔ Are any sentences confusing because the words that the modifiers refer to are missing?

TEACHING MODIFIER
ERRORS
Have students get out a
piece of paper and draw
pictures representing the
following sentences:
"Picking flowers, my
nose became red and
itchy," and "I chased the
dog wearing my under-
wear." Collect the pic-
tures, and point out to
the students that most of
them drew the pictures
incorrectly (most of
them will—especially for
the first example).

Explain that literally
the first sentence says
the nose was picking the
flowers and the second
says the dog was wearing
the underwear.

Showing students how
misplaced modifiers
change the meaning of
sentences can help them
identify their own modi-
fier errors.

■ For more sample sen-
tences, see the Instruc-
tor's Resource Manual,
Section II, Part II.

As you know, a modifier describes another word or group of words. Some-times, however, a modifier is too far from the words it refers to (*misplaced modifier*), or the word it refers to is missing altogether (*dangling modifier*). As a result, the sentence is confusing.

Notice how the modifiers work in the following paragraph by David Macaulay.

> Using a keyboard to control a complex computer program is awkward and slow. The advent of the mouse and icons makes a computer much easier to use and also gives programs much greater flexibility. The mouse is a controller that is moved over a mat or desktop. As it moves, electric pulses inform the computer of its exact change in position. The computer responds by shifting a cursor over the picture in the same direction as the mouse. The computer can be given commands by moving the mouse so that the cursor points to an icon, and then "clicking" its switch. The command represented by the selected icon is then carried out.

In this paragraph, David Macaulay describes how a computer mouse works. Before continuing in this chapter, take a moment to describe something that you know a great deal about. Save your work because you will use it later in the chapter.

> **Writing Assignment: How It Works**
>
> Think of something that you use every day and are very familiar with. Choose something like a guitar, a pager, or a microwave. Could you describe it to someone else? How does it work? What does a person have to do to use it? Write a paragraph describing the process of operating or using this object.

> **Revising Your Writing**
>
> Revise the first draft of your paragraph before you focus on editing. Use the Revising Checklist on pages 24–25 to help you with your revision. Make sure your paragraph has a good topic sentence, is well developed, and is well organized. Then check your paragraph for unity and coherence.

TEACHING ON THE WEB

Exploring and Discussing: Have students find various cartoons on the Web. How often do cartoonists use modifier errors to enhance the humor of their cartoons? How do modifiers change meaning? In what ways do the unclear modifiers add to the humor?

TEACHING ON THE WEB

Mosaics Web Site: To learn more about modifier errors, students can go to www.prenhall.com/ mosaics.

MISPLACED MODIFIERS

A modifier should be placed as close as possible to the word or words it modifies, but this does not always happen. A **misplaced modifier** is too far from the word or words it refers to, making the meaning of the sentence unclear. Look at these examples.

Misplaced: The gardener prunes the tree that grows in the backyard **in May.**

(Does the tree in the backyard grow only in May? Probably not. But the gardener prunes it only in May. So the modifier *in May* needs to be moved closer to the word it actually modifies.)

Correct: **In May,** the gardener prunes the tree that grows in the backyard.

Misplaced: I need to upgrade the computer in that office **that doesn't have a mouse.**

(It is the computer, not the office, that doesn't have a mouse. So the modifier *that doesn't have a mouse* needs to be moved closer to the word it modifies.)

Correct: I need to upgrade the computer **that doesn't have a mouse** in that office.

Certain modifiers that limit meaning are often misplaced, causing problems. Look at how meaning changes by moving the limiting word *only* in the following sentences:

Only Rachel plans to meet Sally for lunch at The Pepper. (No one but Rachel will meet Sally.)

Rachel **only** plans to meet Sally for lunch at The Pepper. (Rachel plans to meet her but might not show up.)

Rachel plans **only** to meet Sally for lunch at The Pepper. (Rachel plans to meet Sally for lunch and do nothing else.)

Rachel plans to meet **only** Sally for lunch at The Pepper. (Rachel plans to meet no one but Sally.)

Rachel plans to meet Sally **only** for lunch at The Pepper. (Rachel does not plan to meet for any other reason.)

Rachel plans to meet Sally for lunch **only** at The Pepper. (Rachel plans to have lunch there but no other meals.)

Rachel plans to meet Sally for lunch at The Pepper **only.** (Rachel does not plan to meet at any other place.)

Here is a list of common limiting words.

almost	hardly	merely	only
even	just	nearly	scarcely

Reviewing Misplaced Modifiers

What is a misplaced modifier?

A modifier that is not as close as possible to the word it refers to

How can you correct a misplaced modifier?

Place it as close as possible to the word or words it refers to.

Practice 1 Identifying Put a C next to the sentence if the underlined modifier is as close as possible to the words it modifies.

1. ______ The bank called me about a canceled check <u>at work</u>.
2. __C__ We drove to the farmer's market <u>on the corner</u>.
3. ______ Jermaine left his jersey on the back porch <u>for the big game</u>.

4. _____ Steve told Lisa that <u>to lose weight</u> she had no motivation.

5. __C__ The book <u>by John Steinbeck</u> is on the counter.

6. __C__ Shannon's son and my nephew are <u>on the same baseball team</u>.

7. _____ I heard a funny noise when I was in the garage <u>that sounded like a cat</u>.

8. _____ Jackie told Ryan <u>in a magazine</u> about a compatibility quiz.

9. _____ We made cookies in the kitchen <u>with lots of chocolate chips</u>.

10. __C__ Carrie waited <u>until the last minute</u> to start the project.

Practice 2 Identifying   Underline the misplaced modifiers in each of the following sentences.

1. Anne lost a filling while shopping <u>from a molar</u>.

2. I told them that we would have lunch today in the park <u>last weekend</u>.

3. <u>As a young child</u>, my parents tried not to spoil me.

4. Paul sold his bike to me after he got a new one as a present <u>for $150</u>.

5. Eunice used shampoo on her hair <u>from the beauty salon</u>.

6. The best movie ever made was *Jaws* <u>in 3D</u>.

7. Thomas told Renee that to pass the exam <u>she would be wise</u>.

8. I need to check out the book about Edgar Allen Poe <u>with the blue spine</u>.

9. The basketball team held a car wash <u>from our college</u>.

10. My diary is in the closet <u>under my collection of quarters</u>.

Practice 3 Correcting   Correct the modifier errors in Practice 2 by rewriting each incorrect sentence.

1. *While shopping, Anne lost a filling from a molar.*

2. *Last weekend, I told them that we would have lunch today in the park.*

3. *My parents tried not to spoil me as a young child.*

4. *Paul sold his bike to me for $150 after he got a new one as a present.*

5. *Eunice used shampoo from the beauty salon on her hair.*

6. *The best movie ever made in 3-D was Jaws.*

7. _Thomas told Renee that she would be wise to pass the exam._ _____

8. _I need to check out the book with the blue spine about Edgar Allen Poe._ _____

9. _The basketball team from our college held a car wash._ _____

10. _My diary is under my collection of quarters in the closet._ _____

🌿 Practice 4 Completing   Fill in each blank in the following paragraph with a modifier. Include at least two phrases. _Answers will vary._

When Stephanie was born, her parents owned a (1) _____ car that had many miles on it. They took many vacations in the car, even going (2) _____ one year. It was a dependable car, but it was very small and (3) _____. Needless to say, when Stephanie came along, her parents realized their need for (4) _____ transportation. They (5) _____ started shopping around for (6) _____ roomy vehicles that would fit her baby car seat and still have room for (7) _____. One salesman talked them into a minivan, which they initially thought was (8) _____. Eventually, they came to (9) _____ the car and found it was perfect for them. Sixteen years later, when Stephanie got her driver's license, the (10) _____ became her car, and her parents bought a new Toyota.

🌿 Practice 5 Writing Your Own

A. Write a sentence of your own for each of the following modifiers. _Answers will vary._

1. after the rain _____

2. since we arrived _____

3. while making dinner _____

4. before she saw him _____

5. though we couldn't hear it _____

B. Write five sentences of your own using modifiers correctly, and underline the modifiers in each sentence. _Answers will vary._

1. _____

2. _____

3. _____

4. _____

5. _____

DANGLING MODIFIERS

Modifiers are "dangling" when they have nothing to refer to in a sentence. **Dangling modifiers** (starting with an *-ing* word or with *to*) often appear at the beginning of a sentence. Here is an example.

> **Dangling:**   **Surfing the Internet,** my computer mouse is very helpful.

A modifier usually modifies the words closest to it. So the phrase *Surfing the Internet* modifies *my computer mouse.* But my mouse doesn't surf the Internet. In fact, there is no logical word in the sentence that the phrase modifies. It is left dangling. You can correct a dangling modifier in one of two ways—by inserting the missing word that is being referred to or by rewriting the sentence.

> **Correct:**   **Surfing the Internet, I** find my computer mouse very helpful.

> **Correct:**   **When I am surfing the Internet,** my computer mouse is very helpful.

> **Dangling:**   **To play the lottery,** a ticket must be bought.

> **Correct:**   **To play the lottery, you** must buy a ticket.

> **Correct:**   You must buy a ticket if you want **to play the lottery.**

> **Dangling:**   The bag for charity was full **after going through our old clothes.**

> **Correct:**   **After going through our old clothes, we** had a full bag for charity.

> **Correct:**   **After we went through our old clothes, we** had a full bag for charity.

> **Correct:**   The bag for charity was full **after we went through our old clothes.**

❧ Practice 6 Identifying   Put a C next to the sentence if the under-lined modifier is correct.

1. _____ To determine the winner, the contest has a panel of five judges.

2. _____ Taking a shower, the power went out in our house.

3. _C_ Waiting for the news, the man started to sweat.

4. _____ Holding the child, the cold weather made me wish I had a blanket.

5. _C_ To prevent sunburn, Tina applied sunscreen.

6. _____ Before walking the dog, the garage needed to be swept out.

7. _C_ To give up smoking, I had to get the support of my friends.

8. _C_ While walking to the bus stop, Jennifer told Aaron she would meet him after class.

9. _C_ Doing my psychology homework, I fell asleep.

10. _____ Watching television, the popcorn was falling between the sofa cushions.

❧ Practice 7 Identifying   Underline the dangling modifiers in each of the following sentences.

1. Thinking the team would never win the tournament, the calendar marked the big day.

2. To remain in this fraternity, dues must be paid.

3. While drawing in the coloring book, the crayons broke.

4. Before jumping in the pool, the diving board was very slippery.

5. To visit South America, a passport must be purchased.

6. Flying first class in the commercial jet, the seat would not recline.

7. To upgrade the computer, more memory was installed.

8. To change the oil in my car, the filter must be replaced.

9. After waiting in line for an hour, the post office worker closed her window.

10. To feed the children dinner, macaroni and cheese was prepared.

Practice 8 Correcting   Correct the modifier errors in Practice 7 by rewriting each incorrect sentence. *Answers may vary.*

1. _Thinking the team would never win the tournament, I marked the calendar for the big day._

2. _To remain in this fraternity, members must pay their dues._

3. _While drawing in the coloring book, the child broke the crayons._

4. _Before jumping in the pool, the swimmer noticed that the diving board was very slippery._

5. _A traveler must purchase a passport to visit South America._

6. _Flying first class in the commercial jet, the passenger found that the seat would not recline._

7. _I installed more memory to upgrade the computer._

8. _When I change the oil in my car, I must also replace the filter._

9. _After customers waited in line for an hour, the post office worker closed her window._

10. _To feed the children dinner, I prepared macaroni and cheese._

Practice 9 Completing   Fill in each blank in the following paragraph with a modifier. Include at least two phrases. *Answers will vary.*

(1) _____, everything at Macy's goes on sale. The salespeople run around frantically, preparing (2) _____ clothes and other items. Hundreds of (3) _____ people show up at the doors, often arriving before the store opens. Within a few hours, shoppers are (4) _____, and all of the beautifully arranged items become (5) _____. I personally witnessed one of these big sales when (6) _____. It was (7) _____ to see the number of people

fighting over everything in sight. I wondered if they really needed the items or were just (8) _____. After I made my few purchases, I left (9) _____. I was glad to be out of the confusion and back (10) _____.

❄ Practice 10 Writing Your Own

A. Write a sentence of your own for each of the following phrases. *Answers will vary.*

1. clear and sunny _____

2. taking my coat _____

3. to communicate with my parents _____

4. getting a haircut _____

5. to visit Paris _____

B. Write five sentences of your own using phrases, and underline the phrases. *Answers will vary.*

1. _____

2. _____

3. _____

4. _____

5. _____

CHAPTER REVIEW

You might want to reread your answers to the questions in the review boxes before you do the following exercises.

❄ Review Practice 1 Reading   Referring to the paragraph by David Macaulay on page 324, list 10 modifiers the author used correctly. *Answers will vary.*

_____

_____

_____

_____

_____

_____

_____

_____

_____

Review Practice 2 Identifying   Underline any misplaced or dangling modifiers in the following sentences.

1. Joanne told Sam that she would take him to dinner tonight <u>last Wednesday</u>. *(Last Wednesday, Joanne told Sam . . .)*

2. <u>Checking the time</u>, the clock said it was exactly 1:00 p.m. *(When I checked the time, the clock said . . .)*

3. <u>Fishing in the lake</u>, the boat sprang a leak. *(While we were fishing in the lake . . .)*

4. <u>To iron your shirts</u>, spray starch is needed. *(You need spray starch to iron your shirts.)*

5. My souvenirs are on the table <u>from Florida</u>. *(My souvenirs from Florida are on the table.)*

6. We made the floral arrangements from my garden <u>with lots of daffodils</u>. *(. . . the floral arrangements with lots of daffodils from my garden.)*

7. <u>To turn off the television</u>, the remote must be used. *(To turn off the television, you must use the remote.)*

8. <u>Scanning pictures from our vacation</u>, my printer broke. *(While I was scanning . . .)*

9. <u>Moving the furniture for the carpet cleaners</u>, the sofa landed on my toe. *(When I moved the furniture . . .)*

10. Peter just bought a classic Mustang from a used-car dealer <u>with white racing stripes</u>. *(. . . a classic Mustang with white racing stripes from . . .)*

Review Practice 3 Correcting   Correct the misplaced or dangling modifiers in Review Practice 2 by rewriting the sentences. *See Review Practice 2.* *Answer may vary.*

EDITING A STUDENT PARAGRAPH

Following is a paragraph written by Steven Banks in response to the writing assignment in this chapter. Read the paragraph, and underline as many modifiers as you can. Don't forget modifiers of more than one word.

Here are the corrected modifier errors:

My favorite invention is the toaster oven. The toaster with a glass door is in the kitchen. Every morning it is used to make toast and bagels. Being the oldest of four children, I find it is usually very difficult to prepare a quick breakfast for everyone. But the toaster is very helpful and easy to use. I first determine the appropriate cook time and set the dial on the chosen temperature. Opening the glass door, I place the toast or bagel on the rack inside. Then the door is shut, and the lever on the front is pressed down. After the toaster cooks for the specified time, a bell will ring to signal that the food is ready to eat. I will be moving into the dorms next quarter, and yesterday my mom promised to buy a new toaster oven for me. I just know that having a toaster oven in my dorm room will earn me a reputation as a great cook.

My <u>favorite</u> invention is the toaster oven. The toaster is in the kitchen [with a glass door]. [To make toast and bagels], <u>every</u> morning it is used. [Being the oldest of four children], it is <u>usually</u> <u>very</u> <u>difficult</u> <u>to prepare a quick breakfast for everyone</u>. But the toaster is <u>very helpful</u> and <u>easy to use</u>. [To determine the appropriate cook time], the dial must be set on the <u>chosen</u> temperature. [Opening the glass door], the rack <u>inside</u> is <u>where the toast or bagel is placed</u>. Then the door is shut, and the lever on the front is pressed <u>down</u>. [After cooking for the specified time], a bell will ring to signal that the food is <u>ready to eat</u>. I will be moving into the dorms <u>next</u> quarter, and my mom promised <u>to buy a new toaster oven for me</u> [yesterday]. I just know that <u>having a toaster oven in my dorm room</u> will earn me a reputation <u>as a great cook</u>.

Collaborative Activity

Team up with a partner, and put brackets around the seven modifier errors (five dangling modifiers and two misplaced modifiers). Then, working together, use what you have learned in this chapter to correct these errors. Rewrite the paragraph with your corrections. *See student paragraph for errors. Corrections are in the margin.*

❧ EDITING YOUR OWN PARAGRAPH

Now go back to the paragraph you wrote and revised at the beginning of this chapter, and underline as many modifiers as possible.

Collaborative Activity

Exchange paragraphs with your partner, and put brackets around the modifier errors that you find in your partner's paragraph.

Individual Activity

On the Error Log in Appendix 6, record any modifier errors that your partner found in your paragraph. To complete the writing process, correct these errors by rewriting your paragraph.

Unit 4 Review
Modifiers

🌾 **Unit Practice 1 Identifying**   In each of the following sentences, underline the adverbs and adjectives that are used incorrectly. Put brackets around any misplaced or dangling modifiers.

1. That was the <u>bestest</u> meal I have ever eaten. *(best)*

2. You did <u>good</u> on this report, so I think you'll get a pay raise. *(well)*

3. [To bake a cake] a greased pan is needed. *(To bake a cake, you need a greased pan.)*

4. Fred started shopping here because the clerks are <u>more friendlier</u> than in any other store. *(friendlier)*

5. Devon <u>couldn't never</u> understand geometry, no matter how hard he studied it. *(couldn't)*

6. [Jogging to the dock] the boat left without us. *(As we were jogging to the dock, ...)*

7. I tried <u>real</u> hard, but I just couldn't move that rock by myself. *(really)*

8. Melanie showed off her new purchase at the mall with Sarah [wearing her new jacket] *(Melanie, wearing her new jacket,)*

9. Of all the students in the class, Jade is the <u>more intelligent</u>. *(most intelligent)*

10. I left the wallet on the cafeteria table [that I got from my sister] *(I left the wallet that I got from my sister ...)*

11. Sit <u>quiet</u> so that you don't disturb anyone. *(quietly)*

12. You couldn't sing <u>more worse</u> than Toni. *(worse)*

13. [Looking under the bed] my shoes were right in front of me. *(Looking under the bed, I saw that my shoes ...)*

14. I <u>couldn't barely</u> hear what you were whispering. *(could barely)*

15. Between Sam and Luke, Sam is the <u>tallest</u>. *(taller)*

■ For additional material about teaching modifiers, for journal entries, and for various tests, see the *Instructor's Resource Manual*, Section II, Part II.

ADDITIONAL
WRITING TOPIC
Let your students expand into well-developed essays the paragraphs they wrote in one of the unit chapters.

16. She did <u>bad</u> on the test, so she wants to do an assignment for extra credit. *(badly)*

17. Having lost his job, Mike <u>didn't have nowhere</u> to go. *(didn't have anywhere)*

18. I heard the song we requested at the concert [in the car] *(In the car, I heard . . .)*

19. There are 14 houses on this block, and mine is by far the <u>bigger</u>. *(biggest)*

20. I think it would be <u>more better</u> if you sat with your family and I with mine. *(better)*

🌿 Unit Practice 2 Correcting   Correct the adjective, adverb, and modifier errors in Unit Practice 1 by rewriting each incorrect sentence. *See Unit Practice 1. Answers may vary.*

🌿 Unit Practice 3 Identifying   In the following paragraph, underline the adverbs and adjectives that are used incorrectly. Put brackets around any misplaced or dangling modifiers.

During my first year of college, I wrote for the campus newspaper [about our sports teams]. I was assigned to cover the men's basketball games, the women's swim meets, and all of the tennis matches. Needless to say, I was kept quite busy going to <u>real</u> exciting sports events. Of the three types, I thought the swim meets were <u>more fun</u>. Cheri and Julia were the two swim coaches, and they were so cooperative. The only problem I had was keeping up with the deadlines. [To get an article published in a weekly paper], a draft had to be submitted by Tuesday evening. Wednesday the editors reviewed it for corrections or changes, and Thursday it was laid out for press. This tight schedule <u>didn't leave no</u> room for procrastination; however, it made me a better writer. Because the deadlines were so strict, I had no choice but to sit down with my pen and paper. Something even <u>more better</u> was that I learned how to take good notes. [Listening for important details], my notes were very organized. I also learned how to manipulate the tone of my articles, making them sound positive even when the teams weren't doing so <u>good</u>. Writing for the paper was the <u>most toughest</u> experience I've had, but it was also the most rewarding.

🌿 Unit Practice 4 Correcting   Correct the adjective, adverb, and modifier errors in Unit Practice 3 by rewriting the paragraph. *Answers will vary.*

UNIT WRITING ASSIGNMENTS

1. Where is this scene? Imagine what kinds of animals live in this area. What is the weather like? Do people live here also? Imagine that you are camping here, and write about a typical day in this area.

2. What is your personal writing process? What do you do to prepare yourself for writing? What are your favorite prewriting techniques? What do you look for in revision? Describe your writing process from beginning to end, using as many details as possible.

3. We all have our idiosyncrasies, especially when it comes to doing everyday tasks. How do you go about doing an everyday task, such as washing laundry or driving to school? Write about the process you go through to perform this activity.

4. Describe the first major holiday that you can remember. Who was there? What happened? How did you feel? Write about the holiday using as many details as you can.

5. Create your own assignment (with the assistance of your instructor), and write a response to it.

Unit 5 Punctuation

Can you imagine streets and highways without stoplights or traffic signs? Driving would become a life-or-death adventure as motorists made risky trips with no signals to guide or protect them. Good writers, like conscientious drivers, prefer to leave little to chance. They observe the rules of punctuation to ensure that their readers arrive at their intended meaning. Without punctuation, sentences would run together, ideas would be unclear, and words would be misread. Writers need to use markers, like periods, commas, and dashes, to help them communicate as efficiently and effectively as possible.

Look at the difference punctuation makes in the meaning of the following letter.

Dear John:

I want a man who knows what love is all about. You are generous, kind, thoughtful. People who are not like you admit to being useless and inferior. You have ruined me for other men. I yearn for you. I have no feelings whatsoever when we're apart. I can be forever happy—will you let me be yours?

Susan

Dear John,

I want a man who knows what love is. All about you are generous, kind, thoughtful people, who are not like you. Admit to being useless and inferior. You have ruined me. For other men, I yearn. For you, I have no feelings whatsoever. When we're apart, I can be forever happy. Will you let me be?

Yours, Susan

As you know, punctuation is as important as the words that come between the marks. But this concept is difficult to get across to students. The "Dear John" letter in the unit introduction is an attempt to prove that together punctuation and words can help your students communicate clearly and efficiently.

This unit will help you write the love letter you actually want to write—with the punctuation that gets your message across. It will also provide you with guidelines for using the following punctuation.

End Punctuation

 Checklist for Using End Punctuation

- ✔ Does each sentence end with a period, a question mark, or an exclamation point?
- ✔ Are question marks used when asking questions?
- ✔ Do sentences that exclaim end with exclamation points?

TEACHING END
PUNCTUATION
Distribute a lively, animated paragraph with the end punctuation taken out. Read the paragraph aloud to the class to show how dull the paragraph is without the punctuation.

Then hand out the paragraph with the punctuation inserted, and ask three or four students to read the paragraph with a lot of enthusiasm. This shows students how end punctuation defines parameters, but it also demonstrates the variety with which people voice punctuation marks.

■ For sample paragraphs, see the *Instructor's Resource Manual*, Section II, Part II.

End punctuation signals the end of a sentence in three ways: The period ends a statement, the question mark signals a question, and the exclamation point marks an exclamation.

Notice how the end punctuation works in the following paragraph by Nigel Hawkes.

> On another occasion, the 66-year-old Pope threatened to have the artist physically thrown down from the scaffolding if he did not work faster. "When will it be ready?" demanded Julius. "When it is ready," replied Michelangelo shortly. The Pope flushed with anger and mimicked, "When it is ready! When it is ready!" He then raised his walking stick in rage and struck Michelangelo on the shoulder.

In this paragraph, author Nigel Hawkes describes an emotional conversation that took place between Michelangelo Buonarroti and Pope Julius II. Before continuing in this chapter, take a moment to record an emotional event in your life. Save your work because you will use it later in this chapter.

Writing Assignment: Emotions

Think of an event in your life when your emotions were raging. You might have been extremely happy, sad, excited, confused, or frustrated. What was taking place? Why was the event so emotional? Who else was involved? Write a paragraph telling about what happened and what was said. Try to remember as many details as you can.

Revising Your Writing

Revise the first draft of your paragraph before you focus on editing. Use the Revising Checklist on pages 24–25 to help you with your revision. Make sure your paragraph has a good topic sentence, is well developed, and is well organized. Then check your paragraph for unity and coherence.

TEACHING ON THE WEB

Exploring and Discussing: Have students go to on-line chat rooms and participate in a conversation. How does end punctuation play a role in these on-line conversations? How important is end punctuation to the tone of the messages?

TEACHING ON THE WEB

Mosaics Web Site: To learn more about end punctuation, students can go to www.prenhall.com/mosaics.

PERIOD

A period is used with statements, mild commands, and indirect questions.

Statement:	Michelangelo painted the Sistine Chapel.
Command:	Paint the Sistine Chapel.
Indirect Question:	I wonder if he had any help painting the Sistine Chapel.

It is also used with abbreviations and numbers:

Abbreviations:	Mrs. Baker lives at 7901 Broad St., next door to Dr. Janet Rodriguez.
Numbers:	$15.85 10.5 $659.95 .075

REVIEWING PERIODS

What are the three main uses of a period?

To mark the end of statements, mild commands, and indirect questions

What are two other uses of a period?

With abbreviations and numbers

⚘ Practice 1 Identifying   Add missing periods to each of the following sentences when necessary.

1. The geometry class is too full.
2. Dr. Hunter is my dentist.
3. I wonder if there is another piece of cake.
4. I made $250.65 at my yard sale this weekend.
5. I can't remember if I mailed that check.
6. Keep your hands to yourself.
7. Ms. Foster bought a new BMW.
8. Sales tax is now 7.25% throughout most of California.
9. Geoff didn't want to go.
10. My grandmother is selling her house on Maple St. to move to Orange Ave.

⚘ Practice 2 Identifying   Put an X next to each sentence that contains a period error.

1. __X__ I am taking the day off *(.)*
2. _____ I want to know what you are doing.
3. __X__ I can sell the chair for $1500, or about two hours of work. *($15.00)*
4. __X__ I wonder if Mr Thompson can help me. *(Mr.)*
5. __X__ Will you be at Seventh St and Pine Ave this afternoon? *(St., Ave.)*
6. __X__ My checking account has a balance of $105,90. *($105.90)*
7. _____ Dr. Edwards, please check my blood pressure.
8. __X__ Dr Ross is my math instructor. *(Dr.)*
9. _____ We need to take the trash out tonight.
10. __X__ I work for the US ambassador to Ecuador. *(U.S.)*

⚘ Practice 3 Correcting   Correct the punctuation errors in Practice 2 by rewriting each incorrect sentence. *See Practice 2.*

1. _____

2. _____

3. _____

4. _____

5. _____

6. _____

7. _____

8. _____

9. _____

10. _____

✿ Practice 4 Completing   Add periods to the following paragraph.

The woman, Mrs. Chambers, rushed into the emergency room. She was 38 weeks pregnant and going into labor. Mr. Chambers had been sitting at home while his wife ran errands. He had no idea what was going on until he received a call from St. Vincent's Hospital, telling him that his wife had been admitted. Dr. Bustamonte delivered their baby within the hour, and Mr. Chambers arrived just in time. Unfortunately, in his hurry to get to the hospital, Mr. Chambers forgot the camcorder, the camera, and even a change of clothes for his wife. But aside from those minor details, the family went home with a healthy little boy and a bill for $1,569.88.

✿ Practice 5 Writing Your Own

A. Write a sentence of your own for each of the following directions. *Answers will vary.*

1. a statement about Mr. Guerra

_____

2. an indirect question about Jefferson St.

_____

3. a statement about $934.59

_____

4. a command to do the laundry

_____

5. an indirect question about the weather

_____

B. Write five sentences of your own—two statements, two commands, and one indirect question—using periods correctly. *Answers will vary.*

1. _____
2. _____
3. _____
4. _____
5. _____

QUESTION MARK

The question mark is used after a direct question.

> **Question Mark:** What do you know about Michelangelo?
>
> **Question Mark:** "What do you know about Michelangelo?" the teacher asked.

REVIEWING QUESTION MARKS

What is the main role of a question mark?

To indicate that a question is being asked

Give an example of a question.

Examples will vary.

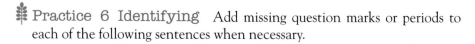 Practice 6 Identifying   Add missing question marks or periods to each of the following sentences when necessary.

1. You can sit here if you want to.

2. "Do you think this dress is too purple?" she asked.

3. I heard you remembered my birthday.

4. Is there a reason for this bill?

5. "Can you help me with my Spanish homework?" Marshall asked.

6. Marsha wondered, "What should I wear today?"

7. Why won't my Gerber daisies stay alive?

8. I wonder what his address is.

9. Is Greg still the one in charge of this program?

10. "Where will you be living?" I asked.

Practice 7 Identifying   Put an X next to each sentence that contains a question mark error.

1. ___X___ Are you kidding. (. *should be ?*)

2. ___X___ I wonder if Steve registered for this class? (? *should be .*)

3. _____ Janie asked, "What is taking so long?"

4. ___X___ This cannot happen today? (? *should be .*)

5. _____ What seems to be the problem?

6. ___X___ I can't remember if Kimo is allergic to dairy products? (? *should be .*)

7. ___X___ "Would you like something to drink?" the waitress asked? (*second ? should be .*)

8. _____ You are planning to be there, right?

9. ___X___ I can't believe you haven't cleaned this room? (? *should be .*)

10. ___X___ Tiffany asked the teacher what she meant? (? *should be .*)

Practice 8 Correcting   Correct the punctuation errors in Practice 7 by rewriting each incorrect sentence. *See Practice 7.*

1. _____

2. _____

3. _____

4. _____

5. _____

6. _____

7. _____

8. _____

9. _____

10. _____

🌱 Practice 9 Completing   Add question marks to the following paragraph.

Being a professional photographer is not a glamorous job. Sometimes I ask myself, "Why are you doing this? because it definitely isn't easy. On more than one occasion, I have had to work with uncooperative people, and I wonder silently, "Why are they here if they don't want to smile for me?Didn't they make this appointment?Didn't they call *me* for *my* services? Nonetheless, I keep taking their pictures. At least three times I've asked men, "Will you please take the toothpick out of your mouth? And they look at me as if they really think the toothpick makes them look sexy. Can you imagine how uncivilized that is?However, when I wake up each morning, I really do look forward to seeing who will come through my studio door. I've had the opportunity to capture a baby's first smile, the proud sparkle in a new bride's eye, and a grandmother's soft touch as she read to her grandson. Now, what other job could give me that for my résumé?

🌱 Practice 10 Writing Your Own

A. Write a sentence of your own for each of the following questions. *Answers will vary.*

1. a question about gardening

_____

2. a question Frank asked about his car tires

_____

3. a question about breakfast

_____

4. a question Toni asked about computer paper

_____

5. a question Matt asked about basketball

_____

B. Write five direct questions of your own, using question marks correctly.
Answers will vary.

1. _____

2. _____

3. _____

4. _____

5. _____

EXCLAMATION POINT

The exclamation point indicates strong feeling. If it is used too often, it is not as effective as it could be. You shouldn't use more than one exclamation point at a time.

> **Exclamation Point:**   Never!
> **Exclamation Point:**   I can't believe it!
> **Exclamation Point:**   That is insulting!
> **Exclamation Point:**   "That is insulting!" he said.

REVIEWING EXCLAMATION POINTS

What is the main use of an exclamation point?

To show strong emotion   _____

Give an example of an exclamation.

Examples will vary.   _____

Practice 11 Identifying   Add missing exclamation points to each of the following sentences where necessary.

1. "Not in my house!" the mother yelled.

2. Get over it!

3. "You won ten dollars!" I said in astonishment.

4. Shame on you!

5. "Two points!" he screamed.

6. Get off my foot!

7. "One more chance!" she begged.

8. Come back!

9. We made it!

10. "He finally asked me out!" she exclaimed.

❊ Practice 12 Identifying Put an X next to each sentence that contains an exclamation point error.

1. __X__ Did you tell me the truth! *(! should be ?)*

2. _____ Don't you dare!

3. _____ Yea, we won!

4. _____ "Thank God!" she said.

5. __X__ What have you been doing in here! *(! should be ?)*

6. __X__ Can you tell me how to get to New Mexico! *(! should be ?)*

7. __X__ "It's going to explode," the man shouted! *(, should be ! ; ! should be .)*

8. __X__ Mandy told the disc jockey, "My favorite artist is Whitney Houston!" *(! should be .)*

9. _____ Get off my bike!

10. __X__ "That's it," Shannon screamed! *(, should be ! ; ! should be .)*

❊ Practice 13 Correcting Correct the punctuation errors in Practice 12 by rewriting each incorrect sentence. *See Practice 12.*

1. _____

2. _____

3. _____

4. _____

5. _____

6. _____

7. _____

8. _____

9. _____

10. _____

✷ Practice 14 Completing   Add exclamation points to the following paragraph.

The last baseball game I saw was between the Texas Rangers and the Seattle Mariners during the summer of 2001. I am a big fan of the Rangers, even during their bad seasons. Posters saying "Go Rangers!" hang proudly on my bedroom walls. Sometimes I even bring them to the games. During this particular game, the Rangers were up by one run at the bottom of the ninth inning. Seattle was at bat, and there were already two outs. Doug Davis was pitching for the Rangers, and Ichiro Suzuki was at bat. "Strike him out!" I yelled from my seat, but the first pitch was a ball. "No way!" I screamed. "That's a horrible call!" Yet the next pitch was another ball. I couldn't believe it! The bases were empty, and this was looking like a victory for Texas, but Davis was going to give it away. "Throw a strike!" I shouted at the top of my lungs, and finally he did. "Two more, Davis!" I begged. Whoosh! The pitch flew by Ichiro at the speed of light, and the ump called out, "Strike!" One more pitch went out—whoosh! "Strike three!" yelled the ump, and the stands erupted in applause. Victory for the Rangers! That was one of the happiest days of my life.

✷ Practice 15 Writing Your Own

A. Write a sentence of your own for each of the following exclamations.
   Answers will vary.

1. an exclamation about cockroaches

   _____

2. an exclamation about childbirth

   _____

3. an exclamation by Terry about a broken ankle

   _____

4. an exclamation by Steve about a touchdown

   _____

5. an exclamation about bad food

   _____

B. Write five sentences of your own expressing strong feelings, using exclamation points correctly. *Answers will vary.*

1. _____

2. _____

3. _____

4. _____

5. _____

CHAPTER REVIEW

You might want to reread your answers to the questions in the review boxes
before you do the following exercises.

Review Practice 1 Reading   Refer to the paragraph by Nigel Hawkes
on page 340 to do the following exercises.

1. Rewrite the following sentence to make it an indirect question.

    "When will it be ready?" demanded Julius.

    Julius asked when it would be ready.

2. Rewrite the following statement to make it a direct question.

    He then raised his walking stick in rage and struck Michelangelo on the
    shoulder.

    Did he then raise his walking stick in rage and strike Michelangelo on the shoulder?

3. List the two uses of exclamation points.

    The Pope flushed with anger and mimicked, "When it is ready! When it is ready!"

Review Practice 2 Identifying   Underline the periods, question
marks, and exclamation points that are used incorrectly in the following
sentences.

1. Have you seen my little brother. *(. should be ?)*

2. "Go?" Marcus yelled to Chris, who was preparing to bungee-jump at the
    fairgrounds. *(? should be !)*

3. "Will you come help me paint my house!" Vernon asked. *(! should be ?)*

4. Get out of my way. *(. should be !)*

5. Can you open this jar of pickles for me_ *(. should be ?)*

6. I wonder if Tom knows his zipper is down_? *(? should be .)*

7. "Yea_?" Isabel screamed when she learned she was pregnant. *(? should be !)*

8. My porch light is burned out_? *(? should be .)*

9. "Could you repeat that_!" she asked. *(! should be ?)*

10. I can't remember where I left my wallet_? *(? should be .)*

🌱 Review Practice 3 Correcting   Correct the punctuation errors in Review Practice 2 by rewriting the incorrect sentences. *See Review Practice 2.*

🖋 EDITING A STUDENT PARAGRAPH

Following is a paragraph written and revised by Marina Jones in response to the writing assignment in this chapter. Read the paragraph, and underline each of her periods, question marks, and exclamation points.

Last summer, I belonged to a book club_. It was full of nice people, and I became good friends with many of the ones my age?|Unfortunately, the club was growing too rapidly, and soon there were too many new members_. When that happened, the structure of the club fell apart?| Instead of discussing books, the people would get together just to eat munchies and complain about things!| Soon the leaders sent out a survey, asking the club members for comments and suggestions_. I thought this would be my chance to explain how uncomfortable I was feeling!|They asked things like "What kinds of things could we do to make it a better?|club!|" and I answered all of the survey questions honestly_. What I didn't expect was that one of the club leaders took all of my answers personally, and she was suddenly very mad at me_. I was confused by her response, and I asked myself, "What could I possibly have said wrong?" She told me that my answers were sarcastic and mean_. I was shocked?| "How!|" I tried to ask her, but she kept avoiding me_. When I finally met with her, she began to cry_. "You hurt me?|" she yelled, and I was still in shock_. I apologized profusely and tried to understand, and eventually I think she forgave me_. Still, I don't think I'll be going back to that book club again_.

Here is the correct punctuation:

.

.

.

.

(no punctuation)

?

.

?

!

Collaborative Activity

Team up with a partner, and put brackets around the nine end punctuation errors in Marina's paragraph. Then, working together, use what you have learned in this chapter to correct these errors. Rewrite the paragraph with your corrections. *See student paragraph for errors. Corrections are in the margin.*

🍃 EDITING YOUR OWN PARAGRAPH

Now return to the paragraph you wrote and revised at the beginning of this chapter, and underline your periods, question marks, and exclamation points.

Collaborative Activity

Exchange paragraphs with your partner, and circle any errors in end punctuation that you find in your partner's paragraph.

Individual Activity

On the Error Log in Appendix 6, record any end punctuation errors that your partner found in your paragraph. To complete the writing process, correct these errors by rewriting your paragraph.

Commas

⬚ Checklist for Using Commas

- ✔ Are commas used to separate items in a series?
- ✔ Are commas used to set off introductory material?
- ✔ Is there a comma before *and, but, for, nor, or, so,* and *yet* when they are followed by an independent clause?
- ✔ Are commas used to set off interrupting material in a sentence?
- ✔ Are commas used to set off direct quotations?
- ✔ Are commas used correctly in numbers, dates, addresses, and letters?

The comma is the most frequently used punctuation mark, but it is also the most often misused. Commas make reading sentences easier because they separate the parts of sentences. Following the rules in this chapter will help you write clear sentences that are easy to read.

Look at some commas at work in the following paragraph by Deborah Tannen.

> I broke the class into small groups to discuss the issues raised in the readings and to analyze their own conversational transcripts. I devised three ways of dividing the students into groups: one by the degree program they were in, one by gender, and one by conversational style, as closely as I could guess it. This meant that when the class was grouped according to conversational style, I put Asian students together, fast talkers together, and quiet students together. The class split into groups six times during the semester, so they met in each grouping twice. I told students to regard the groups as examples of interactional data and to note the different ways they participated in the different groups. Toward the end of the term,

TEACHING COMMAS
Create 10 sentences that contain comma errors. Put each sentence on a small poster board so that you have 10 poster boards. Then create a duplicate set of poster boards. Divide the class into two teams. Place a set of 10 poster boards in front of each team with the sentences facing down.

Begin a tag team relay in which each team uses a marker to fix or supply the commas. When the first person finishes the first sentence, he or she hands the marker to the next person, who moves to the next sentence. The second person places commas in the second sentence and then hands the marker to the next person, and so on. Time the tag teams.

When the students have completed all the sentences, check to make sure that all the commas are correctly placed. Add five seconds

■ For sample sentences, see the *Instructor's Resource Manual*, Section II, Part II.

TEACHING ON THE WEB

Exploring and Discussing: Have students access your college's newspaper on-line (or the newspaper from a college near you). Then have the students choose one article and underline comma errors in it. How many comma errors did students find? Have students complete to see who can find the largest number of different types of errors in a single article. How do the comma errors distract readers from the message in the article?

TEACHING ON THE WEB

Mosaics Web Site: To learn more about commas, students can go to www.prenhall.com/ mosaics.

to the team's time for each incorrect or missed comma. The team to finish with the lowest time wins.

I gave them a questionnaire asking about their class and group participation.

In this paragraph, Deborah Tannen describes how she organizes student group activities based on the students' individual personalities. Before continuing in this chapter, take a moment to record some of your own observations. Save your work because you will use it later in this chapter.

Writing Assignment: Classroom Behavior

What are some of your observations about classroom behavior? What behaviors characterize the students in your English class? Are the dynamics of your English class different from the dynamics of your other classes? What differences and similarities do you see? What conclusions can you draw from these observations? Write a paragraph comparing the students in two of your classes.

Revising Your Writing

Revise the first draft of your paragraph before you focus on editing. Use the Revising Checklist on pages 24–25 to help you with your revision. Make sure your paragraph has a good topic sentence, is well developed, and is well organized. Then check your paragraph for unity and coherence.

COMMAS WITH ITEMS IN A SERIES

Use commas to separate the items in a series. This means that you should put a comma between all items in a series.

Series: The class required that we read 2 novels, 20 short stories, and 12 poems.

Series: The students exchanged their essays, read them, and gave each other suggestions.

Series: Tonight I need to finish an essay, read a short story, and answer the questions on page 15.

Sometimes this rule applies to a series of adjectives in front of a noun, but sometimes it does not. Look at these two examples.

| **Adjectives with Commas:** | The long, boring lecture is finally over. |
| **Adjectives without Commas:** | The last red encyclopedia is checked out of the library. |

Both of these examples are correct. So how do you know whether or not to use commas? You can use one of two tests. One test is to insert the word "and" between the adjectives. If the sentence makes sense, use a comma. Another test is to switch the order of the adjectives. If the sentence still reads clearly, use a comma between the two words.

Test 1: The **long and boring** lecture is finally over.   **OK, so use a comma**

Test 2: The **boring, long lecture** is finally over.   **OK, so use a comma**

Test 1: The **last and blue** encyclopedia is checked out of the library.   **NO comma**

Test 2: The **blue last** encyclopedia is checked out of the library. **NO comma**

REVIEWING COMMAS WITH ITEMS IN A SERIES

Why use commas with items in a series?

To separate the items

Where do these commas go?

After all items in the series except the last

Practice 1 Identifying   Add missing commas to each of the following sentences where necessary.

1. Emily Dickinson, Robert Frost, and T. S. Eliot are my favorite poets.

2. My two-year-old son loves to watch Elmo videos, read picture books, and color with crayons.

3. Jeffery plans on going out to dinner, ordering an expensive meal, and enjoying a glass of wine on his birthday.

4. Marty discovered that he's allergic to roses, daffodils, and mums.

5. Maggie has two dogs, four cats, and eight goldfish.

6. We studied *The Tempest, A Midsummer Night's Dream,* and *Twelfth Night* in my Shakespeare class.

7. On their vacation, they visited the Grand Canyon, Yellowstone National Park, and Old Faithful.

8. I stayed up too late last night studying, visiting with my friends, and cleaning my dorm room.

9. My brother, my sister, and my cousin started their own business.

10. Christine can play shortstop, rover, and second base.

Practice 2 Identifying   Put an X next to the sentence if any commas in the underlined part of the sentence are used incorrectly.

1. _____ If I win the lottery, I will go to Paris, buy a new house, and pay off my student loans.

2. __X__ My best friend can play tennis golf and, racquetball. *(tennis, golf, and racquetball)*

3. __X__ Charise's fat brown puppy is chewing on my sandals. *(fat, brown)*

4. _____ The piano, the desk, and the entertainment center need to be dusted.

5. __X__ I gave my old jeans, my leather jacket and the television to charity. *(jacket, and)*

6. __X__ When we went to the hockey game, we ate ice cream popcorn and red licorice. *(ice cream, popcorn, and)*

7. _____ Every day, Debra goes to work, goes to night school, and works out at the gym.

8. _____ *Third Watch, ER,* and *NYPD Blue* are all very interesting TV dramas.

9. __X__ The old red barn needs to be painted. *(old, red)*

10. __X__ The salmon the prime rib, and the crab legs are this restaurant's signature dishes. *(salmon, the prime rib)*

Practice 3 Correcting   Correct the comma errors in Practice 2 by rewriting each incorrect sentence. *See Practice 2.*

1. _____

2. _____

3. _____

4. _____

5. _____

6. _____

7. _____

8. _____

9. _____

10. _____

❊ Practice 4 Completing   Add the missing commas to the following paragraph.

When the strangers arrived in the quiet town, they saw a private village, a brick silo, and a white house. Next to the house was a pigpen, a chicken yard, and a granary. Hard mud filled the pigpen, but there were no pigs. The doors of the house were dirty, the rain gutters were hanging from the rooftops, and two windows were broken. Beyond the barn was a small garden of geraniums, roses, and azaleas. The house appeared to be occupied by a young couple, two small boys, and a teenage girl. The scattered toys in the front yard gave the strangers this impression. It didn't look like anyone was home, but the strangers hoped the residents wouldn't be gone long. They just wanted a warm meal, a soft bed, and a pleasant conversation for one night.

❊ Practice 5 Writing Your Own

A. Write a sentence of your own for each of the following series. *Answers will vary.*

1. three kinds of animals

_____

2. three places to spend money

_____

3. three occupations

_____

4. three things to do at the beach

_____

5. three things to buy at the grocery store

_____

B. Write five sentences of your own using commas correctly to separate items in a series. *Answers will vary.*

1. _____

2. _____

3. _____

4. _____

5. _____

COMMAS WITH INTRODUCTORY WORDS

Use a comma to set off an introductory word or group of words from the rest of its sentence. If you are unsure whether to add a comma, try reading the sentence with your reader in mind. If you want your reader to pause after the introductory word or phrase, you should insert a comma.

Introductory Word:	**Actually,** the class was more interesting than I thought it would be.
	Yes, I finished my essay.
Introductory Phrase:	**To save time,** I did my homework during my lunch break.
	All in all, this is a very competitive group.
Introductory Clause:	**When the professor wrote on the chalkboard,** we began taking notes.
	As the papers were being passed out, everyone was nervous.

REVIEWING COMMAS WITH INTRODUCTORY WORDS

Why use commas with introductory words, phrases, and clauses?

To set them off from the rest of the sentence

How can you tell if a comma is needed?

Read the sentence to see if you want your reader to pause after the introductory words.

🌾 **Practice 6 Identifying**   Add missing commas to each of the following sentences where necessary.

1. If I'm lucky, we will be getting married in May.

2. Just because you asked, I'll tell you the whole story.

3. Well, Rebecca isn't choosing sides right now.

4. When we were in class, someone belched very loudly.

5. Your best option is perhaps to talk to him.

6. Basically, there is no other way to get there.

7. As they were walking, the man tripped over his shoelaces.

8. Having completed his homework, Ned went to bed.

9. In what was for her a noble gesture, she volunteered to help.

10. Ultimately, there will be one winner.

🌾 **Practice 7 Identifying**   Put an X next to the sentence if any commas in the underlined part of the sentence are used incorrectly.

1. _____ <u>To be totally honest,</u> I've never liked math classes.

2. ___X___ <u>Of course</u> I'd love to help you with that project. *(Of course,)*

3. ___X___ <u>Hoping, to see some changes</u> we all voted in the last student body election. *(Hoping to)*

4. ___X___ <u>When they asked, for my opinion,</u> I spoke honestly. *(When they asked for my opinion,)*

5. _____ <u>Because Camille was with me,</u> I felt brave.

6. ___X___ <u>Not knowing, what we were up against,</u> we were a little nervous. *(Not knowing what we were up against,)*

7. _____ <u>When she was tired,</u> Sara drank lots of coffee.

8. _____ <u>Thank goodness,</u> the hardest part is over.

9. ___X___ <u>Fortunately Mike,</u> is on the panel too. *(Fortunately, Mike is)*

10. ___X___ <u>In hindsight</u> that was a bad decision. *(In hindsight,)*

🌾 **Practice 8 Correcting**   Correct the comma errors in Practice 7 by rewriting each incorrect sentence. *See Practice 7.*

1. _____

2. _____

3. _____

4. _____

5. _____

6. _____

7. _____

8. _____

9. _____

10. _____

✸ Practice 9 Completing   Add the missing commas to the following paragraph.

Finally, our squad is ready for the big cheerleading competition. Being one of the 10 men on the team, I always feel lots of pressure and anxiety. The women count on us to lift, hold, and catch them without a flaw. Really, it's not just dropping the girls that I worry about. Every minor mistake takes points away from our total score. When I was in high school, cheerleading was just for girls. Now that I'm in college, I have a whole different view. The cheerleading squad depends on big, strong men, and the best squads seem to have the most men. Unfortunately, it is often difficult to recruit men to cheer. For some reason, many people don't think it's a "manly" thing to do. Personally, I can't think of anything more manly than catching a petite cheerleader in a short skirt and swinging her up over my head. It always makes me think of Tarzan and Jane.

✸ Practice 10 Writing Your Own

A. Write a sentence of your own for each of the following introductory words, phrases, or clauses. *Answers will vary.*

1. Well _____

2. When I was in junior high _____

3. After the song started _____

4. Honestly _____

5. To be more specific _____

B. Write five sentences of your own using commas correctly to set off intro-
    ductory words, phrases, or clauses. *Answers will vary.*

1. _____

2. _____

3. _____

4. _____

5. _____

COMMAS WITH INDEPENDENT CLAUSES

**Use a comma before *and, but, for, nor, or, so,* and *yet* when they join two
independent clauses.** Remember that an independent clause must have
both a subject and a verb.

Independent Clauses:	The instructor put us in small groups, **and** she gave us a new assignment.
Independent Clauses:	The essay was difficult to read, **but** I learned some new vocabulary words.

HINT: Do not use a comma when a single subject has two verbs.

No
comma
↓

    s   v   v

The instructor put us in small groups and **gave** us a new assignment.

Adding a comma when none is needed is one of the most common errors in
college writing assignments. Only if the second verb has its own subject
should you add a comma.

Comma
↓

    s   v   s   v

The instructor put us in small groups, and **she gave** us a new
assignment.

REVIEWING COMMAS WITH INDEPENDENT CLAUSES

Name three coordinating conjunctions.

Answers will vary.

_____

When should you use a comma before a coordinating conjunction?

When it joins two independent clauses

_____

> *Should you use a comma before a coordinating conjunction when a single subject has two verbs?*
>
> *No—only if the second verb has its own subject*

🌿 Practice 11 Identifying   Add missing commas to the following sentences where necessary.

1. We made a batch of cookies, and we ate too much dough.

2. I wasn't happy about the decision, nor did I appreciate their rude comments.

3. Justin waited by the phone, yet it never rang.

4. We bought lots of new clothes, but many things shrank in the wash.

5. This will be my last night at this job, or I'm going to go crazy.

6. The coin collection is in the closet, so I think it is in a safe place.

7. I looked for Christina, but I didn't see her.

8. I am going to the beach, for that is the only place where I can relax.

9. My computer crashed, so I'm glad I have a backup.

10. Sharon used to dream of being an astronaut, but she realized that she's afraid of heights.

🌿 Practice 12 Identifying   Put an X next to the sentence if any commas in the underlined part of the sentence are used incorrectly.

1. __X__ Mom went to the outlet <u>mall and</u> she bought a new jacket for me.
   (mall, and)

2. __X__ My car ran out of <u>gas but</u> the gas gauge said I had a full tank. *(gas, but)*

3. _____ Greg organized a local baseball <u>league and</u> did lots of fund-raising.

4. __X__ I can't stay <u>long for</u> I have a paper to write. *(long, for)*

5. __X__ My brother is out with his <u>girlfriend or</u> he's working late tonight.
   (girlfriend, or)

6. _____ Junior is usually late to <u>class, but</u> he's always prepared.

7. __X__ I've been <u>dieting yet</u> I haven't lost any weight. *(dieting, yet)*

8. __X__ I'm going to order either the chicken <u>parmesan, or</u> the fettucine Alfredo. *(parmesan or)*

9. _____ James is taking a trip to <u>Missouri, and</u> he's visiting his grandparents.

10. __X__ I have a doctor's appointment in 20 <u>minutes so</u> I have to leave right now. *(minutes, so)*

🌾 Practice 13 Correcting   Correct the comma errors in Practice 12 by rewriting each incorrect sentence. *See Practice 12.*

1. _____

2. _____

3. _____

4. _____

5. _____

6. _____

7. _____

8. _____

9. _____

10. _____

🌾 Practice 14 Completing   Add the missing commas to the following paragraph.

The trainers at the Los Angeles Zoo watch the animals closely, so they are usually prepared for anything. One of the elephants, Orion, was becoming extremely overweight, and the trainers began to worry about him. Orion was very intelligent, but he was also very lazy. The trainers started him on a cardiovascular exercise program, and within a few months, Orion lost 600 pounds. Then the trainers worried that the exercise might be too much, for Orion was 42 years old. They wondered if his heart would be able to take all of this activity, so they called in some veterinarians. The vets brought in an ultrasound machine, but they could not detect Orion's heartbeat. They decided that either his heart was too deep for the ultrasound to pick up or his sternum was too thick and made the ultrasound machine useless. Eventually, the vets found other instruments, and they determined that Orion was a very healthy elephant. This was a very challenging experience, yet it was also very helpful. The vets and trainers learned a great deal about the elephant's anatomy, and that will help them deal with Orion in the future.

Practice 15 Writing Your Own

A. Write a sentence of your own using each of the following coordinating conjunctions with two independent clauses. *Answers will vary.*

1. and _____

2. so _____

3. but _____

4. or _____

5. yet _____

B. Write five sentences of your own using commas correctly with independent clauses and coordinating conjunctions. *Answers will vary.*

1. _____

2. _____

3. _____

4. _____

5. _____

COMMAS WITH INTERRUPTERS

Use a comma before and after a word or phrase that interrupts the flow of a sentence. Most words that interrupt are not necessary for understanding the main point of a sentence. Setting them off makes it easier to recognize the main point.

Word: I didn't study for the exam, **however,** because I had to work late.

The exchange student, **Frida,** is from Sweden.

Phrase: The city with the most hotels, **according to this travel journal,** is Las Vegas.

This book, ***The Long Valley,*** is a collection of Steinbeck's short stories.

James Whitaker, **the chair of the English Department,** is retiring.

A very common type of interrupter is a clause that begins with *who, whose, which, when,* or *where* and is not necessary for understanding the main point of the sentence:

Clause: The new instructor**, who came here from UC Berkeley,** is teaching the American literature class.

Because the information "who came here from UC Berkeley" is not necessary for understanding the main idea of the sentence, it is set off with commas.

Clause: The public library**, which is downtown,** provides several books on tape.

The main point is that the public library provides books on tape. Since the other information isn't necessary to understanding the sentence, it can be set off with commas.

HINT: Do *not* use commas with *who, whose, which, when,* or *where* if the information is necessary for understanding the main point of the sentence:

My brother **who joined the Navy** came home for Christmas.

Because the information in the *who* clause is necessary to understand which brother came home for Christmas, you should not set it off with commas.

HINT: Do not use commas to set off clauses beginning with *that*:

The movie theater **that is on Elm Street** is showing *Jurassic Park III*.

REVIEWING COMMAS WITH INTERRUPTERS

Why should you use commas to set off words and phrases in the middle of a sentence?

To make the main point easier to recognize

When should you use commas with who, whose, which, when, *or* where?

When the interrupting words are not necessary for understanding the main point.

When should you not *use commas before these words?*

When the information is necessary to the point of the sentence

🌿 **Practice 16 Identifying**   Add missing commas to each of the following sentences where necessary.

1. I'm driving my car, a Nissan Sentra, on a long road trip.

2. The alligator tamer, Steve, is crazy.

3. I will take a nap, which I'm looking forward to, before the big party.

4. Gardening, Sue's favorite pastime, is very hard work.

5. Yvonne read that book, *Martin Eden*, in her literature class.

6. I need to get a tan, obviously, before I leave for Hawaii.

7. Paint the house, please, before our relatives get here.

8. The best restaurant in town, according to this article, is Fish Lips on Truxton Avenue.

9. I need the credit card that is in your wallet, Honey, to buy a pair of shoes.

10. Basketball is the best sport, however, for exercise.

🌿 **Practice 17 Identifying**   Put an X next to the sentence if there are any comma errors in the underlined part of the sentence.

1. ___X___ I bought this <u>car however,</u> because of the extended warranty. *(car, however,)*

2. _____ Jimmy's favorite <u>character, Buzz Lightyear,</u> is from *Toy Story*.

3. ___X___ <u>Pink, a female music group</u> is in concert this weekend. *(Pink, a female music group,)*

4. ___X___ The <u>vacuum cleaner which I hate,</u> is in the hall closet. *(vacuum cleaner, which I hate,)*

5. _____ My <u>aunt, who made this bread,</u> lives in New Mexico.

6. ___X___ The <u>remote control, that is on the coffee table,</u> works both the TV and the VCR. *(remote control that is on the coffee table works)*

7. ___X___ I need to go to the <u>office which is on the north side of the building</u> to get the tickets. *(office, which is on the north side of the building,)*

8. _____ My next-door <u>neighbor, whose cat always torments mine,</u> works for the school district.

9. ___X___ Jack has been dating <u>Lisa the girl from Texas</u> for about five months. *(Lisa, the girl from Texas,)*

10. _____ You are the <u>one, of course,</u> who will win this election.

🌾 Practice 18 Correcting   Correct the comma errors in Practice 17 by rewriting each incorrect sentence. *See Practice 17.*

1. _____
2. _____
3. _____
4. _____
5. _____
6. _____
7. _____
8. _____
9. _____
10. _____

🌾 Practice 19 Completing   Add the missing commas to the following paragraph.

Doing laundry is my favorite household chore. I have to sort the clothes of course before I throw them all into the washing machine, but I am very picky about what items can be washed together. I put the colors the dark ones in one pile, and the whites go in another. But there are in-between colors like tans and beiges that I cannot put in either stack. Those colors get their own pile. The whites and only the whites are washed in hot water, and sometimes I will put in a little bleach. The colors are always washed in warm or cold usually cold because I don't want the colors to "bleed." I love my washing machine which was quite expensive because it can handle very large loads. Four people live in this house, so believe me their laundry stacks up quickly. Most of the other chores like washing dishes and dusting I will gladly give away, but save the laundry for me.

🌾 Practice 20 Writing Your Own

A. Write a sentence of your own using each of the following phrases or clauses as interrupters. *Answers will vary.*

1. who was 16 years old _____

2. however _____

3. of course _____

4. which changes every year _____

5. whose bike is in my garage _____

B. Write five sentences of your own using commas correctly with interrupting phrases or clauses. *Answers will vary.*

1. _____

2. _____

3. _____

4. _____

5. _____

COMMAS WITH DIRECT QUOTATIONS

Use commas to mark direct quotations. A direct quotation records a person's exact words. Commas set off the exact words from the rest of the sentence, making it easier to understand who said what.

Direct Quotation: The instructor said, "The exam will be next Friday."

Direct Quotation: "The exam will be next Friday," the instructor said.

Direct Quotation: "The exam," said the instructor, "will be next Friday."

HINT: If a quotation ends with a question mark or an exclamation point, do not use a comma. Only one punctuation mark is needed.

NOT   "What was the question?," he asked.

Correct: "What was the question?" he asked.

REVIEWING COMMAS WITH DIRECT QUOTATIONS

Why should you use commas with a direct quotation?

To help the reader understand who said what

> *Should you use a comma if the quotation ends with a question mark or an exclamation point? Why or why not?*
>
> No—only one punctuation mark is needed.
> _____

🌿 **Practice 21 Identifying**   Add missing commas to the following sentences where necessary.

1. "Yea, Dodgers!" they screamed.

2. "We'll meet you at the park," Nancy said.

3. Tina quietly whispered, "Don't eat the rice."

4. "I can't see where I'm going," said Wanda.

5. "When you get to Real Road," he said, "turn right."

6. "I can't find my lucky pencil," she said sadly.

7. "If you've finished your homework," said the teacher, "pass it forward."

8. Rachel screamed, "A spider is on my head!"

9. "We need more envelopes for this office," said the receptionist.

10. "Take me to your leader," commanded the alien.

🌿 **Practice 22 Identifying**   Put an X next to the sentence if there are any comma errors in the underlined part of the sentence.

1. _____ Shawn said, "I think this is a good day for tennis."

2. ___X___ "Take me dancing" said Helen Hunt's character in *As Good As It Gets*. *(dancing,")*

3. ___X___ "I can't believe" she said, "that you are going to miss the big event." *(believe," she said, "that)*

4. _____ "We got the loan!" Diane shouted in glee.

5. ___X___ Julian asked "Where are we supposed to meet?" *(asked, "Where)*

6. ___X___ "Do these pants make me look fat?," she asked. *(fat?" she)*

7. _____ "Go to work," he said, "and I'll take you to dinner when you get home."

8. _____ "If you insist," she said, "then that's the way it will be."

9. ___X___ Tammy <u>shouted "Get</u> back in line!" *(shouted, "Get)*

10. _____ "Is this fish <u>fresh?"</u> I asked the waitress.

🌾 Practice 23 Correcting   Correct the comma errors in Practice 22 by rewriting each incorrect sentence. *See Practice 22.*

1. _____

2. _____

3. _____

4. _____

5. _____

6. _____

7. _____

8. _____

9. _____

10. _____

🌾 Practice 24 Completing   Add the missing commas to the following paragraph.

"I'm looking for some plants for my garden," Annabel told the man at the nursery. "What kinds of plants did you have in mind?" he asked her. "Well, something that can tolerate heat," she said, "because my garden gets lots of sun." "If you want flowers," he said, "roses are always nice, and these petunias would do well." Annabel thought about them and said, "I need something that spreads out, too, like a ground cover." "Oh," he said, "I have just the thing for you! Try this verbena." "Will it spread out pretty far?" she asked. "Absolutely," he assured her, "and it will be full of little flowers." "I'll take it," she said, pulling out her checkbook.

🌾 Practice 25 Writing Your Own

A. Write a sentence of your own for each of the following quotations.
Answers will vary.

1. a direct quotation about the weather

_____

2. a direct quotation about your job

_____

3. a direct quotation about television

_____

4. a direct quotation about dinner

_____

5. a direct quotation about attending class regularly

_____

B. Write five sentences of your own using commas correctly with direct quotations. *Answers will vary.*

1. _____
2. _____
3. _____
4. _____
5. _____

OTHER USES OF COMMAS

Use commas in the following ways.

Numbers:	What is 2,667,999 divided by 10,300?
Dates:	Mike and Melissa were married on August 1, 2000, in Cincinnati.
Addresses:	Nicole moved from Lamont, California, to 8900 New Fork Lane, Aspen, CO 81615.
Letters:	Dear Alyson,
	Yours truly,

REVIEWING OTHER USES OF COMMAS

Give one example of commas in each of the following situations: Examples will vary.

Numbers: _____

Dates: _____

Addresses: _____

Letters: _____

Why are these commas important?

They clarify information in everyday writing.

🌾 Practice 26 Identifying   Add missing commas to the following where necessary.

1. The murder took place near 4000 Chester Avenue.

2. More than 55,600 excited fans rushed onto the field.

3. February 14, 2001, was the worst Valentine's Day I have ever had.

4. My car needs a new transmission, but it will cost over $1,200.

5. We had $3,565 in tax deductions last year.

6. Quincy is looking into buying a house at 355 Park Way.

7. Dear Mark,

8. The next assessment exam is on May 5, 2003.

9. Our new address is 4800 Jackson Place, Richmond, VA 84955.

10. Sincerely yours,

🌾 Practice 27 Identifying   Put an X next to the sentence if there are any comma errors in the underlined part of the sentence.

1. __X__ My grandmother lives at 3,230 Eureka Street. *(3230)*

2. _____ On June 10, 2004, I will graduate from this university.

3. _____ The boys are camping in Denver, Colorado.

4. __X__ This stadium holds 300,00 people. *(30,000)*

5. _____ We moved from Jackson, Mississippi, to Oakland, California.

6. __X__ We're getting married on December 3 2003. *(3, 2003)*

7. __X__ I only paid $1566 for my new bedroom furniture. *($1,566)*

8. _____ There are approximately <u>450,000</u> people living in this city.

9. __X__ William built a house at <u>2244 Knoxbury Street, Miami, FL, 33459</u>. *(FL 33459)*

10. __X__ The winner of the contest will receive <u>$5000,00</u> in prize money. *($500,000)*

Practice 28 Correcting   Correct the comma errors in Practice 27 by rewriting each incorrect sentence. *See Practice 27.*

1. _____

2. _____

3. _____

4. _____

5. _____

6. _____

7. _____

8. _____

9. _____

10. _____

Practice 29 Completing   Add the missing commas to the following paragraph.

My cousin joined the Marines on June 20, 1996, and after boot camp, he was sent to Okinawa, Japan. At this base, he worked in communications. Since he was such a quick learner, he advanced in rank very quickly. Soon he was responsible for more than 1,500 other Marines. His paychecks were not very much—approximately $2,000 each month—however, he was single and didn't have any big bills. After three years and many other tours, the Marines asked him if he was planning to stay in the service. He had a great reputation, and they wanted him to keep advancing in rank. My cousin thought about it for a long time, but he decided that he would be happier back in the civilian world. After his discharge, he bought a house in Topeka, Kansas, and fell in love with a beautiful girl. Several of my cousin's Marine friends were at their wedding on November 16, 2001, to express their support.

✿ Practice 30 Writing Your Own

A. Write a sentence of your own for each of the following items. *Answers will vary.*

1. your current address

    _____

2. the date you were born

    _____

3. the number of students at your school

    _____

4. the amount of money you would like to make in one year

    _____

5. the address of your campus library

    _____

B. Write five sentences of your own using commas correctly with numbers, dates, and addresses. *Answers will vary.*

1. _____
2. _____
3. _____
4. _____
5. _____

CHAPTER REVIEW

You might want to reread your answers to the questions in the review boxes before you do the following exercises.

✿ Review Practice 1 Reading   Refer to the paragraph by Deborah Tannen on pages 353–354 to do the following exercises.

1. List the two sentences that use commas to separate items in a series.

    I devised three ways of dividing the students into groups: one by the degree program

    they were in . . .

> *This meant that when the class was grouped according to conversational style, I put*
>
> *Asian students . . .*

2. List one introductory phrase that is set off with a comma.

   > *Toward the end of the term, I gave them a questionnaire asking about their class and*
   >
   > *group participation.*

3. List the sentence that uses a comma with two independent clauses.

   > *The class split into groups six times during the semester, so they met in each grouping*
   >
   > *twice.*

4. Rewrite the following sentence from the paragraph with an interrupter and commas.

   I broke the class into small groups to discuss the issues raised in the readings.

   > *Answers will vary.*

5. Rewrite the following sentence from the paragraph to make it a direct quotation, using commas correctly.

   I told students to regard the groups as examples of interactional data and to note the different ways they participated in the different groups.

   > *Answers will vary.*

6. Add another sentence to the following sentence, using commas correctly with numbers or dates.

   Toward the end of the term, I gave them a questionnaire asking about their class and group participation.

   > *Answers will vary.*

✿ Review Practice 2 Identifying   Underline the incorrect and missing commas in each of the following sentences.

1. When we went to the store_we forgot to buy milk. *(store,)*

2. Matt tried to move the refrigerator, but it was too heavy.

3. Fortunately_this is the last chemistry class that I have to take. *(Fortunately,)*

4. "Really" she said, "I never meant to hurt, your feelings." *(Really, . . . hurt your feelings)*

5. I sat next to Carter, my best friend_at the concert. *(friend,)*

6. We started this class on September 5_2001. *(September 5, 2001)*

7. Chaney brought chips_salsa, and soft drinks to the party. *(chips,)*

8. The_empty_deserted farmhouse₁ caught fire yesterday. *(empty, . . . farmhouse caught)*

9. We need to raise $100_500 in donations. *($100,500)*

10. I found the special paper_pen_and ink₁ that I need at a stationery store. *(paper, pen, and ink that)*

✿ Review Practice 3 Correcting   Correct the comma errors in Review Practice 2 by rewriting each incorrect sentence. *See Review Practice 2.*

1. _____

2. _____

3. _____

4. _____

5. _____

6. _____

7. _____

8. _____

9. _____

10. _____

✎ EDITING A STUDENT PARAGRAPH

Following is a paragraph written and revised by Marla Anderson in response to the writing assignment in this chapter. Read the paragraph, and think about where commas should be.

The students in my English class and the students in my theater class are very different. In theater, the students just won't be quiet and settle down. This is probably because the theater students are talkative, outgoing people. Usually, the class gets out of hand, which I don't like. When it gets really bad, it sounds like there's 1000 people in one small classroom. Sometimes I just want to yell, "Shut up!" The students in my English class,^{4} however,^{4} are very quiet and serious. They usually listen well,^{1} pay close attention to the teacher,^{1} and maintain order in the class. I think I probably learn more in this class,^{3} but it can get boring at times. I'll just be glad when June 10,^{6}2000,^{6}comes because then I'll be a certified social worker,^{3}and I'll be finished with my degree.

Collaborative Activity

Team up with a partner, and find the 14 missing commas in Marla's paragraph. Then, working together, use what you have learned in this chapter to label each error from the list below.

1   Commas with items in a series
2   Commas with introductory words
3   Commas with independent clauses
4   Commas with interrupters
5   Commas with direct quotations
6   Commas with numbers, dates, addresses, and letters

Finally, rewrite the paragraph with your corrections. *See student paragraph.*

❧ EDITING YOUR OWN PARAGRAPH

Now return to the paragraph you wrote and revised at the beginning of this chapter. Underline each of your commas.

Collaborative Activity

Exchange paragraphs with your partner, and underline any comma errors that you find in your partner's paragraph.

Individual Activity

Using the six rules governing comma usage, identify the rule for each of the comma errors your partner found in your paragraph. On the Error Log in Appendix 6, record your comma errors. Finally, to complete the writing process, correct these errors by rewriting your paragraph.

Apostrophes

✐ Checklist for Using Apostrophes

✔ Are apostrophes used correctly in contractions?

✔ Are apostrophes used correctly to show possession?

The *apostrophe* looks like a single quotation mark. Its two main purposes are to indicate where letters have been left out and to show ownership.

Let's watch some apostrophes at work in the following paragraph by Alan Monroe.

> Someone has said, "Let me hear a voice, and I'll tell you what sort of person he or she is." This statement is, of course, exaggerated; nonetheless, its essential truth is borne out both by common experience and by scientifically conducted experiments. The tone of people's voices varies from normal when they're angry, excited, sleepy, or terrified. Habits of temperament such as nervousness, irritability, or aggressiveness likewise seem to be reflected in one's habitual speaking voice; people are inclined, therefore, to judge one's personality largely on the sound of the voice. A person whose tones are too sharp and nasal is often thought of as being a nagging person. A person whose voice is harsh and guttural is judged to be crude and rough. Weak, thin voices suggest weakness in character. These judgments may, at times, be absolutely contrary to fact; more often they're close to the truth. But whether true or false, such judgments are important in that they color the listener's attitude toward all that the speaker does or says. They're often a major factor in determining the first impression speakers make on their audience.

In this paragraph, Alan Monroe discusses the importance of a speaker's voice. Before continuing in this chapter, take a moment to discuss your feelings about talking in public. Save your work because you will use it later in this chapter.

Writing Assignment: Talking in Public

Do you feel comfortable talking in front of other people? Are there certain situations that make you uneasy? What about classroom situations? Do you like to answer questions and participate in class discussions? Are you the kind of person who tends to dominate discussions, or are you the one who will sit on the sidelines and listen? Write a paragraph describing your reactions when you have to talk in public.

Revising Your Writing

Revise the first draft of your paragraph before you focus on editing. Use the Revising Checklist on pages 24–25 to help you with your revision. Make sure your paragraph has a good topic sentence, is well developed, and is well organized. Then check your paragraph for unity and coherence.

MARKING CONTRACTIONS

Use an apostrophe to show that letters have been omitted to form a contraction. A **contraction** is the shortening—or contraction—of one or more words. Our everyday speech is filled with contractions.

I will   = I'll (*w* and *i* have been omitted)

do not = don't (*o* has been omitted)

let us   = let's (*u* has been omitted)

Here is a list of commonly used contractions.

Some Common Contractions

I am	= I'm		*we have*	= we've
I would	= I'd		*we will*	= we'll
I will	= I'll		*they are*	= they're
you have	= you've		*they have*	= they've
you will	= you'll		*do not*	= don't
he is	= he's		*did not*	= didn't
she will	= she'll		*have not*	= haven't
it is	= it's		*could not*	= couldn't

HINT: Two words that are frequently misused are *it's* and *its*.

it's = contraction: it is (*or* it has)   **It's** my birthday today.

its = pronoun: belonging to it   **Its** wings need to be clipped.

To see if you are using the correct word, say the sentence with the words *it is*. If that is what you want to say, add an apostrophe to the word.

> **?**   I wonder if **its** on the dresser.
> **Test:** I wonder if **it is** on the dresser.   **YES, add an apostrophe**

This sentence makes sense with *it is*, so you can write *it's*.

> **Correct:** I wonder if **it's** on the dresser.
> **?**   The horse stomped **its** hoof.
> **Test:** The horse stomped **it is** hoof.   **NO, so no apostrophe**

This sentence does not make sense with *it is*, so you should not use the apostrophe in *its*.

> **Correct:** The horse stomped **its** hoof.

REVIEWING CONTRACTIONS

What is the purpose of an apostrophe in a contraction?

To show that letters have been omitted

Write five contractions, and tell which letters have been omitted.

Answers will vary.

_____   _____

_____   _____

_____   _____

_____   _____

_____   _____

What is the difference between it's and its?

It's stands for it is or it has, and its is a possessive pronoun.

Practice 1 Identifying   Add missing apostrophes to the following sentences where necessary.

1. My husband wonders why babies don't come with instruction manuals.
2. Sylvia won't be attending the class reunion.
3. They're going to Mustang Island for the weekend.
4. You shouldn't have said that.
5. Gretchen said she's feeling much better now.
6. Isn't it funny that we were in the same class all semester and never knew it?
7. If you could help me with this, I'd really appreciate it.
8. We've been so busy lately that we forgot to RSVP for the party.
9. Elise can't make it tonight, but she'll be there tomorrow.
10. It's a funny thing that our chicken always lays its eggs in my dad's boot.

Practice 2 Identifying   Put an X next to the sentence if an apostrophe is missing or used incorrectly.

1. _____ You've got to leave before my parents get home.
2. _____ My sister said that she's applying to UCLA.
3. __X__ I think wel'l be able to make it. *(we'll)*

4. ___X___ Amber did'nt have a ride to class. *(didn't)*
5. ______ We're going to the mountains on Friday.
6. ___X___ Its a nice day today. *(It's)*
7. ______ He said they've been here before.
8. ___X___ Can you write the report while Im making the display? *(I'm)*
9. ___X___ The cat knocked it's bowl over last night. *(its)*
10. ___X___ Hows this plan going to work? *(How's)*

Practice 3 Correcting Correct the apostrophe errors in Practice 2 by rewriting each incorrect sentence. *See Practice 2.*

1. ______________________________
2. ______________________________
3. ______________________________
4. ______________________________
5. ______________________________
6. ______________________________
7. ______________________________
8. ______________________________
9. ______________________________
10. ______________________________

Practice 4 Completing Add apostrophes to the contractions in the following paragraph.

Gordon Foster couldn't drive fast enough to pick up his wife, Betsy, from the airport. She'd been at a conference in Tennessee for five days, and he couldn't wait to see her again. She's one of the nutritionists for the city's hospital, and they're always being sent to meetings and lectures out of state. When she's gone, Gordon can't stand it. They've only got two children, and the kids are now in high school, so it's not that he's stuck changing diapers or preparing bottles. He just doesn't like being without Betsy. Sometimes she'll shake her head and laugh at how dependent Gordon is. But it's pretty obvious that she enjoys being missed so much.

🌾 Practice 5 Writing Your Own

A. Write a sentence of your own for each of the following contractions.
Answers will vary.

1. he's _____

2. they'll _____

3. couldn't _____

4. doesn't _____

5. we'd _____

B. Write five sentences of your own using apostrophes correctly in contractions. *Answers will vary.*

1. _____

2. _____

3. _____

4. _____

5. _____

SHOWING POSSESSION

1. **For a singular word, use 's to indicate possession or ownership.**
You can always replace a possessive with *of* plus a noun or pronoun.

the team's leader	= the leader *of the team*
Edward's car	= the car *of Edward*
the teacher's rules	= the rules *of the teacher*
tomorrow's weather	= the weather *of tomorrow*

2. **For plural nouns ending in -s, use only an apostrophe.**

the students' books	= the books *of the students*
the sisters' bedroom	= the bedroom *of the sisters*
the writers' convention	= the convention *of the writers*
the tourists' hotel	= the hotel *of the tourists*

3. **For plural nouns that do not end in -s, add 's.**

the men**'s** bathroom   = the bathroom *of the men*

the children**'s** toys   = the toys *of the children*

the women**'s** tea party   = the tea party *of the women*

Reviewing Possessives

How do you mark possession or ownership for a singular word?

Add 's to the word.

How do you mark possession or ownership for a plural word that ends in -s?

Add an apostrophe after the -s ending.

How do you mark possession or ownership for a plural word that doesn't end in -s?

Add 's to the word.

✱ Practice 6 Identifying   Add missing apostrophes to each of the following sentences when necessary.

1. Janet's last day at work will be Wednesday.

2. From here on, this receptionist's job includes filing documents.

3. All of the neighborhood boys' bicycles need to stay out of the street.

4. My cousin's car is in the shop.

5. Thomas's pencil is on my desk.

6. Fran made cookies for Secretaries' Day.

7. This team's 12 wins put it in second place.

8. The lawyer's briefcase hit me in the leg as I walked by.

9. I never could understand Mr. Davidson's sense of humor.

10. The dentist's drill needs to be sterilized after each patient.

✱ Practice 7 Identifying   Put an X next to the sentence if an apostrophe is missing or used incorrectly.

1. _____ Jennifer's dad is on his way to Boston.
2. __X__ Dustin wrecked his moms car last night. *(mom's)*
3. __X__ The two dog's food dish is full of bugs. *(dogs')*
4. __X__ Marks walls are covered with Post-it Notes. *(Mark's)*
5. __X__ My one brothers' dream is to climb Mount Everest. *(brother's)*
6. __X__ Uncle Bobs' boat sank in Lake Eerie. *(Bob's)*
7. _____ They broke into their friend's room and left a present.
8. __X__ Can you see the childrens' department from here? *(children's)*
9. _____ The many customers' complaints have been reviewed.
10. __X__ Are you going to Eddies' birthday party? *(Eddie's)*

✿ Practice 8 Correcting   Correct the apostrophe errors in Practice 7 by rewriting each incorrect sentence. *See Practice 7.*

1. _____
2. _____
3. _____
4. _____
5. _____
6. _____
7. _____
8. _____
9. _____
10. _____

✿ Practice 9 Completing   Add apostrophes to the possessive nouns in the following paragraph.

Last year we spent Mother's Day at the Rollerama with my little sister. We decided that our family's time together was important, so we promised each other we would stay together all day. Beth's passion is to roller-skate. Dad's passion is not to roller-skate. I was somewhere in the middle, and Mom was just enjoying the day's activities. The roller rink's entrance fee was waived that day, and all the other prices were discounted. My sister's friends were there, and I was embarrassed to be there. But I have to admit that I had fun.

❀ Practice 10 Writing Your Own

A. Create possessive nouns from the following phrases, and write a sentence of your own for each one. *Sentences will vary.*

1. the program of the children *(children's program)*

   _____

2. the dress code of the school *(school's dress code)*

   _____

3. the lunch break of the workers *(workers' lunch break)*

   _____

4. the cookies of the grandmother *(grandmother's cookies)*

   _____

5. the problems of Susanna *(Susanna's problem)*

   _____

B. Write five sentences of your own using apostrophes correctly in possessive nouns. *Answers will vary.*

1. _____
2. _____
3. _____
4. _____
5. _____

COMMON APOSTROPHE ERRORS

Two common errors occur with apostrophes. The following guidelines will help you avoid these errors.

No Apostrophe with Possessive Pronouns

Do not use an apostrophe with a possessive pronoun. Possessive pronouns are possessive without an apostrophe, so they do not need an apostrophe.

		Correct
NOT	his'	his
NOT	her's or hers'	hers
NOT	it's or its'	its
NOT	your's or yours'	yours
NOT	our's or ours'	ours
NOT	their's or theirs'	theirs

No Apostrophe to Form the Plural

Do not use an apostrophe to form a plural word. This error occurs most often with plural words ending in *-s*. An apostrophe indicates possession or contraction; it does *not* indicate the plural. Therefore, a plural word never takes an apostrophe unless it is possessive.

NOT	The **bike's** are in the garage.
Correct:	The **bikes** are in the garage.

NOT	He bought a new pair of **shoe's** yesterday.
Correct:	He bought a new pair of **shoes** yesterday.

NOT	I saw eight hockey **game's** this season.
Correct:	I saw eight hockey **games** this season.

Reviewing Apostrophe Errors

List three possessive pronouns.

Answers will vary. _____   _____   _____

Why don't possessive pronouns take apostrophes?

They are possessive without apostrophes. _____

What is wrong with the apostrophe in each of the following sentences?

The last float in the parade is our's. The pronoun ours is possessive without an apostrophe.

There must be 100 floats' in the parade. Floats is plural only, not possessive.

❧ **Practice 11 Identifying**   Add missing apostrophes in the following sentences where necessary.

1. We help with Dad's projects whenever he's around.

2. My boss's files are a mess!

3. I thought your presentation was great, but I really enjoyed Misty's and hers.

4. Kyle's going to his grandfather's house.

5. Dust Susan's lamps while I'm cleaning out her refrigerator.

6. My new parrot used to be theirs, but now it's Sydney's.

7. Winston received five awards at yesterday's ceremony.

8. I thought I had good penmanship until I saw Terrence's.

9. If the neighbor's dog barks at you, give him a treat.

10. One of those chairs' legs is broken.

❧ **Practice 12 Identifying**   Put an X next to the sentence if an apostrophe is missing or used incorrectly.

1. __X__ That new car is her's. *(hers)*

2. _____ I lost my handouts, so I had to borrow theirs.

3. __X__ There were four nails' in my front tire. *(nails)*

4. __X__ This is my paper, but can I see your's? *(yours)*

5. __X__ Jackson ordered pizza's for our meeting. *(pizzas)*

6. __X__ Office Depot has computer's on sale. *(computers)*

7. _____ Do you have his telephone number?

8. __X__ These book's are going to the basement. *(books)*

9. _____ You can sit at any of the tables in this room.

10. __X__ When they ran out of their soft drinks, I offered to share our's. *(ours)*

❧ **Practice 13 Correcting**   Correct the apostrophe errors in Practice 12 by rewriting each incorrect sentence. *See Practice 12.*

1. _____

2. _____

3. _____

4. _____

5. _____

6. _____

7. _____

8. _____

9. _____

10. _____

🌿 Practice 14 Completing   Correct the apostrophe errors in the following paragraph.

After breakfast, Sam walked around the cabin. Bug's had come in through the hole in the screen door, and Sam squashed some of them with his' bare hand's. The cabin was especially quiet, so he began looking through the cabinet's in the kitchen. He was hungry, but he didn't want to bother any of the other campers'. He found a jar of grape jelly that was labeled "Homemade by Marci," and he tasted it. He also found some homemade biscuit's that he knew were her's too, but he didn't think she'd mind if he ate them. When he'd just about filled his' stomach, Marci walked into the room. She smiled at him and gave him two napkin's to wipe the jelly off of his face.

🌿 Practice 15 Writing Your Own

A. Write a sentence of your own for each of the following possessive pronouns. *Answers will vary.*

1. hers _____

2. its _____

3. his _____

4. yours _____

5. theirs _____

B. Write five sentences of your own using apostrophes correctly. *Answers will vary.*

1. _____

2. _____

3. _____

4. _____

5. _____

CHAPTER REVIEW

You might want to reread your answers to the questions in the review boxes before you do the following exercises.

❋ Review Practice 1 Reading   Refer to the paragraph by Alan Monroe on page 378 to do the following exercises.

1. List four contractions from the paragraph.

   I'll _____   *they're* _____

   they're _____   *they're* _____

2. List four possessive nouns with apostrophes.

   people's _____   *one's* _____

   one's _____   *listener's* _____

3. List two possessive pronouns.

   its _____   *their* _____

4. List four plural nouns that end in *-s*.

   Answers will vary. _____   _____

   _____   _____

❋ Review Practice 2 Identifying   Underline the words missing apostrophes or the words in which apostrophes are used incorrectly in each of the following sentences.

1. <u>Terrys</u> piano needs to be tuned. *(Terry's)*

2. The library's <u>hour's</u> change every six <u>month's</u>. *(hours, months)*

3. Some of the <u>actor's</u> <u>werent</u> familiar with their lines. *(actors, weren't)*

4. <u>Im</u> going to the mall to buy <u>pant's</u> like <u>your's</u>. *(I'm, pants, yours)*

5. My <u>geranium's</u> <u>havent</u> bloomed yet. *(geraniums, haven't)*

6. <u>Its</u> impossible to see those <u>planet's</u> without a telescope. *(It's, planets)*

7. <u>Shes</u> going to Magic Mountain for the day. *(She's)*

8. The <u>waters</u> too cold for swimming right now. *(water's)*

9. My <u>principals</u> wife is good <u>friend's</u> with my aunt. *(principal's, friends)*

10. I <u>shouldnt</u> have told you about that new house of <u>their's</u>. *(shouldn't, theirs)*

Review Practice 3 Correcting   Correct the apostrophe errors in Review Practice 2 by rewriting the sentences. *See Review Practice 2.*

1. _____

2. _____

3. _____

4. _____

5. _____

6. _____

7. _____

8. _____

9. _____

10. _____

EDITING A STUDENT PARAGRAPH

Following is a paragraph written and revised by Willie Perkins in response to the writing assignment in this chapter. Read the paragraph, and underline each of his words with apostrophes.

I like to talk, especially when I have an audience. <u>I'm</u> usually the one coming up with conversation <u>topic's</u>, trying to make people laugh, and "breaking the ice." Sometimes in a classroom situation, though, its different. I dont mind answering <u>question's</u> that the instructor poses, but sometimes Im afraid that Ill say the wrong thing and make a fool of myself. The difference is that in social situations, <u>I'm</u> not being judged. <u>Everyone's</u> trying to be <u>friend's</u> and have

Here are the corrections:
it's
don't
I'm
I'll
I'm
instructor's
students'
it's

fun. In a classroom, the instructor is waiting to see if I know

what Im talking about. The instructor's always judging
    X

me, but that's the instructors job. Though I'm not always
                          X

the one to dominate class discussion's, I do like to partici-

pate in them. I'd much rather we talk in groups than listen

to lectures. I like to hear other students opinions, because
                                          X

sometimes they'll bring up very interesting points. Al-

though talking in front of people can sometimes be intimi-

dating, its a very good way to learn about yourself.
        X

Collaborative Activity

Team up with a partner, and mark an X above the eight words that are missing apostrophes in Willie's paragraph. Place a second underline under the
four plural nouns that use apostrophes incorrectly. Then, working together,
use what you have learned in this chapter to correct these errors. Rewrite the
paragraph with your corrections. *See student paragraph. Corrections are in the margin.*

❧ EDITING YOUR OWN PARAGRAPH

Now return to the paragraph you wrote and revised at the beginning of this
chapter. Underline each word that contains an apostrophe.

Collaborative Activity

Exchange paragraphs with your partner, and circle any missing or misplaced
apostrophes that you find in your partner's paragraph.

Individual Activity

On the Error Log in Appendix 6, record the apostrophe errors that your
partner found in your paragraph. To complete the writing process, correct
these errors by rewriting your paragraph.

Quotation Marks

Checklist for Using Quotation Marks

✔ Are quotation marks used to indicate someone's exact words?

✔ Are all periods and commas inside quotation marks?

✔ Are words capitalized correctly in quotations?

✔ Are quotation marks used to indicate the title of a short work, such as a short story or a poem?

Quotation marks are punctuation marks that work together in pairs. Their most common use is to indicate someone's exact words. They are also used to indicate the title of a short piece of writing, such as a short story or a poem.

Note how quotation marks are used in the following paragraph by Anna Quindlen.

> My husband, a bred-in-the-bone Boyfriend, was terrified of this aspect of having children, convinced that on the morning after our first son was born he would awaken with a drawerful of pajamas and cardigan sweaters and the urge to say things like, "Now, son, I think we should have a little talk about that." Not a chance. His most recent foray into fatherhood was to teach both his children the words to "You Give Love a Bad Name." The eldest can also play air guitar along with the song. On the one hand, I hate "You Give Love a Bad Name," although my children sing it rather well. On the other hand, my husband would not think twice about scandalizing a Confederate ball by bidding $150 in gold to dance with me. And, like Scarlett, when someone said, "She will not consider it, sir," I know what I would say without a moment's hesitation: "Oh, yes, I will."

TEACHING
QUOTATION MARKS
Present the class with an excerpt from a play (one with numerous stage directions and comments) written as one long paragraph with no quotation marks to distinguish the spoken language from the stage directions. Have a student read the excerpt from the play. Students will see how difficult distinguishing the stage remarks from the words is and will then understand the value of marking direct quotations.

Then have students work in groups of three or four to punctuate the paragraph correctly by adding quotation marks and proper spacing.

■ For sample paragraphs, see the *Instructor's Resource Manual*, Section II, Part II.

In this paragraph, Anna Quindlen writes about music's role in her marriage. Before continuing in this chapter, take a moment to record your ideas about music. Save your work because you will use it later in this chapter.

Writing Assignment: Music

Are you interested in music? Do you play music or enjoy listening to it? How has music affected you personally? Has it helped you make friends, or has it helped you learn more about yourself? Write a paragraph explaining your thoughts about music and the role it plays in your life.

Revising Your Writing

Revise the first draft of your paragraph before you focus on editing. Use the Revising Checklist on pages 24–25 to help you with your revision. Make sure your paragraph has a good topic sentence, is well developed, and is well organized. Then check your paragraph for unity and coherence.

DIRECT QUOTATIONS

Use quotation marks to indicate a direct quotation—someone's exact words. Here are some examples. They show the three basic forms of a direct quotation.

Direct Quotation: "This is a great song," said the teenager.

Here the quoted words come first.

Direct Quotation: The teenager said, "This is a great song."

Here the quoted words come after the speaker is named.

Direct Quotation: "This," the teenager said, "is a great song."

In this example, the quoted words are interrupted, and the speaker is named in the middle. This form emphasizes the beginning words.

INDIRECT QUOTATIONS

If you just talk about someone's words, you do not need quotation marks. Look at these examples of **indirect quotations.** Indirect quotations usually use the word *that*, as in *said that*. In questions, the wording is often *asked if*.

> **Direct Quotation:**   "I'm joining a rock band," said Rick.

These are Rick's exact words, so you must use quotation marks.

> **Indirect Quotation:**   Rick **said that** he is going to join a rock band.

This sentence explains what Rick said but does not use Rick's exact words. So quotation marks should not be used.

> **Direct Quotation:**   "There will be a jazz concert next weekend," said Donna.
>
> **Indirect Quotation:**   Donna **said that** there will be a jazz concert next weekend.
>
> **Direct Quotation:**   "Could you sing at my wedding?" Sharon asked.
>
> **Indirect Quotation:**   Sharon **asked if** I could sing at her wedding.

REVIEWING QUOTATION MARKS WITH QUOTATIONS

How do you show that you are repeating someone's exact words?

Put the words in quotation marks

What is an indirect quotation?

An explanation of someone's words but not the exact words

 Practice 1 Identifying   Add missing quotation marks to the following sentences where necessary.

1. Nadia said, "I really liked visiting with you yesterday."

2. Murphy asked, "Can we start this project tonight?"

3. I called the phone company and said, "My phone has been disconnected."

4. "Take me to the game with you," Stefan begged.

5. "This is the only afternoon," I said, "when we can get these things finished."

6. "Are you ready?" they asked us.

7. The firefighters yelled to the woman, "Jump out the window!"

8. Charles told me, "He didn't do well on the last test."

9. "Stand up and cheer!" yelled the cheerleaders.

10. "This dip is outstanding," I told her.

🌿 Practice 2 Identifying   Put an X next to the sentence if quotation marks are missing or used incorrectly.

1. ___X___ "Run! yelled the first base coach. *("Run!")*

2. ___X___ Robert said, The apple pie "tastes delicious." *("The apple pie tastes delicious.")*

3. _____ "Going to the movies," she said, "is my favorite pastime."

4. ___X___ Angela asked if "we could help her with her car." *(no quotation marks needed)*

5. ___X___ Jackie replied, "Of course, you are invited. *(invited.")*

6. _____ "Is this the best you could do?" I asked.

7. ___X___ "Give me one reason," he said, why I should believe you." *(said, "why)*

8. ___X___ Nicole said "that she wanted to see Big Ben." *(no quotation marks needed)*

9. ___X___ "Can I get you something to drink? the hostess asked. *(drink?")*

10. _____ "Don't forget," she said, "that we have a test tomorrow."

🌿 Practice 3 Correcting   Correct the quotation mark errors in Practice 2 by rewriting each incorrect sentence. *See Practice 2.*

1. _____

2. _____

3. _____

4. _____

5. _____

6. _____

7. _____

8. _____

9. _____

10. _____

🌱 Practice 4 Completing Add quotation marks to the following paragraph.

Kevin had the day off, so he called Marty and asked, "Do you want to play golf today?" "Well, I don't know," said Marty. "What do you mean?" asked Kevin. Marty explained, "I promised my girlfriend we'd go to the beach." "The beach?" Kevin said. "Well, it's our six-month anniversary," Marty said. "You don't count months for anniversaries," Kevin responded, "because anniversaries mark only years." Marty didn't follow his logic. "The word is related to the word *annual*, which means yearly," Kevin continued, "so you don't owe her anything until you have dated for one year." Marty thought for a minute and then replied, "I think you should be the one to explain that to my girlfriend." "No thanks," Kevin replied. "I'd have better luck finding someone else to golf with!"

🌱 Practice 5 Writing Your Own

A. Write a sentence of your own for each of the following items. *Answers will vary.*

1. a question Margaret asked

_____

2. a statement spoken by a police officer

_____

3. an exclamation spoken by Randy

_____

4. an indirect question that Tabitha asked

_____

5. a statement spoken by the plumber

_____

B. Write five sentences of your own using quotation marks correctly. *Answers will vary.*

1. _____

2. _____

3. _____

4. _____

5. _____

CAPITALIZING AND USING OTHER PUNCTUATION MARKS WITH QUOTATION MARKS

Quotation marks are used around sentences or parts of sentences. Therefore, when you are quoting someone's exact sentences, begin with a capital letter and use appropriate end punctuation—a period, a question mark, or an exclamation point. You do not need to capitalize the first word of a quotation if it is only part of a sentence. Here are some examples.

"This is a very good band," he said.

She said, "Turn up the stereo."

Capitalize the first letter of the words being quoted, and put a period at the end of the sentence if it is a statement. Separate the spoken words from the rest of the sentence with a comma.

He yelled, "Stop that car!"

"Why are you leaving?" she asked.

If the quotation ends with a question mark or an exclamation point, use that punctuation instead of a comma or a period.

"Yes," said the guitar player, "we will give you a concert."

In a quotation that is interrupted, capitalize the first word being quoted, but do not capitalize words in the middle of the sentence. Use a comma both before and after the interruption. End with a period if it is a statement.

My mom told me to relax and "have faith."

You do not need to capitalize the first word of a quotation that is only part of a sentence.

HINT: Look at the examples again. Notice that periods and commas always go *inside* the quotation marks.

NOT   "No**"**, he said, "this isn't the way to Woodstock**"**.

Correct: "No**,"** he said, "this isn't the way to Woodstock**."**

REVIEWING CAPITALIZATION AND PUNCTUATION
WITH QUOTATION MARKS

When you quote someone's exact words, why should you begin with a capital letter?

Because the word begins a sentence

Where do commas go in relation to quotation marks? Where do periods go?

Both commas and periods go inside quotation marks.

Practice 6 Identifying   Add missing punctuation to the following sentences where necessary. Check for proper capitalization also.

1. "These are the best cookies I have ever eaten,"she remarked.

2. "What happened to Jeremy?"Terry asked.

3. Patty smiled and said,"thanks so much for coming by to see me."

4. "Take this class with me,"said my friend.

5. Rachel exclaimed, "I passed the test!"

6. "Could you drop these off for me?"Greta asked.

7. The nurse instructed,"Lie down on your side."

8. "Ouch! My ankle's broken!"screamed Tim.

9. "I think I'm feeling sick,"said Holly.

10. "We're meeting at lunch in the cafeteria,"he said.

Practice 7 Identifying   Put an X next to the sentence if it contains capitalization or punctuation errors.

1. __X__ "Give up", he said as he tackled his opponent. *(up,")*

2. _____ Rudolfo complained, "There's no more turkey in the refrigerator."

3. __X__ "Walk me to my car, she said, "so I can talk to you." (car,")

4. _____ The tree trimmer asked, "How long has that tree been infected?"

5. __X__ "Have you seen," I asked, "That new horror movie?" (asked, "that)

6. __X__ "If you leave," she told him, don't come back." (him, "don't)

7. __X__ My neighbor asked, "can we borrow your wheelbarrow?" (asked, "Can)

8. _____ Landon said, "My fraternity is having a big fund-raiser."

9. __X__ Michael greeted his guests and said, "welcome to my home." (said, "Welcome)

10. _____ "This," she said, "is my favorite part of the game."

🌱 Practice 8 Correcting   Correct the errors in Practice 7 by rewriting each incorrect sentence. *See Practice 7.*

1. _____
2. _____
3. _____
4. _____
5. _____
6. _____
7. _____
8. _____
9. _____
10. _____

🌱 Practice 9 Completing   Add quotation marks and other necessary punctuation to the following paragraph.

I took my tomcat to a local pet groomer and asked her, "How much would it cost to get this cat bathed?" "Well, does he have fleas?" she asked. "Not that I know of," I replied. "Then that will make it cheaper," she said "because he won't need to be dipped." "Dipped?" I asked. "Yes," she explained, "we have a flea dip that is really effective on cats, but it's more expensive." "Well, I think he only needs a normal bath," I said. "Actually," she said, "he's pretty clean already. I think he just needs a good brushing." "OK," I said, "how much would that cost?" She stroked my cat's back and answered, "I'll do it for $20."

🌾 Practice 10 Writing Your Own

A. Write a sentence of your own for each of the following direct quotations.
Answers will vary.

1. "Get off the bus!"

   _____

2. "Maureen is coming over for dinner."

   _____

3. "Are you sure we have ice cream?"

   _____

4. "Hand me that book."

   _____

5. "You need a new tennis racket."

   _____

B. Write five sentences of your own using quotation marks correctly. *Answers will vary.*

1. _____
2. _____
3. _____
4. _____
5. _____

QUOTATION MARKS AROUND TITLES

Put quotation marks around the titles of short works that are parts of larger works. The titles of longer works are put in italics (or underlined).

Quotation Marks	Italics/Underlining
"The Wild Swans" (short story)	*Hans Andersen's Fairy Tales* (book)
"Mud Master" (poem)	*The Collected Poems of Wallace Stevens* (book)
"There's Your Trouble" (song)	*Wide Open Spaces* (CD)
"Losing Weight the Easy Way" (magazine article)	*Parenting* (magazine)

"Power Bills on the Rise"
(newspaper article)

Orange County Register
(newspaper)

"The Inferno" (episode on a
TV show)

Third Watch (TV show)

REVIEWING QUOTATION MARKS WITH TITLES

When do you put quotation marks around a title?

When it is a short work that is part of a larger work

When do you italicize (or underline) a title?

When it is a longer work

 Practice 11 Identifying   Add missing quotation marks in the following sentences where necessary.

1. Last night's episode of *LA Law* was called "The Verdict."

2. *People* magazine ran an article called "Hollywood Threatens Strike!"

3. The Oates story "A Good Man Is Hard to Find" was made into a movie last summer.

4. We always sing "Hit Me with Your Best Shot" when we go to the karaoke bar.

5. "Wedding Bells Are Ringing" was a great article in February's *Brides Magazine*.

6. Mark Twain wrote the essay "How to Tell a Story" after he wrote the book *The Adventures of Huckleberry Finn*.

7. The *Boston Globe* conducted a survey asking people about the president's new bill.

8. Aretha Franklin's best song ever was "Respect."

9. "Birches" by Robert Frost was published in 1916.

10. Every time I hear "I Will Remember You" on the radio, I cry.

 Practice 12 Identifying   Put an X next to the sentence in which the titles are punctuated incorrectly.

1. __X__ "Beloved" is my favorite novel by Toni Morrison. *(Beloved)*

2. _____ When I hear the Beach Boys sing "Surfin' USA," it makes me want to go to the beach.

3. __X__ I read some good gardening advice in Making Roses Your Friends in *American Gardener Magazine*. *("Making Roses Your Friends")*

4. __X__ The "Denver Herald" ran an article on the recent snowstorm. *(Denver Herald)*

5. __X__ I can't wait to watch "Frasier" tonight. *(Frasier)*

6. _____ "Success Is Counted Sweetest" is a popular poem by Emily Dickinson.

7. __X__ "The Weakest Link" is having the "Celebrity Episode" next Thursday night. *(The Weakest Link)*

8. _____ "Brown-Eyed Girl" is the theme song for our charity event.

9. __X__ Xavier read a great article in "Newsweek" about the recent election. *(Newsweek)*

10. _____ My literature class studied Hawthorne's short story "Young Goodman Brown" this quarter.

Practice 13 Correcting   Correct the quotation mark errors in Practice 12 by rewriting each incorrect sentence. *See Practice 12.*

1. _____

2. _____

3. _____

4. _____

5. _____

6. _____

7. _____

8. _____

9. _____

10. _____

🌿 **Practice 14 Completing**　Place quotation marks around the titles of short works, and underline the titles of long works in the following paragraph.

　　　Marjorie Clemens is a popular celebrity agent in Hollywood. She spotted the band Four Up when it was playing in a small hometown talent show. The group sang "Hangin' with My Girl," and Marjorie just knew it would be a hit. She put Four Up in contact with Arista Records, who released the album <u>Just Four Fun</u> only a few months later. Soon all of the teen magazines, such as <u>Bop</u> and <u>Teen Dream</u>, were printing articles about Four Up. The guys were stunned by their overnight success as they read articles titled "Four Up Not Coming Down" and "Americans Want These Guys Four Keeps." Three years later, a journalist named Walt Gentry worked with them on a book he titled <u>One, Two, Three, Four Up: Counting on Our Fans</u>. But just when the group had become a household name, the lead singer, Eric Bassy, left for a solo career. Music fans all over America were in tears as they read "Four Up Is One Down" across the front page of the newspapers.

🌿 **Practice 15 Writing Your Own**

A. Write a sentence of your own for each of the following titles. Make up a title if you can't think of one. *Answers will vary.*

1. a short story _____

2. a song title _____

3. a newspaper article _____

4. a poem _____

5. a magazine article _____

B. Write five sentences of your own using quotation marks correctly. *Answers will vary.*

1. _____

2. _____

3. _____

4. _____

5. _____

CHAPTER REVIEW

You might want to reread your answers to the questions in the review boxes before you do the following exercises.

❊ **Review Practice 1 Reading**   Refer to the paragraph by Anna Quindlen on page 393 to do the following exercises.

1. List the three direct quotations in the paragraph.

   . . . to say things like, "Now, son, I think we should have a little talk about that."

   And, like Scarlett, when someone said, "She will not consider it, sir," I know what I would say . . .

   . . . without a moment's hesitation: "Oh, yes, I will."

2. List the one song title in the paragraph.

   "You Give Love a Bad Name"

❊ **Review Practice 2 Identifying**   Mark an X above each place where punctuation is used incorrectly or missing.

1. Seth is watching his favorite video, I said. *("Seth . . . video,")*
2. Austin asked Can I borrow your shower? *(asked, "Can . . . shower?")*
3. Arlene titled her essay The Truth About Being Twenty. *(essay, "The . . . Twenty.")*
4. When we arrived at the hotel, the valet asked if "we wanted him to park the car." *(if we wanted . . . car.)*
5. Zane memorized Roethke's poem My Papa's Waltz for his English class. *("My . . . Waltz")*
6. When Mother Teresa died, the *New York Times* ran an article with the headline Saint Taken Home. *("Saint . . . Home.")*
7. When you get back she said let's go out to dinner. *("When . . . back," she said, "let's . . . dinner.")*
8. Edgar said that "we could meet at his house." *(that we could . . . house.)*
9. We sang Happy Birthday to Fran in class today. *("Happy Birthday")*
10. I read an article in *Tennis Weekly* titled How Venus Williams Stays in the Game. *("How . . . Game.")*

❊ **Review Practice 3 Correcting**   Correct the quotation marks and other punctuation errors in Review Practice 2 by rewriting each of the sentences.

✎ EDITING A STUDENT PARAGRAPH

Following is a paragraph written and revised by Scott Flores in response to the writing assignment in this chapter. Read the paragraph, and underline each of his quotation marks.

Listening to music is my favorite way to relax. The only instrument that I can play is my stereo, but I like to play it nice and loud. I really enjoy alternative rock bands, such as Blink-182. I listen to the band's CD "Cheshire Cat" almost every single day. "Touchdown Boy" is my favorite song, even though my mother hates the lyrics. She always screams, "Turn that music down!" But all of my friends like the music too. In fact, I didn't realize that Blink-182 had so many fans. I went to a concert last month and saw about 20 people from my school standing in the audience. I've heard people say, "Classical music is the best," but I believe that all music is an expression. It's both an expression of the artist and an expression of the person or people listening to it. With that in mind, I'd say that alternative rock expresses my personality best.

Collaborative Activity

Team up with a partner, and underline twice the six quotation mark errors (including the missing quotation marks) in Scott's paragraph. Then, working together, use what you have learned in this chapter to correct these errors. Rewrite the paragraph with your corrections. *See student paragraph for errors and corrections.*

❧ EDITING YOUR OWN PARAGRAPH

Now return to the paragraph you wrote and revised at the beginning of this chapter. Underline each of your quotation marks.

Collaborative Activity

Exchange paragraphs with your partner, and circle any quotation mark errors that you find in your partner's paragraph.

Individual Activity

On the Error Log in Appendix 6, record any quotation mark errors that your partner found in your paragraph. To complete the writing process, correct these errors by rewriting your paragraph.

Other Punctuation Marks

✐ Checklist for Using Semicolons, Colons, Dashes, and Parentheses

- ✔ Are semicolons used to join two closely related complete sentences?
- ✔ Are long items in a series that already contains commas separated by semicolons?
- ✔ Are colons used correctly to introduce a list?
- ✔ Are dashes used to emphasize or further explain a point?
- ✔ Are parentheses used to include additional, but not necessary, information?

This chapter explains the uses of the semicolon, colon, dash, and parentheses. We'll look at these punctuation marks one by one.

Note how the following paragraph by Joan Didion uses those punctuation marks correctly.

> But Las Vegas seems to offer something other than "convenience"; it is merchandising "niceness," the facsimile of proper ritual, to children who do not know how else to find it, how to make the arrangements, how to do it "right." All day and evening long on the Strip, one sees actual wedding parties, waiting under the harsh lights at a crosswalk, standing uneasily in the parking lot of the Frontier while the photographer hired by The Little Church of the West ("Wedding Place of the Stars") certifies the occasion, takes the picture: the bride in a veil and white satin pumps, the bridegroom usually in a white dinner jacket, and even an attendant or two, a sister or a best friend in hot-pink *peau de soie,* a flirtation veil, a carnation nosegay. "When I Fall in Love It Will Be Forever," the organist

TEACHING OTHER PUNCTUATION MARKS
Before class, put a series of sentence parts and punctuation marks on small pieces of cardboard. The sentence parts should include clauses, phrases, and single parts of speech.

Assign several pieces of cardboard to each student, and have the students begin by wearing one card. Then have students who are sentence parts stand in front of the class to form a sentence. For example, six students might make the following sentence:

I went bike riding
  (independent clause)
after my classes
  (prepositional phrase)
because that sport gives me a complete workout (dependent clause)
thighs/abs/lungs/heart
  (words)

Then have the people who are punctuation marks go to the correct places in the sentence (for example, a colon after *workout* and commas after *thighs*, *abs*, and *lungs*). By moving students around, show them how punctuation changes when certain words, phrases, and clauses are rearranged, added, or inserted.

■ For more words, phrases, and clauses, see the *Instructor's Resource Manual*, Section II, Part II.

TEACHING ON THE WEB

Exploring and Discussing: Have students find a magazine article on-line. Then have them rewrite portions of the article by changing the punctuation to include semicolons, colons, parentheses, and dashes. How does the inclusion of these punctuation marks alter the way people will view the message of the article? Does the new punctuation make the article more or less clear?

TEACHING ON THE WEB

Mosaics Web Site: To learn more about other punctuation, students can go to www.prenhall.com/mosaics.

plays, and then a few bars of Lohengrin. The mother cries; the stepfather, awkward in his role, invites the chapel hostess to join them for a drink at the Sands. The hostess declines with a professional smile; she has already transferred her interest to the group waiting outside. One bride out, another in, and again the sign goes up on the chapel door: "One moment please—Wedding."

In this paragraph, Joan Didion describes a Las Vegas wedding. Before continuing in this chapter, take a moment to record your thoughts about some rituals in your life. Save your work because you will use it later in this chapter.

Writing Assignment: Rituals in Your Life

What rituals have you participated in or observed? How did you feel about these rituals? Why do we have rituals? What one ritual holds special memories for you? Write a paragraph explaining this ritual to your class.

Revising Your Writing

Revise the first draft of your paragraph before you focus on editing. Use the Revising Checklist on pages 24–25 to help you with your revision. Make sure your paragraph has a good topic sentence, is well developed, and is well organized. Then check your paragraph for unity and coherence.

SEMICOLONS

Semicolons are used to separate equal parts of a sentence. They are also used to avoid confusion when listing items in a series.

1. **Use a semicolon to separate two closely related independent clauses.** An independent clause is a group of words with a subject and a verb that can stand alone as a sentence. You may use a semicolon instead of a coordinating conjunction (*and, but, for, nor, or, so, yet*) or a period. Any one of the three options would be correct.

	Independent	Independent

Semicolon: Carter wants to buy a new truck; he took one for a test drive yesterday.

Conjunction: Carter wants to buy a new truck, **so** he took one for a test drive yesterday.

Period: Carter wants to buy a new truck. **He** took one for a test drive yesterday.

2. **Use a semicolon to join two independent clauses that are connected by such words as** *however, therefore, furthermore, moreover, for example,* **or** *consequently.* Put a comma after the connecting word.

	Independent	Independent

Semicolon: Studying for exams is hard work; **however,** getting good grades is important.

Semicolon: You promised to help me paint the house; **therefore,** I expect you to be here.

Semicolon: She had a weakness for sweets; **for example,** she couldn't resist chocolate candy.

3. **Use a semicolon to separate items in a series when commas are already part of the list.**

NOT   To avoid leaving anyone out, we invited all of our friends from high school, college, and work, my mother's bridge club, and my father's tennis buddies.

Correct: To avoid leaving anyone out, we invited all of our friends from high school, college, and work; my mother's bridge club; and my father's tennis buddies.

REVIEWING SEMICOLONS

How are semicolons used between two independent clauses?

To separate the clauses

How are semicolons used with items in a series?

To separate the items when commas are included

❦ **Practice 1 Identifying**   Add missing semicolons or other punctuation to the following sentences where necessary.

1. We went to the drive-in; we ordered the cheeseburger special.

2. Monica borrowed $5 from me; she needed lunch and bus fare.

3. This weekend, we need to spray the trees, bushes, and flowers for bugs; paint the fence; and wash the car.

4. This book has been on the best-seller list for a month, but I didn't think it was very good.

5. The curtains need to be cleaned; however, I think I can put them in the washing machine.

6. Bathe the baby; put him in a new diaper, socks, and pajamas; and fix him a bottle.

7. Catherine took that picture when she was in Italy; it became her favorite.

8. We threw Diane a big baby shower; consequently, she had lots of thank-you notes to write.

9. Please bring me an aspirin; I have a horrible headache.

10. I don't agree with his teaching methods; furthermore, I won't be taking any more classes from him.

❦ **Practice 2 Identifying**   Put an X next to the sentence if it contains errors with semicolons.

1. _____ My house caught fire; I lost all of my pictures from elementary school.

2. __X__ We have saved more than $3,000, therefore; it is time that we took a big vacation. *($3,000; therefore,)*

3. __X__ We need to leave right now the movie; starts in five minutes. *(leave right now; the movie starts)*

4. _____ Jonathan is our strongest runner; he should be the first man in our relay team.

5. __X__ Mr. Jeffries raises corn; wheat; and oranges on his farm. *(corn, wheat, and oranges)*

6. _____ Deena works at Stairway to Beauty; she cuts hair and does nails.

7. __X__ Our toilet overflowed and flooded our carpet, consequently, our insurance premium was raised. *(carpet; consequently,)*

8. ___X___ The sale items include the furniture, appliances, and bedding; some of the ceiling fans, and the patio furniture. *(fans; and)*

9. ___X___ I vacuumed the carpets, but; I didn't polish the hardwood floors. *(carpets, but I didn't)*

10. ___X___ We have two orange cats in our neighborhood, however, I think one of them belongs to Mrs. Ayala. *(neighborhood; however,)*

🌿 **Practice 3 Correcting**   Correct the punctuation errors in Practice 2 by rewriting each incorrect sentence. *See Practice 2.*

1. _____
2. _____
3. _____
4. _____
5. _____
6. _____
7. _____
8. _____
9. _____
10. _____

🌿 **Practice 4 Completing**   Add semicolons to the following paragraph.

This summer, my friend Laura had to have knee surgery. She's a very active person;she dances and plays volleyball constantly. She has had to sit still for two weeks now, which is almost impossible for her. She is one of those people who can't quit moving;she's always in constant motion. If she's not dancing around while she's talking to you, she's sitting in an odd position;she's extremely limber. I don't know how much longer she has to stay off her knee;I hope it's not long. I think she'll go crazy soon;I can already see her dancing in her mind.

🌿 **Practice 5 Writing Your Own**

A. Write a sentence of your own of each of the following types. *Answers will vary.*

1. two closely related independent clauses joined with a semicolon

_____

2. two independent clauses joined by the word "nonetheless"

_____

3. a list that has items with commas

_____

4. two independent clauses joined by the word "however"

_____

5. two independent clauses joined by the words "for example"

_____

B. Write five sentences of your own using semicolons correctly. *Answers will vary.*

1. _____

2. _____

3. _____

4. _____

5. _____

COLONS

The main use of the **colon** is to introduce a list or thought. Here are some examples:

Colon: Bring the following items with you to the beach**:** a swim-suit, a towel, sun block, and sunglasses.

Colon: The mall opened several new stores**:** The Gap, Bath and Beauty, Victoria's Secret, and Old Navy.

Colon: The answer is clear**:** Take the trip.

The most common error with colons is using one where it isn't needed. Do not use a colon after the words *such as* or *including*. A complete sentence must come before a colon.

NOT   Use only primary colors, **such as:** blue, green, yellow, and red.

Correct: Use only primary colors, **such as** blue, green, yellow, and red.

NOT   They traveled to many places this summer, **including:** New Mexico and Arizona.

Correct: They traveled to many places this summer, **including** New Mexico and Arizona.

In addition, you should not use a colon after a verb or after a preposition. Remember that a complete sentence must come before a colon.

NOT   The best forms of cardiovascular exercise **are:** tennis and aerobics.

Correct: The best forms of cardiovascular exercise **are** tennis and aerobics.

NOT   Put the clothes **in:** the closet, the dresser, or the armoire.

Correct: Put the clothes **in** the closet, the dresser, or the armoire.

REVIEWING COLONS

What is the main use of a colon?

To introduce a list

Why should you not use a colon after such words as is or of?

A colon must come after a complete sentence.

※ Practice 6 Identifying Add missing colons to the following sentences where necessary.

1. Grandpa served in three wars: World War II, Korea, and Vietnam.

2. My favorite slush flavors are bubble gum, grape, and cherry.

3. We bought three new pieces of furniture: a dresser, an armoire, and a desk.

4. The ending of this book was awful: disappointing, predictable, and pathetic.

5. Could you hand me a pencil, a pen, and some paper?

6. We have three choices for the movie tonight: *Kiss of the Dragon, America's Sweethearts,* or *The Score.*

7. I'll take some food: a hot dog, a jumbo pretzel, and an ice-cream cone.

8. My favorite NHL teams are the Dallas Stars, the San Jose Sharks, and the Chicago Blackhawks.

9. Yolanda only has three classes left to take: chemistry, astronomy, and statistics.

10. I want to have a career in law enforcement, teaching, or accounting.

Practice 7 Identifying   Put an X next to the sentence if it contains colon errors.

1. __X__ We need to bring these things with us, as well as: the sodas, the chips, and the hot dogs. *(delete colon)*

2. __X__ Nathan has: three goals, graduate from college, get accepted by Harvard law school, and meet Judge Ito. *(has three goals:)*

3. __X__ My father always told me to: take pride in myself, believe in my abilities, and trust my instincts. *(delete colon)*

4. _____ Computers are good for many things: they speed communication, they organize finances, and they format important documents.

5. _____ I learned a great deal in this class: how to proofread, how to check spelling, and how to use colons.

6. __X__ My best friends are: Shawna, Kay, and Margie. *(delete colon)*

7. __X__ I knew she was lying when she: started playing with her hair, wouldn't look me in the eyes, and tried to change the subject. *(delete colon)*

8. _____ If you forget everything else, remember the following things: Be patient, try your best, and forgive yourself.

9. __X__ Darren left four things: on the nightstand—his wallet, his glasses, his passport, and his keys. *(four things on the nightstand:)*

10. __X__ On our vacation, we are going to: Disneyland, Lake Tahoe, and Mount Rushmore. *(delete colon)*

Practice 8 Correcting   Correct the colon errors in Practice 7 by re-writing each incorrect sentence. *See Practice 7.*

1. _____

2. _____

3. _____

4.   _____

5.   _____

6.   _____

7.   _____

8.   _____

9.   _____

10. _____

🌼 Practice 9 Completing   Add colons to the following letter.

Dear Howard,

   Here are our choices for dinner tonight:barbecue the tri-tip in the freezer, heat the leftover lasagna in the fridge, or order a pizza. If you decide on barbecue, I'll need you to do a few things:sweep off the back porch, refill the propane tank at the hardware store, and go to the market for barbecue sauce. There are only three brands of barbecue sauce I like. They are Hunts, El Paso, and O'Malley's. Thank you so much for this help. If you decide on pizza, make sure you tell them to add my favorite veggies:mushrooms, bell peppers, and olives. If you have any questions, please call me at work. I should be home for dinner.

Thanks again,

Vera

🌼 Practice 10 Writing Your Own

A. Write a sentence of your own for each of the following directions, using colons correctly. Remember that a complete sentence must come before a colon. *Answers will vary.*

1. three reasons to eat fast food

   _____

2. three colors in your bedroom

   _____

3. three things on a to-do list

   _____

4. three sports cars you would like to drive

_____

5. three reasons to own a computer

_____

B. Write five sentences of your own using colons correctly. *Answers will vary.*

1. _____

2. _____

3. _____

4. _____

5. _____

DASHES AND PARENTHESES

Use dashes to emphasize or draw attention to a point.

> **Dash:**   Nancy pinpointed her biggest source of stress—her husband.

In this example, the beginning of the sentence introduces an idea, and the dash then sets off the answer.

> **Dash:**   Faithfulness and honesty—these are the keys to a lasting relationship.

In this example, the key words are set off at the beginning, and the explanation follows. Beginning this way adds some suspense to the sentence.

> **Dashes:**   Patrick gave me a very nice birthday gift—a crystal vase—and I was quite impressed.

The dashes divide the sentence into three distinct parts, which makes the reader pause and think about each part.

While dashes set off material that the writer wants to emphasize, **parentheses** do just the opposite: **Use parentheses to set off information that is interesting or helpful but not necessary for understanding the sentence.**

> **Parentheses:**   My second cousin **(who owns an auto parts store)** is coming to visit.

> **Parentheses:**   The best coffee in town **(if you don't mind waiting in line)** is at a coffeehouse called Common Grounds.

Parentheses are also used to give a person's life span and to number items in a sentence. They are always used in pairs. Here are some examples:

Parentheses: Charles Dickens **(1812–1870)** wrote the long novel *Bleak House.*

Parentheses: I have three important errands today: **(1)** pick up the dry cleaning, **(2)** mail the bills, and **(3)** order the flowers.

REVIEWING DASHES AND PARENTHESES

What is the difference between dashes and parentheses?

Dashes emphasize information, and parentheses set off unnecessary but helpful

information.

When do you use dashes?

To emphasize or draw attention to a point

When do you use parentheses?

To set off information that isn't necessary to the main point of a sentence

---

Practice 11 Identifying Figure out whether the underlined words require dashes or parentheses, and add them to the following sentences where necessary.

1. My brother has one love in his life—<u>tennis shoes</u>.

2. We made a foolish purchase <u>(an old Model-T)</u> and ended up spending too much money restoring it.

3. This restaurant <u>(owned by Vietnamese people)</u> serves great French food.

4. <u>Photography</u>—that is the one thing I can do well.

5. Tillie <u>(who lives next door to my mother)</u> fell yesterday and broke her hip.

6. Lisa opened her mailbox to find the surprise of her life—<u>a check for $500,000</u>.

7. Richard opened his new office in the Haberfeld Center <u>(the tall brick building)</u> to attract more customers.

8. Mary is staying at my house so she can (1) feed my dogs, (2) water my houseplants, and (3) pick up my mail.

9. Bernadette Bradley (1816–1880) was one of the founders of this city.

10. My computer (a Compaq Presario) cost $1,200 when I bought it.

Practice 12 Identifying   Put an X next to the sentence if it contains errors with dashes or parentheses.

1. __X__ I wanted to buy this jacket (but I didn't have enough money).
(jacket—but . . . money.)

2. _____ Mandy (who plays tennis with my brother) is going to Yale next year.

3. _____ There is only one solution—take more time off work.

4. __X__ Greta made a good point—and I agree—Bill should not be in charge of that department. *(point, and I agree: Bill)*

5. __X__ Charles Divine lived (from 1919 to 1988). *(delete parentheses)*

6. __X__ (Courage and respect) these are two things I look for in a man.
(delete parenthesis, add dash after "respect")

7. _____ We gave Tom a television—a big-screen TV—so that he could enjoy the Super Bowl.

8. _____ The highest priorities are (1) the customer complaints, (2) the late bills, and (3) this month's invoices.

9. _____ I could sum up all of my problems with two words—money management.

10. _____ Movies and music—two things every American teen is interested in.

Practice 13 Correcting   Correct the punctuation errors in Practice 12 by rewriting each incorrect sentence. *See Practice 12.*

1. _____

2. _____

3. _____

4. _____

5. _____

6. _____

7. _____

8. _____

9. _____

10. _____

✤ Practice 14 Completing   Add dashes or parentheses around the underlined words in the following paragraph.

When Dad found Skipper (or rather, Skipper found Dad) , it was a hot summer day in my southern Kentucky hometown. For most of his life, Dad had never cared for pets, but the sight of that skinny, flea-infected puppy seemed to open his heart. Filthy and smelly—that's how I described Skipper when I first saw him. Skipper was curled up in the corner of an abandoned warehouse (the old Carter's Machinery building) that Dad's company was preparing to tear down. Dad carried Skipper to his truck and drove him to the neighborhood vet (who usually treated large farm animals) . The vet gave Dad something for the fleas (Bug-Out Flea Dip) and some vitamins to add to his food. He told Dad that Skipper was lucky to be found. If he'd been on the streets much longer, he would have surely picked up some kind of an infection—and most likely would have died. After a couple of weeks in our home, Skipper began to look healthy again. It took several flea baths (at least four) to get rid of the fleas, but Skipper didn't mind. As soon as Skipper was back on his feet, Dad began taking him to work with him. In no time, there was only one word to describe them—inseparable.

✤ Practice 15 Writing Your Own

A. Write a sentence of your own of each of the following types. *Answers will vary.*

1. a sentence that uses dashes to set off key words at the end

_____

2. a sentence that uses dashes to set off key words at the beginning

_____

3. a sentence that uses dashes to divide the sentence into three parts

_____

4. a list of three things using parentheses around the numbers

_____

5. a sentence that places the years of someone's life in parentheses

_____

B. Write five sentences of your own using dashes and parentheses correctly.
Answers will vary.

1. _____

2. _____

3. _____

4. _____

5. _____

CHAPTER REVIEW

You might want to reread your answers to the questions in the review boxes before you do the following exercises.

Review Practice 1 Reading   Refer to the paragraph by Joan Didion on pages 407–408 to do the following exercises.

1. List the two sentences with semicolons, and explain the rule that applies to each. *Answers may vary.*

    ". . . other than 'convenience'; it is merchandising niceness . . ."

    Rule: *Use semicolons to separate two closely related independent clauses.*

    "The mother cries; the stepfather, awkward in his role, . . ."

    Rule: *Use semicolons to separate two closely related independent clauses.*

2. List the two sentences with colons, and explain the rule that applies to each.

    "the photographer . . . takes the picture: the bride in a veil . . ."

    Rule: *Use colons to introduce a list.*

    "the sign goes up on the chapel door: 'One moment please—Wedding.'"

    Rule: *Use colons to introduce a thought.*

3. List the sentence with a dash, and explain the rule that applies to it.

    "'One moment please—Wedding'"

    Rule: *Use dashes to emphasize or draw attention.*

4. List the sentence with parentheses, and explain the rule that applies to it.

"(Wedding Place of the Stars)" _____

Rule: ___*Use parentheses to set off interesting but unnecessary information.*___

Review Practice 2 Identifying   Underline the semicolons, colons, dashes, and parentheses used incorrectly in the following sentences.

1. Sinclair Lewis—1885–1951—was an American author who won the Nobel Prize in 1930. *(Lewis (1885–1951) was)*

2. There are only three things I will do when I'm on vacation; check my e-mail, buy groceries, and read the paper. *(vacation:)*

3. She was crying for an hour today: however, she wouldn't tell us why. *(today;)*

4. Devon was wearing pants in my favorite color today (teal blue). *(today— teal blue.)*

5. Frank: who never forgets anything: locked his keys in the car. *(Frank (who ... anything))*

6. Cookies and cupcakes: are my biggest weakness. *(cupcakes are)*

7. (This chair comes in four colors) navy, black, brown, or beige. *(This chair ... colors:)*

8. My two-year-old is a very good climber (today I found him on the refrigerator)! *(climber—today ... refrigerator!)*

9. We have to meet Mark, Julie, and Craig: walk to the park: and set up the volleyball net. *(Craig; ... park;)*

10. This class requires that we—1, read two novels, 2, write five essays, and 3, do eight hours of community service. *(we (1) read ... , (2) write ... , and (3) do ...)*

Review Practice 3 Correcting   Correct the errors in Review Practice 2 by rewriting the sentences.

EDITING A STUDENT PARAGRAPH

Following is a paragraph written and revised by Angela Houston in response to the writing assignment in this chapter. Read the paragraph, and underline each of her semicolons, colons, dashes, and parentheses.

My family used to have the same routine from Christmas Eve to Christmas Day. This ritual started sometime when I was young (maybe around the time I was 10 or 11).

On Christmas Eve: my sister, my brother, and I would get to open one present from under the tree. We were allowed to choose it; we had to get approval before we could actually open it; just in case it was an expensive gift. We loved getting a taste of Christmas before the day arrived. That night, we would set out a plate of cookies for Santa and some carrots for Rudolph--which we later learned was for Dad and Sparky the dog. We were supposed to go to bed early--after all, Santa doesn't come when children are awake. But I usually decided to do my spring cleaning early and cleaned my room until I was too tired to keep my eyes open. Then (like clockwork) my little brother would wake us up at 3:30 a.m., excited to begin the day. This was the best part of the day: waking up our parents, opening our gifts, and enjoying the morning with the family. My mom would make homemade doughnuts; the best around; before we would all go back to bed for a nap. Later that evening, we would eat a wonderful dinner and just celebrate the holiday and our family; I miss those days.

Collaborative Activity

Team up with a partner, and place a second underline beneath the 10 punctuation errors in Angela's paragraph. Then, working together, use what you have learned in this chapter to correct these errors. Rewrite the paragraph with your corrections. *See student paragraph for errors. Corrections will vary.*

❧ EDITING YOUR OWN PARAGRAPH

Now return to the paragraph you wrote and revised at the beginning of this chapter. Underline each of your semicolons, colons, dashes, and parentheses.

Collaborative Activity

Exchange paragraphs with your partner, and circle any punctuation errors that you find in your partner's paragraph.

Individual Activity

On the Error Log in Appendix 6, record any punctuation errors that your partner found in your paragraph. To complete the writing process, correct these errors by rewriting your paragraph.

Unit 5 Review
Punctuation

🌾 **Unit Practice 1 Identifying**   Underline the punctuation errors in the following sentences.

1. I wonder if I left the lights on? *(on.)*

2. "Where's my credit card" yelled the woman in the store! *(card?" ... store.)*

3. The gardener mowed the grass; raked the leaves; and pruned the hedges this afternoon. *(grass, ... leaves, ...)*

4. We studied all night long; but we still missed several questions on the exam. *(long,)*

5. There are five yellow house's on my block. *(houses)*

6. Are you ready yet. *(yet?)*

7. The magnets on my refrigerator door are from: London, Paris, and Venice. *(no colon)*

8. I can't believe they wo'nt take personal checks here. *(won't)*

9. When he was a little boy; he ran around in his front yard naked. *(boy,)*

10. My great-grandfather, Sylvester Martin—1870–1950—founded this hardware store. *(Martin (1870–1950) founded)*

11. Are you going to be here for a few more minutes! *(minutes?)*

12. Please turn off (the television) before you leave the room. *(no parentheses)*

13. "If you can't find me, Paul said, I'm probably in the library." *(me," Paul said, "I'm)*

14. I went to the post office; which is near my office; and mailed those letters. *(office, which ... office, and)*

■ For additional material about teaching punctuation, for journal entries, and for various tests, see the *Instructor's Resource Manual,* Section II, Part II.

ADDITIONAL WRITING TOPIC
Let your students expand into well-developed essays the paragraphs they wrote in one of the unit chapters.

15. At 5:00 p.m., we need to pick up Sharon, Camilla, and Tony, drive to the restaurant, and reserve a table for six. *(Tony; . . . restaurant; . . .)*

16. The best desserts to bring are: lemon cream pie, chocolate brownies, or peach cobbler. *(no colon)*

17. <u>Shell</u> be here in about 10 minutes. *(She'll)*

18. Gary is riding his bike today because (his car ran out of gas). *(no parentheses)*

19. This weekend I plan to—1—visit my sister, —2—make cookies for Eddie, and —3—finish this needlepoint. *(to (1) visit . . . , (2) make . . . , and (3) finish . . .)*

20. "Did you drive or fly to Boston" asked Sheryl? *(Boston?" asked Sheryl.)*

✙ Unit Practice 2 Correcting   Correct the punctuation errors in Unit Practice 1 by rewriting each sentence. *See Unit Practice 1.*

✙ Unit Practice 3 Identifying   Underline the punctuation errors in the following paragraph.

Here are the corrections:
house.
it—finally
children, so
lots of hamburgers
   (no colon)
arrive,
job," they said.
friends, who works with
   my wife, was
house; the
wasn't
"Wow!" I exclaimed.

In July, we bought our very first house? There was only one word to describe it (finally). My wife and I have three small children; so it was about time for this move. We had a house-warming party on August 1, and we asked all of our friends to come see the new place. About 30 people said they would stop by, so we bought lots of: hamburgers, hot dogs, and sodas. When people started to arrive; they immediately told us how beautiful the house was. "You guys have really done a great job, they said." One of our friends—who works with my wife—was especially impressed that we did all of the landscaping ourselves. We really enjoyed visiting and showing off our new house, the party was over before we knew it. It was'nt until everyone had left that I saw what a mess they had made. There were spills on the carpet and glasses of punch left in every room. Napkins and trash had been dropped in the strangest places. "Wow" I exclaimed! "I think our house has been officially warmed!"

✙ Unit Practice 4 Correcting   Correct the punctuation errors in Unit Practice 3 by rewriting the paragraph. *Corrections are in the margin.*

UNIT WRITING ASSIGNMENTS

1. Who are these people? What sport do they play? Where is this scene? Imagine that you just watched one of their games, and write about what happened. Did they win or lose? What was the score? Did anything unusual or unexpected happen during the game?

2. How do you unwind? When you have a particularly stressful day, what do you do to relax? Do you read a book, listen to music, watch television, or do something else? Write about the steps you take to get rid of stress.

3. There are some natural differences between men and women, but most often we hear about the stereotypes. The reality is that women are *not* born to be better cooks or housekeepers than men, and men are *not* the only ones capable of repairing cars. What are some of the gender stereotypes that you have personally proved wrong? For example, are you a female who has a talent for math but an aversion to needlepoint? Are you a male who doesn't mind ironing his own shirts, but you cannot change the oil in your car? Describe one of your talents, interests, or dislikes that contradicts the stereotypes for your gender.

4. If you won an all-expense-paid vacation anywhere in the world, where would you go? If you knew that whatever you wanted to do at your vacation spot would be absolutely free, what would you do? What would you like to see if you only had the chance? Write about this vacation place and the activities you would find there. Use as many details as possible.

5. Create your own assignment (with the help of your instructor), and write a response to it.

Unit 6 Mechanics

The mechanical aspects of a sentence are much like the mechanical features of a car, an appliance, or a clock. They are some of the smallest—yet most important—details in a sentence. In writing, the term "mechanics" refers to capitalization, abbreviations, and numbers. We usually take these items for granted, but when they are used incorrectly, a sentence, just like a mechanical appliance with a weak spring, starts to break down.

Following a few simple guidelines will help you keep your sentences running smoothly and efficiently. They are explained in two chapters:

Chapter 25: Capitalization
Chapter 26: Abbreviations and Numbers

Students need to understand that although mechanical errors in sentences are minor, they shake the foundation of a sentence. The message becomes confusing and therefore starts to break down communication.

Following a few simple guidelines will help your students keep their sentences running smoothly and efficiently.

Capitalization

Checklist for Editing Capitalization

✔ Are all proper nouns capitalized?
✔ Are all words in titles capitalized correctly?
✔ Have you followed the other rules for capitalizing correctly?

Because every sentence begins with a capital letter, capitalization is the best place to start discussing the mechanics of good writing. Capital letters signal where sentences begin. They also call attention to certain kinds of words, making sentences easier to read and understand.

Notice how capitalization shows where a sentence begins and calls attention to specific words in the following paragraph.

On a bus trip to London from Oxford University where I was earning some graduate credits one summer, a young man, obviously fresh from a pub, spotted me and as if struck by inspiration went down on his knees in the aisle. With both hands over his heart he broke into an Irish tenor's rendition of "Maria" from *West Side Story*. My politely amused fellow passengers gave his lovely voice the round of gentle applause it deserved. Though I was not quite as amused, I managed my version of an English smile: no show of teeth, no extreme contortions of the facial muscles—I was at this time of my life practicing reserve and cool. Oh, that British control, how I converted it. But "Maria" had followed me to London, reminding me of a prime fact of my life: You can leave the island, master the English language, and travel as far as you can, but if you are Latina, especially one like me who obviously belongs to Rita Moreno's gene pool, the island travels with you.

TEACHING
CAPITALIZATION
Show students copies of real e-mail messages that contain no capitalization whatsoever. At the same time, show students copies of chat room conversations where people who type in all caps are told to "stop yelling."

Have students rewrite the e-mails with correct capitalization.

After the exercise, talk to students about how capitalization marks sentence boundaries.

■ For sample sentences, see the *Instructor's Resource Manual*, Section II, Part II.

TEACHING ON
THE WEB
Exploring and Discussing: Have students find information about author bell hooks on-line. Why doesn't she capitalize the first letters of her name? Why does the capitalization mean so much to her? What

does this say about the importance of capitalization overall?

TEACHING ON THE WEB

Mosaics Web Site: To learn more about capitalization, students can go to www.prenhall.com/mosaics.

In this paragraph, the young man makes an assumption about author Judith Ortiz Cofer based on her appearance. Before continuing in this chapter, take a moment to write about your experiences with snap judgments. Save your work because you will use it later this chapter.

Writing Assignment: Snap Judgments

Have you ever made a snap judgment about another person, or has someone ever assumed something false about you based on appearance? What was the judgment? What were the physical clues that led to the conclusion made? How did this make you or the other person feel? What did you learn from the experience? Write a paragraph focusing your thoughts on these questions.

Revising Your Writing

Revise the first draft of your paragraph before you focus on editing. Use the Revising Checklist on pages 24–25 to help you with your revision. Make sure your paragraph has a good topic sentence, is well developed, and is well organized. Then check your paragraph for unity and coherence.

CAPITALIZATION

Correct capitalization coupled with correct punctuation add up to good, clear writing. Here are some guidelines to help you capitalize correctly.

1. **Capitalize the first word of every sentence, including the first word of a quotation that forms a sentence.**

> We are vacationing in Hawaii.
> "We are vacationing in Hawaii," he said.
> He said, "We are vacationing in Hawaii."

Do not capitalize the second part of a quotation that is split.

> "We are vacationing," he said, "in Hawaii."

2. **Capitalize all proper nouns. Do not capitalize common nouns.**

Common Nouns	Proper Nouns
person	George Washington
state	Texas

building	Eiffel Tower
river	Columbia River
airplane	*Spruce Goose*

Here are some examples of proper nouns.

People:	Cindy, Marilyn Monroe, Jack Nicholson
Groups:	Russians, New Yorkers, Cherokees, Canadians, Vietnamese
Languages:	Latin, Gaelic, German
Religions, Religious Books, Holy Days:	Taoism, Baptist, Upanishads, Bible, Lent, Good Friday, Chanukah
Organizations:	American Kennel Club, Independent Party, American Association of University Women, National Council of Teachers of English
Places:	Yosemite National Park, New Orleans, Orange County, Bunker Hill, Sunset Boulevard, Highway 99, London Bridge, Tampa International Airport
Institutions, Agencies, Businesses:	North High School, Harvard University, UCLA Harbor Hospital, Pacific Bell
Brand Names, Ships, Aircraft:	Adidas, Dr Pepper, *Spirit of St. Louis*

3. **Capitalize titles used with people's names or in place of their names.**

> Mr. Judson L. Montgomery, Ms. Christy Waldo, Dr. Crystal Reeves
> Aunt Janet, Grandpa Bill, Cousin Margaret, Sis, Nana

Do not capitalize words that identify family relationships.

NOT	I talked with **my** Grandfather last month.
Correct:	I talked with **my** grandfather last month.
Correct:	I talked with Grandfather last month.

4. **Capitalize the titles of creative works.**

Books:	*The Stand*
Short Stories:	"Barn Burning"
Plays:	*Tea Party*

Poems:	"Icarus"
Articles:	"Ah, Happiness"
Magazines:	*Life*
Songs:	"Come Together"
Albums or CDs:	*Abbey Road*
Films:	*Gladiator*
TV Series:	*King of the Hill*
Works of Art:	*The Woman in the Red Hat*
Computer Programs:	Endnotes

Do not capitalize *a, an, the,* and short prepositions unless they are the first or last word in a title.

5. **Capitalize days of the week, months, holidays, and special events.**

   Monday, September, Mother's Day, the Fourth of July, Ramadan, Halloween

Do not capitalize the names of seasons: *summer, fall, winter, spring.*

6. **Capitalize the names of historical events, periods, and documents.**

   D-Day, the Battle of Wounded Knee, the Age of Enlightenment, the War of the Roses, the Seventies, the Bill of Rights

7. **Capitalize specific course *titles* and the names of language courses.**

   Sociology 401, Physics 300, French 202, Economic History

Do not capitalize a course or subject you are referring to in a general way unless the course is a language.

   my math course, my English course, my German course, my economics course

8. **Capitalize references to regions of the country but not words that merely indicate direction.**

   If you travel west from the Midwest, you will end up in the West.

9. **Capitalize the opening of a letter and the first word of the closing.**

   Dear Dr. Rogers, Dear Sir

   Fondest regards, Sincerely

Notice that a comma comes after the opening and closing.

REVIEWING CAPITALIZATION

Why is capitalization important in your writing?

It signals the beginning of a sentence and calls attention to certain kinds of words so

that sentences are easier to read and understand.

What is the difference between a proper noun and a common noun?

Common nouns are everyday words; proper nouns name specific people and things.

 Practice 1 Identifying   Underline the correctly capitalized word or phrase in each of the following sentences.

1. According to (<u>Mom</u>, mom), butter is better than margarine.

2. The letter ended with (<u>Love, Thelma</u>; love, Thelma).

3. Sue's (Grandmother, <u>grandmother</u>) was a full-blooded (<u>Crow</u>, crow) (<u>Indian</u>, indian).

4. Your (<u>Nike</u>, nike) shoes are under the couch.

5. My (Husband, <u>husband</u>) is a member of the (<u>Democratic Party</u>, democratic party), and I am a member of the (<u>Republican Party</u>, republican party).

6. In our (Physics, <u>physics</u>) class, we are learning (<u>Newtonian</u>, newtonian) math.

7. You must travel (North, <u>north</u>) from here to get to the (<u>East Coast</u>, east coast).

8. Last (Summer, <u>summer</u>), we ran a (Marathon, <u>marathon</u>) for the (<u>American Cancer Society</u>, american cancer society).

9. Even though (*The Simpsons*, *the simpsons*) has been canceled, I can still watch the (Reruns, <u>reruns</u>) on the (<u>Fox</u>, fox) network.

10. My favorite computer game is (<u>Diablo II</u>, diablo II), but for some reason it will only run on my (<u>Gateway</u>, gateway) computer.

 Practice 2 Identifying   Put an X next to the sentence if the underlined words are capitalized incorrectly.

1. __X__ Uncle John used to live in <u>Cairo</u>, Egypt, before he moved to Flower <u>street</u> in Willis, Texas. *(Street)*

2. _____ After graduating from <u>Permian High School</u>, I attended college at <u>South Coast University</u>.

3. __X__ when I was 13 years old, my dog ran away. *(When)*

4. __X__ The letter from <u>father</u> began, "<u>dear</u> son." *(Father, Dear)*

5. __X__ "We should leave," she said "<u>Before</u> the rain starts." *(before)*

6. _____ Sandra shopped at <u>Kmart</u> for some <u>Martha Stewart</u> bathroom accessories, some <u>Coca-Cola</u>, and a Dixie Chicks CD.

7. __X__ For <u>christmas</u>, I got season tickets to the <u>red sox</u> games. *(Christmas, Red Sox)*

8. __X__ I bought <u>aunt</u> Eustice a Liz Claiborne outfit. *(Aunt)*

9. __X__ In <u>anthropology</u> 400, we are studying the <u>paleolithic</u> <u>age</u>. *(Anthropology, Paleolithic, Age)*

10. _____ "Go <u>west</u>, young man," is a famous saying.

🌿 Practice 3 Correcting   Correct the capitalization errors in Practice 2 by rewriting each incorrect sentence. *See Practice 2.*

1. _____
2. _____
3. _____
4. _____
5. _____
6. _____
7. _____
8. _____
9. _____
10. _____

🌿 Practice 4 Completing   Fill in each blank in the following sentences with a word that makes sense and capitalize when necessary. *Answers will vary.*

1. Before _____ left the country, he made sure he had his _____ watch and shoes.

2. When we lived in _____, we saw the _____.

3. Jane's _____, George, used to work for the _____.

4. In _____ 405, we are studying the _____ age.

5. According to my _____ instructor, _____ was famous for his efforts.

6. People from _____ think their state is the best.

7. Travel _____ on _____ to reach _____.

8. This _____, we will celebrate _____.

9. "Everybody needs a few basic necessities," he said, "_____."

10. I belong to the _____, which helps needy families every _____.

🌱 **Practice 5 Writing Your Own**   Write 10 sentences of your own that cover all nine of the capitalization rules. *Answers will vary.*

1. _____

2. _____

3. _____

4. _____

5. _____

6. _____

7. _____

8. _____

9. _____

10. _____

CHAPTER REVIEW

You might want to reread your answers to the questions in the review boxes before you do the following exercises.

🌱 **Review Practice 1 Reading**   Refer to the paragraph by Judith Ortiz Cofer on page 427 to do the following exercises.

1. List the capitalization rule that applies to each of the following words from the professional paragraph.

Capitalized Words	Rule Number
On	1
London	2
Oxford University	2
Irish	2
"Maria"	4
West Side Story	4
English	2
British	2
Latina	2
Rita Moreno's	2

❊ **Review Practice 2 Identifying**   Underline the capitalization errors in the following sentences.

1. I would love a dress like the one <u>marilyn monroe</u> wore when she sang "<u>diamonds are</u> a <u>girl's best friend</u>." *(Marilyn Monroe, Diamonds, Girl's Best Friend)*

2. The letter began, "<u>dear</u> Mary," and then said, "You must turn <u>North</u> on <u>bombay</u> street." *(Dear, north, Bombay Street)*

3. Kim took pictures of the <u>empire state building</u>. *(Empire State Building)*

4. My <u>Mother</u> always makes me chocolate chip cookies when I'm feeling blue. *(mother)*

5. We have been learning about <u>taoism</u> in <u>chinese politics</u> 403. *(Taoism, Chinese Politics)*

6. <u>latin</u> may be considered a <u>Dead Language</u>, but it is still beneficial to <u>english</u> majors. *(Latin, dead language, English)*

7. Aunt <u>betty</u> is a member of MADD, <u>mothers against drunk driving</u>. *(Betty, Mothers Against Drunk Driving)*

8. We had dinner with <u>senator</u> Williams to celebrate <u>mardi gras</u>. *(Senator, Mardi Gras)*

9. Since *the x-files* came out, more people are convinced that the <u>Government</u> is covering up the existence of alien beings. *(X-files, government)*

10. The death of thousands of <u>native americans</u> along the <u>trail</u> of <u>tears</u> was a terrible waste of human life. *(Native Americans, Trail of Tears)*

🌱 **Review Practice 3 Correcting**   Correct the capitalization errors from Review Practice 2 by rewriting each incorrect sentence. *See Review Practice 2.*

1. _____

2. _____

3. _____

4. _____

5. _____

6. _____

7. _____

8. _____

9. _____

10. _____

🍃 EDITING A STUDENT PARAGRAPH

Following is a paragraph written and revised by Susan Miller in response to the writing assignment in this chapter. Read the paragraph, and underline each capital letter.

I have always been small--not just short, but small. When we lived in the new jersey, mom used to have to pick me up and put me on the school bus. I was too small to manage what appeared to be a mountain of a step. Because I was so small, others naturally made false judgments about my age and my intellect. On my first day at Willis High School, I knew no one. I had just finished my english literature class and was fumbling with *the complete works of william shakespeare* at my locker trying to remember the combination when a very polite young man came up to me. His name was richard marquez, and he asked me if I was lost. "No," I said, "But thank you." Obviously he didn't believe me because he then told me that the junior high school was just South of the high school--and he was serious! This was my d-day, the day I recognized just how others saw me, and it was devastating. I guess somewhere in the back of

Here is the correct capitalization:
New Jersey
Mom
English
*The Complete Works of
    William Shakespeare*
Richard Marquez
but
south
D-Day

my mind I always assumed people took me seriously, even though they often thought I was five years younger than I looked. I learned a valuable lesson on that day. But I have since learned another valuable lesson about my size–people often underestimate me, and that gives me an advantage.

Collaborative Activity

Team up with a partner, and underline twice the 14 words in Susan's paragraph that are capitalized incorrectly. Then, working together, use what you have learned in this chapter to correct the errors. Rewrite the paragraph with your corrections. *See student paragraph for errors. Corrections are in the margin.*

EDITING YOUR OWN PARAGRAPH

Now return to the paragraph you wrote and revised at the beginning of this chapter. Underline the capitalized words in your own writing.

Collaborative Activity

Exchange paragraphs with your partner, and circle any capitalization errors that you find in your partner's paragraph.

Individual Activity

On the Error Log in Appendix 6, record any capitalization errors that your partner found in your paragraph. To complete the writing process, correct these errors by rewriting your paragraph.

CHAPTER 26

Abbreviations and Numbers

✐ Checklist for Using Abbreviations and Numbers

- ✔ Are titles before and after proper names abbreviated correctly?
- ✔ Are government agencies and other organizations abbreviated correctly?
- ✔ Are numbers *zero* through *nine* spelled out?
- ✔ Are numbers 10 and over written as figures (10, 25, 1–20, 324)?

Like capitalization, abbreviations and numbers are also mechanical features of writing that help us communicate what we want to say. Following the rules that govern their use will make your writing as precise as possible.

Notice how the consistent use of abbreviations and numbers moves the following paragraph along.

> The educational dimensions of the risk before us have been amply documented in testimony received by the commission. For example,
>
> - International comparisons of student achievement, completed a decade ago, reveal that on 19 academic tests American students were never first or second and, in comparison with other industrialized nations, were last seven times.
> - Some 23 million American adults are functionally illiterate by the simplest tests of everyday reading, writing, and comprehension.

TEACHING ABBREVIATIONS AND NUMBERS
Have students work in groups of three or four to write a paragraph that is filled with abbreviation and number errors. Have them be as inventive as possible yet still make the paragraph coherent.
Have the groups exchange paragraphs and try to decipher the paragraphs they now have. Point out how distracting abbreviations and numbers can be when they are not used correctly.
■ For a sample paragraph, see the *Instructor's Resource Manual*, Section II, Part II.

TEACHING ON THE WEB
Exploring and Discussing: Have students find an on-line catalog that sells numerous items. Then have them

write out numbers that are figures or put into figures numbers that are spelled out for a few of the items being sold. Also have students abbreviate words that they feel could be shortened. Do these changes make the catalog more difficult to read and understand? Why is it important to follow abbreviation and number rules?

TEACHING ON THE WEB

Mosaics Web Site: To learn more about abbreviations, students can go to www.prenhall.com/mosaics.

- About 13 percent of all 17-year-olds in the United States can be considered functionally illiterate. Functional illiteracy among minority youth may run as high as 40 percent.

- Average achievement of high school students on most standardized tests is now lower than it was when Sputnik was launched [1957].

- Over half the population of gifted students do not match their tested ability with comparable achievement in school.

- The College Board's Scholastic Aptitude Tests (SATs) demonstrate a virtually unbroken decline from 1963 to 1980. Average verbal scores fell over 50 points, and average mathematics scores dropped nearly 40 points.

- College Board achievement tests also reveal consistent declines in recent years in such subjects as physics and English.

- Both the number and proportion of students demonstrating superior achievement on the SATs (i.e., those with scores of 650 or higher) have also dramatically declined.

- There was a steady decline in science achievement scores of U.S. 17-year-olds as measured by national assessments of science in 1969, 1973, and 1977.

In this paragraph, David Gardner explains that the U.S. system of public education is not doing its job well. Before continuing in this chapter, take a moment to write about how well prepared you are for college. Save your work because you will use it later in this chapter.

Writing Assignment: How Ready Are You?

How ready are you for college work? Did your high school prepare you adequately for the classes you are now taking? Do you feel confident in your basic skills (reading, writing, and math)? What would you like to change about your academic background? What would you keep the same? Write a paragraph discussing these issues in reference to your high school.

Revising Your Writing

Revise the first draft of your paragraph before you focus on editing. Use the Revising Checklist on pages 24–25 to help you with your revision. Make sure your paragraph has a good topic sentence, is well developed, and is well organized. Then check your paragraph for unity and coherence.

ABBREVIATIONS

Writers often turn to abbreviations to save time and effort. However, relatively few abbreviations are acceptable in writing. The following rules will help you use abbreviations correctly in your writing.

1. **Abbreviate titles before proper names.**

   Mr. Jason Best, **Mrs.** Baker, **Ms.** Susan Elias, **Dr.** George Carlton, **Rev.** Sid Peterson, **Gov.** Gray Davis, **Sgt.** Milton Santos

Abbreviate religious, governmental, and military titles when used with an entire name. Do *not* abbreviate them when used only with a last name.

NOT   We support **Gov.** Wilson.
Correct: We support **Governor** Wilson.
Correct: We thought that **Gov.** Lionel Wilson would be supported.

Professor is not usually abbreviated.

2. **Abbreviate academic degrees.**

   B.S.   (Bachelor of Science)
   A.A.   (Associate of Arts)
   E.M.T   (Emergency Medical Technician)

3. **Use the following abbreviations with numbers.**

   a.m. *or* A.M.   p.m. *or* P.M.   B.C. and A.D.

4. **Abbreviate *United States* only when it is used as an adjective.**

   NOT   The **U.S.** is a capitalist society.
   Correct: The **United States** is a capitalist society.
   Correct: The **U.S.** president will address the people today.

5. **Abbreviate the names of certain government agencies, businesses, and educational institutions by using their initials without periods.**

CIA (Central Intelligence Agency)
DMV (Department of Motor Vehicles)
AMA (American Medical Association)
USC (University of Southern California)
KCEOC (Kern County Economic Opportunity Corporation)

6. **Abbreviate state names when addressing mail or writing out the postal address. Otherwise, spell out the names of states.**

Christy moved to 504 Frontier Street, New York, **NY** 10011.
Christy moved to New York, **New York.**

REVIEWING ABBREVIATIONS

When you write, are you free to abbreviate any words you want?

No, relatively few abbreviations are acceptable in writing.

Practice 1 Identifying   Underline the correct choice in each of the following sentences.

1. (Prof., <u>Professor</u>) Stockton teaches English 305.
2. (Sgt., <u>Sergeant</u>) Williams was the toughest instructor I've ever had.
3. If the president needed to find someone's telephone number, he or she could ask the (<u>CIA</u>, Central Intelligence Agency) for help.
4. They visited (TX, <u>Texas</u>) last summer.
5. This is the year 2001 (<u>A.D.</u>, a.d.).
6. Ginny's brother is going to be an (<u>E.M.T.</u>, emer. med. tech.).
7. When Sally was little, she lived at 511 Arbor Drive, Lafayette, (<u>LA,</u> Louisiana).
8. The (U.S., <u>United States</u>) has one of the highest standards of living in the world.

9. The driver was passing the (<u>YMCA</u>, Young Man's Christian Association) when he slammed on his brakes.

10. The (<u>AMA</u>, A.M.A.) does not support tobacco smoking.

❧ **Practice 2 Identifying**   Put an X next to the sentence if the underlined word is incorrect.

1. _____ <u>Mr.</u> Hewett helped settle the crowd down.

2. __X__ My family migrated to the <u>U.S.</u> in the early 1800s. *(United States)*

3. __X__ <u>Rev.</u> Thomas performed the marriage ceremony. *(Reverend)*

4. _____ <u>Florida</u> is a wonderful state for a vacation.

5. __X__ Your new address is 121 Bennington Avenue, Iowa City, <u>Iowa</u> 54321. *(IA)*

6. __X__ When I woke up, the alarm clock read 3:30 <u>ante</u> <u>meridiem</u>. *(A.M. or a.m.)*

7. __X__ <u>Prof.</u> Angus will be the guest speaker at the ceremony. *(Professor)*

8. __X__ This company reports all earnings to avoid an audit by the <u>I.R.S.</u> *(IRS)*

9. __X__ I plan to get my <u>Associate of Arts</u> degree at a community college before attending a four-year university. *(A.A.)*

10. __X__ The <u>United States</u> Supreme Court will rule today. *(U.S.)*

❧ **Practice 3 Correcting**   Correct the errors you identified in Practice 2 by rewriting each incorrect sentence. *See Practice 2.*

1. _____

2. _____

3. _____

4. _____

5. _____

6. _____

7. _____

8. _____

9. _____

10. _____

🌿 Practice 4 Completing   Fill in each blank in the following sentences with either an abbreviation or a word that makes sense. *Answers will vary.*

1. _____ Lang will be taking over this class for the rest of the quarter.

2. Brian decided to attend college at _____.

3. In four years, you could have your _____ in English, history, or philosophy.

4. _____ Williams is head of the mission from our church.

5. It is a myth that everything is bigger in the state of _____ than anywhere else.

6. The _____ is a somewhat controversial organization.

7. The U.S. _____ is strong this year.

8. The letter was addressed to 1011 Sunny Boulevard, Los Angeles, _____.

9. We moved from Spain to the _____ more than five years ago.

10. Jason was going over 75 _____ when the police officer pulled him over.

🌿 Practice 5 Writing Your Own

A. Write a sentence of your own for each of the following abbreviations.
   Answers will vary.
1. Gov. _____
2. a.m. _____
3. CBS _____
4. CA _____
5. U.S. _____

B. Write five sentences of your own covering at least five of the six abbreviation rules. *Answers will vary.*

1. _____
2. _____
3. _____
4. _____
5. _____

NUMBERS

Most writers ask the same question about using numbers: When should a number be spelled out, and when is it all right to use numerals? The following simple rules will help you.

1. **Spell out numbers from *zero* to *nine*. Use figures for numbers 10 and over.**

   I own **two** houses.

   My sister has **11** dogs and **15** cats living on her ranch.

Do not mix spelled-out numbers and figures in a sentence if they refer to the same types of items. Use figures for all numbers in that case.

NOT   I have **three** reports, **11** files, and **two** memorandums to finish today.

Correct: I have **3** reports, **11** files, and **2** memorandums to finish today.

2. **For very large numbers, use a combination of figures and words.**

   The company's profits this fiscal year were **$21 million**.

   His cabin in the mountains cost **$1.1 million**.

3. **Always spell out a number that begins a sentence.** If this becomes awkward, reword the sentence.

   Twenty-five apples fell from the tree.

   A total of **25** apples fell from the tree.

4. **Use figures for dates, addresses, ZIP codes, telephone numbers, identification numbers, and time.**

   On July **22, 1998**, we relocated to **2504** Box Drive, Bryan, TX **77805**.

Scott's old telephone number was **(661) 399-3405**.

My Social Security number is **101-112-1314**.

The alarm went off at **4:30** a.m.

5. **Use figures for fractions, decimals, and percentages.**

Mix **1/2** cup of butter and **2** tablespoons of vanilla in a saucepan.

His GPA is **3.8**.

Only **10** percent of the people polled were in favor of the measure.

Notice that *percent* is written out and is one word.

6. **Use figures for exact measurements, including amounts of money. Use a dollar sign for amounts over $1.**

The backyard is **20** feet by **22** feet.

She paid **$10.99** for her shorts—**99 cents** more than I paid.

7. **Use figures for the parts of a book.**

Chapter **9**   page **119**   Exercise **7**   questions **2** and **8**

REVIEWING NUMBERS

What is the general rule for spelling out numbers as opposed to using numerals?

Spell out numbers zero through nine, and use figures for 10 and over.

✱ Practice 6 Identifying   Underline the correct choice in the following sentences.

1. I cannot make this recipe because I do not have (<u>1/2</u>, a half) cup of milk.

2. They found (<u>4</u>, four) silver coins, 15 gold coins, and (<u>3</u>, three) pieces of jewelry in the old chest.

3. Walk about (<u>3</u>, three) miles up the road, and you should see the sign.

4. This warehouse, which measures approximately (<u>5,000</u>, five thousand) square feet, is up for sale.

5. My brother has (2, <u>two</u>) motorcycles and a car, whereas I have neither.

6. The instructor assigned Chapters (<u>10 and 11</u>, ten and eleven) for reading.

7. Our phone rang at (2:30, two thirty) in the morning.

8. The yearlong charity drive earned a little over ($1.5 million, one and a half million dollars).

9. In (2001, two thousand and one), we renewed our marriage vows.

10. (10,000, Ten thousand) people attended the rally.

❀ Practice 7 Identifying   Put an X next to the sentence if the underlined number is in the incorrect form.

1. ___X___ We caught 3 fish for supper. *(three)*

2. ___X___ Clear off an area measuring twenty feet by thirty feet. *(20, 30)*

3. _____ Approximately 2.9 percent of his sentences were compound-complex.

4. ___X___ 9 people perished in the flood. *(Nine)*

5. ___X___ Please read Chapter Two for the discussion next week. *(2)*

6. _____ I was born on December 22, 1978.

7. _____ Thirty people showed up for the surprise party.

8. ___X___ The address is two, three, nine Woodrow Avenue. *(239)*

9. ___X___ Only five percent of the people exposed actually got sick. *(5)*

10. ___X___ They paid over two thousand dollars for their new carpet. *($2,000)*

❀ Practice 8 Correcting   Correct the errors in Practice 7 by rewriting each incorrect sentence. *See Practice 7.*

1. _____

2. _____

3. _____

4. _____

5. _____

6. _____

7. _____

8. _____

9. _____

10. _____

Practice 9 Completing   Fill in each blank in the following sentences with a number or figure that makes sense. *Answers will vary.*

1. _____ new recruits joined the army today.

2. My telephone number is _____.

3. I have _____ brothers and sisters and _____ cousins.

4. The construction on this building to bring it up to code will cost _____ million.

5. In the future, my GPA will be _____.

6. Over _____ percent of the incoming freshmen are from out of state.

7. I woke up at _____ today.

8. The dorm measures _____ feet by _____ feet.

9. Did you complete Exercises _____ and _____?

10. This new CD cost _____.

Practice 10 Writing Your Own   Write 10 sentences of your own that cover all seven of the number rules.
Answers will vary.

1. _____

2. _____

3. _____

4. _____

5. _____

6. _____

7. _____

8. _____

9. _____

10. _____

CHAPTER REVIEW

You might want to reread your answers to the questions in the review boxes before you do the following exercises.

❖ **Review Practice 1 Reading**   Refer to the paragraph by David Gardner on pages 437–438 to do the following exercises.

1. List an abbreviation from the paragraph that follows each of the following abbreviation rules.

    Rule 4: _U.S. 17-year-olds_

    Rule 5: _SAT (Scholastic Aptitude Tests)_

2. List all the numbers from the paragraph that follow each of the following number rules.

    Rule 1: _seven, 19, 17, 50, 40, 650_

    Rule 2: _23 million_

    Rule 4: _1957, 1963–1980, 1969, 1973, 1977_

    Rule 5: _13 percent, 40 percent_

❖ **Review Practice 2 Identifying**   Underline the abbreviation and number errors in each of the following sentences. Some sentences contain more than one error.

1. There are only <u>5</u> new houses being built with a <u>ten</u>-by-<u>twelve</u> entryway. *(five, 10, 12)*

2. I couldn't imagine living anywhere but the <u>U.S.</u> *(United States)*

3. Over <u>three hundred thousand</u> claims were handled this month. *(300,000)*

4. <u>Sen.</u> Wood earned his <u>Bachelor of Science</u> degree at the same university that my dad attended. *(Senator, B.S.)*

5. <u>4</u> contestants claimed to have the winning number. *(Four)*

6. The new telephone number is <u>three, nine, eight, four, four, five, four</u>. *(398-4454)*

7. Benjamin fled the country to avoid the <u>Internal Revenue Service</u>. *(IRS)*

8. The recipe on page <u>one hundred twenty</u> calls for <u>one-eighth</u> cup of chili powder. *(120, 1/8)*

9. Jim rides his bike <u>forty</u> miles to work each day. *(40)*

10. The best Cajun food comes from <u>LA</u>. *(Louisiana)*

🌿 Review Practice 3 Correcting   Correct the abbreviation and number errors in Review Practice 2 by rewriting each incorrect sentence. *See Review Practice 2.*

✎ EDITING A STUDENT PARAGRAPH

Following is a paragraph written and revised by Ashley Knight in response to the writing assignment in this chapter. Read the paragraph, and underline all the capitalized words, abbreviations, and numbers.

Here are the corrections:

high school
three
CIA
high school
university
M.A.
degree
teachers
4,000
100 percent

When I graduated from High School, I thought I was prepared for college. What I discovered was that this was not so. But I think this is as much my fault as it was my school's. I knew 3 years ago I wanted to work for the Central Intelligence Agency or the FBI. And even though I did what was required of me in High School, I never learned how to study because my grades were decent enough without having to worry about it. Now I'm at a University, and I wish I had better study skills to help me manage my time better here. I'll never get my Master of Arts Degree at the rate I'm going. People in my high school were aware that many students were barely trying but making OK grades, yet they never really taught us to be prepared for crash-course study skills lessons. Of course, it's difficult for Teachers to keep an eye on four thousand students. To have learned these skills would have made my life one hundred % easier.

Collaborative Activity

Team up with a partner, and put a second underline below the 10 capitalization, abbreviation, and number errors in Ashley's paragraph. Then, working together, use what you have learned in this chapter to correct these errors. Rewrite the paragraph with your corrections. *See student paragraph for errors. Corrections are in the margin.*

🌿 EDITING YOUR OWN PARAGRAPH

Now return to the paragraph you wrote and revised at the beginning of this chapter. Underline all of your capitalized words, abbreviations, and numbers.

Collaborative Activity

Exchange paragraphs with your partner, and circle any capitalization, abbreviation, number, and figure errors that you find in your partner's paragraph.

Individual Activity

On the Error Log in Appendix 6, record any mechanics errors that your partner found in your paragraph. To complete the writing process, correct these errors by rewriting your paragraph.

Unit 6 Review
Mechanics

■ For additional material about teaching mechanics, for journal entries, and for various tests, see the *Instructor's Resource Manual*, Section II, Part II.

ADDITIONAL WRITING TOPIC

Let your students expand into well-developed essays the paragraphs they wrote in one of the unit chapters.

❈ **Unit Practice 1 Identifying**   Underline the capitalization, abbreviation, and number errors in each of the following sentences. Some sentences contain more than one error.

1. "<u>hey</u>, you," the boy shouted, "<u>Throw</u> me the ball." *(Hey, throw)*

2. When Kimmie was eight, she moved from the <u>midwest</u> to the <u>south</u>. *(Midwest, South)*

3. <u>Rev.</u> Dunn wrote many satirical sermons. *(Reverend)*

4. You can purchase a duplicate title for your car at the <u>Department of Motor Vehicles</u>. *(DMV)*

5. While visiting Alaska, we sampled <u>9</u> different types of fish. *(nine)*

6. Since I gave up television for Lent, I decided to occupy myself with J. R. R. <u>tolkien's</u> <u>*lord* of the *rings*</u> trilogy. *(Tolkien's, Lord, Rings)*

7. I have always wanted to work for the <u>Central Intelligence Agency</u>. *(CIA)*

8. Last spring, Barney bought his <u>Mother</u> a family <u>bible</u> for <u>mother's</u> <u>day</u>. *(mother, Bible, Mother's Day)*

9. The politician spent over <u>two million dollars</u> on her campaign. *($2 million)*

10. Around <u>three thirty</u> this afternoon, you will need to add <u>two and a half</u> cups of stewed tomatoes to the soup simmering on the stove. *(3:30, 2½)*

11. This picture of my <u>Dog</u> <u>ralph</u> is hilarious. *(dog, Ralph)*

12. Last night, I got ahead in my <u>Sociology</u> class by reading Chapters <u>Twenty</u> through <u>Twenty-Five</u>. *(sociology, 20, 25)*

13. The new playground will measure <u>one hundred</u> feet by <u>one hundred and fifty</u> feet. *(100, 150)*

14. After the <u>dallas</u> <u>cowboys</u> game, <u>grandpa</u> Roland asked for his slippers and his <u>english</u> tea. *(Dallas, Cowboys, Grandpa, English)*

15. I am currently pursuing my <u>Master of Arts</u> degree in psychology. *(M.A.)*

16. He signed the letter, "<u>your</u> secret admirer." *(Your)*

17. <u>250</u> people were hired for the job. *(Two hundred fifty)*

18. The <u>U.S.</u> offers many trade opportunities to other nations. *(United States)*

19. In <u>history</u> 401, we are studying the <u>war</u> of 1812. *(History, War)*

20. The state of <u>NV</u> was the first to legalize gambling. *(Nevada)*

🌿 **Unit Practice 2 Correcting**   Correct the errors in Unit Practice 1 by rewriting each incorrect sentence.

1. _____
2. _____
3. _____
4. _____
5. _____
6. _____
7. _____
8. _____
9. _____
10. _____
11. _____
12. _____
13. _____
14. _____
15. _____
16. _____
17. _____
18. _____

19. _____

20. _____

🌿 **Unit Practice 3 Identifying**   Underline the capitalization, abbreviation, and number errors in the following paragraph.

Here are the corrections:
spring
United States
French
Uncle
north
IRS
p.m.
French
Mrs.
1950s
1
Getting Along in Life
three
$1 million
One
458–21–7938
A.A.
3
Mrs.
$10
Oregon

In the Spring of 1999, I was out of the U.S. trying to get some much needed relaxation away from phones, work, and television. I was staying in the french countryside at uncle Mike's small villa. Unfortunately, I was unavoidably detained and could not mail my taxes in on time. Once I realized the problem, I drove North to the nearest town to call the Internal Revenue Service. But it was a holiday, and the post office was closed. I had to make the same trip the following day at 4:00 post meridiem. My french 307 class was apparently a waste of time because the lady on the other side of the counter, Missus Ideaux, who was wearing clothes from the nineteen-fifties, and I could not communicate. I followed the advice in Chapter one of my psychology text (*getting along in life*) when I counted to 3, took a deep breath, and tried once again to explain that I needed a phone. I finally reached someone at the IRS who told me that I owed over one million dollars. "1 million dollars!" I screamed. "Are you sure you have the right Social Security number?" I asked. "It's four, five, eight, two, one, seven, nine, three, eight." "Ah, yes," returned the voice on the other end. "Here is your record. You're a student getting an Associate of Arts degree. I'll make a note in your file, but you'll have to pay a three percent penalty fee and fill out some paperwork when you return to the United States." I said that was fine and hung up the phone. But before I could leave, Missus Ideaux asked for ten dollars for the phone call, which I gladly paid. Boy, was I glad to get back to my home in OR, where there is a phone in every room.

🌿 **Unit Practice 4 Correcting**   Correct the errors in Unit Practice 3 by rewriting the paragraph. *See the margin.*

UNIT WRITING ASSIGNMENTS

1. Who do you think the people are in the picture on the next page? What is the mood of the picture? Where do you think these people are going? Are they on an adventure or just walking for pleasure? Do they have a long way to walk? Use your imagination to create the details.

2. Most of us know people who go about life in dramatically different ways, such as parents disciplining their children or friends handling relationships. Compare two people you know who have different approaches to the same task. Explain how each goes about the task and why.

3. You have been asked to write a short article for your local newspaper about the best fast-food restaurants in town. Which restaurants are they, and why are they the best? You might want to consider the atmosphere, the service, the price, and the food.

4. When we are children, play is an important part of our day. But as we get older, responsibilities soon take up most of our spare time, and our "play" changes. Now that you are an adult, what do you do for playtime? How has this changed from childhood, if at all? Why? What were the benefits of play as a child? As an adult?

5. Create your own assignment (with the help of your instructor), and write a response to it.

Unit 7 Effective Sentences

At one time or another, you have probably been a member of a team. You may have actively participated in sports somewhere or been a part of a close-knit employee group. Or maybe you have taken part in classroom discussion groups or special projects that required your cooperation with your peers. Whatever the situation, teamwork is important in many everyday situations. To be a good team member, you must perform your individual duties with others in mind as you also work.

Sentences, too, require good teamwork to be successful. Each individual word, phrase, or clause has to express its own meaning but must also work together with other words, phrases, and clauses toward the common goal of communicating a clear message. In this unit, three chapters will help you write successful sentences that work in harmony with each other to say exactly what you want to say in the best way possible:

Writing effective sentences lets students use all their communication skills to show others their thoughts, ideas, and abilities. Students also need to know that their writing is often all that future employers see before an interview, so sentence skills are especially important in job applications. The chapters in this unit will help your students write successful sentences that work together in harmony.

Varying Sentence Structure

 Checklist for Varying Sentence Patterns

✔ Do you add introductory material to vary your sentence patterns?

✔ Do you occasionally reverse the order of some subjects and verbs?

✔ Do you move sentence parts to add variety to your sentences?

✔ Do you sometimes use questions and exclamations to vary your sentence structure?

The way your ideas are received has a great deal to do not only with what you say but also with how you say it. Reading the same sentence pattern over and over can become very monotonous for your readers. Look at the following example.

> I have longed to be independent. I have a part-time job and a full-time college career. I will be moving into my new apartment soon. I have already begun to shop for secondhand furniture. I am very excited about this change in my life.

This paragraph has some terrific ideas, but they are expressed in such a monotonous way that the readers might doze off. What this paragraph needs is variety in its sentence structure.

Notice how varying sentence structures can liven up writing:

> This is truly the land of opportunity, and I would have enjoyed its bounty even if I hadn't walked into Miss Hurd's classroom in 1953. But she was the one who directed my grief and pain into writing, and if it weren't for her I wouldn't have

TEACHING VARYING
SENTENCE
STRUCTURE
Put students into groups
of three or four, and
provide them with a
paragraph made up of
simple sentences. All
groups should receive
the same paragraph.
Have each group
make its paragraph more
lively by using the guidelines in this chapter to
vary the sentence struc-
ture.
Then have the groups
read their paragraphs to
the rest of the class, and
let the students decide
which paragraph is most
exciting. Why did they
choose the paragraph
they did?
■ For sample
paragraphs, see the
*Instructor's Resource
Manual*, Section II,
Part II.

become an investigative reporter and foreign correspondent, recorded the story of my mother's life and death in *Eleni* and now my father's story in *A Place for Us,* which is also a testament to the country that took us in. She was the catalyst that sent me into journalism and indirectly caused all the good things that came after. But Miss Hurd would probably deny this emphatically.

In this paragraph, Nicholas Gage is explaining how a teacher changed his life by helping him discover his true potential. Before continuing in this chapter, take a moment to write about a time when you discovered something new about yourself. Save your work because you will use it later in this chapter.

Writing Assignment: Self-Discovery

Have you ever had one of those moments when you realize something about yourself that you had not previously known? What was the situation? Were you tempted into doing something you never thought you would do, or did you discover a hidden personality trait? How did you react to the situation? Have your feelings changed since your discovery? Write a paragraph explaining this discovery.

Revising Your Writing

Revise the first draft of your paragraph before you focus on editing. Use the Revising Checklist on pages 24–25 to help you with your revision. Make sure your paragraph has a good topic sentence and is well developed. Then check your paragraph for unity, organization, and coherence.

In this chapter, we will be working on your sentence variety. Here are some ideas for keeping your readers awake and ready to hear your good thoughts.

1. Add some introductory words to your sentences so that they don't all start the same way.

   Ever since I turned 17, I have longed to be independent. **Now** I have a part-time job and a full-time college career. **In addition,** I will be moving into my new apartment soon. I have already begun to shop for secondhand furniture. I am very excited about this change in my life.

🌿 **Practice 1 Identifying**   Put an X next to the sentence if the under-lined words are introductory words, phrases, or clauses.

1. __X__ <u>When I was little</u>, I liked pickles and peanut butter.

2. _____ <u>Tigger</u>, the kitten, destroyed the couch.

3. _____ <u>Your car</u> is located down aisle 5A.

4. __X__ <u>However</u>, I think I can manage to raise the money.

5. __X__ <u>Even though Marciella didn't want to go</u>, she went to provide moral support.

6. _____ <u>Shonell's</u> gum pops every time that she chews it.

7. __X__ <u>Initially</u>, no one grasped the strategy.

8. __X__ <u>Although some of the results remain mysterious</u>, the process is now well understood.

9. __X__ <u>Therefore</u>, denying her feelings led to complete chaos.

10. __X__ <u>In the beginning</u>, everyone loved the old house.

🌿 **Practice 2 Identifying**   Underline the sentence in each pair that can be turned into an introductory word, phrase, or clause.

1. <u>It was late that night</u>. The car started making bizarre noises.

2. Rolando was almost hit by a car. <u>He was walking in the middle of the street</u>.

3. Benjamin tried to sneak out of the dorm. <u>It was 2:00 a.m.</u>

4. Fermin complained too much. <u>The instructor gave him extra work</u>.

5. I was nervous to start college. <u>It was the beginning of the semester.</u>

6. <u>There was a tornado yesterday</u>. The tornado destroyed several homes.

7. <u>It was spring</u>. They feel in love.

8. <u>Bring me the telephone</u>. I will make the phone call for you.

9. <u>Judith won't do it</u>. I will.

10. <u>Mario thought he smelled a cow</u>. It was actually a pig.

✻ Practice 3 Correcting   Combine the sentences in Practice 2 by turning the sentence you underlined into an introductory word, phrase, or clause.
Answers will vary.

1. _____
2. _____
3. _____
4. _____
5. _____
6. _____
7. _____
8. _____
9. _____
10. _____

✻ Practice 4 Completing   Fill in each blank in the following sentences with introductory words, phrases, or clauses that make sense. *Answers will vary.*

1. _____, the strawberries are not ripe enough to eat.
2. _____, I just got out of my seat and walked out of the room.
3. _____, let's make a pie instead.
4. _____, her hair turned a pale shade of green.
5. _____, the shoes were too small for her very large feet.
6. _____, you must close all the shutters and lock the windows.
7. _____, someone will have to compromise.
8. _____, you will find an old chest with clothes from the 1800s.
9. _____, everyone toured Europe except me.
10. _____, she does enjoy taking long walks at twilight.

✻ Practice 5 Writing Your Own

A. Write a sentence of your own using each of the following as introductory words, phrases, or clauses. *Answers will vary.*

1. yesterday _____
2. after the day ended _____

3. during the night _____

4. since my brother left _____

5. at the store _____

B. Write five sentences of your own containing an introductory word, phrase, or clause. Underline the introductory words. *Answers will vary.*

1. _____

2. _____

3. _____

4. _____

5. _____

2. Reverse the order of some subjects and verbs. For example, instead of *I am very excited*, try *Am I ever excited!* You can also add or drop words and change punctuation to make the sentence read smoothly.

Ever since I turned 17, I have longed to be independent. Now I have a part-time job and a full-time college career. In addition, I will be moving into my new apartment soon. I have already begun to shop for secondhand furniture. **Am I ever** excited about this change in my life!

✿ Practice 6 Identifying   Put an X next to the sentence if the subject and verb have been reversed.

1. __X__ Out from behind the door popped a strange man.

2. __X__ In the back of the trunk is a surprise for you.

3. _____ Jeremy taught the dog to play dead.

4. __X__ Am I really happy to see you!

5. __X__ Lovely is the well-mannered person.

6. __X__ "This is really confusing," thought Jerome.

7. __X__ Out of the fog arose a ghostly figure.

8. __X__ Completely satisfied was I.

9. _____ The pennies fell from the purse.

10. __X__ Before the test is the time to ask questions.

🌾 **Practice 7 Identifying**   Underline the subjects and verbs that can be reversed in the following sentences.

1. <u>I am</u> so relieved. *(Am I ever relieved!)*

2. <u>Those men were</u> very hungry. *(Very hungry were those men!)*

3. <u>A twig is caught</u> in the spokes of the tire. *(Caught in the spokes of the tire is a twig.)*

4. Most infants can smile by three months of age.

5. <u>Her steps were</u> determined and purposeful. *(Determined and purposeful were her steps.)*

6. I couldn't remember my telephone number.

7. <u>The gifts are hidden</u> in the closet. *(Hidden in the closet are the gifts.)*

8. <u>He was</u> extremely bored. *(Was he extremely bored!)*

9. <u>The apples and milk are</u> in the refrigerator. *(In the refrigerator are the apples and milk.)*

10. <u>Rebecca almost forgot</u> her ten-year anniversary. *(Her ten-year anniversary Rebecca almost forgot.)*

🌾 **Practice 8 Correcting**   Reverse the subjects and verbs in Practice 7 when possible by rewriting each sentence. *See Practice 7.*

1. _____

2. _____

3. _____

4. _____

5. _____

6. _____

7. _____

8. _____

9. _____

10. _____

🌾 **Practice 9 Completing**   Fill in each blank in the following sentences with a subject or verb that makes sense. *Answers will vary.*

1. Forceful and clear was _____.

2. Through the small lane _____ a herd of sheep.

3. Out of the smoke _____ the _____.

4. In the garage _____ your new car.

5. _____ I ever so grateful.

6. From the tree _____ the _____.

7. Calm and collected was the _____.

8. To the ground burned the old _____.

9. On my father's land are many _____.

10. Happy _____ the person who can forgive.

Practice 10 Writing Your Own

A. Write a sentence of your own using the following reversed subjects and verbs. *Answers will vary.*

1. am I _____

2. was the cow _____

3. jumped the children _____

4. asked Jay _____

5. is the person _____

B. Write five sentences of your own with subjects and verbs reversed. Underline the subjects and verbs in each sentence. *Answers will vary.*

1. _____

2. _____

3. _____

4. _____

5. _____

3. Move some parts of the sentences around. Experiment to see which order works best.

   Ever since I turned 17, I have longed to be independent. Now I have a part-time job and a full-time college career. In addition, **soon** I will be moving into my new apartment. I have already begun to shop for secondhand furniture. Am I ever excited about this change in my life!

🌿 Practice 11 Identifying   Put an X next to the sentence if the underlined words can be moved.

1. __X__ <u>To get Seth to agree</u>, Becca bribed him with sweets.

2. _____ <u>Fear</u> can make people do strange things.

3. __X__ Samantha got very little sleep last night <u>because of all the traffic on the streets</u>.

4. _____ Cats are much cleaner <u>than dogs</u>.

5. __X__ <u>Despite your great attitude</u>, some people still complained.

6. __X__ I got a haircut <u>before the big date</u>.

7. __X__ <u>To pass the driving test</u>, you should first practice driving.

8. __X__ <u>However</u>, he said that he would certainly make an effort.

9. _____ The computer's low hum <u>almost put me to sleep</u>.

10. _____ <u>My friends</u> are always giving me advice.

🌿 Practice 12 Identifying   Underline the parts of the following sentences that can be moved.

1. My favorite recipe, <u>though</u>, calls for 3 cups of sugar. *(sugar, though.)*

2. <u>Initially</u>, the phone wouldn't stop ringing. *(ringing initially.)*

3. <u>Consequently</u>, I do feel fine today. *(today, consequently.)*

4. We looked marvelous, <u>except for the rain and mud trailing down our bodies</u>. *(Except for the rain and mud trailing down our bodies, we looked marvelous.)*

5. <u>Even if you beg and plead</u>, I am still going to say no. *(I am still going to say no, even if you beg and plead.)*

6. <u>To help with the chores</u>, I mowed the backyard. *(I mowed the backyard to help with the chores.)*

7. Our house guest <u>finally</u> agreed to go home. *(Finally, our)*

8. <u>After that first kiss</u>, we knew we were meant to be together. *(We knew we were meant to be together after that first kiss.)*

9. <u>Before doing the errands</u>, will you please balance the checkbook? *(Will you please balance the checkbook before doing the errands?)*

10. He stood there <u>as if he was waiting for something to happen</u>. *(As if he was waiting for something to happen, he stood there.)*

🌿 Practice 13 Correcting   Rewrite the sentences in Practice 12 by moving the words you underlined. *See Practice 12. Answers may vary.*

1. _____

2. _____

3. _____

4. _____

5. _____

6. _____

7. _____

8. _____

9. _____

10. _____

Practice 14 Completing   Rewrite the following paragraph by moving words and phrases around. *Answers will vary.*

At night, I always read. I love to find new places when I read that I will travel to someday. Once I discovered a boiling lake in the jungles of Dominica. By accident, I learned about a Mayan cave in Belize that was discovered by a young man's dog while it was chasing a large rat. Just yesterday, I read about 250-pound codfish in the Great Barrier Reef in Australia. I love to read to take my mind to these places before I can afford to see them in person. Forever, I will love traveling through books.

Practice 15 Writing Your Own

A. Write a sentence of your own for each of the words, phrases, and clauses here. *Answers will vary.*

1. however _____

2. in the summer _____

3. before you speak _____

4. when the sun comes up _____

5. after I study _____

B. Vary the structure of the sentences you wrote in Practice 15A by moving portions of each sentence around and rewriting it. Underline the words you moved. *Answers will vary.*

1. _____

2. _____

3. _____

4. _____

5. _____

4. Use a question, command, or exclamation occasionally.

Ever since I turned 17, I have longed to be independent. **Have you ever longed to be independent?** Now I have a part-time job and a full-time college career. In addition, soon I will be moving into my new apartment. I have already begun to shop for secondhand furniture. Am I ever excited about this change in my life!

✻ Practice 16 Identifying   Identify each of the following sentences as a statement (S), a question (Q), a command (C), or an exclamation (E). Add the appropriate end punctuation.

1. __S__ Margery has a strange phobia.

2. __C__ Finish these reports before the end of the week.

3. __E__ Hey, you just took my seat!

4. __Q__ Why are you sitting in the dark?

5. __Q__ Which way did the horse run?

6. __S__ Yes, I would like some more iced tea.

7. __S__ Jim will be in San Francisco on Tuesday.

8. __C__ Walk the dog.

9. __E__ You are awesome!

10. __Q__ How do I start this machine?

✻ Practice 17 Identifying   Label the sentences in the following paragraph as statements (S), questions (Q), commands (C), or exclamations (E) in the following paragraph.

There are so many different genres of music. __S__ Just pick one. __C__ Progressive, alternative, rap, and country are just a few. __S__ And there are even divisions of music within genres. __S__ Have you ever heard of new country? ___*Q*___ It's a blend of rock and country. ___*S*___ Or have you ever heard of classic rock? ___*Q*___ Out of the 1960s and 1970s came that type. ___*S*___ Or have you ever heard of retroactive, big band, gansta rap, light jazz, metal, acid rock, and so on? ___*Q*___ There are just too many of them to count! ___*E*___ You choose. ___*C*___

Practice 18 Correcting   Change each of the sentences in Practice 16 from a statement, question, command, or exclamation into another type of sentence. *Answers will vary.*

1. _____
2. _____
3. _____
4. _____
5. _____
6. _____
7. _____
8. _____
9. _____
10. _____

Practice 19 Completing   Fill in each blank in the following sentences to make each into a statement, question, command, or an exclamation, and add the correct punctuation. *Answers will vary.*

1. Wow! That was _____
2. Explain _____
3. What was _____
4. Take this _____
5. Hey, _____
6. I like _____
7. You just _____
8. How did he _____

9. Which of these _____

10. She felt _____

❋ Practice 20 Writing Your Own

A. Rewrite each of the following sentences, making them into the sentence type indicated in parentheses. *Answers may vary.*

1. How many questions are there? (statement) _There are ten questions._

2. What did you do? (exclamation) _You did that!_

3. Take me to your superior. (question) _Could you take me to your superior?_

4. Do I like candy? (statement) _I like candy._

5. Will you deliver this to the Smiths? (command) _Deliver this to the Smiths._

B. Write five sentences of your own, making at least one a statement, one a question, one a command, and one an exclamation. *Answers will vary.*

1. _____

2. _____

3. _____

4. _____

5. _____

REVIEWING WAYS TO VARY SENTENCE PATTERNS

Why is varying sentence patterns important in your writing?

Sentence variety keeps the readers interested.

Name four ways to vary your sentence patterns.

Add introductory words and phrases.

Reverse the order of some subjects and verbs.

Move some parts of your sentences around.

> Use a question, a command, or an exclamation occasionally.
>
> **What other kinds of sentences besides statements can you use for variety?**
>
>   _questions_   _commands_   _exclamations_

CHAPTER REVIEW

You might want to reread your answers to the questions in the review boxes before you do the following exercises.

Review Practice 1 Reading   Refer to the paragraph by Nicholas Gage on pages 455–456 to do the following exercises.

1. List two introductory words from the paragraph.

   But

   But

2a. Record a sentence from the paragraph whose subject and verb can be reversed.

   Answers will vary.

2b. Write this sentence with its subject and verb reversed.

   Answers will vary.

3a. List two sentences that have words that can be moved.

   Answers will vary.

3b. Write these two sentences in another way, moving at least one word in each one.

   Answers will vary.

4. Add one question, one command, and one exclamation to the paragraph.

   Answers will vary.

🌱 Review Practice 2 Identifying   Underline the words or groups of words that have been added or moved in each revised sentence. Then use the list below to tell which rule you applied to the sentence.

Rule

1. Add introductory words.
2. Reverse the order of subject and verb.
3. Move parts of the sentence around.
4. Use a question, command, or exclamation occasionally.

1. We laughed in the rain.

   ___1___ <u>Last night</u>, we laughed in the rain.

2. They decided to fly instead of drive due to the terrible conditions of the road.

   ___3___ <u>Due to the terrible conditions of the roads</u>, they decided to fly instead of drive.

3. You fit all those clothes in that tiny suitcase.

   __2 or 4__ <u>How</u> did you fit all those clothes in that tiny suitcase?

4. It was spring. We were competing in the biggest game of our lives.

   ___1___ <u>During the spring</u>, we competed in the biggest game of our lives.

5. The bird flew out of the house.

   ___2___ <u>Out of the house</u> flew <u>the bird</u>.

6. Indeed, she felt happy to have survived the weekend.

   ___3___ She felt happy <u>indeed</u> to have survived the weekend.

7. You should listen more carefully.

   ___4___ Listen more carefully.

8. The man came lumbering down the lane.

   ___2___ <u>Lumbering down the lane</u> <u>came the man</u>.

9. I found my keys.

   __1 or 4__ <u>Yippee</u>, I found my keys!

10. Since then, everyone has gotten along fantastically.

    ___3___ Everyone has gotten along fantastically <u>since then</u>.

🌿 **Review Practice 3 Correcting**   Vary the structure of the following sentences with at least three of the four ideas you learned in this chapter. Rewrite the paragraph with your changes. *Answers will vary.*

> Good hairdressers are hard to find. They should be good listeners. That's the first step to pleasing customers. They should also be able to visualize what their customers want. The best hairdressers always make suggestions about what will or will not look good on a person. They should do what the customer wants, though, since the customer is always right. They also need to be interested in their customers' lives.

✒ EDITING A STUDENT PARAGRAPH

Following is a paragraph written and revised by Gabriel Alvarez in response to the writing assignment in this chapter. Read the paragraph, and check it for sentence variety. *Student responses will vary.*

> While practicing with my band, I found out that the other band members thought I was a bit too serious, even mean at times. They said that I was "cool" and everything, but when it came to practicing music, my personality changed. They were even afraid to voice their opinions to me for fear of my reaction. I thought this was odd because I'm usually considered an easygoing person. I have often heard people say that I don't play around when it comes to my tunes. They are right. I take music very seriously. But I had no idea how seriously. I guess it took someone else to make me realize this. I will try to be more polite. I don't regret this part of my personality. If I didn't take our practices seriously, there would be no practice. The band needs someone to be in charge, and that's me. And besides, my personality changes back once practice is over.

Collaborative Activity

Team up with a partner, and put brackets around any sentence in Gabriel's paragraph that could use some variety in its structure. Then add at least one introductory element; reverse the order of one subject and verb; move some parts of a sentence around; and create at least one question, command, or exclamation. Rewrite the paragraph with your changes. *Answers will vary.*

🌿 EDITING YOUR OWN PARAGRAPH

Now return to the paragraph you wrote and revised at the beginning of this chapter. Check it for sentence variety.

Collaborative Activity

Exchange paragraphs with your partner, and put brackets around any sentence that could use some variety in your partner's paragraph.

Individual Activity

Apply at least two of the guidelines you learned in this chapter to your own writing. To complete the writing process, revise any sentences that your partner marked in your paragraph by rewriting your paragraph.

Parallelism

Checklist for Using Parallelism

✔ Can you use parallelism to add coherence to your sentences and paragraphs?

✔ Are all items in a series grammatically balanced?

When sentences are parallel, they are balanced. That is, words, phrases, or clauses in a series start with the same grammatical form. Parallel structures make your sentences interesting and clear.

Notice how parallel structures create smooth and interesting writing:

> To be fair, it's simplistic to dump all the woes of education on mothers and fathers. Some apathetic teachers, autocratic principals, narrow-minded school boards, lifeless textbooks, suffocating policies, and ridiculous rules must share the blame. Besides, our children are growing up in a society that's only willing to pay lip service to the need for first-class schools.
>
> Yet none of these problems compares with the disappearance and disarray of parents. During more than a decade of reporting and writing about Florida schools, I have met hundreds of dedicated teachers with the same horror stories: parents who never set foot on school grounds, who don't show up for conferences, who insult and sometimes threaten teachers, who show little interest in what's happening to their children, and who sometimes don't seem to care if their kids are actually going to school. Over and over, teachers tell me, parents say: "Hey, you're the expert. You deal with it."

TEACHING
PARALLELISM
Draw a picture of two
sets of train tracks that
run parallel to each
other. Draw a second
picture of two sets of
train tracks that eventu-
ally cross each other.
Ask students the follow-
ing question: If both
tracks have trains head-
ing toward each other
and you were on one of
the trains, which set of
tracks would you prefer
your train to be on? Of
course students will
choose the parallel
tracks. Ask them to dis-
cuss their choice.
  Now explain to stu-
dents that when sen-
tences are not parallel,
they are often like two
trains heading for each
other and about to col-
lide. Then discuss how
faulty parallelism can
wreck an idea just as
trains not on parallel
tracks can collide.

In this paragraph, Thomas French discusses who's to blame for the problems in public schools. Before continuing in this chapter, take a moment to write about a time you blamed someone or something for your own actions. Save your work because you will use it later in this chapter.

Writing Assignment: The Blame Game

Have you ever blamed something or someone other than yourself for a problem when in fact you were to blame? What was the situation? Who was involved? What did you do and why? How did your actions make you feel? Write a paragraph describing the situation and the outcome.

Revising Your Writing

Revise the first draft of your paragraph before you focus on editing. Use the Revising Checklist on pages 24–25 to help you with your revision. Make sure your paragraph has a good topic sentence and is well developed. Then check your paragraph for unity, organization, and coherence.

Parallel structure gives your sentences order and continuity. It helps your readers navigate through your ideas and understand what you are saying. Notice how difficult the following paragraph is to understand because the items in a series are not grammatically parallel.

> Susan had her summer all planned out. She was going to read as many romance novels as possible, will work in her garden, and will be taking piano lessons. Then her brother called her and asked if she could stay at his house for a month while he and his wife vacationed in Florida. Now she is taking care of the children, feeding the dog, and the elderly neighbor.

Words and phrases in a series should be parallel, which means they should start with the same type of word. Parallelism makes your sentence structure smoother and more interesting. Look at this sentence, for example.

NOT   She was going to **read** as many romance novels as possible,

will work in her garden, and

will be taking piano lessons.

Parallel: She **will read** as many romance novels as possible,

                    will work in her garden, and

                    will be taking piano lessons.

Parallel: She was going to **read** as many romance novels as possible,

                    work in her garden, and

                    take piano lessons.

Here is another sentence that would read better if the parts were parallel:

NOT   Now she is **taking** care of the children,

                    feeding the dog, and

                    the elderly neighbor.

Parallel: Now she is **taking** care of the children,

                    feeding the dog, and

                    looking after the elderly neighbor.

Parallel: Now she is taking care of **the children,**

                    the dog, and

                    the elderly neighbor.

Now read the paragraph with these two sentences made parallel or balanced.

Susan had her summer all planned out. She was going to read as many romance novels as possible, work in her garden, and take piano lessons. Then her brother called her and asked if she could stay at his house for a month while he and his wife vacationed in Florida. Now she is taking care of the children, the dog, and the elderly neighbor.

REVIEWING PARALLELISM

What is parallelism?

Starting words, phrases, and clauses in a series with the same grammatical form

Why should you use parallelism in your writing?

To make your writing interesting and clear

🌿 Practice 1 Identifying   Underline the parallel structures in each of the following sentences.

1. They <u>baked me a cake</u>, <u>sang me a song</u>, and <u>bought me presents</u> for my birthday.

2. <u>Kiara</u>, <u>Jayda</u>, <u>Robin</u>, and <u>Laura</u> were voted most likely to succeed.

3. I'm feeling even more <u>confused</u>, <u>frustrated</u>, and <u>lost</u> than before.

4. When you <u>get dressed up in those clothes</u>, <u>fix your hair like that</u>, and <u>wear your sunglasses</u>, you look like a movie star.

5. Edgar plans to <u>rehearse with his band</u>, <u>watch James Bond movies</u>, and <u>surf the waves</u> this summer.

6. <u>Walk across the street</u>, <u>turn left</u>, and <u>proceed straight ahead</u> to your destination.

7. The secretary phoned to ask <u>if we could prepare the minutes</u> and <u>if we could give a small speech</u> for the meeting.

8. <u>In the cupboard</u>, <u>behind the boxes</u>, and <u>to the right</u> are the blank Christmas cards from last year.

9. Lori believed <u>that she would win the contest</u> and <u>that she would go to the finals</u>.

10. Since you are so <u>patient</u>, <u>kind</u>, and <u>generous</u>, you should be in charge of the children.

🌿 Practice 2 Identifying   Put an X next to the sentence if the underlined structures are not parallel.

1. _____ On vacation, we plan to <u>hike in the mountains</u>, <u>swim in the ocean</u>, and <u>dance under the stars</u>.

2. __X__ She always turns red whenever someone <u>smiles at her</u> or <u>paying her a compliment</u>. *(pays her a complement)*

3. _____ He ordered *Time*, the *New York Times*, and the *Los Angeles Times* for his boss.

4. _____ The frog jumped <u>on the dresser</u>, <u>across the table</u>, and <u>out the window</u>.

5. __X__ <u>Biking</u>, <u>talk to friends</u>, and <u>to eat pizza</u> are some of my favorite things to do. *(talking to friends, and eating pizza)*

6. __X__ After the television has been turned off, after the children have been tucked into bed, and the dog has been let out for the night, I can finally go to bed. *(after the dog has been let out for the night)*

7. __X__ I believe in you because you are loyal, dedicated, and kept my secrets. *(are dedicated, and keep my secrets)*

8. _____ Because the car was not running and because the rain hadn't stopped, we decided to stay home.

9. __X__ To start your research, you should surf the Net, peruse the library, and you will need to interview people. *(and interview people)*

10. __X__ Kendra was so stressed out today that she put the Windex in the refrigerator, put the milk in the cupboard, and the remote in the medicine cabinet. *(put the remote in the medicine cabinet)*

✳ Practice 3 Correcting   Correct the parallelism errors in Practice 2 by rewriting each incorrect sentence. *See Practice 2. Answers may vary.*

1. _____
2. _____
3. _____
4. _____
5. _____
6. _____
7. _____
8. _____
9. _____
10. _____

✳ Practice 4 Completing   Fill in the blanks in each of the following sentences with parallel structures. *Answers will vary.*

1. The pictures on the wall are by _____, _____, and _____.

2. We thought that you _____ and that you _____.

3. In spite of the _____, _____, and _____, Jerome managed to finish his final on time.

4. He _____, _____, and _____.

5. Because Shane _____ and _____, Marianne agreed to marry him.

6. The penny rolled _____, bounced _____, and landed _____.

7. The most _____, _____, and _____ person in the world just asked me out on a date.

8. This _____, _____, and _____ essay should be published.

9. It tasted like _____, _____, and _____.

10. You will find your grandmother's handmade quilts in the garage, _____, and _____.

Practice 5 Writing Your Own

A. Write a sentence of your own for each of the following parallel structures. *Answers will vary.*

1. that you should have apologized and that you should try to make it up

   _____

2. through the hedges, across the stream, and over the hill

   _____

3. every time he sees her, talks to her, or mentions her name

   _____

4. blue, red-gold, and off-white

   _____

5. read, sun-bathe, and garden

   _____

B. Write five sentences of your own using parallel structures, and underline the parallel structures. *Answers will vary.*

1. _____

2. _____

3. _____

4. _____

5. _____

CHAPTER REVIEW

You might want to reread your answers to the questions in the review boxes before you do the following exercises.

Review Practice 1 Reading   List the two parallel structures from the paragraph by Thomas French on page 471.

1. _apathetic teachers, autocratic principals, narrow-minded school boards, lifeless textbooks, suffocating policies, and ridiculous rules_

2. _parents who never set foot on school grounds, who don't show up for conferences, who insult and sometimes threaten teachers, who show little interest in what's happening to their children, and who sometimes don't seem to care if their kids are actually going to school_

Review Practice 2 Identifying   Underline the faulty parallel structures in the following sentences.

1. Jake enjoys golfing, jogging, and <u>playing tennis</u>. *(tennis)*

2. We always take the path through the woods, around the old haunted house, and <u>run across the meadow</u>. *(across the meadow)*

3. Minnie taught Adrian how to bait a hook, cast a lure, and <u>avoiding falling into the river</u>. *(avoid falling into the river)*

4. She will eat only organic foods, wear only all-natural clothes, and <u>uses only natural beauty products</u>. *(use only natural beauty products)*

5. Zach said that the banquet was at 6:00 p.m. and that <u>served at 6:30 was dinner</u>. *(dinner was served at 6:30)*

6. If you lay your clothes out the night before, gather your materials and set them on the table, and <u>if you will wake up a bit earlier</u>, you should be able to make it to work on time. *(wake up a bit earlier)*

7. Please fill the car with gas, get a receipt, and <u>I would love some donuts</u>. *(get some donuts)*

8. Take the rugs outside, hang them on the clothesline, and <u>the dust needs to be beaten out of them</u>. *(beat the dust out of them)*

9. Tonight Rosa plans to surprise her husband by making a romantic dinner, putting on some soft jazz, and <u>get her parents to watch the kids</u>. *(getting her parents to watch the kids)*

10. On the drums, you first begin with the stride, then the main beat, and <u>the counterbeat comes next</u>. *(then the counterbeat)*

❧ Review Practice 3 Correcting   Correct the faulty parallel structures in Review Practice 2 by rewriting each sentence. *See Review Practice 2.*

✎ EDITING A STUDENT PARAGRAPH

Following is a paragraph written and revised by Jessie Santillion in response to the writing assignment in this chapter. Read the paragraph, and underline her words, phrases, and clauses in a series.

Here are the corrected parallel structures:
<u>pull the weeds in the flowerbeds</u>, make up the beds, and iron some clothes
raced out of the room, <u>flew down the hall</u>, and skidded to a halt
smoldering, hissing, and <u>smoking</u>
stamped the fire out, <u>grabbed the white oval rug from my room</u>, and covered up my crime
dropped her fork, gasped for breath, and <u>turned her stricken eyes toward our mother</u>
crying, pleading, and <u>begging</u>

When I was 8 years old, I set the carpet on fire. It all started when Dad asked me to do some chores: <u>pulling the weeds in the flowerbeds</u>, ^X <u>make up the beds</u>, and <u>iron some clothes</u>. After I finished pulling the weeds and making the beds, I went into the laundry room to do some ironing. When I got there, I found that LaVonne, my eldest sister, had left the iron on. I proceeded to do my ironing until the phone rang. I <u>raced out of the room</u>, <u>down the</u> ^X <u>hall I flew</u>, and <u>skidded to a halt in front of the phone</u>. (It was always a race to see who could get to the phone first.) By the time I made it back to the ironing, the carpet was <u>smoldering</u>, <u>hissing</u>, and <u>smoked</u>. ^X In my haste, I must have knocked the iron over. I <u>stamped the fire out</u>, <u>grab the white oval rug</u> from my room, and <u>covered up my</u> ^X <u>crime</u>. That night at dinner, Mom casually asked about the carpet in the laundry room. LaVonne <u>dropped her fork</u>, ^X <u>gasped for breath</u>, and <u>her stricken eyes turned toward</u>

our mother. Obviously, LaVonne thought she had done the deed. I chose to remain silent. LaVonne got grounded for two months. But before the weekend came, my conscience began to devour my innocence, and so I confessed. But Mom didn't believe me! And even after crying, pleading, and I begged, Mom still didn't believe me--or so she said. In hindsight, I think that she knew that I was the criminal all along and that my conscience was punishment enough. Since that day, I have always thought twice about blaming others for my actions.

Collaborative Activity

Team up with a partner, and put an X above the six items in Jessie's paragraph that are not parallel to the other items in their series. Then, working together, use what you have learned in this chapter to correct these errors. Rewrite the paragraph with your corrections. *See student paragraph for errors. Corrections are in the margin.*

❧ EDITING YOUR OWN PARAGRAPH

Now return to the paragraph you wrote and revised at the beginning of this chapter. Underline any words, phrases, and clauses in a series.

Collaborative Activity

Exchange paragraphs with your partner, and put an X above any structures in your partner's paragraph that are not parallel with others in their series.

Individual Activity

On the Error Log in Appendix 6, record any parallelism errors that your partner found in your paragraph. To complete the writing process, correct these errors by rewriting your paragraph.

Combining Sentences

✐ Checklist for Combining Sentences

> ✔ Do you combine sentences to avoid too many short, choppy sen-
>   tences in a row?
> ✔ Do you use different types of sentences?

Still another way to add variety to your writing is to combine short, choppy sentences into longer sentences. Combining sentences changes the rhythm of a paragraph and stimulates your readers' interest.

Notice how different types of sentences add variety and interest to the following paragraph.

> I liked Grandma the best, though, when she told me about my mama, because it was a part of Mama that I had never seen or been close to. I didn't know that when Mama was a little girl a photographer came one day to take a picture of her and her sister in a pony cart. I couldn't imagine that they had to bribe them into good behavior by giving them each a coin. In the picture Mama is crying and biting her coin in half. It was a dime, and she wanted the bigger coin—the nickel—given to her sister. Somehow, I thought that Mama was born knowing the difference between a nickel and a dime. (Erma Bombeck, "Mother")

In this paragraph, Erma Bombeck explores her changing perceptions of her mother. Before continuing in this chapter, take a moment to write about how your own perception of someone has changed. Save your work because you will use it later in this chapter.

Writing Assignment: Perceptions

We've all had moments when we discover something new about ourselves, but what about others? Have you ever been shocked to learn something about someone you thought you knew well? For example, when did you discover that one of your parents or guardians was actually human—that he or she could cry, feel pain, be silly, act immature, or make a mistake? What happened to change your view of this person? What did you discover about this person? How did this discovery make you feel? Write a paragraph explaining your changing perceptions.

Revising Your Writing

Revise the first draft of your paragraph before you focus on editing. Use the Revising Checklist on pages 24–25 to help you with your revision. Make sure your paragraph has a good topic sentence and is well developed. Then check your paragraph for unity, organization, and coherence.

How does combining sentences raise the level of the essay? Why is it important that sentences be combined?

TEACHING ON THE WEB

Mosaics Web Site: To learn more about combining sentences, students can go to www.prenhall.com/ mosaics.

Simple sentences can be combined to make three other types of sentences: compound, complex, and compound-complex.

SIMPLE SENTENCES

A **simple sentence** consists of one independent clause. Remember that a clause has a subject and a main verb.

In the following examples, notice that a simple sentence can have more than one subject and more than one verb. (For more on compound subjects and compound verbs, see Chapter 7.)

s   v

I have many opportunities for the future.

s   s   v

Ed and Jim took the dogs for a walk.

s   s   v   v

Margarita and I shop and gossip at the mall.

> REVIEWING SIMPLE SENTENCES
>
> **What does a simple sentence consist of?**
>
> *One independent clause*
>
> **Write a simple sentence.**
>
> *Answers will vary.*

❋ Practice 1 Identifying Underline the subjects once and the verbs twice in the following simple sentences.

1. The phone and the doorbell rang at the same time.
2. The carpenter measured and then cut the wood.
3. You can choose from many career opportunities.
4. The doe and her fawn were startled and ran away.
5. The math problem frustrated and confused me.
6. We wasted much time.
7. The skaters and the bikers joined forces and cleaned up the park.
8. The Kilpatricks and the McLoughlins sponsored the event.
9. The sun's light felt warm and comforting.
10. Juan and Tim smiled at the girls.

❋ Practice 2 Identifying Put an S next to the sentence if it is a simple sentence. Remember to look for subjects and verbs first.

1. __S__ Marvin reconfigured the computer's memory.
2. __S__ My sister and my mother will be spending the weekend at an exclusive spa.
3. _____ Michael and Kim volunteer at the local shelter, and their friends provide homes for foster children.
4. _____ He calculated the distance between home and school, and she biked there.
5. __S__ The neighbor's dogs barked all night long and annoyed me greatly.

6. _____ The child hugged his stuffed bear tightly, and he cried for a long time after his mother left.

7. _S_ Our house and landscape were designed and built by a close friend.

8. _____ Many people are turning to solar energy; others insist on gas and electricity.

9. _S_ They played Monopoly and visited all day.

10. _____ When I'm ready to leave, the suitcase and carry-on will be sitting by the door, and the taxi will be here.

🌾 Practice 3 Correcting   Make 10 simple sentences out of the sentences in Practice 2 that are not simple. *Answers will vary.*

1. _____
2. _____
3. _____
4. _____
5. _____
6. _____
7. _____
8. _____
9. _____
10. _____

🌾 Practice 4 Completing   Fill in the blanks in each of the following sentences with subjects and verbs that complete the simple sentences. *Answers will vary.*

1. _____ and _____ chased the ice-cream truck around the corner.

2. Yolanda's _____ and _____ _____ with her over the weekend and _____ the following Monday.

3. The _____ and _____ have fallen behind the bookshelf.

4. Most people _____ mild peppers to the hotter ones.

5. A _____ just bit me.

6. The fans _____ and _____ for the football team.

7. The stereo's _____ went dead.

8. Mom and Dad _____ everything and _____ to the door.

9. Your _____ is about to run outside.

10. Your _____ and _____ in your bedroom are _____ and _____ to be let out.

✿ Practice 5 Writing Your Own

A. Write a simple sentence of your own for each of the following subjects and verbs. *Answers will vary.*

1. laughing and singing _____

2. the dog and cat _____

3. the red sports car _____

4. are skipping and whistling _____

5. gasped _____

B. Write five simple sentences of your own, and underline the subjects and verbs. *Answers will vary.*

1. _____

2. _____

3. _____

4. _____

5. _____

COMPOUND SENTENCES

A **compound sentence** consists of two or more independent clauses joined by a coordinating conjunction (*and, but, for, nor, or, so,* or *yet*). In other words, you can create a compound sentence from two (or more) simple sentences.

Simple:	Amy enjoys reading.
Simple:	Amy can read very quickly.

       S   V   S   V

Compound: Amy enjoys reading, **and** she can read very quickly.

Simple:	He loves to cook for people.
Simple:	He owns his own restaurant.

        S   V   S   V

Compound: Charles loves to cook for people, **so** he owns his own
         restaurant.

Simple:	Natasha and Christy wanted to stay in a fancy hotel.
Simple:	They didn't have enough money.

       S   S   V

Compound: Natasha and Christy wanted to stay in a fancy hotel,

        S   V

       but they didn't have enough money.

HINT: As the examples show, a comma comes before the coordinating conjunction in a compound sentence.

REVIEWING COMPOUND SENTENCES

What does a compound sentence consist of?

 Two or more independent clauses

Write a compound sentence.

 Answers will vary.

Practice 6 Identifying Underline the independent clauses once and the coordinating conjunctions twice in each of the following compound sentences.

1. The dinner looked great, and it tasted even better.
2. The marble sculpture fell during the earthquake, and it broke into many pieces.

3. It is 110 degrees outside, <u>and</u> our air conditioning is not working.

4. The tennis player served the ball, <u>but</u> it hit the net.

5. He cannot give you a ride to the store, <u>nor</u> can he pick up the dry cleaning.

6. You can work late today, <u>or</u> you can come in on Saturday.

7. Frank pushed the car with all his strength, <u>yet</u> he could not get it out of the mud.

8. We ran out of bait, <u>so</u> we used fake worms instead.

9. One of the engines failed on the airplane, <u>but</u> the other engines made up for the loss of power.

10. The dog chased the cat, <u>but</u> the cat quickly ran up a tree.

🌱 **Practice 7 Identifying**   Underline the independent clauses in the following sentences once, and underline any coordinating conjunctions twice. Then label the sentence either simple (S) or compound (C).

1. __C__   Dean went to the Bahamas, <u>and</u> he snorkeled there for the first time.

2. __S__   Jeremy was worried about his weight.

3. __C__   John liked the shirt, <u>but</u> his girlfriend didn't.

4. __C__   The computer cannot think for itself, <u>nor</u> can it solve every problem.

5. __S__   The lock on the door was bolted.

6. __C__   The sail was raised, <u>and</u> soon the boat was out at sea.

7. __S__   My dictionary does not provide definitions of slang words.

8. __C__   The cat kept sharpening its claws on my new couch, <u>so</u> I bought a scratching post.

9. __S__   Cruise lines tend to overfeed passengers.

10. __S__   Aunt Rosa's roses usually take first place at the fair.

🌱 **Practice 8 Correcting**   Using the sentences in Practice 7 that are not compound, make 10 compound sentences. *Answers will vary.*

1. _____

2. _____

3. _____

4. _____

5. _____

6. _____

7. _____

8. _____

9. _____

10. _____

✣ Practice 9 Completing   Combine each pair of simple sentences into a compound sentence. *Answers will vary.*

1. Michelle loves to shop. She doesn't have any money. *(but)*

2. The mascot broke his leg. He couldn't perform at tonight's game. *(so)*

3. The storm blew down the power lines. We missed our favorite television show. *(and)*

4. I am very hungry. There is no food in the refrigerator. *(but)*

5. He didn't have much experience. He got the job anyway. *(but)*

6. Cheryl cannot eat strawberries. She cannot drink milk. *(and)*

7. Ants have a complex social structure. Each type of ant has a specific task within the structure. *(and)*

8. Sparky, my dog, has been hit by lightning three times. He survived each episode. *(yet)*

9. Mr. Dupré is an excellent teacher. He enjoys working with students. *(for)*

10. Chris spoke harshly to his girlfriend. Now he regrets it. *(and)*

✣ Practice 10 Writing Your Own

A. Write a compound sentence of your own by adding a coordinating conjunction and an independent clause to each of the following sentences. *Answers will vary.*

1. The gophers are digging holes in the yard.

   _____

2. We got a new DVD player.

   _____

3. Sequoia National Forest is a protected area.

_____

4.   Sydney is really good at spelling.

_____

5. Scientists are working on a cure for cancer.

_____

B. Write five compound sentences of your own, and underline the subjects and verbs. *Answers will vary.*

1. _____
2. _____
3. _____
4. _____
5. _____

COMPLEX SENTENCES

A **complex sentence** is composed of one independent clause and at least one dependent clause. A **dependent clause** begins with either a subordinating conjunction or a relative pronoun.

Subordinating Conjunctions

after	because	since	until
although	before	so	when
as	even if	so that	whenever
as if	even though	than	where
as long as	how	that	wherever
as soon as	if	though	whether
as though	in order that	unless	while

Relative Pronouns

who	whom	whose	which	that

You can use subordinating conjunctions and relative pronouns to make a simple sentence (an independent clause) into a dependent clause. Then you can add the new dependent clause to an independent clause to produce a complex sentence that adds interest and variety to your writing.

How do you know which simple sentence should be independent and which should be dependent? The idea that you think is more important should be the independent clause. The less important idea will then be the dependent clause.

Following are some examples of how to combine simple sentences to make a complex sentence.

Simple: David has a demanding job.

Simple: David really enjoys his job.

                                      Dep   Ind

Complex: **Though** David has a demanding job, he really enjoys it.

This complex sentence stresses that David enjoys his job. That the job is demanding is of secondary importance.

                              Ind   Dep

Complex: David has a demanding job, **though** he really enjoys it.

In this complex sentence, the fact that David's job is demanding is the important point, so it is stated in the independent clause.

Simple: Jack loves to go deep-sea fishing.

Simple: Jack is my brother.

                      Ind   Dep   Ind

Complex: Jack, **who** is my brother, loves to go deep-sea fishing.

This complex sentence answers the question "Who loves to go deep-sea fishing?" The information about Jack being the brother is of secondary importance.

                            Ind   Dep

Complex: My brother is Jack, **who** loves to go deep-sea fishing.

This complex sentence answers the question "Who is your brother?" The information that he loves to go deep-sea fishing is secondary.

┌───┐
│   │
│   REVIEWING COMPLEX SENTENCES   │
│   │
│   *What does a complex sentence consist of?*   │
│   │
│   *An independent clause and at least one dependent clause*   │
│   ───   │
│   │
│   *Write a complex sentence.*   │
│   │
│   *Answers will vary.*   │
│   ───   │
│   │
└───┘

Practice 11 Identifying   Identify the underlined part of each sentence as either an independent (Ind) or a dependent (Dep) clause.

1. ___Ind___ Even though he enjoys working with small children, <u>they try his patience sometimes</u>.

2. ___Dep___ Thomas, <u>who won the election</u>, is now the dorm monitor.

3. ___Dep___ <u>Before you leave for work</u>, make sure the iron is turned off.

4. ___Ind___ <u>She always sneezes</u> whenever she is around daffodils.

5. ___Dep___ There is the mouse <u>that you have been trying to catch</u>!

6. ___Dep___ Of course you can attend the wedding, <u>provided that you are invited</u>.

7. ___Ind___ <u>I wonder</u> how I can improve my grades.

8. ___Dep___ Cassandra is the employee <u>whose attendance is perfect</u>.

9. ___Ind___ <u>The winner of the beauty contest is Sandy Grain</u>, who is also my sister.

10. ___Ind___ <u>We are celebrating</u> because we passed our final exams.

Practice 12 Identifying   Underline the independent clauses once and the dependent clauses twice in each of the following sentences.

1. Your proposal, which is beautifully written, was accepted.

2. My favorite singer is Sting, who also has a B.A. in English literature.

3. Have the carpets cleaned before the new furniture arrives.

4. Aiden appreciated Joan's efforts to cheer him though he still felt sad.

5. Although I do want to go, I have a deadline to meet.

6. In life, <u>you never know</u> <u>whom you might meet.</u>

7. <u>Ann believes</u> <u>that she is the best candidate for the position.</u>

8. <u>Even if the sun comes out from behind the clouds,</u> <u>it's still going to be cold.</u>

9. <u>If they try to jump over that stream,</u> <u>they are probably going to fall in.</u>

10. <u>The air conditioning is set to 72 degrees</u> <u>so that the computers will run properly.</u>

🌿 Practice 13 Correcting   Write the sentences in Practice 12 as either simple or compound sentences. You can change words when necessary.
Answers will vary.

1. _____

2. _____

3. _____

4. _____

5. _____

6. _____

7. _____

8. _____

9. _____

10. _____

🌿 Practice 14 Completing   Finish each of the following sentences, and label the new clause either dependent (Dep) or independent (Ind). *Answers in blanks will vary.*

1. __Dep__ My cousin, _____, won the lottery.

2. __Dep__ Here are the rods and reels _____.

3. __Dep__ Thomas left the lights on _____.

4. __Ind__ Even if the show ends by 9:00, _____.

5. __Ind__ Whenever it snows, _____.

6. __Ind__ _____, although he really doesn't like it.

7. __Dep__ The presents _____ are already in the mail.

8. __Dep__ I invested money in a CD _____.

9. __Dep__ Before _____, make sure that the car is filled with gas.

10. __Ind__ _____ how you finished your work so quickly.

❈ Practice 15 Writing Your Own

A. Write a dependent clause using each of the following subordinating conjunctions and relative pronouns. *Answers will vary.*

1. that _____

2. whose _____

3. after _____

4. whereas _____

5. unless _____

B. Write five independent clauses to combine with the dependent clauses you wrote in Practice 15A to make five complex sentences. *Answers will vary.*

1. _____

2. _____

3. _____

4. _____

5. _____

COMPOUND-COMPLEX SENTENCES

If you combine a compound sentence with a complex sentence, you produce a **compound-complex sentence.** That means your sentence has at least two independent clauses (to make it compound) and at least one dependent clause (to make it complex). Here are some examples.

Simple: James likes to sail.

Simple: He is going to Cancun this summer.

Simple: He is looking forward to sailing in Cancun.

Compound-	Ind	Ind
Complex:	James likes to sail, **and** he is going to Cancun	

Dep

this summer, **which** he is looking forward to.

Simple:	She is selling her old house.
Simple:	Her house has only one bedroom.
Simple:	She plans to buy a bigger house.

Compound-	Ind	Dep
Complex:	She is selling her old house, **which** has only one	

Ind

bedroom, **and** she plans to buy a bigger house.

Simple:	These cookies look delicious.
Simple:	The cookies are very hot.
Simple:	The cookies just came out of the oven.

Compound-	Ind	Ind
Complex:	These cookies look delicious, **but** they are very hot	

Dep

since they just came out of the oven.

HINT: Notice that we occasionally have to change words in combined sentences so that they make sense.

REVIEWING COMPOUND-COMPLEX SENTENCES

What does a compound-complex sentence consist of?

At least two independent clauses and one dependent clause

Write a compound-complex sentence.

Answers will vary.

Practice 16 Identifying   Identify the underlined part of each sentence as either an independent (Ind) or a dependent (Dep) clause.

1. __Dep__ Alyssa, who is a practical joker, left a pail of paint over the door, and she also put a fake mouse in the sheets.

2. __Ind__ Even though I like to be alone sometimes, I do enjoy others' company, and I can make small talk.

3. __Dep__ Golf is a difficult game, but it can be mastered if a person has patience.

4. __Dep__ The man looked as if he was going to burst out laughing, yet he just gasped and wheezed into his napkin.

5. __Ind__ They have been married for five years, and they are very happy together even though both have very different personalities.

6. __Dep__ While the boss was out of the office, the employees did a little redecorating, yet they resisted the urge to play hooky.

7. __Ind__ Whether you believe it or not, Harvey really did send you an invitation, and he really does like you.

8. __Dep__ The antique-white dress, which belonged to my grandmother, is lovely, and I plan to have it altered for my wedding.

9. __Ind__ We caught several bass and catfish, but they were too small for supper, so we threw them back in the lake.

10. __Ind__ When the tire blew, he quickly pulled the car over to the side of the road, and then he called AAA.

❋ Practice 17 Identifying   Underline the independent clauses once and the dependent clauses twice in each of the following sentences.

1. Manny, who is a wonderful father, spends much time with his children, and he even takes them to work with him on occasion.

2. The books that you ordered over the Internet are in the mail, and they should reach you within three days.

3. These CDs, which I borrowed from a friend, are the best, and I am going to buy them for myself.

4. She whipped up a quick meal, and then she jumped in the bathtub when the phone rang.

5. After you accept your diploma, you should turn and smile for the camera, but you shouldn't make any silly faces.

6. We are planning the roast for our retiring chair, and we are going to pre-pare a slide show <u>because we have some hilarious pictures of everyone.</u>

7. <u>Even though the weather is horrible outside,</u> <u>Luke insists on going on the trip, and</u> <u>he will not back down.</u>

8. <u>She asked him</u> <u>how he managed to escape without a lecture,</u> and <u>then she filed the information away for future use.</u>

9. <u>Once the liquid comes to a rolling boil,</u> <u>remove the mixture from the stove,</u> but <u>don't allow it to cool too quickly.</u>

10. <u>The person</u> <u>who gets the job</u> <u>must have experience with phone systems, and he or she must also have great customer service skills.</u>

🌿 **Practice 18 Correcting**   Write the sentences in Practice 17 as either simple, compound, or complex sentences. You can change words when necessary. *Answers will vary.*

1. _____

2. _____

3. _____

4. _____

5. _____

6. _____

7. _____

8. _____

9. _____

10. _____

🌿 **Practice 19 Completing**   Write two compound-complex sentences for each set of sentences. You may have to change some of the words to make the new sentences clear. *Answers will vary.*

1. I need a new computer.

   I broke my last computer.

   I plan to order a computer from Gateway.

_____

_____

2. The tea was lukewarm.
   I was thirsty.
   I drank the tea.

_____

_____

3. Bob owns a vintage Harley Davidson.
   Bob has been a biker for 10 years.
   Bob likes to ride in the mountains.

_____

_____

4. Joshua loves to eat Reese's Peanut Butter Cups.
   He has a process for eating Reese's Peanut Butter Cups.
   Joshua will not share his Reese's Peanut Butter Cups.

_____

_____

5. Crystal has an infectious sense of humor.
   Crystal laughs all the time.
   Crystal makes others laugh too.

_____

_____

❀ Practice 20 Writing Your Own

A. Expand the following clauses into compound-complex sentences. *Answers will vary.*

1. I know the man who was the last person to arrive

_____

2. I was reading a really good book

_____

3. They bought the house that you decorated

_____

4. I am a free spirit, and I love to travel

   _____

5. so that the rain wouldn't come through the roof

   _____

B. Write five compound-complex sentences of your own, and underline the independent clauses once and the dependent clauses twice in each sentence. *Answers will vary.*

1. _____

2. _____

3. _____

4. _____

5. _____

CHAPTER REVIEW

You might want to reread your answers to the questions in the review boxes before you do the following exercises.

Review Practice 1 Reading   Refer to the paragraph by Erma Bombeck on page 480 to do the following exercises.

1. List the simple sentence from the paragraph.

   In the picture Mama is crying and biting her coin in half.

2. List the one compound sentence from the paragraph.

   It was a dime, and she wanted the bigger coin—the nickel—given to her sister.

3. List the four complex sentences from the paragraph.

   I liked Grandma the best, though, when she told me . . . never seen or been close to.

   I didn't know that when Mama . . . her and her sister in a pony cart.

   I couldn't imagine that they had to bribe them into good behavior by giving each of them a coin.

   Somehow, I thought that Mama was born knowing the difference between a nickel and a dime.

4. Combine some of the sentences in the professional paragraph to create a compound-complex sentence.

Answers will vary.

_____

_____

❧ Review Practice 2 Identifying   Underline the independent clauses once and the dependent clauses twice in each of the following sentences. Then label each sentence simple (S), compound (C), complex (CX), or compound-complex (CCX). The following definitions will help you.

Simple	= one independent clause
Compound	= two or more independent clauses joined by *and, but for, nor, or, so,* or *yet*
Complex	= one independent clause and at least one dependent clause
Compound-complex	= at least two independent clauses and one or more dependent clauses

1. ___C___ They often attend auctions, but they rarely bid on the antiques.

2. ___S___ Erin is always joking with people.

3. ___CX___ He cooked dinner, washed the dishes, and mowed the lawn while she watched television.

4. ___CCX___ He said that you were a trustworthy employee, and he recommended that we hire you.

5. ___CX___ Most people who are allergic to bees developed the allergy after their second sting.

6. ___S___ The car sputtered and died.

7. ___C___ This printer can print in many different colors, and it can act as a fax too.

8. ___CCX___ We brought extra water, freeze-dried food, and heavy-duty sleeping bags, and we made sure that the first-aid kit was stocked.

9. ___C___ A. C. Bradley is a well-known Shakespearean critic, and he is often cited in research papers.

10. ___CX___ Whenever Sarah gets that silly smile on her face, she is thinking about her fiancé.

❧ Review Practice 3 Writing Your Own   Combine each set of sentences to make the sentence pattern indicated in parentheses. You may need to change some wording in the sentences so they make sense. The list of sentence types in Review Practice 2 may help you with this exercise.

Answers will vary.

1. The plane may not arrive on time. We will miss our next connection. (complex)

2. Joey left for Spain. Joey got a new passport. Joey brushed up on his Spanish. (compound-complex)

3. Whole-wheat muffins or bagels are tasty. Whole-wheat muffins or bagels are healthy. (simple)

4. You had to suffer through the lecture. The lecture was extremely boring. You had to catch a plane back home. (compound-complex)

5. The phone lines were down. Cathy used her cell phone. Cathy cut the conversation short to save money. (compound-complex)

6. Simone discussed the upcoming election. Craig discussed the upcoming election. (simple)

7. Nurses have difficult jobs. Most nurses find their work worthwhile. (compound)

8. Many people entered the drawing. Only one person won. (complex)

9. You always laugh. People laugh with you. (complex)

10. Mindy and Jennifer will build a fire in the fireplace. Dave and Voni will begin supper. (compound)

✎ EDITING A STUDENT PARAGRAPH

Following is a paragraph written and revised by Tim Robertson in response to the writing assignment in this chapter. Read the paragraph, and underline the independent clauses once and the dependent clauses twice.

> I found out that my older brother Mike was actually a member of the human race. It was the day when he fixed my bike. I was 6 years old. Mike was 13. I thought that he knew everything. Mike was a distant god in my eyes. It was a Saturday morning. The chain had come loose on my bike. I was crying in the garage. Mike came out. He saw me crying and said that he would fix my bike. I watched for a while. Then I got bored. Most 6-year-olds get bored easily. I went inside to find other entertainment. Soon I was in the garage again. "Are you finished yet?" I asked

Here are the sentence types:

I found out that my older brother Mike was actually a member of the human race. (CX)

It was the day when he fixed my bike. (CX)

I was 6 years old. (S)

Mike was 13. (S)

I thought that he knew everything. (CX)

Mike was a distant god in my eyes. (S)

It was a Saturday morning. (S)

The chain had come loose on my bike. (S)

I was crying in the garage. (S)

Mike came out. (S)

He saw me crying and said that he would fix my bike. (CX)

I watched for a while. (S)

Then I got bored. (S)

Most 6-year-olds get bored easily. (S)

I went inside to find other entertainment. (S)

Soon I was in the garage again. (S)

"Are you finished yet?" (S)

I asked him. (S)

"No," he said. (S)

I repeated this routine four times within 30 minutes. (S)

On the fourth time, Mike yelled, (S) "No, I am not finished yet. (S)

If you don't stop bugging me, I'm going to throw the chain in the garbage!" (CX)

I ran screaming to my room. (S)

I slammed the door. (S)

Not five minutes later, Mike came into my room. (S)

He sat on my bed. (S)

It was lumpy from years of jumping. (S)

He pulled me onto his lap and gave me a big hug. (S)

"You know that I really do love you," he said, "even when you bug me." (CCX)

Mike and I had seven years separating us. (S)

Mike never seemed to have time for me. (S)

I thought that I was simply someone whom he tolerated. (CX)

On that day, however, my perspective of Mike changed. (S)

He was no longer just a distant god. (S)

He was my big brother too. (S)

him. "No," he said. I repeated this routine four times within 30 minutes. On the fourth time, Mike yelled, "No, I am not finished yet. If you don't stop bugging me, I'm going to throw the chain in the garbage!" I ran screaming to my room. I slammed the door. Not five minutes later, Mike came into my room. He sat on my bed. It was lumpy from years of jumping. He pulled me onto his lap and gave me a big hug. "You know that I really do love you," he said, "even when you bug me." Mike and I had seven years separating us. Mike never seemed to have time for me. I thought that I was simply someone whom he tolerated. On that day, however, my perspective of Mike changed. He was no longer just a distant god. He was my big brother too.

Collaborative Activity

Team up with a partner, and label each of Tim's sentences S (simple), C (compound), CX (complex), or CCX (compound-complex). Then, working together, use what you have learned in this chapter to add variety to the paragraph by combining some of the sentences. Make at least two compound, two complex, and two compound-complex sentences. Rewrite the paragraph with your revisions. *Sentence types are in the margin. Revised paragraphs will vary.*

EDITING YOUR OWN PARAGRAPH

Now return to the paragraph you wrote and revised at the beginning of this chapter. Underline the independent clauses once and the dependent clauses twice.

Collaborative Activity

Exchange paragraphs with your partner, and label each of your partner's sentences S (simple), C (compound), CX (complex), or CCX (compound-complex).

Individual Activity

To complete the writing process, add variety in your sentence patterns by combining some of the sentences in your paragraph.

Unit 7 Review
Effective Sentences

🌿 **Unit Practice 1 Identifying** Label each of the following sentences simple (S), compound (C), complex (CX), or compound–complex (CCX).

1. _____ My boyfriend likes to go to the movies a lot.

   _____ He always wants to see blood-and-guts movies.

   _____ Someday I'll sneak in a romance, a drama, or seeing a comedy.

2. _____ I am ready for summer break.

   _____ I took too many units this quarter, unfortunately.

   _____ I hope that I can keep up my hectic pace through finals.

3. _____ I love to shop for groceries, cook meals, and baking.

   _____ Thank goodness my roommate loves to clean.

   _____ We decided to keep peace by doing these chores for each other.

4. _____ Monday is my favorite day of the week.

   _____ Most people think that this is very strange.

   _____ I love starting a new week, making new decisions, and my troubles are left behind me.

5. _____ My favorite brother is moving to my town.

   _____ I love being with my brother.

   _____ Being together will be like old times.

🌿 **Unit Practice 2 Varying** Rewrite each of the sentences in Unit Practice 1 using one of the following techniques to add variety to them.
Answers will vary.

■ For additional material about teaching effective sentences, for journal entries, and for various tests, see the *Instructor's Resource Manual*, Section II, Part II.

ADDITIONAL WRITING TOPIC
Let your students expand into well-developed essays the paragraphs they wrote in one of the unit chapters.

1. Add some introductory words to your sentences so that they don't all start the same way.

2. Reverse the order of some subjects and verbs.

3. Move some parts of the sentences around.

4. Use a question, command, or exclamation occasionally.

1. _____

_____

_____

2. _____

_____

_____

3. _____

_____

_____

4. _____

_____

_____

5. _____

_____

_____

Unit Practice 3 Making Parallel   Correct any items in a series that are not parallel in the sentences you wrote in Unit Practice 2 by rewriting each series in parallel form. *Answers will vary.*

1. *. . . a romance, a drama, or a comedy.* _____

2. _____

3. *. . . to shop for groceries, cook meals, and baking.* _____

4. *. . . starting a new week, making new decisions, and leaving my troubles behind me.*

5. _____

🌿 **Unit Practice 4 Combining**   Combine sentences in Unit Practice 1
using as many of the changes you made in Unit Practices 2 and 3 as possible.
Answers will vary.

1. _____
   _____

2. _____
   _____

3. _____
   _____

4. _____
   _____

5. _____
   _____

UNIT WRITING ASSIGNMENTS

1. What is this ad about? What is the unspoken message in this picture?
   Are you persuaded by this ad? Why or why not?

2. You have been asked to prepare a speech for your English class about
   writing. Use your experience as a writer to persuade your audience that
   writing is beneficial for many different reasons. Be sure to explain what
   the benefits are and why they are benefits. You may even want to narrow
   your topic to one type of writing.

3. You have decided to use your yard skills and mow the lawns in your neighborhood to make money during the summer. This job fits with your summer classes, and you can work as much or as little as you want. How do you plan to approach your customers? What will you do to demonstrate your talents? What will you say? Explain your approach and the reasons for your choices.

4. Create your own assignment (with the help of your instructor), and write a response to it.

Unit 8 Choosing the Right Word

Choosing the right word is like choosing the right snack to satisfy your appetite. If you don't select the food you are craving, your hunger does not go away. In like manner, if you do not choose the right words to say what is on your mind, your readers will not be satisfied and will not understand your message.

Choosing the right word depends on your message, your purpose, and your audience. It also involves recognizing misused, nonstandard, and misspelled words. We deal with the following topics in Unit 8:

Chapter 30: Standard and Nonstandard English
Chapter 31: Easily Confused Words
Chapter 32: Spelling

Choosing the right words is sometimes part of the drafting stage for students and sometimes part of the revising or editing stage. It involves recognizing nonstandard, misused, and misspelled words. Students should understand that choosing the right word is an essential part of the final product and the impression that the writing makes on its readers.

Standard and Nonstandard English

🖉 Checklist for Choosing the Right Word

> ✔ Do you consistently use standard English in your paper?
> ✔ Is your paper free of nonstandard, ungrammatical words?
> ✔ Have you changed any slang to standard English?

Choosing the right words for what you want to say is an important part of effective communication. Look, for example, at the following sentences. They all have generally the same message, expressed in different words.

I am studying to become a nurse, the reason being that I want to help people.

I be studying to be a nurse, so I can help people.

I'm pounding the books so I can be a good nurse.

I am pursuing a degree in nursing so that I can help others in need.

Which of these sentences would you probably say to a friend or to someone in your family? Which would you most likely say in a job interview? Which would be good for a college paper?

The first three sentences are nonstandard English. They might be said or written to a friend or family member, but they would not be appropriate in an academic setting or in a job situation. Only the fourth sentence would be appropriate in an academic paper or in a job interview.

Notice in the following paragraph how the consistent use of standard English makes a message smooth and coherent.

Just last week, I was walking down the street with my mother, and I again found myself conscious of the English I was using, the English I do use with her. We were talking about the price of new and used furniture, and I heard myself saying this: "Not waste money that way." My husband was with us as well, and he didn't notice any switch in my English. And then I realized why. It's because over the twenty years we've been together I've often used that same kind of English with him, and sometimes he even uses it with me. It has become our language of intimacy, a different sort of English that relates to family talk, the language I grew up with.

In this paragraph, Amy Tan discusses the different types of English she uses depending on the situation. Before continuing in this chapter, take a moment to record your thoughts on your language use in a typical day. Save your work because you will use it later in this chapter.

TEACHING ON THE WEB

Mosaics Web Site: To learn more about standard and nonstandard English, students can go to www. prenhall.com/mosaics.

Writing Assignment: Languages

How many languages do you speak and write? What is your native language? How do you adjust your English to different people and different situations? Why do you adjust your language in these ways? Write a paragraph describing your language use in a typical day. Do your adjustments in language suit the different purposes and people in your life?

Revising Your Writing

Revise the first draft of your paragraph before you focus on editing. Use the Revising Checklist on pages 24–25 to help you with your revision. Make sure your paragraph has a good topic sentence and is well developed. Then check your paragraph for unity, organization, and coherence.

STANDARD AND NONSTANDARD ENGLISH

Most of the English language falls into one of two categories—either *standard* or *nonstandard*. **Standard English** is the language of college, business, and the media. It is used by reporters on television, by newspapers, in most magazines, and on Web sites created by schools, government, business, and organizations. Standard English is always grammatically correct and free of slang.

Nonstandard English does not follow all the rules of grammar and often includes slang. Nonstandard English is not necessarily wrong, but it is more appropriate in some settings (with friends and family) than others. It is not appropriate in college or business writing. To understand the difference between standard and nonstandard English, compare the following paragraphs.

Nonstandard English

I just got a new pad and went to the grocery store to stock the fridge with some grub. Since I only had 40 bucks to my name, I knew I oughta play it cool and just stick to the list: milk, eggs, cereal, soda, bread, peanut butter, and jelly. Irregardless of my good intentions, I sorta lost it in the frozen food section. By the time I got outta that section, I must of picked up one of each kind of food—pizza, corn dogs, burritos, pies, and apple turnovers. And somewheres underneath all that stuff were the bread and the eggs. I was real embarrassed when I go to check out cuz I didn't have enough money and I had to put some of the stuff back. At that moment, I realized I was a long ways from home.

Standard English

I just got a new apartment and went to the grocery store to stock the refrigerator with some food. Since I had only $40, I knew I had to stick to my list: milk, eggs, cereal, soda, bread, peanut butter, and jelly. Regardless of my good intentions, I made too many selections in the frozen food section. By the time I got out of that aisle, I must have picked up one of each kind of food—pizza, corn dogs, burritos, pies, and apple turnovers. And somewhere underneath all that food were the bread and the eggs. I was really embarrassed when I went to check out because I didn't have enough money and I had to put some of the items back. At that moment, I realized I was a long way from home.

In the rest of this chapter, you will learn how to recognize and correct ungrammatical English and how to avoid slang in your writing.

REVIEWING STANDARD AND NONSTANDARD ENGLISH

Where do you hear standard English in your daily life?

On TV, in the media, in schools, in newspapers

What is nonstandard English?

English that does not follow the rules of grammar and usage.

Give two examples of nonstandard English.

Answers will vary.

NONSTANDARD ENGLISH

Nonstandard English is ungrammatical. It does not follow the rules of standard English. The academic and business worlds expect you to be able to recognize and avoid nonstandard English. This is not always easy because some nonstandard terms are used so often in speech that many people think they are acceptable in writing. The following list might help you choose the correct words in your own writing.

ain't

> **NOT** He **ain't** leaving until tomorrow.
>
> **Correct:** He **isn't** leaving until tomorrow.

anywheres

> **NOT** Susie can't find her glasses **anywheres.**
>
> **Correct:** Susie can't find her glasses **anywhere.**

be

> **NOT** I **be** really good at art.
>
> **Correct:** I **am** really good at art.

For additional help with *be*, see Chapter 11, "Verb Tense."

being as, being that

> **NOT** Justin will not be joining the study group tonight, **being as** his car broke down.
>
> **Correct:** Justin will not be joining the study group tonight, **because** his car broke down.

coulda/could of, shoulda/should of

NOT   She **could of** made the sauce with cream instead of milk.

Correct: She **could have** made the sauce with cream instead of milk.

different than

NOT   This sandwich is no **different than** that sandwich.

Correct: This sandwich is no **different from** that sandwich.

don't

NOT   Tanya **don't** eat properly because she likes sweets too much.

Correct: Tanya **doesn't** eat properly because she likes sweets too much.

For additional help with *do*, see Chapter 11, "Verb Tense."

drug

NOT   I **drug** the rug across the floor.

Correct: I **dragged** the rug across the floor.

enthused

NOT   Jim was **enthused** about his GPA.

Correct: Jim was **enthusiastic** about his GPA.

everywheres

NOT   My little sister follows me **everywheres.**

Correct: My little sister follows me **everywhere.**

goes

NOT   Then Nancy **goes,** I'm taking the bus.

Correct: Then Nancy **says,** "I'm taking the bus."

Correct: Then Nancy **said** she was taking the bus.

has/have/had

NOT   My cat **have** only three toes.

Correct: My cat **has** only three toes.

For additional help with *have*, see Chapter 11, "Verb Tense."

hisself

NOT	Evan made **hisself** sick on peanut butter.
Correct:	Evan made **himself** sick on peanut butter.

in regards to

NOT	I got your memo **in regards to** the changes.
Correct:	I got your memo **in regard to** the changes.

irregardless

NOT	**Irregardless** of your healthy lifestyle, you still need to lower your cholesterol.
Correct:	**Regardless** of your healthy lifestyle, you still need to lower your cholesterol.

kinda/kind of, sorta/sort of

NOT	This tastes **kinda** sweet, **sorta** like cherries.
Correct:	This tastes **rather** sweet, **much** like cherries.

most

NOT	**Most** everyone is going.
Correct:	**Almost** everyone is going.

must of

NOT	I **must of** left my backpack in the park.
Correct:	I **must have** left my backpack in the park.

off of

NOT	Michael skated **off of** the ramp.
Correct:	Michael skated **off** the ramp.

oughta

NOT	Sometimes you **oughta** say please and thank you.
Correct:	Sometimes you **ought to** say please and thank you.

real

NOT	She was **real** glad to see us.
Correct:	She was **really** glad to see us.

somewheres

> **NOT**   His books are **somewheres** in that dirty room.
>
> **Correct:** His books are **somewhere** in that dirty room.

suppose to

> **NOT**   They were **suppose to** meet us here.
>
> **Correct:** They were **supposed to** meet us here.

theirselves

> **NOT**   The children hid **theirselves** throughout the house.
>
> **Correct:** The children hid **themselves** throughout the house.

use to

> **NOT**   I **use to** work while listening to music.
>
> **Correct:** I **used to** work while listening to music.

ways

> **NOT**   We are lost and a long **ways** from home.
>
> **Correct:** We are lost and a long **way** from home.

where . . . at

> **NOT**   **Where** is the remote control **at?**
>
> **Correct:** **Where** is the remote control?

REVIEWING NONSTANDARD ENGLISH

What is one reason using nonstandard English in written work is easy to do?

We hear it so often we think it is standard

Give four examples of nonstandard English; then correct them.

Examples will vary.

🌿 **Practice 1 Identifying**   Put an X next to the sentence if the underlined words are ungrammatical.

1. __X__ <u>Being that</u> it is such a beautiful day, we should take our lunch on the patio.

2. __X__ Alyssa <u>don't</u> like to be tickled.

3. _____ She <u>used</u> to drink coffee every morning.

4. __X__ We <u>ain't</u> going to fail this test.

5. _____ Jake bought <u>himself</u> a dirt bike.

6. __X__ The crowd was <u>enthused</u> about his speech.

7. __X__ Those dogs <u>oughta</u> be on a leash.

8. __X__ My cell phone goes <u>everywheres</u> I go.

9. _____ The computer was <u>supposed</u> to come with a color printer.

10. __X__ <u>Most everyone</u> likes your idea.

🌿 **Practice 2 Identifying**   Underline the ungrammatical words or phrases in each of the following sentences.

1. Mom was <u>real</u> mad when I left the milk out. *(really)*

2. They made <u>theirselves</u> a promise to spend more time together. *(themselves)*

3. We have wandered a long <u>ways</u> from the path. *(way)*

4. Your wallet could be <u>anywheres</u> in the backyard. *(anywhere)*

5. The plant <u>have</u> only two blooms. *(has)*

6. <u>Irregardless</u> of how much time you spent on your paper, it still needs revision. *(Regardless)*

7. <u>Somewheres</u> out there is the perfect car for me. *(Somewhere)*

8. Where is the phone <u>at</u>? *(omit at)*

9. You could <u>of</u> taken the freeway instead of the back roads. *(have)*

10. The receptionist must <u>of</u> written down the wrong phone number. *(have)*

🌿 **Practice 3 Correcting**   Correct the standard English errors in Practice 2 by rewriting each incorrect sentence. *See Practice 2.*

1. _____

2. _____

3. _____

4. _____

5. _____

6. _____

7. _____

8. _____

9. _____

10. _____

Practice 4 Completing   Fill in each blank in the following sentences with standard English using the list at the beginning of this chapter.

1. The girl's behavior is very different _____*from*_____ the boy's.

2. With his teeth, the puppy _____*dragged*_____ his toy across the living room.

3. Then William _____*said*_____ that he would do the job.

4. They received the letter in _____*regard*_____ to the board meeting.

5. He fell _____*off*_____ the sidewalk and sprained his ankle.

6. My little sister didn't realize that she wasn't _____*supposed*_____ to eat the mud pies.

7. The cake _____*isn't*_____ ready yet.

8. I _____*am*_____ very fond of seafood.

9. That smells _____*rather*_____ bad, _____*much*_____ like garbage.

10. The dog has buried my keys _____*somewhere*_____ in the backyard.

Practice 5 Writing Your Own

A. Write a sentence of your own for each of the following words and phrases. *Answers will vary.*

1. should have _____

2. in regard to _____

3. ought to _____

4. must have _____

5. dragged _____

B. Write five sentences of your own using at least five of the standard English examples at the beginning of this chapter. Underline the standard English examples. *Answers will vary.*

1. _____

2. _____

3. _____

4. _____

5. _____

SLANG

Another example of nonstandard English is **slang,** popular words and expressions that come and go, much like the latest fashions. For example, in the 1950s, someone might call his or her special someone *my steady*. In the 1970s, you might hear a boyfriend or girlfriend described as *foxy*, and in the 1980s, *stud* was a popular slang term for males. Today your significant other might be your *homegirl* or *lady*. These expressions are slang because they are part of the spoken language that changes from generation to generation and from place to place. As you might suspect, slang communicates to a limited audience who share common interests and experiences. Some slang words, such as *cool* and *neat*, have become part of our language, but most slang is temporary. What's in today may be out tomorrow, so the best advice is to avoid slang in your writing.

Reviewing Slang

What is slang?

Popular words and expressions that come and go _____

Give two examples of slang terms that were popular but aren't any longer.

Examples will vary. _____   _____

Give two examples of slang terms that you and your friends use today.

Examples will vary. _____   _____

🌿 **Practice 6 Identifying**   Put an X next to the sentence if the underlined word is slang.

1. __X__ Your leather jacket is <u>slammin'</u>.

2. __X__ This is good <u>grub</u>.

3. __X__ Cordelia's talking <u>smack</u> again.

4. __X__ I'm making <u>big bucks</u> now.

5. _____ Sam will leave when he is <u>ready</u>.

6. __X__ Let's <u>chill</u> at the library for a while.

7. _____ <u>Talk to me</u> about your decision.

8. __X__ We don't allow <u>scrubs</u> in our dorm.

9. _____ You deserve <u>praise</u> for your efforts.

10. _____ The hostess was <u>very</u> gracious.

🌿 **Practice 7 Identifying**   Underline the slang words or phrases in the following sentences.

1. These CDs are <u>da bomb</u>. *(the best)*

2. Everyone knows Jason is a <u>player</u>. *(Jason dates many girls.)*

3. She's <u>down with</u> the plan. *(She agrees with)*

4. You have to <u>get your groove on</u> at the party. *(dance)*

5. <u>Me and my dawgs</u> are going to the show. *(My friends and I)*

6. <u>Keep it real</u>. *(Don't be fake.)*

7. <u>I got your back</u>. *(I'll watch out for you.)*

8. I <u>dig</u> your new <u>ride</u>. *(I like your new car)*

9. <u>Give it to me straight</u>. *(Tell me the truth.)*

10. What's <u>crackin'</u>? *(What's going on?)*

🌿 **Practice 8 Correcting**   Correct the slang errors in Practice 7 by rewriting each sentence. *See Practice 7. Answers may vary.*

1. _____

2. _____

3. _____

4. _____

5. _____

6. _____

7. _____

8. _____

9. _____

10. _____

Practice 9 Completing   Translate each of the following slang expressions into standard English. *Answers may vary.*

1. go with the flow *be cooperative*
2. yawning in technocolor *vomiting*
3. get outta here *leave*
4. pump it up *create more energy or excitement*
5. toasts your brain *gives you a headache*
6. homies *friends*
7. five-finger discount *theft*
8. keep it on the DL *keep it a secret*
9. give him props *give him proper respect*
10. give big ups *praise*

Practice 10 Writing Your Own

A. List five slang words or expressions, and use them in sentences of your own. *Answers will vary.*

1. _____

2. _____

3. _____

4. _____

5. _____

B. Rewrite each sentence from Practice 10A using standard English to replace the slang expressions. *Answers will vary.*

1. _____

2. _____

3. _____

4. _____

5. _____

CHAPTER REVIEW

You might want to reread your answers to the questions in the review boxes before you do the following exercises.

Review Practice 1 Reading   Rewrite the paragraph by Amy Tan on page 507 in nonstandard English.

Answers will vary.

_____

_____

_____

_____

_____

_____

Review Practice 2 Identifying   Underline any nonstandard English and slang in the following sentences.

1. We're really <u>rolling</u> now. *(moving)*

2. She <u>must of</u> forgotten that we were going to have lunch today. *(must have)*

3. The monkeys at the zoo acted <u>real hyper</u> when they saw us. *(really excited)*

4. That's <u>jacked up</u>. *(very wrong or unfair)*

5. You don't understand, <u>man</u>. *(drop "man")*

6. <u>Somewheres</u> out there is the girl for you. *(Somewhere)*

7. <u>Peep</u> this. *(Watch/Look at)*

8. Where is the sugar <u>at</u>? *(omit at)*

9. Just back that train up. *(rethink that idea or statement)*

10. This ain't the best idea. *(isn't)*

🌿 **Review Practice 3 Correcting**   Correct the nonstandard English and slang in Review Practice 2 by rewriting each sentence. *See Review Practice 2.*

🪶 EDITING A STUDENT PARAGRAPH

Following is a paragraph written and revised by Jamie Franks in response to the writing assignment in this chapter. Read the paragraph, and look for any nonstandard English or slang.

Unfortunately, I now only speak one language. I say "now" because I use to speak Spanish until I was 3, but I have lost all memory of the language. In a way, however, the statement that I only speak one language is false, because I kinda speak two languages--a form of English I use with adults and a form of English I use with my friends. And believe me, one is definitely different than the other. When I speak to my friends, I go, "Dude, I went to a phat party last night. Carly was chillin' with a hottie named Dan. Man, she was beat." Of course, I ain't gonna say this to my grandma. I would say, "I went to a great party last night. A girl named Carly spent time with a good-looking guy named Dan, but she wasn't very attractive." Irregardless of the situation, it be real disrespectful, in some ways, to talk to adults in slang being that they don't understand, but it's also not proper. But I wouldn't talk in proper English all the time to my friends because we'd eventually never communicate. I'd be left behind somewheres in the conversation. So I do believe that language is important, and I do believe I speak two languages. They just both happen to be English.

Here are the standard English corrections:
used to
kind of
different from
say
Hey
great
spending time
good-looking guy
Boy
wasn't very attractive
am not
going to
Regardless
is
really
because
somewhere

Collaborative Activity

Team up with a partner, and underline the 17 nonstandard and slang expressions in Jamie's paragraph. Then, working together, use what you have learned in this chapter to correct these errors. Rewrite the paragraph with your corrections. Don't change any words in the quotations. *See student paragraph for errors. Corrections are in the margin.*

🌿 EDITING YOUR OWN PARAGRAPH

Now return to the paragraph you wrote and revised at the beginning of this chapter. Look for any nonstandard English or slang.

Collaborative Activity

Exchange paragraphs with your partner, and underline any nonstandard or slang expressions that you find in your partner's paragraph.

Individual Activity

On the Error Log in Appendix 6, record any nonstandard English errors your partner found in your paragraph. To complete the writing process, correct these errors by rewriting your paragraph.

CHAPTER 31

Easily Confused Words

Checklist for Easily Confused Words

✔ Is the correct word chosen from the easily confused words?

✔ Are the following words used correctly: *its/it's*, *their/there/they're*, *to/too/two*, *who's/whose*, *your/you're?*

Some words are easily confused. They may look alike, sound alike, or have similar meanings. But they all play different roles in the English language.

Notice how the careful selection of words helps convey meaning in the following paragraph.

> Do you consistently write more than necessary in e-mail messages? Are you swamping your readers with too many details? Do you give so much information—important, unimportant, and in no particular order—that your reader cannot easily conclude what matters and what does not? A poll published in *Oregon Business* found that 26 percent of respondents spend an hour each day reading and replying to their e-mail; 14 percent spend more than an hour. So, do everything possible to compose messages that will help your reader save time. Some guidelines include the following: (1) Limit messages to one screen so the reader will not have to scroll down, and (2) use numbers, bullets, etc., to highlight key points.

In this excerpt, Mark Hansen gives some practical advice about communicating through e-mail. Before continuing in this chapter, take a moment to respond to his suggestions. Save your work because you will use it later in this chapter.

Eye have run this poem
   threw it;
I am shore your pleased
   two no.
Its letter perfect awl the
   weigh;
My chequer told me sew!

**TEACHING ON
THE WEB**

Exploring and Discussing:
Have students review past
e-mail messages. How
many confused word
errors can they find from
people who posted
messages in haste? What
do these errors say about
the people who posted
them? Notice what
opinions we form about
people who make these
errors.

**TEACHING ON
THE WEB**

Mosaics Web Site: To
learn more about easily
confused words, students
can go to www.prenhall.
com/mosaics.

Writing Assignment: The Joys of Technology

Letter writing is a ritual from the past. Very few people take the time to write and mail letters when they have access to faster or more convenient means of communication. What is your experience with modern communication technology? How does e-mail fit into your life? Are you keeping up with the latest changes? How does technology affect your studies? Your job? Where do you think technology will be in a few years? Write a paragraph explaining your thoughts on these questions.

Revising Your Writing

Revise the first draft of your paragraph before you focus on editing. Use the Revising Checklist on pages 24–25 to help you with your revision. Make sure your paragraph has a good topic sentence and is well developed. Then check your paragraph for unity, organization, and coherence.

This chapter will help you choose the right words for your sentences.

EASILY CONFUSED WORDS, PART I

a/an: Use *a* before words that begin with a consonant. Use *an* before words that begin with a vowel (*a, e, i, o, u*).

> **a** letter, **a** cookie, **a** fax
>
> **an** answer, **an** eon, **an** animal

accept/except: *Accept* means "receive." *Except* means "other than."

> I **accept** your apology.
>
> I found all the marbles **except** the black one.

advice/advise: *Advice* means "helpful information." *Advise* means "give advice or help."

> His **advice** is sound.
>
> He **advises** me on financial matters.

affect/effect: *Affect* means "influence." *Effect* means "bring about" or "a result."

> This decision will **affect** the final outcome.

> The new law will **effect** important reforms.

> The **effect** was caused by changes in weather patterns.

already/all ready: *Already* means "in the past." *All ready* means "completely prepared."

> Sarah has **already** received her shots.

> They were **all ready** to leave when the car broke down.

among/between: Use *among* when referring to three or more people or things. Use *between* when referring to only two people or things.

> The doctors discussed the diagnoses **among** themselves.

> She lives **between** those two houses.

bad/badly: *Bad* means "not good." *Badly* means "not well."

> That rash on your arm looks **bad.**

> He performed **badly** on his driving test.

> He felt **bad** about the ruined sweater.

beside/besides: *Beside* means "next to." *Besides* means "in addition (to)."

> I sat **beside** a large oak tree.

> **Besides** smelling bad, the sneakers were covered with mud.

brake/break: *Brake* means "stop" or "the parts that stop a moving vehicle." *Break* means "shatter, come apart" or "a rest between work periods."

> She put her foot on the **brake** as soon as she saw the dog.

> I saw the vase **break** when it hit the floor.

> I like my job, but I look forward to my lunch **break.**

breath/breathe: *Breath* means "air." *Breathe* means "taking in air."

> Take a deep **breath** and count to 10.

> If you **breathe** too quickly, you could hyperventilate.

choose/chose: *Choose* means "select." *Chose* is the past tense of *choose*.

> You **choose** the restaurant.

> He **chose** to go with his friends.

REVIEWING WORDS THAT ARE EASILY CONFUSED, PART I

Do you understand the differences in the sets of words in Part I of the list?

Answers will vary.

_____

Have you ever confused any of these words? If so, which ones?

Answers will vary.

_____

🌿 Practice 1 Identifying   Underline the correct word in each of the following sentences.

1. Can you offer any (<u>advice</u>, advise) on this problem?

2. Your actions will (<u>affect</u>, effect) the outcome.

3. The class talked quietly (<u>among</u>, between) themselves.

4. If you keep bending that twig, you are going to (brake, <u>break</u>) it.

5. The puppy (choose, <u>chose</u>) a spot in front of the oven to sleep.

6. That looks like (<u>a</u>, an) weather balloon, not a spaceship.

7. She is not a (<u>bad</u>, badly) child, just mischievous.

8. Please (advice, <u>advise</u>) me on upcoming courses.

9. The horses are (already, <u>all ready</u>) to be ridden.

10. The (affects, <u>effects</u>) of your actions were impossible to foresee.

🌿 Practice 2 Identifying   Put an X next to the sentence if the under-lined word is incorrect.

1. __X__ <u>Among</u> the two of us, we can cook a great meal. *(Between)*

2. _____ I <u>already</u> gave to that charity.

3. __X__ The <u>affect</u> was subtle. *(effect)*

4. __X__ Sometimes the air we <u>breath</u> is not healthy. *(breathe)*

5. _____ The dog food is <u>beside</u> the dog's bowl.

6. __X__ She was so nervous that she sang <u>bad</u>. *(badly)*

7. _____ You should listen to your mother's <u>advice</u>.

8. __X__ Please don't <u>brake</u> my heart. *(break)*

9. __X__ <u>A</u> ant just crawled up my pant leg. *(An)*

10. __X__ Yesterday you <u>choose</u> the red one, but now you want the blue one.
    (chose)

Practice 3 Correcting   Correct the word errors in Practice 2 by rewriting each incorrect sentence. *See Practice 2.*

1. _____

2. _____

3. _____

4. _____

5. _____

6. _____

7. _____

8. _____

9. _____

10. _____

Practice 4 Completing   Fill in each blank in the following sentences with a correct word that makes sense from Part I of the list of easily confused words.

1. Anna did ____accept____ your invitation to lunch.

2. ____A____ dictionary is a good reference tool.

3. The loan officer has ____already____ left for the day.

4. ____Between____ those two students sits my mother.

5. Why did Martin ____choose____ to move to Ohio?

6. My accountant gives me good ____advice____ regarding stocks.

7. That dog has turned ____bad____, so don't pet him.

8. His yawning ____affects____ the rest of us.

9. Mints will sweeten your ____breath____.

10. ____Except____ for balancing the checkbook and going to the grocery store, I don't have any plans for today.

🌾 **Practice 5 Writing Your Own**   Use each of the following pairs of words correctly in a sentence of your own. *Answers will vary.*

1. choose/chose

_____

_____

2. breath/breathe

_____

_____

3. bad/badly

_____

_____

4. beside/besides

_____

_____

5. advice/advise

_____

_____

EASILY CONFUSED WORDS, PART II

coarse/course: *Coarse* refers to something that is rough. *Course* refers to a class or a route.

This cornmeal is **coarse.**

My future **course** is clear.

desert/dessert: *Desert* refers to dry, sandy land or means "abandon." *Dessert* refers to the last course of a meal.

The **desert** has many strange animals.

He **deserted** the army.

The strawberry shortcake **dessert** was the best I ever had.

HINT: You can remember that dessert has two s's if you think of *strawberry shortcake.*

does/dose: *Does* means "performs." *Dose* refers to a specific portion of medicine.

> He **does** the yard work, and I do the housework.

> A large **dose** of cranberry juice will clear up that infection.

fewer/less: *Fewer* refers to things that can be counted. *Less* refers to things that cannot be counted.

> Now that I am older, I have **fewer** really good friends.

> I have **less** time for play now that I am in college.

good/well: *Good* modifies nouns. *Well* modifies verbs, adjectives, and adverbs. *Well* also refers to a state of health.

> Jane is a **good** instructor.

> She did **well** on the state exam.

> My goldfish is swimming sideways; he must not feel **well.**

hear/here: *Hear* refers to the act of listening. *Here* means "in this place."

> The child didn't speak until he was 4 because he couldn't **hear** well.

> **Here** are the Easter eggs from last year—yuck!

it's/its: *It's* is the contraction for *it is* or *it has*. *Its* is possessive.

> **It's** the best solution.

> The water buffalo flicked **its** tail at the flies.

knew/new: *Knew* is the past tense of *know*. *New* means "recent."

> He **knew** about the **new** television set.

know/no: *Know* means "understand." *No* means "not any" or is the opposite of *yes*.

> **No,** I didn't **know** that you had lived overseas.

lay/lie: *Lay* means "set down." (Its principal parts are *lay, laid, laid*.) *Lie* means "recline." (Its principal parts are *lie, lay, lain*.)

> She **lays** material out before cutting it.

> He **laid** down the heavy firewood.

> My mom **lies** on the couch to watch her soaps.

> They **lay** under the stars.

(For additional help with *lie* and *lay*, see Chapter 10, "Regular and Irregular Verbs.")

loose/lose: *Loose* means "free" or "unattached." *Lose* means "misplace" or "not win."

Ben knocked his tooth **loose.**

I'm fighting hard not to **lose** this game.

passed/past: *Passed* is the past tense of *pass. Past* refers to an earlier time or means "beyond."

Brittany **passed** us in her car, but she didn't see us.

We can learn about ourselves from the **past.**

Suddenly, a bird swooped **past** me.

REVIEWING WORDS THAT ARE EASILY CONFUSED, PART II

Do you understand the differences in the sets of words in Part II of the list?

Answers will vary.

Have you ever confused any of these words? If so, which ones?

Answers will vary.

 Practice 6 Identifying   Underline the correct word in each of the following sentences.

1. We are studying Egypt's (passed, <u>past</u>).

2. Put the gifts (hear, <u>here</u>).

3. Everybody (<u>knew</u>, new) about the surprise but you.

4. Jimmie flew (passed, <u>past</u>) me on his bike.

5. Jerome always (<u>does</u>, dose) well in art.

6. You must not (loose, <u>lose</u>) your pass, or you will not be allowed back in.

7. The bird lifted (it's, <u>its</u>) wings in the wind.

8. Martin's suggestions are (<u>good</u>, well) ideas.

9. Now that summer is almost over, there are (<u>fewer</u>, less) blooms on the rose bushes.

10. The ship sailed on a northern (coarse, <u>course</u>).

 Practice 7 Identifying   Put an X next to the sentence if the underlined word is incorrect.

1. ___X___ Be careful because your pants are really <u>lose</u> and might fall off.
(loose)
2. ___X___ <u>Its</u> time for you to make your entrance. *(It's)*
3. ___X___ The <u>dessert</u> can be a beautiful place if you know where to look.
(desert)
4. ___X___ The <u>knew</u> uniforms are still in their boxes. *(new)*
5. ___X___ The <u>does</u> she took was too strong. *(dose)*
6. _____ Her language was <u>coarse</u> and uncalled for.
7. _____ Speak louder since I can't <u>hear</u> you.
8. ___X___ There is <u>fewer</u> water in your cup than in mine. *(less)*
9. ___X___ Ben's presentation in class went <u>good</u>. *(well)*
10. _____ Since Tabitha just moved here, she doesn't <u>know</u> anybody.

Practice 8 Correcting Correct the word errors in Practice 7 by rewriting each incorrect sentence.

1. _____
2. _____
3. _____
4. _____
5. _____
6. _____
7. _____
8. _____
9. _____
10. _____

Practice 9 Completing Fill in each blank in the following sentences with a correct word that makes sense from Part II of the list of easily confused words.

1. The maximum ____dose____ is 2 tablespoons.
2. They are taking a ____course____ together.
3. We could ____hear____ the class laughing all the way down the hall.
4. ____Dessert____ wines go well with fruit and cheeses.

5. The _____*less*_____ time you spend editing, the more mistakes you're likely to make.

6. Candice doesn't want to go to the party because she doesn't _____*know*_____ how to dance.

7. Craig always _____*lays*_____ a blanket down for the baby.

8. _____*It's*_____ perhaps the funniest thing I've seen all day.

9. This cap is too _____*loose*_____ for this jar.

10. I love to _____*lie*_____ in the sun and read a good novel.

🌿 Practice 10 Writing Your Own   Use each of the following pairs of words in a sentence of your own. *Answers will vary.*

1. know/no

_____

_____

2. passed/past

_____

_____

3. fewer/less

_____

_____

4. good/well

_____

_____

5. it's/its

_____

_____

EASILY CONFUSED WORDS, PART III

principal/principle: *Principal* means "main, most important," "a school official," or "a sum of money." A *principle* is a rule. (Think of principle and rule—both end in -*le*.)

My **principal** reason for attending college is to get a good job.

Our **principal** was strict but kind.

Sometimes it's hard to live by one's **principles.**

quiet/quite: *Quiet* means "without noise." *Quite* means "very."

We have to be **quiet** so we don't disturb the others.

I found the book **quite** fascinating.

raise/rise: *Raise* means "increase" or "lift up." *Rise* means "get up from a sitting or reclining position."

Do not **raise** the lid on the stew; it's simmering.

As the temperature **rises,** so does everyone's temper.

set/sit: *Set* means "put down." *Sit* means "take a seated position."

You can **set** those anywhere you like.

Barbie can **sit** and watch TV for hours.

(For additional help with *sit* and *set,* see Chapter 10, "Regular and Irregular Verbs.")

than/then: *Than* is used in making comparisons. *Then* means "next."

I am older **than** my aunt.

Allen smelled the daisies, and **then** he sneezed.

their/there/they're: *Their* is possessive. *There* indicates location. *They're* is the contraction of *they are*.

Their coats are in the entryway

We went **there** first.

They're all happy for you.

threw/through: *Threw,* the past tense of *throw,* means tossed. *Through* means "finished" or "passing from one point to another."

The quarterback **threw** the ball.

Are you **through** with studying?

The mouse ate **through** the cupboard wall.

to/too/two: *To* means "toward" or is used with a verb. *Too* means "also" or "very." *Two* is a number.

Diane always goes **to** the reunion **to** catch up on the gossip.

The coffee was **too** strong.

We have **two** children.

wear/were/where: *Wear* means "have on one's body." *Were* is the past tense of *be. Where* refers to a place.

You can **wear** casual clothes but not shorts or jeans.

Where were those candles?

weather/whether: *Weather* refers to outdoor conditions. *Whether* expresses possibility.

Whether you believe it or not, you can trust the **weather** to stay sunny.

who's/whose: *Who's* is a contraction of *who is* or *who has. Whose* is a possessive pronoun.

Who's going to determine **whose** display is the best?

your/you're: *Your* means "belonging to you." *You're* is the contraction of *you are.*

Your actions will tell others if **you're** a loyal friend or not.

REVIEWING WORDS THAT ARE EASILY CONFUSED, PART III

Do you understand the differences in the sets of words in Part III of the list?

Answers will vary.

Have you ever confused any of these words? If so, which ones?

Answers will vary.

🌿 Practice 11 Identifying   Underline the correct word in each of the following sentences.

1. The (<u>principal</u>, principle) of our old high school has accepted another position.

2. (Set, <u>Sit</u>) in this chair until the doctor can see you.

3. She'd rather eat worms (<u>than</u>, then) have to watch this movie.

4. Are you (quiet, <u>quite</u>) sure that's what you want to do?

5. (Their, <u>There</u>, They're) are many decisions to be made.

6. They went (<u>to</u>, too, two) the wrecking yard to hunt for spare parts.

7. Kendra and Parker (<u>were</u>, wear, where) thrilled about the pregnancy.

8. Walk (threw, <u>through</u>) those doors, and turn left.

9. The (<u>weather</u>, whether) has turned unexpectedly cold.

10. When you (raise, <u>rise</u>) in the morning, don't forget to do your exercises.

❈ Practice 12 Identifying   Put an X next to the sentence if the underlined word is incorrect.

1. ___X___ I was <u>quiet</u> upset when I got to the station and couldn't find my train. *(quite)*

2. ___X___ Few of us are able to live strictly by our <u>principals</u>. *(principles)*

3. _____ That was <u>too</u> much information to digest at once.

4. ___X___ Allow the dough to <u>raise</u> for one hour. *(rise)*

5. ___X___ <u>Their</u> asking a lot of questions that I cannot answer. *(They're)*

6. _____ <u>Who's</u> giving Sheila a ride to the airport?

7. _____ Make sure the children <u>wear</u> their coats.

8. ___X___ The snake slithered underneath the bed, and <u>than</u> I ran screaming out the door. *(then)*

9. _____ <u>Your</u> hair is snagged on a tree limb.

10. ___X___ I'm never going to make it <u>threw</u> this traffic on time. *(through)*

❈ Practice 13 Correcting   Correct the word errors in Practice 12 by rewriting each incorrect sentence. *See Practice 12.*

1. _____

2. _____

3. _____

4. _____

5. _____

6. _____

7. _____

8. _____

9. _____

10. _____

❋ **Practice 14 Completing**   Fill in each blank in the following sentences with a correct word that makes sense from Part III of the list of easily confused words.

1. ____*Your*____ shoes are untied.

2. You must be ____*quiet*____ in this hospital ward.

3. If you ____*set*____ those books on that table, they are going to fall.

4. The students have prepared ____*their*____ orals in advance.

5. ____*Whose*____ watch is this?

6. ____*Raise*____ the hood of the car very carefully.

7. Benjamin always eats what she cooks for him, ____*whether*____ he likes it or not.

8. There are ____*two*____ letters in the mailbox for Jamie.

9. The reporter listened intently, and ____*then*____ she took out her pen and notebook.

10. What was Gregory thinking when he ____*threw*____ that rock at the beehive?

❋ **Practice 15 Writing Your Own**   Use each of the following pairs of words in a sentence of your own. *Answers will vary.*

1. quiet/quite

_____

_____

2. their/there/they're

_____

_____

_____

3. threw/through

_____

_____

4. than/then

_____

_____

5. raise/rise

_____

_____

CHAPTER REVIEW

You might want to reread your answers to the questions in the review boxes before you do the following exercises.

Review Practice 1 Reading   List the nine words that could be confused from the paragraph by Mark Hansen on page 521.

than	your	an
too	does	their
no	a	to

Review Practice 2 Identifying   Underline the words used incorrectly in each of the following sentences.

1. It is <u>to</u> hot in here to pay attention. *(too)*

2. Beverly <u>choose</u> to tour Europe for a year before attending college. *(chose)*

3. My mom cannot <u>except</u> the fact that I am an adult. *(accept)*

4. It looks like <u>its</u> going to be another long day. *(it's)*

5. Peter will be getting a <u>rise</u> next month. *(raise)*

6. The kids <u>new</u> they could talk us into agreeing. *(knew)*

7. What will be the <u>affect</u> if we mix these two chemicals? *(effect)*

8. You must be absolutely <u>quite</u>, or else we are going to get caught. *(quiet)*

9. <u>Whose</u> going to call the fire department? *(Who's)*

10. Owen dropped his <u>desert</u> down the front of his shirt. *(dessert)*

🎋 Review Practice 3 Correcting   Correct the words used incorrectly in Review Practice 2 by rewriting each incorrect sentence. *See Review Practice 2.*

🍃 EDITING A STUDENT PARAGRAPH

Following is a paragraph written and revised my Maki Okuta in response to the writing assignment in this chapter. Read the paragraph, and underline the words that may be confused.

Here are the corrected confused words:

affected
through
weather
choose
then
where
their
It's
quite
badly
here
to

    The technological age has arrived, and people who don't learn what technology has <u>too</u> offer will soon be left behind. The biggest way technology has <u>effected</u> every-one's lives is <u>threw</u> the Internet. The Internet has brought the world <u>to</u> every person's doorstep. If a person in Hong Kong wants <u>to</u> find out the <u>whether</u> at Catalina Island, he or she could go find the information on the Web. If a person wants <u>to</u> buy a house, <u>chose</u> a college, or even find a hus-band or wife, <u>than</u> a click of the mouse is all it takes. Pretty soon, all people will <u>know</u> <u>were</u> <u>their</u> kids are, can check on the house from work, or can turn on <u>there</u> heat in the car from inside the house. <u>Its</u> really <u>quiet</u> amazing. People who are frightened <u>bad</u> by technology need <u>to</u> learn <u>to</u> under-stand it because <u>it's</u> <u>hear</u> <u>too</u> stay. And soon it will be a part of every aspect of our lives.

Collaborative Activity

Team up with a partner, and add a second underline below the 12 confused words used incorrectly in Maki's paragraph. Then, working together, use what you have learned in this chapter to correct these errors. Rewrite the paragraph with your corrections. *See student paragraph for errors. Errors are double-underlined.*

EDITING YOUR OWN PARAGRAPH

Now return to the paragraph you wrote and revised at the beginning of this chapter. Underline the words that may be confused.

Collaborative Activity

Exchange paragraphs with your partner, and put an X above any words used incorrectly that you find in your partner's paragraph.

Individual Activity

On the Spelling Log in Appendix 7, record any word errors that your partner found in your paragraph. To complete the writing process, correct these errors by rewriting your paragraph.

CHAPTER 32

Spelling

✐ Checklist for Identifying Misspelled Words

> ✔ Do you follow the basic spelling rules?
> ✔ Are all words spelled correctly?

If you think back over your education, you will realize that your teachers think spelling is important. There is a good reason they feel that way: Spelling errors send negative messages. Misspellings seem to leap out at readers, creating serious doubts about the writer's abilities in general. Because you do not always have access to spell-checkers—and because spell-checkers cannot catch all spelling errors—improving your spelling skills is important.

Notice how good spelling makes an author seem trustworthy.

> I remember the spelling books that we used—the color, size, and shape of the books; how the words to be learned were grouped on the page. And I can remember how hard I tried to learn these words, doing just what my teacher said—printing the words over and over again, spelling a word to myself with my eyes closed and then opening my eyes to check if I was right, spelling the words for my parents before bed, going over them again and again right before the test. I can also remember what it was like to take the spelling tests—a piece of wide-margined paper and a pencil, the teacher saying the words aloud, fear and anxiety. I struggled to remember how to spell each word. Erase. No matter how I spelled a word, it looked wrong. Fear. I crossed out, printed over, went back, tried again. "One minute left." Anxiety. When my spelling papers came back they were covered with red marks, blue marks, check marks,

---

TEACHING SPELLING
Create a word search game (single letters in columns and rows of approximately 20 letters each), and provide students with a list of misspelled words. Tell students that the correctly spelled words are the words they are searching for inside the word search game. The first student to uncover all the correctly spelled words wins.

■ For sample word search games, see the *Instructor's Resource Manual*, Section II, Part II.

TEACHING ON THE WEB
Exploring and Discussing: Have students find information about the state of spelling in America. Why are we such poor spellers? What does the research think Americans should do to become better spellers? What do readers often think about people who

correction marks, and poor grades. It was so humiliating, and it was always the same. No matter how much I prepared or how hard I tried, I couldn't spell most of the words. And no matter how many spelling tests I took and failed, there were always more spelling tests to take and fail. We got a new book of spelling words at the beginning of each term.

In this paragraph, Mark Levensky describes his anxiety over spelling tests. Before continuing in this chapter, take a moment to write about your own spelling ability. Save your work because you will use it later in this chapter.

misspell words? Why is spelling considered an important symbol of our reading and writing ability?

TEACHING ON THE WEB

Mosaics Web Site: To learn more about spelling, students can go to www.prenhall.com/ mosaics.

Writing Assignment: What Spelling Reveals

Our spelling tells a lot about us. Spelling mistakes on personal notes say we're sloppy and we don't even take time to proofread. What are your experiences with spelling? Are you a good or bad speller? What experiences have you had with your strengths or weaknesses in spelling? Write a paragraph describing your experiences and feelings.

Revising Your Writing

Revise the first draft of your paragraph before you focus on editing. Use the Revising Checklist on pages 24–25 to help you with your revision. Make sure your paragraph has a good topic sentence and is well developed. Then check your paragraph for unity, organization, and coherence.

SPELLING HINTS

The spelling rules in this chapter will help you become a better speller. But first, here are some practical hints that will also help you improve your spelling:

1. Start a personal spelling list of your own. Use the list of commonly misspelled words on pages 546–552 as your starting point.
2. Study the lists of easily confused words in Chapter 31.
3. Avoid all nonstandard expressions (see Chapter 30).

4. Use a dictionary when you run across words you don't know.

5. Run the spell-check program if you are writing on a computer. Keep in mind, however, that spell-check cannot tell if you have incorrectly used one word in place of another (such as *to* instead of *too* or *two*).

Reviewing Hints for Becoming a Better Speller
....

Name two things you can do immediately to become a better speller.

Answers will vary.

Why can't you depend on a spell-check program to find every misspelled word?

Because it won't find confused words that are spelled correctly

---

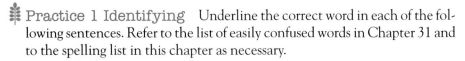 Practice 1 Identifying   Underline the correct word in each of the following sentences. Refer to the list of easily confused words in Chapter 31 and to the spelling list in this chapter as necessary.

1. The flames will (<u>fascinate</u>, fascinat) you if you stare at them long enough.

2. They received a (<u>bicycle</u>, bycicle) for two as a wedding present.

3. (Seperate, <u>Separate</u>) the egg yokes from the whites carefully.

4. The union has agreed to (<u>cooperate</u>, coopperate).

5. I learned (<u>grammar</u>, grammer) in junior high school, but I forgot most of it by the time I got to college.

6. You can (succed, <u>succeed</u>) at anything as long as you put your mind to it.

7. My father is a (genuse, <u>genius</u>) and a member of Mensa.

8. Public spelling bees used to (embarass, <u>embarrass</u>) me.

9. Dora's cat is a bit (<u>weird</u>, wierd)—he likes to take baths.

10. In the movie, the (<u>villain</u>, villian) gets away.

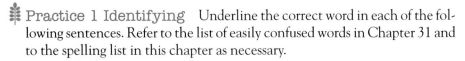 Practice 2 Identifying   Underline the misspelled words in each of the following sentences. Refer to the spelling list in this chapter as necessary.

1. There are <u>undoutedly</u> more people living in the United States now than ever before. *(undoubtedly)*

2. Ouch! I bit my <u>tonge</u>. *(tongue)*

3. The cotton candy made my tooth <u>ach</u>. *(ache)*

4. Because Alyssa is allergic to wasps, we called the <u>ambulence</u> immediately. *(ambulance)*

5. Many <u>soldeirs</u> who fought in the war died from disease. *(soldiers)*

6. The original masterpiece was lost.

7. Beverly was jealous of Evan's new Mustang convertible.

8. If you drink and drive, you will lose your <u>lisence</u>. *(license)*

9. The Louisiana bayous are a dangerous place for the inexperienced.

10. Even though <u>Febrary</u> is a cold month, it is filled with warmth on Valentine's Day. *(February)*

Practice 3 Correcting   Correct the spelling errors in Practice 2 by rewriting each incorrect sentence. *See Practice 2*

1. _____

2. _____

3. _____

4. _____

5. _____

6. _____

7. _____

8. _____

9. _____

10. _____

Practice 4 Completing   Fill in each blank in each of the following sentences with hints that help with spelling.

1. Use a _____*dictionary*_____ to look up words you don't know.

2. You can always use the _*spell-check program*_ on your computer, but you should remember that it cannot correct confused words, only misspelled words.

3. Start a _____*spelling list*_____ to help you remember words you commonly misspell.

4. Study the lists of ___confused words___ in Chapter _____31_____.

5. Try to avoid all ___nonstandard___ English.

✿ Practice 5 Writing Your Own

A. Choose the correctly spelled word in each pair, and write a sentence of your own for it. Refer to the spelling list in this chapter as necessary. *Sentences will vary.*

1. <u>banana</u>/bannana _____

2. volunter/<u>volunteer</u> _____

3. desision/<u>decision</u> _____

4. oposit/<u>opposite</u> _____

5. <u>recommend</u>/recomend _____

B. Write five words that you often misspell, and use each in a sentence of your own. Underline these words. *Answers will vary.*

1. _____

2. _____

3. _____

4. _____

5. _____

SPELLING RULES

Four basic spelling rules can help you avoid many misspellings. It pays to spend a little time learning them now.

1. **Words that end in -e:** When adding a suffix beginning with a vowel (*a, e, i, o, u*), drop the final *-e*.

        ache + ing   = aching
        challenge + ed = challenged
        value + able   = valuable

    When adding a suffix beginning with a consonant, keep the final *-e*.

        aware + ness   = awareness
        improve + ment = improvement
        leisure + ly   = leisurely

2. **Words with *ie* and *ei*:** Put *i* before *e* except after *c* or when sounded like *ay* as in *neighbor* and *weigh*.

-*c* + *ei*	(no -*c*) + *ie*
receive	anxiety
receipt	niece
deceive	convenience
neighbor	fiery

3. **Words that end in -*y*:** When adding a suffix to a word that ends in a consonant plus y, change the y to *i*.

    silly + er = sillier
    cry + ed   = cried
    shy + er   = shier

4. **Words that double the final consonant:** When adding a suffix starting with a vowel to a one-syllable word, double the final consonant.

    big + est = biggest
    quit + er = quitter
    bet + ing = betting

With words of more than one syllable, double the final consonant if (1) the final syllable is stressed and (2) the word ends in a single vowel plus a single consonant.

    beget + ing   = begetting
    permit + ing = permitting
    uncap + ed   = uncapped

The word "travel" has more than one syllable. Should you double the final consonant? No, you should not, because the stress is on the first syllable (**tra** vel). The word ends in a vowel and a consonant, but that is not enough. Both parts of the rule must be met.

REVIEWING FOUR BASIC SPELLING RULES

What is the rule for adding a suffix to words ending in -e (such as date + ing)?

Drop the final -e when adding a suffix that begins with a vowel, and keep the -e when

adding a suffix that begins with a consonant.

What is the rule for spelling ie *and* ei *words (such as* receive, neighbor, *and* friend*)?*

Put i before e except after c or when sounded like ay as in neighbor and weigh.

When do you change -y *to* i *before a suffix (such as* sunny + est*)?*

When the word ends in a consonant plus y

When do you double the final consonant of a word before adding a suffix (such as cut, begin, *or* travel + ing*)?*

When a one-syllable word ends in a consonant or when words of more than one syllable

have the stress on the final syllable and end in a vowel plus a consonant

🌿 Practice 6 Identifying   Underline the correct word in each of the following sentences.

1. Art Fry (<u>conceived</u>, concieved) the idea for Post-it Notes while working at MIT.

2. In the (begining, <u>beginning</u>), Sandra found the class difficult.

3. Nancy has a strange hobby; she visits (<u>cemeteries</u>, cemeterys) and makes rubs of the headstones.

4. He (<u>seized</u>, seizd) the opportunity when it came.

5. Not studying will give you (<u>grief</u>, greif) on the day of the exam.

6. The (groceryes, <u>groceries</u>) are still in the car.

7. There were (<u>approximately</u>, approximatly) 70 applicants for the position.

8. Charles is (<u>getting</u>, geting) his hair cut.

9. Darn, I didn't have the (wining, <u>winning</u>) ticket.

10. We are (<u>temporarily</u>, temporaraly) staying with my aunt.

🌿 Practice 7 Identifying   Underline the misspelled words in each of the following sentences.

1. Upon reaching the door, I hesitated when I heard the strange noise.

2. My father <u>accompanyed</u> me on my first date. *(accompanied)*

3. The lieutenant ordered us to peel potatoes.

4. Before they agreed to buy the house, they asked that the <u>cieling</u> be re-paired. *(ceiling)*

5. The mountain climbers faced many difficulties.

6. The oceanographer is mapping out the ocean floor.

7. The <u>elaboratness</u> of the room was overwhelming. *(elaborateness)*

8. Now that Veronica has been accepted at Yale, she is <u>happyer</u>. *(happier)*

9. Let the dog smell your hand before you begin <u>peting</u> him. *(petting)*

10. I had problems <u>unwraping</u> the plastic from the CD. *(unwrapping)*

Practice 8 Correcting   Correct the spelling errors in Practice 7 by rewriting each incorrect sentence. *See Practice 7.*

1. _____

2. _____

3. _____

4. _____

5. _____

6. _____

7. _____

8. _____

9. _____

10. _____

Practice 9 Completing   Complete each of the following spelling rules.

1. When adding a suffix beginning with a vowel to a word that ends in *-e*, ___*drop the final -e*___.

2. Put *i* before *e* except after ____*c*____ or when sounded like ____*ay*____ as in ___*neighbor and weigh*___.

3. When adding a suffix starting with a ____*vowel*____ to a one-syllable word, ____*double*____ the final consonant.

4. When adding a suffix to a word the ends in a consonant plus y, change the ____*y*____ to ____*i*____.

5. With words of more than one syllable, ____double____ the final consonant if (1) the final syllable is ____stressed____ and (2) the word ends in
a single ____vowel____ plus a single ____consonant____.

🌿 Practice 10 Writing Your Own

A. Choose the correctly spelled word in each pair, and write a sentence of
your own for it. Refer to the spelling list in this chapter as necessary.
Sentences will vary.

1. believing/believeing _____

2. audience/audeince _____

3. tried/treid _____

4. seting/setting _____

5. weigh/wiegh _____

B. Write five words that you often misspell, and use them each in a sentence of your own. *Answers will vary.*

1. _____

2. _____

3. _____

4. _____

5. _____

COMMONLY MISSPELLED WORDS

Use the following list of commonly misspelled words to check your spelling
when you write.

abbreviate	accommodate	ache
absence	accompany	achievement
accelerate	accomplish	acknowledgment
accessible	accumulate	acre
accidentally	accurate	actual

address	autumn	cafeteria
adequate	auxiliary	calendar
advertisement	avenue	campaign
afraid	awkward	canoe
aggravate	baggage	canyon
aisle	balloon	captain
although	banana	career
aluminum	bankrupt	carriage
amateur	banquet	cashier
ambulance	beautiful (50)	catastrophe
ancient	beggar	caterpillar
anonymous	beginning	ceiling
anxiety	behavior	cemetery
anxious	benefited	census
appreciate	bicycle	certain
appropriate	biscuit	certificate
approximate	bought	challenge
architect	boundary	champion
arithmetic	brilliant	character
artificial	brought	chief
assassin	buoyant	children
athletic	bureau	chimney
attach	burglar	coffee
audience	business	collar
authority	cabbage	college

column	cozy	dissatisfied
commit	criticize	divisional
committee	curiosity	dormitory
communicate	curious	economy
community	curriculum	efficiency
comparison	cylinder	eighth
competent	dairy	elaborate
competition	dangerous	electricity (150)
complexion	dealt	eligible
conceive (100)	deceive	embarrass
concession	decision	emphasize
concrete	definition	employee
condemn	delicious	encourage
conference	descend	enormous
congratulate	describe	enough
conscience	description	enthusiastic
consensus	deteriorate	envelope
continuous	determine	environment
convenience	development	equipment
cooperate	dictionary	equivalent
corporation	difficulty	especially
correspond	diploma	essential
cough	disappear	establish
counterfeit	disastrous	exaggerate
courageous	discipline	excellent
courteous	disease	exceptionally

excessive	geography	immortal
exhaust	gnaw	impossible
exhilarating	government	incidentally
existence	graduation	incredible
explanation	grammar	independence
extinct	grief (200)	indispensable
extraordinary	grocery	individual
familiar	gruesome	inferior
famous	guarantee	infinite
fascinate	guess	influential
fashion	guidance	initial
fatigue	handkerchief	initiation
faucet	handsome	innocence
February	haphazard	installation
fiery	happiness	intelligence
financial	harass	interfere
foreign	height	interrupt
forfeit	hesitate	invitation
fortunate	hoping	irrelevant
forty	humorous	irrigate
freight	hygiene	issue
friend	hymn	jealous
fundamental	icicle	jewelry
gauge	illustrate	journalism
genius	imaginary	judgment
genuine	immediately	kindergarten

knife	marriage	nuisance
knowledge	material	obedience **(300)**
knuckles	mathematics	obstacle
laboratory **(250)**	maximum	occasion
laborious	mayor	occurred
language	meant	official
laugh	medicine	omission
laundry	message	omitted
league	mileage	opportunity
legible	miniature	opponent
legislature	minimum	opposite
leisure	minute	original
length	mirror	outrageous
library	miscellaneous	pamphlet
license	mischievous	paragraph
lieutenant	miserable	parallel
lightning	misspell	parentheses
likable	monotonous	partial
liquid	mortgage	particular
listen	mysterious	pastime
literature	necessary	patience
machinery	neighborhood	peculiar
magazine	niece	permanent
magnificent	nineteen	persistent
majority	ninety	personnel
manufacture	noticeable	persuade

physician

pitcher

pneumonia

politician

possess

prairie

precede

precious

preferred

prejudice

previous

privilege

procedure

proceed

pronounce

psychology

publicly

questionnaire

quotient

realize

receipt

recipe

recommend

reign

religious

representative **(350)**

reservoir

responsibility

restaurant

rhyme

rhythm

salary

satisfactory

scarcity

scenery

schedule

science

scissors

secretary

seize

separate

significant

similar

skiing

soldier

souvenir

sovereign

spaghetti

squirrel

statue

stomach

strength

subtle

succeed

success

sufficient

surprise

syllable

symptom

technique

temperature

temporary

terrible

theater

thief

thorough

tobacco

tomorrow

tongue

tournament

tragedy

truly

unanimous

undoubtedly

unique

university **(400)**

usable

usually

vacuum	volunteer	wreckage
valuable	weather	writing
various	Wednesday	yacht
vegetable	weigh	yearn
vehicle	weird	yield
vicinity	whose	zealous
villain	width	zoology **(425)**
visible	worst	

REVIEWING COMMONLY MISSPELLED WORDS
....

Why is spelling important in your writing?

   Answers will vary.
_____

Start a personal spelling log of your most commonly misspelled words.

_____   _____   _____   _____

_____   _____   _____   _____

_____   _____   _____   _____

_____   _____   _____   _____

❋ Practice 11 Identifying   Underline the correct word in each of the following sentences.

1. The gas (<u>gauge</u>, guage) was almost on empty.

2. Sean's uncle is a (<u>tobacco</u>, tabaco) farmer.

3. The (labortory, <u>laboratory</u>) was destroyed in the fire.

4. The choir sang a gospel (<u>hymn</u>, hym) to open the graduation ceremony.

5. You should see a doctor about that (coff, <u>cough</u>).

6. Up to three (<u>absences</u>, absenses) will be excused.

7. (Icicycles, <u>Icicles</u>) make beautiful prisms that reflect light.

8. The sea is (<u>visible</u>, visable) from atop that cliff.

9. (Yeild, <u>Yield</u>) the right-of-way to oncoming traffic.

10. Her nephew can speak five (<u>languages</u>, langages).

❧ Practice 12 Identifying   Underline the misspelled words in each of the following sentences.

1. Driving is a <u>privelege</u>, not a right. *(privilege)*

2. Special <u>scisors</u> are made for left-handed people. *(scissors)*

3. Though the twins are not identical, they are similar-looking.

4. My <u>knowlege</u> is lacking in this area. *(knowledge)*

5. Dean recommends the Chinese restaurant on Blossom Avenue.

6. The doctor had to <u>reschedle</u> my appointment. *(reschedule)*

7. Real <u>sucess</u> isn't gained through money. *(success)*

8. I accidentally ran over my bicycle with my car.

9. Yes, Martha is <u>familar</u> with linear math. *(familiar)*

10. Alisha's <u>stomache</u> hurts. *(stomach)*

❧ Practice 13 Correcting   Correct the spelling errors in Practice 12 by rewriting each incorrect sentence. *See Practice 12.*

1. _____
2. _____
3. _____
4. _____
5. _____
6. _____
7. _____
8. _____
9. _____
10. _____

❧ Practice 14 Completing   Fill in each blank in the following sentences with a word that makes sense from the spelling list in this chapter. *Answers will vary.*

1. The _____ was caught at the airport.

2. The _____ stars look like diamonds.

3. My _____ is bothering me.

4. His new house is rather _____.

5. The show *Who's Line Is It, Anyway?* always makes people _____.

6. I filled out the _____ even though it was very long.

7. Take a picture of that _____.

8. Cassidy met her future husband in _____.

9. Don't worry; your mismatched socks aren't _____.

10. For a doctor, your writing is quite _____.

Practice 15 Writing Your Own

A. Choose the correctly spelled word in each pair, and write a sentence for each one. Refer to the spelling list in this chapter as necessary. *Sentences will vary.*

1. appreciate/apprecate _____

2. laundry/landry _____

3. mariage/marriage _____

4. excellent/excelent _____

5. oposite/opposite _____

B. Choose five words from the spelling list in this chapter that you often misspell, and use each in a sentence of your own. Underline these words. *Answers will vary.*

1. _____

2. _____

3. _____

4. _____

5. _____

CHAPTER REVIEW

You might want to reread your answers to the questions in the review boxes before you do the following exercises.

🌾 **Review Practice 1 Reading**   Refer to the paragraph by Mark Levensky on pages 538–539 to do the following exercises.

1. List two words from the paragraph that have nonstandard versions.

   From Paragraph   **Nonstandard**

   Answers will vary.
   _____   _____

   _____   _____

2. List two words from the paragraph that are easily confused with other words.

   From Paragraph   **Easily Confused Word**

   Answers will vary.
   _____   _____

   _____   _____

3. List two words from the paragraph that might be easily misspelled.

   From Paragraph   **Misspelling**

   Answers will vary.
   _____   _____

   _____   _____

🌾 **Review Practice 2 Identifying**   Underline the misspelled words in each of the following sentences. Refer to the spelling list in this chapter as necessary.

1. There is a <u>terrable</u> flu going around. *(terrible)*
2. My kitten's <u>curosity</u> landed him in the toilet. *(curiosity)*
3. Who says chocolate isn't an <u>essintial</u> food group? *(essential)*
4. That smells <u>delicous</u>. *(delicious)*
5. The show will air <u>tommorrow</u>. *(tomorrow)*
6. <u>Catapillars</u> may be cute, but they wreak havoc in my garden. *(Caterpillars)*
7. I may be an <u>amature</u> baseball player today, but I plan to play professional ball in a few years. *(amateur)*
8. The bread <u>nife</u> is in the third drawer. *(knife)*
9. She has all the <u>symtoms</u> of someone in love. *(symptoms)*
10. That perfume is just <u>sutle</u> enough. *(subtle)*

🌿 Review Practice 3 Correcting   Correct the spelling errors in Review Practice 2 by rewriting each sentence. *See Review Practice 2.*

✎ EDITING A STUDENT PARAGRAPH

Following is a paragraph written and revised by Sabrina Patrova in response to the writing assignment in this chapter. Read the paragraph, and look for any misspelled words. Do not count words that are misspelled intentionally.

Here are the corrected spelling errors:

usually
embarrassing
breaths
tried
whether
know
achievements
happily
neighbor
anxiety
quitter

I'm an average speller. Just like everybody else, I usualy confuse "effect" with "affect" or "accept" with "except," have difficulty remembering if an ending should be "-ant" or "-ent," or have difficulty remembering those weird words (like "weird") that don't follow the "i before e except after c" rule. But for the most part, I tend to get by with my spelling--until I'm asked to spell in public. When someone asks me to spell a word, even the simplest word like "of," my brain freezes. (I once spelled "of" ove!) But this problem becomes most embarassing when I'm called to the chalkboard to write. My heart starts to pound. My palms get sweaty. I try counting to 10. I try taking deep breathes. I have even tryed to quickly go over the spelling rules in my mind as I approach the board. But it doesn't matter weather I no the spelling rules or not. My spelling knowledge vanishes somewhere between my desk and the board. Now, I consider myself a fairly intelligent person. My achievments are many. Yet I always look foolish in these moments, no matter how brilliant my ideas. But happyly--or perhaps sadly--I have learned that I'm not alone. Many others suffer from the same phobia. My nieghbor calls it "fear of public spelling." Perhaps we should join forces and start a support group, because until someone figures out a way to rewire or recondition the brain, I don't know how to overcome this problem. I know what spelling errors say about me: "You're lazy," "You can't write," "Your anxeity got the better of you." Even though these statements aren't true, I still hate the messages. But I'm no quiter. I'll continue that long walk to the front of the class whenever I hear, "Sabrina, could you come to the board and . . ."

Collaborative Activity

Team up with a partner, and underline the 11 misspelled words in Sabrina's paragraph. Then, working together, use what you have learned in this chapter to correct these errors. Rewrite the paragraph with your corrections. *See student paragraph for errors. Corrections are in the margin.*

❦ EDITING YOUR OWN PARAGRAPH

Now go back to the paragraph you wrote and revised at the beginning of this chapter. Look for misspelled words.

Collaborative Activity

Exchange paragraphs with your partner, and underline any misspelled words that you find in your partner's paragraph.

Individual Activity

On the Spelling Log in Appendix 7, record any spelling errors that your partner found in your paragraph. To complete the writing process, correct these errors by rewriting your paragraph.

Unit 8 Review
Choosing the Right Word

🌿Unit Practice 1 Identifying   Underline the words used incorrectly in each of the following sentences.

1. <u>Everywheres</u> I look, I see smiling, happy faces. *(Everywhere)*

2. Today, Carol will <u>chose</u> a major. *(choose)*

3. These physics problems are <u>frying my brain</u>. *(extremely hard)*

4. Surely Tom <u>exaggerrated</u> the story. *(exaggerated)*

5. He <u>ain't</u> going to like your plan. *(isn't)*

6. <u>Its</u> been a very long and exhausting day. *(It's)*

7. It's been <u>a</u> eon since I've seen you. *(an)*

8. <u>Being that</u> it is so hot outside, let's go ice-skating. *(Since)*

9. Carlie has a vast <u>awarness</u> of herself. *(awareness)*

10. The package was <u>unwraped</u> when Scott bought it. *(unwrapped)*

11. We're going to <u>rock the house</u> tonight. *(have fun)*

12. The fake blood and gore looked <u>grusome</u> in the moonlight. *(gruesome)*

13. That is <u>to</u> much information for me to process at the moment. *(too)*

14. Mac was very <u>enthused</u> about winning the door prize. *(excited, enthusiastic)*

15. Jan's new boyfriend is a <u>hottie</u>. *(cute guy)*

16. The little girl <u>cryed</u> for her lost kitten. *(cried)*

17. In the <u>dessert</u>, the temperature drops dramatically at night. *(desert)*

18. With her fair skin, she <u>oughta</u> wear sunscreen. *(ought to)*

For additional material about teaching choosing the right word, for journal entries, and for various tests, see the *Instructor's Resource Manual.*

ADDITIONAL WRITING TOPIC

Let your students expand into well-developed essays the paragraphs they wrote in one of the unit chapters.

558

19. Don't touch that pan—it's <u>firy</u> hot. *(fiery)*

20. Everyone can fit in the truck <u>accept</u> the dog. *(except)*

🌿 Unit Practice 2 Correcting   Correct the errors in Unit Practice 1 by rewriting each incorrect sentence. *Answers may vary.*

1. _____
2. _____
3. _____
4. _____
5. _____
6. _____
7. _____
8. _____
9. _____
10. _____
11. _____
12. _____
13. _____
14. _____
15. _____
16. _____
17. _____
18. _____
19. _____
20. _____

🌿 Unit Practice 3 Identifying   Underline the words used incorrectly in the following paragraph.

<u>Being that</u> my brother got a chemistry set for his birthday one summer, I <u>figureed</u> it was time to take up science. Scott, my brother, <u>played around</u> with the set a couple of times, and <u>than</u> he forgot about

it, so I <u>five-fingered</u> it. I remember waiting for the weekend to come, for the nights when everyone was asleep and no one could censure me and the experiments could begin. The secrecy of those nighttime rituals made me feel <u>sorta</u> like an ancient goddess performing sacred rites while the world <u>slept</u> and the moon shone <u>threw</u> my window. I was <u>quiet</u> lax when it came to the rules—who needed instructions? <u>Needless</u> to say, there were a few accidents in my <u>labortory</u>. But the joy of discovery and the thrill of creating were addictive. I never set out to actually create anything specific. The lure was the adventure itself. Now I get the same thrill from journal writing. I can mix new ingredients, feelings, and ideas and see where they take me. I can explore any crazy notion that comes into my head because there is no censorship: I am the <u>audeince</u>. Occasionally, my writing becomes flammable, and if I survive the flame, I'm left with illumination. Sometimes I wait for the night to come, and when everybody is asleep and the moonlight from the window casts a glow on my computer, I write. Again I am a goddess, only this time the chemical reaction happens within my heart, my mind, my psyche, my soul. My new discovery is myself. I <u>be</u> the creator and the created.

❋ Unit Practice 4 Correcting   Correct the errors in Unit Practice 3 by rewriting the paragraph. *Answers are in the margin.*

UNIT WRITING ASSIGNMENTS

1. What is the child tying to persuade her parent to do in the picture? What do you think the child's strategy is? Is the child effective in persuading the parent? Why or why not?

2. Are you aware of listening to the languages that are spoken around you? Are the languages different? What can you tell from people's tone of voice even when you don't speak the language? Think of a time you went to an amusement park or a public place where you heard many different languages. What were your observations? What were the differences among the speakers? What were the similarities?

3. You have just taken the Pepsi challenge. What brand of soda—Pepsi or Coca-Cola—did you choose? Prepare an article for your college newspaper comparing the two sodas and arguing why one soda is better than the other.

4. At one time or another, we have all been let down by our computer's spell-check, and yet many of us continue to use only the computer's tools to find words used incorrectly in our papers. Why is relying only on spell-check not a good editing habit? Can spell-check catch every word used incorrectly? Why or why not? Should an author use other methods along with the computer? If so, what methods?

5. Create your own assignment (with the help of your instructor), and write a response to it.

P · A · R · T

III

PARAGRAPHS: SENTENCES IN CONTEXT

Studying their own writing puts students in a position to see themselves as language users, rather than as victims of a language that uses them.

—DAVID BARTHOLOMAE

Part III focuses on the paragraph. Even though you have been working with sentences and paragraphs throughout this text, this section makes sure you know how to write a successful paragraph, step by step. It provides both a professional and a student model for you to work with. Then it helps you apply specific revising and editing guidelines to a student paragraph and to your own writing.

Recognizing a Paragraph

As you have learned, a **paragraph** is a series of sentences that develop, illustrate, or explain a single topic. Paragraphs differ in organization and content, but they share several features that set them apart from other forms of writing. The first and perhaps easiest way to recognize a paragraph is to look at its form. You will see (as with the next paragraph) that the first line of a new paragraph is indented, signaling to the reader that a new topic is being introduced.

Second, paragraphs have a controlling idea that is expressed in a **topic sentence,** which is usually the first sentence of the paragraph. The rest of the paragraph includes **details** that explain the topic sentence. Finally, a paragraph has a **concluding sentence** that sums up the information in the paragraph.

The following paragraph, by K. C. Cole, is from an essay titled "Calculated Risks." It explains how we can learn from taking some well-chosen risks.

> Of course, risk isn't all bad. Without knowingly taking risks, no one would ever walk out the door, much less go to school, drive a car, have a baby, submit a proposal for a research grant, fall in love, or swim in the ocean. It's hard to have any fun, accomplish anything productive, or experience life without taking risks—sometimes substantial ones. Life, after all, is a fatal disease, and the mortality rate for humans, at the end of the day, is 100 percent.

Before continuing, take a moment to record some of your own thoughts and observations on taking risks. Save your work because you will use it later in Part III.

Bring in several paragraphs that have strong topic sentences. Divide students into groups of three or four, and have them identify the topic sentences and supporting details of two or three paragraphs. Have them discuss as a group how well the details go with the topic sentences.

TEACHING ON THE WEB

Exploring and Discussing: Have students look at paragraphs that are on Web pages. How good are the topic sentences in some of the paragraphs they find? What makes some good and others not so good? If they're not good, what is wrong, and how can they be improved?

Writing Your Own Paragraph

Think of a risk you took that taught you a valuable lesson. What was the situation? In what way was it a risk? What did you gain from it? In what ways did it help you? Write a paragraph explaining how this risk turned out to be a valuable experience in your life.

CHAPTER

34

How to Write
a Successful Paragraph

The key to a successful paragraph is well-built sentences—sentences that are clear and complete. In this book, you have learned how to write good sentences. Even when you wrote paragraphs in previous chapters, we focused on the sentences within those paragraphs. Now you will learn how to build an effective paragraph around a single topic. The following guidelines can serve as a blueprint for writing a paragraph on any subject.

1. **Choose a subject that can be covered in a single paragraph.** Sometimes you will be given a subject to write on, and other times you will be asked to choose your own topic. If you can select your own topic, write on something you know about. If you aren't a baseball fan, you probably shouldn't write about baseball. Instead, make a list of what's on your mind and what interests you. Here, for instance, is one student's list:

> All types of music
>
> Movies
>
> Psychology
>
> Summer jobs
>
> Basketball

Next, be sure your subject can be covered in only one paragraph. That is, your topic should not be too general. Suppose the student who made the list decided to write on movies. That topic is far too general for a paragraph. In fact, whole books are written on movies. So she narrows her topic to science-fiction movies. But that's still too general. So she narrows still further to Steven Spielberg's science-fiction movies and eventually to his movie *A.I.* She finally decides to write a paragraph on why *A.I.* was Steven Spielberg's greatest science-fiction movie.

K. C. Cole, the author of the model paragraph in Chapter 33, is a science writer. She brings both math and science to life in her articles. So she might have started with a general topic like "mathematics" and then narrowed it to "statistics about people." Since this topic is still too broad for a paragraph, she probably narrowed her scope again to "risks" and finally to "calculated risks that let us have some fun in life." Now she has a topic that can be covered in a single paragraph.

2. **Write a topic sentence for your paragraph.** Your topic sentence should express the controlling idea—or the main point—of your paragraph. Although the topic sentence can be either the first or last sentence of its paragraph, making it the first is preferable because it tells the reader what your paragraph will be about.

A topic sentence has two parts: a limited topic and a statement about that topic. The statement gives your opinion on the topic. Here are some examples.

Topic	Limited Topic	Statement
Friendship	What makes a good friend	A good friend is a good listener.
Athletics	Basketball is fun to watch.	Basketball is fun to watch because it is fast.

K. C. Cole's topic sentence is the first sentence in her paragraph: "Of course, risk isn't all bad." Like all good topic sentences, it has two parts— a limited topic ("risk") and a statement about that topic ("isn't all bad"). She makes this statement so she can talk about the value of some risks.

3. **Develop your paragraph with details and examples that support your topic sentence.** At this point in writing your paragraph, think of yourself as a lawyer. You have stated your position in the topic sentence, and you now need details and examples to prove your point. If you aren't sure what supporting details will work best, try turning your topic sentence into a question. The way you answer this question will give you the details and examples you need.

If Cole turned her topic sentence into a question, it might be, "Are risks all bad?" She then answers this question in her paragraph with clear details and examples. She explains that everyday activities such as walking out the door, going to school, driving a car, having a baby, submitting a proposal, falling in love, and swimming in the ocean involve taking risks. By furnishing specific, concrete examples of risks we all take every day, Cole leads the reader to her main point—that risks have value.

4. **Organize your supporting details and examples.** Once you know which details and examples best support your topic sentence, you need to think about how you will organize them. What should come first? Second? Last? How you organize your ideas depends on your purpose. Here are some examples:

- *Chronological (time) order:* If you are retelling an important story, you should start at the beginning and tell the story as it happened, in chronological or time order.
- *Chronological (step-by-step) order:* If you are telling how to do something or how something happened, you should explain step by step, in a logical time sequence.
- *Spatial order:* If you are describing something physical, you will probably move from one area or location to another, such as from top to bottom, left to right, inside to outside—or the reverse.
- *From one extreme to another (least to most or most to least):* If you are using details and examples to support a specific point, they need to be organized in some meaningful way. You should suit your order to your purpose—for example, from least important to most important, from funniest to least funny, from least frustrating to most frustrating, or from most exciting to least exciting.

In the model paragraph, K. C. Cole arranges her examples from least to most dangerous. Walking out the door every day involves the least amount of risk compared to her other examples; swimming in the ocean is the most dangerous of her examples.

5. **Write a concluding sentence.** The last step in drafting your paragraph is to write a concluding sentence, a sentence that sums up what you have said in your paragraph. Summing up does not mean repeating. You should never write a concluding sentence that repeats what you have just said. Instead, aim to give the reader a feeling that the paragraph comes to a natural close. Since paragraphs are usually part of longer pieces of writing, a concluding sentence often sums up one paragraph and hints at what will come next.

K. C. Cole concludes her paragraph with two sentences. The first sums up what she said in the paragraph by explaining how the examples she lists contribute to the quality of our lives: "It's hard to have any fun, accomplish anything productive, or experience life without taking risks—sometimes substantial ones." The final sentence then brings the paragraph to a close and puts the idea of risks into a larger perspective: "Life, after all, is a fatal disease, and the mortality rate for humans, at the end of the day, is 100 percent."

6. **Revise and edit your paragraph.** Writing is a process, and you will realize as you write that your ideas grow, develop, and change. In your effort to communicate your ideas to others, you may find a better way of saying something or come up with a more appropriate example. Therefore, after you draft your paragraph, read it over again, asking yourself the following questions:

- Does the topic sentence clearly state your topic and your position on it?
- Do you give enough specific details and examples?
- Do the sentences in your paragraph support your topic sentence?
- Have you arranged your ideas in a way that makes sense?
- Have you summed up your ideas in a concluding sentence?

After you have revised your paragraph for content, you can begin editing your paragraph—checking grammar, punctuation, mechanics (capitalization, abbreviations, and numbers), and spelling. As a successful writer, Cole no doubt revised and edited her paragraph—probably more than once.

Paragraphs at Work

To practice recognizing the working features of a paragraph, read the following three paragraphs taken from essays in Part IV of this text. Then answer the questions after each paragraph.

FROM "A GIANT STEP" BY HENRY LOUIS GATES Jr. (p. 600)

In this paragraph, Gates writes about some ugly, heavy orthopedic shoes that he is finally able to put aside. Notice the various writing strategies that make this paragraph work so well.

> We had been together since 1975, those shoes and I. They were orthopedic shoes built around molds of my feet, and they had a 2¼-inch lift. I had mixed feelings about them. On the one hand, they had given me a more or less even gait for the first time in 10 years. On the other hand, they had marked me as a "handicapped person," complete with cane and special license plates. I went through a pair a year, but it was always the same shoe, black, wide, weighing about four pounds.

1. What is the subject of this paragraph?

   The author is describing his orthopedic shoes
   _____

2. What is its topic sentence?

   We had been together since 1975, those shoes and I.
   _____

   Does the topic sentence state the author's position on the subject?

   Yes; he introduces the shoes and implies his position of having mixed feelings about

   them.
   _____

3. Does the author include enough details and examples to support the topic
    sentence? _____Yes_____

    List at least three supporting details: *Answers may vary.*

    A 2¼-inch lift on his shoes

    His even gait for 10 years with the shoes

    Labeled "handicapped" with the shoes

4. Are the supporting details organized as effectively as possible? Label their
    method of organization.

    They are organized from least to most important, which is effective for his subject.

5. How does the author conclude the paragraph?

    By vividly describing what the shoes look like

    Does the final sentence actually bring the essay to a close?

    Yes; he is looking back on the experience.

FROM "A QUESTION OF TRUST" BY SHERRY HEMMAN HOGAN (p. 609)

> Some 12 years later, and newly divorced, quite a few hand-
> kerchief sessions with Dad were in order as my daughter and I
> faced a whole new life together. After heart-wrenching discus-
> sions at Mom and Dad's, my search for a tissue invariably ended
> with my father's familiar offer. Then, concerned about my going
> home to a dark house, my parents established a routine for their
> peace of mind as well as mine. Within minutes of my arrival, I
> would always call to say, "Hi, Dad. It's me. I'm home."

1. What is the subject of this paragraph?

    How a young woman relied on her parents for emotional support during a rough time.

2. What is its topic sentence?

    Some 12 years later, and newly divorced, quite a few handkerchief sessions with Dad

    were in order as my daughter and I faced a whole new life together.

    Does the topic sentence state the author's position on the subject?

    Yes; it shows that she needed her dad for support.

3. Does the author include enough details and examples to support the topic sentence? _Yes_

    List at least three supporting details: *Answers may vary.*

    The offer of a handkerchief

    Parents' concern about the author driving home in the dark

    Calling her parents

4. Are the supporting details organized as effectively as possible? Label their method of organization.

    Yes; they are organized chronologically.

5. How does the author conclude the paragraph?

    By showing her parents' concern for her well-being

    Does the final sentence actually bring the paragraph to a close?

    Yes; it brings that part of the story to an end with the exact words Hogan said.

FROM "FERRYING DREAMERS TO THE OTHER SIDE" BY TOMÁS ROBLES (p. 618)

Before we get to the immigration checkpoint, we get out of the car and let the driver continue north. The drivers have their papers, so they can pass through the checkpoint. Then we walk into the countryside. It's dark, but we know where we're going. There are power lines that we use to guide us. We go on together, walking and walking, for five or six hours. There are lots of rattlesnakes, and you can die if they bite you. We walk on through the brush until we get to a place to rest. Then one person—only one—goes out to the road to see if the drivers are there yet. When they arrive, we get back in the cars, and off we go to Houston.

1. What is the subject of this paragraph?

    Taking illegal immigrants into the United states

2. What is its topic sentence?

    Before we get to the immigration checkpoint, we get out of the car and let the driver continue north.

Does the topic sentence state the author's position on the subject?

Yes; it lets us know that the writer is part of the illegal activity.

3. Does the author include enough details and examples to support the topic sentence? *Yes*

List at least three supporting details: *Answers may vary.*

Drivers' papers

Walk through the countryside

Power lines as guides

4. Are the supporting details organized as effectively as possible? Label their method of organization.

Yes; they are organized spatially.

5. How does the author conclude the paragraph?

By making it across the border and toward Houston

Does the final sentence actually bring the paragraph to a close?

Yes; it ends this phase of the crossing.

Revising and Editing a Student Paragraph

Here is a paragraph written by Josh Ellis, a college student. As you read it, figure out what Josh's main idea is, and think of ways he might convey this idea more fully.

> [1]We all deal with boredom in different ways. [2]Unfortunately, most of us has to deal with it far to often. [3]Most people deal with boredom. [4]By trying to distract themselves from boring circumstances. [5]Myself, I'm a reader. [6]So at the breakfast table over a bowl of cereal, I read the cereal box, the milk carton, the wrapper on the bread. [7]Also, waiting in a doctor's office, I will gladly read weekly newsmagazines of three years ago, a book for 5-year-olds, advertizements for drugs, and even the physician's diplomas on the walls. [8]That's my recipe for beating boredom, what's yours?

This paragraph is Josh's first draft, which now needs to be revised and edited. First, apply the Revising Checklist below to Josh's draft so that you are working with his content. When you are satisfied that his ideas are fully developed and well organized, use the Editing Checklist on page 577 to correct his grammar and mechanics errors. Answer the questions after each checklist. Then write your suggested changes directly on Josh's draft.

Revising Checklist

TOPIC SENTENCE
✔ Does the topic sentence convey the paragraph's controlling idea and appear as the first or last sentence?

DEVELOPMENT

✔ Does the paragraph contain *specific* details that support the topic sentence?

✔ Does the paragraph include *enough* details to explain the topic sentence fully?

UNITY

✔ Do all the sentences in the paragraph support the topic sentence?

ORGANIZATION

✔ Is the paragraph organized logically?

COHERENCE

✔ Do the sentences move smoothly and logically from one to the next?

Topic Sentence

✔ Does the topic sentence convey the paragraph's controlling idea and appear as the first or last sentence?

1. What main idea does Josh communicate in his paragraph?

   We each deal with boredom in our own way.

2. Put brackets around Josh's topic sentence. Does it introduce his main idea? *No*

3. Rewrite it, if necessary, to introduce all the ideas in Josh's paragraph?

   Here is one possibility: I deal with boredom in my own unique way.

Development

✔ Does the paragraph contain *specific* details that support the topic sentence?

✔ Does the paragraph include *enough* details to explain the topic sentence fully?

1. Does Josh's paragraph contain specific details that support his topic sentence? *Yes*

2. List two of his details. *Answers will vary.*

_____

_____

3. Make one detail more specific than it already is.

4. Does Josh's paragraph have enough details to make his point? __Yes__

5. Add another detail to Josh's paragraph. *Answers will vary.*

Unity

> ✔ Do all the sentences in the paragraph support the topic sentence?

1. Read each of Josh's sentences with his topic sentence (revised, if necessary) in mind.

2. Drop or rewrite any of his sentences that are not directly related to his topic sentence. *All sentences relate to the topic sentence.*

Organization

> ✔ Is the paragraph organized logically?

1. List Josh's details to see if his paragraph is arranged logically.

Reading at the breakfast table: cereal box, milk carton, bread wrapper

Reading at the doctor's office: old newsmagazines, children's book, ads for drugs,

physician's diplomas

2. Move any details that are out of order. *All details are in order.*

Coherence

> ✔ Do the sentences move smoothly and logically from one to the next?

1. Circle two transitions Josh uses. For a list of transitions, see page 36. *Answers will vary.*

2. Explain how one of these makes Josh's paragraph easier to read.

   Answers will vary.

Now rewrite Josh's paragraph with your revisions.

✐ Editing Checklist

SENTENCES

✔ Does each sentence have a main subject and verb?

✔ Do all subjects and verbs agree?

✔ Do all pronouns agree with their nouns?

✔ Are modifiers as close as possible to the words they modify?

PUNCTUATION AND MECHANICS

✔ Are sentences punctuated correctly?

✔ Are words capitalized properly?

WORD CHOICE AND SPELLING

✔ Are words used correctly?

✔ Are words spelled correctly?

Sentences

✔ Does each sentence have a main subject and verb?

For help with subjects and verbs, see Chapter 7.

---

1. Underline the subjects once and the verbs twice in your revision of Josh's paragraph. Remember that sentences can have more than one subject-verb set.

2. Does each of Josh's sentences have at least one subject and verb that can stand alone? _No_

3. Did you find and correct Josh's fragment? If not, find and correct it now. For help with fragments, see Chapter 8. *Sentence 4.*

4. Did you find and correct Josh's run-on sentence? If not, find and correct it now. For help with run-ons, see Chapter 9. *Sentence 8.*

✔ Do all subjects and verbs agree?

For help with subject-verb agreement, see Chapter 12.

---

1. Read aloud the subjects and verbs you underlined in your revision of Josh's paragraph.

2. Correct any subjects and verbs that do not agree. *Sentence 2*

✔ Do all pronouns agree with their nouns?

For help with pronoun agreement, see Chapter 16.

---

1. Find any pronouns in your revision of Josh's essay that do not agree with their nouns. *All pronouns agree with their nouns.*

2. Correct any pronouns that do not agree with their nouns.

✔ Are modifiers as close as possible to the words they modify?

For help with modifier errors, see Chapter 19.

---

1. Find any modifiers in your revision of Josh's essay that are not as close as possible to the words they modify. *There are no modifier errors.*

2. Rewrite sentences if necessary so that modifiers are as close as possible to the words they modify.

Punctuation and Mechanics

✔ Are sentences punctuated correctly?

For help with punctuation, see Chapters 20–24.

---

1. Read your revision of Josh's paragraph for any errors in punctuation.

2. Make sure the fragment and run-on you revised are punctuated correctly.

✔ Are words capitalized properly?

For help with capitalization, see Chapter 25.

---

1. Read your revision of Josh's paragraph for any errors in capitalization.
   All capitals are correct.
2. Be sure to check his capitalization in the fragment and run-on you revised.

Word Choice and Spelling

✔ Are words used correctly?

For help with confused words, see Chapter 31.

---

1. Find any words used incorrectly in your revision of Josh's paragraph.

2. Correct any errors you find. *to/too (sentence 2)*

✔ Are all words spelled correctly?

For help with spelling, see Chapter 32.

---

1. Use spell-check and a dictionary to check the spelling in your revision of Josh's paragraph.

2. Correct any misspelled words. *advertizements/advertisements (sentence 7)*

Now rewrite Josh's paragraph again with your editing corrections.

Revising and Editing Your Own Paragraph

Now you are ready to revise and edit the paragraph that you wrote in Chapter 33. The checklists here will help you apply what you have learned to your own writing.

✐ Revising Checklist

TOPIC SENTENCE

☐ Does the topic sentence convey the paragraph's controlling idea and appear as the first or last sentence?

DEVELOPMENT

☐ Does the paragraph contain *specific* details that support the topic sentence?

☐ Does the paragraph include *enough* details to explain the topic sentence fully?

UNITY

☐ Do all the sentences in the paragraph support the topic sentence?

ORGANIZATION

☐ Is the paragraph organized logically?

COHERENCE

☐ Do the sentences move smoothly and logically from one to the next?

Have students send an essay they wrote in your class to an on-line writing lab (OWL) for revising and editing feedback. Have students include a printout of the OWL's comments when they turn in their final draft of the essay, and have them reflect on the on-line tutorials by answering the following questions.

1. What was the most important learning experience from the OWL?
2. What was the least important learning experience from the OWL?
3. How can an OWL be beneficial with papers you may be writing for other classes?

For a complete list of OWLs, go to wca.syr.edu/NWCA/ NWCAOWLS.html. One of the best is owl.english.purdue.edu.

Topic Sentence

TEACHING ON THE WEB

Research: Have students log on to the following sites to help them with revising and editing. How are these sites helpful for both revising and editing?

www.prenhall.com/
    mosaics
www.prenhall.com/troyka

> ☐ Does the topic sentence convey the paragraph's controlling idea and appear as the first or last sentence?

1. What is the main idea you are trying to convey in your paragraph?
2. Put brackets around your topic sentence. Does it communicate your main idea?
3. Rewrite it, if necessary, to introduce all the ideas in your paragraph?

Development

> ☐ Does the paragraph contain *specific* details that support the topic sentence?
>
> ☐ Does the paragraph include *enough* details to explain the topic sentence fully?

1. Does your paragraph contain specific details that support your topic sentence? List three of your details.

   _____

   _____

   _____

2. Make one detail more specific than it already is.
3. Does your paragraph have enough details to make your point?

   _____

4. Add another detail to your paragraph.

Unity

> ☐ Do all the sentences in the paragraph support the topic sentence?

1. Read each of your sentences with your topic sentence (revised, if necessary) in mind.

2. Drop or rewrite any of your sentences that are not directly related to your topic sentence.

Organization

> ☐ Is the paragraph organized logically?

1. List your details to see if your paragraph is organized logically.

_____   _____

_____   _____

_____   _____

2. Move any details that are out of order.

Coherence

> ☐ Do the sentences move smoothly and logically from one to the next?

1. Circle two transitions you use. For a list of transitions, see page 36.
2. Explain how one of these makes your paragraph easier to read.

_____

Now rewrite your paragraph with your revisions.

✐ Editing Checklist

SENTENCES
☐ Does each sentence have a main subject and verb?
☐ Do all subjects and verbs agree?
☐ Do all pronouns agree with their nouns?
☐ Are modifiers as close as possible to the words they modify?

PUNCTUATION AND MECHANICS
☐ Are sentences punctuated correctly?
☐ Are words capitalized properly?

WORD CHOICE AND SPELLING
☐ Are words used correctly?
☐ Are words spelled correctly?

Sentences

☐ Does each sentence have a main subject and verb?
For help with subjects and verbs, see Chapter 7.

1. Underline the subjects once and the verbs twice in your revised paragraph. Remember that sentences can have more than one subject-verb set.

2. Does each of your sentences have at least one subject and verb that can stand alone?

3. Correct any fragments you find. For help with fragments, see Chapter 8.

4. Correct any run-on sentences you find. For help with run-ons, see Chapter 9.

☐ Do all subjects and verbs agree?
For help with subject-verb agreement, see Chapter 12.

1. Read aloud the subjects and verbs you have underlined in your revised paragraph.

2. Correct any subjects and verbs that do not agree.

☐ Do all pronouns agree with their nouns?
For help with pronoun agreement, see Chapter 16.

1. Find any pronouns in your revised paragraph that do not agree with their nouns.

2. Correct any pronouns that do not agree with their nouns.

☐ Are modifiers as close as possible to the words they modify?
For help with modifier errors, see Chapter 19.

1. Find any modifiers in your revised paragraph that are not as close as possible to the words they modify.

2. Rewrite sentences if necessary so that your modifiers are as close as possible to the words they modify.

Punctuation and Mechanics

☐ Are sentences punctuated correctly?
    For help with punctuation, see Chapters 20–24.

1. Read your revised paragraph for any errors in punctuation.

2. Make sure any fragments and run-ons you revised are punctuated correctly.

☐ Are words capitalized properly?
    For help with capitalization, see Chapter 25.

1. Read your revised paragraph for any errors in capitalization.

2. Be sure to check your capitalization if you revised any fragments or run-ons.

Word Choice and Spelling

☐ Are words used correctly?
    For help with confused words, see Chapter 31.

1. Find any words used incorrectly in your revised paragraph.

2. Correct any errors you find.

☐ Are words spelled correctly?
    For help with spelling, see Chapter 32.

1. Use spell-check and a dictionary to check the spelling in your revision.

2. Correct any misspelled words.

Now rewrite your paragraph again with your editing corrections.

Ideas for Writing

Guidelines for Writing a Paragraph

1. Choose a subject that can be covered in a single paragraph.
2. Write a topic sentence for your paragraph.
3. Develop your paragraph with details and examples that support your topic sentence.
4. Organize your supporting details and examples.
5. Write a concluding sentence.
6. Revise and edit your paragraph.

1. Imagine that you are in this setting waiting for someone. Whom are you waiting for? Why are you in this particular place? What is the reason for

Have your students complete one of the following writing projects, each representing one of the eight multiple intelligences: (1) verbal and linguistic, (2) musical, (3) logical and mathematical, (4) visual and spatial, (5) bodily and kinesthetic, (6) intrapersonal, (7) interpersonal, and (8) naturalistic.

THEME: THE WORKPLACE

1. Some people research the origins of words, trace the use of slang, or focus on different types of English in the United States. Does this kind of work interest you? What other jobs focus on language? Why are these jobs important, and how do they ultimately affect everyone?

2. Many jobs exist that deal with music in some way. If you wanted to work with music and could create your ideal job, what would it be?

Why is this job ideal? Is it possible for you to someday have this job or something closely related to it?

3. Computer technology is still a fast-growing field. Where do you think this field will be in 5 years? 10 years? 20 years? What do you think computers will someday be capable of doing? Will they eventually replace human workers?

4. No matter what is happening in the world, people always love to be entertained. Many careers deal with entertaining the public. If you could have a job that entertains people, what would it be, and why would you want this job?

5. Many people play sports in high school and college but decrease their physical activity dramatically when they start their careers. How can former athletes keep the jobs they have worked so hard to secure and also maintain the level of fitness they desire in their lives?

6. Some people do not work well with others and prefer an isolated job. If someone had these preferences, what kind of job would you recommend? What can someone do that would not put him or her in contact with other people and would still allow the person to have a fulfilling career?

7. Some people can't stand the idea of working alone. Being alone for hours on end would be

your meeting? Put yourself in this scene, and talk about your reasons for being there.

2. Write a paragraph describing your ideal work environment. What factors make it ideal? Why is it a good environment for you to work in?

3. Tell about a time you were blamed for a mistake you did not make. What were the circumstances? Why were you blamed? Did you ever clear your name?

4. Create your own assignment (with the help of your instructor), and write a response to it.

Revising Workshop

Small Group Activity (5–10 minutes per writer): In groups of three or four, each person should read his or her paragraph to the other members of the group. Those listening should record their reactions on a copy of the Peer Evaluation Form on page 675. After your group goes through this process, give your evaluation forms to the appropriate writers so that each writer has two or three peer comment sheets for revising.

Paired Activity (5 minutes per writer): Using the completed Peer Evaluation Forms, work in pairs to decide what you should revise in your paragraphs. If time allows, rewrite some of your sentences, and have your partner check them.

Individual Activity: Rewrite your paragraph, using the revising feedback you received from other students.

Editing Workshop

Paired Activity (5–10 minutes per writer): Swap papers with a classmate, and use the editing portion of your Peer Evaluation Form to identify as many grammar, punctuation, mechanics, and spelling errors as you can. Mark the errors on the student paragraph using the editing symbols on the inside back cover. If time allows, correct some of your errors, and have your partner check them.

Individual Activity: Rewrite your paragraph again, using the editing feedback you received from other students. Record your grammar, punctuation, and mechanics errors in the Error Log (Appendix 6) and your spelling errors in the Spelling Log (Appendix 7).

Reflecting on Your Writing

When you have completed your own paragraph, answer these five questions:

1. What was most difficult about this assignment?
2. What was easiest?
3. What did you learn about writing by completing this assignment?
4. What do you think are the strengths of your paragraph? What are its weaknesses?
5. What did you learn from this assignment about your own writing process—about preparing to write, about writing the first draft, about revising, and about editing?

unappealing to these people. What career would you recommend to someone who wanted to be around people constantly? Why would this be the perfect job for this type of person?

8. Some people want an outdoor job. They think working indoors is the equivalent of being locked up. Think of three jobs that involve working primarily outdoors, and explain to someone who loves nature why these are the jobs he or she should seriously consider.

P · A · R · T

IV

FROM READING TO WRITING

The best writing is rewriting.

—E. B. White

Part IV is a collection of essays that demonstrate the rhetorical modes you are studying in this book. Each chapter focuses on a different rhetorical strategy and includes two essays showing the strategy at work with other strategies. Following each essay are questions to check your understanding of the selection. By charting your correct and incorrect responses to these questions in Appendix 1, you can track your general level of reading comprehension.

Describing

When you **describe,** you create a picture in words to show your reader something you have seen, heard, or done. The following essays describe events, actions, and thoughts so clearly that we can experience them for ourselves through words. "A Day in the Homeless Life," written by Colette Russell, describes her daily activities, joys, frustrations, and humiliations as a homeless person. In "Casa: A Partial Remembrance of a Puerto Rican Childhood" by Judith Ortiz Cofer, the author discusses the daily ritual of the women in her family.

Colette Russell

A DAY IN THE HOMELESS LIFE

SUMMARY
In this essay, Russell describes the grim reality of a typical day in her life as a homeless person.

READABILITY
5.1

Focusing Your Attention

1. We all own things that we would never part with. What are your prize possessions? If you had to live in a shelter or on the streets, what would you take with you?

2. In the essay you are about to read, the writer describes in vivid detail her daily routine as a homeless person. If you suddenly became homeless, where would you go? What would you do to get food, shelter, and comfort?

Expanding Your Vocabulary

The following word is important to your understanding of this essay.

invariably: without ever changing (paragraph 2)

"Good morning, ladies. It's 5 a.m. Time to get up." Ceiling lights were suddenly   1
ablaze. This message boomed repeatedly until nearly everyone was out of bed.

Two toilets and three sinks for 50 women; no toilet paper in the morning, in-   2
variably. Three tables with benches bordered by beds on two sides were our day
room, dining room, and lounge.

Breakfast usually arrived at 5:45 a.m., too late for those who were in the day-   3
labor van pools. They went to work on empty stomachs, and they were the ones
needing food the most.

Breakfast generally consisted of rolls and sausage and juice until it ran out.   4
The coffee was unique: It didn't taste like coffee, but that's what we had to drink.

At 6:30 a.m. we were ordered to go down to the lobby, where we joined 50   5
other women either standing or sitting on wooden benches awaiting the light of
day. Some talked to themselves. Some shouted angrily. Some sat motionless.
Some slept sitting up. Some jumped up and down, walking away and then returning. Some chain-smoked.

All of us had our belongings with us. Carrying everything every step of the   6
way every day was hard on the arms, and I felt it was a dead giveaway that I was
homeless.

At 7:30 a.m. the clothing room opened. It was shocking to be told, "Throw   7
away what you're wearing after you get a new outfit." No laundry, just toss out
yesterday's garments. We were allotted five minutes to paw through racks looking for articles that fit.

I was always happy to see 8:30 a.m. roll around. Grabbing my bags, I headed   8
down Berkeley Street away from the jam-packed, smoke-filled "holding cell." Always I felt guilty at not going to work like everyone else who hurried by as I approached the business district.

The main library was my daily stop. I positioned myself at a table where I   9
could watch the clock: We had to return to the shelter before 4 p.m. to get in line
for a bed. Otherwise we might miss out.

Reading was the high point of the day. Escape into a book. There was relative   10
privacy at a library table. It was heavenly. I hated to leave.

The clock signaled the task of trudging back, at 3:45 p.m., with even heavier   11
bags. The bags, of course, were no heavier; they just seemed heavier.

Back in the "yard" I joined the group already assembled. Some women never   12
left the grounds, staying all day in the small yard by the building. God forbid.
With the appearance of a staff member, we would form a line as the staffer prepared a list of our names and bed requests.

I was always glad when the lights went out at 9 p.m. and I could climb into   13
bed (a bottom sheet and a blanket—no top sheet) and close my eyes and pretend
I wasn't there but back in my apartment on the West Coast.

3. She was "always glad when the lights went out at 9 p.m." because once it was dark, she could "close my eyes and pretend I wasn't there but back in my apartment on the West Coast" (para. 13).

Thinking Critically About Purpose and Audience

4. Russell's dominant impression is one of despair. When she talks about the lack of toilets, sinks, and toilet paper, readers understand that her life has very little to celebrate.

5. Russell writes this essay for a general audience. Anyone can appreciate this essay, whether homeless or not.

6. Russell wants readers to understand what being homeless is like, and she wants readers to know that respectable people can be homeless. She probably hopes people will understand people in her situation by reading her essay. The details students choose to answer this question will vary.

Thinking Critically About Sentences

7. Answers will vary. Here are the questions in the essay:

"Who knew they were there?" (para. 14)

"Even if I were to do day labor at $4 per hour and clear $28 or so a day, how many weeks would it take me to save enough for first and last month's rent

14   Twice I was robbed. Once a bag was taken. Another time my new blue underpants disappeared out of one of my bags. Who knew they were there?

15   Even if I were to do day labor at $4 per hour and clear $28 or so a day, how many weeks would it take to save enough for first and last month's rent on an apartment plus deposit and enough to pay for initial utilities? I was too depressed to even try to work and took frequent breaks to sit down while doing kitchen volunteer work. I was tired all the time.

16   The true stories I heard were heartbreaking. Which was the sadder?

17   One young woman with no skills and no job training had been OK financially until her CETA job ended—the program was abolished—and the YWCA raised its weekly room rate. She couldn't afford a room and couldn't find a job. She'd been in shelters for three or four years. I marveled that she was still sane. She did crossword puzzles while waiting everywhere.

18   Another older lady had held the same job for 10 years and would still have been working had not the corporation, without notice, closed up shop. She was 59 years old and out of a job, with a little severance pay and no help to find new work. She tried but was unsuccessful in finding a new job. She exhausted her savings after her unemployment ran out. One June day in 1987, she found herself homeless. No money for rent.

19   Both of these women are intelligent, honest, pleasant, clean, and neatly dressed. And both are penniless and homeless. How will they escape the shelters? Will they?

20   I got by, all right, by keeping my mouth shut around the staff and talking only with two or three women whom I knew to be sane and sociable. I was lucky. Two and a half months after I'd first gone into a shelter, my son rescued me. I was on the verge of madness, so hungry for a little privacy and peace that I was afraid I'd start screaming in my sleep and be shunted off to a mental ward.

21   Now I've got a job paying more than I've ever earned. But I remember those days and nights.

22   No one should have to live like that. Too many do—and will, I fear, unless and until we who do have homes and jobs help them end their eternal, living nightmare.

Thinking Critically About Content

1. List one detail from this essay for each of the five senses: seeing, hearing, touching, tasting, and smelling. How do these details *show* rather than *tell* the readers what a homeless life is like?

2. Why do you think the writer describes the lives of other homeless women in addition to her own?

3. Why was Russell "always glad when the lights went out at 9 p.m." (paragraph 13)?

Thinking Critically About Purpose and Audience

4. What do you think is Russell's dominant impression in this essay? Which details in paragraph 2 help create this dominant impression?

5. Who do you think is Russell's audience? Do you think people who have never been homeless can appreciate her descriptions?

6. What attitude do you think Russell wants her readers to have toward homeless people as a result of reading her essay? On what details do you base your answer?

Thinking Critically About Sentences

7. Find two sentences that are questions in Russell's essay. How do these questions help you understand the writer's attitude about the shelter?

8. What is the topic sentence of paragraph 9? Is it a good topic sentence for the details in that paragraph?

9. Write one or more complete sentences describing Russell's inner feelings about homelessness.

Judith Ortiz Cofer

CASA: A PARTIAL REMEMBRANCE OF A PUERTO RICAN CHILDHOOD

Focusing Your Attention

1. Think of a ritual that you are very familiar with, such as putting up holiday decorations, hanging the hammock for summer, or sitting on the porch in the evening. What do you like best about these rituals? Why are they important to you?

2. In the essay you are about to read, a young girl tells us about the ritual the women in her family have of sitting around and talking in the late afternoon. Think of a ritual that is important in your life, and list the sights, sounds, smells, textures, and tastes that you associate with this ritual.

Expanding Your Vocabulary

The following words are important to your understanding of this essay.

café con leche: coffee with milk (paragraph 1)

embellishing: enhancing (paragraph 2)

SUMMARY

Cofer describes an afternoon she spent with her family, where she listened to the grown-ups retell a story of a village woman who was left at the altar.

READABILITY

8.0

on an apartment plus deposit and enough to pay for initial utilities?" (para. 15)
"Which was the sadder?" (para. 16)
"How will they escape the shelters? Will they?" (para. 19)
These questions help readers understand that Russell genuinely has no answers.
8. The topic sentence of paragraph 9 is "The main library was my daily stop" (sentence 1). This is a good topic sentence because the other sentences focus on her time in the library.
9. Answers will vary.

histrionic: dramatic (paragraph 3)

conclave: private gathering (paragraph 3)

impassively: unemotionally, casually (paragraph 3)

ironic: unexpectedly amused (paragraph 3)

ministrations: aid (paragraph 3)

matriarchal: motherly (paragraph 3)

hombres: men (paragraph 4)

pueblo: village (paragraph 4)

haciendas: country homes (paragraph 4)

plait: braid (paragraph 5)

La Escuela San José: the San Jose School (paragraph 5)

La Loca: the crazy lady (paragraph 6)

bodega: grocery store (paragraph 6)

pasteles: meat pies (paragraph 6)

Gringa: white female (paragraph 7)

chameleons: people with changeable moods or habits (paragraph 7)

realm: domain (paragraph 7)

epithet: name, title (paragraph 8)

conspiratorially: mischievously (paragraph 9)

finca: property, estate (paragraph 9)

collaborators: people who band together (paragraph 10)

mesmerizing: hypnotic (paragraph 10)

denouement: conclusion (paragraph 11)

promesa: promise (paragraph 11)

lamented: agonized (paragraph 11)

infectious: spreading from one person to another (paragraph 13)

1　At three or four o'clock in the afternoon, the hour of *café con leche,* the women of my family gathered in Mamá's living room to speak of important things and retell familiar stories meant to be overheard by us young girls, their daughters. In Mamá's house (everyone called my grandmother Mamá) was a large parlor built by my grandfather to his wife's exact specifications so that it was always cool, facing away from the sun. The doorway was on the side of the house so no one could walk directly into her living room. First they had to take a little stroll through and around her beautiful garden where prize-winning orchids grew in the trunk of an ancient tree she had hollowed out for that purpose. This room was furnished with several mahogany rocking chairs, acquired at the births of her children, and one intricately carved rocker that had passed down to Mamá at the death of her own mother.

It was on these rockers that my mother, her sisters, and my grandmother sat 2 on these afternoons of my childhood to tell their stories, teaching each other, and my cousin and me, what it was like to be a woman, more specifically, a Puerto Rican woman. They talked about life on the island, and life in *Los Nueva Yores,* their way of referring to the United States from New York City to California: the other place, not home, all the same. They told real-life stories though, as I later learned, always embellishing them with a little or a lot of dramatic detail. And they told *cuentos,* the morality and cautionary tales told by the women in our family for generations: stories that became a part of my subconscious as I grew up in two worlds, the tropical island and the cold city, and that would later surface in my dreams and in my poetry.

One of these tales was about the woman who was left at the altar. Mamá liked 3 to tell that one with histrionic intensity. I remember the rise and fall of her voice, the sighs, and her constantly gesturing hands, like two birds swooping through her words. This particular story usually would come up in a conversation as a result of someone mentioning a forthcoming engagement or wedding. The first time I remember hearing it, I was sitting on the floor at Mamá's feet, pretending to read a comic book. I may have been eleven or twelve years old, at that difficult age when a girl was no longer a child who could be ordered to leave the room if the women wanted freedom to take their talk into forbidden zones, nor really old enough to be considered a part of their conclave. I could only sit quietly, pretending to be in another world, while absorbing it all in a sort of unspoken agreement of my status as silent auditor. On this day, Mamá had taken my long, tangled mane of hair into her ever-busy hands. Without looking down at me and with no interruption of her flow of words, she began braiding my hair, working at it with the quickness and determination that characterized all her actions. My mother was watching us impassively from her rocker across the room. On her lips played a little ironic smile. I would never sit still for *her* ministrations, but even then, I instinctively knew that she did not possess Mamá's matriarchal power to command and keep everyone's attention. This was never more evident than in the spell she cast when telling a story.

"It is not like it used to be when I was a girl," Mamá announced. "Then, a man 4 could leave a girl standing at the church altar with a bouquet of fresh flowers in her hands and disappear off the face of the earth. No way to track him down if he was from another town. He could be a married man, with maybe even two or three families all over the island. There was no way to know. And there were men who did this. Hombres with the devil in their flesh who would come to a pueblo, like this one, take a job at one of the haciendas, never meaning to stay, only to have a good time and to seduce the women."

5   The whole time she was speaking, Mamá would be weaving my hair into a flat plait that required pulling apart the two sections of hair with little jerks that made my eyes water; but knowing how grandmother detested whining and *boba* (sissy) tears, as she called them, I just sat up as straight and stiff as I did at La Escuela San José, where the nuns enforced good posture with a flexible plastic ruler they bounced off of slumped shoulders and heads. As Mamá's story progressed, I noticed how my young Aunt Laura lowered her eyes, refusing to meet Mamá's meaningful gaze. Laura was seventeen, in her last year of high school, and already engaged to a boy from another town who had staked his claim with a tiny diamond ring, then left for Los Nueva Yores to make his fortune. They were planning to get married in a year. Mamá had expressed serious doubts that the wedding would ever take place. In Mamá's eyes, a man set free without a legal contract was a man lost. She believed that marriage was not something men desired, but simply the price they had to pay for the privilege of children and, of course, for what no decent (synonymous with "smart") woman would give away for free.

6   "María La Loca was only seventeen when *it* happened to her." I listened closely at the mention of this name. María was a town character, a fat middle-aged woman who lived with her old mother on the outskirts of town. She was to be seen around the pueblo delivering the meat pies the two women made for a living. The most peculiar thing about María, in my eyes, was that she walked and moved like a little girl though she had the thick body and wrinkled face of an old woman. She would swing her hips in an exaggerated, clownish way, and sometimes even hop and skip up to someone's house. She spoke to no one. Even if you asked her a question, she would just look at you and smile, showing her yellow teeth. But I had heard that if you got close enough, you could hear her humming a tune without words. The kids yelled out nasty things at her, calling her *La Loca,* and the men who hung out at the bodega playing dominoes sometimes whistled mockingly as she passed by with her funny, outlandish walk. But María seemed impervious to it all, carrying her basket of *pasteles* like a grotesque Little Red Riding Hood through the forest.

7   María La Loca interested me, as did all the eccentrics and crazies of our pueblo. Their weirdness was a measuring stick I used in my serious quest for a definition of normal. As a Navy brat shuttling between New Jersey and the pueblo, I was constantly made to feel like an oddball by my peers, who made fun of my two-way accent: a Spanish accent when I spoke English, and when I spoke Spanish I was told that I sounded like a *Gringa.* Being the outsider had already turned my

brother and me into cultural chameleons. We developed early on the ability to blend into a crowd, to sit and read quietly in a fifth story apartment building for days and days when it was too bitterly cold to play outside, or, set free, to run wild in Mamá's realm, where she took charge of our lives, releasing Mother for a while from the intense fear for our safety that our father's absences instilled in her. In order to keep us from harm when Father was away, Mother kept us under strict surveillance. She even walked us to and from Public School No. 11, which we attended during the months we lived in Paterson, New Jersey, our home base in the states. Mamá freed all three of us like pigeons from a cage. I saw her as my liberator and my model. Her stories were parables from which to glean the *Truth*.

"María La Loca was once a beautiful girl. Everyone thought she would marry 8 the Méndez boy." As everyone knew, Rogelio Méndez was the richest man in town. "But," Mamá continued, knitting my hair with the same intensity she was putting into her story, "this *macho* made a fool out of her and ruined her life." She paused for the effect of her use of the word "macho," which at that time had not yet become a popular epithet for an unliberated man. This word had for us the crude and comical connotation of "male of the species," stud; a *macho* was what you put in a pen to increase your stock.

I peeked over my comic book at my mother. She too was under Mamá's spell, 9 smiling conspiratorially at this little swipe at men. She was safe from Mamá's contempt in this area. Married at an early age, an unspotted lamb, she had been accepted by a good family of strict Spaniards whose name was old and respected, though their fortune had been lost long before my birth. In a rocker Papá had painted sky blue sat Mamá's oldest child, Aunt Nena. Mother of three children, stepmother of two more, she was a quiet woman who liked books but had married an ignorant and abusive widower whose main interest in life was accumulating wealth. He too was in the mainland working on his dream of returning home rich and triumphant to buy the *finca* of his dreams. She was waiting for him to send for her. She would leave her children with Mamá for several years while the two of them slaved away in factories. He would one day be a rich man, and she a sadder woman. Even now her life-light was dimming. She spoke little, an aberration in Mamá's house, and she read avidly, as if storing up spiritual food for the long winters that awaited her in Los Nueva Yores without her family. But even Aunt Nena came alive to Mamá's words, rocking gently, her hands over a thick book in her lap.

Her daughter, my cousin Sara, played jacks by herself on the tile porch outside 10 the room where we sat. She was a year older than I. We shared a bed and all our family's secrets. Collaborators in search of answers, Sara and I discussed everything we heard the women say, trying to fit it all together like a puzzle that, once assembled, would reveal life's mysteries to us. Though she and I still enjoyed taking part in boys' games—chase, volleyball, and even *vaqueros,* the island version of cowboys and Indians involving cap-gun battles and violent shoot-outs under the mango tree in Mamá's backyard—we loved best the quiet hours in the afternoon when the men were still at work, and the boys had gone to play serious baseball at the park. Then Mamá's house belonged only to us women. The aroma of coffee perking in the kitchen, the mesmerizing creaks and groans of the rockers, and the women telling their lives in *cuentos* are forever woven into the fabric of my imagination, braided like my hair that day I felt my grandmother's hands teaching me about strength, her voice convincing me of the power of storytelling.

11   That day Mamá told how the beautiful María had fallen prey to a man whose name was never the same in subsequent versions of the story; it was Juan one time, José, Rafael, Diego, another. We understood that neither the name nor any of the *facts* were important, only that a woman had allowed love to defeat her. Mamá put each of us in María's place by describing her wedding dress in loving detail: how she looked like a princess in her lace as she waited at the altar. Then, as Mamá approached the tragic denouement of her story, I was distracted by the sound of my Aunt Laura's violent rocking. She seemed on the verge of tears. She knew the fable was intended for her. That week she was going to have her wedding gown fitted, though no firm date had been set for the marriage. Mamá ignored Laura's obvious discomfort, digging out a ribbon from the sewing basket she kept by her rocker while describing María's long illness, "a fever that would not break for days." She spoke of a mother's despair: "that woman climbed the church steps on her knees every morning, wore only black as a *promesa* to the Holy Virgin in exchange for her daughter's health." By the time María returned from her honeymoon with death, she was ravished, no longer young or sane. "As you can see, she is almost as old as her mother already," Mamá lamented while tying the ribbon to the ends of my hair, pulling it back with such force that I just knew I would never be able to close my eyes completely again.

12   "That María's getting crazier every day." Mamá's voice would take a lighter tone now, expressing satisfaction, either for the perfection of my braid, or for a story well told—it was hard to tell. "You know that tune María is always humming?" Carried away by her enthusiasm, I tried to nod, but Mamá still had me pinned between her knees.

13   "Well, that's the wedding march." Surprising us all, Mamá sang out, "Da, da, dara . . . da, da, dara." Then lifting me off the floor by my skinny shoulders, she would lead me around the room in an impromptu waltz—another session ending with the laughter of women, all of us caught up in the infectious joke of our lives.

Thinking Critically About Content

1. What happened to María La Loca after she was left at the altar?
2. Find at least one detail for each of the five senses. Does Cofer draw on any one sense more than the others?

3. Why does the narrator believe in "the power of storytelling" (paragraph 10)?

Thinking Critically About Purpose and Audience

4. What dominant impression does Cofer create in this essay?

5. Who do you think Cofer's primary audience is?

6. Explain your understanding of this essay's title.

Thinking Critically About Sentences

7. How does the addition of Spanish words to Cofer's sentences help you understand her main ideas?

8. Find a sentence that *shows* rather than *tells* her story. Explain your choice.

9. Write one or more complete sentences about the type of wedding you have had or hope to have.

5. Cofer's audience is general, but unmarried women will probably most identify with this essay.
6. Answers will vary.

Thinking Critically About Sentences

7. The mixture of Spanish and English words helps enforce the idea that the narrator lives part of the time in Puerto Rico and part of the time in the United States.
8. Answers will vary.
9. Answers will vary.

Writing Topics: Describing

Before you begin to write, you might want to review the writing process in Part I.

1. In the first essay, Colette Russell draws on impressions from all the senses to show her readers what her life is like on the streets. Think of a tough situation that you have been through. Describe the situation, drawing on as many of the senses as possible— seeing, hearing, touching, smelling, and tasting—so that your reader can experience the problem as you did.

2. How much do you like rituals? Write a description of your favorite personal ritual with vivid details that make your readers feel as if they are participating in the activity with you.

Narrating

Narration, or storytelling, is an interesting way of getting someone's attention and sharing thoughts and experiences. To understand how to write your own narrative essay, you may find it helpful to read some samples. The first essay, "A Giant Step" by Henry Louis Gates Jr., explains his handicap and his coping skills for dealing with it. In the next essay, "The Struggle to Be an All-American Girl," Elizabeth Wong discusses her desire to become "more American."

Henry Louis Gates Jr.

A GIANT STEP

Focusing Your Attention

1. The world is full of people who are considered heroes. Who in your life do you consider a hero? Explain your answer.
2. In the essay you are about to read, Henry Louis Gates Jr. tells a story about a pair of shoes that are very important in his life. Think of an object that is important to you, and explain its role in your life.

Expanding Your Vocabulary

The following words are important to your understanding of this essay.

orthopedic: medically corrective (paragraph 7)

incurred: brought upon oneself (paragraph 8)

delinquent: troublemaker (paragraph 10)

psychosomatic: all in the mind (paragraph 27)

pathology: illness (paragraph 28)

immobilized: prevented from moving (paragraph 31)

SUMMARY

In this essay, Gates recounts how he became disabled and how he was treated directly after the injury. He then discusses his life with his disability and the surgery that ultimately corrects his handicap.

READABILITY

5.8

orthotics: custom-designed shoes (paragraph 34)

amnesiac: forgetful (paragraph 40)

furtive: secret (paragraph 44)

Imelda Marcos: the wife of a former Philippine dictator known for her large collection of shoes (paragraph 44)

"What's this?" the hospital janitor said to me as he stumbled over my right shoe.   1

"My shoes," I said.   2

"That's not a shoe, brother," he replied, holding it to the light. "That's a brick."   3

It *did* look like a brick, sort of.   4

"Well, we can throw these in the trash now," he said.   5

"I guess so."   6

We had been together since 1975, those shoes and I. They were orthopedic   7
shoes built around molds of my feet, and they had a $2\frac{1}{4}$-inch lift. I had mixed feelings about them. On the one hand, they had given me a more or less even gait for the first time in 10 years. On the other hand, they had marked me as a "handicapped person," complete with cane and special license plates. I went through a pair a year, but it was always the same shoe, black, wide, weighing about four pounds.

It all started 26 years ago in Piedmont, W.Va., a backwoods town of 2,000   8
people. While playing a game of touch football at a Methodist summer camp, I incurred a hairline fracture. Thing is, I didn't know it yet. I was 14 and had finally lost the chubbiness of my youth. I was just learning tennis and beginning to date, and who knew where that might lead?

Not too far. A few weeks later, I was returning to school from lunch when, out   9
of the blue, the ball-and-socket joint of my hip sheared apart. It was instant agony, and from that time on nothing in my life would be quite the same.

I propped myself against the brick wall of the schoolhouse, where the school   10
delinquent found me. He was black as slate, twice my size, mean as the day was long and beat up kids just because he could. But the look on my face told him something was seriously wrong, and—bless him—he stayed by my side for the two hours it took to get me into a taxi.

"It's a torn ligament in your knee," the surgeon said. (One of the signs of what   11
I had—a "slipped epithysis"—is intense knee pain, I later learned.) So he scheduled me for a walking cast.

I was wheeled into surgery and placed on the operating table. As the doctor   12
wrapped my leg with wet plaster strips, he asked about my schoolwork.

"Boy," he said, "I understand you want to be a doctor."   13

14   I said, "Yessir." Where I came from, you always said "sir" to white people, unless you were trying to make a statement.

15   Had I taken a lot of science courses?

16   "Yessir. I enjoy science."

17   "Are you good at it?"

18   "Yessir, I believe so."

19   "Tell me, who was the father of sterilization?"

20   "Oh, that's easy, Joseph Lister."

21   Then he asked who discovered penicillin.

22   Alexander Fleming.

23   And what about DNA?

24   Watson and Crick.

25   The interview went on like this, and I thought my answers might get me a pat on the head. Actually, they just confirmed the diagnosis he'd come to.

26   He stood me on my feet and insisted that I walk. When I tried, the joint ripped apart and I fell on the floor. It hurt like nothing I'd ever known.

27   The doctor shook his head. "Pauline," he said to my mother, his voice kindly but amused, "there's not a thing wrong with that child. The problem's psychosomatic. Your son's an overachiever."

28   Back then, the term didn't mean what it usually means today. In Appalachia, in 1964, "overachiever" designated a sort of pathology: the overstraining of your natural capacity. A colored kid who thought he could be a doctor—just for instance—was headed for a breakdown.

29   What made the pain abate was my mother's reaction. I'd never, ever heard her talk back to a white person before. And doctors, well, their words were scripture.

30   Not this time. Pauline Gates stared at him for a moment. "Get his clothes, pack his bags—we're going to the University Medical Center," which was 60 miles away.

31   Not great news: the one thing I knew was that they only moved you to the University Medical Center when you were going to die. I had three operations that year. I gave my tennis racket to the delinquent, which he probably used to club little kids with. So I wasn't going to make it to Wimbledon. But at least I wasn't going to die, though sometimes I wanted to. Following the last operation, which fitted me for a metal ball, I was confined to bed, flat on my back, immobilized by a complex system of weights and pulleys. It was six weeks of bondage—and bedpans. I spent my time reading James Baldwin, learning to play chess, and quarreling daily with my mother, who had rented a small room—which we could ill afford—in a motel just down the hill from the hospital.

32   I think we both came to realize that our quarreling was a sort of ritual. We'd argue about everything—what time of day it was—but the arguments kept me from thinking about that traction system.

I limped through the next decade—through Yale and Cambridge . . . as far   33
away from Piedmont as I could get. But I couldn't escape the pain, which increased as the joint calcified and began to fuse over the next 15 years. My leg
grew shorter, as the muscles atrophied and the ball of the ball-and-socket joint
migrated into my pelvis. Aspirin, then Motrin, heating pads and massages, became my traveling companions.

Most frustrating was passing store windows full of fine shoes. I used to   34
dream about walking into one of those stores and buying a pair of shoes. "Give
me two pairs, one black, one cordovan," I'd say. "Wrap 'em up." No six-week
wait as with the orthotics in which I was confined. These would be real shoes.
Not bricks.

In the meantime, hip-joint technology progressed dramatically. But no sur-   35
geon wanted to operate on me until I was significantly older, or until the pain
was so great that surgery was unavoidable. After all, a new hip would last only
for 15 years, and I'd already lost too much bone. It wasn't a procedure they
were sure they'd be able to repeat.

This year, my 40th, the doctors decided the time had come.   36

I increased my life insurance and made the plunge.   37

The nights before my operations are the longest nights of my life—but   38
never long enough. Jerking awake, grabbing for my watch, I experience a delicious sense of relief as I discover that only a minute or two have passed. You
never want 6 A.M. to come.

And then the door swings open. "Good morning, Mr. Gates," the nurse says.   39
"It's time."

The last thing I remember, just vaguely, was wondering where amnesiac   40
minutes go in one's consciousness, wondering if I experienced the pain and
sounds, then forgot them, or if these were somehow blocked out, dividing the
self on the operating table from the conscious self in the recovery room. I didn't
like that idea very much. I was about to protest when I blinked.

"It's over, Mr. Gates," says a voice. But how could it be over? I had merely   41
blinked. "You talked to us several times," the surgeon had told me, and that
was the scariest part of all.

Twenty-four hours later, they get me out of bed and help me into a "walker."   42
As they stand me on my feet, my wife bursts into tears. "Your foot is touching
the ground!" I am afraid to look, but it is true: the surgeon has lengthened my
leg with that gleaming titanium and chrome-cobalt alloy ball-and-socket-joint.

"You'll need new shoes," the surgeon says. "Get a pair of Dock-Sides; they   43
have a secure grip. You'll need a $3/4$-inch lift in the heel, which can be as dis-
creet as you want."

I can't help thinking about those window displays of shoes, those elegant   44
shoes that, suddenly, I will be able to wear. Dock-Sides and sneakers, boots

and loafers, sandals and brogues. I feel, at last, a furtive sympathy for Imelda Marcos, the queen of soles.

45   The next day, I walk over to the trash can, and take a long look at the brick. I don't want to seem ungracious or unappreciative. We have walked long miles together. I feel disloyal, as if I am abandoning an old friend. I take a second look.

46   Maybe I'll have them bronzed.

Thinking Critically About Content

1. What is Gates's injury? How did it happen?

2. Why do you think Gates tells the readers about the school delinquent? According to the essay, what is the significance of the delinquent's actions on the day Gates's hip comes out of its socket?

3. When referring to his shoes at the end of the essay, why do you think Gates says, "Maybe I'll have them bronzed" (paragraph 46)?

Thinking Critically About Purpose and Audience

4. Why do you think Gates calls this essay "A Giant Step"?

5. What do you think Gates's purpose is in this essay? Explain your answer.

6. Out of 46 paragraphs, Gates uses 20 of them to describe his medical examination by the first doctor. Why do you think Gates spends so much time on this aspect of the story?

Thinking Critically about Sentences

7. How do the sentences in paragraphs 15–24 help you understand the prejudice of the doctor treating Gates?

8. Find two sentences in the essay that contain dialogue, and explain what they add to Gates's essay.

9. Write one or more complete sentences that Gates's mother might have said to her son when his problem was finally diagnosed.

Thinking Critically About Purpose and Audience

4. This essay is called "A Giant Step" because of the enormous "step" Gates thinks he took when he had the surgery. He knew he might have only one chance to have this surgery.

5. Gates wrote this essay to inform readers of his ordeal and to show them that people can overcome adversity, even under the worst situations.

6. Gates spends so much time writing about his medical examination because he wants his readers to see that his injury was compounded by the prejudice of a white doctor.

Thinking Critically About Sentences

7. These paragraphs help show the prejudice of the doctor because the doctor is asking Gates valid questions—for a doctor trying to help a patient in pain—but the doctor uses this information to judge that Gates is overreacting.

8. Answers will vary.

9. Answers will vary.

Elizabeth Wong

THE STRUGGLE TO BE AN ALL-AMERICAN GIRL

Focusing Your Attention

1. Imagine moving to a country where you don't know the language. Imagine going to school in a foreign country. How much of your

SUMMARY

In this essay, Wong describes her life at a Chinese school when heritage would you like to keep, and how much of your new culture would you like to adopt? Why?

2. The essay you are about to read talks about adopting the language and customs of a new country. How difficult do you think it would be to learn a new language? How difficult would understanding a new culture be? How are language and culture related?

Expanding Your Vocabulary

The following words are important to your understanding of this essay.

stoically: unemotionally (paragraph 1)

defiant: resistant (paragraph 3)

maniacal: insane (paragraph 3)

Nationalist Republic of China: Taiwan (paragraph 5)

kowtow: bow (paragraph 6)

ideographs: pictorial symbols (paragraph 7)

raunchy: crude (paragraph 8)

pedestrian: ordinary and dull (paragraph 8)

fanatical: enthusiastic (paragraph 10)

pidgin: flawed (paragraph 10)

smatterings: pieces (paragraph 10)

It's still there, the Chinese school on Yale Street where my brother and I used to 1 go. Despite the new coat of paint and the high wire fence, the school I knew 10 years ago remains remarkably, stoically the same.

Every day at 5 P.M., instead of playing with our fourth- and fifth-grade friends 2 or sneaking out to the empty lot to hunt ghosts and animal bones, my brother and I had to go to Chinese school. No amount of kicking, screaming, or pleading could dissuade my mother, who was solidly determined to have us learn the language of our heritage.

Forcibly, she walked us the seven long, hilly blocks from our home to school, 3 depositing our defiant tearful faces before the stern principal. My only memory of him is that he swayed on his heels like a palm tree, and he always clasped his impatient twitching hands behind his back. I recognized him as a repressed maniacal child killer, and knew that if we ever saw his hands we'd be in big trouble.

she was young and her desire to become more American.

READABILITY

8.0

ANSWERS TO QUESTIONS
Thinking Critically About Content

1. Answers will vary. The following are examples.

"instead of playing with our fourth- and fifth-grade friends or sneaking out to the empty lot to hunt ghosts and animal bones, my brother and I had to go to Chinese school" (para. 2)

"The room smelled like Chinese medicine,

and imported faraway mustiness. Like ancient mothballs or dirty closets. I hated that smell. I favored crisp new smells. Like soft French perfume that my American teacher wore in public school" (para. 4)

"I had better things to learn than ideographs copied painstakingly in lines that ran right to left. . . . Nancy Drew, my favorite book heroine, never spoke Chinese" (para. 7)

All of Wong's comparisons show that she prefers the American way of life over the Chinese.
2. The essay begins when Wong describes her schooling at age 10. By the end of the essay, she is an adult.
3. At the time Wong was granted the "cultural divorce," it reflects a happy time because she can finally focus on becoming more American. Later, when she says, "At last, I was one of you; I wasn't one of them. Sadly, I still am" (para. 14), the reader realizes she now thinks this divorce was a sad occasion.

Thinking Critically About Purpose and Audience

4. Wong wrote this essay to show the importance of retaining cultural identity. She probably wrote it for people who want to give up part of

4   We all sat in little chairs in an empty auditorium. The room smelled like Chinese medicine, an imported faraway mustiness. Like ancient mothballs or dirty closets. I hated that smell. I favored crisp new scents. Like the soft French perfume that my American teacher wore in public school.

5   There was a stage far to the right, flanked by an American flag and the flag of the Nationalist Republic of China, which was also red, white, and blue but not as pretty.

6   Although the emphasis at the school was mainly language—speaking, reading, writing—the lessons always began with an exercise in politeness. With the entrance of the teacher, the best student would tap a bell and everyone would get up, kowtow, and chant, "Sing san ho," the phonetic for "How are you, teacher?"

7   Being ten years old, I had better things to learn than ideographs copied painstakingly in lines that ran right to left from the tip of a *moc but,* a real ink pen that had to be held in an awkward way if blotches were to be avoided. After all, I could do the multiplication tables, name the satellites of Mars, and write reports on *Little Women* and *Black Beauty.* Nancy Drew, my favorite book heroine, never spoke Chinese.

8   The language was a source of embarrassment. More times than not, I had tried to disassociate myself from the nagging loud voice that followed me wherever I wandered in the nearby American supermarket outside Chinatown. The voice belonged to my grandmother, a fragile woman in her seventies who could outshout the best of the street vendors. Her humor was raunchy, her Chinese rhythmless, patternless. It was quick, it was loud, it was unbeautiful. It was not like the quiet, lilting romance of French or the gentle refinement of the American South. Chinese sounded pedestrian. Public.

9   In Chinatown, the comings and goings of hundreds of Chinese on their daily tasks sounded chaotic and frenzied. I did not want to be thought of as mad, as talking gibberish. When I spoke English, people nodded at me, smiled sweetly, said encouraging words. Even the people in my culture would cluck and say that I'd do well in life. "My, doesn't she move her lips fast," they would say, meaning that I'd be able to keep up with the world outside Chinatown.

10   My brother was even more fanatical than I about speaking English. He was especially hard on my mother, criticizing her, often cruelly, for her pidgin speech—smatterings of Chinese scattered like chop suey in her conversation. "It's not 'What it is,' Mom," he'd say in exasperation. "It's 'What *is* it, what *is* it, what *is* it!'" Sometimes Mom might leave out an occasional "the" or "a," or perhaps a verb of being. He would stop her in mid-sentence: "Say it again, Mom. Say it right." When he tripped over his own tongue, he'd blame it on her: "See, Mom, it's all your fault. You set a bad example."

What infuriated my mother most was when my brother cornered her on her 11
consonants, especially "r." My father had played a cruel joke on Mom by assign-
ing her an American name that her tongue wouldn't allow her to say. No matter
how hard she tried, "Ruth" always ended up "Luth" or "Roof."

After two years of writing with a *moc but* and reciting words with multiples 12
of meanings, I finally was granted a cultural divorce. I was permitted to stop
Chinese school.

I thought of myself as multicultural. I preferred tacos to egg rolls; I enjoyed 13
Cinco de Mayo more than Chinese New Year.

At last, I was one of you; I wasn't one of them. Sadly, I still am. 14

Thinking Critically About Content

1. Wong includes many comparisons between American and Chinese
   cultures in her essay. Find two comparisons, and explain how they
   show Wong's desire to become "more American."

2. What do you think the time span is from the beginning to the end of
   this essay? Explain your answer.

3. In paragraph 12, Wong states, "I finally was granted a cultural divorce.
   I was permitted to stop Chinese school." Do these two sentences
   reflect a happy or sad moment in Wong's life? Explain your answer.

Thinking Critically About Purpose and Audience

4. Why do you think Wong wrote this essay? Who did she probably
   write it for?

5. Wong explains different Chinese customs in her essay. How do these
   explanations help the reader understand Wong's "struggle to be an
   all-American girl"?

6. Why do you think Wong included the information about her brother
   criticizing her mother? How does this section affect the entire essay?

Thinking Critically About Sentences

7. Wong focuses on her struggle to become an American girl. What
   does the last sentence of the essay—"Sadly, I still am"—suggest about
   this struggle?

8. Look at paragraph 9. What is the topic sentence? Do you think the
   remainder of the sentences in the paragraph support this topic
   sentence? Explain your answer.

9. Write one or more complete sentences describing how you think
   Wong now wishes she had felt about Chinese schooling.

their heritage to adopt
someone else's.
5. By describing the dif-
ferent customs, Wong is
showing readers a definite
division between certain
American and Chinese
customs. She shows the
readers through this
division that her struggle
was difficult.
6. Wong probably in-
cluded the information
about her brother criti-
cizing her mother because
she wanted to show read-
ers how embarrassed they
both were when their
mother spoke improper
English—to the point
where her brother would
get angry with their
mother. This helps
readers see how desper-
ately Wong wanted
to become more
American.

*Thinking Critically
About Sentences*
7. The last sentence sug-
gests that Wong now
realizes how foolish
she felt to give up her
Chinese way of life.
8. "In Chinatown, the
comings and goings of
hundreds of Chinese on
their daily tasks sounded
chaotic and frenzied"
(sentence 1) is the topic
sentence of paragraph 9.
The remainder of the
sentences support this
topic sentence because
the topic sentence opens
the door to a discussion
about the "chaotic and
frenzied" language of the
Chinese.
9. Answers will vary.

Writing Topics: Narrating

Before you begin to write, you might want to review the writing process in Part I.

1. Gates's essay reminds us that we all have handicaps and problems in life—some more visible and obvious than others. Tell a story that summarizes one of your problems. Include in the story how you are dealing or have dealt with the problem.

2. Is culture always part of heritage? Can they be different? How engrained is your culture in you? Write a narrative that highlights an important part of your cultural heritage.

CHAPTER 41

Illustrating

Illustrating is giving examples to make a point. The following essays develop their main ideas primarily through examples. The first, "A Question of Trust" by Sherry Hemman Hogan, uses a handkerchief to represent some special lessons she learned about trust. In "Mortality," author Bailey White demonstrates with many examples her love of an old car and her insistence on keeping it running.

Sherry Hemman Hogan

A QUESTION OF TRUST

Focusing Your Attention

1. Think of someone special in your life. Why does this person mean so much to you?
2. In the essay you are about to read, a father's handkerchief becomes an important symbol to his daughter. Think of an object that reminds you of someone special. Explain why this object is important and what your associations are with this object.

Expanding Your Vocabulary

The following words are important to your understanding of this essay.

treacherous: dangerous (paragraph 1)

mariner: sailor, navigator (paragraph 1)

waterworks: tears (paragraph 4)

admonition: warning (paragraph 4)

SUMMARY
Hogan illustrates through many examples the significance of her father's handkerchief in this essay.

READABILITY
6.1

invariably: never changing (paragraph 9)

undaunted: fearless (paragraph 14)

1   When in treacherous waters, the mariner trusts the reliable beam of the lighthouse to guide his passage. My dependable beacon was my father's handkerchief. He didn't care for fancy French silk or Italian lace and had no need for those with elaborately embroidered initials. Dad preferred plain white cotton, the best buy from the local five-and-dime.

2   The uses of Dad's handkerchief were innumerable. It was a white flag hanging from the car window when the old station wagon overheated on vacation, filled with five squabbling kids, a dog, a cat, and two worn-out parents. The handkerchief, ever ready for back-seat disasters, sponged up melted Popsicles and oozing egg-salad sandwiches.

3   Amazing that a simple piece of cloth can evoke so many memories. It bound the wound of my favorite kitten after a close encounter with the neighbor's dog, then handled my sniffles too. It was Dad's amateur magician's prop for his disappearing-nickel trick. The first time I ever saw my dad cry, the crumpled cloth wiped his tears after he carried the lifeless body of his beloved German shepherd, Princess, out to her grave.

4   As a teen distraught over a crush on a boy, my waterworks ceased only when Dad offered me his handkerchief with the tender admonition "Here, take mine. You never seem to have one when you need it."

5   I remember going to him when I was 20 just before leaving on my first solo adventure, a trip to Europe. As the big moment arrived, I was scared, not so sure I was ready to be independent after all. The tears came as I confronted leaving everything I knew: my family, my home, my friends, and my boyfriend.

6   "You'll see, this is going to be one of the best experiences of your life," Dad said reassuringly as he handed me his familiar cotton square. "Trust me," he added with a wink.

7   Three years in France and Africa was, indeed, the greatest journey of my life. And upon returning, my first sight scanning through the throngs at Kennedy Airport was Dad's white handkerchief waving over the crowd.

8   It would make many appearances throughout my life—never more movingly than when my mom wept into it with joy at the triumphant birth of my daughter, Shannon, following two miscarriages.

9   Some 12 years later, and newly divorced, quite a few handkerchief sessions with Dad were in order as my daughter and I faced a whole new life together. After heart-wrenching discussions at Mom and Dad's, my search for a tissue

invariably ended with my father's familiar offer. Then, concerned about my going home to a dark house, my parents established a routine for their peace of mind as well as mine. Within minutes of my arrival, I would always call to say, "Hi, Dad. It's me. I'm home."

My father was then fighting his own battle, a 12-year war with prostate can- 10
cer. By Christmas, 1997, the illness had taken over his body. Knowing that we could lose him any time, we did our best to make it a joyous occasion. But when asked what he needed for presents, Dad could only say with a wry grin, "There's nothing I need where I'm going. Everything's provided for."

Still, we had to get him *something*. After a discussion with my sisters and   11
brother, I suggested handkerchiefs—he still kept a fresh one with him every day. I went to a boutique and bought some beautiful, expensive linen ones with the initial *R* for Robert, his first name, embroidered in brilliant black, red, and silver. Then, knowing my father, I ran to a discount store to purchase a few of the cheap variety. At home I placed them in three different gift boxes.

For the first time in 55 years, my parents were separated, living in two constant-   12
care rooms near each other in a retirement home. From his favorite chair, Dad opened the trio of gaily wrapped packages. "Well, what do you know!" he said each time, giving us the impish smile we cherished. "Just what I needed."

Setting aside the elegantly initialed linens, he chose a bargain hanky and   13
waved the familiar flag. "*This* is how I built that little nest egg for your mother," he said. "I'll only use the expensive ones for very important occasions."

Dad knew his time was short. As was his way, everything was prepared,   14
including his obituary. Undaunted, he and I spent several evenings writing it together. On a stormy night in January, I brought him the final draft. While he reclined in his favorite chair, I began to read aloud. Although strong during all our discussions, I could no longer suppress my emotions looking into the eyes that had seen me through 45 years. The tears just would not stop.

With tremendous effort, he squeezed my hand. "I'm ready to move on, Sher.   15
You know that. But look after your mother, okay?"

"You've . . . always been there for me, Dad," I barely choked out.   16

"And I always will be, just in a different way," he said. "Trust me."   17

I rooted in my purse for a tissue. Smiling, Dad said gently, "I've got lots of   18
these—thanks to you. Now dry your tears and blow your nose, okay? A good, hard one." He glanced out at the blustery weather. "You shouldn't have stayed so late. Driving may be tricky. Why don't you call me when you get in?"

During the ten-minute drive home, his words *trust me* echoed in my heart.   19
He was the most trustworthy person I knew. If he said something, he meant it. I felt far more peaceful now, but still found my voice catching when I phoned him as soon as I arrived. "Hi, Dad . . . I'm home." *Would this be the last time he would hear those words from me?*

ANSWERS TO
QUESTIONS
*Thinking Critically
About Content*
1. The handkerchief represents security for Hogan. She recounts how her father helped her feel secure every time he gave her his handkerchief.
2. Hogan's father always said "Trust me" when Hogan needed his advice. He says this just before he dies because he wants Hogan to know that he will look after her and that she will be OK even after he dies.
3. After she mysteriously finds the expensive handkerchief, Hogan remembers the words from Emerson that her dad spoke: "All I have seen teaches me to trust the Creator for all I have not seen." She realizes that her dad is where he is supposed to be and he will indeed watch out for her. She unpacks the Easter decorations as a symbol of this new understanding of her father.

*Thinking Critically
About Purpose
and Audience*
4. Hogan's purpose is to entertain. She uses examples from her life to show people not to take things for granted.
5. Hogan probably had a general audience in mind when she wrote this essay.
6. The phone call always signaled to her parents that she would be safe. In paragraph 19, she spoke this knowing she may

20   It was. Dad passed away just ten days later. We knew he was ready.

21   In the weeks after the funeral, we did our best to stay strong for Mom. One of the most difficult chores was clearing out his room, which held so many reminders. My mom had no extra space in her room. So Dad's chair found a home in my living room, where Shannon, now 18, adopted it as her favorite spot to snuggle, nap, and do homework. Her grandfather had been her hero too.

22   Eight weeks after Dad's death, Friday, March 13, the permanence of such a major loss hit. This date, gloomy for the superstitious, was always one of optimism for our family. My father was born on the 13th day of September in 1919, and he assured us from childhood that it was a lucky day.

23   This Friday the 13th, however, provided no reason to celebrate; Dad was no longer with us. Yes, I knew that he was in a better place, but the father I could always rely on was gone.

24   Even the promise of spring, due to arrive in just seven days, seemed too much to hope for. Easter, the essence of rebirth, was only a month away, but I couldn't even bring myself to unpack the decorations. I felt lifeless, as I had during other crises. And to whom had I gone then? Dad.

25   In tears, I called my sister. "Dad always helped me through things like this. He had the answers."

26   "Talk to him, Sher," she said gently. "I do all the time."

27   I hung up, tears still streaming down my face. I wandered aimlessly around the living room and scrabbled in an empty box of Kleenex. Then I talked to him. "Oh, Dad. I know you're in a better place. I have that faith, mostly because of you. But I miss you so much. And I just wish I *knew* that you're all right."

28   Silence. Nothing. I felt worse. Sobbing uncontrollably, I could feel grief washing through my entire body. My hands turned icy cold, and I started to shake all over.

29   That's when I saw it. Out of the corner of my eye, a big square of white peeked from beneath Dad's chair. "What on earth is that?" I mumbled, impatient because I had just tidied the room that morning.

30   Stooping to pick it up, I stared through the fog of tears. It was one of Dad's new handkerchiefs with the embroidered design. I clutched it, stroking the elegant black letter *R*.

31   I took a few deep breaths and tried to calm myself. My mind worked. I clean this room every morning, I thought. I vacuum the entire rug, moving this chair, twice a week. Where on earth did this come from?

32   I felt pretty silly. But when we'd emptied Dad's room, I had carefully explored that chair, collecting pens and paper clips and other odds and ends that had slipped between the seat and armrests. Once in my living room, that chair had been lovingly cleaned. It had been bounced upon by my neighbors' grandkids

and survived my daughter's slumber party with seven teenage girls scrambling in and out of it throughout the night. So why had the handkerchief shown up now?

I paced through the house, shaking my head. This, I could not explain.   33

"All I have seen teaches me to trust the Creator for all I have not seen." I   34
could almost hear Dad quoting Emerson. And then his own words to me at Christmas came back: "I'll only use the expensive ones for very important occasions."

Gently tucking the embroidered cloth in my pocket with new resolve, I   35
retrieved the Easter decorations: the bunnies, eggs and butterflies—all symbols of creation, new life and rebirth, the very promise of spring.

Yes, I could trust that spring would arrive—it always does. And I could trust   36
the words of my father.

That handkerchief, which so mysteriously appeared, now has a treasured   37
place on my desk. It's a reminder that perhaps some things in life are better left unexplained. Leaps of faith can be very good exercise for the healing heart.

As far as I was concerned, it was Dad's way of sending me a message. It was   38
his way of saying, "Hi, Sher. It's me. I'm okay. I'm home."

Thinking Critically About Content

1. What does the handkerchief represent in this essay? Explain your answer.
2. Why does Hogan's father say, "Trust me," just before he dies (paragraph 17)?
3. Why does Hogan finally unpack the Easter decorations at the end of the essay?

Thinking Critically About Purpose and Audience

4. What do you think Hogan's purpose is in this essay?
5. What audience do you think Hogan had in mind when she wrote this essay?
6. What is important about the phone call to her father, saying, "Hi, Dad . . . I'm home" (paragraphs 9 and 19)? What other references to *home* are important in the essay?

Thinking Critically About Sentences

7. List the examples the author uses in paragraph 2. Does the paragraph's topic sentence introduce them adequately? Explain your answer.

never speak to her father again, and it was her way of telling him she would be safe when he was gone. Some additional references to *home* include the following:

"I confronted leaving everything I knew: my family, my home, my friends, and my boyfriend" (para. 5)

"Then, concerned about my going home to a dark house, my parents established a routine for their peace of mind as well as mine" (para. 9)

"Hi Sher. It's me. I'm okay. I'm home." (para. 38)

They depict *home* as a safe, secure place.

Thinking Critically About Sentences

7. The topic sentence is "The uses of Dad's handkerchief were innumerable." This sentence adequately introduces the rest of the sentences because it provides Hogan a way to introduce her examples:

"It was a white flag hanging from the car window when the station wagon overheated on vacation, filled with five squabbling kids, a dog, a cat, and two worn-out parents."

It was "ever ready for backseat disasters, sponged up melted Popsicles and oozing egg-salad sandwiches."

8. The short sentences help emphasize her grief; it is quick and immediate, and the short words demonstrate this well.
9. Answers will vary.

8. In paragraph 28, Hogan uses very short sentences. How do these sentences help illustrate her mood in this paragraph?

9. Write one or more complete sentences from the father's point of view about the relationship he had with his daughter.

Bailey White

MORTALITY

SUMMARY

White illustrates her long relationship with her car in this humorous essay, providing examples that show her love for the car.

READABILITY

5.2

Focusing Your Attention

1. Think of an item like an old shirt or pair of jeans that you want to keep forever, even though it might wear out. Explain why this item is important to you.

2. The essay you are about to read talks about a special relationship between a car and its owner. If you could have any car, what car would you choose? Why? Explain your answer.

Expanding Your Vocabulary

The following words are important to your understanding of this essay.

disintegrated: fell to pieces (paragraph 5)

odometer: distance gauge (paragraph 5)

fire wall: wall between the engine and the passenger compartment of a vehicle (paragraph 6)

slopped: poured (paragraph 10)

ominous: alarming (paragraph 11)

internal combustion: burning fuel inside an engine (paragraph 13)

hurtling: moving at a great speed (paragraph 13)

amble: walk (paragraph 22)

1   It really makes you feel your age when you get a letter from your insurance agent telling you that the car you bought, only slightly used, the year you got out of college, is now an antique. "Beginning with your next payment, your insurance premiums will reflect this change in classification," the letter said.

2   I went out and looked at the car. I thought back over the years. I could almost hear my uncle's disapproving voice. "You should never buy a used car," he had

told me the day I brought it home. Ten years later I drove that used car to his funeral. I drove my sister, Louise, to the hospital in that car to have her first baby, and I drove to Atlanta in that car when the baby graduated from Georgia Tech with a degree in physics.

"When are you going to get a new car?" my friends asked me.   3

"I don't need a new car," I said. "This car runs fine."   4

I changed the oil often, and I kept good tires on it. It always got me where I   5 wanted to go. But the stuffing came out of the backseat and the springs poked through, and the dashboard disintegrated. At 300,000 miles the odometer quit turning, but I didn't really care to know how far I had driven.

A hole wore in the floor where my heel rested in front of the accelerator, and   6 the insulation all peeled off the fire wall. "Old piece of junk," my friends whispered. The seat-belt catch wore out, and I tied on a huge bronze hook with a fireman's knot.

Big flashy cars would zoom past me. People would shake their fists out the   7 windows. "Get that clunker off the road!" they would shout.

Then one day on my way to work, the car coughed, sputtered, and stopped,   8 "This is it," I thought, and I gave it a pat. "It's been a good car."

I called the mechanic. "Tow it in," I said. "I'll have to decide what to do." After   9 work I went over there. I was feeling very glum. The mechanic laughed at me. "It's not funny," I said. "I've had that car a long time."

"You know what's wrong with that car?" he said. "That car was out of gas."   10 So I slopped a gallon of gas in the tank and drove ten more years. The gas gauge never worked again after that day, but I got to where I could tell when the gas was low by the smell. I think it was the smell of the bottom of the tank.

There was also a little smell of brake fluid, a little smell of exhaust, a little   11 smell of oil, and after all the years a little smell of me. Car smells. And sounds. The wonderful sound when the engine finally catches on a cold day, and an ominous *tick tick* in July when the radiator is working too hard. The windshield wipers said "Gracie Allen Gracie Allen Gracie Allen." I didn't like a lot of conversation in the car because I had to keep listening for a little skip that meant I needed to jump out and adjust the carburetor.

I kept a screwdriver close at hand—and a pint of brake fluid, and a new   12 rotor, just in case. "She's strange," my friends whispered. "And she drives so slow."

I don't know how fast I drove. The speedometer had quit working years ago.   13 But when I would look down through the hole in the floor and see the pavement, a gray blur, whizzing by just inches away from my feet, and feel the tremendous heat of internal combustion pouring back through the fire wall into my lap, and hear each barely contained explosion just as a heart attack victim is able to hear his own heartbeat, it didn't feel like slow to me. A whiff of brake fluid would remind me just what a tiny thing I was relying on to stop myself

ANSWERS TO QUESTIONS
Thinking Critically About Content
1. Answers will vary. The following are examples.

"But the stuffing came out of the backseat and the springs poked through, and the dashboard disintegrated. At 300,000 miles the odometer quit turning." (para. 5)

"A hole wore in the floor where my heel rested in front of the accelerator, and the insulation all peeled off the fire wall." (para. 6)

"The seat-belt catch wore out, and I tied on a huge bronze hook with a fireman's knot." (para. 6)

2. She decided to buy a new car after her old car was reclassified as an antique by her insurance company. She drove the old one for so long because it had become her friend; she knew every quirk about the car and enjoyed driving it the way it was.

3. She can be talking about either. It could be a reference to the car because the car is still working after so many years. Or she might be talking about herself because she realizes if a car can hold on that long, she might be able to as well.

Thinking Critically About Purpose and Audience

4. White calls her essay "Mortality" because she wrote an essay about a car that should actually have broken down long ago but is still alive.

from hurtling along the surface of the earth at an unnatural speed, and when I finally arrived at my destination, I would slump back, unfasten the seat belt hook with trembling hands, and stagger out. I would gather up my things and give the car a last look. "Thank you, sir," I would say. "We got here one more time."

14   But after I got that letter, I began thinking about getting a new car. I read the newspaper every night. Finally I found one that sounded good. It was the same make as my car, but almost new. "Call Steve," the ad said.

15   I went to see the car. It was parked in Steve's driveway. It was a fashionable wheat color. There was carpet on the floor, and the seats were covered with a soft, velvety-feeling stuff. It smelled like acrylic and vinyl and Steve. The instrument panel looked like what you would need to run a jet plane. I turned a knob. Mozart's Concerto for Flute and Harp poured out of four speakers. "But how can you listen to the engine with music playing?" I asked Steve.

16   I turned the key. The car started instantly. No desperate pleadings, no wild hopes, no exquisitely paired maneuvers with the accelerator and the choke. Just instant ignition. I turned off the radio. I could barely hear the engine running, a low, steady hum. I fastened my seat belt. Nothing but a click.

17   Steve got in the passenger seat, and we went for a test drive. We floated down the road. I couldn't hear a sound, but I decided it must be time to shift gears. I stomped around on the floor and grabbed Steve's knee before I remembered it had automatic transmission. "You mean you just put it in 'Drive' and drive?" I asked.

18   Steve scrunched himself way over against his door and clamped his knees together. He tested his seat belt. "Have you ever driven a car before?" he asked.

19   I bought it for two thousand dollars. I rolled all the windows up by mashing a button beside my elbow, set the air-conditioning on "Recirc," and listened to Vivaldi all the way home.

20   So now I have two cars. I call them my new car and my real car. Most of the time I drive my new car. But on some days I go out to the barn and get in my real car. I shoo the rats out of the backseat and crank it up. Even without daily practice my hands and feet know just what to do. My ears perk up, and I sniff the air. I add a little brake fluid, a little water. I sniff again. It'll need gas next week and an oil change.

21   I back it out, and we roll down the road. People stop and look. They smile. "Neat car!" they say.

22   When I pull into the parking lot, my friends shake their heads and chuckle. They amble into the building. They're already thinking about their day's work. But I take one last look at the car and think what an amazing thing it is, internal combustion. And how wonderful to be still alive!

Thinking Critically About Content

1. Using examples from the essay, describe the kind of car White drove.

2. Why did White decide to buy a new car? Why do you think she drove the old one for so long?

3. Whom is White talking about when she says, "And how wonderful to be still alive!" (paragraph 22)—the car or herself? Explain your answer.

Thinking Critically About Purpose and Audience

4. Why do you think White calls her essay "Mortality"?

5. What type of reader do you think would most understand and appreciate this story?

6. What specific examples about the car were most interesting to you? In what ways do these examples help you understand White's attachment to the car?

Thinking Critically About Sentences

7. The topic sentence of paragraph 20 is "So now I have two cars." Do all of the other sentences in this paragraph explain this main idea? Explain your answer.

8. What do the sentences in dialogue form in paragraphs 12 and 13 add to the essay?

9. Write one or more complete sentences about how the car might feel about White's attachment to it.

5. Anyone can appreciate this story because of its humor, but people who are particularly attached to a car, like White, might appreciate it best.
6. Answers will vary.

Thinking Critically About Sentences
7. The sentences in paragraph 20 all support the paragraph's topic sentence. Sentence 2 talks about both cars. Sentence 3 refers to the new car, and sentences 4–10 refer to White's "real car."
8. In paragraph 12, the dialogue provides a different point of view in the essay—that of White's friends regarding White. In paragraph 13, White is thanking her car, which makes her relationship with her car more real.
9. Answers will vary.

Writing Topics: Illustrating

Before you begin to write, you might want to review the writing process in Part I.

1. Like the handkerchief in Hogan's essay, what objects carry special emotional value for you? Explain what one of these objects represents in your life.

2. After reading White's essay, what do you think are the main characteristics of the relationship between a car and its owner? How does this relationship develop? Do you have a similar relationship with your car, bike, motorcycle, feet, or bus pass? Explain your answer.

42

Analyzing a Process

Process analysis is a form of explaining. The essays you are about to read demonstrate both types of process analysis: how to do something and how something happened. They both tell what comes first, second, and so on. The first essay, "Ferrying Dreamers to the Other Side" by Tomás Robles, tells how illegal immigrants from Mexico are smuggled across the Texas border. In the second essay, "The Burden of Race," Arthur Ashe, one of the world's greatest tennis players, explains the effect that race has had on his life soon after he finds out he has AIDS.

Tomás Robles

FERRYING DREAMERS TO THE OTHER SIDE

Focusing Your Attention

SUMMARY

This essay outlines Robles's method of smuggling Mexicans into the United States.

READABILITY
4.0

1. Think about the journey from your car or dorm room to the classroom you now sit in. In order, list every action you had to take to get to your seat. Don't forget to list small details like walking up stairs or opening doors.

2. The essay you are about to read describes the process of smuggling Mexican immigrants across the Texas border. Explain why you think people would risk their lives and leave their families and possessions behind to come to the United States.

Expanding Your Vocabulary

The following words are important to your understanding of this essay.

> *pateros:* smugglers (paragraph 2)
>
> **coyote:** smuggler (paragraph 8)
>
> **Matamoros:** a city in Mexico (paragraph 8)

mordida: payoff (literally, bite) (paragraph 12)

La Migra: Immigration (paragraph 13)

wetback: illegal immigrant (paragraph 13)

gringos: Americans (paragraph 20)

First I look at you. I study you. Then I know whether or not you're going to cross   1
to the other side.

When people arrive, they're afraid. If I see that you've just stepped off the bus   2
and I ask if you want to get to the other side, you're not going to say yes. You're
uncertain. You'll think to yourself, "Who is this guy? Is he a criminal? A policeman?" So you'll tell me, "No, I am not going to cross. I'm just here to visit some
relatives." Now, when a lot of *pateros* hear this, they'll just walk away. Not me. I
say, "You know what? Whatever you want to do, my job is to cross people over to
the other side, and I won't charge you a nickel until we get there."

I just keep talking. I don't stop. It's the *patero* who talks the best that gets the   3
most people. I say, "It doesn't matter to me if you've got no money. All you need
is a telephone number of someone over there, a relative or someone else who can
pay your way. Here, I'll cover your food and lodging. I'll give you a place to sleep
and everything. I won't charge you a penny until we've crossed over. Do you
have the number of someone on the other side?"

Then you'll look at me and say, "Okay, I want to cross. How much do you   4
charge?"

"Six hundred dollars from here to Houston. Everyone charges the same. But   5
listen, we can't talk here. It's dangerous with all these police. I live just one block
away. Let's go to my house. You can wash up. I'll buy you something to eat and
we can talk some more."

Then you follow me, see, and we keep talking. Once you're at my house,   6
you're mine. That's how it works. Before we cross the border, you give me the
telephone number of someone on the other side, and we call. If they say, "We
don't have any money" or "We don't know him," that's it, there's no deal. That's
how we arrange things.

We put you up in a hotel until we've gathered ten, twelve, or fifteen people.   7
Sometimes it takes two or three days. We won't carry just two or three people
across. It isn't worth it. We need at least eight, because we never work alone. We
usually cross over with three or four *pateros*. When we've got everyone together,
we tell them, "At four o'clock we're going to cross the river. You'll have to leave
your suitcases here. This isn't a vacation. You're going to cross with just a shirt
and a pair of pants. Okay?"

8   Then we say, "If they catch us, don't tell them who's carrying you across. If they ask who helped you cross or which one's the coyote, you just say, 'Nobody's carrying us across. We're all just looking for work.' That way, if Immigration finds us, they'll just send us back across the border, back to Matamoros. They won't jail us and we'll cross over again. If Immigration catches us, they'll ask for our names. We'll give them fake names, and if they catch us again, we'll give them different names. They never remember us."

9   Once we've talked this over and everyone understands, we take a taxi that drops us off close to the river. On the Mexican side, the police patrol the river on horseback. If they see us, they'll come over to check us out.

10   "Listen, we're just going over to Brownsville to earn a little money."

11   "Okay, just give us a little something so we can buy a drink."

12   So we give them a little money and they let us pass. If we're caught by police who know we're *pateros,* we're screwed. They'll make us pay them one, two, maybe three hundred dollars. If we don't pay them, they'll arrest us for some crime we've never committed. They won't just charge us with being *pateros.* They'll charge us with assault and really screw us. . . . We have to work with them. After we give them their *mordida,* they'll let us pass.

13   Then we go on to the river. We take off our clothes and put them in a bag. We get in the water and cross the river naked. If we crossed wearing clothes, when we got to the other side we'd be wet and people would notice. If La Migra sees that, they'll say, "Look, there goes another wetback," and they'll nail you.

14   Sometimes we cross people who don't know how to swim. We buy inner tubes and put the people inside. They get nervous, but I tell them, "Don't worry if you can't swim. Just hold on tight to one of my feet." They'll grab on to my foot, and I'll swim across the river using my hands. It's about thirty feet across, but when the water's high, the current gets strong. If you know what you're doing, it's easy, but if not, it can be dangerous. Lots of people drown.

15   On the American side of the river, there are bandits who carry knives and guns. They'll wait for you and catch you as you get out of the water, naked. They'll tear open your bag looking for money. They'll check your socks and your shoes. They look everywhere. If you've got good boots, nice pants, or a decent shirt, they'll steal them. Sometimes they take everything. Other times they beat you up or threaten you with knives. That's happened to me many times. I've got a knife wound on my leg, another one over there, and another here. Look at all these scars. Look at how they've sliced me up.

16   Once we've crossed the river, we walk calmly into Brownsville. Then we call up some friends who drive taxis. We put five people in each taxi and carry them to a hotel. We get one room for everybody. The next day, around three or four in the morning, we wake everyone up. We divide the group between three cars. That way if the police or Immigration stop us on the way, they'll only catch one

ANSWERS TO QUESTIONS
Thinking Critically About Content

1. From a *patero's* point of view, the following are steps in the process for illegally crossing from Mexico to the United States.

   a. Find a person who wants to cross the border illegally.
   b. Put the person up in a hotel until 10 to 15 people are gathered, which can take two to three days.
   c. Take a taxi close to the river and bribe the police if necessary.
   d. Go to the river, put all clothes in a bag, and cross the river naked.
   e. Once everyone is safely across the river, dress and walk calmly into Brownsville.
   f. Stay in a hotel until around 3 or 4 the next morning, when people are divided and put into three cars.
   g. Get out of the car before the checkpoint so the driver,

group and the other two will make it through to Houston. We lose less money if we split up, because when they catch you, they arrest the driver, confiscate the car, and send everyone back to the other side.

Before we get to the immigration checkpoint, we get out of the car and let the   17 driver continue north. The drivers have their papers, so they can pass through the checkpoint. Then we walk into the countryside. It's dark, but we know where we're going. There are power lines that we use to guide us. We go on together, walking and walking, for five or six hours. There are lots of rattlesnakes, and you can die if they bite you. We walk on through the brush until we get to a place to rest. Then one person—only one—goes out to the road to see if the drivers are there yet. When they arrive, we get back in the cars and off we go to Houston.

Then we drive to a special house. Our boss meets us there. We gather every-   18 one into the house, park the cars, close the door, and then start calling the phone numbers, one by one. "Okay, we've got your nephew here"—or your son, your brother, whoever. "Come on over with the money." They come over and pay us. We give them the person and off they go. There's times when they don't want to pay or when they only have three or four hundred dollars. Sometimes they'll give us rings, watches, or bracelets. If they don't have anyone who can pay and nothing to give us, we take the people back to Matamoros. If there's someone who'll buy the people off of us, we'll sell them.

Our boss collects the money, and when everyone's gone he divides it up.   19 He takes his cut and everyone else gets a share. Then we go to the best bar in Houston and get drunk. We take a lot of chances on the road—the police might catch us, Immigration might send us back. Who knows? We might drown in the river or someone might kill us. So we celebrate to make up for everything we've gone through. We drink and drink until the table is covered with beer bottles. We have girls on all sides of us, sitting on our laps, dancing. We have a great time. Nothing but *pateros* and women. There in that bar, for one night, we're all kings.

I know that what I do is illegal, but it's man who invented these laws, not   20 God. It's the American government that doesn't want us to pass people to the other side. They don't want us to be with you, the gringos. I'm not doing anything wrong. I'm not robbing, beating, or killing anyone. I'm not working against God. Where these people are from, they earn so little they can't even support their families. So even though what I do is illegal, in the end it's actually good. I'm helping people to better themselves, to realize their dreams.

I'm ready for whatever might happen. If today or tomorrow they kill me, or   21 a snake bites me, or they crush the life out of me, my kids will have money in the bank. Every day, I risk my life for my family. It's an adventure being a *patero,* a beautiful life—to know the road, to cross the river. If tomorrow something were to happen to me, who cares? In the end, every man suffers for the life he leads.

with the proper papers, can get through.

h. Walk five or six hours in the countryside using power lines as a guide until its safe to get back into the car.

i. Go to Houston to a special house, where the boss calls friends and family of the immigrants to come and pay for the passage.

j. Divide up the money, and get drunk to celebrate not getting caught by Immigration or killed by robbers.

2. The authorities probably already know the tricks the *pateros* use, but Robles's essay may give authorities some insight into the lengths to which people will go to get into the United States.

3. From Robles's tone, he sounds as though he is providing a necessary service, but because of the lying and cheating he does to avoid detection, jail, and death, he is probably aware that it is not honorable.

Thinking Critically About Purpose and Audience

4. He probably told this story for money. He also seems to think that he is too clever to get caught.

5. People in border towns would most likely appreciate this essay most because they can identify

with the immigration problem and the information is interesting.
6. Answers will vary.

Thinking Critically About Sentences
7. Answers will vary. The following are examples.
"Six hundred dollars from here to Houston." (para. 5)
"We put you up in a hotel until we've gathered ten, twelve, or fifteen people." (para. 7)
"Sometimes it takes two or three days." (para. 7)
"They'll make us pay them one, two, maybe three hundred dollars." (para. 12)
8. Robles is stating that if he dies a tragic death, it will be because he lived a dangerous and tragic life, just as people who live heroic lives deserve heroic deaths.
9. Answers will vary.

Thinking Critically About Content

1. List the steps of the process that Robles explains.

2. On the basis of the information given in this essay, do you think authorities can now catch *pateros* like Robles? Explain your answer.

3. Do you think Robles believes he is providing an honorable service to the Mexican people? Why or why not?

Thinking Critically About Purpose and Audience

4. Why do you think Robles tells readers how he illegally smuggles Mexicans across the border?

5. Who do you think would most appreciate reading Robles's story? Explain your answer.

6. Which step of this process is most interesting to you? Why? In what ways is this step important to the process?

Thinking Critically About Sentences

7. Find three sentences that contain specific numbers. What do these details add to your understanding of Robles's smuggling process?

8. Explain the meaning of the last sentence in the essay: "In the end, every man suffers for the life he leads." Do you think it is a good ending for this essay? Explain your answer.

9. In one or more complete sentences, write down what you think an immigration officer would say to Robles if they met.

Arthur Ashe

THE BURDEN OF RACE

SUMMARY
In this passage from *Days of Grace*, Ashe explains how prejudice and racism in this country often cast a shadow over his life.

READABILITY
8.8

Focusing Your Attention

1. Have you or anyone you know ever experienced prejudice of any sort? What were the circumstances?

2. In the excerpt you are about to read, Arthur Ashe tells about a time he faced a difficult racial situation. Have you ever had to deal publicly with any kind of prejudice? What did you do? How did it make you feel?

Expanding Your Vocabulary

The following words are important to your understanding of this essay.

probing: penetrating (paragraph 1)

groping: struggling (paragraph 1)

onerous: hard to bear (paragraph 8)

baffled: puzzled (paragraph 9)

inevitably: unavoidably (paragraph 9)

fatalistic: accepting of whatever happens (paragraph 11)

self-pitying: feeling sorry for oneself (paragraph 11)

cynical: scornful (paragraph 11)

maudlin: overly sentimental (paragraph 11)

literally: actually (paragraph 13)

metaphorically: symbolically, figuratively (paragraph 13)

USTA: United States Tennis Association (paragraph 13)

mar: ruin (paragraph 14)

hypersensitivity: extreme sensitivity (paragraph 14)

nuances: subtle shades of meaning or feeling (paragraph 14)

clamorous: loud (paragraph 14)

sullied: disgraced, ruined (paragraph 19)

pensive: thoughtful (paragraph 27)

Eurocentric: viewing all cultures through the lens of European culture (paragraph 30)

I had spent more than an hour talking in my office at home with a reporter for 1 *People* magazine. Her editor had sent her to do a story about me and how I was coping with AIDS. The reporter's questions had been probing and yet respectful of my right to privacy. Now, our interview over, I was escorting her to the door. As she slipped on her coat, she fell silent. I could see that she was groping for the right words to express her sympathy for me before she left.

"Mr. Ashe, I guess this must be the heaviest burden you have ever had to 2 bear, isn't it?" she asked finally.

I thought for a moment, but only a moment. "No, it isn't. It's a burden, all 3 right. But AIDS isn't the heaviest burden I have had to bear."

4   "Is there something worse? Your heart attack?"

5   I didn't want to detain her, but I let the door close with both of us still inside. "You're not going to believe this," I said to her, "but being black is the greatest burden I've had to bear."

6   "You can't mean that."

7   "No question about it. Race has always been my biggest burden. Having to live as a minority in America. Even now it continues to feel like an extra weight tied around me."

8   I can still recall the surprise and perhaps even the hurt on her face. I may even have surprised myself, because I simply had never thought of comparing the two conditions before. However, I stand by my remark. Race is for me a more onerous burden than AIDS. My disease is the result of biological factors over which we, thus far, have had no control. Racism, however, is entirely made by people, and therefore it hurts and inconveniences infinitely more.

9   Since our interview (skillfully presented as a first-person account by me) appeared in *People* in June 1992, many people have commented on my remark. A radio station in Chicago aimed primarily at blacks conducted a lively debate on its merits on the air. Most African Americans have little trouble understanding and accepting my statement, but other people have been baffled by it. Even Donald Dell, my close friend of more than thirty years, was puzzled. In fact, he was so troubled that he telephoned me in the middle of the night from Hamburg, Germany, to ask if I had been misquoted. No, I told him, I had been quoted correctly. Some people have asked me flatly, what could you, Arthur Ashe, possibly have to complain about? Do you want more money or fame than you already have? Isn't AIDS inevitably fatal? What can be worse than death?

10   The novelist Henry James suggested somewhere that it is a complex fate being an American. I think it is a far more complex fate being an African American. I also sometimes think that this indeed may be one of those fates that is worse than death.

11   I do not want to be misunderstood. I do not mean to appear fatalistic, self-pitying, cynical, or maudlin. Proud to be an American, I am also proud to be an African American. I delight in the accomplishments of fellow citizens of my color. When one considers the odds against which we have labored, we have achieved much. I believe in life and hope and love, and I turn my back on death until I must face my end in all its finality. I am an optimist, not a pessimist. Still, a pall of sadness hangs over my life and the lives of almost all African Americans because of what we as a people have experienced historically in America, and what we as individuals experience each and every day. Whether one is a welfare recipient trapped in some blighted "housing project" in the inner city or a former Wimbledon champion who is easily recognized on the streets and whose home

is a luxurious apartment in one of the wealthiest districts of Manhattan, the sadness is still there.

In some respects, I am a prisoner of the past. A long time ago, I made peace 12 with the state of Virginia and the South. While I, like other blacks, was once barred from free association with whites, I returned time and time again, under the new rule of desegregation, to work with whites in my hometown and across the South. But segregation had achieved by that time what it was intended to achieve: It left me a marked man, forever aware of a shadow of contempt that lays across my identity and my sense of self-esteem. Subtly the shadow falls on my reputation, the way I know I am perceived; the mere memory of it darkens my most sunny days. I believe that the same is true for almost every African American of the slightest sensitivity and intelligence. Again, I don't want to overstate the case. I think of myself, and others think of me, as supremely self-confident. I know objectively that it is almost impossible for someone to be as successful as I have been as an athlete and to lack self-assurance. Still, I also know that the shadow is always there; only death will free me, and blacks like me, from its pall.

The shadow fell across me recently on one of the brightest days, literally and 13 metaphorically, of my life. On August 30, 1992, the day before the U.S. Open, the USTA and I together hosted an afternoon of tennis at the National Tennis Center in Flushing Meadows, New York. The event was a benefit for the Arthur Ashe Foundation for the Defeat of AIDS. Before the start, I was nervous. Would the invited stars (McEnroe, Graf, Navratilova, et al.) show up? Would they cooperate with us or be difficult to manage? And on the eve of a Grand Slam tournament, would fans pay to see light-hearted tennis? The answers were all a resounding yes (just over ten thousand fans turned out). With CBS televising the event live and Aetna having provided the air time, a profit was assured. The sun shone brightly, the humidity was mild, and the temperature hovered in the low 80s.

What could mar such a day? The shadow of race, and my sensitivity, or per- 14 haps hypersensitivity, to its nuances. Sharing the main stadium box with Jeanne, Camera [Ashe's wife and young daughter], and me, at my invitation, were Stan Smith [a former tennis champion], his wife Marjory, and their daughter Austin. The two little girls were happy to see one another. During Wimbledon in June, they had renewed their friendship when we all stayed near each other in London. Now Austin, seven years old, had brought Camera a present. She had come with twin dolls, one for herself, one for Camera. A thoughtful gesture on Austin's part, and on her parents' part, no doubt. The Smiths are fine, religious people. Then I noticed that Camera was playing with her doll above the railing of the box, in full view of the attentive network television cameras. The doll was the problem, or rather, the fact that the doll was conspicuously a blond. Camera owns dolls of all colors, nationalities, and ethnic varieties. But she was now on national television playing with a blond doll. Suddenly I heard voices in my head, the voices of irate listeners to a call-in show on some "black format" radio station. I imagined insistent, clamorous callers attacking Camera, Jeanne, and me:

15   "Can you believe the doll Arthur Ashe's daughter was holding up at the AIDS benefit? Wasn't that a shame?"

16   "Is that brother sick or what? Somebody ought to teach that poor child about her true black self!"

17   "What kind of role model is Arthur Ashe if he allows his daughter to be brainwashed in that way?"

18   "Doesn't the brother understand that he is corrupting his child's mind with notions about the superiority of the white woman? I tell you, I thought we were long past that!"

19   The voices became louder in my head. Despite the low humidity, I began to squirm in my seat. What should I do? Should I say, To hell with what some people might think? I know that Camera likes her blond dolls, black dolls, brown dolls, Asian dolls, Indian dolls just about equally; I know that for a fact, because I have watched her closely. I have searched for signs of racial partiality in her, indications that she may be dissatisfied with herself, with her own color. I have seen none. But I cannot dismiss the voices. I try always to live practically, and I do not wish to hear such comments on the radio. On the other hand, I do not want Austin's gift to be sullied by an ungracious response. Finally, I act.

20   "Jeanne," I whisper, "we have to do something."

21   "About what?" she whispers back.

22   "That doll. We have to get Camera to put that doll down."

23   Jeanne takes one look at Camera and the doll and she understands immediately. Quietly, cleverly, she makes the dolls disappear. Neither Camera nor Austin is aware of anything unusual happening. Smoothly, Jeanne has moved them on to some other distraction.

24   I am unaware if Margie Smith has noticed us, but I believe I owe her an explanation. I get up and go around to her seat. Softly I tell her why the dolls have disappeared. Margie is startled, dumbfounded.

25   "Gosh, Arthur, I never thought about that. I never ever thought about anything like that!"

26   "You don't have to think about it," I explain. "But it happens to us, in similar situations, all the time."

27   "All the time?" She is pensive now.

28   "All the time. It's perfectly understandable. And it certainly is not your fault. You were doing what comes naturally. But for us, the dolls make for a bit of a problem. All for the wrong reasons. It shouldn't be this way, but it is."

29   I return to my seat, but not to the elation I had felt before I saw that blond doll in Camera's hand. I feel myself becoming more and more angry. I am angry at the

---

ANSWERS TO QUESTIONS

Thinking Critically About Content

1. Ashe attended a special event the day before the U.S. Open in New York, which was a benefit for the Arthur Ashe Foundation for the Defeat of AIDS. The event was almost ruined when Ashe overreacted to a blonde doll his daughter was playing with. Ashe was afraid that people would criticize him for letting his daughter have a white doll, so he took the doll away from her. Later, he was embarrassed that he felt he needed to modify his child's behavior.

2. Ashe believes that race is more of a burden than AIDS because AIDS "is the result of biological factors over which we, thus far, have had no control" whereas racism "is entirely made by people, and therefore it hurts and

force that made me act, the force of racism in all its complexity, as it spreads into the world and creates defensiveness and intolerance among the very people harmed by racism. I am also angry with myself. I am angry with myself because I have just acted out of pure practicality, not out of morality. The moral act would have been to let Camera have her fun, because she was innocent of any wrongdoing. Instead, I had tampered with her innocence, her basic human right to act impulsively, to accept a gift from a friend in the same beautiful spirit in which it was given.

Deeply embarrassed now, I am ashamed at what I have done. I have made Camera adjust her behavior merely because of the likelihood that some people in the African American community would react to her innocence foolishly and perhaps even maliciously. I know I am not misreading the situation. I would have had telephone calls that very evening about the unsuitability of Camera's doll. Am I being a hypocrite? Yes, definitely, up to a point. I have allowed myself to give in to those people who say we must avoid even the slightest semblance of "Eurocentric" influence. But I also know what stands behind the entire situation. Racism ultimately created the state in which defensiveness and hypocrisy are our almost instinctive responses and innocence and generosity are invitations to trouble.

This incident almost ruined the day for me. That night, when Jeanne and I talked about the excitement of the afternoon, and the money that would go to AIDS research and education because of the event, we nevertheless ended up talking mostly about the incident of the dolls. We also talked about perhaps its most ironic aspect. In 1954, when the Supreme Court ruled against school segregation in *Brown* v. *Board of Education,* some of the most persuasive testimony came from the psychologist Dr. Kenneth Clark concerning his research on black children and their pathetic preference for white dolls over black. In 1992, the dolls are still a problem.

Once again, the shadow of race had fallen on me.

Thinking Critically About Content

1. What event does Arthur Ashe attend, and why is it so important to him? What almost ruins his day at this event?
2. Why does Ashe say that race has been more of a burden in his life than AIDS?
3. What do you think Ashe means by the final sentence in the essay: "Once again, the shadow of race had fallen on me"?

Thinking Critically About Purpose and Audience

4. In your opinion, what is Arthur Ashe's purpose in this essay? Explain your answer.

inconveniences infinitely more" (para. 8).
3. Ashe says this because even on the heels of a highly successful AIDS benefit, all he can think about is his reaction to the dolls. Race has once again cast a shadow over him.

Thinking Critically About Purpose and Audience

4. Ashe wants people to understand what it is like to be black. His story about the doll and his explanations throughout the essay allow readers to understand what he dealt with on a daily basis.
5. This essay was probably written primarily for multiethnic audiences. People from ethnic minorities can most likely identify with Ashe's story, but it also opens the eyes of those who don't understand what being a minority in America is like.
6. On the surface, he tells Marjory Smith about the dolls so she won't think he was rude for taking the dolls away. But on some level, he truly wants Smith to understand her error and open her eyes to the problems that plague African Americans.

Thinking Critically About Sentences

7. The writer's point of view is that members of minority groups have to deal with issues every day that are hard to understand by the white population.

8. The topic sentence in paragraph 12 is "In some ways, I am a prisoner of the past" (sentence 1). All the sentences in this paragraph support this topic sentence because they explain how the history of African Americans casts a shadow on who they are today. He believes that white people look at black people and see the African-American history in their skin.

9. Answers will vary.

5. Do you think this essay was written primarily for African-American audiences or for multiethnic audiences? Explain your answer.

6. Why did Ashe decide to tell Marjory Smith his reasons for wanting the doll out of the view of the television cameras?

Thinking Critically About Sentences

7. Describe in a complete sentence the writer's point of view toward racism.

8. What is the topic sentence of paragraph 12? Do all the sentences in that paragraph support this topic sentence? Explain your answer.

9. Write one or more complete sentences that represent what you think Marjory Smith might have been thinking when Ashe explained his reasons for removing the dolls.

Writing Topics: Analyzing a Process

Before you begin to write, you might want to review the writing process in Part I.

1. Think of something in life that you want as much as the immigrants in Robles's essay want to come to the United States. Then explain your plan for achieving this goal or accomplishing this mission you have set for yourself.

2. What is your biggest "burden" at this point in your life? Why is it a burden? How are you coping with it?

Comparing and Contrasting

Comparing and contrasting involve finding similarities and differences between two or more items. The essays in this chapter demonstrate this type of thinking. The first example, "Boy in Blue Tutu," written by Lisen Stromberg compares her son, a 3-year-old "cross-dresser," with a neighborhood tomboy in order to question our stereotyping of young children. Then, in "The Ugly Truth About Beauty," Dave Barry humorously compares and contrasts the "beauty regimens" that men and women go through before they face the public.

Lisen Stromberg

BOY IN BLUE TUTU

Focusing Your Attention

1. Describe what you were like as a child. If you are a male, did you play baseball and collect bugs? If you are a female, did you wear dresses and play with dolls? Or did you do what you wanted and dress as you liked, regardless of your gender? Explain your answer.

2. The essay you are about to read talks about the criticism a young boy receives when he prefers dress-up and ballet to "boy activities." If you had a son who wanted to play dress-up or host tea parties as a child, would you try to discourage his behavior? If you had a daughter who wanted to play baseball and collect bugs, would you discourage her? Explain your answers.

SUMMARY
Stromberg discusses her son's fascination with girls' clothes and toys in this essay, making readers think about the differences in the way society treats people like her son and how they treat tomboys.

READABILITY
6.2

Expanding Your Vocabulary

The following words are important to your understanding of this essay.

prances: dances around (paragraph 1)

empathetic: accepting and understanding (paragraph 4)

repression: restrictions (paragraph 8)

adolescence: the teenage years (paragraph 8)

Ritalin: medication to treat hyperactivity in children (paragraph 8)

rambunctious: noisy, rowdy (paragraph 8)

docile: tame, meek, mild (paragraph 8)

reels: spins (paragraph 8)

taunting: scornful reproaches, sarcastic remarks (paragraph 9)

intervention: interference (paragraph 10)

1   My son is a cross-dresser. Most mornings he gets up, puts on a hand-me-down dress, wraps an old pillowcase around his head with a ribbon (to create his "long blond hair"), and prances around singing "The hills are alive with the sound of music." My son is 3 years old.

2   At the toy store, he does not want a Batman doll. "I want Batgirl," he cries. When he begs to play with his friend Margo, it is because she has an extensive collection of Barbie dolls and outfits in which he can dress them.

3   He loves preschool for the teachers, but also for the wonderful selection of tutus, party shoes, and costume jewelry. His grandmother received the shock of her life when she went to pick him up at school one day and he was wearing a blue tutu with beaded gold slippers. His teacher tells us that he is "highly in touch with his feminine side."

4   Not everyone is so empathetic. "Boys should be playing baseball, not Barbie," my mother-in-law exclaims. "He keeps taking my daughter's Cinderella slippers!" my neighbor tells my other neighbor, who then tells me. Strangers ask, "So when do you think he will grow out of it?" and "How does your husband feel?"

5   I've tried to explain to these people that my son approaches life with a unique flair. He loves soccer, and he often plays in a silk cape that flutters in the wind when he runs. My husband can't wait for Little League to start because our son can already hit the ball out of the backyard. Our son can't wait for baseball, either, but for a different reason: He says the cleats are "just like tap shoes."

6   No one seems to be the least bit disturbed about my son's friend Gillian. At the age of 5, she refuses to wear dresses, plays T-ball and soccer, and is skilled at

climbing trees and collecting bruises. Gillian is a tomboy. "Isn't she cute?" a friend exclaims to me. But my son, I remind myself, is not cute when he dresses up and re-enacts the glass slipper scene from *Cinderella*.

If Gillian is a tomboy because she likes to do boylike things, does that make my son a janegirl? As far as I can tell, there isn't an equivalent word in the English language. More importantly, while it's OK—even cute—for a girl to "behave like a boy," my son's "girlish" behavior is viewed as less than acceptable. Watching my son grow up, I have begun to ask myself: What is normal? My son also loves trucks, cars, and trains. Last fall, during his terrible twos, he was accused of being a bully because he bit a girl at the playground. How can a child go from bully to sissy in just 12 months? 7

While our sex-role stereotypes have expanded for girls, they have contracted for boys. We're doing research to help ensure that girls will excel in math, overcome the repression of adolescence, and get elected to corporate boards. I'm thrilled. Trust me: I have a 1-year-old daughter. But what about my son? It is not just in my house that the days of "boys will be boys" seem to be over. Prescriptions for Ritalin are at an all-time high, and, increasingly, boys are expected to be less rambunctious and more docile—that is, be more like girls. My mind reels: Is society saying that a 3-year-old boy should be more like a man, but a 12-year-old should be more like a girl? 8

Sometimes, I have to admit, even I am embarrassed by my son's behavior. His recent declaration to my father-in-law that he wants to be a ballet dancer when he grows up almost created a family feud. When the father of one of his preschool classmates unintentionally called him a girl—he was wearing that blue tutu—I cringed just a little. And I am often confused about the messages I'm sending him. I don't mind if he wants to wear pink lipstick to a birthday party—"Mom, you wear lipstick when you dress up!" he reminds me—but how do I protect him from the taunting that inevitably will occur as he ages? 9

I come back to my original question: What is normal? My husband and I are learning all too early in our son's life that the boundaries of normalcy are narrow. On the other hand, my son, who at the moment is pretending to be Belle from *Beauty and the Beast*, complete with pearl-drop earrings, doesn't know this yet. With luck and a little parental intervention, he won't for a long time. Until then, Beauty, at least in our household, will reign. 10

Thinking Critically About Content

1. What is Stromberg comparing and contrasting in this essay?

2. Why does Stromberg feel that people should call her son a "jane-girl"?

3. Why do you think Stromberg is not concerned with her son's behavior when everyone around her is?

son's behavior and then justifies why these comments are wrong.

Thinking Critically About Sentences

7. "Not everyone is so emphatic" introduces the idea that not everyone is as accepting as she is about her son's interests. This sentence lets Stromberg talk next about people who don't approve of her son.

8. The writer believes society should not criticize young boys who display a "feminine" side and treat them as fairly as people treat young girls who display a "masculine" side.

9. Answers will vary.

Thinking Critically About Purpose and Audience

4. Although this essay was originally published in a parenting magazine, do you think readers who aren't parents can appreciate it? Explain your answer.

5. Why do you think Stromberg wrote an essay telling readers about her son's "cross-dressing"?

6. What attitude do you believe Stromberg wants readers to have toward people who assign stereotypes to young children? In what ways does the essay help you come to this conclusion?

Thinking Critically About Sentences

7. What new idea does the topic sentence of paragraph 4 introduce? How does the first sentence in paragraph 4 help Stromberg develop this comparison-and-contrast essay?

8. Describe in one sentence the writer's point of view toward stereotypes.

9. Write one or more complete sentences about the writer's son from the point of view of the writer's mother-in-law.

Dave Barry

THE UGLY TRUTH ABOUT BEAUTY

SUMMARY

In this essay, Barry takes a humorous look at the difference in the way men and women deal with their appearance.

READABILITY

9.0

Focusing Your Attention

1. How much time do you spend getting ready in the morning? What is your daily routine?

2. The essay you are about to read compares males' and females' focus on their appearance. The media often feature actors and actresses who are too thin to be healthy. How much do you believe Hollywood is responsible for causing eating disorders in teenagers? Explain your answer.

Expanding Your Vocabulary

The following words are important to your understanding of this essay.

> **stud muffins:** cute guys (paragraph 4)
>
> **regimen:** routine (paragraph 5)
>
> **dispensed:** distributed (paragraph 8)

genetic mutation: creature resulting from an unusual change in DNA (paragraph 8)

demeaning: degrading, insulting (paragraph 9)

bolster: boost, increase (paragraph 9)

If you're a man, at some point a woman will ask you how she looks.   1

"How do I look?" she'll ask.   2

You must be careful how you answer this question. The best technique is to   3
form an honest yet sensitive opinion, then collapse on the floor with some kind of
fatal seizure. Trust me, this is the easiest way out. Because you will never come
up with the right answer.

The problem is that women generally do not think of their looks in the same   4
way that men do. Most men form an opinion of how they look in seventh grade,
and they stick to it for the rest of their lives. Some men form the opinion that they
are irresistible stud muffins, and they do not change this opinion even when their
faces sag and their noses bloat to the size of eggplants and their eyebrows grow
together to form what appears to be a giant forehead-dwelling tropical caterpillar.

Most men, I believe, think of themselves as average-looking. Men will think   5
this even if their faces cause heart failure in cattle at a range of 300 yards. Being
average does not bother them; average is fine, for men. This is why men never
ask anybody how they look. Their primary form of beauty care is to shave themselves, which is essentially the same form of beauty care that they give to their
lawns. If, at the end of his four-minute daily beauty regimen, a man has managed
to wipe most of the shaving cream out of his hair and is not bleeding too badly,
he feels that he has done all he can, so he stops thinking about his appearance
and devotes his mind to more critical issues, such as the Super Bowl.

Women do not look at themselves this way. If I had to express, in three words,   6
what I believe most women think about their appearance, those words would be
"not good enough." No matter how attractive a woman may appear to be to others, when she looks at herself in the mirror, she thinks: woof. She thinks that at
any moment a municipal animal-control officer is going to throw a net over her
and haul her off to the shelter.

Why do women have such low self-esteem? There are many complex psycho-   7
logical and societal reasons, by which I mean Barbie. Girls grow up playing with
a doll proportioned such that, if it were a human, it would be seven feet tall and
weigh 81 pounds, of which 53 pounds would be bosoms. This is a difficult appearance standard to live up to, especially when you contrast it with the standard
set for little boys by their dolls . . . excuse me, by their action figures. Most of the

ANSWERS TO
QUESTIONS
*Thinking Critically
About Content*

1. Answers may vary. The
following are examples.

Men think they are average-looking, whereas women never think they look good enough.

For most men, shaving is their entire beauty regimen, whereas women will spend a fortune trying to look like Barbie.

Girls grow up playing with Barbie, while men grow up playing with "hideous-looking" action figures (para. 7).

2. Barry believes there is no safe answer to this question. The woman will think the man is either horrible for telling her the truth or horrible because she thinks he is lying to her.

3. Men don't care much about their appearance because most of them are not raised to think it is important. Women, by contrast, are often raised thinking that Barbie is ideal, and many women try to attain that ideal their entire lives.

Thinking Critically About Purpose and Audience

4. Barry writes this essay because he wants to point out that most women never feel good about themselves, and no matter how hard men try, they cannot convince women of their true beauty.

5. Barry wrote to a general audience, but men are probably his primary audience.

6. Barry included this reference to Cindy

action figures that my son played with when he was little were hideous-looking. For example, he was very fond of an action figure (part of the He-Man series) called "Buzz-Off," who was part human, part flying insect. Buzz-Off was not a looker. But he was extremely self-confident. You could not imagine Buzz-Off saying to the other action figures: "Do you think these wings make my hips look big?"

8   But women grow up thinking they need to look like Barbie, which for most women is impossible, although there is a multibillion-dollar beauty industry devoted to convincing women that they must try. I once saw an Oprah show wherein supermodel Cindy Crawford dispensed makeup tips to the studio audience. Cindy had all these middle-aged women applying beauty products to their faces; she stressed how important it was to apply them in a certain way, using the tips of their fingers. All the women dutifully did this, even though it was obvious to any sane observer that, no matter how carefully they applied these products, they would never look remotely like Cindy Crawford, who is some kind of genetic mutation.

9   I'm not saying that men are superior. I'm just saying that you're not going to get a group of middle-aged men to sit in a room and apply cosmetics to themselves under the instruction of Brad Pitt, in hopes of looking more like him. Men would realize that this task was pointless and demeaning. They would find some way to bolster their self-esteem that did not require looking like Brad Pitt. They would say to Brad: "Oh *yeah?* Well what do you know about *lawn care,* pretty boy?"

10   Of course many women will argue that the reason they become obsessed with trying to look like Cindy Crawford is that men, being as shallow as a drop of spit, *want* women to look that way, to which I have two responses:

1. Hey, just because *we're* idiots, that does not mean *you* have to be; and

2. Men don't even notice 97 percent of the beauty efforts you make anyway. Take fingernails. The average woman spends 5,000 hours per year worrying about her fingernails; I have never once, in more than 40 years of listening to men talk about women, heard a man say, "She has a nice set of fingernails!" Many men would not notice if a woman had upward of four hands.

11   Anyway, to get back to my original point: If you're a man, and a woman asks you how she looks, you're in big trouble. Obviously, you can't say she looks bad. But you also can't say that she looks great, because she'll think you're lying, because she has spent countless hours, with the help of the multibillion-dollar beauty industry, obsessing about the differences between herself and Cindy Crawford. Also, she suspects that you're not qualified to judge anybody's appearance. This is because you have shaving cream in your hair.

Thinking Critically About Content

1. What are three comparisons or contrasts that Barry makes between men and women?

2. Why does Barry believe that "if you're a man, and a woman asks you how she looks, you're in big trouble" (paragraph 11)?

3. Why do you think men care so little about their appearance?

Thinking Critically About Purpose and Audience

4. Why do you think Barry writes an essay comparing and contrasting men's and women's beauty regimens?

5. What type of audience do you think Barry had in mind when he wrote this essay? Explain your answer.

6. Why do you think Barry included in paragraph 10 his two responses to the issue that men want women to look like Cindy Crawford? What do you think he is trying to tell women in these responses?

Thinking Critically About Sentences

7. Look at the quotations in paragraphs 2, 6, and 7. How do these quotations help you understand what Barry is trying to say in this essay?

8. Describe in a complete sentence the writer's point of view.

9. Write one or more complete sentences that explain your opinion of some other problems men and women face today.

Writing Topics: Comparing and Contrasting

Before you begin to write, you might want to review the writing process in Part I.

1. In the first essay, Stromberg talks about the differences she sees in the upbringing of boys and girls in American society. Compare and contrast your upbringing with someone else's. What are the main differences between the two of you? What are the main similarities?

2. Expand on your ideas about other problems men and women face today (in response to question 9 after the Dave Barry essay).

Crawford because he is pointing out that most women alter their looks just to please men. In his two responses, he is telling women that this is not a good idea.

Thinking Critically About Sentences

7. These quotations help readers understand what Barry is trying to say because the quotes are responses of women. Barry is trying to represent women's opinions so that he can convince his readers that his views are accurate.
8. Barry believes that women should not try to change just for the sake of men.
9. Answers will vary.

Dividing and Classifying

Division refers to dividing a single category into many categories, while **classification** moves from many categories to one. They are mirror images of each other. The essays in this chapter demonstrate both division and classification. "Dads," the first essay in this chapter, divides today's fathers into categories that author Annie Murphy Paul feels represent the family today. In the second essay, titled "Why Do We Resist Learning?" John Roger and Peter McWilliams divide and classify students according to personality types that might resist learning in school.

Annie Murphy Paul

DADS

SUMMARY
In this essay, Paul divides today's "dads" into several interesting categories: the Distant Dad, the Disney Dad, the Serial Dad, the Single Dad, and the Stepdad.

READABILITY
8.1

Focusing Your Attention

1. Describe your relationship with your father when you were a child. What aspects of your father's personality do you like the most? What traits do you wish you could change? Why?

2. The essay you are about to read discusses the common traits of the modern father. Before you read this essay, try to define for yourself what characterizes the perfect father. Do you think this perfect father exists? Explain your answer.

Expanding Your Vocabulary

The following words are important to your understanding of this essay.

> **gamut:** range (paragraph 2)
>
> **unambiguous:** clear (paragraph 9)

Brothers Grimm: Jacob Ludwig Carl Grimm (1785–1863) and Wilhelm Carl Grimm (1786–1859), authors of *Grimm's Fairy Tales* (paragraph 14)

gleaned: collected, recovered (paragraph 18)

Once we all knew what a dad was: he was the guy who married mom, who gave 1 you your eyes or your smile or your sense of humor, who made you eat your spinach and do your homework, who was always around somewhere, puttering in the basement or grilling burgers out back.

Not anymore. Today's fathers run the gamut, from sperm-bank donors to 2 superdads—and there are a lot of men in the middle, trying to puzzle out the meaning of modern fatherhood. They're getting some help from psychologists, biologists and sociologists, whose research has something to tell us all about the ties that bind father to child. Here is a family portrait of today's fathers.

The Distant Dad

Throughout the 1980s, the deadbeat dad vied with the welfare queen and the 3 tax-and-spend liberal for the prize of public enemy number one. Now his numbers are on the wane, thanks to stronger child-support enforcement efforts—and we're left with what may be a bigger problem. How do we ensure that these "nonresidential fathers" (the new, more neutral term) contribute time and care as well as money to their kids?

One of the keys lies in what would seem an unlikely place: the women these 4 men have left or been left by. Even in intact families, research shows, mothers act as gatekeepers, supervising access to children. Their authority is further increased when they have primary custody of children, as is still the case in 87% of divorces. A friendly or at least civil relationship between ex-spouses can keep those gates from clanging shut. "Former partners don't have to be intimate or close," declares Constance Ahrons, Ph.D., a sociologist at the University of Southern California. "They just need to be mature enough to separate out marital issues from parenting issues, and put the parenting issues on the front burner."

Some state and local governments are trying to make that effort easier, by re- 5 quiring all divorcing couples with children to draw up a "parenting plan." "It's partly the outcome of the plan that's valuable, the set of decisions that are made about the children and how they will be cared for," says Ross Thompson, Ph.D., psychology professor at the University of Nebraska. "But just as important is the process. In the midst of negotiations to go their separate ways, the couple has to make plans for how they are going to continue to maintain contact."

The Disney Dad

6   Divorced fathers who do stay involved tend to "think that if they fill visits with fun activities, the child will look forward to seeing him," says Thompson. "But the fact is, those kinds of activities can be stressful. They're nice on special occasions, but they're not the basis of an ongoing relationship." Psychologists blame the Disney Dad syndrome on the visitation system itself, with its rigid and unnatural limits on the non-custodial parent's role. "Why should we be surprised when time passes and fewer and fewer fathers maintain contact?" asks Thompson.

7   What's needed is an improved system of shared custody. One new arrangement, now being experimented with by several states, grants responsibility for major decisions—where children go to school, what kind of medical treatment they receive—to both parents, even if the child lives with only one. "If parenting is about anything, it's about deep involvement and intimate contact, being knit into the everyday experience of a child's life," Thompson says. "And how can you do that if you're only visiting?"

The Serial Dad

8   The serial dad is of the love-the-one-you're-with school: he has children with one woman, then moves on to another and yet another, investing his time and money in the family of the moment.

9   These men may never have come to see themselves as fathers in any meaningful way, say sociologists. When fathers feel certain in their abilities as parents, when their place in their children's lives is clear and unambiguous, and when they feel satisfied with their interactions with their children, they are likely to stay involved with their offspring, according to Randy Leite, program coordinator of human development and family science at Ohio State University.

10 Some social scientists believe such confidence can be instilled by actively teaching parenting skills. Across the country, fathering programs like "It's my Child, Too" at Purdue University and "Making Room for Daddies" at the Center for Men in Cambridge, Massachusetts, are teaching men, especially those who are young and unmarried, how to be a father in full.

The Single Dad

11 Single fathers were once an amusing oddity: usually widowers, they were portrayed in popular culture as hopelessly inept with diapers and blushingly awkward with talks about the birds and the bees. But times have changed. According to a report by the Census Bureau, the number of single fathers jumped 25% in three years, from 1.7 million in 1995 to 2.1 million [in 1998].

12 Moreover, many of these men are taking on the role for new reasons: not because their wives have died but because judges have awarded them custody. That change reflects a larger one: Men are increasingly considered capable and

ANSWERS TO
QUESTIONS
*Thinking Critically
About Content*

1. The Distant Dad—one
   who is not around

effective single parents. "It appears that fathers raising children on their own are doing a better job than they were several decades ago," observes Doug Downey, Ph.D., a sociologist at Ohio State University. In fact, the care they provide is almost indistinguishable in its effect from that given by single mothers, as a recent study by Downey demonstrates: on measures of self-esteem, behavior and performance in school, relationships with others, and well-being later in life, children raised by single mothers and single fathers fared virtually the same.

There's a lesson here for fathers in intact familes: they only act like "Dad" because there's a "Mom" to play off of. "Faced with similar structural demands and without another adult with whom to 'do gender,'" notes Downey, "women and men in single-parent households act in less sex-stereotyped ways than their counterparts in mother-father households." 13

The Stepdad

Stepparents of both sexes are an increasingly familiar part of family life: more than 33% of U.S. children are expected to live in a stepfamily by age 18. While cultural fables abound about stepmothers, there are few featuring their male counterparts—but the social science research on them is straight out of the Brothers Grimm. 14

Stepfathers, it turns out, invest fewer resources in their charges, are less involved in their lives, and know less about their thoughts and opinions than biological fathers. Men find it more difficult to raise stepchildren than biological children and become less satisfied with stepfathering once they have had children of their own. Grimmest of all, the work of Martin Daly, Ph.D, and Margo Wilson, Ph.D., both psychology professors at McMaster University in Ontario, indicates that men are much more likely—on the order of 100 times—to abuse and even kill their stepchildren than their genetic offspring. 15

Blame nature for this bleak reality, the researchers say: such behavior is in an evolutionary sense "adaptive." A father looks after the well-being of his child, the theory goes, to ensure that his own genes will be reproduced in turn. A man has no such genetic investment in his stepchildren, who may even take resources from his own children or time from his partner, their mother. 16

Despite the harsh implications of such theories, Daly insists that looked at from another angle, they offer an impressive demonstration of the strength of the father-child bond. "Parental love is the most selfless love we know. You give and give to your kid and get nothing back and you're glad to do it," he says. "It would be very strange if people acted that way toward just any old baby." The fact that the great majority of stepfathers are kind and loving toward their stepchildren is a testament to a bond of another sort: affection, freely chosen and generously given. 17

The Disney Dad—one who always has big, fun activities planned
The Serial Dad—one who has many children from many women and pays attention to the latest family or child
The Single Dad—one who raises his children on his own
The Stepdad—one who raises children who aren't his

2. Paul believes that single dads and stepdads are the best because she talks about how much they give of themselves no matter how difficult that may be. She does not believe distant, Disney, or serial dads are good dads because they are hardly ever around

3. Answers will vary.

Thinking Critically About Purpose and Audience
4. Paul's purpose in this essay is to explain the different types of dads in society today.
5. Paul's original audience may have been parents, especially dads. They might read the essay and take the categorization as a form of advice.
6. These categories show that the family unit is deteriorating somewhat in society. Paul shows how complicated people's lives are and how this complexity affects their parenting abilities.

Thinking Critically About Sentences

7. The following sentences contain statistics:

"Their [mother's] authority is further increased when they have primary custody of children, as is still the case in 87% of divorces" (para. 4)

". . . the number of single fathers jumped 25% in three years, from 1.7 million in 1995 to 2.1 million [in 1998]" (para. 11)

". . . more than 33% of U.S. children are expected to live in a stepfamily by age 18" (para. 14)

". . . men are much more likely—on the order of 100 times—to abuse and even kill their stepchildren than their genetic offspring" (para. 15).

These sentences help readers understand the problems dads face because they give solid evidence of the problems.

8. Answers will vary.

9. Answers will vary.

18   If there's any insight to be gleaned from this gathering of modern father figures, perhaps it's just that: what makes a father may be genetic material, or a monthly check, or a legal document, but what makes a dad is love.

Thinking Critically About Content

1. What types does Paul divide "dads" into? What are the characteristics of each type?

2. What types of dads do you think Paul believes are the best? What types do you think she considers the worst? Explain your answer.

3. Do you agree with Paul's final statement that "what makes a father may be genetic material, or a monthly check, or a legal document, but what makes a dad is love" (paragraph 18)? Explain your answer.

Thinking Critically About Purpose and Audience

4. What do you think Paul's purpose is in this essay?

5. Who do you think is Paul's main audience for this essay? Explain your answer.

6. What do these categories of dads say about the problems facing fathers today? Explain your answer.

Thinking Critically About Sentences

7. Find two sentences that contain statistics. How do these sentences help you understand the problems those types of dads face?

8. Find a topic sentence that you think works well in its paragraph, and explain how the other sentences in that paragraph support this topic sentence.

9. Add another category to Paul's list. Why do you think this should be added? Explain your answer in one or more complete sentences.

John Roger and Peter McWilliams

WHY DO WE RESIST LEARNING?

SUMMARY

Roger and McWilliams divide people into four categories in this essay and then associate these

Focusing Your Attention

1. How do you think your group of friends in high school was viewed by other people? If someone secretly watched you from a distance, how would your group of friends be described?

2. The essay you are about to read discusses various reactions to the process of learning. How important is learning in your life? What energy do you put into learning?

Expanding Your Vocabulary

The following words are important to your understanding of this essay.

tirade: outburst (paragraph 7)

Catch-22: no-win situation (paragraph 13)

reverse psychology: tricking someone into doing something by telling them to do the opposite (paragraph 17)

insinuating: appealing (paragraph 23)

homecoming floats: elaborately decorated vehicles used in parades during certain high school and college celebrations (paragraph 24)

categories with the way people learn.

READABILITY
4.6

___

If we're here to learn, and if we have this seemingly in-built desire to learn 1 (curiosity), why do we resist learning so much? The classic example is the argument that goes, "Listen to me!" "No, you listen to me!" "No, you listen to me!" Et cetera.

It seems that somewhere around the age of eighteen (give or take ten years), 2 something in us decides, "That's it, I've had it, I'm done. I know all I need to know and I'm not learning any more."

Why? 3

Let's return to the idea of the small child being taught about life by its par- 4 ents. Parents are as gods to little children—the source of food, protection, comfort, love.

Also, parents are BIG! They're four to five times bigger than children. Imag- 5 ine how much respect (awe? fear?) you'd have for someone twenty to thirty feet tall, weighing 800 to 1,000 pounds.

Let's imagine a child—two, three—playing in a room. The parents are read- 6 ing, the child is playing, all is well. After an hour or so, CRASH! The child bumps a table and knocks over a lamp.

Where there once was almost no interaction with the parents, suddenly there 7 is a lot—almost all of it negative. "How many times have we told you . . ." "Can't you do anything right?" "What's the matter with you?" "That was my favorite lamp!" Shame, bad, nasty, no good, and so on. This verbal tirade might or might not be reinforced by physical punishment.

8   What does the child remember from an evening at home with the folks? Does the child remember the hours spent successfully (i.e., no broken any-thing) playing while mommy and daddy read, or does the child remember the intense ten minutes of "bad boy," "nasty girl," "shame, shame, shame," after the fall?

9   The negative, of course. It was loud, and it was frightening (imagine a pair of twenty-to-thirty-foot, 1,000-pound gods yelling at you). It was, for the most part, the *only* interaction the child may have had with "the gods" all evening (especially if being put to bed early is part of the punishment).

10   When a child's primary memory of the communication from its parents ("the gods") is no, don't, stop that, shouldn't, mustn't, shame, bad, bad, bad, what is the child being taught about itself? That it can do no good; that it must be alert for failure at every moment, and still it will fail; that it is a disappointment, a letdown, a failure.

11   In short, a child begins to believe that he or she is fundamentally not good enough, destined for failure, and in the way. In a word, unworthy.

12   And there is very little in the traditional educational system to counteract this mistaken belief. If anything, school etches the image even deeper. (If we learned all we needed to know in kindergarten, it was promptly drummed out of us in first grade.) You are taught you must perform, keep up, and "make the grade," or you aren't worth much. If you *do* work hard at making the grades, some authority figure is bound to ask, "Why are you studying all the time? Why aren't you out playing with the other children? What's wrong with you? Don't you have any friends?"

13   Catch-22 never had it so good.

14   Naturally, we can't go around feeling unworthy all the time. It hurts too much. So we invent defenses—behaviors that give the illusion of safety. Soon we notice that others have not only adopted similar defenses, but have taken their defenses to new and exotic levels. The school of limitation is in session.

15   We begin hanging out with other members of the same club. We are no longer alone. In fact, we start to feel worthy. We have comrades, companions, cohorts, compatriots, confidants, confreres, counterparts, and chums.

16   The clubs? There are basically four main chapters of the Let's Hide Away From All the Hurtful Unworthiness Clubs International.

The Rebels

17   The rebels like to think of themselves as "independent." They have, in fact, merely adopted a knee-jerk reaction to whatever "law" is set before them. They are prime candidates for reverse psychology. ("The best way to keep children from putting beans in their ears is to tell them they *must* put beans in their ears.") They conform to nonconformity.

MOST FEARED FORTUNE COOKIE: "A youth should be respectful to his elders."

SLOGAN: "Authority, you tell us that we're no good. Well, authority, *you're* no good."

MOTTO (minus the first two words): ". . . and the horse you came in on!"

If the ones who tell you you're no good are no good, then, somehow, that 18 makes you good. Somehow.

The Unconscious

These are the people who appear not all there because, for the most part, they're 19 not all there. They're not dumb; they're just someplace else: a desert island, a rock concert, an ice cream parlor. They are masters of imagination. They are not stupid. They do their best, however, to *appear* dumb, drugged, or asleep to anyone they don't want to deal with. They want, simply, to be left alone by all authority figures.

FAVORITE FORTUNE COOKIE: "To know that you do not know is the best."

SLOGAN: "You can't expect much from me, so you can't criticize me because, uh, um, what was I saying?"

MOTTO: "Huh?"

The real world picks them apart, so they retreat to a fantasy world of which 20 they can be a part.

The Comfort Junkies

These are the ones who hide in comfort. All that is (or might be) uncomfortable 21 is avoided (unless avoiding it would be more uncomfortable), and all that might bring comfort (food, distractions, TV, portable tape players, drink, drugs) is sought after (unless the seeking after them would be uncomfortable).

MOST FEARED FORTUNE COOKIE: "The scholar who cherishes the love of comfort is not fit to be deemed a scholar."

SLOGAN: "Comfort at any cost! (Unless it's too expensive.)"

MOTTO (taken from Tolkien): "In a hole in the ground there lived a hobbit. Not a nasty, dirty, wet hole, filled with the ends of worms and an oozy smell, nor yet a dry, bare, sandy hole with nothing in it to sit down on or to eat: it was a hobbit-hole, and that means comfort."

They memorize as much of their motto as is comfortable.   22

The Approval Seekers

23   The best way to prove worthiness is to have lots of people telling you how wonderful you are. These people work so hard for other people's approval (preferably) and acceptance (at the very least), they have little or no time to seek their own. But their own doesn't matter. They, after all, are unworthy, and what's the worth of an unworthy person's opinion? These people take the opposite tack of the rebels: rebels deem the opinions of others unworthy; acceptance seekers deem others' opinions *too* worthy. They would run for class president, but they're afraid of a backlash, so they usually win treasurer by a landslide.

> MOST FEARED FORTUNE COOKIE: "Fine words and an insinuating appearance are seldom associated with true virtue."
>
> SLOGAN: "What can I do for *you* today?"
>
> MOTTO: "Nice sweater!"

24   Without such people, homecoming floats would never get built.

25   You've probably been able to place all your friends in their respective clubhouses. If you're having trouble placing yourself, you might ask a few friends. If their opinions tend to agree, you'll have your answer. You may not like it, but you'll have your answer.

26   (NOTE: If you reject the idea that you could possibly fit into any category, you're probably a rebel. If you accept your friend's evaluations too readily, you may be looking for approval. If you forget to ask, maybe you're unconscious. If you're afraid to ask, you may be seeking comfort. If a friend says, "You don't fit in any of these; you seem to transcend them all," that person is probably looking for *your* approval.)

27   Most of us tend to pay some dues to each club at one time or another, about one thing or another. We may, for example, be rebels when it comes to speed limits, unconscious when it comes to income tax, comfort-junkies when it comes to our favorite bad habit, and acceptance-seekers in intimate relationships.

28   These are also the four major ways people avoid learning. The rebels don't need to learn; the unconscious don't remember why they should; the comfortable find it too risky; and the acceptance-seekers don't want to rock any boats. ("Leave well enough alone.") Most of us have our own personal combination of the four—a little of this and a little of that—that have perhaps kept us from learning all we'd like to know.

Thinking Critically About Content

1. What are Roger and McWilliams dividing and classifying in this essay?

2. How do the fortune cookies, slogans, and mottoes help you understand the categories in this essay?

3. What do Roger and McWilliams say have "kept us from learning all we'd like to know" (paragraph 28)?

Thinking Critically About Purpose

4. What do you think Roger and McWilliams's purpose was in writing this essay?

5. What readers would find this essay most interesting? Who else would enjoy reading this essay? Explain your answer.

6. Why do you think Roger and McWilliams ask you to determine which group you fall into? In what way might this exercise benefit you?

Thinking Critically About Sentences

7. How do the four headings help you move through the essay?

8. Explain paragraph 12 in your own words. Does the first sentence state the main idea of the paragraph?

9. Identify which category in the essay your learning style falls into. Explain your answer in one or more complete sentences.

people's behavior will enjoy this essay.
6. They want readers to identify with the group they fall into. To do this will help readers begin to change their behavior.

Thinking Critically About Sentences
7. The subdivisions help show when the authors are talking about a new "type" of people. This helps readers shift focus and transition their thoughts into thinking about a new category.
8. Answers will vary. The first sentence does state the main idea of the paragraph, as long as readers understand that the sentence is referring to the ideas in paragraph 11.
9. Answers will vary.

Writing Topics: Dividing and Classifying

Before you begin to write, you might want to review the writing process in Part I.

1. In the first essay, Paul divides and classifies the behavior of contemporary dads. Using her essay as a reference, explain what category your dad fits into and why he fits there.

2. Using Roger and McWilliams's essay, place your personality in one of their categories, and explain your reasoning.

45

Defining

Definition explains a word, phrase, or idea so that the readers can understand clearly what it is. The essays in this chapter take several different approaches to definition. In the first essay, "The Perfect Trap," Monica Ramirez Basco defines "perfection" and examines its side effects. In the second essay, "Black and Latino," Roberto Santiago defines his ethnic identity as he discovers it through the eyes of others.

Monica Ramirez Basco

THE PERFECT TRAP

SUMMARY
In this essay, Basco defines "perfectionism" by describing what it is, how it interferes with life, and how to overcome it.

READABILITY
8.6

Focusing Your Attention

1. If you could design a perfect person, what physical, mental, and emotional qualities would this person have?

2. The essay you are about to read explains what it means to be a perfectionist: Their schoolwork must be perfect, their appearance must be flawless, and their job performance must be exemplary. What do you think drives them to these goals?

Expanding Your Vocabulary

The following words are important to your understanding of this essay.

agonizing: worrying (paragraph 2)

humiliation: embarrassment, shame (paragraph 3)

procrastination: postponing activities to avoid doing them (paragraph 6)

anorexia nervosa: an abnormal fear of gaining weight (paragraph 12)

bulimia: binge eating followed by vomiting to avoid gaining weight (paragraph 12)

relapse: return of the problem behavior (paragraph 12)

intolerant: unaccepting (paragraph 13)

flaunting: calling attention to (paragraph 13)

genetically: from birth (paragraph 14)

in flux: in a state of change (paragraph 17)

mundane: ordinary, unexciting (paragraph 19)

subordinates: employees (paragraph 19)

plagued: troubled (paragraph 23)

overanxious: very nervous (paragraph 23)

tyranny: oppression, cruelty (paragraph 24)

schemas: patterns (paragraph 25)

catastrophic: disastrous (paragraph 26)

existential: concrete (paragraph 29)

absolute: perfect, ideal (paragraph 30)

hypotheses: assumptions (paragraph 32)

Susan, an interior designer, had been working frantically for the last month trying to get her end-of-the-year books in order, keep the business running, and plan a New Year's Eve party for her friends and her clients. Susan's home is an advertisement of her talent as a designer, so she wanted to make some changes to the formal dining room before the party that would be particularly impressive. It all came together in time for the party and the evening seemed to be going well, until her assistant, Charles, asked her if Mrs. Beale, who owned a small antique shop and had referred Susan a lot of business, and Mr. Sandoval, a member of the local Chamber of Commerce and a supporter of Susan's, had arrived. 1

Susan felt like her head was about to explode when she realized that she had forgotten to invite them to the party. "Oh, no," she moaned. "How could I be so stupid? What am I going to do? They'll no doubt hear about it from someone and assume I omitted them on purpose. I may as well kiss the business good-bye." Though Charles suggested she might be overreacting a little, Susan spent the rest of the night agonizing over her mistake. 2

Susan is an inwardly focused perfectionist. Although it can help her in her work, it also hurts her when she is hard on herself and finds error completely unacceptable. Like many people, she worries about what others will think of her and her business. However, in Susan's case her errors lead to humiliation, distress, sleepless nights, and withdrawal from others. She has trouble letting go 3 and forgiving herself because, in her mind, it is OK for others to make mistakes, but it is not OK for her to make mistakes.

4   Tom, on the other hand, is an outwardly focused perfectionist. He feels OK about himself, but he is often disappointed in and frustrated with others who seem to always let him down. Quality control is his line of work, but he cannot always turn it off when he leaves the office.

5   Tom drove into his garage to find that there was still a mess on the workbench and floor that his son Tommy had left two days ago. Tom walked through the door and said to his wife in an annoyed tone of voice, "I told Tommy to clean up his mess in the garage before I got home." His wife defended their son, saying, "He just got home himself a few minutes ago." "Where is he now?" Tom demanded. "He better not be on the phone." Sure enough, though, Tommy was on the phone, and Tom felt himself tensing up and ordering, "Get off the phone, and go clean up that mess in the garage like I told you." "Yes, sir," said Tommy, knowing that a lecture was coming.

6   For Tom, it seems like every day there is something new to complain about. Tommy doesn't listen, his wife doesn't take care of things on time, and there is always an excuse. And even when they do their parts, it usually isn't good enough, and they don't seem to care. It is so frustrating for Tom sometimes that he does the job himself rather than ask for help, just so he doesn't have to deal with their procrastination and excuses.

7   Tom's type of perfectionism causes him problems in his relationships with others because he is frequently frustrated by their failure to meet his expectations. When he tries to point this out in a gentle way, it still seems to lead to tension and sometimes to conflict. He has tried to train himself to expect nothing from others, but that strategy doesn't seem to work either.

The Personal Pain of Perfectionists

8   The reach for perfection can be painful because it is often driven by both a desire to do well and a fear of the consequences of not doing well. This is the double-edged sword of perfectionism.

9   It is a good thing to give the best effort, to go the extra mile, and to take pride in one's performance, whether it is keeping a home looking nice, writing a report, repairing a car, or doing brain surgery. But when despite great efforts you feel as though you keep falling short, never seem to get things just right, never have enough time to do your best, are self-conscious, feel criticized by others, or cannot get others to cooperate in doing the job right the first time, you end up feeling bad.

10   The problem is not in having high standards or in working hard. Perfectionism becomes a problem when it causes emotional wear and tear or when it keeps you from succeeding or from being happy. The emotional consequences of perfectionism include fear of making mistakes, stress from the pressure to perform, and

self-consciousness from feeling both self-confidence and self-doubt. It can also include tension, frustration, disappointment, sadness, anger, or fear of humiliation. These are common experiences for inwardly focused perfectionists.

The emotional stress caused by the pursuit of perfection and the failure to 11 achieve this goal can evolve into more severe psychological difficulties. Perfectionists are more vulnerable to depression when stressful events occur, particularly those that leave them feeling as though they are not good enough. In many ways, perfectionistic beliefs set a person up to be disappointed, given that achieving perfection consistently is impossible. What's more, perfectionists who have a family history of depression and may therefore be more biologically vulnerable to developing the psychological and physical symptoms of major depression may be particularly sensitive to events that stimulate their self-doubt and their fear of rejection or humiliation.

The same seems to be true for eating disorders, such as anorexia nervosa and 12 bulimia. Several recent studies have found that even after treatment, where weight was restored in malnourished and underweight women with anorexia, their perfectionistic beliefs persisted and likely contributed to relapse. Perfectionism also seems to be one of the strongest risk factors for developing an eating disorder.

Sometimes the pain of perfectionism is felt in relationships with others. Per- 13 fectionists can sometimes put distance between themselves and others unintentionally by being intolerant of others' mistakes or by flaunting perfect behavior or accomplishments in front of those who are aware of being merely average. Although they feel justified in their beliefs about what is right and what is wrong, they still suffer the pain of loneliness. Research suggests that people who have more outwardly focused perfectionism are less likely than inwardly focused perfectionists to suffer from depression or anxiety when they are stressed. However, interpersonal difficulties at home or on the job may be more common.

How Did I Get This Way?

There is considerable scientific evidence that many personality traits are inher- 14 ited genetically. Some people are probably born more perfectionistic than others. I saw this in my own children. My oldest son could sit in his high chair, happily playing with a mound of spaghetti, his face covered with sauce. My second son did not like being covered in goo. Instead, he would wipe his face and hands with a napkin as soon as he was old enough to figure out how to do it. As he got a little older, he kept his room cleaner than his brother. When he learned to write he would erase and rewrite his homework until it was "perfect."

Parental influences can influence the direction or shape that perfectionism 15 takes. Many perfectionists, especially inwardly focused perfectionists, grew up with parents who either directly or indirectly communicated that they were not good enough. These were often confusing messages, where praise and criticism were given simultaneously. For example, "That was nice, but I bet you could do better." "Wow, six A's and one B on your report card! You need to bring that B up to an A next time." "Your choir performance was lovely, but that sound system is really poor. We could hardly hear you."

16   Unfortunately, with the intention of continuing to motivate their children, these parents kept holding out the emotional carrot: "Just get it right this time, and I will approve of you." Some psychological theories suggest over time the child's need to please her parents becomes internalized, so that she no longer needs to please her parents; she now demands perfection from herself.

17   Some perfectionists tell stories of chaotic childhoods where they never seemed to have control over their lives. Marital breakups, relocations, financial crises, illnesses, and other hardships created an environment of instability. One of the ways in which these people got some sense of order in their otherwise disordered lives was to try to fix things over which they had some control, such as keeping their rooms neat and tidy, working exceptionally hard on schoolwork, or attempting to control their younger brothers and sisters. As adults, however, when their lives were no longer in flux, they may have continued to work hard to maintain control.

Are You a Perfectionist?

18 Perfectionists share some common characteristics. They are usually neat in their appearance and are well organized. They seem to push themselves harder than most other people do. They also seem to push others as hard as they push themselves. On the outside, perfectionists usually appear to be very competent and confident individuals. They are often envied by others because they seem to "have it all together." Sometimes they seem perfect. On the inside they do not feel perfect, nor do they feel like they always have control over their own lives.

19   Let's look at some of these characteristics more closely and how they interfere with personal and professional life. Terry, 34, a divorced working mother of two, is a high achiever with high career ambitions. But she can sometimes get hung up on the details of her work. She is not good with figures but does not trust her staff enough to use their figures without checking them herself. She gets frustrated with this mundane work and makes mistakes herself and then becomes angry with her subordinates for doing poor work.

20   Perfectionists also tend to think there is a right way and wrong way to do things. When Joe, a retired Marine Corps drill sergeant, takes his boys fishing, they have a routine for preparation, for fishing, and for cleanup. It is time-efficient, neat, organized. The boys think the "fishing ritual" is overdone, and they resent having to comply.

21   Expecting people to do their best is one thing. Expecting perfection from others often means setting goals that can be impossible to achieve. Brent, 32 and single, has been looking for Ms. Right for 12 years but cannot seem to find her. He

does not have a well-defined set of characteristics in mind. He just has a general impression of an angel, a sexual goddess, a confident, independent, yet thoroughly devoted partner. Blond is preferable, but he's not that picky.

Perfectionists can have trouble making decisions. They are so worried about 22 making the wrong one that they fail to reach any conclusion. If the person is lucky, someone else will make the decision for them, thereby assuming responsibility for the outcome. More often the decision is made by default. A simple example is not being able to choose whether to file income tax forms on time or apply for an extension. If you wait long enough, the only real alternative is to file for an extension.

Along with indecision, perfectionists are sometimes plagued by great diffi- 23 culty in taking risks, particularly if their personal reputations are on the line. Brent is in a type of job were creativity can be an asset. But coming up with new ideas rather than relying on the tried and true ways of business means making yourself vulnerable to the criticism of others. Brent fears looking like an idiot should an idea he advances fail. And on the occasions when he has gone out on a limb with a new concept, he has been overanxious. Brent's perfectionism illustrates several aspects of the way that many perfectionists think about themselves. There can be low self-confidence, fear of humiliation and rejection, and an inability to attribute success to their own efforts.

Breaking Free

To escape the tyranny of perfectionism, you need to understand and challenge 24 the underlying beliefs that drive you to get things "just right."

Each of us has a set of central beliefs about ourselves, about other people and 25 the world in general, and about the future. We use these beliefs or schemas to interpret the experiences in our life, and they strongly influence our emotional reactions. Schemas can also have influence on our choice of actions.

Under every perfectionist schema is a hidden fantasy that some really good 26 thing will come from being perfect. For example, "If I do it perfectly, then . . . I will finally be accepted . . . I can finally stop worrying . . . I will get what I have been working toward . . . I can finally relax." The flip side of this schema, also subscribed to by perfectionists, is that "If I make a mistake," there will be a catastrophic outcome ("I will be humiliated . . . I am a failure . . . I am stupid . . . I am worthless").

Changing these schemas means taking notice of the experiences you have 27 that are inconsistent with, are contrary to, or otherwise do not fit with them. June, who prides herself on being a "perfect" homemaker and mother, believed with 90% certainty that "If I do it perfectly, I will be rewarded." Yet she does a number of things perfectly that others do not even notice. June would tell herself that there would be a reward from her husband or her children for taking the

ANSWERS TO QUESTIONS
Thinking Critically About Content
1. The two types of perfectionists are

inwardly focused and
outwardly focused.
2. Basco thinks perfec-
tionism might be genetic,
but parents often con-
tribute to their children's
perfectionism by criti-
cizing them when they
do not perform perfectly.
Some characteristics of
a perfectionist include
the following (from
para. 18):
"They are usually neat in
   appearance and well
   organized."
"They seem to push
   themselves harder
   than most other
   people do."
"They also seem to push
   others as hard as they
   push themselves."
"On the outside, [they]
   usually appear to
   be very competent
   and confident
   individuals."
"On the inside they do
   not feel perfect, nor
   do they feel like they
   always have control
   over their own lives."
3. Answers will vary.

*Thinking Critically
About Purpose
and Audience*

4. Basco's purpose in
writing this essay is
probably to inform
readers of the problems
with perfectionism and
offer suggestions for
changing perfectionist
behavior.
5. Anyone can under-
stand and benefit
from this essay, but
people who are perfec-
tionists or people who
know perfectionists will

extra time to iron their clothes perfectly. Her son did not even realize his shirts had been ironed. When Mother's Day came, she got the usual candy and flowers. No special treats or special recognition for her extra efforts.

28   When June begins to notice the inaccuracy of her schema, she begins to reevaluate how she spends her time. She decides that if it makes her feel good, then she will do it. If it is just extra work that no one will notice, then she may skip it. She is certain that there are some things she does, such as iron the bedsheets, which no one really cares about. As a matter of fact, June herself doesn't really care if the sheets are ironed. However, she does like the feel of a freshly ironed pillow cover, so she will continue that chore. June has modified her schema. Now she believes, "If you want a reward, find a quicker and more direct way to get it."

29   If your schema centers around more existential goals, like self-acceptance, fulfillment, or inner peace, then you must employ a different strategy. If you believe that getting things just right in your life will lead to acceptance, then you must not be feeling accepted right now. What are the things you would like to change about yourself? What could you do differently that would make you feel better about who you are? If you can figure out what is missing or needs changing, you can focus your energies in that direction.

30   Or you may be motivated to take a different, less absolute, point of view. Instead of "I must have perfection before I can have peace of mind," consider "I need to give myself credit for what I do well, even if it is not perfect." Take inventory of your accomplishments or assets. Perhaps you are withholding approval from yourself.

31   If your schema is that other people's opinions of you are a mirror of your self-worth, you must ask yourself if you know when you have done something well, if you are able to tell the difference between a good performance and a poor performance. If you are capable of evaluating yourself, you do not really need approval from others to feel like you are a valuable worker or a good romantic partner.

32   In general, you must treat your perfectionistic schemas as hypotheses rather than facts. Maybe you are right or maybe you are wrong. Perhaps they apply in some situations, but not in others (e.g., at work, but not at home), or with some people, such as your up-tight boss, but not with others, such as your new boyfriend. Rather than stating your schema as a fact, restate it as a suggestion. Gather evidence from your experiences in the past, from your observations from others, or by talking to other people. Do things always happen in a way that your schemas would predict? If not, it is time to try on a new basic belief.

33   One of my patients described the process as taking out her old eight-track tape that played the old negative schemas about herself and replacing it with a new compact disc that played her updated self-view. This takes some practice, but it is well worth the effort.

Thinking Critically About Content

1. What are the two types of perfectionists?

2. How does Basco think some people become perfectionists? What are some of the characteristics of a perfectionist?

3. Based on Basco's definition of a perfectionist, how much of a perfectionist do you believe you are? Explain your answer.

Thinking Critically About Purpose

4. What do you think is Basco's purpose in writing this essay?

5. What audience do you think would best understand and benefit from reading this essay?

6. Why do you think Basco compares perfectionism to eating disorders? In what ways are the two related?

Thinking Critically About Sentences

7. Describe in a complete sentence the author's point of view toward perfectionism.

8. Find two sentences that give examples of perfectionism in the essay. In what ways do these examples help you understand the definition of "perfectionism"?

9. Write one or two complete sentences explaining whether or not you are a perfectionist.

Roberto Santiago

BLACK AND LATINO

Focusing Your Attention

1. Think of a family member you have always gone to for answers to difficult questions about life. Who is this person, and why did you choose this person?

2. The essay you are about to read focuses on various advantages and disadvantages connected with ethnic identity. How many cultures make up your heritage? Are you fully aware of your ethnic background? What do you wish you knew about your family history?

Expanding Your Vocabulary

The following words are important to your understanding of this essay.

probably appreciate this essay the most.

6. Basco compares perfectionism to eating disorders because the two are very similar; both are concerned with achieving the ideal. The two are related in that eating disorders are a form of perfectionism.

Thinking Critically About Sentences

7. The author believes perfectionism is unhealthy, both for the perfectionists and for the people around them.

8. Examples will vary. The examples in this essay help readers identify with the concept of "perfectionism." If Basco had not provided these examples, readers would have difficulty understanding and relating to this abstract concept.

9. Answers will vary.

SUMMARY

In this essay, Santiago defines what it is like to be the product of interracial parents. His definition focuses mainly on his ethnic status.

READABILITY

8.2

perplexes: confuses (paragraph 1)

East Harlem: a neighborhood of Manhattan, New York (paragraph 2)

boriqua: slang for Puerto Rican (paragraph 3)

moreno: black (paragraph 3)

parody: humorous imitation (paragraph 4)

Indio: Mexican Indian (paragraph 6)

predominant: main, most important (paragraph 6)

determinant: conclusive (paragraph 6)

Piri Thomas: 1928–   , Puerto Rican author (paragraph 6)

bridle path: a path for saddled horses (paragraph 7)

Central Park: the largest park in Manhattan (paragraph 7)

whiffle ball: a ball game (paragraph 7)

solace: comfort (paragraph 9)

pegged: identified (paragraph 11)

iconoclast: a person who challenges others' beliefs (paragraph 11)

1 "There is no way that you can be black and Puerto Rican at the same time." What? Despite the many times I've heard this over the years, that statement still perplexes me. I *am* both and always have been. My color is a blend of my mother's rich, dark skin tone and my father's white complexion. As they were both Puerto Rican, I spoke Spanish before English, but I am totally bilingual. My life has been shaped by my black and Latino heritages, and despite other people's confusion, I don't feel I have to choose one or the other. To do so would be to deny a part of myself.

2   There has not been a moment in my life when I did not know that I looked black—and I never thought that others did not see it, too. But growing up in East Harlem, I was also aware that I did not "act black," according to the African-American boys on the block.

3   My lighter-skinned Puerto Rican friends were less of a help in this department. "You're not black," they would whine, shaking their heads. "You're a *boriqua,* you ain't no *moreno.*" If that was true, why did my mirror defy the rules of logic? And most of all, why did I feel that there was some serious unknown force trying to make me choose sides?

4   *Acting black. Looking black. Being a real black.* This debate among us is almost a parody. The fact is that I am black, so why do I need to prove it?

The island of Puerto Rico is only a stone's throw away from Haiti, and, no fool-   5
ing, if you climb a palm tree, you can see Jamaica bobbing on the Atlantic. The
slave trade ran through the Caribbean basin, and virtually all Puerto Rican citizens have some African blood in their veins. My grandparents on my mother's
side were the classic *negro como carbón* (black as carbon) people, but despite
the fact that they were as dark as can be, they are officially not considered black.

There is an explanation for this, but not one that makes much sense, or dif-   6
ference, to a working-class kid from Harlem. Puerto Ricans identify themselves as
Hispanics—part of a worldwide race that originated from eons of white Spanish
conquests—a mixture of white, African, and *Indio* blood, which, categorically, is
apart from black. In other words, the culture is the predominant and determinant
factor. But there are frustrations in being caught in a duo-culture, where your
skin color does not necessarily dictate what you are. When I read Piri Thomas's
searing autobiography, *Down These Mean Streets,* in my early teens, I saw that
he couldn't figure out other people's attitudes toward his blackness, either.

My first encounter with this attitude about the race thing rode on horseback.   7
I had just turned six years old and ran toward the bridle path in Central Park as I
saw two horses about to trot past. "Yea! Horsie! Yea!" I yelled. Then I noticed one
figure on horseback. She was white, and she shouted, "Shut up, you f——nigger!
Shut up!" She pulled back on the reins and twisted the horse in my direction. I
can still feel the spray of gravel that the horse kicked at my chest. And suddenly
she was gone. I looked back and, in the distance, saw my parents playing whiffle
ball with my sister. They seemed miles away.

They still don't know about this incident. But I told my Aunt Aurelia almost   8
immediately. She explained what the words meant and why they were said. Ever
since then I have been able to express my anger appropriately through words or
action in similar situations. Self-preservation, ego, and pride forbid me from ever
ignoring, much less forgetting, a slur.

Aunt Aurelia became, unintentionally, my source for answers I needed about   9
color and race. I never sought her out. She just seemed to appear at my home
during the points in my childhood when I most needed her for solace. "Puerto
Ricans are different from American blacks," she told me once. "There is no
racism between what you call white and black. Nobody even considers the marriages interracial." She then pointed out the difference in color between my father and mother. "You never noticed that," she said, "because you were not
raised with that hang-up."

Aunt Aurelia passed away before I could follow up on her observation. But   10
she had made an important point. It's why I never liked the attitude that says I
should be exclusive to one race.

My behavior toward this race thing pegged me as an iconoclast of sorts. Chil-   11
dren from mixed marriages, from my experience, also share this attitude. If I have

to beat the label of iconoclast because the world wants people to be in set categories and I don't want to, then I will.

12   A month before Aunt Aurelia died, she saw I was a little down about the whole race thing, and she said, "Roberto, don't worry. Even if—no matter what you do— black people in this country don't, you can always depend on white people to treat you like a black."

Thinking Critically About Content

1. What do you think Santiago is defining in this essay?

2. Why do Santiago's friends in the first part of the essay say that he isn't black?

3. What did Aunt Aurelia teach Santiago about his ethnicity?

Thinking Critically About Purpose and Audience

4. Why do you think Santiago wrote this essay?

5. Who do you think Santiago's primary audience is?

6. Does this essay help you understand your own identity? Explain your answer.

Thinking Critically About Sentences

7. How do the Spanish words sprinkled in some sentences help you appreciate what Santiago is saying? Explain your answer.

8. Explain how the topic sentence works in paragraph 7: "My first encounter with this attitude about the race thing rode on horseback." Do the other sentences in the paragraph support this topic sentence?

9. Write one or more complete sentences describing what you think Santiago's worst struggle has been.

Writing Topics: Defining

Before you begin to write, you might want to review the writing process in Part I.

1. In the first essay, Basco defines perfectionism. Write your own definition of another character trait, such as alcoholism, workaholism, procrastination, or optimism.

2. Using Santiago's method of development through examples, explain your identity.

Analyzing Causes and Effects

Analyzing causes and effects is what we do to make sense out of the world around us. It involves searching for connections and reasons. The essays in this chapter discuss the causes and effects of certain actions or ideas. In the first essay, "How the Navy Changed My Life," Bryan Johnson explains how military discipline and education saved his life. The second essay, "For My Indian Daughter" by Lewis Sawaquat, discusses prejudice and heritage.

Bryan Johnson

HOW THE NAVY CHANGED MY LIFE

Focusing Your Attention

1. Describe a time when someone you know tried to talk you out of an important decision. Did you take his or her advice? Explain the issue and its effect on your life.

2. In the essay you are about to read, education was the beginning of a new life for the author. Describe how you think your college education will change your life. Where do you think you will be, and what do you think you will be doing after you graduate? How will your education help you reach your goals?

Expanding Your Vocabulary

The following words are important to your understanding of this essay.

   sentiments: feelings (paragraph 2)

   abysmal: awful (paragraph 3)

chaise longue: couchlike chair (paragraph 3)

canned: fired from a job (paragraph 3)

quintessential: purest, most perfect (paragraph 3)

Gen-Xer: member of Generation X, born between 1965 and 1985 (paragraph 3)

rack: bed (paragraph 6)

invigorating: exhilarating, stimulating (paragraph 9)

solitude: being alone (paragraph 9)

preconceived notion: preexisting opinion or assumption (paragraph 9)

1 I still remember a good friend's concern when I joined the Navy a year out of high school. "Dude, what are you doin'? You could die or sump'n. You're crazy, bro'."

2   I understood his sentiments. The thought of signing up for military service in post-Vietnam America evoked images of dope-smoking teenagers wandering the jungle. The "praise the Lord and pass the ammunition" days of World War II just didn't seem realistic in 1989. I thought of military enlistment as custom-made for boneheads not bright enough to further their education or talented enough to do anything else.

3   If that was the case, then I fit the mold at 19. I barely graduated from high school with an abysmal 1.8 GPA; my most formidable accomplishment was holding the senior-year record for skipping classes. After high school, I drove a patio-furniture delivery van. I had "quit" my other job as a cashier after being accused of fingering money from the register (truthfully, I just couldn't add or subtract). I could usually be found speeding through a retirement community en route to dropping off a *chaise longue*, giving old people in golf carts the bird when they yelled at me to slow down. Customer complaints were many, and if it weren't for a lack of available delivery boys, I would have been canned. I was the quintessential Gen-Xer, a prime example of why the world was going to pot.

4   Faced with a life of delivering windproof side tables, I decided to give the military a shot. When I bid farewell at the patio store and turned in my van keys, the manager laughed. "You'll be back," he said. I walked out thinking he was probably right.

5   My parents were more relieved than saddened when I left for boot camp. Mom knew those daily confrontations with Dad would end, and the old man thought a military hitch might straighten me out.

Pops couldn't have been more right. After naval boot camp, I was assigned as 6
a "deck ape" on a destroyer, my days filled with backbreaking hours of sanding
and painting in a never-ending battle to preserve the ship's exterior. I learned the
value of an honest day's work but soon began looking for a way out of a dull,
weary routine. I found it that first Christmas home, when I spent my stocking
money on remedial math and reading texts. I returned to the ship with a backpack full of scholarly spoils, and the tiny bulb over my rack burned every night for
almost a year. My hard work paid off when I landed a position standing naviga-
tion watch.

As he showed me how to plot our destroyer's course, my new supervisor said 7
something that made a lasting impression. "If you don't do your job right, don't
pay attention, people could die." Lives were at stake and someone was trusting
me to make good decisions. I was honored. What an odd yet wonderful feeling
that was.

More important, a fire had ignited inside me. I now rose to challenges instead 8
of avoiding them and loved the sense of self-worth I felt at a job well done. I
grabbed at every opportunity thrown my way. I won't soon forget the time I ma-
neuvered the ship's wheel on a course through the Panama Canal or rescued a
trapped dolphin in the Persian Gulf.

While life at sea had many invigorating moments, it could also be very lonely. 9
To fill in those empty hours of solitude, crew members talked with one another,
and we often knew everything about the men we lived and labored with. I
learned that a person's skin color, or where he came from, wasn't a very good in-
dicator of his character. I also realized that my preconceived notion of a military
consisting of losers was completely unfounded. I knew one sailor, for instance,
who could have supported his wife and baby more easily by flipping burgers at
McDonald's. He joined the Navy because he cherished his country's freedom and
wanted to give his time and energy in return.

Despite a worthwhile four years, I decided not to re-enlist and to give college 10
a try. I diligently pursued a B.S. degree and graduated with honors and hopes of
attending medical school.

Yet something was missing. I recalled the pride I had felt in my uniform, a sym- 11
bol of something greater than myself. I applied to the United States' only military
school of medicine and started classes last fall.

Going home these days is a bit like winding back the clock 10 years—old 12
friends look bewildered when I mention that I've rejoined the service. Don't think
I'm offended; I belong to an organization that defends the right of Americans to
have their own opinions.

Although I've put the past behind me, I often wonder what that manager 13
would say if I dropped by the patio store. But then he'd be right; I would be
back—but only to buy a ceramic yard frog.

ANSWERS TO
QUESTIONS
*Thinking Critically
About Content*
1. After getting a taste of knowledge while in the Navy, Johnson wanted to further his education after leaving the Navy.
2. Johnson first joined the Navy because he thought he was not "bright enough to further [his] education, or talented enough to do anything else" (para. 2). He learned the "value of an honest day's work" (para. 6), and he learned about responsibility, honor, and self-worth.
3. Johnson's duties in the Navy will help his medical career because he will demonstrate the same perseverance, diligence, and truth that he learned while he was serving on a destroyer.

*Thinking Critically
About Purpose
and Audience*
4. Johnson wrote this essay to show how the military can help people who think they have nowhere to go in life.

5. People who lead wayward, unambitious, or unfocused lives would most likely understand and appreciate this essay.
6. Johnson includes this information because he wants people to see that it's never too late to change or try to make a better life for yourself. Because Johnson had such a low GPA and was in a job that would lead nowhere, readers understand how important the Navy was in Johnson's life—especially when they realize how much the Navy changed him and his life.

Thinking Critically About Sentences

7. Answers will vary.
8. Johnson believes education is the key to a successful life.
9. Answers will vary.

Thinking Critically About Content

1. What causes Johnson to return to school after joining the Navy?

2. Why did Johnson first join the military? What values did he learn there? How did these values influence his future decisions?

3. How do you think Johnson's duties in the Navy will help him in his medical career?

Thinking Critically About Purpose and Audience

4. Why do you think Johnson wrote this essay?

5. What audience do you think would most understand and appreciate this essay?

6. Why do you think Johnson includes information about his "abysmal" school record and first two jobs? In what ways does this information help you understand the importance of the Navy in Johnson's life?

Thinking Critically About Sentences

7. Summarize this essay in a few sentences. Focus on the causes and effects that Johnson discusses.

8. What is Johnson's point of view toward education?

9. Write one or more complete sentences that Johnson might say to a group of seniors in high school about going to college.

Lewis Sawaquat

FOR MY INDIAN DAUGHTER

SUMMARY

In this essay, Sawaquat describes how he came to understand and appreciate his Indian heritage.

READABILITY

7.0

Focusing Your Attention

1. What do you know about your heritage? Have you or anyone you know ever gone through an identity crisis? If so, what was the situation?

2. The essay you are about to read is a personal memory of the author's Native American roots. What do you know about Native American history in this country? What stories do you know about Native Americans that you can share with your class?

Expanding Your Vocabulary

The following words are important to your understanding of this essay.

guttural: throaty (paragraph 2)

affluent: rich (paragraph 5)

comeuppance: deserved punishment (paragraph 7)

irony: mockery, humor (paragraph 7)

lore: knowledge, teachings (paragraph 8)

powwow: ceremonial meeting (paragraph 9)

iridescent: shimmering, glistening (paragraph 9)

masquerade: disguise oneself (paragraph 10)

culminated: ended, peaked (paragraph 12)

discomfiting: disturbing, frustrating (paragraph 13)

solitude: being alone (paragraph 14)

My little girl is singing herself to sleep upstairs, her voice mingling with the 1 sounds of the birds outside in the old maple trees. She is two, and I am nearly 50, and I am very taken with her. She came along late in my life, unexpected and unbidden, a startling gift.

Today at the beach my chubby-legged, brown-skinned daughter ran laugh- 2 ing into the water as fast as she could. My wife and I laughed watching her, until we heard behind us a low guttural curse and then an unpleasant voice raised in an imitation war whoop.

I turned to see a fat man in a bathing suit, white and soft as a grub, as he 3 covered his mouth and prepared to make the Indian war cry again. He was middle-aged, younger than I, and had three little children lined up next to him, grinning foolishly. My wife suggested we leave the beach, and I agreed.

I knew the man was not unusual in his feelings against Indians. His beach 4 behavior might have been socially unacceptable to more civilized whites, but his basic view of Indians is expressed daily in our small town, frequently on the editorial pages of the county newspaper, as white people speak out against Indian fishing rights and land rights, saying in essence, "Those Indians are taking our fish, our land." It doesn't matter to them that we were here first, that the U.S. Supreme Court has ruled in our favor. It matters to them that we have something they want, and they hate us for it. Backlash is the common explanation of the attacks on Indians, the bumper stickers that say, "Spear an Indian, Save a Fish," but I know better. The hatred of Indians goes back to the beginning when white people came to this country. For me it goes back to my childhood in Harbor Springs, Mich.

Theth

Theft

5 Harbor Springs is now a summer resort for the very affluent, but a hundred years ago it was the Indian village of my Ottawa ancestors. My grandmother, Anna Showanessy, and other Indians like her, had their land there taken by treaty, by fraud, by violence, by theft. They remembered how whites had burned down the village at Burt Lake in 1900 and pushed the Indians out. These were the stories in my family.

6   When I was a boy, my mother told me to walk down the alleys in Harbor Springs and not to wear my orange football sweater out of the house. This way I would not stand out, not be noticed, and not be a target.

7   I wore my orange sweater anyway and deliberately avoided the alleys. I was the biggest person I knew and wasn't really afraid. But I met my comeuppance when I enlisted in the U.S. Army. One night all the men in my barracks gathered together and, gang-fashion, pulled me into the shower and scrubbed me down with rough brushes used for floors, saying, "We won't have any dirty Indians in our outfit." It is a point of irony that I was cleaner than any of them. Later in Korea I learned how to kill, how to bully, how to hate Koreans. I came out of the war tougher than ever and, strangely, white.

8   I went to college, got married, lived in La Porte, Ind., worked as a surveyor, and raised three boys. I headed Boy Scout groups, never thinking it odd when the Scouts did imitation Indian dances, imitation Indian lore.

9   One day when I was 35 or thereabouts, I heard about an Indian powwow. My father used to attend them, and so with great curiosity and a strange joy at discovering a part of my heritage, I decided the thing to do to get ready for this big event was to have my friend make me a spear in his forge. The steel was fine and blue and iridescent. The feathers on the shaft were bright and proud.

10   In a dusty state fairground in southern Indiana, I found white people dressed as Indians. I learned they were "hobbyists," that is, it was their hobby and leisure pastime to masquerade as Indians on weekends. I felt ridiculous with my spear, and I left.

11   It was years before I could tell anyone of the embarrassment of this weekend and see any humor in it. But in a way it was that weekend, for all its silliness, that was my awakening. I realized I didn't know who I was. I didn't have an Indian name. I didn't speak the Indian language. I didn't know the Indian customs. Dimly I remembered the Ottawa word for dog, but it was a baby word, *kahgee*, not the full word, *muhkahgee*, which I was later to learn. Even more hazily I remembered a naming ceremony (my own). I remembered legs dancing around me, dust. Where had that been? Who had I been? "Sawaquat," my mother told me when I asked, "where the tree begins to grow."

12   That was 1968, and I was not the only Indian in the country who was feeling the need to remember who he or she was. There were others. They had powwows,

real ones, and eventually I found them. Together we researched our past, a search that for me culminated in the Longest Walk, a march on Washington in 1978. Maybe because I now know what it means to be Indian, it surprises me that others don't. Of course there aren't very many of us left. The chances of an average person knowing an average Indian in an average lifetime are pretty slim.

Circle

Still, I was amused one day when my small, four-year-old neighbor looked at me as I was hoeing in my garden and said, "You aren't a real Indian, are you?" Scotty is little, talkative, likable. Finally I said, "I'm a real Indian." He looked at me for a moment and then said, squinting into the sun, "Then where's your horse and feathers?" The child was simply a smaller, whiter version of my own ignorant self years before. We'd both seen too much TV, that's all. He was not to be blamed. And so, in a way, the moronic man on the beach today is blameless. We come full circle to realize other people are like ourselves, as discomfiting as that may be sometimes. 13

As I sit in my old chair on my porch, in a light that is fading so the leaves are barely distinguishable against the sky, I can picture my girl asleep upstairs. I would like to prepare her for what's to come, take her each step of the way saying, there's a place to avoid, here's what I know about this, but much of what's before her she must go through alone. She must pass through pain and joy and solitude and community to discover her own inner self that is unlike any other and come through that passage to the place where she sees all people are one, and in so seeing may live her life in a brighter future. 14

Thinking Critically About Content

1. What does Sawaquat see as the origin of the hatred of Native Americans in the United States?

2. What does Sawaquat learn from his first powwow?

3. Why do you think Sawaquat says that his daughter "must pass through pain and joy and solitude and community to discover her own inner self" (paragraph 14)? To what extent do we all need to do this in our lives?

Thinking Critically About Purpose and Audience

4. Why does Sawaquat begin this essay with the story about his daughter on the beach? How does the story make you feel?

5. The author calls paragraphs 5–12 "Theft" and paragraphs 13–14 "Circle." Explain these two subtitles.

6. Who do you think would enjoy this essay the most? Who do you think would benefit most from this essay?

different directions, and finally, withdraw into herself to find the best path for the future—as we must all do in our lives to some extent.

Thinking Critically About Purpose and Audience
4. The story of Sawaquat's daughter helps the reader feel the emotions of a victim of prejudice; it is especially moving because Sawaquat's two-year-old daughter is unaware of the trials to come. Beyond this, answers will vary.
5. The subtitle "Theft" represents what was taken away from Sawaquat during the time that he lost his cultural identity and became, "strangely, white" (para. 7). "Circle" represents the discovery of his cultural identity that has come "full circle" and will be passed on to his daughter.
6. Anyone can enjoy this essay, but Native Americans who have questions about their identity will probably benefit from it the most.

Thinking Critically About Sentences
7. Since this sentence is spoken by a boy too young to know better, it shows how Indians are stereotyped by most people. This young boy had to learn about Indians from his parents or from TV.
8. "I came out of the war tougher than ever and, strangely, white" (last

sentence) is the topic sentence of paragraph 7. The other sentences in paragraph 7 support this topic sentence because they show Sawaquat's progression from being unafraid and Indian to afraid and white.

9. Answers will vary.

Thinking Critically About Sentences

7. Explain the significance of the sentence, "'Then where's your horse and feathers?'" (paragraph 13).

8. What is the topic sentence of paragraph 7? Do all the sentences in that paragraph support this topic sentence? Explain your answer.

9. Write one or more sentences that might represent how Sawaquat's daughter felt when the fat man made whooping sounds on the beach.

Writing Topics: Analyzing Causes and Effects

Before you begin to write, you might want to review the writing process in Part I.

1. In the first essay, Johnson was motivated by a dead-end job to make a dramatic change in his life. Has anything motivated you to make an important change in your life? What were the circumstances?

2. In "For My Indian Daughter," Sawaquat says that his daughter must find her inner self on her own. Do you think you have found your inner self? How did you discover it? Was it painful? How does this discovery help you relate to others?

Arguing

4 7

The purpose of **arguing** is to persuade people to take a certain action or to think or feel a specific way. The essays in this chapter show the power of argument. The first essay, titled "This Has Nothing to Do with You: A Special Message to African-American Collegians," was written by Nikki Giovanni. In it, Giovanni tries to persuade African-American college students to become more aware of their past so they can better understand their future. The second essay, "Appearances Are Destructive" by Mark Mathabane, argues for school uniforms as a solution to some of the problems in today's schools.

Nikki Giovanni

THIS HAS NOTHING TO DO WITH YOU: A SPECIAL MESSAGE TO AFRICAN-AMERICAN COLLEGIANS

Focusing Your Attention

1. What is your family's ancestry? How does knowing about your family's roots help you in your daily life?

2. The essay you are about to read focuses on education as the key to living a good life. How important is education to you? How important is it to your family? Explain your answer.

Expanding Your Vocabulary

The following words are important to your understanding of this essay.

emancipated: free, not a slave (paragraph 1)

viscerally: emotionally (paragraph 1)

couched: vocalized, expressed (paragraph 3)

underground railroad: in the years before the Civil War, a network that helped slaves in the South escape to freedom in the North (paragraph 3)

pondered: considered, thought about (paragraph 4)

illogicality: lack of sense or logic (paragraph 4)

individualistic: selfish (paragraph 9)

1   There is a photograph that I hung in my son's room. It shows a Black man, clearly emancipated . . . not a slave, standing behind a mule. In his right hand he is holding the plow; in his left he has a McGuffey *Reader*. I wanted that picture in my son's room because I wanted him to know, viscerally, who he is and where he comes from. I don't know that the picture made all that much difference to Tom. He would probably have preferred some busty woman in some lewd or obscene pose, but since I am grown and he wasn't, I won the first battle of the walls.

2   The need to read and write is genetically deep. Humans have drawn on cave walls, fashioned language from the animal and natural sounds surrounding us. The need to communicate is basic to humans. Education is still the key.

3   I would not be so naive as to say or think that without formal education people cannot survive or thrive. Black people, especially, have done both. When we were, as a group, forbidden to read and write, when our drums were taken from us, when our religious practices were forbidden, we couched our tales in the spirituals, saying, "Go down, Moses" when Harriet Tubman and the underground railroad were ready to roll; we sang "Steal Away" when we were going to run; we released our sorrow in "Nobody knows the trouble I've seen"; and we shouted our Good News in "I've got a crown up in the Heavens . . . ain't that Good News." No history course can tell me the slaves didn't leave a record. They sang, "Deep River . . . my home is over Jordan." They told us, "You got to walk this lonesome valley." They told us, "Wade in the water . . . God's gonna trouble the water." The slaves left a record; America just doesn't like the fact that "everybody talking 'bout Heaven ain't going there."

4   I guess I just don't understand why this generation is so lost. The young people who are dropping out of school could not understand the fight of our people for literacy, could not understand that one of the main reasons you could get "sold south" was because you could read and write. The young people today must never have sat and read the Constitution, let alone the *Federalist Papers,* or they would surely know how essential the Black presence in the New World was. It's not just that Blacks supplied labor; we supplied the skills that made that labor necessary. What did Europeans know about planting? What did they know about

iron and bronze? Only what we taught them. Who has pondered the illogicality of bringing women to the New World? Slavery had existed and still does exist on earth. No people in their right mind would bring a woman across the seas. The Romans never thought to bring Greek women. Look at slavery in the African continent. You killed and enslaved the men. The women you left behind. Why? Because once you bring the female, you cannot breed the Black out. Look at the Moors in Spain, look at France, Germany, England. Look at Switzerland today with its "Turkish" problem and at what was once West Germany for the same situation. Why did they bring women to America? It's a question needing an answer.

But what has this got to do with you? If you knew that Liberia was founded in 5
1822 to send free and emancipated Blacks there, what does it mean that some stayed because they wanted to and others stayed because they had to? The solution was in the hands of the Americans. Why didn't they take it? How can anyone say the Civil War was not fought over slaves? Of course it was. Free labor cannot compete with slave labor. But why would poor white boys fight for a system that does not benefit them? Perhaps for the same reason Black men fought the Indians with the British, defeating the Black men who fought the Indians with the French. How can you be a Black man and not understand the great job the Black preacher did in getting the slaves one day off? I still hear people saying the preacher is nothing. Where is their sense of history? How would they like to be alive in 1750 or so, trying to convince a planter that on a pretty day, which just happens to be a Sunday, the slaves should be allowed to praise God? What kind of network would we have had without the preacher? What would have happened to our language if the preacher had not been allowed to study the Bible? How would our story have been kept alive if we had not found a song in code?

All I'm saying is this stuff today has nothing to do with us. The drugs, the 6
drive-by shootings, the pregnancies, the dropouts . . . these are not us. We have come through the fires. How can we now be tired? Isn't there an old song that says, "Walk together, children, don't you get weary"? And didn't we sing that in Montgomery, Selma, and all over the South? Why did we do that? For a cup of coffee? For the joy of voting for Lyndon Johnson over Barry Goldwater? We did it for the future. Why now, young Black men, have you decided to live in the present? What happened to the future vision of your grandfathers and great-grandfathers? Why now do you have to go to jail before you take time to commune with yourselves? Why do you have to be on death row before you decide to read a book or study law or heroically save someone's life? Your generation talks a lot about "roles." What "role" will you play in life? Try man. Try responsible man. Try forward-looking man. Try man who learns something the easy way (college) instead of the hard way (prison). Try doing the very difficult job of helping yourself and someone else by building something. Try honoring the very best in yourself instead of the very worst.

ANSWERS TO QUESTIONS
Thinking Critically About Content
1. Giovanni wants young African American students to learn their history so they can understand the plight of past African Americans. Giovanni believes that African Americans today should know why they are benefiting today.
2. Giovanni wants her son to realize that even when African Americans were slaves, they knew the importance of reading and writing.
3. She first uses the word in a negative way—almost synonymous with

"selfish." But then she points out that "pioneers" are always individuals. This word is important to her message because Giovanni wants her readers to understand that being "individualistic" is something to strive for—just as African-American ancestors strove for it.

Thinking Critically About Purpose and Audience

4. Giovanni's purpose in this essay is to persuade young African Americans to learn more about their past so they can actively change the future.
5. All readers can appreciate this essay because no matter what race they are, people can benefit from learning and understanding the past.
6. Giovanni uses the various songs to show how slaves maintained their literacy when they were denied an education. This is how they passed on information to others about the past and present. These examples help readers understand Giovanni's message because they show readers how resourceful the slaves were and how important literacy was to them.

Thinking Critically About Sentences

7. Giovanni uses questions to help show the ignorance of what people understood or now believe about the historical period involving

7   Am I picking on the men? I hope not. I hope I am reminding you that you have a job to do today. I hope I am reminding you that the people who produced you had little reason to dream, yet dream they did. They dreamed that one day you would be judged by the content of your character. They had no doubt that you would pass the test. Something has got to turn around.

8   Clearly the men are going to have to change. Malcolm X was fond of saying, "Show me how a country treats its women, and I'll show you the progress of that nation." We in Black America have turned that around: Show me how men treat each other, and I will show you the future of those people.

9   Those of you, young African-American men, who are struggling in high school and college . . . you are our pioneers. Don't let people tell you it is "individualistic" to try to do something with your life. Frederick Douglass was "individualistic" when he walked off that plantation in Maryland; David Walker was "individualistic" when he wrote his appeal; Marcus Garvey was "individualistic" when he got on that boat in Jamaica and came to America, and the people he organized were "individualistic" in their desire to make a better life. A people can be oppressed, but it takes individuals to seek freedom.

10   It is a wonderful thing to be young and Black today. The world is in the process of redefining itself. Those of you who will make a positive difference are those of you preparing yourself for the future. Your sacrifice is worth it. The slurs you take are worth it. The racists with whom we live have nothing to do with us. We are about our Father's business. We know there are many mansions in His house. We are now looking for keys that open the doors. Don't get down on yourself. Don't let shortsighted people make you feel bad. There is something out there that only the sensibility of African-Americans can understand. "Don't let nobody turn you 'round." Know who you are; then you'll know where you are going.

Thinking Critically About Content

1. What is Giovanni trying to persuade young African-American college students to do?

2. In connection with the rest of the essay, what is the significance of the photograph Giovanni puts in her son's room?

3. In paragraph 9, what does Giovanni mean by "individualistic"? Why is this word important to her message?

Thinking Critically About Purpose and Audience

4. What do you think Giovanni's purpose is in this essay?

5. Do you think readers who are not African-American can appreciate and understand this essay? Explain your answer.

6. Why do you think Giovanni spends so much time in paragraph 3 describing the songs from the slaves? How do these examples help you understand Giovanni's message?

Thinking Critically About Sentences

7. Reread the questions in paragraphs 4, 5, and 6. Explain how you think these sentences help Giovanni make her point.

8. Explain the significance of the last sentence in this essay: "Know who you are; then you'll know where you are going" (paragraph 10). What does this sentence add to the entire essay?

9. Write one or more complete sentences in response to this essay. Address your remarks to Giovanni herself.

slavery. She uses the questions to help persuade young African Americans that they should already know about these questions and answers, so they can learn more about their history.
8. The last sentence sums up the entire article and gives valuable advice: If you know where you've been, then you'll know where you're going.
9. Answers will vary.

Mark Mathabane

APPEARANCES ARE DESTRUCTIVE

Focusing Your Attention

1. Do you think uniforms should be required in high schools today? What problems would uniforms solve? What problems would they create? Explain your answer.

2. The essay you are about to read deals with the importance that high school students give to clothes and appearance. How important are they to you now? How important were they to you in high school? How important are they to other people in your life?

Expanding Your Vocabulary

The following words are important to your understanding of this essay.

apartheid: the policy of racial segregation enforced in South Africa before the 1990s (paragraph 2)

Shangri-Las: paradises (paragraph 2)

distraught: upset (paragraph 4)

ogling: staring at (paragraph 6)

meretricious extravagances: flashy excess (paragraph 8)

civil libertarians: believers in free will (paragraph 10)

SUMMARY

In this essay, Mathabane tries to persuade readers that schools should implement dress codes to produce better academic results.

READABILITY

10.0

diminution: lessening, reduction (paragraph 10)

curtailment: reduction (paragraph 12)

1   As public schools reopen for the new year, strategies to curb school violence will once again be hotly debated. Installing metal detectors and hiring security guards will help, but the experience of my two sisters makes a compelling case for greater use of dress codes as a way to protect students and promote learning.

2   Shortly after my sisters arrived here from South Africa I enrolled them at the local public school. I had great expectations for their educational experience. Compared with black schools under apartheid, American schools are Shangri-Las, with modern textbooks, school buses, computers, libraries, lunch programs, and dedicated teachers.

3   But despite these benefits, which students in many parts of the world only dream about, my sisters' efforts at learning were almost derailed. They were constantly taunted for their homely outfits. A couple of times they came home in tears. In South Africa students were required to wear uniforms, so my sisters had never been preoccupied with clothes and jewelry.

4   They became so distraught that they insisted on transferring to different schools, despite my reassurances that there was nothing wrong with them because of what they wore.

5   I have visited enough public schools around the country to know that my sisters' experiences are not unique. In schools in many areas, Nike, Calvin Klein, Adidas, Reebok, and Gucci are more familiar names to students than Zora Neale Hurston, Shakespeare, and Faulkner. Many students seem to pay more attention to what's on their bodies than in their minds.

6   Teachers have shared their frustrations with me at being unable to teach those students willing to learn because classes are frequently disrupted by other students ogling themselves in mirrors, painting their fingernails, combing their hair, shining their gigantic shoes, or comparing designer labels on jackets, caps, and jewelry.

7   The fiercest competition among students is often not over academic achievements, but over who dresses most expensively. And many students now measure parental love by how willing their mothers and fathers are to pamper them with money for the latest fads in clothes, sneakers, and jewelry.

8   Those parents without the money to waste on such meretricious extravagances are considered uncaring and cruel. They often watch in dismay and helplessness as their children become involved with gangs and peddle drugs to raise the money.

When students are asked why they attach so much importance to clothing, they frequently reply that it's the cool thing to do, that it gives them status and earns them respect. And clothes are also used to send sexual messages, with girls thinking that the only things that make them attractive to boys are skimpy dresses and gaudy looks, rather than intelligence and academic excellence. **9**

The argument by civil libertarians that dress codes infringe on freedom of expression is misleading. We observe dress codes in nearly every aspect of our lives without any diminution of our freedoms—as demonstrated by flight attendants, bus drivers, postal employees, high school bands, military personnel, sports teams, Girl and Boy Scouts, employees of fast-food chains, restaurants, and hotels. **10**

In many countries where students outperform their American counterparts academically, school dress codes are observed as part of creating the proper learning environment. Their students tend to be neater, less disruptive in class, and more disciplined, mainly because their minds are focused more on learning and less on materialism. **11**

It's time Americans realized that the benefits of safe and effective schools far outweigh any perceived curtailment of freedom of expression brought on by dress codes. **12**

Thinking Critically About Content

1. What is Mathabane trying to persuade readers to do in this essay?

2. Why is he so concerned that "Nike, Calvin Klein, Adidas, Reebok, and Gucci are more familiar names to students than Zora Neal Hurston, Shakespeare, and Faulkner" (paragraph 5)?

3. According to Mathabane, in what ways could school dress codes create "the proper learning environment" (paragraph 11)?

Thinking Critically About Purpose and Audience

4. Why do you think Mathabane titles his essay "Appearances Are Destructive"? In what ways does this title influence your reading?

5. What readers would find this essay most interesting? Are there other people who would benefit from reading this essay? Who are they? How would this essay benefit them?

6. Which details in Mathabane's argument are most convincing to you? Which are least convincing? Explain your answer.

Thinking Critically About Sentences

7. Which sentence in paragraph 3 lets us know what Mathabane thinks about school uniforms?

Hurston, Shakespeare, and Faulkner.
3. Dress codes would eliminate teasing about dress among students, would limit the amount of primping in school, and would get rid of the need to discuss clothes during school. Dress codes put a focus on learning rather than on appearances.

Thinking Critically About Purpose and Audience

4. His title represents his belief that appearances are destructive to students' emotions and academics. The title is an attempt to start swaying readers even before they read the first word.
5. High school students and parents of high school students would find this essay most interesting because it directly affects them. But most people will probably be interested in this essay because school issues affect us all.
6. Answers will vary.

Thinking Critically About Sentences

7. The last sentence lets readers know how Mathabane feels about school uniforms because it shows that, without school uniforms, people can become preoccupied with clothes and jewelry.
8. Mathabane uses examples in paragraph 6 to show how students can become preoccupied with themselves and ignore

their classwork. These examples suggest that school uniforms would put the students' minds back in the classroom where thy belong.

9. Answers will vary.

8. How does Mathabane use examples to get his point across in paragraph 6?

9. In one or more complete sentences, record what you imagine the feelings of Mathabane's two sisters were when the other students made fun of their clothes.

Writing Topics: Arguing

Before you begin to write, you might want to review the writing process in Part I.

1. In "This Has Nothing to Do with You: A Special Message to African-American Collegians," Nikki Giovanni tries to persuade her readers that education is the key to freedom for African Americans. What else might bring minorities freedom in American society? Write an argument that presents an alternate idea.

2. Mathabane's essay argues that uniforms would put high school students' attention on academics instead of on clothes. Think of another strategy for getting high school students to put academics above appearance, and try to convince a group of high school students to try your idea.

APPENDIX 1   Critical Thinking Log

Circle the critical thinking questions that you missed after each essay you read. Have your instructor explain the pattern of errors.

Reading	Content	Purpose and Audience	Paragraphs	Number Correct
Describing				
Collette Russell	1 2 3	4 5 6	7 8 9 10	
Judith Ortiz Cofer	1 2 3	4 5 6	7 8 9 10	
Narrating				
Henry Louis Gates	1 2 3	4 5 6	7 8 9 10	
Elizabeth Wong	1 2 3	4 5 6	7 8 9 10	
Illustrating				
Sherry Hemman Hogan	1 2 3	4 5 6	7 8 9 10	
Bailey White	1 2 3	4 5 6	7 8 9 10	
Analyzing a Process				
Arthur Ashe	1 2 3	4 5 6	7 8 9 10	
Tomas Robles	1 2 3	4 5 6	7 8 9 10	
Comparing and Contrasting				
Lisen Stromberg	1 2 3	4 5 6	7 8 9 10	
Dave Barry	1 2 3	4 5 6	7 8 9 10	
Dividing and Classifying				
Annie Murphy Paul	1 2 3	4 5 6	7 8 9 10	
John Roger and Peter McWilliams	1 2 3	4 5 6	7 8 9 10	
Defining				
Monica Ramirez Basco	1 2 3	4 5 6	7 8 9 10	
Roberto Santiago	1 2 3	4 5 6	7 8 9 10	
Analyzing Causes and Effects				
Bryan Johnson	1 2 3	4 5 6	7 8 9 10	
Lewis Sawaquat	1 2 3	4 5 6	7 8 9 10	
Arguing				
Nikki Giovanni	1 2 3	4 5 6	7 8 9 10	
Mark Mathabane	1 2 3	4 5 6	7 8 9 10	

The legend on the reverse side will help you identify your strengths and weaknesses in critical thinking.

Legend for Critical Thinking Log

Questions	Skill
1–2	Literal and interpretive understanding
3–6	Critical thinking and analysis
7–9	Analyzing sentences
10	Writing paragraphs

APPENDIX 2A   Revising
Writing a Paragraph
Peer Evaluation Form

Use the following questions to evaluate your partner's paragraph. Direct your comments to your partner.

Writer: _____   **Peer:** _____

Writing a Paragraph

1. Does the writer choose a subject that can be covered in a single paragraph? Explain your answer.

Topic Sentence

2. Does the topic sentence contain the paragraph's controlling idea? Explain your answer.

Development

3. Does the paragraph contain enough specific details to develop the topic sentence? Explain your answer.

Unity

4. Do all the sentences in the paragraph support the topic sentence? Explain your answer.

Organization

5. Is the paragraph organized so readers can easily follow it? Explain your answer.

Coherence

6. Do the sentences move smoothly and logically from one to the next? Explain your answer.

Writing a Paragraph
Peer Evaluation Form

Use the following questions to help you find editing errors in your partner's paragraph. Mark the errors directly on your partner's paper using the editing symbols on the inside back cover.

Writer: _____   **Peer:** _____

Sentences

1. Does each sentence have a subject and verb?

   Mark any fragments you find with *frag.*

   Mark any run-on sentences you find with *r-o.*

2. Do all subjects and verbs agree?

   Mark any subject-verb agreement errors you find with *sv.*

3. Do all pronouns agree with their nouns?

   Mark any pronoun errors you find with *pro agr.*

4. Are all modifiers as close as possible to the words they modify?

   Mark any modifier errors you find with *ad* (adjective or adverb problem), *mm* (misplaced modifier), or *dm* (dangling modifier).

Punctuation and Mechanics

5. Are sentences punctuated correctly?

   Mark any punctuation errors you find with the appropriate symbol under Unit 5 of the editing symbols (inside back cover).

6. Are words capitalized properly?

   Mark any capitalization errors you find with *lc* (lowercase) or *cap* (capital).

Word Choice and Spelling

7. Are words used correctly?

   Mark any words that are used incorrectly with *wc* (word choice) or *ww* (wrong word).

8. Are words spelled correctly?

   Mark any misspelled words you find with *sp.*

APPENDIX 3 Editing Quotient
Error Chart

Put an X in the square that corresponds to each question that you missed.

	a	b	c	d	e	f	g	h
1								
2								
3								
4								
5								
6								
7								
8								
9								
10								

Then record your errors in the categories below to find out where you might need help.

Fragments   1b_____ 1d_____ 2a_____ 3c_____ 4d_____ 5c_____
     6d_____ 7b_____ 8g_____ 9e_____ 10a_____

Run-ons   1a_____ 1c_____ 2c_____ 3d_____ 4a_____ 5d_____
     6c_____ 7c_____ 8c_____ 9f_____ 10c_____

Subject-verb agreement   2b_____ 2d_____ 9a_____

Verb forms   3a_____ 3b_____

Pronoun reference   8b_____

Pronoun agreement   4b_____ 4c_____ 4e_____

Modifiers   5a_____ 5b_____

End punctuation   6e_____

Commas	6b_____	9d_____	10b_____		
Capitalization	6a_____	9b_____	9c_____		
Abbreviations	8a_____				
Numbers	7a_____				
Confused words	8d_____	8e_____	8f_____	8h_____	10d_____

APPENDIX 4   Error Log

List any grammar, punctuation, and mechanics errors you make in your writing on the following chart. Then, to the right of this label, record (1) the actual error from your writing, (2) the rule for correcting this error, and (3) your correction.

Error Comma	Example I went to the new seafood restaurant and I ordered the lobster.
	Rule Always use a comma before a coordinating conjunction when joining two independent clauses.
	Correction I went to the new seafood restaurant, and I ordered the lobster.
Error	Example
	Rule
	Correction
Error	Example
	Rule
	Correction
Error	Example
	Rule
	Correction
Error	Example
	Rule
	Correction
Error	Example
	Rule
	Correction
Error	Example
	Rule
	Correction
Error	Example
	Rule
	Correction

Error	Example
	Rule
	Correction
Error	Example
	Rule
	Correction
Error	Example
	Rule
	Correction
Error	Example
	Rule
	Correction
Error	Example
	Rule
	Correction
Error	Example
	Rule
	Correction
Error	Example
	Rule
	Correction
Error	Example
	Rule
	Correction

APPENDIX 5   Spelling Log

On this chart, record any words you misspell, and write the correct spelling in the space next to the misspelled word. In the right column, write a note to yourself to help you remember the correct spelling. (See the first line for an example.) Refer to this chart as often as necessary to avoid misspelling the same words again.

Misspelled Word	Correct Spelling	Definition/Notes
there	their	there = place; their = pronoun; they're = "they are"

Credits

Index